D0999905

Letters from Jack London

Letters from Jack London

¶ *Containing an Unpublished Correspondence*

Between London *and* Sinclair Lewis

Edited by King Hendricks and Irving Shepard

Published by The Odyssey Press, New York

TO THE MEMORY OF
ELIZA LONDON SHEPARD

Library of Congress catalog card number: 65-22039

CONTENTS

LIST OF ILLUSTRATIONS
(following page 246)

1. Jack London and his first wife, Bessie.
2. Anna Strunsky.
3. Holograph letter, Jack London to Anna Strunsky.
4. Jack London in Oakland.
5. Bessie London in Oakland.
6. Jack London in 1903.
7. Jack London in 1905.
8. London's daughters.
9. London and his daughters.
10. Portrait of London by Arnold Genthe.
11. Portrait of London by Xavier Martinez.
12. London and part of the Carmel group.
13. Jack and Charmian London.
14. London and Charmian "boxing."
15. Aboard the *Snark*, 1907.
16. Aboard the unfinished *Snark*, 1906.
17. Trial run of the *Snark*.
18. The *Snark*, April, 1907.
19. The Londons in Honolulu.
20. London in South Seas costume.
21. London riding on "The Beauty Ranch."
22. London bungalow.
23. Aboard the *Roamer*, 1914.
24. Aboard the *Roamer*, 1910.
25. The ruins of "Wolf House."
26. Architect's sketch of "Wolf House."
27. Jack London with Joan.
28. London with George Sterling and Stewart Edward White.
29. The Londons in Hawaii, 1916.
30. Newspaper notice of London's death.
31. London shortly before his death.

FOREWORD

AT THE TIME of his death at the age of forty, Jack London had published forty-four volumes: novels, short stories, plays, and essays. Six volumes have been published posthumously. Not included in these fifty books are a number of articles he wrote for newspapers or journals as a war correspondent (Japanese-Russian War, 1904, and the Mexican conflict, 1914) and newspaper reporter of special events.

During his life he also made it a point of discipline to answer all letters in what he called the "mountain of mail." In one of his letters he apologizes for the brevity because he has three hundred letters to answer; in another, nine hundred; and in a third, three thousand. These figures may sound like convenient exaggerations to anyone who has not seen the incredible number of letters to London on file in the Huntington Library, San Marino, California, and at the Ranch, Glen Ellen, California. Naturally, London's mail often accumulated while he was traveling. When he was at sea on the *Snark,* for instance, his letters were forwarded to places where he intended to dock.

After his return from the *Snark* voyage in 1909, he purchased a sloop which he called the *Roamer,* and during the last years of his life he and Charmian took lengthy cruises on San Francisco Bay, often for weeks, during which time his mail was kept for him at the Ranch. Mail also piled up whenever London was away on a newspaper assignment as a reporter or war correspondent, or when business called him away.

It is impossible to establish even an approximation of the number of letters he wrote, but to publish the known letters *in toto* would require several volumes. In compiling the present volume we have had access to more than two thousand letters he wrote and several times as many written to him. We would have more if it were not for the fact that he frequently wrote in longhand or typed the letters himself, particularly during the early years (before 1905), and kept no carbons. Hence, unless the addressees returned the letters or placed them on file in some library, they are not available.

In selecting the letters we have tried to choose those that are most representative of London. We began our series with his first letter to an editor when he was twenty-two years old, at a time when he was on the threshold of his literary career. We know that there are earlier ones but we have not had access to any worthy of inclusion. There are very few to Charmian because, after their marriage in 1905, the Londons were seldom apart. We feel, however, that the letters in this volume will create a fairly accurate image of London, his intellectual and physical vigor, his impetuousness, his dreams and doubts and frustrations.

There is no double-talk in London's correspondence. He wrote exactly what he thought; as he would say, he never "pulled a punch," with the result that he was often brutally frank.

We have attempted always to let him speak for himself. Hence our footnotes are explanatory and not interpretive. Whenever possible we have identified the addressees or persons referred to in the letters. Many, however, are unknown to us, and we can only surmise that they were mere acquaintances or individuals unknown to London who, knowing his reputation as an alms-giver, sent him begging letters; or they were persons who wrote him fan letters, or persons who took issue with him and wrote only to castigate him.

A NOTE ON THE EDITING:

London had the ability to write lucidly and accurately. *His Tramp Diary,* written during his hoboing in 1894 when he was only eighteen years old, before he had attended high school, and written in various places (freight-cars, roundhouses, hobo shacks, jails, etc.) under varying conditions, is remarkable for its sentence structure and mechanical accuracy. Because of this evidence, we have taken the liberty to correct what seem to be obvious type errors.

We have changed his punctuation only as far as it affects titles. London used quotation marks or capitals for all titles, for individual pieces as well as collections. Many of his titles of short stories or essays later became titles of collections. To avoid confusion we have followed the standard practice of italicizing titles of books or independent publications, and quoting titles of short stories, essays, etc.

Each letter has been printed in its entirety, except in one or two cases where we have deleted portions of a long quotation, such as a well-known poem or essay.

ACKNOWLEDGMENTS

It has been impossible to include in this collection all of the letters that we have received from various sources, but we gratefully acknowledge the assistance of the following institutions and individuals. We especially appreciate the assistance of Huntington Library and its staff, notably John E. Pomfret, Director; Robert O. Dugan, Librarian; Herbert C. Schulz, Curator of Manuscripts; Phyllis Rigney and Haydee Noy of the Manuscripts Department; and Mary Isabel Fry, Registrar.

FOREWORD

Alderman Library, University of Virginia, Anne Freudenberg, Assistant Curator of Manuscripts, Elizabeth Ryall, Manuscript Assistant; Brooklyn Public Library, Francis R. St. John, Librarian; Library of Harvard University, W. H. Bond, Curator of Manuscripts; University of Kentucky, Jacqueline Bull, Archivist; Lehigh University Library, The Honeyman Collection, James D. Mack, Librarian; Los Angeles Public Library, Lois M. Jones, Departmental Librarian; Loyola University, Elizabeth M. Cudahy Memorial Library, Genevieve Delana, Associate Librarian; Middlebury College Library, Grace S. Davis, Curator; Mills College Library, Mary Manning Cook, Reference Librarian; Oakland Public Library, Frances H. Buxton, Senior Librarian; San Francisco Public Library, Gladys Hansen, Reference Librarian; Southwest Museum, Ella Robinson, Librarian; University of California at Los Angeles Library, Department of Special Collections, Brooks Whitney; University of Southern California Library, American Literature Collection, Lloyd A. Arvidson, Curator; Utah State University Library, Milton C. Abrams, Librarian; State Historical Society of Wisconsin, Josephine L. Harper, Manuscript Librarian; Wagner College Library, Robert L. Enequist, Librarian; Yale University Library, Collection of American Literature, Donald C. Gallup, Curator; Appleton-Century-Crofts Company, Helen Cohan; The Macmillan Company, R. L. DeWilton, Associate Editor, retired; Utah State University Research Council, D. Wynne Thorne, Director; Hensley C. Woodbridge, Librarian, Murray State College.

We acknowledge particularly and express appreciation to H. Barbara Hendricks for continued assistance in the compiling, selecting, and editing of the letters.

ix

1876-1899

THE EARLY YEARS

CHRONOLOGY

1876: Born January 12, the son of John and Flora Wellman London.

1891: Completion of grade school (eighth grade). Summer work in the cannery. Purchased the *Razzle-Dazzle* and became an oyster pirate on San Francisco Bay.

1892: Served for nearly a year as an officer in the Fish Patrol of San Francisco Bay.

1893: Shipped as seaman aboard the *Sophie Sutherland* to hunt seals in the Japanese waters as far north as the coast of Siberia. The cruise lasted five months. From this came his first publication, the prize-winning essay "Typhoon off the Coast of Japan."

1894: Tramping experiences. Member of Kelly's Army. Tramped east across the United States and returned via Canada. Served prison term for vagrancy in Erie County Penitentiary.

1895: High school. Published some articles in the *Aegis,* the high school paper at Oakland High School.

1896: Attended the University of California for one semester.

1897: March. Left for the Yukon; spent the winter at Dawson.

1898: Returned from the Yukon. Began serious writing.

1899: January. Sold first story, "To the Man on Trail," to *Overland Monthly* magazine. Devoted his entire time and energy to writing. During the year published twenty-four items, including stories and essays.

To Editor of the *Bulletin*[1]

Oakland, Calif.
Sept. 17, 1898

Dear Sir:—

I have returned from a year's residence in the Clondyke [*sic*], entering the country by way of Dyea and Chilcoot Pass. I left by way of St. Michaels, thus making altogether a journey of 2,500 miles on the Yukon in a small boat. I have sailed and traveled quite extensively in other parts of the world and have learned to seize upon that which is interesting, to grasp the true romance of things, and to understand the people I may be thrown amongst.

I have just completed an article of 4,000 words, describing the trip from Dawson to St. Michaels in a rowboat.[2] Kindly let me know if there would be any demand in your columns for it—of course, thoroughly understanding that the acceptance of the manuscript is to depend upon its literary and intrinsic value.

Yours very respectfully,
Jack London

[1]The editor wrote in longhand the following note on the bottom of London's letter and returned it to him: "Interest in Alaska has subsided in an amazing degree. Then, again, so much has been written, that I do not think it would pay us to buy your story." Across the top, in Charmian London's handwriting, is the statement: "This is Jack's first letter to an editor."
[2]Published as, "From Dawson to the Sea."

To Mabel Applegarth[1]

Oakland, Calif.
Nov. 27, 1898

Dear Mabel:—

Forgive my not writing, for I have been miserable and half sick. So nervous this morning that I could hardly shave myself. I knew by Thanksgiving that you were expecting me; but I delayed, hoping to start every day and everyday. And now, I receive a letter from Frank Atherton,[2] telling me that he will arrive either Monday night or Tuesday morning. So if things should come my way, I would be unable to go to College Park till he finishes his visit.

Everything seems to have gone wrong—why, I haven't received my twenty dollars for those essays yet.[3] Not a word as to how I stood in my Civil Exs.[4] Not a word from the *Youth's Companion*,[5] and it means to me what no one can possibly realize.

You seem to misunderstand. I thought I made it perfectly plain, that those squibs of poetry were merely diversions and experiments; yet you say— "But always the same theme." Theme had nothing to do with it; they were studies in structure and versification. Though it took me a long while, I have learned my lesson, and thanks to no one. I made ambitious efforts once. It makes me laugh to look back on them, though sometimes I am nearer to weeping. I was the greenest of tyros, dipping my brush into white-wash and coal-tar, and without the slightest knowledge of perspective, proportion or color, attempted masterpieces—without a soul to say "you are all wrong; herein you err; there is your mistake."

Why, that poem on gold is one of the finest object-lessons in my posses-sion—Ted has it now. I was ambitious in that. With no more comprehension of the aims and principles of poetry than a crab, I proposed or rather, purposed to make something which would be something. I would strike out on new trails; I would improve upon the Spencerian [*sic*] Stanza; I would turn things upside down. So I tried what has been probably tried a thousand times and discarded because it was worthless; one Alexandrine at the end of the stanza was not enough; I added a second. I treated my theme as Dryden or Thompson would have treated it. My elephantine diction was superb—I out-Johnsoned Johnson. I was a fool—and no one to tell me.

So you see, to-day, I am unlearning and learning anew, and as such things are merely principles, you can readily see why I don't care a snap for the theme. I have played Darius Green once, and if my neck is broken a second time it will be my own fault. I shall not be ready for any flights till my flying machine is perfected, and to that perfection I am now applying myself. Until then, to the deuce with themes. I shall subordinate thought to technique till the latter is mastered; then I shall do vice a versa.

I do not know when I can be down—I may be digging sewers or shoveling coal next week. Am glad to hear you are better. Give my regards to every-body.

Good-bye,
Jack

[1]In 1895, while a student at the Oakland High School, London met Fred Jacobs, who introduced him to Bessie Maddern and Ted Applegarth. Shortly afterward, Ted intro-duced him to his sister, Mabel. It was Jack's first serious love affair. He partially tells the story of the romance in *Martin Eden,* where Mabel becomes Ruth Morse.
[2]A boyhood friend.
[3]He had won two prizes, worth ten dollars each, in a Republican Club contest.
[4]Civil Service examinations for the position of Mail Carrier, which he successfully passed.
[5]He had submitted *Where Boys Are Men.*

To Mabel Applegarth

Oakland Park
Nov. 30, 1898

Dear Mabel:—

Am replying at once. As to that medicine: since there is no certainty to my plans, I think it would be best to send up money to me and order to

Owl Drug Co. Send at once, so Frank can take it back with him. He does not go before Saturday, and the chances are that he will stay even longer.

I do appreciate your interest in my affairs, but—we have no common ground. In a general, vaguely general, way, you know my aspirations; but of the real Jack, his thoughts, feelings, etc., you are positively ignorant. Yet, little as you do know, you know more about me than anybody else. I have fought and am fighting my battle alone.

You speak of going to my sister. I know how well she loves me; do you know how? or why? I spent years in Oakland and we saw nothing of each other—perhaps once a year looked on each other's face. If I had followed what she would have advised, had I sought her I would to-day be a clerk at forty dollars a month, a railroad man, or something similar. I would have winter clothes, would go to the theatre, have a nice circle of acquaintances, belong to some horrible little society like the W.R.C.,[1] talk as they talk, think as they think, do as they do—in short, I would have a full stomach, a warm body, no qualms of conscience, no bitterness of heart, no worrying ambition, no aim but to buy furniture on the installment plan and marry. I would be satisfied to live a puppet and die a puppet. Yes, and she would not have liked me half as well as she does. Because I felt that I was or wanted to be something more than a laborer, a dummy; because I showed that my brain was a little bit better than it should have been, considering my disadvantages and lack of advantages; because I was different from most fellows in my station; because of all this she took a liking to me. But all this was secondary; primarily, she was lonely, had no children, a husband who was no husband, etc., she wanted someone to love. A great deal of this same feeling has been lavished upon the W.R.C. for the same reason.

If the world was at my feet to-morrow, none would be happier than she, and she would say she knew it would be so all the time. But until that time —well, she would advise to not think of it, to sink myself in two score years of oblivion with a full belly and no worry, to die as I had lived, an animal. Why should I so study that I may extract joy from reading some poem? She does not and does not miss anything; Tom, Dick and Harry do not, and they are happy. Why should I develop my mind? It is not necessary for happiness. A babble of voices, petty scandals, and foolish nothings, should satisfy me. It does Tom, Dick and Harry, and they are happy.

As long as my mother lives, I would not do this; but with her gone to-morrow, if I knew that my life would be such, that I was destined to live in Oakland, labor in Oakland at some steady occupation, and die in Oakland —then to-morrow I would cut my throat and call quits with the whole cursed business. You may call this the foolish effervescence of youthful ambition, and say that it will all tone down in time; but I have had my share of toning down.

Why, as you have laid down my duty in your letter, if I had followed it what would I have been to-day? I would be a laborer, and by that I mean I would be fitted for nothing else than labor. Do you know my childhood?

When I was seven years old, at the country school of San Pedro, this happened. Meat, I was that hungry for it I once opened a girl's basket and stole a piece of meat—a little piece the size of my two fingers. I ate it but I never repeated it. In those days, like Esau, I would have literally sold my birthright for a mess of pottage, a piece of meat. Great God! when those youngsters threw chunks of meat on the ground because of surfeit, I could have dragged it from the dirt and eaten it; but I did not. Just imagine the development of my mind, my soul, under such material conditions.

This meat incident is an epitome of my whole life. I was eight years old when I put on my first undershirt made at or bought at a store. Duty—at ten years I was on the streets selling newspapers. Every cent was turned over to my people, and I went to school in constant shame of the hats, shoes, clothes I wore. Duty—from then on, I had no childhood. Up at three o'clock in the morning to carry papers. When that was finished I did not go home but continued on to school. School out, my evening papers. Saturday I worked on an ice wagon. Sunday I went to a bowling alley and set up pins for drunken Dutchmen. Duty—I turned over every cent and went dressed like a scarecrow.

Was there any duty owing to me?

Fred worked in the cannery for a short summer vacation—aye, the reward was to be a term at college. I worked in the same cannery, not for a vacation but for a year. For months at a time, during that year, I was up and at work at six in the morning. I took half an hour for dinner. I took half an hour for supper. I worked every night till ten, eleven and twelve o'clock. My wages were small, but I worked such long hours that I sometimes made as high as fifty dollars a month. Duty—I turned every cent over. Duty—I have worked in that hell hole for thirty-six straight hours, at a machine, and I was only a child. I remember how I was trying to save the money to buy a skiff—eight dollars. All that summer I saved and scraped. In the fall I had five dollars as a result of absolutely doing without all pleasure. My mother came to the machine where I worked and asked for it. I could have killed myself that night. After a year of hell to have that pitiful—to be robbed of that petty joy.

Duty—had I followed your conception of duty, I should never have gone to High School, never to the University, never—I should have remained a laborer.

My body and soul were starved when I was a child, cannot they do without a few little luxuries for me at this stage of the game?

Aye, I at least kicked over the traces; but even then, did I wholly run away from duty? Many a goldpiece went into the family. When I returned from seven months at sea, what did I do with my pay day? I bought a second hand hat, some forty-cent shirts, two fifty-cent suits of underclothes, and a second hand coat and vest. I spent exactly seventy cents for drinks among the crowd I had known before I went to sea. The rest went to pay the debts of my father and to the family. When I was working in the jute

6

mills, I received forty dollars pay and at the same time twenty-five dollars from a prize in a literary contest.[2] I bought a ten-dollar suit of clothes and got my watch out of hock. That was all I spent. Two days afterward, I had to soak my watch to get money for tobacco.

How often, as I swept the rooms at High School, has my father come to me at my work and got a half dollar, a dollar, or two dollars? And you know I had a place to put every bit of it myself. Aye, I have had my father come there, when I did not have a cent, and went to the *Aegis*[3] fellows and borrowed it—mortgaged my next month's wages.

Do you know what I suffered during that High School and University period? The imps of hell would have wept had they been with me. Does anyone know? Can anyone know? O the hours I have eaten out my heart in bitterness! Duty—I fought it off for two long years without cessation, and I am glad. You knew me before those two years—did they do me any good?

You say, "It is your duty, if you wish to hold the esteem of those whose approval or companionship is worth having." If I had followed that, would I have known you? If I had followed that, who would I now know whose companionship I would esteem? If I had followed that from childhood, whose companionship would I now be fitted to enjoy?—Tennyson's? or a bunch of brute hoodlums on a street corner?

I cannot lay bare, cannot put my heart on paper, but I have merely stated a few material facts of my life. These may be cues to my feelings. But unless you know the instrument on which they play, you will not know the music. Me how I have felt and thought through all this struggle; how I feel and think now—you do not know. Hungry! Hungry! Hungry! From the time I stole the meat and knew no call above my belly, to now when the call is higher, it has been hunger, nothing but hunger.

You cannot understand, nor never will.

Nor has anybody ever understood. The whole thing has been by itself. Duty said "do not go on; go to work." So said my sister, though she would not say it to my face. Everybody looked askance; though they did not speak, I knew what they thought. Not a word of approval, but much of disapproval. If only someone had said, "I understand." From the hunger of my childhood, cold eyes have looked upon me, or questioned, or snickered and sneered. What hurt above all was that some were my friends—not professed but real friends. I have calloused my exterior and receive the strokes as though they were not; as to how they hurt, no one knows but my own soul and me.

So be it. The end is not yet. If I die I shall die hard, fighting to the last, and hell shall receive no fitter inmate than myself. But for good or ill, it shall be as it has been—alone.

Mabel, remember this: the time is past when any John Halifax Gentleman ethics can go down with me. I don't care if the whole present, all I possess, were swept away from me—I will build a new present; if I am left naked and hungry to-morrow—before I give in I will go on naked and hungry; if I were a woman I would prostitute myself to all men but that I would succeed—in short, I will.

Am sorry that I have devoted so much to myself, and glad that you are better. How I would like to come down, and I shall if things come my way.

Frank has been playing the violin and Johnny⁴ the devil in the room while I have been writing this, so you will forgive its disconnectedness.

Tell Ted I shall write in a couple of days, and ask him to explain more fully what he meant about that hymn which was enclosed.

Yours,

Jack

[1]Women's Relief Corps, of which Eliza Shepard was one-time President.
[2]Prize essay, "Typhoon off the Coast of Japan," *San Francisco Call,* Nov. 12, 1893.
[3]Oakland High School student publication, to which London contributed a number of articles while a student.
[4]Johnny Miller, London's nephew.

To Mabel Applegarth

Oakland, Calif.
Dec. 6, 1898

Dear Mabel:—

Frank is at last gone and I can do a little writing. Why did you not send me what you had written? Were you afraid of hurting my feelings—it seems your previous frankness, extending through several years, had precluded any such possibility.

Ere this you will have received your medicine, for I asked Frank to take it out at once as you needed it. I only hope you are so much better that you don't. It seems too bad; but then, it is better to be sick in winter than in summer.

Sent out in this mail, "trailers" after articles I mailed last September, and which have vanished utterly. Received a letter from the *Overland Monthly.* This is the substance of it:— We have read your MS. ["To the Man on Trail"] and are so greatly pleased with it, that, though we have an enormous quantity of accepted and paid-for material on hand, we will at once publish it in the January number, if—aye, "if you can content yourself with five dollars."

There are between three and four thousand words in it. Worth far more than five dollars, at the ordinary repertorial rate of so much per column. What do you think of that for a first class magazine like the *Overland?* Every magazine has its clique of writers, on whom it depends, and whom it patronizes in preference to all other writers. True, they had to work into that position of preference. Well, a newcomer must excel them in their own fields before he is accepted, or else he must create a new field. Perhaps it

8

was the latter that impressed the editors in favor of my article; but be it what it may, if worthy of publication, it were worthy of proper pay.

You wanted a sample of a villanelle—I wrote the enclosed in fifteen minutes, without even the refrains when I began. It's fine drill, forcing one to be trite, to sum his thought in small compass, to condense. No room for Johnsonian periods there—no verbosity, etc. You can figure out the rhyme and refrain structure.

We are getting ready to sue the Republican Club[1] for our prizes. No word from *Youth's Companion*.

If I could only come down.

Hope this will find you in better health—I hate to think of you lying sick —if you get a chance, read the American translation of *Cyrano de Bergerac;* but read slowly or not at all. Several portions of it were my own thoughts, my own moods.

Give regards to all, and believe me,

Good night,
Jack London

[1]The Oakland Fifth Ward Republican Club held a contest for campaign songs, essays, cartoons, and poems. London won first prize for prose, others won prizes for songs, etc. None was ever paid.

TO MABEL APPLEGARTH

Oakland, Calif.
Xmas Morning [1898]

Dear Mabel:—

About the loneliest Christmas I ever faced—guess I'll write to you. Nothing to speak of, though—everything quiet. How I wish I were down at College Park, if for no more than a couple of hours. Nobody to talk to, no friend to visit—nay, if there were, and if I so desired, I would not be in position to. Hereafter and for some time to come, you'll have to content yourself with my beastly scrawl, for this is, most probably, the last machine made letter I shall send you.

Well, the FIRST BATTLE has been fought. While I have not conquered, I'll not confess defeat. Instead, I have learned the enemy's strongholds and weak places, and by the same I shall profit when the SECOND BATTLE comes off; and by what I learn through that, I will be better fitted for the THIRD BATTLE—and so on, ad infinitum.

The typewriter goes back on the thirty-first of December. Till then I expect to be busy cleaning up my desk, writing business letters of various nature, and finishing the articles I am at present on. Then the New Year, and an entire change of front.

I have profited greatly, have learned much during the last three months.

How much I cannot even approximate—I feel its worth and greatness, but it is too impalpable to put down in black and white. I have studied, read, and thought a great deal, and believe I am at last beginning to grasp the situation—the general situation, my situation, and the correlative situation between the two. But I am modest, as I say, I am only beginning to grasp —I realize, that with all I have learned, I know less about it than I thought I did a couple of years ago.

Are you aware of the paradox entailed by progress? It makes me both jubilant and sad. You cannot help feeling sad when looking over back work and realizing its weak places, its errors, its inanities; and again, you cannot but rejoice at having so improved that you are aware of it, and feel capable of better things. I have learned more in the past three months than in all my High School and College; yet, of course, they were necessary from a preparatory standpoint.

And to-day is Christmas—it is at such periods that the vagabondage of my nature succumbs to a latent taste for domesticity. Away with the many corners of this round world! I am deaf to the call of the East and West, the North and South—a picture such as Fred used to draw is before me. A comfortable little cottage, a couple of servants, a select coterie of friends, and above all, a neat little wife and a couple of diminutive models of us twain—a hanging of stockings last evening, a merry surprise this morning, the genial interchange of Christmas greeting; a cosy grate fire, the sleepy children cuddling on the floor ready for bed, a sort of dreamy communion between the fire, my wife, and myself; an assured, though quiet and monotonous, future in prospect; a satisfied knowledge of the many little amenities of civilized life which are mine and shall be mine; a genial, opti-mistical contemplation—

Ever feel that way? Fred dreamed of it, but never tasted; I suppose I am destined likewise. So be it. The ways of the gods are inscrutable—and do they make and break us just for fun? What a great old world! What a jolly good world! It contains so much which is worth striving for; and nathe-less, so much to avoid. But it's like a great Chinese puzzle—in every little community are to be found the Islands of the Blest, and yet we know not where to look for them. And if we do, our ticket in Life's Lottery bears the wrong number. An auspicious mingling of all the elements which go to make up the totality of human happiness—the capital prize—there are various ways of winning it, and still more various ways of losing it. You may be born into it, you may tumble into it, you may be dragged into it; but verily, you may not knowingly walk into it. The whole thing is a gamble, and those least fitted to understand the game win the most. The most unfortunate gamblers are those who have, or think they have systems to beat the game —they always go broke. The same with life. There are numerous paths to earthly happiness; but to find them, skill in geography or typography is worse than useless.

I shall forsake my old dogmas, and henceforth, worship the true god.

"There is no God but Chance, and Luck shall be his prophet!" He who stops to think or beget a system is lost. As in other creeds, faith alone atones. Numerous hecatombs and many a fat firstling shall I sacrifice—you just watch my smoke (I beg pardon, I mean incense).

I started to write a letter; I became nonsensical; forgive me. I go to dine at my sister's. Happy New Year to all!

Jack

To Corresponding Editor, *Youth's Companion*

Oakland, Calif.
Jan. 7, 1899

Dear Sir:—

Your kind letter of December 29th at hand. I have been quite sick, but am better now. I have vague recollections of what I wrote you, but they are so confused with what passed through my head in the several succeeding days and nights, that I cannot tell of how much I unburdened myself. I was on the verge of breaking down, so I suppose my letter had a strong tinge of hysteria. I had no friend to go to and had to break out on somebody. This working out one's soul is not a pleasant task.

I must thank you for your kindness in replying as you did. But first, a word in explanation, or rather, extenuation. You say: "The chapters should not exceed thirty-five hundred words in length, should be at least five and not more than seven in number. . . ." One objection to my MS.[1] was the excessive length of the chapters, a length never permissible save in "very special instances." Five of my seven chapters were within fifty of three thousand words; one exceeded that number by one hundred and fifty words; and another sank to about twenty-six hundred. Surely the double-spacing could not have led to a mistaken estimate of length.

I understand and appreciate your urging me to not make writing my means of livelihood. Enclosed ad. is the one I am at present running in the local papers. Have been trying for work constantly. In the midst of *Youth's Companion* MS., broke off to take Civil Service Examinations for the Post Office.[2] They are very slow at Washington, however, for I have yet to receive my standing in the same. I think I did very well.

Yet to me all work will be but a means to an end. I may labor till I am old and decrepit; but periods of idleness and sickness eating into the savings of labor and frugality, will have placed me in the proper position for the poor house. No, no; I have seen too much labor and too many laborers, not to understand the game. Some day I shall hit upon my *magnum opus*. And then, if my struggling expression at last finds tongue, I will not have to go to the poor house because my muscles can no longer work. And if not— well, so be it.

11

Again thanking you, I promise some day, if the gods are propitious, to drop into Boston-town and shake hands with you.

Very truly yours,
Jack London

[1]*Where Boys Are Men*. Never published under this title.
[2]Passed the examinations but never accepted an appointment.

To Mabel Applegarth

Oakland, Calif.
Jan. 28, 1899

My dear Mabel:—

Right in the neck—don't mention it. 'Tisn't exactly right to ask for criticism, and then criticize—I understand that, but, well, I wanted to show the point of view by which I worked. I was wrong in doing it, and besides, did it rather rudely. Still, I believe you're none the worse for it. I wish I could talk with you; I might explain better.

One other thing. I don't know whether you share this belief with Ted, but think you do—that I do not take time enough; do not let a thing cool; do not write and write and rewrite; do not, in short, exhibit the peculiar, or rather, exercise the peculiar methods of the lapidary. To this, I believe, you attribute the weakness of the characters I have drawn. Two other possibilities arise. First, as I stated before, the lack of effect may be laid to your egregious ignorance of such types. Secondly, the fault may lie with me, but not in the trick of the hand or phrase. The latter may do their work very thoroughly, admirably, and through no weakness on their part, produce a puerile result. This then, is due to insincerity of vision on my part; and all the polishing of the MS. will never succeed in bettering it. You see what I am driving at. I am sure what I have written reflects almost perfectly the thought, the image in my mind. I know, if I draw the complete character of Malemute Kid in one short story, all *raison d'être* of a Malemute Kid[1] series ceases.

Am very sorry to hear you are worse; and you had been so hopeful, too. Hope my last letter had no bad effect—if it stirred you up, as it evidently did Ted, it was really criminal on my part. Forgive me. Though I guess you know already what a rough-shod barbarian I am, even at my best. At least you cannot say I am anything but candid. Unless Ted mentions it, don't let him know you know I was lectured—it's only Jack, anyway.

By the way, forgot to tell you in last letter, that I stand first on the eligible list for carriers. My percent was 85.38. My postman tells me I stand a good show for appointment. At first one goes on as extraman, making about forty-five dollars per month. After about six months of that he becomes regular with sixty-five dollars. But the whole year may elapse before I get anything at all.

Ted is getting along all right—nothing to be feared.

You are unusually prejudiced against Ella Wheeler Wilcox; Ted Shares it with you; I am sure your mother does too; and hence, with no further search, you fan each other's distaste. Tell me what you think of the following—style and thought:

"The effect of the sweetly good woman upon man is like the perfume of a flower that grew in his childhood's garden, or a strain of music heard in his youth. He is ashamed of his grosser appetites when he is in her presence. He would not like her to know of his errors and vices. He feels like another man when near her and realizes that he has a spiritual nature. Yet as the effect of the strain of music or the perfume of the flower is necessary, so often her influence ceases when he is absent from her, unless she be the woman who rules his life."

"Now!" cried the reviewers, "here is a pedestal for you—up you go!"

"Gentlemen," blubbered Patient Merit, "you are too kind—but, help me up!"

"And they helped him up."

"And when he was well posed they proceeded to throw potsherds at him."

Speaking of magnificent, glance at the use of the following adjective by Frederic Harrison, one of the famous English literati: "Mr. Ruskin once hazarded the GLORIOUS paradox that Cary's *Dante* was better reading than Milton's *Paradise Lost*."

Speaking of marriage—the following is what Zangwill calls Spinoza's "aphorism on marriage": "It is plain that Marriage is in accordance with Reason, if the desire is engendered not merely by external form, but by a love of begetting children and wisely educating them; and if, in addition, the love both of husband and wife has for its cause not external form merely, but chiefly liberty of mind."

John Keats wrote to Miss Jeffry: "One of the reasons that the English have produced the finest writers in the world is that the English world has ill treated them during their lives and fostered them after their deaths."

What do you think of it? Don't harbor the idea for a minute that I deem myself in that category. I consider myself a clumsy apprentice, learning from the master craftsmen and striving to get my hand in.

It's midnight, and I'm going to mail this before I turn in, so you must put up with a very dry letter. Ted is over in 'Frisco, gone to the theatre I believe. I shall read in bed till his return. If the *Overland, Black Cat,*[2] and Republicans pay me next week, within a couple of days of each other, I may be able to come down. Good night Mabel,

Jack

[1]A character who appears in a collection of stories *The Son of the Wolf.*
[2]*Overland Monthly* had published "To the Man on Trail," and *Black Cat* had accepted "A Thousand Deaths."

TO CLOUDESLEY JOHNS[1]

Oakland, Calif.

Feb. 10, 1899

Dear sir:—

What an encouragement your short note was! From the same I judge you can appreciate one's groping in the dark on strange trails. It's the first word of cheer I have received (a cheer, far more potent than publisher's checks).

If a strong chin and a perhaps deceptive consciousness of growing strength, will aid in the fulfillment of your prophecy,[2] it may to a certain extent be realized. Yes, my name is Jack London—rather an un-American heritage from a Yankee ancestry, dating beyond the French and Indian Wars.

Thanking you for your kindness,

I am,

Very truly yours,

Jack London

[1]Cloudesley Johns was a contemporary, a struggling writer and a Socialist. This letter began an extensive correspondence.
[2]Johns wrote in the margin: "I prophesied greatness, and told him not to disappoint me. He won't."

TO CLOUDESLEY JOHNS

Oakland, Calif.

Feb. 22, 1899

Dear sir:—

Pardon my not sending postal acknowledging receipt of MS. You see, the same did not arrive till the last mail, and I am replying at once. "Charge it to the Company" or "Buzzard & Co.," would make fair titles to your story. I would prefer the first; yet I think you could cudgel your brains a little and find still better. But at the outset, it were well I explained the utter impossibility of my rendering a fair judgment on the style of anything, except it be printed or type-written. One standard I can apply to written MS. —that of ear by reading aloud. But my own stuff stands or falls by the eye, by the look of it. Hence, it must be printed or typed. But, in turn, you must understand what I mean when I say judging by the eye. You know, when one first begins to scan or write verse, he unavoidably has recourse to counting on his fingers; but, as he becomes proficient, he gradually and unconsciously gets out of the habit—in the same way, sight gives me the swing and the structure.

But to return: your story is virile, has the smack of rough life and real life about it. Here's what I would recommend: cut out all direct reference to the Norton-Drake Co., and spend another thousand words in making real men out of your Mexicans, who are puppets, and in amplifying the characters of M'Carthy and O'Connel. The last two are real, but make them more so, go into the psychology of it, into the racial delineation a little more. In short, give us a little more of their mental attitudes, temperaments, etc.

It's hard to explain what I mean. Thus, for the Mexicans— Statistics are not emotional, when stated in statistical manner. Don't say the Co. treated the men this way or cheated them that way. Let the reader learn these facts through the minds of the men themselves, let the reader look at the question through their eyes. There are a variety of ways by which to do this—the most common would be to have them talk with each other. Let them carambo' and speak out the bitterness of their hearts, the injustice they suffer or think they suffer from the Co., the hatred they bear their bosses etc., etc. You see what I mean.

Again, put us more in sympathy with M'Carthy. Show us more clearly his sterling qualities which I know you had in your mind at the time. Remember, the reader does not know him; you do. To you, every action of M'Carthy is the action of the M'Carthy you know; to the reader, only of the M'Carthy you have described, etc.

As to Norton-Drake Co., though half the world declaims against them, there are many novels written with a purpose. It is not the legitimate field of such literary productions. A journalistic article (3000 words), expositional and sensational, and not in the form of a story, would be the proper method in attacking and exposing such a company—and it should be done through the columns of the press. You know there is an eternal fitness of things.

Don't mention your Co. or R. R. by name—give them fictitious names, or better still, be wholly abstract. Any fool will be able to read between the lines.

Keep yourself wholly out of the story—I noticed a number of "I"'s.— they jar. Let it be all third person.

Don't permit repetition (it is sometimes allowable, but rarely). P—I—3 Par.—in four words, "waves" appears twice—change to billows, anything else.

(individual taste) following sentence—I should change "and the railroad ran through."

Next sen.—strike out "and" following "cut." You have another in the same period and can afford it.

"Got" is a good solid standby, but you use it too frequently—substitute "been," etc., once in a while.

3 par. P. 3, see if you can duplicate the sentence with any of other modern writers? Too much colon and semicolon. (my op.)

P. 4—would you consider Norton-Drake Co., a singular noun?—if so, shouldn't "have" be "has"?

P. 5—Let the Mexicans speak of the killing of two bosses, as also of facts laid down on previous page. If not colloquially, introduce the reader to the same, still using the attitude, or way of the men's looking at it, for a medium.

P. 6—"But that"—hurts the tongue and ear—possible change: "but a buzzard will return # # #; this is a fact # # #."

P. 6—Strike out "of which we can have no conception"— While you cannot elucidate the why or how, you, in same sentence, you clearly do conceive the possibility of such a thing.

P. 7—3 line—strike out second "that."

Use the relative pronoun "which" for "that," once in a while. There is great latitude allowed in the use of "that," but it may be overstepped.

Your style occasionally reminds me of Bierce.

P. 10—"he knew that he had"—strike out "that."

P. 11—I would not be so ghastly with that intestine, strike out "and hung down" (my taste only, yet I appreciate such things for I have seen much of them).

I like O'Connel's turning, dying, and his last words to M'Carthy;—a true stroke and a strong stroke.

P. 12—how many ribs can a knife pass between?

Some vivid, realistic work in "the living half of the ghastly thing squirmed, etc." The fact of limbs being dead through broken back.

In conclusion: you have powerful material in this tale, strong types, racial contrasts, primal instincts, etc. I would advise rewriting entirely. Try and sway the readers more with sympathy for the actors in the tragedy, etc. Now the tale, as it is, isn't bad; but I advocate this because there are such possibilities in it. I know I have botched the whole thing, that you will mistake what I mean, and swear at me a dozen times for being such an ass, etc. But what would you? I never did any criticising, anyway; so I just say what I think—hence, you gain sincerity of me, if nothing else. If I could talk with you for a few minutes it would all be so much clearer.

Will send this off this mail. "Zebro" goes to-morrow's mail. Oh! one thing —I would advise you to soften your terseness a little, at least to remove an occasional jerky place.

Tender my thanks to your mother[1] for her short note; and tell her I can thoroughly appreciate rush. Agree with you as to "Old Don's Honor,"—I mean "Lucky Find." The former was a good subject, poorly treated—illustrations redeemed it however, in its effect on reader. Thanks for tip to "Western Press"; I have some of my earlier, immature work with them now. Suppose I'll someday call my present work just as immature. I look forward to that day anyway.

Will take advantage of tip to *Vanity Fair*. Yes; I have noticed certain phenomena of pessimism about you. As to foto of myself. You shall be one of a number of friends who wait and wait in vain for a likeness of yours truly. My last posed foto was taken in sailor costume with a Joro girl in Yokohama. Have but one. But I'll do this: tell you all about me. 23 years of age last January. Stand five foot seven or eight in stocking feet—sailor life shortened me. At present time weigh 168 lbs; but readily jump same pretty close to 180 when I take up outdoor life and go to roughing it. Am clean shaven—when I let 'em come, blonde moustache and black whiskers —but they don't come long. Clean face makes my age enigmatical, and equally competent judges variously estimate my age from twenty to thirty. Greenish-grey eyes, heavy brows which meet; brown hair, which, by the way, was black when I was born, then came out during an infantile sickness and returned positively white—so white that my Negress nurse called me "Cotton Ball." Face bronzed through many long-continued liaisons with the sun, though just now, owing to bleaching process of sedentary life, it is positively yellow. Several scars—hiatus of eight front upper teeth, usually disguised with false plate. There I am in toto. Now reciprocate—your age has puzzled me most of all. Sometimes I would feel like placing you at twenty, and other times at forty.

Tell me what you think of enclosed verse, and kindly return—was written a long time ago, but have no outside criticism. Get your mother's criticism too, that is, if she is not too busy. I just dabble in verse occasionally, sort of vacation.

Must shut down if I catch this mail.

Believe me,

Sincerely yours,
Jack London

---

[1]Mrs. Jeanie Peet, writer and sculptress. One time stepmother of Percy MacKaye.

To CLOUDESLEY JOHNS

Oakland, Calif.
Feb. 27, 1899

Dear Sir:—

Since you have taken an interest in my work, I hope you will not be disappointed with my non-appearance in the March number of *The Overland*. The editor has but recently returned from New York, and I had been waiting to see him personally. He has been pleased with my work, and if I can keep up the standard, will handle more.

I cannot express the effect of hearing that what I have written has pleased others, for you know, of all people in the world, the author is the least competent to judge what he produces. At least, such is my opinion. When I have finished a thing I cannot, as a rule, tell whether it is good or trash.

When I first looked over the printed "White Silence," I was sick at heart, felt that it was a most miserable performance, and was heartily ashamed that it had escaped the waste-paper basket. Yet it seems its effect on others was different.

My life has been such a wandering one that there are great gaps in my reading and education, and I am so conscious of them that I am afraid of myself—besides, in the course of a sketch, I become saturated with the theme till at last it palls upon me.

I appreciate, in a way, the high praise of being likened to Tourgenieff. Though aware of the high place he occupies in literature, we are as strangers. I think it was in Japan I read his *House of Gentlefolk;*[1] but that is the only book of his I have ever seen—I do not even know if the title is correct. There is so much good stuff to read and so little time to do it in. It sometimes makes me sad to think of the many hours I have wasted over mediocre works, simply for want of better.

I can only thank you for your kindness; it has put new life into me and at the same time placed a few landmarks on the uncharted path the beginner must travel. Would you tell me of the error you mentioned? The compositors made some bad mistakes, the worst being a willful change in the title, and a most jarring one. It was plainly typewritten "To the Man on Trail"; this they printed "To the Man on the Trail." What trail? The thing was abstract.

Yours sincerely,
Jack London

[1] *A Nest of Gentlefolk.*

To Mabel Applegarth

Oakland, Calif.
Feb. 28, 1899

Dear Mabel:—

Yours came to hand not half an hour ago. Am very sorry to hear of Ted's illness, and I can appreciate just about how well worn out everyone is. Now as to my coming down. If absolutely necessary, telegraph, and I will be there. Yet much as I would like to, my hands are so full and there is so much to be done, that I could not be just to my family and myself did I come when it was not absolutely necessary. You know how we are living from hand to mouth, nothing coming in except what is earned, even yet much of my stuff is in pawn and bills running galore.

And I wish to turn out some good work in this coming month, for I expect a call from the Post Office in April if not sooner. As to the good work—I will explain. James Howard Bridge, Editor of the *Overland,* has at last returned. He at once sent for me. I went last Saturday. This is the essence of our conversation:

While advising the majority of candidates for the magazine field to seek other pursuits, he would not do so in my case. I showed the proper touch, only needing bringing out. Different people had been asking about me, Sunday Editors of the *Examiner,* etc. He had bought the Feb. *Overland* on the train West, and was quite taken with my "White Silence." Said it was the most powerful thing which had appeared in the magazine for a year; but he was afraid it was a fluke and perhaps it would be impossible for me to repeat it, etc. Now to his proposition. The *Overland* prints forty pages of advertisements at thirty dollars per page, while *McClure's* prints one hundred pages at three hundred dollars per page; yet printing, plates, paper, mail service, etc., cost just as much for the *Overland.* The only thing the *Overland* could scale down was the writers, and these it had to. While not in position to pay me well, he thought he could give me most valuable returns for my work. If I sustained the promise I had given, he would give me a prominent place in the pages of his magazine, see that the newspapers, reviews, etc., puffed me, and inaugurate a boom to put my name before the public. You can readily see how valuable this would be—putting future employment into my hands from publications which could afford to pay well. Yet the best he could do would be $7.50 per sketch. It would take too long to go over all we said. I may be called over again any day.

You understand my position, I hope; yet frankly, should it be necessary you know you can call upon me. As I expect it to rain this week, the roads will be impassable and I will have to have recourse to Ferry to Alviso.

Had to laugh on hearing you had not seen my letter to Ted, and that your mother had read it to him. I wonder if she read it verbatim. There were some rather stiff things in it, not personal, but stiff for a woman to read to a man as coming from a third party.

From what I have told you above, you may see that things are brightening, only as yet in the future. I may not fulfill expectations, break down, and have to still further develop before I come out; and if I do not, even present success is a matter of much waiting. Enclosed letter from Cloudesley Johns, return with what you think of it. Don't think I've got the swellhead. I was sick at heart when I read printed "White Silence," and I yet fail to see anything in it. Give my regards to all, not excepting a good share to yourself, and believe me ready to come if you cannot get along without me.

Jack

To Cloudesley Johns

Oakland, Calif.
Mar. 7, 1899

My dear sir:—

How I appreciate your complaining of your friends when they say of your work, "Splendid, "Excellent," etc. That was my one great trouble. The farther I wandered from the beaten track, (I mean the proper trend of modern style and literary art), the more encomiums were heaped upon me —by my friends. And believe me, the darkness I strayed into was heartbreaking. Surely, I have since thought, they must have seen where I was blind. So I grew to distrust them, and one day, between four and five months ago, awoke to the fact that I was all wrong. Everything crumbled away, and I started, from the beginning, to learn all over again. At first I was completely lost—had no conception even of the relative values of the comma, colon, and semicolon. Since then have been digging.

Just previous to your letter I ran across "The Voice of the Juice" in a heap of old magazines. Was struck with it at the time. Did not see the "Celestial Crime," but the "Glen Echo Mystery" was a most miserable affair. Have never read any of Morrow's work. But I do join with you, and heartily, in admiration of Robert Louis Stevenson. What an example he was of application and self development! As a storyteller there isn't his equal; the same might almost be said of his essays. While the fascination of his other works is simply irresistible, to me, the most powerful of all is his "Ebb Tide." There is no comparison possible between him and that other wonderful countryman of his; there is no common norm by which we may judge them. And I see I do not share with you in my admiration of Kipling. He touches the soul of things. "He draws the Thing as he sees it for the God of Things as they Are." It were useless for me to mention all my favorites of his; let one example suffice. "The Song of the Banjo," and just one line from it. Away in the wilderness where younger sons are striving for hearth and saddle of their own, the banjo is singing, reminding them of the world from which they are exiled.

> "........ ... confess;
> I am torture, I am town, I am all that ever went
> with evening dress!"

How often, a thousand miles beyond the bounds of civilization, thirsting for a woman's face, a daily paper, a good book, or better music,—sick for the charms of the old life—have I had that line recalled by the tumpy tum of a banjo, epitomizing the whole mood.

> "I am torture, I am town, I am all that ever went with
> evening dress!"

How prosaic and lame my explanation of it seems; it's a feeling, only to be understood by one who has undergone.

No; I appreciate how educating my roving has been. At the same time I am sorry that my years could not have been condensed in some magic way, so as to have introduced an equal amount of the scholar's life. That's the trouble of having one's nature dominated by conflicting impulses.

O yes; I have children constantly footing it to the "silent sullen peoples" who run the magazines! The *Overland* has taken a fancy to my Northland tales. My experience with them has been prompt publication; but their pay is small—especially at first. "The Son of the Wolf" was sent to them a week ago; they will have it out in the April number, if possible, illustrated by Dixon. I have seen some of his Indian work and think he's just the man for my types; but I do not know him.

Speaking of the *Black Cat;* sometime since, they accepted a pseudo-scientific tale from me. I want to warn you, in case it comes out in the next year or so, that it was written several years ago—so you will forgive it. I hardly remember what it is like. The title is enough—"By a Thousand Deaths."

Another friend made the same criticism of "sole speck of life." I was saturated with my thought—on the relation of the soul to infinity, etc.—was dealing with the soul of Malemute Kid and did not at the time recognize the dogs. Such slips are liable, since, like you, I can't revise manuscript. My favorite method of composition is to write from fifty to three hundred words, then type it in the Ms. to be submitted. Whatever emendations are made, are put in in the course of typing or inserted with ink in the Ms. I may learn the lapidary's art some day. Have at last learned to compose first, to the very conclusion, before touching pen to paper. I find I can thus do better work.

I have not seen any of your work, nor your mother's either—have done very little reading in the last several years. But I would like to see some. Could you send me some: I can easily return should you have no duplicates. And I warn you, I am as harsh on others as I expect them to be on me. This primrose dalliance among friends never leads anywhere. I once had a friend[1]—we went to college and did much of our studying together —with whom we could candidly discuss each other, holding back nothing. But he lies dead in Manila now. Yet once in a while even he got angry when I expressed my opinion too plainly.

Happened to have the December *Land of Sunshine*. Looked at Mary Hallock Foote's[2] story and saw the mistake you mentioned. Do they pay well? Kind of hard the way they hold a fellow's work back!

How are you off for humor? To save my life, while I can appreciate extremely well, I cannot develop a creative faculty for the same. Am starting out in a few minutes for a run to San Jose on my wheel; expect to stay over two or three days. So pardon abrupt close,

Sincerely yours,
Jack London

[1]Fred Jacobs, who, as an enlisted man during the Spanish-American War, died on a transport en route to Manila.
[2]Author of *Led-Horse Claim*.

21

To Cloudesley Johns

Oakland, Calif.
Mar. 15, 1899

Dear Sir:—

I see I have mistaken your name—an illustration of my habitual care-lessness. Shall not occur again. I agree with you that R. L. S. never turned out a foot of polished trash, and that Kipling has; but—well, Stevenson never had to worry about ways or means, while Kipling, a mere journalist, hurt himself by having to seek present sales rather than posthumous fame. Stevenson received from his people 93 pounds, I believe, per year. Think of it! forty dollars a month, with no one to care for but himself, and in a country where that forty dollars was equal in purchasing power to nearly eighty, here.

How those lines, prefacing one of K's tales, have haunted me!

> O Thou who hast builded the world!
> O Thou who hast lighted the sun!
> O Thou who hast darkened the Tarn!
>   Judge Thou
> The sin of the Stone that was hurled
> By the Goat from the light of the Sun,
> As She sinks in the mire of the Tarn,
>   Even now—even now—even now!

Kipling has his hand upon the "fatted soul of things."

Speaking of humor—find enclosed triolets, the first, and also the last, I ever attempted. Perhaps there's no market for such things. *Judge* and *Life* refused them, and I quit.[1]

So you have completed a novel? Lucky dog! How I envy you! I have only got from ten to twenty mapped out, but God knows when I'll ever get a chance to begin one, much less finish it. I have figured that it is easier to make one of from thirty-five to sixty thousand words and well written, than one three or four times as long and poorly written. What do you think about it? Tell me about yours, how long it is, theme, etc.

Last November I spent a couple of hours over the last ten or twelve num-bers of *Short Stories*. Of all I went through, there is only one I can remem-ber anything about. I skimmed through most, skipped many, and only read those which attracted. The one I recollect, I think must be that of your mother's. I don't know, now, what drew me to it, but anyway I read it. Doesn't it deal with a great wood-chopping peasant with an airy fairy crea-ture of a wife, and situated in France somewhere at the close of the Hun-dred Years' War? Do not remember the divisions you mention as having been mangled by the editor, so I may be mistaken. The contrast of the man and wife and their love was well done, and the touch about the children which might have come was most pathetic—gave me the shivery sensation at the base of the spine, which is always mine when deeply touched or stirred. If that was not your mother's, and you have read it, you will surely remember it.

As you say, "Zebro" is not bad of its kind. The one trouble is that the literature of the times demands so much of that kind. It has unity, and the part of Zebro is well simulated. Interest is sustained, and I doubt if very many would anticipate. Am afraid I am hypercritical on this last point. Have worried so about being anticipated myself, that I always, self-consciously, set myself down to discover a writer's point in advance. I'll wager you can handle the same thing far better to-day. Still, you threw in a few hints of atmosphere, and how many things do we read which are totally devoid of that essential?

By the way, should you happen to have no duplicate you will wish it returned. Let me know. I like to be in possession of everything of my own— a sort of crystallization of one's labor, very pleasant to contemplate. Now that you speak of it, I remember "The Ape, the Idiot and Other People"— had forgotten author. No; I shall not go into *Century* Competition. Am not a grad. Left in my Sophomore year for Klondike, and don't think I shall ever return. Struck the following some time ago:

"Now!" cried the reviewers, "here is a pedestal for you—up you go!"

"Gentlemen," blubbered Patient Merit, "you are too kind!—but help me up."

"And they helped him up!"

"And when he was well posed they proceeded to throw potsherds at him."

Very sincerely,
Jack London

---

[1]London kept a record of the materials that he submitted to magazines which he called *Magazine Sales Record*. There are four notebooks. No. 1 covered Sept., 1898 to May, 1900; No. 2, May, 1900 to Feb., 1903; No. 3, Feb., 1903 to Feb., 1909; No. 4, May, 1909 to his death. According to his *Magazine Sales No. 1,* London wrote four "triolets," entitled "He Chortled with Glee," "Just Over the Way," "When He Came In," and "Trying to Miss His Trip to Hades." Altogether the four were submitted to eighteen different publishers between January 23, 1899 and April, 1900. *Town Topics* published "He Chortled with Glee," April 20, 1899, and "When He Came In," April 26, 1900. He records that he received one dollar for the first. It may be assumed that he received the same amount for the second.

To Cloudesley Johns

Oakland, Calif.
Mar. 30, 1899

My dear friend:—

Three or four months on the edge of the desert, all alone—how I envy you; and again, how I thank heaven I am not in a similar position. What a glorious place it must be in which to write: That's one of the drawbacks of my present quarters. Everybody comes dropping in, and I haven't the heart to turn them away. Every once in a while, some old shipmate turns up. With but one exception, this is their story: just returned from a long voyage; what a wonderful fellow Jack London is; what a good comrade he always was; never liked anybody in all the world so much; have a barrel of curios aboard which will bring over in a couple of days for a present; big payday coming; expect to get paid off to-morrow—"Say, Jack old boy, can you lend us a couple of dollars till to-morrow?" That's the way they always wind up. And then I scale them down about half, give them the money and let them go. Some I never hear from again; others come back the third and fourth time.

But I have the fatal gift of making friends without exertion. And they never forget me. Of course they are not of the above calibre; but I'd just as soon give them the money and let them go, as to have them eat up my time as they always do. Among my feminine friends I am known as "only Jack." 'Nough said. Any trouble, tangles, etc., finds me called upon to straighten out. Since Saturday morning I have spent my whole time for one of them, and have accomplished what she and her friends failed to do in five years. This evening I shall finally settle the whole thing to her satisfaction;—but look at the time I have lost. Of course, remuneration is out of the question; but it will have so endeared me to her, that she'll call again the next time she gets into a scrape. And so it goes—time—time—time. How precious the hours are!

But I should not be unjust. The other afternoon I met an old friend on the car. Delighted to see me; must go back to the "society" again. I finally promised to go down the following night; but lo, he had spread the news among other friends who had not seen me for two long years. I really did not think they or people in general ever had cared so much for me, and I was ready to weep with sheer happiness at the sincerity of their delight on again seeing me. Couldn't escape; the whole night was lost among them; supper had been ordered, other forgotten friends invited; etc.

And to me, the strangest part is, that while considering myself blessed above all with the best of friends, I know that I have never done anything to deserve them or to hold them. Mind you the crowd I have reference to in previous paragraph, has never received a favor of me, nor is bound to me by the slightest social, racial, or perhaps intellectual tie. And so it goes.

But I have been isolated so much, that I can no longer bear to be torn away for long at a time from the city life. In this particular you will see thankfulness at not filling your position. Yet you may keep in touch with the world with those trains ever passing.

I suppose you see many of the genus hobo, do you not? I, too, was a tramp once, and beat my way by the most approved methods from Ocean to Ocean, begging my meals from door to door. I remember, one night, leaving a swell function in Michigan and crossing the Lake to Chicago. There, the following morning found me hustling at back doors for a breakfast. That night I made over two hundred miles into Ohio before they finally put me off the train. I wonder what the young lady whom I took into supper would have thought, had she seen me anywhere from twelve to twenty-four hours after.

How I chatter—all about self! I hope your sentiments about my criticism have not been disguised; I was prepared for most anything. The story is good; but I am so prone to see what might be done, that I cannot refrain from suggesting. I cannot re-write; but in turn, I write more slowly. I used to go at it like a hurricane, but found I failed to do myself justice, and gradually grew out of the bad habit. After sending criticism, and being reminded by the same of Bierce, I dug up *Soldiers and Civilians*. I notice in his work the total absence of sympathy. They are wonderful in their way, yet owe nothing to grace of style; I might almost characterize them as having a metallic intellectual brilliancy. They appeal to the mind, but not the heart. Yes; they appeal to the nerves, too; but you will notice in a psychological and not emotional manner. I am a great admirer of him, by the way, and never tire of his Sunday work in the *Examiner*.

Quite an encouraging letter, that of the Western Press. It is evident your work has struck them. Would like to read said article. Pity their pay is so small; but you may, like many another, realize more on the work when collected and presented to the public between covers. What field (I mean what papers) does that Syndicate cover?

It's very kind of you to surrender the western leadership to me; no more do I deserve it; our styles, methods, etc., are so utterly different, that such procedure would be absurd. But we shall do like Antony and Octavian—divide the world between us. What say you? I must confess your letters are refreshing, have a smack of personality, and a unique personality, about them. You at least would not be lost in the common herd. A strong will can accomplish anything—I believe you to be possessed of the same—why not form the habit of studying? There is no such thing as inspiration, and very little of genius. Dig, blooming under opportunity, results in what appears to be the former, and certainly makes possible the development of what original modicum of the latter which one may possess. Dig is a wonderful thing, and will move more mountains than faith ever dreamed of. In fact, dig should be the legitimate father of all self-faith.

Thanks for criticism of poem—merely an experiment, you know. However, I don't exactly agree with you about "absurd." I know the technical accent is on the second syllable, while the accent of either syllable is really indistinguishable as to importance. It was not till after I had completed it that I noticed the debt owing to Omar Kayam [*sic*]. And by the way, what do you think of Le Gallienne:[1] As a writer, I like him. As a man, I have no respect for him, dislike him; yet I know nothing about him as a man. Perhaps it's the ideas I got of the man, Le Gallienne, from reading his work. In his version of the "Rubaiyat," I was especially struck by the following, describing his search for the secret of life:

> "Up, up where Parrius' hoofs stamp heaven's floor,
> My soul went knocking at each starry door,
> Till on the stilly top of heaven's stair,
> Clear-eyed I looked—and laughed—and climbed no more."

But I prefer Fitzgerald's.

It is well you appreciate the virtue in lack of wealth, and you seem to be all the better for it. Here's what wealth would have done for me: it would have turned me into a prince of good fellows, and, barring accidents, would have killed me of strong drink before I was thirty.

We are at one in many things. I, too, have worked like a horse, and eat like an ox; but as to the work—while no comrade can ever say Jack London shirked in the slightest, I hate the very thought of thus wasting my time. It's so deadening—I mean hard labor. We agree as to aversion to getting married; but not so as to women one might link oneself to for life. I am sure I have met a thousand such. As passionate as you, with probably less curb, I think I must have been created for some polygamous country. While I have a strong will, I deliberately withhold it when it happens to clash with desire. I simply refuse to draw the curb. When I was just sixteen I broke loose and went off on my own hook.[2] Took unto myself a mistress of the same age, lived a year of wildest risk in which I made more money in one week than I do in a year now, and then, to escape the inevitable downward drift, broke away from everything and went to sea.[3] My one great weakness is the study of human nature. Knowing no God, I have made of man my worship; and surely I have learned how vile he can be. But this only strengthens my regard, because it enhances the mighty heights he can bring himself to tread. How small he is, and how great he is! But this weakness, this desire to come in touch with every strange soul I meet, has caused me many a scrape.

I may go to Paris in 1900; but great things must occur first. I liked the story you sent. No sentimental gush, no hysteria, but the innate pathos of it! Who could not feel for Mrs. Anerton? Our magazines are so goody-goody, that I wonder they would print a thing as risque and as good as that. This undue care to not bring the blush to the virgin cheek of the American young girl, is disgusting. And yet she is permitted to read the daily papers!

Ever read Paul Bourget's comparison of the American and French young women?

Excuse poor typing, for I get seated and rattle it off. Don't take the care with correspondence as I do with regular composition.

Yours sincerely,

Jack London

[1]Richard Le Gallienne, a contemporary English journalist, essayist, poet, novelist. Father of Eva Le Gallienne.
[2]A reference to his oyster pirating. He bought the *Razzle Dazzle* from French Frank and when he took possession he found French Frank's girl had remained aboard.
[3]Reference to his voyage on the sealing vessel the *Sophie Sutherland*.

To CLOUDESLEY JOHNS

Oakland, Calif.
April 17, 1899

My dear friend:—

Am afraid you will suffer offense every time I write to you. I never wrote a letter yet without forcing myself to it, and I never completed one without sighing a great sigh of relief. As a correspondent I shall never shine. But O how dearly I love to read the letters which come to me from those who little know how I dislike answering. And I never would answer, did I not know they would also cease. I like to write business letters of from one to six lines —can turn so many out in the course of half an hour, you know. Lassalle, the brilliant German Jew, friend to Bismarck and mainly responsible for the latter's State Socialism,—well, Lassalle made and maintained a rule that even his most favored correspondent must write him twice for his once. He broke with one of his best friends because that friend refused to yield to the imposition. And I don't blame the friend; at the same time I envy Lassalle the result of his nerve.

You will notice "The City of the Dreadful Night." He wrote a later article under that title, discarding the first. It is very powerful, if I recollect correctly, for I read it a number of years ago. I have sought it often since, but always vainly. I see you are opposed to Jingoism. Yet I dare not express my views, for to so do myself adequate justice, would require at least one hundred thousand words. An Evolutionist, believing in Natural Selection, half believing Malthus' "Law of Population," and a myriad of other factors thrown in, I cannot but hail as unavoidable, the Black and the Brown going down before the White.

I see, after stating that I would not express my views, I have done the contrary. Will shut up at once.

Have you ever done anything with the San Francisco *Argonaut?* I see most of the stuff they print (usually an original short story each week), (2000 to 3500 words), is after your method, as exemplified in "Zebro" and "The Norton-Drake." Have never sent them any of my stuff, deeming it utterly different from what they required.[1]

27

Town Topics has accepted a two eight-line stanza humorous fancy.[2] Have you ever dealt with them? What do they pay?

So you grow a-weary of the social whirl. Ditto here—only because it eats up so much time. To satisfy my various sides I should be possessed of at least a dozen astral selves, and even then my composite self would be well worked out. Temporary embarrassment led me into hypothecating my dress suit some months ago. You have no idea how easy it is to decline invitations after doing a thing like that. I think I shall allow it to remain, though I greatly fear it may be constantly rented out at so much per night. Most likely it was luckier than its master and shone with 'Frisco's swelldom at the late seismic disturbance—commonly known as the grand opera. Well, if mine uncle does that, it at least will not suffer from moths.

What an acerbitous tongue, or rather, pen, you have in handling topics such as the Virginia Fair and Vanderbilt foregathering. I greatly enjoy it, and have taken the liberty to read certain portions of the same to friends. I mean of your letters. The Fair-Vanderbilt, of course, in its entirety.

What a delightful, fascinating woman, the mother of Ab must have been. Find enclosed review of Gertrude Atherton's *Daughter of the Vine*. I see the current *Argonaut* half intimates that it's a sort of free version of some tale published in their columns some years ago. Enjoyed your "April" and "May"—nearly wore it out by carrying around in my pocket. You've a most virile swing to it.

And you are a man who writes jokes, who has written jokes—a real live man! Well, well. I used to think the joke writer a fictitious personage, a sort of solar myth. I once wrote a joke and sent it the rounds—it must have been a very poor joke. Now that the joke writer is a flesh and blood contemporary, I shall write another and start it off.[3] By the way, to satisfy a curious mortal, what was the "Four-in-hand" worth? "Sam Davis has dropped the Pen for the Toga"—was it published in the *Examiner?* May I know what they paid for it? And may I retain it a week longer to send to a friend? I see the last is supererogatory—I shall have to retain it. From "The Trust Magnate," I imagine we come together somewhat on our political and economic views.

James Creelman has been branded for some time as an autotheist of the most pronounced type. Enclosed cable from him was published in the *Examiner*. A couple nights later it was parodied by a *Bulletin* reporter. I thought the latter neat.

I concede that a natural proficiency is requisite, but add that not one in a hundred will develop without the requisite dig and plenty of it. I like those four lines from Chas. Holt, the infallible rover poet. Too bad such men are not more plastic. I was once shipmates with a Holt. He was drowned with all hands the following year, and I just missed being with them by a miracle.

I differ from you. I honestly can't think of an enemy I possess on either side of the grave. Yet I am very prone to read the law in unmistakable terms, and on occasion, have thrashed the very best of my friends. But in the latter case, only did it when they needed it very badly; and believe me, it always did them good, and made our friendship the better. But enemies—bah! There is no necessity. Lick a man, when it comes to the pinch, or be licked, but never hold a grudge. Settle it for once and all, and forgive.

All my life I have sought an ideal chum—such things as ideals are never attainable, anyway. I never found the man in whom the elements were so mixed that he could satisfy, or come anywhere near satisfying my ideal. A brilliant brain—good; and then the same united with physical cowardice—nit. And vice versa. So it goes and has gone. From what I have learned of you, you approach as nearly as any I have met. But, personality, as reflected by pen and paper, and personality face to face, are two very different things. But I imagine you to have the two main things I have sought.

We agree as to Le Gallienne—pray tell me how you reached your conclusions—I can't for the life of me see how I gained mine.

Next letter shall send you "A Look into the Gulf," by Markham, father of "Man with the Hoe." Bierce considers it genuine poetry, while he characterizes Man with hoe as sand-lot-ism. Don't agree with him. The look into the gulf is excellent. It is away to a friend just now.

It's a great thing, this coming to believe "that the universe can continue to exist and operate in a satisfactory manner, without the perpetuation of one's own individuality." I am an agnostic, with one exception: I do believe in the soul. But in the latter case, I can only see with death, the disintegration of the spirit's individuality, similar to that of the flesh. If people could come to realize the utter absurdity, logically, of the finite contemplating the infinite!

I realize the truth in your criticism of ringing the changes on Malemute Kid, but I had started out with that intention, and made arrangements with the *Overland* accordingly. But you will notice in the "Son of the Wolf" that he appears only cursorily. In the June tale he will not appear at all, or even be mentioned. You surprise me with the aptness of your warning, telling me I may learn to love him too well myself. I am afraid I am rather stuck on him—not on the one in print, but the one in my brain. I doubt if I ever shall get him in print. Your criticism is so true that I shall be delighted to not debate the question with you.

Several technical mistakes in "The Improved Exit." Which is neither here nor there, as Kipling would say. No; they did not go all the way to Klondike for salmon; but it was an important factor to existence to such as lived in the country—especially was it fed to the dogs through the long winters. The salmon run two and three thousand miles up the Yukon and its tributaries to spawn—finest salmon in the world. They are so exhausted by the long trip that they never get back to salt water again, dying in the fall as the river freezes up. They are so thick on some of the tributaries, and the bears come to feed upon them in such quantities that Indians shun such spots, as not being conducive to long life. In summertime, the dogs are worthless as far as sledding goes; so they turn them loose to shift for themselves. They make good livings and get fat, fishing for the salmon. They are very intelligent.

Don't agree with you regarding your criticism of face torn away by bear.

Had forgotten Kipling's "Truce," but anyway it does not matter. Many men are killed yearly, up there, and many more fearfully mangled. If we should allow the successful men to copyright any topic they once happen to camp upon, what the devil would you and I and a very numerous tribe do? Thanks for yellow flag. Don't think I can turn away my friends so easily. Happened to mention in similar postals to yours that I was sick and busy, and at once received a couple of offers to come and take care of me, read to me, etc. Say! I answered very next mail, for fear they would not wait and come anyway.

How can I thank your mother for her criticism of my effusion. You see I am experimenting along those lines, and a blazed trail or a guide will save many mistakes. It was just what I needed. I shall certainly cut out last stanza, altogether, and remodel the penultimate one so that it will become the finish. Shall also, some day when the mood is on me, change the whole thing as per criticism. I can no more say how valuable your mother's advice was than can I thank her for it. It was very, very kind of her, to say the least.

I return hers to you—what a fascinating letter she writes!

Dead wall? Who doesn't strike dead walls? I have spent a day at a time, and then quit, with absolutely nothing to show. Don't believe in writing rapidly any more. Write a tenth as much and strive to make it ten times as good.

Ran across these lines of Helen Hunt Jackson, have been haunting me ever since.

> "His thoughts were song, his life was singing,
>   Men's hearts like harps he held and smote,
> But ever in his heart went ringing,
>   Ringing the song he never wrote."

Remember "Tragedy of the Muse"? also letter with superscription of "dear you"? A very interesting woman who writes me regularly, began to use that phrase on me. And I was struck by it, and appropriated it. She also had read aforementioned tale and drawn it from that source.

O, if you only saw the pile of letters I must answer after this! They've been piling up for ten days.

I know I have forgotten something, but will have to let it slide.

Yours, as ever, sincerely,

Jack London

[1]Here is an inconsistency between his letter and his *M. S. 1*. According to the latter he submitted "The Way of War" to *Argonaut* on Feb. 27, 1899. It was rejected, and subsequently sent to sixteen journals, the last one being *The Boston Globe*, Nov. 15, 1899. It was then marked "Retired."
[2]The poem "If I Were God One Hour" was published in *Town Topics*, May 11, 1899.
[3]His *M. S. 1* shows that six jokes were sent to magazines. After six rejections *Town Topics* published "Egg without Salt" Joke No. 1, Aug. 15, 1899. He received fifty cents for it.

To Cloudesley Johns

Oakland, Calif.
April 22, 1899

My dear friend:—

Not to be thought of. When such time comes that I think I require two for one, I'll hire a secretary and let him write my alternate letters. I remember "Thomas the Doubter," now. A friend of mine quoted portions of it one night, but I was just dozing off and failed to follow him. It is very good, and how one can, in the face of it, stomach such things as the infinite mercy of the most infinitely merciless of creators, is more than I can understand. Pardon the double superlative—"most infinite." By the way, is "infinite" capable of comparison? And again: your mother was wrong, at least I believe so, concerning "while."
"wile" means a trick, stratagem, seduction, etc.
"while" means to loiter, to cause time to pass away pleasantly and without irksomeness.

"Master of His Fate" is something I have been trying to get hold of for a long while. Of course, philosophically, it is but part true; but it is often better to cast out such considerations when dealing with such subjects in any other save a philosophical way. I see, from present selections, that you enjoy tilting against the established theology.

Have you read *Cyrano de Bergerac?* I saw it ably staged last year, and have a pirated edition of it. I was greatly taken with it, and if you have not read it, and would care to, I'll send it down. What say? Shall retain selections till next I write you, as I wish to take off a couple of them.

I sometimes fear that, while I shall surely develop expression some day, I lack in origination. Perhaps this feeling is due to the fact that almost every field under the sun, and over it too, has been so thoroughly exploited by others. Sometimes I hit upon a catchy title, and just as sure as I do I find someone else has already used it. Which reminds me of a talented young fellow I met in the Klondike. Several of his librettos are running at the present time. He told me that his first opera was named *La Sonambula* and he speedily discovered that over a hundred others had been composed with similar titles. Then he composed one, *The Juke-Jukes,* only to be informed that several portions were direct infringements of portions of operas already staged. They offered to stage it at a cost of not less than twenty thousand, if he would make the requisite alterations, but he refused. I don't know what has happened to the same since. But so it goes. Look at the meters other men have rendered classic, and thus debarred the coming generations from for all time. What would happen to you or I, should we compose an epic in the measure of "Hiawatha"? And pray, where in the devil are we to originate new schools of fiction?

Did you ever notice that typewriting was not conducive to good letter-writing? "The Gila Monster" smacks of just the flavor of most of the stories I see in the *Argonaut*. And some of them are very clever. From the way you remark on *Town Topics* it is evident you have had an experience with them. Tell us about it. I forgot to say that they had also taken triolet, "He chortled with glee." Guess I won't bother with any more of such work. Too much strain for such small returns. The only reason I ever venture such things is a desire to practice up thinking in meter. And the more rigid or more intricate structures are good training.

Ha! ha! You demand comfort in place of conventionality, eh? Ditto here. To-morrow I shall put on a white shirt, and I shall do it under protest. I wear a sweater most of the time, and pay calls, etc., in a bicycle suit. My friends have passed through the stage of being shocked, and no matter what I should do henceforth, would, I know, remark "It's only Jack." I once rode a saddle horse from Fresno to the Yosemite Valley, clad in almost tropical nudity, with a ballroom fan and a silk parasol. It was amusing to witness the countryside turn out as I went along. Some of my party who lagged behind heard guesses hazarded as to whether I was male or female. The women of the party were tenderly nurtured, and I hardly know if they have recovered yet, or if their proprieties rather have yet come down to normal. In fact, there was only one I failed to disturb, and he was the rugged old Chinese cook—nothing shocked him except the Mariposa Big Trees. Coming unexpectedly upon the first one, he could not conceal his astonishment, but blurted forth "Gee Klist! Chop'm up four foot ties, make'm one dam railroad!" After we arrived in the Valley he stayed in camp—he was rather set in his ideas, and considered the natural phenomena as innovations which should not be countenanced for a moment.

As to evening dress, I think many a man looks extremely well in it. Of course, not all by a large majority. I like that clean feeling of well fitting clothes, etc.—which is strange for one who has passed through as many dirty periods as I have. But there are very few women I care to see in decollete (or however you spell it). As to the breeding of cripples—I shall try to get something uncompressed before marrying, and then, if I have to take her off to a desert isle, I'll see that no compression goes on while she is carrying any flesh and bone of mine. Barrenness is a terrible thing for a woman; but the paternal instinct is so strong in me that it would almost kill me to be the father of a child not physically or mentally sound. Sometimes I think, because this is so very strong in me, that I am destined to die childless. I can understand a Napoleon divorcing a Josephine, even casting aside state reasons. At the same time, I could not do likewise under similar circumstances. I can condone in others what I haven't the heart, or have too much heart to do myself.

How one wanders on!

"Carvajal the Thorough" was good. If I am correct, Markham will never see forty-five again. He became a father about two weeks and a half ago.

I send his "Look into the Gulf." To me it is a wonderful piece of work. Tell us what you think of it; keep it as long as you wish; but, don't fail to send it back in the end.

I also send you some of my schoolboy work. Stuff written years ago. I found it accidentally, to-day, rummaging through an old trunk down in the basement. I had not seen it in years, and had forgotten its very existence. It is but a modicum of what I wrote during that period, but is fairly representative. Through reading it you may gain a comprehension of one of my many sides, though of course you must take into consideration my youth at the time of writing, if you should try to weigh my presentation of the subjects in hand. People thought I would outgrow that condition and fall back into the conservative way of thinking. I am happy to say they were mistaken. But believe me, while a radical, I am not fanatical; nor am I anything but normal, and fallible, in all affairs of reason. Emotion is quite another matter. The trouble is so few understand Socialism or its advocates. But I shall cut this short, else I will be delivering a diatribe on the dismal science.

I see Edith Wharton, writer of the "Tragedy of the Muse," is just bringing out a volume of short stories in which that piece figures—Scribners, I think are the publishers. How the short story is growing in importance in modern literature! It almost seems the novel is destined to become extinct within a generation or two. I envy you your abnormal memory. I grasp easily, but memorize only in a fairly average sort of way. I am sure there are thousands of books I have read, the very titles of which are forgotten.

There is only one kind of infallibility that I can tolerate, nay, I can enjoy it, and that is the infallibility of the goodnatured fool. As for cowardice in man: I can forgive the errors of a generation of women far more easily than one poltroon of the opposite gender.—

> "In the fell clutch of circumstance
> I have not winced nor cried aloud,
> Under the bludgeoning of chance
> My head is bloody, but unbowed."

Such, in all things, is what I admire in men. The "fine frenzy" of the poet can arouse no greater number of tingles along my spine than a Captain going down on the bridge with his ship; the leading of a forlorn hope; or even a criminal who puts up a plucky fight against overwhelming odds. Perhaps that is why I can have no regard for men of Richard Le Gallienne's ilk. Virility in a man, first and always. Say what you will, I love that magnificent scoundrel, Rupert of Hentzau. And a man who can take a blow or insult unmoved, without retaliating—Paugh!—I care not if he can voice the sublimest sentiments, I sicken.

To me, the "Sea of Serenity" looks like a job. Markham received a somewhat similar boom about the time he brought out "The Man with the Hoe," but it happened in his case that he richly deserved it. Take for instance:

> "Slave of the wheel of labor, what to him
> Are Plato and the swing of Pleiades?
> What the long reaches of the peaks of song—
> Rebuild in it the music and the dream, etc."

I send with this, Fawcett's[1] "Anarchy," which same return. It is very powerful. "Summer in Arcady": isn't it in that that the young college fellow who had returned to the farm, gets the best of the girl and immediately marries her? I read it a long while ago, and know it to be one of Allen's.[2] Have not read "Old King Solomon's Coronation." Will look it up. As to "The thousand Lines" really, while appreciating your kindness, I cannot find it possible to tackle it. To tell you the truth, I don't feel able to; have often thought about trying such work, and as often said "Some day." And I am spending so much time, just now, reading up my history, that I couldn't sandwich the time in which to study up that, and in my case it would require an immense amount of reading, for I am awfully shaky on such things; besides, I am going through Shelley, just now, with a young lady who has an insatiable thirst for things English. Have never thought of my favorite short story—think I would have to make up a list of my "hundred best." And now, in a most unsatisfactory, crowded way, good night, or rather, good morning.

Jack London

---

[1]May refer to Edgar Fawcett, 1847-1904, novelist, poet, playwright, essayist.
[2]James Lane Allen, 1849-1925.

To CLOUDESLEY JOHNS

Oakland, Calif.
April 30, 1899

My dear friend:—

My turn to be charged with blunders. For one who uses Uncle Sam's mails as I do, such ignorance is inexcusable, but to tell the truth, I did not think more than one cent was demanded on the magazine which caused you so much trouble. For that matter, I suppose you have paid postage due on more than one letter of mine? Let us know if you have.

Your several poetical selections have been loaned to a lady friend, so I shall have to still further delay return. Yes; I like the form of refusal you sent me. Here you will find a couple I received the middle of this week. Disagree with both as a matter of course. Can't see any other ending, in the nature of things, to the *McClure* Ms., While *Frank Leslie's*—well, that poor young American girl who mustn't be shocked, nor receive anything less insipid than mare's milk—she seems to rule our destinies. Please return, also Kipling's "For to Admire."

Another case of anticipation, Holt's "Quantum Mutatus." I have been storing away ideas for some months now, for a reply to "O Why Should the Spirit of Mortal Be Proud," and only waiting a little better knowledge of poesy before attempting it.

Those Humors of the composing-room were great, [and] many a hearty laugh have they caused since coming into my possession. Your idea concerning the plot of a story taking a minor place, may apply, in part, to *McClure's* criticism—that is, they wanted more action and a final event to what was really a spirited or very strong sketch. As for *Munsey* and the rest of that ilk, they must really know how vicious their action is in calling for the stories they do.

I can't agree with you regarding *Cyrano*. Perhaps it is because I have seen it staged, but I think the ending is logical, well done, and most fitting. That last scene, where he staggers to his feet, crying that he must meet Death still afoot and sword in hand, is to me superb, to the very wind-up, where he doffs his casque in Christ's fair halls with untarnished plume.

And what effective meters Kipling found! So you like the "Dipsy Chantey"? Ever compared it with his "First Chantey"? I don't remember whether that's its name or not. Are you familiar with his "Lost Legion," beginning:

> "In the legion of the lost ones, in the cohort of the damned,
>   Of his brethren in their sorrows overseas,
> Sings a gentleman of England, cleanly bred, machinely crammed,
>   And a trooper of the Empress if you please."

So you, also, are a socialist? How we are growing! I remember when you could almost count them on one's great toes in Oakland. Job Harriman is considered to be the best popular socialist speaker on the Coast; Austin Lewis the best historical, and [Frank] Strawn-Hamilton the best philosophical. The latter has just gone to his old home in Mississippi, where he remains till December. Then he will go to Washington to fill a private secretaryship under some legislative relative. He spent 48 straight hours with me a couple of days before he went. He has a marvelous brain, one, I think, which could put that of Macaulay's to shame. He has served no less than twenty-nine sentences for vagrancy, to say nothing of the times turned up on trial, in the several years preceding his joining the socialists. As interesting a character in his way as your Holt, who, by the way, I would like to run across. The world is full of such, only the world does not generally know it. But I don't agree with you regarding the death stroke to individuality coming with the change of system.

There will always be leaders, and no man can lead without fighting for his position—leaders in all branches. Sometimes I feel as you do about it, but not for long at a time.

I see we at least agree about courage. A man without courage is to me the most despicable thing under the sun, a travesty on the whole scheme of creation. Have not read "Shrewsbury"—is it good? And who wrote it?

You misunderstood me. It was the very strength of paternal desire, coupled with the perversity of things, which made me feel doubtful of ever realizing it. The things we wish the most for usually pass us by—at least that has been my experience. He who fears death usually dies, unless he is too contemptible, and then the gods suffer him to live on and damn his fellow creatures.

Yes; I would like to see that collection of magazine stories you spoke of. Is there any of the work of Lillian Corbett Barnes in it? I have seen nothing of hers. Has she done much? See Frank Norris has been taken up by *McClures*. Have you read his *Moran of the Lady Letty?* It's well done.

My mother also wishes to be cremated. I think it is the cleanest and healthiest, and best; but somehow, I don't care what becomes of my carcass when I have done with it. As for being buried alive—he's a lucky devil who can die twice, and no matter how severe the pang, it's only for a moment. I am sure the pain of dissolution can be no greater than the moment when the forceps are laid upon a jumping tooth. If it is greater, then it must be stunning in its effect.

Do you remember Robert Louis Stevenson moralizing on death in his *Inland Voyage?* It is a beautiful expansion of "Eat, drink, and be merry, for to-morrow we die."

You asked about the age of Prof. Markham: I saw him down at the Section last Sunday night, when David Starr Jordan spoke on "The Man Who Was Left." He (Markham) is a noble looking man, snow white hair and beard, and very close to sixty. I send you a miserable reporter's account of the meeting, in which nobody or nothing is done justice.

You really must pardon this letter; my mind is dead for the time being. Have been reading a little too heavily. Just as a sample, I shall give you a list of what I am at present working on, to say nothing of three daily papers, and a stagger of an attempt at current literature.

Saint-Amand's *Revolution of 1848*.
Brewster's *Studies in Structure and Style*.
Jordan's *Footnotes to Evolution*.
Tyrell's *Sub-Arctics*.

and Böhm-Bawerk's *Capital and Interest*—this latter is a refutation of Karl Marx's theory of values, as determined or measured by labor. He (Böhm-Bawerk) contends that "final-utility" is the only logical measure of value. Very interesting, I assure you.

36

Good night—by the way, I have forgotten to inform you that an un-
welcome guest has annoyed me all evening, and is now getting ready to
crawl into bed. This has bothered me not a little. He is such a fool. (As soon
sleep with a snake as a man.)

Jack London

To CLOUDESLEY JOHNS

Oakland, Calif.
May 18, 1899

My dear friend:—

Back again at the machine. How one grows to miss it! And you did not
mention my scrawl—said scrawl feels slighted. At last I return clippings of
yours, which have traveled not a little. Find with this, two other selections
from W. E. Henley. Return me "Machine-made Fame" by Bailey Millard.
Keep the rest. Barry Pain's criticism of Kipling and Bierce is very good,
coming, as it does, from an avowed lover of Bierce.

I do most heartily agree with you as regards drowning. My stock
statement is that I should prefer hanging to drowning. From this you may
infer that I, as a strong swimmer, have had some experience. One notable
instance was similar to the one you mention as happening to you: that of
being dragged down by another, who, perhaps, wasn't worth saving. It
happened to me by the dock, with a crowd above but not a boat or boathook
to be had, and the tide very low—twenty feet nearly from the water to the
top of the wharf. I was about sixteen, and the lad I was trying to pull out, a
wharf-rat of about twelve or thirteen. Really, I saw nothing of my past life,
nor beautiful scenes, nor blissful sensations. My whole consciousness was
concentrated upon the struggle, my sensation upon the awful feeling of
suffocation. Another time, I fought a lonely battle in the ocean surf on a
coral beach. Carelessly going in swimming from a sheltered nook, I had
drifted too far out and along the shore, and not having the strength to stem
my way back, was forced to a landing on the open beach. Not a soul in
sight. The seas would swat me onto the beach and jerk me clear again. I'd
dig hand and foot into the sand, but fail to hold. It was a miracle that I
finally did pull out, nearly gone, in a fainting condition, and pounded into
a jelly-like condition.

Another hard struggle was the result of a drunken attempt at suicide—
rather, the chance came my way, and I drunkenly embraced it. I was not
seventeen, yet, in the town of Benecia, midway on the Carquinez Straits,
when it happened. Had been sowing wild; been on a straight drunk for
three weeks, with but few intermittent spaces of partial sobriety. Fell
overboard going aboard a yacht, with the "blues" heavy upon me, and
decided to quit the whole thing There is a terrific current in those Straits
and I went down with the ebb tide. Passing the Solano wharf, where there

were lights and people, I cunningly kept silent so as to avoid rescue. It was past two in the morning. Clear of interruption, I lifted my voice to the stars in my own dirge and quite enjoyed the thought of saying good-bye to the whole works. As you know, it doesn't take much paddling to keep afloat. But the cold water sobered me after a while, and I decided to rescue myself. Undressed and struck out. But went on down the line. As daylight broke, I was in that nasty stretch of water where the Carquinez Straits meet the Straits of Vallejo. And I was about gone, paddling as the man in the *"Black Cat"*[1] paddled, with the land breeze sending each snappy little wave into my mouth. Was still keeping afloat mechanically, when a couple of fishermen from Vallejo picked me up, and can dimly recollect being hauled over the side.

No, drowning is not a pleasant shuffle.

Have not read "Shrewsbury." Have you read Tounsend's "Jimmy Fadden Explains"? If you have not, will send it along when I finish it, which may be quite a little while off. Miriam Michelson, whose "Zojas" I send you, is a space-writer on the *San Francisco Bulletin*. She is a young woman, and is doing some magazine work, besides.

As with you, socialism was evolutionary, though I came to it quite a while ago. You say, "that to retain a leadership one must possess, or acquire, all the virtues which society and politics demand of their favorites—hypocrisy, insincerity, deceit, etc." Robt. Louis Stevenson was a man looked up to, a leader of certain very large classes, in certain very fine ways. I am sure he lacked those virtues. So it would be in all the arts, sciences, professions, sports, etc. Of course, to-day this is already to a certain extent true; but accident of birth (through possibilities of development), and the necessary patronage of wealth, badly mar them. Of course, I realize you mainly applied your statement to politics. But have you ever figured how much of this fawning and low trickery, etc., is due to party politics; and with the removal of party politics and the whole spoils system from the field, cannot you figure a better class of men coming to the fore as political leaders—men, whose sterling qualities to-day prevent them crawling through the muck necessary to attain party chieftainship? It's an endless topic, and were better left alone, being only good when tongues may war unceasingly.

I will give you an idea of the "Lost Legion" from memory, so pardon gaps. The refrain tells the story of gentlemen rankers in India.

> "In the Legion of the Lost Ones, in the cohort of the damned,
>   Of his brethren in their sorrow overseas,
> Sings a gentleman of England, cleanly bred, machinely crammed,
>   And a trooper of the Empress, if you please."
>
> *   *   *   *   *   *   *

How do you like it? Have only given you the complete stanzas which I happened to recollect. There is no end to Kipling, simply no end.

As to the Post Office—I grant red tape, etc., galore; but say, what would it cost me to send a letter to Harold, were the P.O. in the hands of a private corporation?

Though bound to disagree on some points, I can hardly give you to understand how I value your criticism. You have a mind of your own, and you speak your mind. I suffer from a plethora of friends who say "Good," "very good," etc. At least know that I do appreciate. Let me explain my position toward the *Overland*. Last fall I wrote them concerning doing work for them. Was unacquainted with them. Reply was to the effect that they suffered from a press of matter. Sent them anyway, sometime later, a Klondike tale, then a second ("White Silence"), with the proposition of a series. Editor was away. Skipped a month, till one day he sent for me, and arrangements for the series were made. Have not been to the office since, nor seen any of them. So I have to go on with the tales. But, a couple of days prior to reception of yours in which you speak concerning this matter, I wrote *Overland* people, telling them I thought a couple more would finish the series. In reply, they wished me to keep it up. I shall give several more, and then quit. I realize keenly the truth of all that you said, and heartily thank you for the same.

How concisely you analyzed the lack of Unity in the May tale!—a lack of Unity which you may see is recognized in the very title, "The Men of Forty Mile." The sub-heading was not of my doing, as were none of the others. I wonder what you will think of "In a Far Country," which comes out in June number, and which contains no reference to Malemute Kid or any other character which has previously appeared. As I recollect my own judgment of it, it is either bosh, or good; either the worst or the best of the series I have turned out. I shall await your opinion of it with impatience.

I can sympathize with you in your isolation out there on the edge of the desert, deputies non-forthcoming, and teeth waxing clamorous.

Am happy I warned you in advance of the *Black Cat*[1] tale. Yes, rather ponderous verbiage—suffer from that a little and not a very little little, in present work. Apropos of "Thousand Deaths," I enclose the following freak letter which speaks for itself.

Have you read *Prisoner of Zenda?*, and if so, have you read *Rupert of Hentzau,* its sequel? If not, I can send it to you.

We live and learn. With such letters as this, the stereotyped forms of ending have always tortured me. I now comprehend the beauty of yours and make haste to adopt it.

Jack London

---

[1]"A Thousand Deaths," *Black Cat Magazine,* May, 1889. In his Ms. record London says, "first money received for a story from a magazine."

To Cloudesley Johns

Oakland, Calif.
June 7, 1899

Dear friend:—

"If a time came when you should know even the subject of what I should write, then my letters would cease to interest you."

Pray tell me, do you do that often?

I thoroughly appreciated and enjoyed your description of your youthful environment and your grandfather's mistaken altruistic efforts; but—from what I read I was given to understand that all this was merely a discursion and that presently you would pick up the thread again. You even had the effrontery to insinuate at the close of said discursion that while I had most probably forgotten said thread, you certainly had not. And then you picked up the thread, threw in all the elements for a climax, and then wound up in above quoted manner. Don't do it again.

O I have been busy. Have been going out more than at any other time in the past eight months; have been studying harder than ever in my life before; and having been turning out more copy than hitherto. Finding that I must go out more and that I was becoming stale and dead, I have really ventured to be gay in divers interesting ways.

Yes; the time for Utopias and dreamers is past. Co-operative colonies, etc., are at the best impossible (I don't mean religious ones), and never was there less chance for their survival than to-day. From your attitude regarding the populace, I find I really must quote you some more, from Jordan's *Care and Culture of Men:*

"Some there are among us who wish we had a heaven-descended aristocracy, an aristocracy of brains at least, who could take these things out of the people's hands, out of your hands and mine, and make them and keep them right. I do not feel thus. It is better that the people should suffer, with the remedy in their own hands, than that they should be protected by some power not of themselves. Badly though the people may manage their own affairs, the growth of the race depends upon their doing it. We would rather the people would rule ill through choice than that they should be ruled well through force. The Reign of Terror gives more hope for the future than the reign of the good King Henry. The story of the decline and fall of empires is the story of the growth of man." And again he says: "In these times it is well to remember that we come of hardy stock. The Anglo-Saxon race, with its strength and virtues, was born of hard times. It is not easily kept down; the victims of oppression must be of some other stock. We who live in America, and who constitute the heart of this republic, are the sons and daughters of him that overcometh. Ours is a lineage untainted by luxury, uncoddled by charity, uncorroded by vice, uncrushed by oppression. If it were not so, we would not be here to-day. When this nation was born, the day of the government of royalty and aristocracy was fast drawing to a close. Hereditary idleness had steadily done its work, and the sceptre was already falling from nerveless hands. God said: 'I am tired of kings; I suffer them no more.' And when the kings had slipped from their tottering thrones, as there was no one else to rule, the sceptre fell into the hands of common men."

While I am about it, I must give this from Carlyle: "For a man to have died who might have been wise and was not, this I call a tragedy."

And this reply of Agassiz to a Boston publisher: "I have no time, sir, to make money."

I think I have the very thing for you, "The Soul of Man under Socialism," by Oscar Wilde. I have not had a chance to read it myself, yet, but as soon as I do will forward it to you. Same volume contains in addition, "The Socialist Ideal—Art" by Wm. Morris, author of "Earthly Paradise," etc., and "The Coming Solidarity," by W. C. Owen.

Haven't got to "Chimmie Fadden" yet. Will send along "Book News" in a couple of days. O how I am rushed for reading.

So I stuck it into you for a couple of stamps? Won't do it again, now that I know. But I fail to get it into my head yet—U. S. loses the postage due, who the devil gains it?

Apropos of leading essay mentioned above, the writer, I am told, goes on to contend that true individualism cannot, or rather, rarely flourishes under the present system; a contention which I have also always made.

By the way, have you a letter from some fellow of Asbury Park, to me relating to my *Black Cat* yarn? It's in a blue envelope, if I remember aright.

Your brother's letter seems characteristic of your breed. He must be quite an interesting correspondent.

Of course you were correct about the wrong use of interrogation point in sonnet. I had never noticed it. Find enclosed a take-off on Stephen Crane's style, which, in turn, I deem to be a take-off on that of Walt Whitman's. Whiled away a few minutes on it, just for fun.

Francis S. Saltus was a genius who did much, died young, but remained practically unknown because he could not tolerate the prevailing monotheism which happens to not be a monotheism. Don't judge his work to be similar to what I have sent you. He was very versatile, a profound scholar and linguist, wrote over five thousand poems in various languages, made innumerable translations, and did an infinite quantity of newspaper work under the pseudonym of Cupid Jones.[1] In his "Moods of Madness,"— of which he has many—, have you never noticed the effect of words "sonorous, liquid, superb, immense"?

Jack London

---

[1]Among his titles: *Honey and Gall,* 1873; *The Crazy History of the United States,* 1887; *The Witch of Endor,* 1891.

To Cloudesley Johns

Oakland, Calif.
June 12, 1899

My dear friend:—

Yes; I agree with you, "In a Far Country" should have been the best of the series, but was not. As to the clumsiness of structure, you have certainly hit it. I doubt if I shall ever be able to polish. I permit too short a period— one to fifteen minutes—to elapse between the long-hand and the final MS. You see, I am groping, groping, groping for my own particular style, for the style which should be mine but which I have not yet found.

As to plagiarism: you seem very hyper-sensitive on the subject. Know thou, that "In a Far Country" was written long after I read your "Norton-Drake Co." Yet I had no thought of the coincidence till you mentioned it. Great God! Neither you nor I have been the first to make use of a broken back, nor, because of this fact, should we be debarred from using it. How many broken legs, broken necks, broken hearts, etc., have been worked up, over and over again? Take, for instance, why I happened to make use of that incident. I had to kill the two men off, one had to kill the other; I did not wish the other to die at once, because of his dying it was my intention to make the conclusion. I cast about me, and a broken back suggested itself. Take "White Silence." How many have made use of a falling tree? For instance, Captain Kettle in June *Pearson's,* the Doctor who helped him run away from the Congo Free State in the stolen steamer, has to be killed, and is killed by a falling tree.

I see no reason in the world why you should cut the broken back out of "Charge It to the Company."

The questionable moral! A la *Munsey.* Say, I saw a clever turn to the chaste Young American girl idea, regarding reading—"books one would not like to see one's mother read." Did you ever try to read the *Argosy?* I tried it the other day, but simply broke down and couldn't; my mind absolutely refused. Pardon brevity. I have been writing this and entertaining half a dozen friends at the same time. Really don't know what I have been saying.

Jack London

To Cloudesley Johns

Oakland, Calif.
July 5, 1899

My dear friend:—

So, at last, you are getting your long-delayed vacation? Good! So you hiked part of the way? Do you ride underneath? or do they chase a fellow from the rods also. Must be pretty strict down that way. Ah! city life is the only life after all—there you meet people; as a rule you meet vegetables in the country. I really become heart-sick, if I mingle too long with our agrarian population. Of course, there are striking exceptions.

Have you been following the papers of late? Have you noticed the crisis in Belgium? By latest reports the King has capitulated, giving to the Socialists and Republicans a most welcome victory. Have you noticed the troubles in Italy, where the parliament endeavored to pass a bill for a secret ballot on all labor questions. The Socialist members replied that it were far better to vote secretly on all other questions. They were a minority; what could they do when this damnable bill came up to be acted upon? They did the only possible thing—prevented the ballot by force, and this they will continue till the parliament is dissolved. Consider the effect of all this on the people. Preventing the passing of the bill till the next election means the return of a far greater number of Socialist members, which means, in turn, a lessening of the chances of the bill's passage. O we're booming. Do you notice a socialist leader has taken his seat in President Loubet's new cabinet? The two million socialist votes that this leader represented stands for an organized machine which prevented the rise of a new imperialism, and will forever more prevent such a rise.

It would be nice to see you; drop in on me when you come this way, and partake of my blanket, board, and hobbies. The last I give you fair warning against. Nor will I promise to introduce you in local society, for I have abandoned that with my dress suit. Takes too much time. Remember Omar Khayyam's "O make haste"? "Life's none so long," as Kipling says in his "Sestina of the Tramp Royal."

Where am I to draw the line?—At the White. From the family unit, through the tribal dawning, to the race aggregation, you may trace the rise of an altruism, very similar for all its various manifestations. The line stops there. If a man would save an animal from pain, another kind of altruism is brought to bear; the same if he saves a nigger, or a red, a yellow, or a brown. But let Mr. White meet another white hemmed in by dangers from the other colors—these whites will not need to know each other—but they will hear the call of blood and stand back to back. Nor does it matter if one be a genius and the other a poor wretch cursed by congenital defectives, an hereditary inefficient—they will none the less hear the call, feel the bond, and answer. Better conditions (toward which we are constantly moving) from the cradle, will engender better antenatal conditions—these will act and react upon each other to the lifting of the race. Culture, training, eradication of acquired inefficiency (hereditary inefficiency kills itself off in short order when deprived of accessions from environment), all these factors will tend toward the weeding out, the clarifying of the race. Nursing the inferior whites, segregating the hopelessly vicious and idiotic so that they may not breed, and developing those that are not so, draws its own line. To-day, the very opposite prevails as regards the lower classes; that is no reason it should always be so. Mind you, we must come to understand that nature has no sentiment, no charity, no mercy; we are blind puppets at the play of great, unreasoning forces; yet we may come to know the laws of some of the forces and see our trend in relation to them. These forces generated the altruistic in man; the race with the highest altruism will endure— the highest altruism considered from the standpoint of merciless natural law, which never concedes nor alters. The lesser breeds cannot endure. The Indian is an example, as is the black man of the Australian Bush, the South Sea Islander, the inhabitant of the Sub-Arctics, etc.

Apparently I am inconsistent. A man's duty is as his conscience dictates. We are, taken as a whole, blind factors in the action of natural selection among the races of men. England, as a whole, to-day does not consider the trend of her whole policy of generations to be inimical to the very existence of the lesser breeds. Yet her whole course is leading slowly up to that. She does not know it, hence, her duty lies in line with the dictates of her national conscience as reflected by her representative citizens. By that conscience she should have behaved better by her East Indian Empire; by conscienceless nature she has been permitted to do neither more nor less than evolution made possible and demanded. Remember, pain and pleasure, life and death, extinction and survival, all that concerns the individual, does not concern nature. She has no concerns; she does not reason; she does not feel; she is not to be swayed by a hair's breadth from her undeviating course.

Perhaps you will enjoy Rose-Soley's criticism of Frank Norris, and Frank Norris's rejoinder.

Just got home this morning, and have been hard at it ever since. Have written fifteen hundred words of a new story, transacted all my business, started a few more of my returned children on the turf (as you put it),[1] and am now winding up the last letter of my correspondence. Go away again on Friday for a jaunt on wheels down country with a young lady[2] whom I have been promising for some time. She made me a call to-day and fore-closed. We stop with mutual friends along the way. By the way, is mutual used correctly in preceding sentence?

In "Priestly Prerogative," I wish to call your attention to a case of editorial mutilation. I stated (type-written) that the advent of this woman meant a new hegira in their lives. Mr. Editor finds fault with the word and substitutes "era." Now the words are utterly different in their significance, and the substitute makes bosh. Hegira meaning a new period to date from, as, for instance, when I left Harold; "era" meaning the period lying between the hegira and the present. Damn Editors!

Keep us informed of your movements.

Jack London

---

[1]A reference to his practice of sending manuscripts in sequence from one publisher to another.
[2]Bessie Maddern, his first wife, whom he married April 7, 1900.

To Cloudesley Johns

Oakland, Calif.
July 29,1899

My dear friend:—

Trip knocked out in the middle. Whole lot of company came to house—very small house. But shall make another try of it the latter part of this month. Well, we had some of our fun anyway.

Guests are at last gone, and am too flabbergasted to get to work. Have all kinds of work awaiting me, too. Did you ever write a yarn of, say, twelve thousand words, every word essential to atmosphere, and then get an order to cut out three thousand of those words, somewhere, somehow? That's what the *Atlantic* has just done to me.[1] Hardly know whether I shall do it or not. It's like the pound of flesh. Say, am hammering away at that *Cosmopolitan* Essay,[2] at spare intervals, have two of the five thousand words finished. Am thoroughly satisfied, as far as I have gone, which is saying a good deal for me— Am usually sick at this stage, and it's such dry dissertative stuff after all.

Many thanks for short story collection. All of Zangwill's I had read before —isn't he wonderful in his way? Kipling's I had read before, "King Solomon of Kentucky," [by G. L. Allen] also, and "A Matter of Interest"—what a clever style and treatment [R. W.] Chambers has!—"Survival of the Fittest" —just read this latter in a number of Morgan Robertson's tales collected under *Spun-Yarn*. Also read Crane's "Flannagin" and several others I do not just recollect. "Perfect" was among the new ones, but a few of which I have yet read. I anticipate much delight in tackling them. For which my heartiest thanks. But to return to that "Perfect"—I was unusually struck with it—the woman who wrote it knew women, and say, she did know men— things she dealt in, and the methods with which she dealt, are among the many things I am deficient in and must develop.

What is the work you are so interested in, which may permit you to arrive here in a month, or will not for a year? It must be a Magnum Opus, which the month means desertion, the year achievement. Drop in on us when you do come. Small house, but usually plenty of fair steak, chops, etc., in the larder. I am a heavy eater, but a plain one, fruit, vegetables and meat, and plenty of them, but with small regard for pastries, etc. If you're a sweet tooth you will not receive accommodation here except in the fruit line and the candy stores.

O, by the way, just to show how this business of placing MSS. is a despairing one. Long years ago—three, anyway, I wrote a synopsis of "The Road," under that title, describing tramps and their ways of living, etc. It has been everywhere—every syndicate and big Sunday edition refused it as a feature article; but I kept it going. And lo, to-day, came a note of acceptance of same from the *Arena*.[3] Think I'll resurrect some of my old retired third rate work and send it to *Harpers, Century,* etc. That is, if there is any chance of their accepting what tenth class publications have refused. Ever had similar experiences—tell me of them.

And say, when a third rate magazine publishes something of yours, and you wait thirty days after publication for pay, and then dun them, and then they do not even answer your note, what do you do? Is there any way of proceeding against them? Or must one suffer dumbly? Tell me, tell me—I'd like to make it hot for some of those Eastern sharks.

And with these pay-on-acceptance fellows, did you ever get your check at the same time you were notified of acceptance? They always make me an offer, first, and then I needs must sit idly and grow weary and sick at heart waiting during the period between my closing with offer and the arrival of the all-needful. What has been your experience? There's a whole lot of those mysteries I'd like to solve.

Have shoved your picture up on the wall; now don't throw anything; but all my friends I have shown it to, have somewhere along the line of their considerations made the remark, "artistic." I myself likened it at once to such likenesses I have seen of Mark Twain. One other, a young lady, also independently remarked the same. I have but one fault to find with you, supposing your mother to have portrayed you correctly, and that is, your chin. Your chin, beginning from and including the lower lip, I must confess I do not like. It belies the rest of the face which seems so strong. It almost has the touch of effeminacy about it which I so detest to see in men. And yet, from your letters I have always derived the opposite conclusion—that you were strongly masculine. It had seemed there was so much in you, of rudeness, roughness, wildness, hurrah-for-hell sort of stuff, such as I possess —a certain affinity, you see. I can't reconcile the two. Perhaps your mother did not get that portion of it just right; and perhaps you give the lie inwardly to your exterior. Well, well, so be it. Gave you the nice stuff first, and then frankly gave you hell for what may not be yours.

As you say, I am firm. I may sometimes appear impatient at nothing at all, and all that; but this everybody who has had a chance to know me well have noticed: things come my way even though they take years; no one sways me, save in little things of the moment; I am not stubborn but I swing to my purpose as steadily as the needle to the pole; delay, evade, oppose secretly or openly, it's all immaterial, the thing comes my way. To-day I have met my first serious wall. For three long years the fight has been on; to-day it balances; is a deadlock; I may have met my master; I may not; the future will tell, and one or the other of us will break—and on top of it all I may say it concerns neither my interest nor theirs, nothing except the personal vanity and the clash of our wills. "I won't" and "I will" sums the whole thing up.

Firm? But I am firm in foolishness, as well as other things. Take things more seriously than you? Bosh! You don't know me. Ask my very intimate friends. Ask my creditors. Pshaw—let this illustrate: a very dear friend, a woman charming enough to be my wife and old enough to be my mother, discovered that my most precious possession, my wheel, was hocked. You know I only live for the day. She at once put up the all-needful so that I might regain it. She could well afford it, so that was all right; but mark you, she virtually had a lien upon it. Well, to top it—had been extravagant on the strength of receiving money which did not materialize. Creditors waxed clamorous; a few dollars judiciously scattered among them would have eased things; but credit exhausted; along comes a particularly nice person for a good time. A very nice person who wished to see things; wheel hypothecated and things seen for some forty odd hours. This is me all the time and all over—seriously take things of life—does it look like it? Pshaw. Ask those who know me.

And I am firm in my foolishness.

I am glad you took Jordan in the right way. He is, to a certain extent, a hero of mine. He is so clean, and broad, and wholesome. Would to God he were duplicated a few thousand times in the U.S. Working for a sheep-skin! That's what most fools do who go in for education, and most of the rest are geniuses and cranks, who get the kernel and then don't or won't use it.

Well, fiction is the strongest lever, eh? Take the French Revolution, alone —"that tragedy," as John Morley says, "the fifth act of which is yet dark." Those are not his exact words, however. Here are three books, none fiction, not all read to-day, and, for that matter, false and frail from start to finish when viewed through the cold glasses of to-day's knowledge. Pick me in any period three lovers of fiction which have accomplished a tithe of what they did. Here they are: Montesquieu's *Esprit de Loies,* Jean Jacques Rousseau's *Contract Social,* and Diderot and his *Encyclopedia.*

As for my writing historles and works on economics—I may, some day— but I have little ambition to do so. The same may be said of any kind of writing under the sun. My only wish that way is the all-needful—it seems the easiest way. Had I an assured income, my ambition would be for music, music, music. As it is, impossible—I bend.

I have not read *Bab Ballads,*[4] who are they by? I shall look them up. Yes, I was laughing at some of the *Call's* absurdities concerning Ingersoll. I never cared for the man's work myself, while at the same time appreciating the enormous power he was for good among most men. He has done immense work for sanity, normality, sensibility, etc., among his fellows; but, to me, he was not deep enough. However, what I liked in him most of all was his life; they at least have not dared to attack that.

O that England which you do not understand! Let me quote lengthily from Jordan. I just ran across it a couple of days ago, and its effect is still strong. It is from his anti-expansion Essay "Lest we Forget," first in his latest book called *Imperial Democracy.*

"Let us look for a moment at the policy of England. The United States is great through minding her own business; England through minding the business of the world. In the Norse Mythology the Mitgart Serpent appears in the guise of a cat, an animal small and feeble, but in reality the mightiest and the most enduring of all, for its tail goes around the earth, growing down its own throat, and by its giant force it holds the world together. England is the Mitgart Serpent of the nations, shut in a petty island; as Benjamin Franklin said, 'an island which compared to America is but a stepping stone in a brook with scarce enough of it above water to keep one's shoes dry.' Yet, by the force of arms, the force of trade, and the force of law she has become the ruler of the earth. It is English brain and English muscle which hold the world together.

"NO OTHER AGENCY OF CIVILIZATION HAS BEEN SO POTENT AS ENGLAND'S ENLIGHTENED SELFISHNESS. Her colonies are of three orders—friendly nations, subject nations, and military posts. The larger colonies are little united states. They are republics and rule their own affairs. The subject nations and the military posts England rules by a rod of iron, because no other rule is possible. Every year England seizes new posts, opens new ports, and widens the stretch of her empire. But of all this Greater Britain, England herself is but a little part, the ruling head of a world-wide organism. What does he know of England who only England knows? No doubt as Kipling says, England

> "thinks her empire still
> 'Twixt the Strand and Holborn Hill."

but the Strand would be half empty were it not that it leads outward to Cathay. The huge business interests of Greater Britain are the guarantee of her solidarity. All her parts must hold together.

"In similar relation to the Mother Country, America must stand. GREATER ENGLAND HOLDS OVER US THE OBLIGATIONS OF BLOOD, AND THOUGHT, AND LANGUAGE, AND CHARACTER. ONLY THE SAXON UNDERSTANDS THE SAXON. ONLY THE SAXON AND THE GOTH KNOW THE MEANING OF FREEDOM. 'A sanction like that of religion,' says John Hay, 'enforces our partnership in all important affairs.' Not that we should enter into formal alliance with Great Britain. We can get along well side by side, but never tied together. When England suggests a union for attack and defense, let us ask what she expects to gain from us. Never yet did England offer us the hand in open friendliness, in pure good faith, not hoping to get the best of the bargain. THIS IS THE ENGLISH GOVERNMENT, WHICH NEVER ACTS WITHOUT IN-TERESTED MOTIVES. But the English people are our friends in every real crisis, and that without caring over much whether we be right or not. War with England should be forever impossible. THE NEED OF THE COMMON RACE IS GREATER THAN THE NEED OF THE NATIONS. THE ANGLO-SAXON RACE MUST BE AT PEACE WITHIN ITSELF. NOTHING IS SO IMPORTANT TO CIVILIZATION AS THIS. A WAR BETWEEN ENGLAND AND AMERICA FOUGHT TO THE BITTER END MIGHT SUBMERGE CIVILIZATION. WHEN THE WAR SHOULD

BE OVER AND THE SMOKE CLEARED AWAY THERE WOULD BE BUT ONE NATION LEFT, AND THAT, RUSSIA."

"The need of the common race is greater than the need of the nations."— Don't you see, understand how inevitable all this is? Do you appreciate, and if so, can you condemn "This is the English government, which never acts without interested motives"? Great God! why shouldn't it! I needs must smile at the petty Joshuas who rise up to-day, confronting movements and evolutions born a thousand, aye, ten thousand centuries agone, and crying out with puny silliness "Stop! Worm that I am, I bid you stop!" Pshaw!

The maggots!—small wonder they have the nerve to claim themselves gods! they would do anything in the face of that. Let me quote just one sentence from an essay of my own:

"Natural selection, undeviating, pitiless, careless alike of the individual or the species, destroyed or allowed to perpetuate, as the case might be, such breeds as were unfittest or fittest to survive."

And, let me add, will continue to do so.

As the sheet is not used up, let me quote another sentence from same article,

"Drawing his strength and knowledge from the dugs of competition, he early learned the great lesson: THAT HIS STRENGTH LAY IN NUMBERS, IN UNITY OF INTERESTS, IN SOLIDARITY OF EFFORT—IN SHORT, IN COMBINATION AGAINST THE HOSTILE ELEMENTS OF HIS ENVIRONMENT."

Go ahead! Command the sun, moon and stars to stand still, you maggots, you gods! It were easier for a grasshopper to stop the lightning express

Good night,
Jack London

[1]The reference is to "An Odyssey of the North."

[2]"What a Community Loses by the Competitive System."

[3]The entry in *Magazine Sales* reads "[*Arena*] offer of $10.00 Cash. Ten dollars in subscriptions, and one dozen copies of Number in which published. Returned as unavailable under amended policy of new owners March 10/00." The title *The Road* London later used for a collection of stories of "tramping experiences."

[4]*Collection of Humorous Ballads* by W. S. Gilbert, published in 1869. Basis of some of the Gilbert and Sullivan Operas.

To Cloudesley Johns

Oakland, Calif.
Aug. 10, 1899

Dear Friend:—

Same old tale. Wound off one visitor the first of last week, to receive at once two more—they have just now gone home. I'll get even with them yet so that even their letters, much less themselves shall not reach me. I see you have been suffering a similar affliction.

Say! Remember telling me that if I got a check from *Town Topics* to frame it? After acceptance I let them slip for several months, then wrote them a nice little note of enquiry—five lines—and behold! They dug up a dollar for that triolet—"He Chortled with Glee," and two twenty-five for the poem "If I Were God One Hour." You mentioned *The Owl* as a snare and delusion. Well, they haven't got the best of me yet, at least that's all I can say. You know I wrote long ago a lot of stuff upon which I wasted many stamps. Nor would I retire it if hope of getting my postage back still lived. And I must say I have succeeded in disposing of quite a lot of rubbish that way by sending it to the way down publications. *The Owl* published a skit of mine a couple of months ago ["The Handsome Cabin Boy"]. When they made the offer for it, I almost fainted—One Dollar and Fifty cents for two thousand words. But it more than paid for the stamps I had wasted on the thing, and gave promise of release from at least one of my early night-mares, so I closed with the offer. They have not yet paid me. Then the question arises: why should they have made such a miserable offer if they intended to take the whole works? And one answer suggests itself: that from very shame at the smallness of the selling price, the author would refrain from making any trouble in the event of non-payment. However, I am devoid of that kind of shame.

Yes, I cut the story for the *Atlantic*. There were 12,250 words; but while they wanted it reduced three thousand, I only succeeded in getting it down to an even ten thousand. So I don't know what they will do about it. They seem very nice people from their letters, but that, however, remains to be substantiated by something solid. Have also sent Houghton, Mifflin & Co., collection of tales [*The Son of the Wolf*].

I closed with a cash offer of ten dollars, and five yearly subscriptions with the *Arena,* so probably it is all right with them. Say, it's great, learning the inner nature of some of these concerns!

O but I do take myself seriously. My self-estimation has been made in very sober moments. I early learned that there were two natures in me. This caused me a great deal of trouble, till I worked out a philosophy of life and struck a compromise between the flesh and the spirit. Too great an ascendancy of either was to be abnormal, and since normality is almost a fetish of mine, I finally succeeded in balancing both natures. Ordinarily they are at equilibrium; yet as frequently as one is permitted to run rampant, so is the other. I have small regard for an utter brute or for an utter saint.

A choice of ultimate happiness in preference to proximate happiness, when the element of chance is given due consideration, is, I believe, the wisest course for a man to follow under the sun. He that chooses proximate happiness is a brute; he that chooses immortal happiness is an ass; but he that chooses ultimate happiness knows his business.

So Cervantes overthrew Knight Errantry, eh? So we are told by the bellelettristic (or however it should be spelled) triflers of the past several generations. But I say not so. The specialization of industry, aided by the Overthrow of Constantinople and the spread of the "New Learning," gave time and space for the rise of the free cities, which, in turn, increased the kingly prerogative, softened the rigor of feudal dues, smashed the power of the feudal lords, broke down barriers, centralized power, increased trade, exploration, etc., spread civilization, destroyed the baronial power and increased that of the state, pitted a bourgeois aristocracy against a mediaeval one, etc., etc., and somewhere along and all along the line swept knight-errantry out of existence. The Knight of Mancha (or am I quoting from Irving?) simply softened the blow to the nobility, or rather, reconciled them to the fact that knight-errantry was of little use in a work-a-day world. I have rattled this off too quick to do it justice.

Do you remember when Philip the Fair went up against the burghers of the Low Countries? Why, those petty tradesmen could not fight, he said, regarding his steel-clad flowers of chivalry with proud eyes. And do you remember how Philip the Fair and his Knights came back? With their tails between their legs. The damned burghers could fight after all. Little things like that, illustrative of the changing order of things, go to show what really did overthrow Knight-errantry.

I doubt if even you would consider the novel avowedly with a purpose to be real literature. If you do, then let us abandon fiction altogether and give the newspaper its due, for the fixing or changing of public opinion especially on lesser things. But Spencer's *First Principles* alone, leaving out all the rest of his work, has done more for mankind, and through the ages will have done far more for mankind, than a thousand books like *Nicholas Nickleby, Hard Cash, Book of Snobs,* and *Uncle Tom's Cabin.* Why, take the enormous power for human good contained in Darwin's *Origin of Species* and *Descent of Man.* Or in the work of Ruskin, Mill, Huxley, Carlyle, Ingersoll.

Those *Bab Ballads* are rich—I shall look them up. Received to-day your second installment of magazine stories. Many thanks; shall preserve them until you appear on the scene. Am not reading much fiction just now; but within several days shall get through much of the heavier stuff I am now on, and then I won't do a thing to those tales of yours.

As to "that retired stuff"—many thanks for your kind offer; but really, I shall never resurrect it again. Whenever I get to thinking too much of myself I simply look some of it up, and am at once reduced to a more becoming modesty. No, it's put away for good. I have very little out, just now. And it's growing less all the time. It will soon catch me up, I'm afraid, if I don't get down and dig.

If you have not already seen it, I think you will appreciate Bierce's article on the *Call's* editorial writer who wrote divers things concerning Ingersoll.

Well, say, hold on a minute. Let me explain. But first let me say how glad I was that you liked "The Wife of a King." But I was candid, though I cannot for the life of me remember what "shameful comparison" I made in letter to you concerning it. This is the way it happened. I had the most terrific dose of blues I ever was afflicted with in my life. I couldn't think of anything original, so I made a composite of three retired Mss., slapped them together, as I at the time considered, haphazard, with the crudest of dovetailing. Shipped the result off in disgust, and forgot all about it, save a most uncomfortable sense of general dissatisfaction. And for the first time, when I looked upon it printed, I was not wholly disgusted with myself —not because it was the best I had done, but because I had rated it so low that disappointment or disgust seemed impossible. Thanks for sending me "Three and an Extra." I had read it a long while ago, but forgotten its existence. There is quite a similarity, and, as you stated, quite a dissimilarity.

Are there any phases of humanity, under any combinations which have not already been exploited? Yet I think I have for some time had an entirely original field in view, so why should I ask. But who knows. That "Theorist" of yours seems to cause lots of trouble. I should think the only way to write a novel would be to do it at a fair rate per day, and then ship off at once. If I can only get ahead of the game, I'm going to jump back to Jerusalem in the time of Christ, and write one giving an entirely new interpretation of many things which occurred at that time. I think I can do it, so that while it may rattle the slats of the Christians they will still be anxious to read it.

Good night,
Jack London

To Cloudesley Johns

Oakland, Calif.
Sept. 6, 1899

My dear friend:—

Back again, but not yet settled down. Have blown myself for a new wheel ('99 Cleveland), and hence, between appearing at weddings in knickerbockers and rampaging over the country with bloomer-clad lassies, and celebrating the return of the California's I have been unable to chase ink. The way I happened to get said wheel is an illustration of how little rhyme or reason there is in placing Mss. Some time ago I wrote an avowedly hack article for an agricultural paper, expecting to receive five dollars for the same, and to receive it anywhere from sixty to ninety days after acceptance. But it was rejected and, being short at the time, I was correspondingly dejected. But straight away I shipped off the Ms. to *The Youth's Companion* ["King of the Mazy May"], and lo and behold, without any warning, they forwarded me a check for thirty-five dollars—eleven dollars per thousand. How's that for luck?

Yes; I received some time ago that *Scroll* publishing scheme. Did you ever get something similar from a projected magazine which called itself *The Columbia Poeticia* [*sic*]? It agreed to publish *all* the poetry sent it by its subscribers. And if I remember rightly, to pay for it in some sort of way.

Don't weep over what the *National* did—they pay poorly. Sometime ago they accepted one of my ancient efforts, for which they gave five yearly-subscriptions, and five dollars cash, pay on publication. I expect it to come out in the September number. God bless the publishers. If the gods should smile upon me and some day put me on my feet, I won't do a thing to them —I mean some of these cheap-John publishers, not the gods.

I am awaiting the outcome of a little affair with *The Editor,* with great curiosity. James Knap—whatever the rest of his name is, lists them in his 500 Places to Sell MSS. thus: "pay liberally." Feeling rather nervy one day, I sent them a skit of 1700 words of advice to young authors. But I did not tell them how to sell their wares, or to file material, or to dun gracefully, etc. The title will explain better: "On the Writer's Philosophy of Life." They accepted Ms. with promise to pay on publication, said publication to be early. What I am curious about is to see what they consider liberal pay,[1] Or will they expect me to take it out in trade? As I have never yet submitted Mss. anywhere for advice, I don't think I'll begin now. Well, we'll see what we'll see.

Oh! Chapple, Joe Chapple, of the *National,* writes a fellow the most beautiful letters when buying things for a song. Did you ever receive one of his?

To save my life I cannot think of a title for those four lines of Jeanie Peet's. You see that hits me on origination, where I'm weak.

If I am not mistaken, I, in my last to you, or at some time when telling you of Weissman, I said: "do not mistake the meaning of acquired characters." You have muddled "acquired characters" with "fixed characters," it is these latter which are hereditary. Language is an acquired character; a Semitic nose a fixed character. The one is acquired in the lifetime of the individual, the other inherited from an ancestor. No; I wouldn't write that refutation of Weissman if I were you.

I simply misunderstood you when you asked me if I had ever seen a similar title to "A Tragedy of Errors." I naturally thought on the instant of what had suggested it, but what I thought you were in quest of, was as to whether it had not already been suggested to and been used by some other writer.

Go it for the *Black Cat!* I cannot even think of a suitable plot— my damnable lack of origination you see. I think I had better become an interpreter of the things which are, rather than a creator of the things which might be. Many thanks for articles you sent. Did you take especial note of that article by Ray Stannard Baker on Dr. See's new law of temperature? I am afraid the old nebulae theory still holds notwithstanding. Here is his law which you will probably recollect: Constant divided by radius equals temperature. Or, as he states it, "the temperature of a gaseous star varies inversely as the radius." But the compression of a gas is always accomplished under pressure—where is the pressure which compresses the sun? This question merely suggests itself, I have not taken the time to test its stability. Compression does not generate heat, as he conceives it; it merely radiates heat, forces it out, away from, much as one would squeeze the water out of a wet sock. One can not very well assert that the more water he squeezed out of the wet sock the wetter the wet sock became, surely not. Yet this seems to me an analogous assertion to that made by Dr. See. As the article is, it is a splendid bit of pseudo-science, but there is nothing substantial to it.

Trippler's liquid air has interested me not a little; but as yet I fail to see how he has got around the law of THE CONSERVATION OF ENERGY; yet he asserts that with three pounds of liquid air he can generate ten, a surplusage of seven pounds. If this is so, then one may say that at last the lever and the fulcrum by which man may move the earth has at last been discovered. I guess not.

Well, time is flying; I've got a visitor, as usual, spending a few days with me, and as I hear the tinkle of his bicycle bell approaching, I must cut off. But just you watch my smoke some of these days—I intend shaking every mortal who knows me and going off all by myself. So there, now!

Jack London

[1]Received $5.00.

To CLOUDESLEY JOHNS

Oakland, Calif.
Sept. 12, 1899

My dear friend:—

Between engagements, visitors, and friends, I have not yet succeeded in doing a tap. And to-morrow I start out on that postponed trip of mine to Stanford University and Mt. Hamilton, to say nothing of way points. And when I return from that I am going to lock myself up.

You say, in reference to the *McClure's* note, "Is there any editor, I wonder, who wants something besides merely stories?" Why my dear fellow, I am constantly on the lookout for editors who want stories, and I move to amend your query by striking out "something besides merely."

Now for a question: Suppose *McClure's* had accepted that study of yours. Would they have published it in the magazine, or would it have come out in some newspaper through the syndicate? I am always afraid to send *McClure's* anything that I consider good, for fear they will publish it through the syndicate, which syndicate I know nothing about. Can you enlighten me?

As to the *Black Cat* story: I am in such a state of anarchy, and have so much I wish to do, that I can not see my way to tackling your proposition. As it is, the period of the closing of the contest is so very far away that I am not figuring on it at all. I do not even know whether I shall go in for it. Perhaps I may try them with some of my unaccepted stuff.

So one's vocabulary is inherited. Well, well. Would you kindly amplify that statement a little, giving me the data you base it upon. If you can actually prove it you can turn the scientific world upside down. A certain monarch once isolated some babes upon a tower, where they were fed, etc., but allowed no vocal intercourse with the world. It was an experiment. When they had grown up it was found that they were simply idiots. Beyond a few inarticulate sounds by which they expressed the primary passions, they did not speak. Beyond the necessary actions correlated with mere existence they were idiots. Having received no vocabulary from their kind they were unable to think.

No man ever received one word from an ancestor by means of heredity.

I don't know where I'm at regarding the "Tragedy of Errors." I guess you're right, however. You misunderstood Trippler. The heat forced from the air does go somewhere. It is carried off by running water which is piped through the machine. This raised the question in my mind. how much energy would be required on shipboard to pump this running water for the liquid air engine. Of course, in a city, the energy which causes the water to run is supplied by the water company.

Does rotation cause compression? Figure it out.

How I envy you working away at your novel. I am most anxious to have a try at one myself. If I can only get far enough ahead of the game, I certainly shall.

You see, I have a family to support, and that's hell when a man's young and single. Say, what do you know of "The Western Press,"[1] down San Diego way? Sometime ago I sent them one of my failures. When the regulation thirty days was up, I sent a trailer. No answer. Sept 1, I sent a second trailer, this time stamped and addressed envelope enclosed. Still no answer. As I had a "return" on the outside, I know they must have received it. Is this usual with them? Have they gone out of business, broken up, etc.?

Shall do better by you regarding letter-writing, sometime. As it is, I'm not worth a rap for anything. The other day I chased a word several hours and failed to find it. And then, yesterday, lying out in the sand by the edge of the ocean, it came of its own free will, when my mind was many many leagues away. "Exotic" was the word. Such a simple word, but O the trouble it cost me!

Jack London

Am going to try my luck at backhand from now on. How do you like it? Or do you think it possible for me to improve?

J. G. L.[2]

[1]Apparently means the Western Associated Press, an organization of Western and Mid-western papers formed in 1862 in reaction to the monopoly of wire news by Western Union and New York A.P. The group grew in strength and finally made a settlement with the large wire services, but by their rebellion encouraged similar responses in other areas.
[2]While London never used his middle name (Griffith) he frequently signed with his three initials.

To CLOUDESLEY JOHNS

Oakland, Calif.
Sept. 20, 1899

Dear Cloudesley:—

Back again. Had a glorious time. Stopped over at Stanford, where I met several students I knew, sat under the various profs., etc. And looked through the thirty-six inch reflector on top of Mt. Hamilton. There we saw the moon, Saturn and his rings, and quite a number of bourgeois pigs. Yes, they were pigs, dressed like tourists. My companion and I, after seeing them, were exceeding proud of the fact that we were mere proletarians.

"The Quarry Foreman," is good, unqualifiedly good. And altogether different to "Zebro." It is strong, has unity, and the character is strong in conception and handled with bold, deft strokes. You haven't a bit of kick a-coming. Again I say it is good. Perhaps one or two touches may be slightly amateurish, but if so, they are very slightly so. Somehow, I have a vague feeling that the very last line or so might be bettered, bettered by some extremely slight change, perhaps only in the order of the words, perhaps in some simple modification. But beyond this, one can have nothing but praise for it. If that was done a year and a half ago I should like to see some of your later work.

The June *Black Cat* has a $350 prize yowl, and the September number a $500 one. There are no others since May. Thanks for information about *Truth*. They pay on acceptance I suppose? Is the announcement you sent something new? or is it of long standing?

Ah, therein you differ from me—it's money I want, or rather, the things money will buy; and I could never possibly have too much. As to living on practically nothing—I propose to do as little of that as I possibly can. Remember, it's the feed not the breed which makes the man.

As to vocabulary—a person will write as they think. A small vocabulary will limit their thought. If they don't think they will not write; if they think slovenly, they will write slovenly. Let me illustrate by quoting from you. "I have met many people who have little memory, and who are sluggish thinkers, with more extensive vocabularies than mine. Mind you, I know all those words, but I do not, cannot, use them—they are not in my vocabulary."

Now what have you done? You have stated that you knew "all these words," that is to say, that they were in your vocabulary. If you know them, they certainly are in your vocabulary. Then in the next breath you say they are not in your vocabulary. You did not mean that, but you wrote it slovenly—why? Because you thought it slovenly. Had you stopped and thought carefully before you put it on paper, you would have clearly realized the distinction you wished to make, and you would have clearly written it thus: "I know all these words, but I do not, cannot, use them—they are not in my WORKING VOCABULARY."

Again, let me criticise you. You say, "I don't know whether or not this sounds reasonable to you; but for myself, I am as sure of its truth as one can be sure of anything in this ridiculous world where every age contradicts the theories of that preceding it."

Now you did not stop to think that out before you wrote it. If you had you would not have voiced falsehoods which your sober judgment would not countenance. You know that the work of Euclid, a score of centuries old, has not once been contradicted; that Newton's Laws are still with us; that the teachings of Bruno, Galileo and a host of others have not been contradicted. Of course they have been modified. But that is another story. The test of truth is: Will it work? Will you trust your life to it? Every day you behold working or trust your life to things which are directly the result of previous theorizing. Had you stopped to think this out, you would not have set your reason aside for a brilliant generalization.

In your writing I note many words, modern in their origin, which had little or no general use at the period you were conceived. Yet you use them. They were of course "acquired." Had you passed your whole life in solitude you would have had no vocabulary; had you been conceived just as you were and raised in the best Russian circles, you would have had a large Russian vocabulary, not one word of which you would have inherited from your lines of ancestors. Had you been raised in entirely different portions of the United States to those in which you were, you certainly would have many idioms, etc., which were not entailed.

As an artisan cannot work without tools, so a man cannot think without a vocabulary, and the greater his vocabulary the better fitted he is to think. Of course, an ass may acquire the tools of an artisan and be unable to work with them, so with words. But that does not interfere with the broad statement I have laid down.

As to your illustration of J. E. Seeley's spelling— In no court of justice, by no philosopher or scientist would such be permitted to pass as evidence. Do not make the mistake so common with women and lesser men, of taking a coincidence for a cause. To the Egyptian in his rainless land, the rising of the Nile was considered the greatest thing in the world, the most important. Now it happened that this rising of the Nile was marked by the rising in the heavens of the Dog-star Sirius. This was merely a coincidence, but the

Egyptians mistook it for a cause, and worshipped the star because it caused the inundations. From this it was but a step to wander on into all the absurdities of astrology. If one star ruled terrestrial affairs, all stars must have influence, and if with things, then certainly with men.

Of a surety, if a cerebral structure of an ancestor which renders him an idiot or a Kleptomaniac is transmitted to you, you will resemble him in that, to a greater or less degree as excited or mollified by environment. So with, color blindness, for instance, or a thousand and one other similar things. But a vocabulary does not come under this head at all, except that the cerebral formation inherited may be limited as regards memory or quantity of words. Yet this, however, will not affect what certain words go to make up that quantity. So many words may be acquired up to the limit, and then the acquirement of words will virtually cease.

Having done nothing but lecture, I shall now chop off.

Jack London

To Cloudesley Johns

Oakland, Calif.
Sept. 26, 1899

Dear Cloudesley:—

At last am at work; have completed my day's stint; am now clearing up my correspondence; and as soon as I finish this shall be off and away for a scorch on my wheel. Then to-night comes my studying as usual.

Did I ever mention a Ms. I received in response to a trailer, which same Ms. had been O.K.'d and blue-pencilled? Well, such happened to me sometime ago. Without removing marks or anything I shipped it off to *The Youth's Companion*. There were fifteen hundred words to it ["Pluck and Pertinacity"]. Last week a check comes for twenty-five. Say, I'm having lots of luck with the *Companion,* sending them my old, almost-ready-to-be-retired stuff. Have you ever tried them? They pay good and promptly. Though such work won't live it at least brings the ready cash.

Do you do any work for Tillotson & Sons? Either my work is deteriorating or else they have lowered their rates, for I find them paying less each time.

No; I did not like your "Quarry Foreman," through comparison with "Zebro"; but for itself. How I envy you when you say that you do not write for publication. There is certainly far greater chance for you to gain the goal you have picked out, than for me who am in pursuit of dollars, dollars, dollars. Yet I cannot see how I can do otherwise, for a fellow must live, and then there are also others depending upon him. However, once and awhile I shall make it a point to sit down and deliberately not write for publication.

"Because of your indifference to everything when compared with your work, and your habit of sacrificing everything which interferes with it"—ye Gods! that's the spirit to go at it with! You certainly should get there.

Have begun to isolate myself from my friends—a few at a time. But those I have managed to dispense with are easy ones. I can't see my way clear to the others except by running away. But instead of the desert I'll take to sea. Many who know me, ask why I, with my knowledge of the sea, do not write some sea fiction. But you see I have been away from it so long that I have lost touch. I must first get back and saturate myself with its atmosphere. Then perhaps I may do something good.

I am afraid that brother of yours has imbibed just a little of your confounded pessimism. That's bad. Viewing this world through the eyes of science I can see no reason at all why a person should be the slightest bit pessimistic. Why it's all good, considering man's relation to it.

Jack London

P.S. Did I inform you that at last I am once more an uncle. It was born nearly a month ago—a ten month's child[1]—nails long enough to cut.

J. G. L.

[1]Eliza Shepard's only child—Irving.

To CLOUDESLEY JOHNS

Oakland, Calif.
Oct. 3, 1899

Dear Cloudesley:—

That was good, that fable by Charles Battell Loomis. As you did not say return, I've sent it along the line. Is that the Loomis who edits the *Land of Sunshine?* or are there two Loomises? Or does the other fellow spell his name Lumis?[1] Or is it just some tangle of my own wits?

I think your explanation of your own particular pessimism (if pessimism it may be called), tallies very much with mine.

Therein we differ—dissipation is alluring to me. Last Sunday I went off with a very nice young lady [Bessie Maddern] on a bicycle trip up to Mill Valley among the redwoods at the base of Mount Tamalpais. To do this we had to go to 'Frisco and take the ferry to Sausalito, and from thence to destination via pedals. Any number of lively young 'Frisco people take the same outing on Sundays, except that they do not ordinarily or even extraordinarily go on bikes. They patronize the railroad. Well, on the back trip to 'Frisco, a bunch of them took the deck and raised hell generally, to the shocking of many of the more sedate passengers. Am happy to state, however, that the girl I was with, while the kingdoms of the earth could not have lured her into getting up and doing likewise, at least highly enjoyed the performance. All of which is neither here nor there. But for myself, I was attacked by all kinds of feelings. Why, my longing was intense to jump in and join them after the fashion of my wild young days, and go on after we arrived at 'Frisco and make the night of it which I knew they were going to make. Alluring? I guess yes.

59

And then again, I could feel how I had grown away from so much of that —lost touch. I knew if I should happen to join them, how strangely out of place it would seem to me—duck-out-of-water sort of feeling. This made me sad; for, while I cultivate new classes, I hate to be out of grip with the old. But say, it wouldn't take me long to get my hand in again. Just a case of lost practice.

By the way, my companion on that trip is somewhat of an amateur photographer, and the camera usually accompanies us on our trips. We have been waiting for a rainy day for developing and printing the shots we have taken—she's got some kind of a film or plate, or whatever it is, which does not require the sun for printing. Well, when we work them up, if there are any good ones of myself, I'll ship them along.

Have been going on chess drunks of late. Did you ever yield to the toils of the game?—toils in more ways than one. It's a most fascinating game, and one which has devoured well nigh as many of my hours as cards. However, I've done very little chess in the last year or so, and this is merely a temporary relapse.

Having also been feasting my soul with some of the new books: Kipling galore, Bullen's *Sea Idyls,* Grant Allen's *Adventures of Miss Gayly,* and among others, Beatrice Harraden's *Fowler.* It's a strange sort of a work, but it dealt with or worked out a character which is the exact composite of two living models with whom I am acquainted. While no portion of the three hundred and odd pages may lay claim to special excellence, the thing as a whole is unusually well done. Read it when you get a chance. You have probably got an idea of it from the reviews. If you have not, I'll just say that it deals with a sort of creature who is not a man, and who at the same time is not a woman either—a sort of eunuch sort of thing, with a pair of pants on. Well, this creature is the fowler. He is a libertine—but not a physical but a metaphysical one. Women always feel safe with him—physically; and in this their intuition prompts them aright. But he assails their minds, which same he debauches thoroughly. It is a strange idea, but one which after all is not so uncommon in real life.

Am now doing a thousand words per day, six days per week. Last week I finished 1100 words ahead of the required amount. To-day (Tuesday), I am 172 ahead of my stint. I have made it a rule to make up next day what I fall behind; but when I run ahead, to not permit it to count on the following day. I am sure a man can turn out more, and much better in the long run working this way, than if he works by fits and starts. How do you find it?

How time flies! Here is Christmas at hand, and Paris approaching[2]—ah! I wonder if the gods will smile so that I may go!

Jack London

[1]Charles Fletcher Lummis edited *Land of Sunshine.*
[2]He hoped to visit Paris in 1900.

Oakland, Calif.
Oct. 24, 1899

Dear Cloudesley:—

Everything in confusion, visitors still here. So you're a chess player. And it's the one form of dissipation which has any attraction for you. As I can hardly look upon it in that light concerning myself, I can but conclude that you are by far the better player. Why I have never met a good player— spent all my time teaching beginners, and you know nothing is worse for chess than that. And besides, I have never had the time to devote to it. For a year at a stretch I never see a board, and then, for a few short weeks I happen to mildly indulge. As I have not taken the time to learn properly, so I cannot play an intensive game; instead, I play viciously, not more than four moves ahead at the best, and endeavor to break up combinations as fast as my opponent forms them—that is, first, if they are threatening; and second, if the slightest and most insignificant gain will accrue to myself, such as the getting of another piece of mine in position by a trade, or by double-banging my opponent's pawns, or preventing his castling by forcing him to move his king in a trade. For the sake of this latter, when the gambit goes my way, I always trade queens. But a heavy player, once growing accustomed to my play, doesn't do a thing to me. So be it. I shall never learn chess.

Last article published by me had, among other typographical errors, "something fresh for the jaded care of the world," instead of "something fresh for the jaded ear of the world." On second thought it might have been worse.

Think you could train yourself into becoming a hermit? For me that would be far harder than to train myself to become a suicide. I like to rub against my kind, with a gregarious instinct far stronger than in most men. A hermitage—synonym for hell. I would also like to kill a few of my kind once in a while, which same I think I would do rather than to isolate myself.

O, speaking of the fotos—was initiated in the art of developing them last Sunday; expect to print and mount them next Sunday; and then expect one.

So we both suffer from a plethora of sketches. Damn plots; I don't think I could construct a decent one to save my life. And who, of the best short story writers, do write stories which are nearer stories than sketches. If a study is a sketch (and so the magazine editors seem to deem it), then under the generic term "story," few, very very few pen products of not more than six thousand words can be placed. What think you? Beyond the short detective story, did you ever see one first class short yarn which would answer the American magazine classification?

Lucrative mediocrity—I know, if I escape drink, that I shall be surely driven to it. By God! if I have to dedicate my life to it, I shall sell work to

Frank A. Munsey. I'll buck up against them just as long as I can push a pen or they can retain a Ms. reader about the premises. Just on general principles, you know.

I remember Stevenson's reference in his letters to "The White Nigger," but I think it is an unpublished fragment. I have never seen anybody who has read it, or who knew of anybody else reading it. Am reading Stevenson's *Virginibus Puerisque* just now. Find in this mail his *Inland Voyage*. Return it when you have finished, as I wish to pass it along. It has just arrived. Have read it myself. Get such books for "Bull Durham" tobacco tags. Have sent for his *Silverado Squatters*—don't think much of it from previous reading, but it was a long time ago, and I did it too hurriedly, I'm afraid. If you haven't read it I'll send it along later.

So you try experiments in letter writing. I never do nor never have. Haven't the slightest idea what I'm going to say when I sit down—just hammer it out as fast as I can. And right well am I pleased when I have finished the hateful task. I wouldn't do it at all, no more than I would work, were it not for the compensation. As for you, I get more originality in your letters than from all my rest put together—rather jerky and jagged but refreshing and interesting. Believe me, I'm not fishing for a loan.

O I don't blame them. I'd write rot myself—if somebody would only pay me for it. There's the rub. Have been reading Jacob's *More Cargoes*.[1] You have surely seen some of his magazine work, haven't you? Also have been going through Kendricks Bangs' *The Dreamers* and *The Bicyclers and Other Farces*. He's clever and humorous, in a mild sort of way.

Have been digging at Norman's *Eastern Question,* preparatory to a certain economic dissertative article I intend writing—Asia touches one of the phases I wish to deal with. Besides, I have gone through Curzon's similar work, and wish to take up soon Beresford's *Break-up of China*. Am going through Drummond on evolution, Hudson on psychology, and reviewing Macaulay and De Quincey in the course of English in Minto which I am giving to a friend—the photographer. She's well up in the higher math, etc., but not in general culture—coaches in the exact sciences for would-be university students, etc. Say, that reviewing does a fellow good. I had no idea how hazy I had gotten.

Society will never injure me—the world calls too loudly for that.

Good night,
Jack London

[1]*Many Cargoes,* 1896, Wm. W. Jacobs.

To Cloudesley Johns

Oakland, Calif.
Oct. 31, 1899

Dear Cloudesley:—

Am ignorant of Eliza Otis, though I have a hazy recollection that the 'Frisco papers have laughed at her somewhere during the last several months.

So it seems my immature judgment of *Silverado Squatters* has been substantiated by another Stevenson lover. Guess I won't re-read it with so much else clamoring for my attention.

Say, by a still mate do you mean a smothered mate?

So you deem the world as fair a synonym for hell as I do hermitage. Can't see it. There are some redeeming features. As long as there is one good woman in it, or man either, it will not hold. Why I remember, once, when for several weeks I meditated profoundly on the policy of shuffling off. Seemed the clouds would never break. But at last they did, and I doubt if you could imagine the cause of my sweetened mood. A memory of a day, of an hour—nay, a few paltry minutes—came back to me, of a time almost lost in the dim past. I remembered—what? A woman's foot. We were by the sea; in a dare, we went in wading; had to stick our feet in the hot sand till they dried; and it was those few moments which came back to me, dripping with "sweetness and light." Hell. Nay, not so long as one woman's foot remains above ground.

Don't think I'm in love. Simply sentiment. Don't get that way often.

Well, I can't construct plots worth a damn, but I can everlastingly elaborate. Why, some time since, I started in to write a twenty-five hundred word article on "Housekeeping in the Klondike." In choice of theme I had been forced to narrow, being aware of my miserable predilection. And lo, before I had got into full swing, I found that the whole article could be comfortably taken up in a discussion of bread-making. And, still narrowing, it was soon apparent that this should be divided, one single sub-head to be discussed, viz. sour-dough bread-making. And so it goes. Never did a person need the gift of selection more than I.

Wow! How you love society! So that's the way to obtain lucrative imbecility. But, why should one wish to produce lucrative work? Because he needs the cash. And, how under the sun can one cultivate society (the necessary preliminary) when he hasn't the cash? Which reminds me of a point in the opera *Satanella*. Having squandered his patrimony, the young fellow secludes himself in a ramshackle castle, his last remaining possession, reputed to have been last used several centuries previously by an alchemistic ancestor. He (the young fellow) discovers the wizard's book of formulas, incantations, etc. "Now," says he, "I will discover how to make gold and thus rehabilitate my fortunes." Turning to the index, "Ah! 'How to make gold,' page—." He turns to the page and reads, " 'How to make gold. First, take some silver—' "

He breaks off abruptly and meditates. He has no silver. Then a bright idea strikes him. Returning to the index he looks up the recipe for the making of silver, and then turns to the proper page.

" 'How to make silver—first, take some gold—' "

Have just completed Horace Vachell's *The Procession of Life.* Have you read it? Was quite interesting, but not of the first water. I believe he wrote *The Quicksands of Pactolus,* a serial, in the *Overland,* sometime ago. And by the way, did you ever read that boyhood classic, *Phaeton Rogers?* Rossiter Johnston, who edits the Whispering Gallery of the *Overland,* is the author of it. I must have read it twelve or fourteen years ago.

Many thanks for information concerning the *Press* prizes. I had not heard of them. And think, perhaps, that I shall try my hand at some of them. Let me know whether it's the N.Y. City *Press* or the Albany. Have you heard of the *National* prizes? They're not particularly enticing. Don't remember now, but think—yes one must be a subscriber—and they're not very large.

My *Atlantic* story will come out, I believe, in the January number. Received a check for one hundred and twenty dollars yesterday for it, with a year's subscription thrown in. They are very slow, but very painstaking. They even questioned the propriety of using my given name—unconventional.[1] But they came around all right.

Have heard nothing more concerning my collection. They do take their time about it. Nothing from the *Cosmopolitan* prize essay either.

How do you like my new machine? Haven't got used to it yet. Came to-day. When I get married, guess I'll have to marry a type-writer girl. I do most heartily hate the job.

So the poor little Boers have risen in their might. God bless them! I can admire their pluck, while at the same time laughing at their absurdity. There be higher things than formal logic or formal ethics. When a detached, antiquated fragment of a race attempts to buck that race, a spectacle is presented at once pitiful and impotent. Fools, to think that man is the object of his own volition, inasmuch that a few of him may oppose the many in a movement which does not spring from the individual but from the race, and which received its inception before even they had differentiated from the parent branch! As well might a grasshopper buck the flying express— mean lightning express.

Find enclosed a story by Jacobs. Also an opportunity for such budding genius which requires naught but a "name,"—which article the stony-hearted publishers will not permit it to possess.

Jack London

---

[1]"An Odyssey of the North." The Editor asked if "Jack London" was a pseudonym.

To Cloudesley Johns

Oakland, Calif.
Nov. 11, 1899

Dear Cloudesley:—

Ha! ha! The mendicant *Overland,* eh? It's my belief that said mendicancy is no new departure. They may, however, have become more nervy. I doubt if they would have made such a munificent offer, had you been situated nearer at hand. They would have made you a cheap offer instead. That's the way I found them. For "To the Man on Trail," I received five dollars (agreed upon). Then you will notice that in the following month I did not publish. I was waiting to see Bridge with the idea of getting a series published —that is, if I could get better rates. This he agreed to, but they were nothing to boast of—sold at a song. And then it kept me busy dunning them for my paltry due. They only pay for the two or three best articles each month—so I am informed. A glance at the remainder will show the type of contributor. It is said that *The Overland* broke the publishing House of Valentine up, and before that, some other publisher. I have it on hearsay, that Charles Green, the late associate editor and present incumbent of the Oakland Free Library librarianship, was behind something like a couple of thousand salary with them.

Think of it! Of the seven articles they published of mine, I never received the pay for one without excessive dunning—in person and by letter. Did your "Post No. 12" come back? If so, did they have anything to say? I am interested in this little racket of yours, for the third of this month I sent them a Ms. ["The Wisdom of the Trail"]. Said Ms. had been declined in the East till it was positively filthy. From the first class magazines it always had brought with rejection a complimentary letter and expressed desire to see more of my work. But they were evidently afraid of it, and of me. Of course, second rate publications had nothing to say. However, it was so worn out, that I could not in common decency send it east again, and I was too lazy to retype it. So I sent it to the *Overland,* stating the case, and informing them that they could have it for twenty-five dollars. In the face of this proposition to you I am wondering how they will act upon it.

My only experience in asking gratuitous contributions, was with the *S. F. Call.* I assured them that I, like themselves, was in such absorbing pursuit of the shekels that I couldn't think of it; that it would be as hard for me to give it to them for nothing as it would be for them to pay me for publishing it. They couldn't send me back the Ms. But they did the proofs. Hadn't waited to see if I was willing. Then I watched for them. Had saved the correspondence. If they'd dared to publish it I had full intentions of being paid or of sueing them for all it was worth—advertisement, if nothing else.

"This is the beginning of the end—you'll see—and within ten years the British Empire will have followed its predecessors, the Greek, the Roman, and the French." Well, well, well. I'd like to talk with you for a few moments. It's simply impossible to take it up on paper. The day England goes under, that day sees sealed the doom of the United States. It's the Anglo-Saxon people against the world, and economics at the foundation of the whole business; but said economics only a manifestation of the blood differentiations which have come down from the hoary past.

This movement, dimly felt and working in strange ways is not to be stopped in a day, or by a lesser people, or by a bunch of the same which have become anachronisms. The Boers are anachronisms. There is no place for them in the whirl of the world unless they whirl with it.

You say, if subjugated they will still be Boers. Do you remember the Norman invasion of England? How long the Saxons held strictly apart? And how in the end, the Saxon, as a Saxon, vanished from the face of the earth? Took several centuries, but it was accomplished.

Why the British Empire is going back, but not to dissolution. I can only conceive, taking all the factors into consideration, that it is only a temporary affair. The big and increasing adverse balances of trade are striking her hard just now. But they are easily understood. To pay them she is being forced to get rid of her holdings in foreign funds and stock. But it is not for long. But why is it? With the whole world, teeming with natural and undeveloped resources, England, the supremacy of the seas and the best enlightenment of the world hers, leaped at once into the van of the trading nations—this at the time of the industrial revolution, at the end of the last century and the beginning of this. This revolution the rise of modern capitalism and the change from domestic manufacture to capitalistic or factory manufacture.

England was in the lead, and developed a capacity for supplying the markets of the world. This gave her great foreign holdings. Then the newer nations began to compete with her. Prussian beet sugar, heavily subsidized, knocked out England's East and West Indian cane sugars—not for home consumption but for world consumption. The U.S. for instance, in manufactures, is selling everywhere. Same with most countries. Beresford plaintively cries that China is beginning to manufacture, and that England must look sharp if she wishes to sell them the machinery by which to do so. But what does this mean? That in a short while, China will not even have to buy her machinery. And again, that instead of consuming her product, there will be surplus product, cheaper than England's—will England buy it? Who will? All countries are getting in a similar position.

But—England, having led the van, feels now the pinch first; but the others are racing into the same pickle. Only a little while. As it is, absolutely necessary, is the fight for foreign markets. Forced upon the world, inevitably, is an era of great colonial empire—but for a little while. Wish I could talk it over with you. Am knocking it out at lightning speed and cannot present it consecutively, fully—or logically.

I don't envy you the 240,000 words you have to type. I'd quit writing forever if such a dismal fate should come up against me. Don't think I'd have the fortitude to face it. What's your brother fitting himself for? You say he is cramming for Stanford.

Fifty 1 d. stamps—that's sufficient for twenty-five ordinary Mss. isn't it? Have been thinking of trying the English market myself, but have been always delaying getting the stamps.

How can you begin two more novels? And how many have you still unfinished? Pshaw! I envy you. I can't see my way clear to commence my first. Got an acceptance from the *Review of Reviews*—do you know how they pay? And say, besides *Munsey's* and Tillotson and Sons, what is the storiette market? Are there many other publications that make a specialty of them?

I believe Brett Harte wrote a story of a natural fool who got along nicely till he struck it rich. I'm hard at it. Am just finishing an ambitious Klondike yarn which is a failure, and before the twenty-fifth of this month have to write and read up for two essays and prepare for a speech before the Oakland Section. Haven't addressed an audience for three years; it'll seem strange.

I have asked half a dozen well-read friends, but none of them have heard of the "Spider-ship" idea. Nor have I. It seems good, and with your Biercian power of handling the nasty and weird you ought to make something good out of it. Go ahead.

With poem which I did not enclose, I send another by Rudyard K. Ship us it back and tell what you think.

How's that for Teutonic construction?

That *Truth-Seeker* isn't a softe hiytter—this is not archaic English. I meant that it is not a soft hitter. Still, while I like good virile English, I believe that all discretion and good taste should not be cast to the wind. Vituperation does not make converts; It is not logic; it has no appeal to the intellectual person; the bigot is but hardened in his iniquity by it. Some Swedish woman protests, from the highest, purest motives, if totally mistaken in her views; and the T. S. [*Truth Seeker*] slaps it into her without mercy. And the persons concerned her own dead mother or father—I forget which. I don't mind blasphemy; but that, to my mind, is greater than blasphemy is to the Christians. If I had a sister, mother, or dear friend who had been treated as she has been, and if the T. S. editor was within walking distance, I'd thrash him or he'd thrash me.

A truly noble mind would not descend to that. O, when it comes to strong, well equipped men, in the rough and tumble of life, I don't mind how hard they hit back and forth; but this is not such an instance. Eternal fitness, you know.

Why my dear fellow, you, who would rather sing your country's songs, are somewhat didactic after all, controversial, etc. I'm afraid there's too much of Father Adam in you to be nothing but a singer.

I can't help but wonder that you took five dollar's worth of the paper for "The God that Failed." Where the devil else could you have sent it?—

outside of the infidel publications? I wonder what *Munsey's* thought on receiving it? O, I have it—you could have simply changed the ending and had his prayer answered. Then a myriad of Sunday School papers would have clamored for it. You might even have had it printed as a tract and sold several hundred thousand. It's all in the ending you see.

Joshing aside, I think it all right. Logically handled. How your description on scene and man's physical actions reminds me of Bierce!—a certain, bald, but essentially perspicuous method. Nothing ambiguous; nothing requiring a second reading to assure one of the writer's meaning. Do you wish this copy of the T. S. back? Or do you want the answer to an anarchist?

Critical I always am when it comes to dissertative work, but in said "letter," I cannot find one objection. Whatever you have stated, I agree with. Though I do not know how deep you would go into it, as far as it went it was correct. Why don't you get in and systematically ground yourself in history, economics, biology, and the kindred branches? Omnivorous reading will never do it. System you must have if any really available good is to come.

As to your suggestion regarding the finish of "To the Man on Trail"; I had never been satisfied with that ending, though too lazy to even think for an instant of attempting to better it. Your ending could not be bettered, and I shall hasten to take advantage of it. Many thanks for same. It will then leave one with a pleasant taste in the mouth. The alliterative effect you mention strikes my gaudy ear; I shall certainly use it. I want you to read my "Odyssey of the North," when it comes out. Nov. *Atlantic,* bills it for December. But editors told me not till January.

Jack London

To Cloudesley Johns

Oakland, Calif.
Nov. 21, 1899

Dear Cloudesley:—

Hard at it—mostly history and economics. And yet I don't work a tithe of what you work. Why should you work seventeen hours a day? As regards your writing you positively should not do more than six—four were better. But any excess of six cannot be good stuff. Of course, the arrival of typewriter with a huge stack of work to run through accounts for overtime now. But before the arrival of the typewriter what were you doing with those seventeen hours? Writing?—impossible to turn out good work at such rate. Then what? as I do not think you would persistently turn out bad work. What then? what did you do with the other eleven hours? Say four for cooking, eating, etc., and three for post-office duties, what of the other four? Read? What? Aye, there's the rub. I shall take the liberty of forwarding to you by this mail some presumptious advice I was lately guilty of. A certain portion, in line with preceding paragraph, applies to you, which same I leave to your discrimination to discover. Compositors mixed the tenses on me, besides divers other mistakes. All of which amounts to nil. I dashed it off at a white heat any way. The *Editor* has itself listed as "paying liberally." I thought I'd find out what they conceived "liberal" to mean. They were also listed as paying—no they were not either. They said on acceptance that I would receive pay promptly on publication. I dunned them the other day and am still waiting returns. Kindly return *Editor* to me as I wish file to be complete.

I read *Edwin Drood* when I was a little fellow, and was so disgusted at the break-off that I have never possessed an atom of respect for it since. You see, I can remember nothing about it save something to do with a Lascar and with an opium den. Tell me, am I mistaken in those two items? Have I dug them up from something else?

You write very differently than do I. Every day sees what I have composed, all typed and ready to be submitted. I never polish. I write anywhere from ten to two hundred words in long hand, glance over it, and slap it through the machine. Then I repeat the maneuver.

I never pity anybody but myself. Life is too short.

The Overland declined my offer on specious grounds. Twenty-five dollars was stiff under the circumstances. However, I have placed a yarn with them to come out in the Christmas number. O they're great people, of great heart; but heart and finance do not usually go together. Let us know how you come out with them.

Many thanks for English stamps; I shall proceed to exploit them. And you, I suppose you will gather the sinews of war from the mother country, exploiting her as she is exploiting the world. Apropos of this I send clippings by Bierce, etc. I admire Bierce for the stand he takes. Very few American educated people have little else but rancor for England—a rancor which is bred by the school histories and the school traditions. All of which are utterly wrong.

I have to laugh when you call Kipling "a narrow hide-bound, childishly pettish, mean, little man." Not that some of it is not true (or whatever I mean), but at the thought of the clipping I enclose with this. Any masculine who delights in taking down a woman's back hair will find a warm welcome in my heart. And especially so of a man who would in any way merit some of the adjectives you have showered upon him. He really is a man, you know. Yes, by Jove, he is. Why I could have hugged him—supposing it to be true, and as it seems to me if there is but one scrap of truth in the whole sensation-article, that one is the back hair episode.

Find return of Wilson's letter. Keep me informed of the outcome. I'd like to see them tackle you.

Find, with *Editor,* when it comes along, some more proofs of yours truly, taken down by the sounding sea. Also one of the young woman who sometimes accompanies me in my far from conventional rambles [Bessie Maddern]. Last Sunday, threatening rain, we wandered off into the hills cooked our dinner (broiled steak, baked sweet potatoes, coffee, etc., crab, French bread, and a patty of dairy butter), and were a couple of gypsies. To-morrow we may jump on our wheels and ride off forty or fifty miles. And yesterday we may have taken in the opera and dined fashionably. Never the same, except the camera, which same I am slowly mastering.

Haven't much of an opinion on the "Odyssey." Cutting out nearly three thousand words in the beginning, descriptive of the camp, the mailmen, dig-drivers, and policemen, cut me up as well. Luckily I refused to touch the "Odyssey" proper at all. I think it is good, though I only half realized what I conceived it to be. Be sure and tell me what you think of it.

O I was only joshing about the "God that Failed." What I evidently failed to convey was that it was so blasphemous that I couldn't possibly see where you could have rid yourself of it had you rejected the offer of the *Truth-seeker*.

Yes; I read *A New Magdalen* when I was about twelve, and then shocked a very nice young lady by starting to discuss it with her.

Don't know who Rogers is—never heard of him before. But the "Prospector" was good, excellent.

When England is so decadent as to lose her colonies, then England falls. When England falls the United States will be shaken to its foundations, and the chances are one hundred to one that it ever recovers again. Why, England is our greatest purchaser, and our greatest maker of markets, and the only nation which is not deep down hostile to us. Germany, France, Austria and Russia can supply the world with all that the world needs, if only they could get a chance by having England and the United States eliminated from the proposition. And once one were eliminated the ruin of the other were easy. But England is not going to fall. It is not possible. To court such a possibility is to court destruction for the English speaking people. We are the salt of the earth, and it is because we have it in us to frankly say so that we really are so. No hemming or hawing; we state the bald fact. It is for the world to take or leave. Take it may, but it shall always leave us.

Nations do not fall before military prowess. Bad economics or killing competition is what kills them. Rome did not fall before the superior ability of the Germanic tribes. Bad economics had destroyed her warrior class; for centuries her armies had been recruited from among those self-same barbarians. She had ceased to reproduce her own citizens. Nobody cared to have children. She was empty. She did not fall in the end. Simply became empty and was filled up by the flood of emigration from the north. The United States could defend herself against overwhelming odds—aye, in the heyday of economic integrity—but with such things in smash, which also smash the timber of her citizens—why she would assuredly fall.

So? Why the United States never had but one fight in its history; that was when it fought with itself. England never bothered much with her. Read up history and you will find that England's hands were full of other things, and preferring other matters, and she *let* the colonies slip away. Do you really think we whipped the whole of England in the Revolution? Or in 1812, when her hands were full with Napoleon, and she was fighting in every quarter of the globe? Mexico was play. But that civil war was a war, a death grapple. And all hail to the south for the fight it put up against stiff odds.

You little know Canada. Why don't those other European countries, standing by themselves, fall? Because, they are but ostensibly alone. In reality they stand together—whenever it comes to bucking the Anglo-Saxon.

If cash comes with fame, come fame; if cash comes without fame, come cash.

I shall be pleased to see you when you drop in on me. Only I shall not devote myself to trying to knock out of you the fallacies ingrained in your youth. Just let us know a couple of days in advance of your coming. And then come.

I shall send clippings with *Editor*.

Jack London

To Cloudesley Johns

Oakland, Calif.
Dec. 5, 1899

Dear Cloudesley:—

First letter-writing I have done for quite a while. Have been very busy. Have not had an evening at home for nigh on to two weeks, what with suppers, speaking, functions, and last but not least, FOOTBALL. Did you see what we did to Stanford? In case that benighted region in which you reside has not yet received the score, let me have the privilege of blazoning it forth. Thirty to nothing, Berkeley.

It was magnificent, to sit under the blue and gold and [watch] the Berkeley giants wade through the Cardinals, and especially so when one looks back to the times he sat and watched the Stanfordites pile up the score and hammer our line into jelly. Do you care for football? In case you do not, I shall not permit my enthusiasm to bore you further.

Say? I am acquainted with Nan Byxbie, one of the new space-writers on the *Call*. Her name you have probably seen in recent issues if you read that paper. I coached her up in versification and a little bit on style at odd intervals; besides we know each other very well. If the *Call* does not dig up your Ms., shall I see her about it?

Heaven save us from our friends! Last Sunday evening I spoke before the San Francisco Section. Unknown to me, and on the strength of divers newspaper puffs which recently have appeared, they posted San Francisco, and also perpetrated the enclosed handbill. I knew nothing about it till just the moment before I was to go on the platform. Can I sue them for libel? Please return it, as I, also, have a collection.

71

I have not got to your *Truthseekers* yet, nor to anything else, but I will tear out and send you that portion you wish as soon as I read it. My reading table is banked with books and magazines and it makes me shudder every time I look at them.

Am sorry you sent for the December *Atlantic*. The November Number announced the December table of contents, in which was my "Odyssey." But it has been evidently deferred.

So I'm a source of inspiration, eh? I thought that was the prerogative solely of the fair sex. But now that I've gone and inspired you, I don't think I should be defrauded of the fruit of my labor. Go ahead and publish it, but throw some carbon sheets into your typewriter and send me a copy.

228,000 words! Why I verily believe that's more than I have written in all my life (correspondence barred). Of course one should do one's own typing. I do all my polishing on the machine.

You say you are contemplating coming to Oakland somewhere near the end of the year. If you do I am afraid we won't meet each other. I expect to spend my holidays down country, and shall depart thereto as soon as I have caught up in my reading and work. It's a year-old promise, made because of neglect on my part last Christmas, and I cannot break it. If you could delay your coming till January I should be very pleased, for then we would be sure to meet.

I see you do not believe in what is called an adverse balance of trade. Very good. Yet I am sure you apply it in your own case; for the man [who] makes a practice of buying more than his pocket book contains usually goes bankrupt.

Why is it that England has such a grip over the material resources of the world, drawing interest from almost every country under the sun, and with that interest buying the grub of other countries? The answer is simple. Because she spent her spare money by investing it abroad. The man who lives over the contents of his purse never has any money to invest. The United States had to borrow money from abroad to develop a large portion of her resources. These foreign securities drained a huge tide of interest from the States. But the last several years America has been buying back her securities held abroad. And why has she been doing this? or rather, how has she been able to do this? Because her balances of trade had at last grown favorable. If she exports half a billion of dollars more than she imports, this half a billion must be paid to her in gold. And with this gold she has bought back her securities, also had part of it to invest in her own territory and in other countries. O yes, "I know that if we were denied the privilege of sending away a third of our food products we would have less to eat."

O, sure; there never was a fanatic on any subject who did not believe he had logically deduced or induced his conclusions from thoroughly correct premises.

As I said, I was a very little boy when I read *Edwin Drood*. Your criticism of my *Editor* article is exactly my own criticism. We could not disagree on that if we tried. By the way, there were 1750 words in it. The *Editor* was billed to pay liberally, and they told me on acceptance, promptly. It was published last October, I received for it five dollars which came to hand day before yesterday.

O Lord! Good-bye.

Jack London

To Cloudesley Johns

Oakland, Calif.
Dec. 12, 1899

Dear Cloudesley:—

A short letter, for I depart down country. Write me, care Edward Applegarth, Jr.,
  Corner Elm and Asbury sts.,
    San Jose,
      Calif.

I shall come back to Oakland after the holidays. Until then a truce to production and to the machine.

How shall I say? Well, only this, do for goodness sake do some digging at evolution, some real hard digging. As for your theory, pardon my harshness, it is absurd. That self-same evolution, had you studied it in its essentials and not in the popular way, would have prevented you perpetrating the atrocity. What have you done? Builded up a theory on a few false analogies. Us reaching the summit more rapidly—why we have been the slowest, and, to adopt a true analogy, because ours is the highest, is because it has been the slowest, just as man with his fourteen to sixteen years of adolescence is a higher order of being than the dog with its short year of puppyhood. The black has stopped, just as the monkey has stopped. Never will even the highest anthropoid apes evolve into man; likewise the Negro into a type of man higher than any existing. But had you turned the other way you would have found a more youthful race and the only one which can scientifically answer to your hypothesis: namely, the Slav. The Negro, like the Red, has been passed by. The Slav has not yet been reached. He may never be reached.

But don't try to prove things too exclusively by analogy. It is the common belief that death is the correlative of life. That whatsoever lives must die. Yet this is not so. Why the life cells, or rather, germ cells, which leave your body when in the arms of a wanton, lived, yea, they lived when your ancestors were fishes in the sea, when they were reptiles in the dirt, when sex was unknown, when they were nothing but palpitating masses of formless life.

The female is the passive, the male the active factor in the carrying on of the function of reproduction. This is a popular conception. Yet, in the lower forms of life, certain lower forms, not all, the female is far larger than the male, the more predatory and ferocious. She alone possesses the prehensile organs of reproduction. She it is who pursues the resisting male, holds him firmly, rapes him in short, that she may breed her kind. Watch out for analogies.

I started in to write a short letter, and I'll have to. Am going to take a run up to 'Frisco next week from San Jose and I'll find out what Nan Byxbie has discovered relating to your ms. I wrote her about it this mail—I mean manuscript at *Call*.

You mistake. I do not believe in the universal brotherhood of man. I think I have said so before. I believe my race is the salt of the earth. I am a scientific socialist, not a utopian, an economic man as opposed to an imaginative man. The latter is becoming an anachronism.

Nay, nay, bankruptsy (how is it spelled?) is not an ideal state, at least for me. It's horrible, too horrible for words. Give me the millions and I'll take the responsibilities.

Later on I shall forward you an article of mine on the "Question of the Maximum," which contains within it, though not the main theme, the economic basis for imperialism or expansion. This, I know, is directly opposed to the current ethics. But it is the one which will dominate the current ethics.

Good night,
Jack London

P.S. Is the enclosed page the one you wished torn out and sent to you?

J. G. L.

To Anna Strunsky[1]

Oakland, Calif.
Dec. 19, 1899

My dear Miss Strunsky:—

Seems as if I have known you for an age—you and your Mr. Browning. I shall certainly have to re-read him, in the hope after all these years of obtaining a fuller understanding.

What did I start in to write you about, anyway? Oh! First, that toasting the old year out-affair—does it take place on the last Friday or Thursday of the month; and secondly—well, it doesn't matter. I have forgotten.

Please don't carry a wrong impression of my feelings regarding Hamilton.[2] Because I happen to condemn his deficiencies is no reason that I do not appreciate his good qualities, nor that I should not love him. Indeed I do. Do you remember how I said I ran down the street after him on a circus day, cut engagements, etc.? My feelings and personal liking swayed me there; but in summing up the man I set such things to one side and perform the operation with the cold-bloodedness of the economic man. I hope you will understand. My regard for him [is] such that were I to accumulate a treasure I think I would advertise for him in the agony columns throughout the United States and bring him to me, give him a home, a monthly allowance, and let him live out his life whatsoever way he willed.

You said at parting that you also were a literary aspirant. I may be able to help you, perhaps—not in the higher criticism but in the more prosaic but none the less essential work of submitting Mss. Through much travail I have learned the customs of the "silent sullen peoples who run the magazines." Their rates, availability, acceptability, etc. Should you stand in need of anything in this line (economic man), believe me sincerely at your service.

Of course, I do not know what lines you deem yourself best fitted for; however, as I sat there listening to you, I seemed to sum you up somewhat in this way: A woman to whom it is given to feel the deeps and the heights of emotion in an extraordinary degree; who can grasp the intensity of transcendental feeling, the dramatic force of situation, as few women, or men either, can. But, this question at once arose: Has she expression? By this I mean simply the literary technique. And again, supposing that she has not, has she the "dig," the quality of application, so that she might attain it?

In a nut-shell—you have the material, which is your own soul, for a career: have you the requisite action to hew your way to it?

Let me see—I had so much to say, and now I have forgotten it. New Years Day,[3] down country, I read "Andrea del Sarto." Splendid, seems but feeble praise. How delicately and with what virility he touches upon the deepest truths of life. Now, if you will read that to me the next time we are together, I shall understand and appreciate. The good things of life must grow upon one. With each impact they are invested with greater significance. It haunts me that I have the title of the poem wrong. Anyway, it's the "faultless painter."

I was out to Berkeley the other day, taking my friends through, and I was clad in the disreputable comfort of a sweater. It is well we did not meet. Tell me of your new life. My interest is great. Will Berkeley caress you, I wonder? I imagine it to be far colder than Stanford. Why, I cannot tell. It just seems so.

Yours very cordially,

Jack London

P.S. I shall send this by your San Francisco address. Let me have your new one. And also when I may call. The first Fridays in every month, also every week the Mondays, Wednesdays and Sundays are usually engaged, though sometimes, under pressure, I break them.

J. L.

[1]A Russian Jewess whom London met at a Socialist lecture given by Austin Lewis in the fall of 1899. She collaborated with London on the *Kempton-Wace Letters* and later married William English Walling, Socialist writer. She died in late February, 1964.
[2]Frank Strawn-Hamilton, hobo, Socialist, noted as the Socialists' most brilliant speaker.
[3]An apparent incongruity. Original letter is dated Dec. 19, 1899.

To ANNA STRUNSKY

Oakland, Calif.
Dec. 21, 1899

Dear Miss Strunsky:—

Surely am I a barbarian, lacking in cunning of speech and deftness of touch. Perhaps I am only a Philistine. Mayhap the economic man incarnate. At least blundering and rough-shod, lacking even that expression which should properly voice my thoughts. I call for a trial by jury. I throw myself on the mercy of the Court. Nay, after all is said and done, I plead not guilty.

"Somehow it is a new note to me, that of being seen as 'aimless, helpless, hopeless,' and I am uneasy under it all."

I rarely remember what I say in letters, sometimes retaining only vague recollections of what I do not say; but in the present case I am sure I said nothing like the above. I speculated on you as impartially as had you been a hod-carrier, a Hottentot, or a Christ. It was a first speculation; it dealt with but one portion of your being. And as I could not divorce Christ or the Hottentot from the rest of humanity as having nothing in common with it, so I could not divest you of the weaknesses which I know your fellows to suffer from. But such weaknesses are not to be classed under your three-fold caption. 'aimless, helpless, hopeless.' I granted aim. I then asked myself whether you had the qualities by which to realize it. I did not answer that question, for verily I did not nor do I know. I was even more generous. I granted the basic qualities, all-necessary for attainment, and only questioned the existence of the medium by which they could be made to meet with their proper end. And that question I did not answer (to myself) for I did not know, nor do I know.

This is my case. I call for your verdict.

Somehow I am like a fish out of water. I take to conventionality uneasily, rebelliously. I am used to saying what I think, neither more than less. Soft equivocation is no part of me. As had I spoken to a man who came out of nowhere, shared my bed and board for a night, and passed on, so did I speak to you. Life is very short. The melancholy of materialism can never be better expressed than by Fitzgerald's "O make haste!" One should have no time to dally. And further, should you know me, understand this: I, too, was a dreamer, on a farm, nay, a California ranch. But early, at only nine, the hard hand of the world was laid upon me. It has never relaxed. It has left me sentiment, but destroyed sentimentalism. It has made me practical, so that I am known as harsh, stern, uncompromising. It has taught me that reason is mightier than imagination; that the scientific man is superior to the emotional man. It has also given me a truer and a deeper romance of things, an idealism which is an inner sanctuary and which must be resolutely throttled in dealings with my kind, but which yet remains within the holy of holies, like an oracle, to be cherished always but to be made manifest

76

or be consulted not on every occasion I go to market. To do this latter would bring upon me the ridicule of my fellows and make me a failure. To sum up, simply the eternal fitness of things.

All of which goes to show that people are prone to misunderstand me. May I have the privilege of not so classing you?

Nay, I did not walk down the street after Hamilton—I ran. And I had a heavy overcoat, and I was very warm and breathless. The emotional man in me had his will, and I was ridiculous.

I shall be over Saturday night. If you draw back upon yourself, what have I left? Take me this way: a stray guest, a bird of passage, splashing with salt-rimed wings through a brief moment of your life—a rude and blundering bird, used to large airs and great spaces, unaccustomed to the amenities of confined existence. An unwelcomed visitor, to be tolerated only because of the sacred law of food and blanket.

Very sincerely,
Jack London

To Anna Strunsky

Oakland, Calif.
Dec. 27, 1899

My dear Miss Strunsky:—

I am surprised. And pleased beyond measure. So preposterous would it have seemed, that I could not even have canvassed the thought as to your caring for Kipling. Why I could hardly believe my ears when you claimed as among the finest lines of Mandalay, "O ship me somewheres east of Suez, etc." He is so many-sided that the general public finds plenty to admire in him, but your caring for him in other ways—ways in which I thought it possible for but a few world-roughened spirits—astounds me. And puzzles me. How? I ask. How? Not by what right, but by what means have you come to comprehend? Surely, from what little I know of your life, I may safely predicate, absolutely, that you know nothing of much with which he deals, cannot have experienced the feelings or personal conditions he portrays. "Where there aren't no ten commandments and a man can raise a thirst"—How? how? I ask. And then it comes to me this way:—Are you one of those favored spirits who vibrate, by some subtle faculty to states or conditions of which they are in reality ignorant; who, by some occult divination or sympathy may feel with those of which they can know nothing, ring true to that which it would seem is not in them but of which by some incomprehensible way they may partake?

Pardon me for having ventured to analyze you; but mankind is my passion, and the search after potentiality and the realization thereof, my hobby. Thinkers do not suffer from lack of expression; their thought is their expression. Feelers do; it is the hardest thing in the world to put feeling, and deep feeling, into words. From the standpoint of expression, it is easier to write a *Das Capital* in four volumes than a simple lyric of as many stanzas.

A Truce to lecturing. Typewriters, while very excellent in their way, are a very poor medium for conversation. The mouth were better formed for expression than the finger-tips. May I see you next Friday night? Candidly, I may some time steal you or certain portions of you for exploitation between covers, unless you hasten to get yourself copyrighted. Which is to say, preliminarily, that I should like to sum you up some more.

Very cordially yours,

Jack London

To Anna Strunsky

Oakland, Calif.
Dec. 29, 1899

My dear Miss Strunsky:—

Just a line to thank you, for I too, after much unseemly hesitancy, am going away for a few days.

Expression? I think you have it, if this last letter may be any criterion. How have I felt since I received it? How shall I say? At any rate, know this: I do agree, unqualifiedly, with your diagnosis of where I missed and how. If I recollect aright, it was my first and last attempt at a psychological study. I saw that I had much before me yet to gain before I should put my hand to such work. I glanced over several pages just before sending, noted the frightful diction and did not dare go on to the meat of it. I knew, I felt that there was so much which was wrong with it, that the ending was inadequate, etc., and that was all. But you have given me clearer vision, far clearer vision. For my vague feelings of what was wrong, you have given me the why. It is you who are the missionary.

I am down in the dust to Jaky for an unpardonable wrong. But my extenuation is my youth and inexperience. It was absurd at the time I wrote it to think of accomplishing such a thing. It really was false-winged, you see, that flight of mine. Not only have you shown me my main flaw, but you have exposed a second—the lack of artistic selection.

And above all, you have conveyed to me my lack of spirituality, idealized spirituality—I know not if I use the terms correctly. Don't you understand? I came to you like a parched soul out of the wilderness, thirsting for I knew not what. The highest and the best had been stamped out of me. You know my life, typified, mayhap, by the hastily drawn picture of the forecastle. I was troubled. Groping after shadows, mocking, disbelieving, giving my own heart the lie oftentimes, doubting that which very doubt bade me believe. And for all, I was a-thirst. Stiff-necked, I flaunted my physical basis, hoping that the clear water might gush forth. But not then, for there I played the barbarian. Still, from the little I have seen of you my lips have been moistened, my head lifted. Do you remember "It was my duty to have loved the highest; it was my pleasure had I known"? Pray do not think me hysterical. In the bright light of day I might flush at my weakness, but in the darkness I let it pass.

Only, I do hope we shall be friends.

"Only not all Jews haggle and bargain"—there, surely, you did me wrong. My glimmering adumbrations bespoke far more than that. But there—remember I have misunderstood you a score of times and trampled rough-shod over as many sensibilities. Jaky and his wife did exist, did keep a second hand store, were fanatical (?) in their quest after knowledge. I helped them a little in English. Jaky, or his prototype, having abandoned night high school in despair, afterward corresponded with me in order that I might correct his work.

I see this "just a line" has grown. Please do not answer till after your examinations. Know that I pray for the best possible best. And please let me know the outcome, for I shall be as anxious almost as yourself. And further—no—what's the use?

Oh! during the collapse after they are over with, should you run across a January *Atlantic Monthly,* look up my "Odyssey of the North." The first two sections were reduced by nearly three thousand words on request of the editor, and it so broke my heart in cutting them out that I simply mangled it. You see, I had endeavored to supply most of the atmosphere before the odyssey proper began, and such wholesale pruning, months after it was written, took all the spirit out of it. The odyssey proper I strove to invest with a certain rude epic swing—of course it's all idealized.

Again praying that I may be informed of the outcome, just whether it is or it isn't, I am,

Very sincerely,
Jack London

1900-1905

RISE TO FAME

CHRONOLOGY

1900: Married to Bessie Maddern.

Published:[1] *The Son of the Wolf,* Houghton Mifflin Co., April (collected stories).

1901: Birth of first daughter (Joan).

Published: *The God of His Fathers,* McClure, Phillips and Co., May (collected stories).

1902: Trip to London, where he lived among the slums and from which came *The People of the Abyss.* Birth of second daughter (Bess).

Published: *A Daughter of the Snows,* J. B. Lippincott, October (novel).
Children of the Frost, The Macmillan Co., October (collected stories).
The Cruise of the Dazzler, The Century Co., October (juvenile).

1903: Separation from his first wife (Bessie). Purchase of a sloop, the *Spray.*

Published: *The Kempton-Wace Letters,* The Macmillan Co., May (philosophical letters on love, in collaboration with Anna Strunsky).
The Call of the Wild, The Macmillan Co., July (novel).
The People of the Abyss, The Macmillan Co., October (sociological study of London slums).

1904: January to June. In Korea as a war correspondent for Hearst in the Japanese-Russian War.

Published: *The Faith of Men,* The Macmillan Co., May (collected stories).
The Sea Wolf, The Macmillan Co., November (novel).

1905: Divorced from Bessie. Married to Charmian Kittredge. Purchase of the Hill Ranch in Glen Ellen, Sonoma Co., California, the beginning of the "Beauty Ranch." Lecture tour through the Midwest and East. Trip to Jamaica.

Published: *War of the Classes,* The Macmillan Co., April (sociological essays).
The Game, The Macmillan Co., June (novel).
Tales of the Fish Patrol, The Macmillan Co., October (juvenile).

---

[1]Publications in these chronologies will not include serials. For a detailed listing of Jack London's publications see Woodbridge, Hensley C. and John London, *Jack London: a Bibliography,* Georgetown, Calif., The Talisman Press, 1965.

To Anna Strunsky

Oakland, Calif.
Jan. 15, 1900

Dear Miss Strunsky:—

Have been home from my trip and gone away again, just returning last evening to find your letter. Also was tied with a couple of guests, who are now playing chess as many feet away, and appealing as often every minute to my decision. So whatever is choppy please forgive.

I hardly know what I can say on paper, and wish I could have seen you last night. But know this: your idea of education does not end with the sheepskin. That much goes without saying. The university is simply to prepare. The credit one should earn is not a high standard in the college work in itself, but a high standard in the work one is to ultimately do in the world, and for which the university has made fit. It is a matter of common knowledge that the one who captures the prizes for scholarship and the fellowships, rarely does anything in his or her after-life. The fact that he is capable of making of his brain a machine, militates against his being capable of the higher individual initiative in the years to come. Surely you cannot help measuring yourself against your fellows, and surely you cannot find aught to be ashamed of in the ideals which you cherish, the knowledge you have gained, the life you have led and the work you have done for the world—nothing, save that you have failed to be an intellectual machine and to learn—not your lessons (which you have learned)—but the lessons which have been set before you by others. Who are they that they should set these lessons? and who are you that you should receive them? Ah, yes, for the common run of humanity, it is proper that these lessons should be set and learned—but there are other souls which should not be so hampered. And when I see such souls wasting their time over work which is unnecessary or less necessary than other work which they need, which they should be doing, and which if they do not do then they may never do, why it always makes me sad. When you spoke of cramming algebra, simply to gain so many credits to your course, I felt for the moment toward you as I would toward a bright young fellow preparing to bring his razor and his throat in disastrous propinquity. It was all wrong, every bit of it. And in one way I am almost glad that Stanford has turned out as it did. Glad for the soul of Anna Strunsky that it is so. And at the same time sorry am I for the heart of Anna Strunsky, and the pride. Believe me, I do know the suffering entailed, and I do also know that I have not the moral bravery to face the music as you are doing.

But you do know, I know you do, that one's works are not measured by a college career and record but by a whole life, in which the former plays no part save that of preparing. The university, after all, is such a limited audience when the whole world is waiting to hear. You register to-day, at Berkeley. Is it as a special? Heartily I hope so. You escape the trammels, and I know you are well capable of setting your own lessons. But how metallic this all is! I wish I could have seen you last night.

Thank you for "The Feet of the Young Men." I was about to quote from it, but find I must needs quote all, it is so good. Find enclosed the picture of Mary Antin.[1] I wish it were not profile.

It's too distracting, these guests of mine. I must give up writing this. However, let me hear of you, your new address, and when it may be convenient to have me call.

Oh! I also enclose one of Kipling's poems—a favorite of Hamilton's. He had suffered from insomnia himself and so, was never tired of repeating the lines.

Most sincerely,
Jack London

[1]Mary Antin Grabau. Author of *The Promised Land*. Published in English *From Plotzk to Boston*, a description of Jewish life in Poland, in 1899.

To Anna Strunsky

Oakland, Calif.
Jan. 21, 1900

Dear Miss Strunsky:—

O Pshaw!

Dear Anna:—

There! Let's get our friendship down to a comfortable basis. The superscription, "Miss Strunsky," is as disagreeable as the putting on of a white collar, and both are equally detestable. I did not read your last till Friday morning, and the day and evening were taken up. But at last I am free. My visitors are gone, the one back to his desert hermitage, and the other to his own country. And I have much work to make up. Do you know, I have the fatal faculty of making friends, and lack the blessed trait of being able to quarrel with them. And they are constantly turning up. My home is the Mecca of every returned Klondiker, sailor, or soldier of fortune I ever met. Some day I shall build an establishment, invite them all, and turn them loose upon each other. Such a mingling of castes and creeds and characters could not be duplicated. The destruction would be great.

However, I am so overjoyed at being free that I cannot be anything but foolish. I shall, with pitfall and with gin, beset the road my visitors do wander in; and among other things, erect a Maxim rapid-fire gun just within my front door. The sanctity of my fireside shall be inviolate. Or, should my heart fail me, I'll run away to the other side of the world.

Find enclosed, review of Mary Antin's book. Had I not known you I could not have understood the little which I do. Somehow we must ever build upon the concrete. To illustrate: do you notice the same in excerpt from her, beginning, "I thought of tempests and shipwrecks." How I would like to know the girl, to see her, to talk with her, to do a little toward cherishing her imagination. I sometimes weep at the grave of mine. It was sown on arid soil, gave vague promises of budding, but was crushed out by the harshness of things—a mixed metaphor, I believe.

"Like most modern Jewesses who have written, she is, I fear, destined to spiritual suffering." How that haunts one!

Ho! ho! I have just returned from the window. Turmoil and strife called me from the machine, and behold! My nephew [Johnny Miller], into whom it is my wish to inculcate some of the saltiness of the earth, had closed in combat with an ancient enemy in the form of a truculent Irish boy. There they were, hard at it, boxing gloves of course, and it certainly did me good to see the way in which he stood up to it. Only, alas, I see I shall have to soon give him instructions, especially in defense—all powder and flash and snappy in attack, but forgetful of guarding himself. "For life is strife," and a physical coward is the most unutterable of abominations.

Tell me what you think of Ms. It was the work of my golden youth. When I look upon it I feel very old. It has knocked from pillar to post and reposed in all manner of places. When my soul waxes riotous, I bring it forth, and lo! I am again a lamb. It cures all ills of the ego and is a sovereign remedy for self-conceit. "Mistake" is writ broad in fiery letters. The influences at work in me, from Zangwill to Marx, are obvious. I would have portrayed types and ideals of which I knew nothing, and so, trusted myself to false wings. You showed me your earliest printed production last night; reciprocating, I show you one written at the time I first knew Hamilton. I felt I had something there, but I certainly missed it. Some day, putting it at the bottom of the deepest of chests, I shall reattempt it. Tell me the weak points, not of course in diction, etc. Tell me what rings false to you. And be unsparing, else shall I have to class you with the rest of my friends, and it is not complimentary to them if they only knew it.

One has so much to say that the best course is to not say anything. Paper was made for business correspondence and for invitations; while the tongue is too often geared at too high a pitch to adequately carry on its labors.

Very sincerely,
Jack London

P.S. Your Stanford address? I have forgotten it. Is it "Stanford," "Stanford University," or "Palo Alto"?

Oakland, Calif.
Jan. 31, 1900

Gentlemen:

In reply to yours of January 25th. requesting additional biographical data. I see I shall have to piece out my previous narrative, which, in turn, will make this choppy.

My father was Pennsylvania-born, a soldier, scout, backwoodsman, trapper, and wanderer. My mother was born in Ohio. Both came west independently, meeting and marrying in San Francisco, where I was born January 12, 1876. What little city life I then passed was in my babyhood. My life, from my fourth to my ninth years, was spent upon Californian ranches. I learned to read and write about my fifth year, though I do not remember anything about it. I always could read and write, and have no recollection antedating such a condition. Folks say I simply insisted upon being taught. Was an omnivorous reader, principally because reading matter was scarce and I had to be grateful for whatever fell into my hands. Remember reading some of Trowbridge's works for boys at six years of age. At seven I was reading Paul du Chaillu's *Travels,* Captain Cook's *Voyages,* and *Life of Garfield.* And all through this period I devoured what Seaside Library novels I could borrow from the womenfolk and dime novels from the farm hands. At eight I was deep in Ouida and Washington Irving. Also during this period read a great deal of American History. Also, life on a Californian ranch is not very nourishing to the imagination.

Somewhere around my ninth year we removed to Oakland, which, today, I believe, is a town of about eighty thousand, and is removed by thirty minutes from the heart of San Francisco. Here, most precious to me was a free library. Since that time Oakland has been my home seat. Here my father died, and here I yet live with my mother. I have not married—the world is too large and its call too insistent.

However, from my ninth year, with the exception of the hours spent at school (and I earned them by hard labor), my life has been one of toil. It is worthless to give the long sordid list of occupations, none of them trades, all heavy manual labor. Of course I continued to read. Was never without a book. My education was popular, graduating from the grammar school at about fourteen. Took a taste for the water. At fifteen left home and went upon a Bay life. San Francisco Bay is no mill pond by the way. I was a salmon fisher, an oyster pirate, a schooner sailor, a fish patrolman, a longshoreman, and a general sort of bay-faring adventurer—a boy in years and a man amongst men. Always a book, and always reading when the rest were asleep; when they were awake I was one with them, for I was always a good comrade.

Within a week of my seventeenth birthday I shipped before the mast as sailor on a three top-mast sealing schooner. We went to Japan and hunted along the coast north to the Russian side of Bering Sea. This was my longest voyage; I could not again endure one of such length; not because it was tedious or long, but because life was so short. However, I have made short voyages, too brief to mention, and today am at home in any forecastle or stokehole—good comradeship, you know. I believe this comprises my travels; for I spoke at length in previous letter concerning my tramping and Klondiking. Have been all over Canada, Northwest Ty., Alaska, etc., etc., at different times, besides mining, prospecting and wandering through the Sierra Nevadas.

I have outlined my education. In the main I am self-educated; have had no mentor but myself. High school or college curriculums I simply selected from, finding it impossible to follow the rut—life and pocket book were both too short. I attended the first year of high school (Oakland), then stayed at home, without coaching, and crammed the next two years into three months and took the entrance examination, and entered the University of California at Berkeley. Was forced, much against my inclinations, to give this over just prior to the completion of my Freshman Year.

My father died while I was in the Klondike, and I returned home to take up the reins.

As to literary work: My first magazine article (I had done no newspaper work), was published in January, 1899; it is now the fifth story in the *"Son of the Wolf."* Since then I have done work for *The Overland Monthly, The Atlantic, The Wave, The Arena, The Youth's Companion, The Review of Reviews,* etc., etc., besides a host of lesser publications, and to say nothing of newspaper and syndicate work. Hackwork all, or nearly so, from a comic joke or triolet to pseudoscientific disquisitions upon things about which I knew nothing. Hackwork for dollars, that's all, setting aside practically all ambitious efforts to some future period of less financial stringence. Thus, my literary life is just thirteen months old today.

Naturally, my reading early bred in me a desire to write, but my manner of life prevented me attempting it. I have had no literary help or advice of any kind—just been sort of hammering around in the dark till I knocked holes through here and there and caught glimpses of daylight. Common knowledge of magazine methods, etc., came to me as revelation. Not a soul to say here you are and there you mistake.

Of course, during my revolutionary period I perpetrated my opinions upon the public through the medium of the local papers, gratis. But that was years ago when I went to high school and was more notorious than esteemed. Once, by the way, returned from my sealing voyage, I won a prize essay[1] of twenty-five dollars from a San Francisco paper over the heads of Stanford and California Universities, both of which were represented by second and third place through their undergraduates. This gave me hope for achieving something ultimately.

After my tramping trip I started to high school in 1895. I entered the

University of California in 1896. Thus, had I continued, I would be just now preparing to take my sheepskin.

As to studies: I am always studying. The aim of the university is simply to prepare one for a whole future life of study. I have been denied this advantage, but am knocking along somehow. Never a night (whether I have gone out or not), but the last several hours are spent in bed with my books. All things interest me—the world is so very good. Principal studies are, scientific, sociological, and ethical—these, of course, including biology, economics, psychology, physiology, history, etc., etc., without end. And I strive, also, to not neglect literature.

Am healthy; love exercise, and take little. Shall pay the penalty some day.

There, I can't think of anything else. I know what data I have furnished is wretched, but autobiography is not entertaining to a narrator who is sick of it. Should you require further information, just specify, and I shall be pleased to supply it. Also, I shall be grateful for the privilege of looking over the biographical note before it is printed.

Very truly yours,

Jack London

---

[1] "Typhoon off the Coast of Japan," *San Francisco Call.*

To ANNA STRUNSKY

Oakland, Calif.

Feb. 3, 1900

Dear Anna:—

Saturday night, and I feel good. Saturday night, and a good week's work done—hack work of course. Why shouldn't I? Like any other honest artisan by the sweat of my brow. I have a friend [Cloudesley Johns] who scorns such work. He writes for posterity, for a small circle of admirers, oblivious to the world's oblivion, doesn't want money, scoffs at the idea of it, calls it filthy, damns all who write for it, etc., etc.,—that is, he does all this if one were to take his words for criteria. But I received a letter from him recently. *Munsey's* had offered to buy a certain story of him, if he would change the ending. He had built the tale carefully, every thought tending toward the final consummation, notably, the death by violence of the chief character. And they asked him to keep the tale and to permit that character, logically dead, to live. He scorns money. Yes; and he permitted that character to live. "I fell," is the only explanation he has vouchsafed of his conduct.

All of which reminds me—the most cleverly written article of the month is to be found in the February *Atlantic Monthly.* "Journalism as a Basis for Literature," by Gerald Stanley Lee. If you should run across the magazine, read it. In a certain way it eulogizes Kipling, saying, among other things: "The fact that Mr. Kipling is not dead is the most heroically artistic thing about him"; "Kipling is an artist because he respects the passing thing, because he catches the glimmer of the eternal joy upon it and will not let it pass"; "His secret is that he took hold of something that nobody wanted him to do, and did it better that anyone wanted him to do it." His, Mr. Lee's, portrayal of the nineteenth century, "moment-mad," "turning all eternity upside down in the present tense," etc., is a splendid bit of writing, and as true as it is splendid. O you must read it by all means.

In the same magazine, modeled after "Childe Harold to the Dark Tower Came," you will find a poem by Clinton Scollard, called "The Gray Inn."

Find under this cover, Alfred Austin's sonnet. It will bear thinking upon. Perish the thought!—but then, you know, it really will.

I have been looking over my book and find next Thursday evening open. Friday evening I am expecting a letter shortly to decide. It may be free, and it may not. But Thursday evening is. If you are free also, may I call upon you? And please let me know what time in the evening would best suit you.

And if you can have it at hand, may I look at some of your work? If you do, some time I'll reciprocate and let you see some of my dark-hidden earlier productions.

Sometimes I run across some of my pot-boiling work, though as a rule it is lost to me forever. Here are a couple. Please return, as they sometimes serve to chasten one's spirit. I send them to you in much the manner of a lawyer's brief. Do you wonder, turning out such stuff, that I sometimes grow bitter? O, but only for a moment, and then it all seems a joke again. Life is good, isn't it?

Poetry? What wouldn't I give just to be able to sit down and write ambitious work? But then it doesn't pay, and I don't. One must try one's hand for so long in order to get the touch, and the many attempts have no market value. And then, you know, at other times I lose faith in any co-operative commonwealth; cannot see how, after all, there will be incentive. And when I am feeling this way it seems inevitable that new inducements to strive will have to be offered in certain intellectual branches, or else it will fail as far as those branches go. Do you ever have doubts that way?

How one wanders! I shall stop.

Most sincerely yours,

Jack London

P.S. Please let me have your real, condensed address. I find I am incapable of shortening it on the envelope and at the same time retaining the belief that the letter will be safely delivered.

J. G. L.

To Cloudesley Johns

Oakland, Calif.
Feb. 10, 1900

Dear Cloudesley:—

Many thanks for *Philistine*[1] and for clippings. The former I especially enjoyed, nor did I fail to appreciate your vicarious criticism of the dining club. Wow! How he did give it to Harry Thurston Peck. What do *you* think about marriage being made more difficult, and divorce correspondingly easy?

No I won't forget the fotos, though, as yet, nothing important in the way of checks has arrived. However, I have had quite good success with *McClure's*. You remember my mailing that story of a minister who apostatizes ["The God of His Fathers"]? And the vile sinner who did not? *McClure's* accepted it if I would agree to the cutting of the opening and the elimination of certain swear-words. Of course I agreed, as it was an affair of 6000 words. Two days after that came an acceptance, from *McClure's,* of the "Question of the Maximum"[2]—that socialistic essay I read to you. What do you think of that for a rather conservative house? I mean conservative politically. They said, however, that had I written them first concerning the article they would have told me that it was unavailable, but that the article itself was something different, and that they could not let it go. Also promised to publish it between July or August, if not sooner. But, say, I thought they paid on acceptance. That's over 11,000 words and nary a cent. Do you have any idea as to what their rates are? Can they be less than 12 dollars per thousand? They also wanted to see more of my fiction, wanted to have me submit a long story if I had one, and if I had a collection of short stories they wanted to examine them for publication.

Have finished the *Son of the Wolf* proofsheets—251 pages of print in it.

Yes; I have noted the change in the editorship of the *Arena,* but I did not note it until after your kind postal arrived, and it was the postal which made me look it up. I wonder if they will ever pay.

"I have told you that I consider absolute pauperism almost as objectionable as wealth." Now, say, I wonder if you mean it? Of course you are inconsistent. Of course you sacrificed (serially) your name and workmanship by changing the story. And further, you did it for money. You can't defend yourself, you know you can't. Why not come out and [be] brutally frank about it like I am? You are doing the very same thing when you write hack-work, Press or Journal and *Black Cat* prize stories—money, that's all. Simmer yourself down and sum yourself up in a square way for just once. Be consistent, even though you be vile as I in the matter of dollars and cents.

You simply excite my curiosity when speaking as cursorily of your arrest as you did.

Have lost steerage way in the matter of writing. Have done twenty-two hundred words in five days, and gone out every night, and feel as though I can never write again. Isn't it frightful? O Lord! Who wouldn't sell a farm and go to writing! Say, I think I have stuck *Munsey's* with a thirty-two hundred word essay. I wonder if it can be possible? *Wave* has not ponied up yet. Do you want that *Philistine* back again? I have loaned it, and if you do I will get it back, if not, let it pass along the line.

Have evolved new ideas about warfare, or rather, assimilated them. If my article is published soon, upon that subject, I shall send it to you. And, to make it short, war as a direct attainment of an end, is no longer possible. The world has seen its last decisive battle. Economics, not force, will decide future wars. Of course all this is postulated on war between first class powers, or first class soldiers; not frontier squabbles. Nor would I classify the fighting in the Transvaal as a squabble. Unless there is a grave blunder, and unless the British do not too heavily reinforce, it will be found that neither British nor Boers can advance. Whichever side advances, advances to its own destruction. Good-bye.

Jack London

---

[1]*The Philistine: a periodical of protest,* 1895-1915. Edited by Elbert Hubbard from 1896 to end.
[2]In *Magazine Sales No. 1,* London lists "The Question of the Maximum" as having been sent to *North American Review,* Dec. 1, 1899; *Forum,* Dec. 26, 1899; and *McClure's,* Jan. 26, 1900. However, *McClure's* did not publish it.

To Anna Strunsky

Oakland, Calif.
Feb. 13, 1900

Dear Anna:—

To be your taskmaster? Good! I love power, to dominate my fellows. I shall stand over you with a whip of scorpions and drive you to your daily toil. Like Pharaoh of old, I shall hold you in bondage, and in the end, you will send plagues upon me, and amid signs and portents and great tumult, depart, leaving behind a wake of devastation and terror.

A most fascinating outlook, is it not? I love such things, and doubt not that prophecy will be fulfilled. However, fun aside, I'll do it. But, first of all, the first time I have you to myself you must be prepared for a lecture. I'll not be sparing, and promise you I'll handle you without gloves. We'll get right down to the naked facts of life, adjust our compasses and set our course. And then—why if anything happens, it's the fault of the mariners.

I do not know you very well, so I may make mistakes and do you many injustices; so you must forgive all such things in advance. It's safest, you know, to obtain indulgence before you sin. Also, remember this, there will be divers things in which I am unqualified to teach you anything. And also this, that, after all is said and done, everything depends upon yourself.

I shall mail this directly, in the hope that you will receive it before you leave Glenholm Wednesday morning. I would put a special delivery upon it, but the Post Office is too far away. It's too bad that your best day for leisure comes on Wednesday. My Wednesday afternoons and evenings are always taken up. So I shall be unable to come, and believe my sincerity when I state that I regret the fact. However, let me know when I may see you. And if, in the interim, you should perpetrate anything (vernacular for writing), please send it to me. Much wisdom lieth in deliberation.

What am I writing? Letters all morning. Shall now amend a boy's story for the *Youth's Companion* ["Dutch Courage"] which they have accepted on the condition that I change certain things. Isn't that inspiring? However, *McClure's* have become interested in my work, and are begging me to give them first glance at whatever I write. They accepted a 6000 word story of mine ["Grit of Women"] the other day on condition that I should change the opening and eliminate the profanity. I agreed, telling them to go ahead and do it themselves. Gave them *carte blanche,* in fact. Just imagine permitting somebody handling *your* work that way. That is what is called art.

Also, in trying to find a time when I can see you, don't hit upon Sunday. A week from this Tuesday (to-day) or a week from the forthcoming Thursday, would suit me very well, either day or evening. How about you? I am expected out to Glenholm Shrove Tuesday—whenever that is. I don't know, but I've got it down in my book. But that would hardly suit for me to gird on my panoply of war and drag you at my chariot, while if the plagues descended it would certainly make it unpleasant for the theatricals.

Very sincerely,
Jack London

To Anna Strunsky

Oakland, Calif.
Feb. [1900]

Dear Anna:—

There! I hope you do not consider yourself so unconventional as to have merited this boxful of my regard. I blush yet, when I think of Saturday night. You had me on the hip, and scored hard. And I deserved it, every bit. It's wrong to make excuses, but I deserve this. To put it into few words, as I have said before, I am cursed with friends. Believe me, I am not an egotist. Were I, I would not be sending you this box which abounds in frailties and mistakes. But the excuse: I am cursed with friends. I have grown accustomed to their clamoring for my company, and unconsciously feel that my presence (to them) is desirable. This mood is dangerously apt to become chronic. Need I say it so manifested itself Saturday night? And need I say that your company has ever been a great delight to me? That I would not have sought it had I not desired it? That (like you have said of yourself), when you no longer interest me I shall no longer be with you? Need I say these things to prove my candor?

As to the box. Please take good care of the contents. And don't mix them up, please. I haven't written any poetry for months. Those you see are my experiments (studies in structure and meter), and though they be failures I have not surrendered. When I am financially secure, some day, I shall continue with them—unless I have prostituted myself beyond redemption.

To-day I am just learning to write all over again. When you can display as many failures, and have yet achieved nothing, then it is time for you to say that you cannot write. You have no right to say that now. And if you do say so, then you are a coward. Better not begin unless you are not afraid to work, work, work, to work early and late, unremittingly and always.

These are but a few of my failures, poetical and prose. I managed to rummage them out in one pile. I have many more stowed away but cannot take the time to locate them. Unless the house burns down I shall find them someday. And believe me, Anna, I am doing thus to you what I have done to no other person, and sheerly with the desire to encourage you. "O Haru"[1] I once showed to Whitaker[2] for encouragement, but that is all. Other of the attempts, at the time of their perpetration, may have been shown to friends; but no one has seen anything like such a bunch of them. Do you show them to no one. Like the leper, I have exposed my sores; be gentle with me, and merciful in your judgment. And remember, they are for your encouragement. Anna, you have a good brain, also magnificent emotional qualities (this you have doubtless been assured of many times), and in so far you are favored above women in possession. But carry Strawn-Hamilton before you. No system, no application. Carry also Mr. Bamford's[3] quoted warning from Watson's "Hymn to the Sea." Don't apply what you have, wrongly. Don't beat yourself away vainly. Etc. This was not the lecture I intended giving you; that was on other lines.

But Anna, don't let the world lose you; for insomuch that it does lose you, in so much you have sinned.

Jack London

---

[1] Never published.
[2] Herman (Jim) Whitaker, Socialist and writer friend of London's.
[3] Frederick Irons Bamford, organizer of Ruskin Club, old friend and adviser at the public library and a Socialist.

To Cloudesley Johns

Oakland, Calif.
Feb. 17, 1900

Dear Cloudesley:—

Thanks for Julian Ralph's "Picture of New War Problems." Find it herewith returned. If it has interested you, I am sure my article will, for I treat the machinery of war at length, and then go into the economic and political aspects. The world will learn a great lesson from the Transvaal War. I am intending to write an essay entitled "They That Rise by the Sword" shortly. And just you wait till I come out with my "Salt of the Earth."

So, when you are doing your best work you only do about four or five hundred a day. Good. Most good. I hope you will live up to it. I insist that good work can not be done at the rate of three or four thousand a day. Good work is not strung out from the inkwell. It is built like a wall, every brick carefully selected, etc., etc.

You are always working me up with your mysteries. If you are monkeying with established traditions, and at the same time not monkeying with religion, pray let me know what you are monkeying with. If it is so terrible, not even if you were famous, could you get it published save on your own press, nor circulated by any but third-rate distributors. Why Ruskin, at the height of his fame, and turning out his best work in the *Cornhill,* had the series of essays stopped in the middle by Thackeray because they were daring. And daring, mark you, not for their attacks on religion, but for their attacks on the prevailing school of political economy. The same Thackeray refused one of Elizabeth Barrett Browning's best poems because it was *risque.* . . . I'm afraid Thackeray was a snob, a cad, and a whole lot of other things which he in turn has so successfully impaled for the regard of the British reading public.

Herewith from McClure himself. Use it in giving me opinion I asked for in last letter.

Jack London

To Anna Strunsky

Oakland, Calif.
Feb. 20, 1900

Dear Anna:—

You have done me a great wrong. I hardly know whether I can ever forgive you; for you have put into my life a great unrest which will continue for at least a year to come. Yes; out of the largeness of my heart I will forgive you, for I do believe that you did it without malice aforethought. You remember,—O surely you do,—that evening at Glenholm when you told me of Barrie's new story? It's your fault. It was because of you that I looked up the January *Scribner's* and could not lay it down again until I reached "to be continued." Your fault that I did likewise with the February number. Your fault that I am unhinged, my life thrown out of joint, and that I can hardly contain myself until the March number arrives. No; on second thought I shall never forgive you. NEVER!!! But say, isn't "Tommy and Grizel" splendid? Barrie is a master. And in the whimsical delineation of character do you not notice a trace of Dickens at his best?

Now I feel comfortable. Nobody ever "Mr. London's" me, so every time I opened a letter of yours I felt a starched collar draw round my neck. Pray permit me softer neck-gear for the remainder of our correspondence.

Now about Thursday. I have to be down in Oakland at two o'clock in the afternoon. An old chum of mine [Fred Jacobs] (Class of 1900, U.C.), who died on the way to Manila, has come home. I have to attend the funeral. But the morning is free. Can I see you at any time between 9:30 A.M. and 1 P.M.? Tramp if the weather prophet be gracious, or anything you wish. Reply immediately on receipt of this so that I may know.

Most sincerely yours,
Jack London

To Cloudesley Johns

Oakland, Calif.
March 1, 1900

Dear Cloudesley:—

You incorrigible!
Oh do not write for gold alone,
And do not write for fame;
To self be true though still unknown
To all the world your name.
Write on, the message is divine
Since from your soul it springs,
While angels read each glowing line,
And guard you with their wings.

There, now! You can swear at me just as hard as you please. But say, joshing aside, did the person who perpetrated the above do it for gold, or was he a damn fool? Query (?)

I am glad that you have at last discovered *Bab Ballads,* and shall look for them with pleasure, great pleasure. I saw a most complimentary though brief reference to them somewhere the other day. So they are not entirely forgotten. No thanks; Wilson isn't worth a fifty word roast.

"Does Matter Think?," by Wm. H. Maple: Now that is striking and very much like a strayed sheep or lamb in its *Truthseeker* bad company. It is striking and excellent, but why? Because he is a man who has grounded in the fundamentals, and appears striking to those who have not. Why the man positively reeks of Herbert Spencer interpreted by Prof. Haeckel. Not that I am impugning his article; far from it. But he has simply put into his own words what he has learned from them, and he has done well.

Spencer was not openly, that is, didactically favorable to a material basis for thought, mind, soul, etc., but John Fiske has done many queer gymnastics in order to reconcile Spencer, whose work he worships, to his own beliefs in immortality and God. But he doesn't succeed very well. He jumps on Haeckel, with both feet, but in my modest opinion, Haeckel's position is as yet unassailable.

Damn you and your opium. Your analogies are insidiously and invidiously false, and yet you have the nerve to forestall me and deny me the right of so condemning them! Well, well. "You will think this comparison ridiculous if I leave it here, so I will explain that I am not comparing the substances (gold, opium) but the habits, and they are similar." Bah! This is so palpably in error that I am sure on reading it in cold blue type that you cannot fail to see it.

Well, if there is plenty more in your *Theorist* like that which you quoted loosely about love, I don't see why it shouldn't succeed. No; I see not the slightest reason that the book should fail because of such things, but see reasons that (if it keeps up as well throughout), it should prevail. If you should ever get a chance, read Max Nordau's essay, "The Natural History of Love." Its thought is similar to yours, and it also goes down to the physical basis of the physiological basis. God! he does arraign fiction writers and the average man or woman in society on account of their love-making ways, etc.

Am working busily away; have to finish a *McClure's* story, an *Atlantic* story, and my speech before the Oakland Section [of the Socialist Party] for the Eleventh of this month. Then I positively must write a *Black Cat* story. As yet haven't even worked out a plot, or idea. Was going to send them my "Man with the Gash," but *McClure's* accepted it. It was the Ms. which I recently told you of—lost at *Collier's Weekly,* etc., and returned after I had taken a duplicate from the original longhand. Been refused by all sorts of publications and now *McClure's* are to publish it in the magazine. They paid me well. The two stories and essay which they accepted aggregated fifteen thousand words, for which they sent me three hundred dollars—twenty dollars per thousand. Best pay I have yet received. Why certes, if they wish to buy me, body and soul, they are welcome—if they pay the price. I am writing for money; if I can procure fame, that means more money. More money means more life to me. I shall always hate the task of getting money; every time I sit down to write it is with great disgust. I'd sooner be out in the open wandering around most any old place. So the habit of money-getting will never become one of my vices. But the habit of money spending, ah God! I shall always be its victim. I received the three hundred last Monday. I have now about four dollars in pocket, haven't got moved, don't see how I can financially, owe a few debts yet, etc. How's that for about three days?

Am going to 'Frisco to-morrow, when I shall procure your fotos, take one for myself, and send the rest along to Harold.[1] Sorry I have delayed you so long.

Bosh, man, when I come out with my "Salt of the Earth" you will not make me squirm. Naturally I shall look to details in any event; but you, if you were wise, would not attack me on details. Don't you see; if you attack a man verbally on details, and if he is fool enough not to force you down to fundamentals, why you will make him squirm to the vast mass of ordinary unthinking creatures which will applaud you. But a thinking man, would see the shallowness of such attack and go away sorry for the other fellow because he permitted you to attack his details. But, when you attack details in cold print it falls flat. See how flat the *Truthseeker* controversies are to real thinking people. Nobody ever goes down to lay foundations . . . They all seize bricks from the parapets and towers and assault each other vigorously. There is certainly vigor, life, etc., but not intellectual battle. Compare the controversy of men like Spencer and Huxley, etc., etc., to the ordinary newspaper controversies between correspondents. Can't you see the difference? Surely you do.

Apparently you had me on the hip in that little matter regarding how many words to write per day. Let us drop details, and come down to frank opinions. Opinions which are generalized and virtually unqualified. Opinions in few words, voicing your candid belief. Answer me this: Do you think a man can write two or three thousand words as well per day as one thousand? Do you think a man working twelve hours per day at writing can or will turn out as excellent work as though he worked three hours per day? Which will require most going over and polishing, hasty writing and voluminous, or slow writing and not so voluminous? Now, I am not asking you to fly off and tell me the exceptions. I am asking you to generalize all data and all cases which may be known to you under one general head. "The greatest good for the greatest number" sort of a way.

No, no; if you had been at that meeting Whitaker would not have been a worthy foeman for you, but you, attacking his details, would have been an unworthy foeman of his. You would have said nice bright sharp things which would have caught the minds of the popular unthinking audience, and you would have received more applause. But Whitaker's position would not have even been attacked. And you, if you be a thinker, in the silence of your chamber after the excitement had died away, could not possibly assure yourself that you had been true to yourself, to Mr. Whitaker, or to the question discussed. You would know that you had shunned the deeper phases and principles and turned your brain, in the way of the demagogue, to the catching of the popular approval. And if you thought long in the

97

silence of your chamber, and if you have a conscience, you would become ashamed of yourself and what you had done. Such work, whether by priest or politician, has held back this world many a weary year.

You certainly have *Munsey* hard and fast in that "Puritan" story. Of course, only morally, legally they have you.

Let us hear how it comes out. I don't think you could get any magazine to publish such a thing and give names.

Find herewith "Concerning One Wilson." Pardon me, but since it appeared to me that you would not have to send it anywhere I took the liberty of indicating corrections of first page only. I believe such matters count when they catch the editor's eye. It was frightful on Wilson, your letter, and surely the T. S. was wise in not publishing it. If a man, in controversy, becomes undignified, he certainly is beneath your notice, and you likewise lose your dignity if you do notice him. And surely, if he remains dignified, you are the last in the world to become undignified. Life is strife, but it also happens to stand for certain amenities.

I am inclined sometimes to think you are right about Bliss Carman and the Yellow Dwarf. Does he know?

Do you want Loomis's "The Hero Who Escaped" back?

I shall take care of War Clipping, and by next writing shall return "Red Wolf." Pardon my delay in answering, but have been very busy. Nor have I written to anyone till yesterday. Sold *Youth's Companion* a four thousand word story ["The Lost Poacher"] which they say is the best I have yet sent them; that makes two since you were up.

Well, good-bye.

Jack London

---

[1]A small town near the Arizona-California border, where Johns was postmaster.

To CLOUDESLEY JOHNS

Oakland, Calif.
March 10, 1900

Dear Cloudesley:—

How now? Wherefore the blues? Thought such things did not prevail in such a magnificent climate as Harold's. Everybody been jumping upon you at once? I know I have done my share of the jumping; but without animus. Only I wish I had reserved my jumping until you were in the best of spirits. It would have had better effect. Let me know when you are all right again; then I'll do some more.

Honestly, though, rubbing with the world will not harm you if you take the rubs aright. Not only wild and woolly rubbing, but intellectual rubbing. The most healthful experience in the world for you who are rather versatile and universal, would be bumping into specialists who would handle you without gloves. Such has been for me the best education in the world, and I look for it more and more. Man must have better men to measure himself against, else his advance will be nil, or if at all, one-sided and whimsical. The paced rider makes better speed than the unpaced.

I can sympathize with you in your disgust for Harold. A year of it would drive me mad, judging from the pictures. Outside of your own work what intellectual life can you have? You are thrown back upon yourself. Too apt to become self-centered; to measure other things by yourself than to measure yourself by other things. If there were plenty of physical action and adventure (constant) in the Harold life, then for a year or so it would not hurt you. But as it is, it's unhealthful. Man is gregarious, and never more so when intellectual companions are harder to find than mere species companions. Get out by all means, if you feel the call that way. If you do not, then it were wiser not to; for without the call you will but lay up trouble against yourself.

As to being worthy of Whitaker—I simply took your statement of details and figured that you would live up to it. No; I am not contemptuous of you. Rather (frankly) pitiful for you. If I see a man with a good brain who simply won't get down and dig, who won't master fundamentals, I cannot help but pity him. So it is with you. You refuse to systematize yourself; refuse to lay a foundation for your life's work; say that such is not your temperament, etc.; and in short are cowardly. Why, by what right do you say you cannot master first principles? And not only will you not master them, but you persist in holding forth views (no matter how correct they may be), but views which you have no right to hold forth; you have not qualified yourself to hold forth. This action may be forgiven in a youth who is just assailing the world, but not in a man grown. Especially when that man grown has no reason, (valid) to present for not qualifying. It is cowardly to say, "My ancestors made me thus; it is useless for me to try to make myself otherwise."

Forgive me for lecturing you; but my intentions are of the best. I cannot bear to see a man misuse a good brain. Your rabidness against religion is one of the proofs of misuse. If you had discovered the place in this world which by rights you should be able to qualify for, you could not so spend your time. Life is only so long, and to fly against gods and devils is only permissible for very young men who have but received their manumission from superstition. This reaction, for them, is permissible, if they let the reaction work itself out and not become chronic.

Damit! I can't do anything but lecture to-day.

I am only averaging about 350 words per day, now, and can't increase the speed to save me; but, it's either very good work, or else it is trash; in either case I am losing nothing, for I am measuring myself and learning things which will bring returns some future day.

Have to speak Sunday, also Thursday, also very shortly before the Social Democracy of San Jose; so am rushed. Haven't commenced my *Black Cat* story yet; hardly know if I shall have time to enter the competition.

I don't think that Roberts is the writer of the "Prospector." I read or tried to read a volume of short stories by some Canadian writer the other day, and think the man was Roberts. I may be mistaken; but if so, the work is very crude.

Have just finished reading *Forest Lovers* by Maurice Hewlitt. Read it by all means if you ever get a chance. Have made the acquaintance of Charmian Kittredge,[1] a charming girl who writes book reviews, and who possesses a pretty little library wherein I have found all the late books which the public libraries are afraid to have circulate. If you run across *A Man and a Woman,* by Stanley Waterloo, read thou it also. He's the fellow who wrote the *Story of Ab,* the review of which you sent me somewhere about a year ago. The Oakland librarians were studying as to whether they would permit it to circulate or not, and gave it me to read for my judgment. It's good.

If you will read in Spencer's *First Principles* the chapter under the caption of "The Transformation and Equivalence of Forces," you will come pretty close to seeing what god Spencer believed in.

Yours in haste,[2]

[1] Who became his second wife.
[2] Johns wrote across the bottom of the letter, "So much haste he did not even sign it 'Jack' yet he covered more ground than he realized. I want to write some thing about this letter. C. J., 1918."

To CLOUDESLEY JOHNS

Oakland, Calif.
March 15, 1900

Dear Cloudesley:—

Your *Wave* episode reminds me of my *Journal* one. Letter concerning same find herewith and please return. I have sold 2000 words for one dollar and a half; but the work was bad and I would do the same again. But I can't exactly see it when I am offered three fifty for 2200 words of very good work. I wonder what such people think a fellow lives on.

Received *Bab Ballads* but haven't had a chance to run over any of them with the exception of "Gentle Alice Brown." Many thanks for the same. Let me know where to send them in Los Angeles somewhere about the first of April as you indicated. Also received "The Death of Ivan Illiich." Read half way through it on the way down town just now; will tell you how I like it when I have done.

Find herewith two of your own clippings on war. *The Philistine* will be forwarded you shortly from San Jose. Find also some clippings I thought would interest you from my file which I went over the other night. Please return. A recent clipping, "Art Vs. Money," I don't want.

No, no; Cloudesley; you do me wrong. When I say I feel sorry that you with your good brain won't get in and grind, I am not prompted to do so because you deny my gods (this was your explanation). Don't misconstrue my frankness. I said neither more nor less than I thought.

You wax amusingly sarcastic over the first principles I mentioned, as though there was connected with them some great ambiguity or vagueness due to my manner of using them. I know, down in your heart that you knew, in a very general way, what they meant. But let me, for the moment, be concrete.

To be well fitted for the tragedy of existence (intellectual existence), one must have a working philosophy, a synthesis of things. Have you a synthesis of things? Do you write, and talk, and build upon a foundation which you know is securely laid? Or do you not rather build with a hazy idea of "to hell with the foundation." In token of this: What significance do the following generalities have for you:—Matter is indestructible; motion is continuous; Force is persistent; the relations among forces are persistent; the transformation of forces is the equivalence of forces; etc., etc.? And if you do find in these generalities some significance relating to the foundation (way down), of your philosophy of life, what general single idea of the Cosmos do they (which are relative manifestations of the absolute), convey to you? How may you, therefore, without having mastered this idea of law (they are all laws), put down the very basic stone of your foundation? Have you ever thought that all life, all the universe of which you may in any way have knowledge of, bows to a law of continuous redistribution of matter? Have you read or thought that there is a dynamic principle, true of the metamorphosis of the universe, of the metamorphoses of the details of the universe, which will express these ever-changing relations? Nobody can tell you what this dynamic principle is, or why; but you may learn *how* it works. Do you know what this principle is? If you do, have you studied it, ay, carefully and painstakingly? And if you have not done these things, which have naught to do with creeds, or dogmas, with politics or economics, with race prejudices or passions; but which are the principles upon which they all work, to which they all answer because of law; if you have not, then can you say that you have a firm foundation for your philosophy of life?

I never said you could not master first principles; but I did say that you would not, and pitied you. Well?

My dear fellow, if you haven't described to me your temperament, laid such stress upon your heredity, etc., what have you done? You have told me that you can do this in study, that you can't do that in study, etc. O pshaw!

Do you not expose your view of things in all its narrowness, when you say that religion and empire are man's greatest curses? O, but you do. Had you studied that basic law, that law of laws, hinted at above, and studied it as your mind is capable of doing, why then you would not be guilty of such folly as in your statement of man's curses. Don't think all this dogmatic on my part; I simply state it baldly because it would take too much time to show you wherein you err. It will require you to do many weary an hour

101

and night of study (which you can do), to learn it yourself. I couldn't write it in months—that which you require to study to so obtain that result.

"Screaming nonsense!"—my article on war ["The Impossibility of War"]. You amuse me. Permit me to demolish you. What do you know of the new Mauser rifles which are not as yet even in use in South Africa? They have only recently been tested in Holland. Let me demolish you out of your own mouth. Can you conceive of a man pointing, without removing from shoulder, a gun in any given direction for one second, or moving it, during that second at an approximately same elevation for a second? (This isn't sharpshooting, but repelling a rush attack of a body of men.) Also, can you conceive that man is capable of pressing a finger steadily (no clicking, no removing or ejecting of shells on his part) upon a trigger for one second? And can you conceive a man capable of inventing a device, which, under steady pressure, will deliver six blows sufficiently heavy to explode by impact six caps set in the ends of six cartridges? If you cannot conceive these things, then I do sincerely pity you; it would be then the fault of your ancestors.

Did you think that it was necessary for a sharpshooter to shoot so rapidly as all that? Did you think I was fool enough to think so? Cloudesley, Cloudesley! You say that you firmly believe that any position which can be approached at double-quick can be carried at the point of the bayonet by a body twice the strength of the defenders. Cold steel, mind you. Do you happen to know that Hiram Maxim writes his name with a Maxim gun upon a target at two thousand yards? Cold Steel!

You misunderstood the whole trend of my article, which meant first the struggle between first class soldiers of the first class European powers, and said powers are on about an equal war-footing. Secondly, my aim was to show, and I did show, that war being so impossible, that men would not go up against each other to be exterminated, but that a deadlock would happen instead. This bringing in the economic factor. Because I stated that warfare was so deadly, I did not state that it would be applied. Rather would the deadlock occur. Read my article again. You missed the whole drift of it.

Here comes Whitaker, I have to speak over in Alameda in an hour, so must quit.

No; *The Bulletin,* for which thanks, was not written by a friend from data furnished by yours truly. It was simply one of the many advertisements put out from Houghton Mifflin & Co., from the data furnished by myself. But why were you so careful to inform me that the data was furnished by myself? Did you fear I might forget the fact?

I expect to have a try at the *Black Cat* in a couple of days, if only the damned plot will come. Am too busy now to think upon it.

Good-bye, and forgive haste, Most sincerely yours,

Jack London

To Anna Strunsky

Oakland, Calif.
March 15, 1900

Dear Anna:—

"A Creed" is fashioned obviously after the quatrains of Fitzgerald, but is a new production, being culled from "The House of the Hundred Lights."

Did I ever speak with you about "Anarchy?" Or was it someone else?

Regarding box (I am in a rush), please remember that I have disclosed myself in my nakedness—all those vain efforts and passionate strivings are so many weaknesses of mine which I put into your possession. Why, the grammar is often frightful, and always bad, while artistically, the whole boxfull is atrocious. Now don't say I am piling it on. If I did not realize and condemn these faults I would be unable to try to do better. But—why, I think in sending that box to you I did the bravest thing I ever did in all my life.

Say, do you know I am getting nervous and soft as a woman. I've got to get out again and stretch my wings or I shall become a worthless wreck. I am getting timid, do you hear? timid! It must stop. Enclosed letter I received to-day, and it brought a contrast to me of my then "unfailing nerve" and my present nervousness and timidity. Return it, as I suppose I shall have to answer it some day.

Didn't speak last Sunday after all. Fetter made a mistake, or somebody made a mistake, for he got it into his head that he was to speak March 11th, instead of February 11th, as per enclosed syllabus. I have to speak in Alameda to-night—"Question of the Maximum." Might as well work it for all there is in it, before it is published.

Am thinking about moving—getting cramped in my present quarters; but O the turmoil and confusion and time lost during such an operation!

Freda and Mrs. Eppingwell have fought it out, and I have just reached the climax of the scene with Floyd Vanderlip in Freda's cabin.[1] I did not treat it in the way I suggested. Instead of her wasting a sacredly shameful experience upon a man of his stamp, I had her appeal to him sensuously (I think I handled it all right). So the conclusion of the story is only about a day away from now. Then hurrah for the East—if McClure accepts it it will mean about one hundred and eighty dols. He (McClure) sent me a photograph, large and framed, yesterday, and when I could find no free place upon my walls to hang it, I decided to perambulate. Almost wish a fire would come along and burn me out. It would be quicker, you know.

Will write you better next time. Am in a rush. And next week see if you and I can arrange a meeting. Let's hear from you soon.

Hastily,
Jack

---

[1] Episode in "Scorn of Women." First published as a short story.

103

To Anna Strunsky

Oakland, Calif.
May 2, 1900

Dear Anna:—

How sorry I am! Friday I am chairman at the Ruskin Club dinner and cannot possibly escape. Thursday I speak in 'Frisco, and Saturday am bound out to dinner. So there! However, may I put you down for afternoon and dinner on Wednesday, May 9th? Write and let me know if this is convenient.

How enthusiastic your letters always make me feel. Makes it seem as though some new energy had been projected into the world and that I cannot fail gathering part of it to myself. No; God does not punish confidence; but he grinds between the upper and the nether millstone all those of little faith and little heart, and he grinds them very fine. Of course you will succeed—if you will work—and certainly you seem to suffer from a superabundance of energy. Apply this energy, rightly and steadily, and the world will open its arms to you. You are all right; the world is all right; the question is: will you have the patience to gain the ear of the world. You will have to shout loud, for the world is rather deaf, and you may have to shout long. But the world sometimes opens its ears at the first call. May it be thus with you.

Jack

To Cloudesley Johns

Oakland, Calif.
May 2, 1900

Dear Cloudesley:—

I enjoyed your annotations of Paltry Bungler's article,[1] which, of course, I could not consider seriously as a whole. At the same time I must confess that you did strike some true notes. As for Poultney Biglow's[2] article, my opinion of which you asked, I can say that I thought it very good and very honest. I don't believe the man was a hypocrite when he wrote it, and further, it is known that he has been well over the ground he writes about. I thought he was very moderate and quite just, while, naturally, I could not agree with him utterly.

"The White Silence seemed to sneer"—no, I hardly think I find such things complete; they are more thought out. However, to a certain extent their genesis is swayed by the mood of the story or the mood of the setting or the mood of the man, which, certainly, I must also be feeling at the time of writing. No; at the moment I get a good phrase I am not thinking of how much it will fetch in the market, but when I sit down to write I am; and all the time I am writing, deep down, underneath the whole business, is that same commercial spirit. I don't think I would write very much if I didn't have to.

You seem to think that if Russia and England played the Kilkenny cat act, there would be peace in the world and all would be well with us. If that should happen, it would be quickly emulated in part by continental Europe, in so far that the United States would be the cat. But it is not going to happen. You dear Anglophobist, study the statistics of import and export, and find out what country we rely upon mainly for our foreign trade. And tell me what would happen to us were that market destroyed by Russia or any other combination of world powers. Don't allow fancies or prejudices to run away with your thinking apparatus until you have laid the proper economic basis. You will find that economics, not ethics, plays one of the strongest leading parts in the drama of the races.

What the hell did the New York *Press* want all rights for anyway? Am glad you made them come down. I am still waiting pay on the pleasure of Vance[3] of the *Home*. What pay did you say he gave you for that story of yours which he published long ago?

That was a pretty muddle you got yourself into by forgetting that most laconic of letters you wrote me on receipt of news of my intended marriage. I must confess, I, too, was muddled, for one or two letters to come, till you finally straightened yourself out. Ted wanted to know what you would say; so I sent said letter on to him.

Am busy, so will have to quit. Have to speak to-night in 'Frisco, and I am not yet prepared. Also, now that the book is out,[4] have been racing around a good deal in order to do my best for it locally. You understand. Business, you know.

Jack London

Please return "Poor Old Kentucky."
—Did I return you your war clippings you loaned me?

[1]Unidentified.
[2]A political and economic writer, author of *The Children of the Nations.*
[3]Arthur T. Vance, editor of *Woman's Home Companion.*
[4]*The Son of the Wolf.*

To Cloudesley Johns

Oakland, Calif.
June 2, 1900

Dear Cloudesley:—

What do you think of the Boers now? Do you remember their brags that they and their women would die in the last ditch? That they would blow up Johannesburg? Destroy Pretoria? Make a howling desolation of the Transvaal before they were conquered? Do you remember these brags? And if so, what do you think of them now? And how do you incline concerning Ambrose Bierce's statement that the Boers were a warlike people but not a military people. That they had failed in every siege they had attempted. That, were they actually besieged in Pretoria, the British engineering ability alone would have crushed and defeated them. Do you think this so, or not?

Now, Cloudesley, I not only grant, but have sung the praises of the Boers —at least the potential praises. They are strong, most strong. Theirs is the strength of good stock which is stuck close to the soil. There are no one, or two, or three removes among them. They are all close to the soil. They are potentially strong. Three or four generations more, and they will be splendid people. But they are a handful and will be swallowed up—as I have contended all along. A century from now their children's children will unite (they'll be mixed anyway), with the sons' sons of the present Tommy's to conquer more of the world for the Anglo-Saxons. And were they to-day a hundred million instead of a few paltry thousands, why there would be a problem for the world and the Saxon, greater than the Slav. But, unhappily (for your sake and theirs) they are very small and quite lost in the vast centralizing forces now at work in society.

You say you do see further signs of the disintegration of the British Empire—please tell me those signs.

As regards the *Truthseeker*—I stated that some good stuff did stray into it, but that it was like a lamb lying down with the lions, or like a saint among sinners. And further, a person who is capable of doing good stuff should not wander into such bad, narrowsighted, fanatical, flat-headed company. They do do it, but they must not expect praise for it.

Never mind the Texas Pagan—my standpoint stands none the less, and I am sure you must have grasped it—what I said about lack of perspective, not being broad-minded, not understanding the laws of social evolution, etc. There are some people, lamentably, who never will understand, who never will get perspective, but that is no reason that those who have the capacity should not develop it and get a better comprehension of life.

Have you heard anything from the *Black Cat* yet? A fellow I know in 'Frisco was informed by them two weeks ago that he was in the charmed circle—when they wrote him concerning his status and asking if his idea, story, etc., was original in whole and part, and unpublished. I, however, have not heard from them, so am looking for Ms. to come back.

Have sold a couple of hundred more dollars worth of good stuff to *McClure's*—at least I think it is good—"The Grit of Women," and "The Law of Life."

Got the proofsheets of *S. F. Examiner* story in and am correcting them. Probably be published in a Sunday or so. Story, "Which Make Men Remember." If you run across it, tell us what you think of it. It's a newspaper story and maybe a little more.

Ted's grandmother died the other day and was brought up to Oakland for interment. They stopped overnight with me afterward.

So! I am married, and I cannot start to Paris in July, dough or no dough— That's why I got married.

But none the less I heartily envy you your trip. I think maybe I'll take a vacation on the road this summer just for ducks and to gather material, or rather, to freshen up what I have long since accreted.—how would you judge of my use of that last word?

Smart Set? I may go in for one of the lesser prizes. Can't tell yet. *Outing* has asked a bunch of Northland stories of me and I am busy hammering away at them just now.

I should like to look over your "Philosophy of the Road," of which you say you have 17,000 words done. Could you possibly send me up a few sheets of it. The subject is a fascinating one, isn't it.

Jack London

To CLOUDESLEY JOHNS

Oakland, Calif.
June 16, 1900

Dear Cloudesley:—

To commence with, you do me wrong. When you asked if I thought you could do the "Philosophy of the Road," I had no idea of what it was to be, that is, how it was to be treated, and so, did not have the slightest idea concerning whether you could do it or not. Further, when I wrote you, I overlooked that query—that was all. Had I remembered I would have spoken as I have spoken at the head of this paragraph. I do take a little of it back. I did think at the time that by experience you certainly were fitted for it.

It is a fascinating subject. It has itched me for long, and it is often all I can do to keep away from writing on it. However, I have been and am still laying aside notes on it, so that, some day, saturating myself with the life again, I will go ahead. But as you say, it is infinite.

But Cloudesley, do you think you are handling it just right? I don't forget that they were written for "Stories and Sketches of the Road," nor that you say they will have to be re-written; but still I ask, are you going about it right? You are treating it in much the manner Wyckoff treated the *Workers,* "East and West."[1] But he treated it scientifically, and empirically scientifically, if I may use the phrase. And for that matter, he dealt more with the workers than with the tramps; but the method of treatment still applies. As it seems to me, you are too dry. You are not, from your choice of subjects or topics, treating it as he treated it. Therefore your style should be different. You are handling stirring life, romance, things of human life and death, humor and pathos, etc. But God, man, handle them as they should be. Don't you tell the reader the philosophy of the road (except where you are actually there as participant in the first person). Don't you tell the reader. Don't. Don't. Don't. But HAVE YOUR CHARACTERS TELL IT BY THEIR DEEDS, ACTIONS, TALK, ETC. Then, and not until then, are you writing fiction and not a sociological paper upon a certain sub-stratum of society.

And get the atmosphere. Get the breadth and thickness to your stories, and not only the length (which is the mere narration). The reader, since it is fiction, doesn't want your dissertations on the subject, your observations, your knowledge as your knowledge, your thoughts about it, your ideas— BUT PUT ALL THOSE THINGS WHICH ARE YOURS INTO THE STORIES, INTO THE TALES, ELIMINATING YOURSELF (except when in the first person as participant). AND THIS WILL BE THE ATMOSPHERE. AND THIS ATMOSPHERE WILL BE YOU, DON'T YOU UNDERSTAND, YOU! YOU! YOU! And for this, and for this only, will the critics praise you, and the public appreciate you, and your work be art. In short, you will then be the artist; do not do it, and you will be the artisan. That's where all the difference comes in. Study your detestable Kipling; study your Beloved's *Ebb Tide*. Study them and see how they eliminate themselves and create things that live, and breathe, and grip men, and cause reading lamps to burn overtime. Atmosphere stands always for the elimination of the artist, that is to say, the atmosphere is the artist; and when there is no atmosphere and the artist is yet there, it simply means that the machinery is creaking and that the reader hears it.

And get your good strong phrases, fresh, and vivid. And write intensively, not exhaustively or lengthily. Don't narrate—paint! draw! build!— CREATE! Better one thousand words which are builded, than a whole book of mediocre, spun-out, dashed-off stuff.

Think it over and see if you catch what I am driving at. Of course, if you intend what I have called a scientific paper, then don't do anything of these things I have suggested. They would be out of place. But if you intend fiction, then write fiction from the highest standpoint of fiction. Don't be so damnably specific, adding dry detail to dry detail. Put in life, and movement—and for God's sake no creaking. Damn you! Forget you! And then the world will remember you. But if you don't damn you, and don't forget you, then the world will close its ears to you. Pour all yourself into your work until your work becomes you, but nowhere let yourself be apparent. When, in the *Ebb Tide,* the schooner is at the pearl island, and the missionary pearler meets those three desperate men and puts his will against theirs for life or death, does the reader think of Stevenson? Does the reader have one thought of the writer? Nay, nay. Afterwards, when all is over, he recollects, and wonders, and loves Stevenson—but at the time? Not he.

Do the wheels in Shakespeare creak? When Hamlet soliloquizes, does the reader think at the time that it is Shakespeare? But afterwards, ah afterwards, and then he says, "Great is Shakespeare!"

Do you see what I mean? Now please don't fall upon what I have written in spirit other than with which it was written. I've hammered it out hastily and not done it justice, I know, but it has all been sincere.

I can't speak of the good points in the Mss., for I have devoted my space to generalities. But you show a good grasp of psychology, which will or should be a wonderful aid when you get the right method. But I can't go into that. Haven't time. Have to get ready to go out and want to get this off first.

However, let me thank you for sending me the Mss.

I shall not answer the rest of your short letter, though I appreciated it all and would like to.

Jack London

[1]W. A. Wykoff, author of *The Workers; an experiment in reality.* (Vol. 1, *In the East*) (Vol 2, *In the West*).

To ANNA STRUNSKY

Oakland, Calif.
July 31, 1900

Dear Anna:—

Comrades! And surely it seems so. For all the petty surface turmoil which marked our coming to know each other, really, deep down, there was no confusion at all. Did you not notice it? To me, while I said "You do not understand," I none the less felt the happiness of satisfaction—how shall I say?—felt, rather, that there was no inner conflict; that we were attuned, somehow; that a real unity underlaid everything. The ship, new-launched, rushes to the sea; the sliding-ways rebel in weakling creaks and groans; but sea and ship hear them not; so with us when we rushed into each other's lives—we, the real we, were undisturbed. Comrades! Ay, world without end!

And now, comrade mine, how long are those Shakespeare papers to keep you from "Consciousness of Kind"? You know how anxiously I wait the outcome, and how much you must have improved. And Anna, read your classics, but don't forget to read that which is of to-day, the new-born literary art. You must get the modern touch; form must be considered; and while art is eternal, form is born of the generations. And O, Anna, if you will only put your flashing soul with its protean moods on paper! What you need is the form, or in other words, the expression. Get this and the world is at your feet.

And when are we to read "The Flight of the Duchess"?[1] And when are you coming over?

Jack

[1]Jack planned to write a play or novel under this title. The unfinished Ms. is among his papers.

To Anna Strunsky

Oakland Calif.
Sept. 15, 1900

Dear Anna:—

How glad I was to receive Dane Kempton's letter![1] And for the first of all the letters, it was far better than had I dreamed of. It is so hard to commence. Later, ah later, when we have come to realize the characters, then it will be inevitable; the very realization of our personalities will not permit us to wander from the predestined course, or to wonder what the next act or thought should be. If we be at all artistic, and have any sense of proportion in our souls, we cannot err. The living breathing souls we have created shall master us, and dictate to us, mere instruments of their manifestation. Do you see? And hence, now, the beginning, the period of creation, everything depends upon us. Here is where our toil and travail come in.

I shall make carbon copies of all the letters (Dane Kempton's and Herbert Wace's), so that both you and I shall have the complete file on both sides for constant reference. This will be very necessary, I am sure.

You will find I have altered Dane Kempton's letter somewhat, here and there, in little places. But I have striven to do so O so slightly. Only where I deemed strength and ambiguity demanded. For instance: you will notice, page 2, "It was no stepping down from the mountain top." Then you went on with "but rather greater flight, etc." Now it seemed to me a mixed metaphor to commence with, and further, that it weakened by stating the converse. I cannot go further into detail.

But remember, Anna, these alterations are not irrevocable. I must not cramp you for the very truth of it. It is impossible that there be the slightest common ring in the letters of Dane Kempton and the letters of Herbert Wace. We must be ourselves. So see, girl, that whatever alterations I make, I make with this understanding. And in the end, even on such things, your verdict shall be final.

Oh! One thing more. The story hinted at near close of letter—is it the great love story of Dane Kempton's life? And if so, is it good art to bring it in here at the commencement? Or rather should he not be goaded, through my madness of position and because of his great love for me, and his fear —should he not, I say, be goaded or impelled—absolutely, strenuously impelled—to lay naked before us his most sacred possession? Do you catch my drift? Let me hear what you conclude.

Keep up your splendid phrasing. "cramped little note blurted out nothing"; "the joy and the song"; "I seek and find and keep"; "the dear dead"; "frank and demanding"; "glory departed"; "the human hungered"; "fastidiousness of tone"; etc., etc., etc. Keep up, I say, the strength of phrase, but mark well, *don't strain after it*.

I appreciated keenly the suggestion you make of major and minor points, and thank you. And do we both do this to one another. Else will many a splendid point for reply be lost. Keep you a scratch book, and jot down suggestions and notes as they come to you—both for yourself and for me.

There were 615 words in this first letter. The length will pick up (as it should), as we get deeper into it.

The idea of Miss Stebbins[2] writing at end two letters, one to me and one to you, is excellent.

You will note that I have put you into Vernon Chambers,[3] London. Later on you may change to the country—or other places, if you see fit.

As for me—shall we be definite as to what University? And if so, remember I know nothing about Stanford, and hence, verisimilitude of atmosphere would be lacking. I doubt the expediency of making it definite at all; and if so, think Berkeley better. Also, remember thou, I have a little bit of patriotism left in me.

I have a bad cold; have been dosing myself for twelve hours with whiskey; hence there is added unto me a bad headache. When I first received Dane's letter I was just finishing second chapter of novel, so put Dane aside until to-day. To-day or to-morrow I shall make Wace's reply. I want you to see second chapter of Novel [*A Daughter of the Snows*], and pass judgment. Next week, Herbert's first, and Dane's second, should be through the machine; so it were well that you come over again. Wednesday if you can make it. Thursday and Friday I have to speak.

Jack

[1]First reference to the *Kempton-Wace Letters*.
[2]Character in the *Kempton-Wace Letters*.
[3]Fictional setting in *Kempton-Wace Letters*.

To Anna Strunsky

Oakland, Calif.
Oct. 1, 1900

Dear Anna:—

I don't know what you will make of this. At least I have postponed the main issue, of course, while really bringing forward the fundamental issue. In this case I think it better for the reader that we work from the universal to the particular—it will be clearer and arouse more sympathy with all parties concerned.

Behold! I have opened this letter in one mood, written myself into a passionate another mood, and stopped short. Wherefore, to-morrow expect another letter from Herbert Wace.

Your letter was splendid. It made me faint-hearted. So, as usual, I am afraid of the one I have just completed.

I had intended writing you from day to day, but have been so busy and had numerous interruptions. Also, I did not dare read your Dane Kempton

111

letter; for I was in a certain mood in the novel, and it was too great a risk to run to throw myself out of that mood until the chapter was done. The chapter was finished yesterday. And I have worked away at the letters to-day.

Do come over Wednesday (afternoon and night), I am expecting no one in the afternoon, and not that I know of in the evening, and we have so much to discuss.

The appreciation of Grant Allen[1] made me love Richard Le Gallienne. How different from the gutter attack of Robert Buchanan[2] on Kipling and Besant![3]

Am I right in substituting "spasms" for "fits"? And "Elizabeth Barrett" for "Mrs. Browning"? You deliver final judgment, remember.

Top of p. 12. "and" vows have been made for me "in this connection I shall neither sleep nor dream again." Is this not ambiguous? What will the reader think you really mean? Think it over.

Bottom of p. 12. "you still seemed to think defense of an arrangement that made for our separation to be necessary." Poor structure. The reader will absolutely have to go over it 2 or 3 times to get its meaning.

Where shall I look in Wordsworth for "dedicated spirit," etc.?

Remember, on your typed copy of the letters, make all corrections, suggestions, etc., and on margin pencil heavily in blue, red or black so that it will at once attract our attention when we go over.

Have finished "The Ring and the Book," "Half-Rome," "The Other-Half-Rome," and am just opening *Tertium Quid*. It is a revelation to me. How can I ever thank you!

Let us know if you can come Wednesday. Bessie sends love.

Great Haste,

Jack

[1] Author of *The Cruise of the Albatross,* etc.
[2] British poet and novelist. Author of *The Fleshly School of Poetry.*
[3] Sir Walter, British scholar and author.

To ANNA STRUNSKY

Oakland, Calif.

Oct. 3, 1900

Dear Anna:—

If it's bad art, the latter part of letter, it shall be cast out. I introduced it in an effort to further build up Herbert Wace before the main issue is taken up. I hardly know whether I am justified in doing so. I thought also that it might serve to relieve things in a way. The thing really occurred at Berkeley in 1897, Edlin being the socialist in question,—only they did not faze him at all. His indictment stood unchallenged. They were not able to take up defense.

As for the first part of the letter, it should have been finished yesterday, but I was too sick to work on it, and to-day has been almost as bad; so I cannot vouch for the first part even.

I've had a bad cold for a week or so, and it has pulled me down. Then I was poisoned some time ago, and not seeming to work out of my system, I had recourse to powerful medicine and took double and triple quantity. So between the two I was knocked out for a day or so.

While I think of it, Weber tells me he had *Fables in Slang*.[1] Pratt, a mutual friend, is lying in hospital with both ankles broken, and needs reading matter. *Fables* would just suit him. Would it be asking too much for you to mail it over to me?

Come next Monday by all means, to my place. Whitaker will be up. Come in the afternoon, not later than three. If it's windy, all of us will go sailing; if warm, swimming at Alameda; if cold and calm, swimming at Piedmont Baths. What say you?

I must go to San Francisco soon, some day, and will talk over the trip to Land's End later to bring it in on that day.

Bring your Wordsworth with you when you come. What did Hyndman say? Have you the letter? I am indeed gratified.

Quite agree with you, Besant made a worse than poor defense; my blood boiled as I read it and I wanted to rush into the arena myself. He meant well, but—.

Here come some people, so good night,

Jack

[1] By George Ade.

To CLOUDESLEY JOHNS

Oakland, Calif.
Oct. 17, 1900

Dear Cloudesley:—

Yes, I have just been trying the English market myself, these last few weeks, thanks to your English stamps. No, I did not make the mistake in mailing Ms. Find herewith an editorial letter from *Pearson's*. Note the "American flavor."

Didn't I explain my volume of letters? Well, it's this way: A young Russian Jewess of 'Frisco and myself have often quarrelled over our conceptions of love. She happens to be a genius. She is also a materialist by philosophy, and an idealist by innate preference, and is constantly being forced to twist all the facts of the universe in order to reconcile herself with herself. So, finally, we decided that the only way to argue the question out would be by letter. Then we wondered if a collection of such letters should happen to be worth publishing. Then we assumed characters, threw in a real objective love element, and started to work. Of course, don't know yet how it will turn out. We're both doing some very good work—in spots; but we are agreed, in case they merit it, to go over when we are done.

I see you complain against *Tale of Two Cities.* Why, under the sun? What's wrong?

I send you *Berry*[1] in a couple of days. Mr. Whitaker has borrowed it to read, but will bring it back shortly.

I never heard of Kennedy, or his book. How is it there are no reviews anywhere else? I should like to see it some day, and I will when I can raise the price. Clipping (for which same thanks), was from *Sunshine,* I presume?

Find here a poem by 'Gene Field. It's a page which Scribner's send out with his complete works, but which is never bound.

I can't see it. To me *The Rocks*[1] was quite a deal better than *Berry*. Better in handling and better in theme. What think you? Agree with me or with *N.Y. Press?* You have painted the landboomer all right, and the sucker too.

"The widow is gathering nettles for her children's dinner; a perfumed seigneur, delicately lounging in the Oeil de Boeuf, hath an alchemy whereby he will extract from her the third nettle and call it rent."

The above is Carlyle's; let it go. I shall give you better, which is as monstrous as anything he ever wrote (style), and as characteristic. Read it aloud. Don't quarrel with his generalizations in the reading,—just read it aloud. Then find fault with it if you can.

I shall commence excerpts on top of next page.

Jack London

[1]Apparently Johns' Ms.

To Cloudesley Johns

Oakland, Calif.
Dec. 22, 1900

Dear Cloudesley:—

"The Place of Truth"—doesn't such criminal negligence disgust one. There can be no excuse when the whole verse is regular to lose out one complete foot. It's damnable.

Yes, there is a bit of pathos in "The Undertakers." But it is such a little bit, considered from the standpoint of the reader. Don't you see, your pathos is only potential. The story contains all the possibilities of pathos, but those possibilities are not exploited. There are many reasons that they are not.

First, and above all, you approached the thing wrong. There are scores of ways of handling any subject, any situation, only one of which is the best. In my opinion, you did not choose the best. I mean, now, the point of view. Your man who dies is the particular; the world,—your readers, the universal. You, in writing the tale or sketch, meant to apply the particular to the universal. To have been true, to have been artistic, you should have applied the particular, *through the particular,* to the universal. You did not do this. You applied the particular, *through the universal,* to the universal. Let me explain. You took the point of view of the reader, not the main actor in the tragedy. You approached the tragedy and the main actor through the reader, instead of approaching the reader through the tragedy and the main actor. Or, to be plainer (even if I am mixing things up), the reader does not get inside that man and contemplate the whole thing through his soul. The reader stands apart and looks on. And this should not be. For instance, the reader did not look through the man's eyes; the reader did not see, as he saw, or should have seen, the buzzards drifting in.

I cannot be plainer without bringing up something concrete. Yesterday I corrected proofsheets of a story ["The Law of Life"] for *McClure's.* It was written some eight months ago. It will be published in the February number. Do look it up, so that you may understand more clearly what I am trying to explain. It is short, applies the particular to the universal, deals with a lonely death, of an old man, in which beasts consummate the tragedy. My man is an old Indian, abandoned in the snow by his tribe because he cannot keep up. He has a little fire, a few sticks of wood. The frost and silence about him. He is blind. How do I approach the event? What point of view do I take? Why, the old Indian's, of course. It opens up with him sitting by his little fire, listening to his tribesmen breaking camp, harnessing dogs, and departing. The reader listens with him to every familiar sound; hears the last draw away; feels the silence settle down. The old man wanders back into his past; the reader wanders with him—thus is the whole theme exploited through the soul of the Indian. Down to the consummation, when the wolves draw in upon him in a circle. Don't you see, nothing, even the moralizing and generalizing, is done, save through him, in expressions of his experience.

As to the finish of your sketch, you err. You should have chopped off at "and still newcomers wheeled lazily above the buttes, and black specks appeared against the desert sky." That is your proper ending. And have the man lying there, helpless, panting, and watching these black specks. So will the reader lie there, panting, and watch—through his eyes, always through his eyes, looking out from the door of the cabin upon the visible heat. As you have it, the reader does not look out through his eyes, from the door of the cabin. What does the reader do? Why the reader is perched up somewhere on a butte, or in mid air, and looks down and into his eyes and into the cabin door. Don't you see?

I have sent the story off as directed, several days ago; but do, please, consider these things and try to rewrite it, entirely rewrite it.

Again, I know that you can stomach my criticism without offense. Your style—don't be so halty and disconnected. Diversify your sentence structure. Sentence after consecutive sentence of yours are identical in structure, and sometimes almost in length. Quick, snappy sentences, short and crisp and curling, are oftentimes excellent for action. But if, in inaction, or minor action, you have employed them, when you come to major action, great action, they are worthless and worse than worthless.

Still again, as to phrasing. You do not cultivate it enough; you are too bald. Too rarely do you hit upon a good phrase such as "dignified birds of horror." (I could name several others). But too rarely. Sit down and grope after them, hammer them out in sweat and blood, endure your share of the travail of birth. Don't have so many still-borns.

Oh! One other thing, Cloudesley. You are at the same time a miser and a prodigal. You are penurious of words, and spendthrift of substance. The art of omission is of tremendous importance, but must not be misunderstood. Out of the many details, many features, select only the most salient one— but, God, man! when you have selected that one, shove it along for all it is worth. In a sketch, such as yours, a score of major features may be salient, and a thousand minor ones. Yours to select the one major one, and the several minor ones. But then do not neglect the minor, while all the time subordinating them to the major. For instance, how lavish you were with the episode of the spring disappearing and leaving him more lonely. That phase dismissed in a couple of short sentences! Why, you should have taken that up somewhere along near the opening, insinuatingly, craftily, all the time and all the time preparing the poor unconscious reader for it. Let him, in the midst of the vast desert, come to it as to a human for consolation, to stretch beside it and think of the past, to moralize. Weave it into him till it is a part of him,—and then, when it disappears, there is your minor tragedy consummated without ever a word being said for that matter. The tragedy is obvious. The mere statement that it has disappeared is enough. No need to say that he is lonelier; no need, if your preparatory work has been well done. Christ! Pathos! You have all the pathos in the world in that one incident; but you did not bring it out, work it up. It is still only potential. Can you catch what I am driving at?

Yes, after much delay, I captured *Cosmopolitan* prize.[1] I flatter myself that I am one of the rare socialists who have ever succeeded in making money out of their socialism. Apropos of this, I send you a copy of a letter received day before yesterday from Brisben Walker. Of course I shall not accept it. I do not wish to be bound. Which same you do think I am. Not so. McClure's have not bound me, nor will they. I want to be free, to write of what delights me, whensoever and wheresoever it delights me. No office work for me; no routine; no doing this set task and that set task. No man over me. I think McClure's have recognized this, and will treat me accordingly. Aside from pecuniary considerations, I think they are the best publishers, or magazine editors, in their personal dealings that I have run across.

Whites cannot thrive in Philippines. Well, did you ever hear of the control of the tropics, by the dominant white races, from their seats in the temperate zone?—a latter day slavery, if you will. Certainly. The Negro in the South is holding up his hands even now and having the shackles of the new slavery bound upon him. Such is destiny. The exploitation of lesser breeds in non-Caucasian latitudes will become an anachronism—when there are no lesser breeds.

You read "Evolution of Class Struggle." And I found nothing in it with which to disagree. What is that little tract? Only a throwing of the light of the "materialistic conception of history" upon one phase of human development. If you had addressed that portion of your letter, which dealt with the potency of the idea, to Noyes, he would have smiled and told you to go and read Achille Loria's *Economic Foundations of Society,* or Karl Marx's *Das Kapital.* Where do they put the idea? Bah, it is of little account. Whence does the idea come? From the economic structure of the society. Your idea cannot escape coming. It is imperative that it shall come, inevitable. But not come because it is intrinsically an idea, but because it cannot help itself. The thing is too deep for me to go into in a correspondence, but read it up, you. Read also, Draper's *Intellectual Development of Europe,* if you want to know about the materialistic conception of history.

Your idea does not crystallize material conditions, but is crystallized by material conditions. All evolution, all change, is from without, in; not from within, out. The fundamental characteristic of all life is IRRITABILITY. In the other words, capacity for feeling pressures from without. Life itself is an equilibrium, between what is within and what is without. A change from without in the pressures, and the organism's equilibrium is overthrown. Possessing irritability, it may be able to respond to the changed pressure and so establish a new equilibrium. If it does, it continues to live. If it fails, it dies. Life is equilibrium. If all forces which impinged upon organism were constant, you would have a constant organism. There would be no change. And there would be no development. The economic pressure, from without, forces the change, forces the idea, causes the idea.

Yes, do please send me a copy of "The Path of the Destroyer." No, I have seen *Review of Review's* notice of *Cosmopolitan* essay. Thanks just the same.

War—what did I hold? Read up my *Overland* resumé of Bloch's book. I held that war, as a direct means of gaining the desired end, was worthless; that it was now only the indirect means. That behind it was economics, which exerted themselves through it, and accomplished the desired end through it. "Not battles, but famine," I said. I do not ask you to occupy my old ground; for I wish to still occupy it myself. But while we are on this question of occupying ground, let me show you an example of your straddling propensities. In one portion of your present letter you are for "boosting natural selection" out of the way. In another, you say war is a splendid necessity, preventing stagnation, etc. Well, can you reconcile the two statements?

Speaking of illustrations, did you see how beautifully *Ainslie's* did by my story ["The Great Interrogation"] in December number? Incidentally, without asking my permission, here and there they succeeded in cutting out fully five hundred words, which I shall reinsert when published in book form. I suppose the one hundred and twenty-five they paid for it was considered sufficient justification for mangling.

Jack London

[1]With an essay entitled "What a Community Loses by the Competitive System."

To Anna Strunsky

Oakland, Calif.
Dec. 26, 1900

Comrade Mine:—

Thus it was I intended addressing you a Christmas greeting, saying, as it seemed to me, for you, the finest thing in the world. But it was impossible. For a week I have been suffering from the blues, during which time I have not done a stroke of work. Am writing this with cold fingers, at six in the morning—going for a day on the water, fishing, shooting, etc., to see if there are any curative forces left in the universe.

Ah! We refuse not to speak, and yet we speak brokenly and stumblingly! True, too true. The paradox of social existence, to be truthful, we lie; to live true, we live untruthfully. The social wisdom is a thing of great worth—to the mass. For the few it is a torment, upon it they are crucified—not for their salvation, but for the salvation of the mass. I grow, sometimes, almost to hate the mass, to sneer at dreams of reform. To be superior to the mass is to be the slave of the mass. The mass knows no slavery; it is the task master.

But how does this concern you and me? Ah, does it not concern us? We may refuse not to speak, yet we speak brokenly and stumblingly—because of the mass. The tyranny of the crowd, as I suppose Gerald Stanley Lee[1] would put it. As for me, just when freedom seems opening up to me, I feel the bands tightening and the riveting of the gyves. I remember, now, when I was free. When there was no restraint, and I did what the heart willed. Yes, one restraint, the Law; but when one willed, one could fight the law, and break or be broken. But now, one's hands are tied, one may not fight, but only yield and bow the neck. After all, the sailor on the sea and the worker in the shop are not so burdened. To break or be broken, there they stand. But to be broken while not daring to break, there's the rub.

I could almost advocate a return to nature this dark morning. A happiness to me?—added unto me?—Why you have been a delight to me, dear, and a glory. Need I add, a trouble? For the things we love are the things which hurt us as well as the things we hurt. Ah, believe me, believe me, "I have not winced or cried aloud." The things unsaid are the greatest. Surely, sitting here, gathering data, classifying, arranging; writing stories for boys with moral purposes insidiously inserted; hammering away at a thousand words a day; growing genuinely excited over biological objections; thrusting a bit of fun at you and raising a laugh, when it should have been a sob— surely all this is not all. What you have been to me? I am not great enough or brave enough to say. This false thing, which the world would call my conscience, will not permit me. But it is not mine; it is the social conscience, the world's, which goes with the world's leg-bar and chain. A white beautiful friendship?—between a man and a woman?—the world cannot imagine such a thing, would deem it as inconceivable as infinity or non-infinity.

(Thursday morning)

A cold, miserable, shivery day, yesterday, but I brought back a fair catch of fish.

(Friday morning)

So far did I take up the broken screed yesterday, when breakfast called. But before breakfast was over a friend dropped in—most unusual thing. But ere he had been gone five minutes, another dropped in, and another, and then two, and—well, that is the history of the day. Further, received a telephone from Bamford asking me to come and see him, important, and I went.

Now I shall try and finish. I'll come over in the afternoon, Saturday.

(Have just come back from your call at the phone)

So, until to-morrow,

Jack

---

[1]American Congregational Clergyman. Author of *Crowds*.

To Cloudesley Johns

Oakland, Calif.
Jan. 5, 1901

Dear Cloudesley:—

Regarding Talcott Williams on "Change in Current Fiction," must say I cannot agree with him, and that a canvass of the majority of recent books will totally disprove his averages. He says nothing can be done with a book of fifty thousand. *The Son of the Wolf* had only 49,000, and it makes a dollar and a half book of fair size. I hate to go into a book of more than 100,000. What do you think about it?

I stand convicted on the buzzards. My treat. The principle I outlined is all right, though it does not apply in this particular case.

I have written probably one hundred and ten thousand this year, against your ninety-odd; but I think that I loafed or did other things less, and that each thousand took me longer than each of your thousands did you.

To tell you the truth, Cloudesley, I haven't had any decent work published recently—work which I would care to have you read—socialistic essay excepted, and that I was unable to get a whack at in the proofsheets.

Your "plowing" repeated in "Destroyer" sketch is certainly right. "At this season"—wouldn't it damn you. "Not so" is correct. "Not as" is vile grammar. "So" also accompanies the negative. "As," the positive. I am *as good* as you. I am *not so good* as you. That's the rule, anyway, and if I were you I'd fire it into *Home Magazine* editor. Why, sometimes my ear demands that I turn a positive "as" into a "so"; but never have I felt impelled to do the opposite. The bad use of "so" in such instances as this, is chronic with ninety-nine per cent of newspaper men, about ninety of editors, and about fifty of first class writers.

I liked the sketch. I was taken by it right into the country described. Yet I do not think the *motif* was exploited as fully as it might have been or should have been.

I am indeed sorry that I cannot help you out just now. Almost any other time I would have been able to. But, you see, Christmas is just past. Further, a friend [Herman "Jim" Whitaker] has taken up writing with seven children and an undeveloped ability, which said friend I have been helping to finance. Another, both ankles broken badly some time since. Then my mother, to whose pension I add thirty dollars each month, got back in her debts and I have just finished straightening her out to the tune of thirty-six dollars. She just got five more extra ones to-day. And my Mammie Jennie (Negro foster mother) came down upon me for December quarterly payment of interest on mortgage, and delinquent taxes. Furthermore, within a week I expect my wife to be confined. Just the wrong time, Cloudesley, old man. January check *non est,* and I have been going along on borrowed money since before Christmas.

Jack London

To Anna Strunsky

Oakland, Calif.
Jan. 6, 1901

Dear Anna:—

I had intended writing you yesterday, asking you to come over Monday evening and go with me to that equal suffragist club before which Whitaker was to read. Then Tuesday I could have taken your pictures. But I had forgotten Mrs. Cowell's lectures. Then your letter came. Also found out that Monday was not the night and that we would have our regular boxing bout.

So Saturday, but come early, in the morning, so that I may take advantage of the sun. This, then, be the qualification: if I do not telephone you otherwise. Possibly, ere that time, the boy—I do pray for a boy—shall have arrived. In which case, you must come. So, Saturday, early, be it understood, unless I telephone. My birthday. A quarter of a century of breath. I feel very old.

Of the New Comer, I thank you for what you say. It will be in itself a dear consummation. Then must come the patient determining. And, O Anna, it must be make or break. No whining puny breed. It must be great and strong. Or—the penalty must be paid. By it, by me; one or the other. So be.

I shall be glad to go in for the Ibsen circle. I need more of that in my life.

Do bring the two photographic plates from Mrs. Stein's. I am getting soft; I must box more.

Jack

To CLOUDESLEY JOHNS

Oakland, Calif.
Feb. 4, 1901

Dear Cloudesley:—

Not dead, but rushed as usual. Have got down to my regular five hours and a half sleep again and running by the clock. Am just answering a whole stack of letters—you'll say I'm apologizing for not having written sooner—but not so, rather for the shortness of this.

Well, there's no accounting for things. I did so ardently long to be a father, that it seemed impossible that such a happiness should be mine. But it is. And a damn fine, healthy youngster.[1] Weighed nine and a half pounds at birth, which they say is good for a girl. Up to date has shown a good stomach and lack of ailments, for it does nothing but eat and sleep, or lie awake for a straight hour without a whimper. Intend to call her "Joan." Tell me how you like it, what associations it calls up.

Tell me what kind of answer Vance made to your scorcher of Jan. 4th. I am most interested to hear. However, as regards editing the "Destroyer," is there any necessity of drawing me into it. I do not remember what I wrote about it, but nevertheless, if you want to quote me, go ahead. I should rather not, though.

As regards "bumming by force from peoples inhabiting lands we cannot thrive in? Does not our modern slavery serve to deteriorate us, affecting our own government? While counting the profit you must not ignore the loss." —as regarding this I hardly know what to say. Do you not realize that whatever is "is right and wise"? Certainly it may be made wiser and more right in the natural course of evolution (and then again it mayn't), but the point is that it is the best possible under the circumstances. Given so much matter, and so much force, and beginning at the beginning of things as regards this our world, do you not know that it could not have worked out in any other way, nay, not in the least jot or tittle could it have been other than it has. We may make it better; and then again we may not.

As [Dr. Edward A.] Ross somewhere says: "Evolution is no kindly mother to us. We do not know at what moment it may turn against us and destroy

121

us." Don't you see; I speak not of the things that should be; nor of the things I should like to be; but I do speak of the things that are and will be. I should like to have socialism; yet I know that socialism is not the very next step; I know that capitalism must live its life first. That the world must be exploited to the utmost first; that first must intervene a struggle for life among the nations, severer, intenser, more widespread, than any ever before. I should much more prefer to wake to-morrow in a smoothly-running socialistic state; but I know I shall not; I know it cannot come that way. I know that the child must go through its child's sicknesses ere it becomes a man. So, always, remember that I speak of the things that are; not of the things that should be.

Find enclosed *Cosmopolitan* letters. I stood off first one and wrote to *McClure's*. They have agreed to go on with me, giving me utter freedom. So you see, at least they have not bought *me* body and soul. Honestly, they are the most human editors I ever dealt with. When I think about them, it is more as very dear friends, than people I am doing business with.

However, in refusing *Cosmopolitan's* offer,[2] which means giving up freedom, I think I have acted for the best. What think you?

Please return letters.

Jack London

P.S. I send *Fables* this mail. Also "Charge to Company." You fixed the latter up much better, very much better. The former please return quickly, as half a dozen are clamoring for it.

---

[1] Born Jan. 15, 1901.
[2] On Dec. 13, 1900, John Brisben Walker of the *Cosmopolitan Magazine* asked London if he would consider the question of a yearly salary for *Cosmopolitan* to do such work as would be satisfactory after a conference with the editor. "This would contemplate your giving your entire time."

To CLOUDESLEY JOHNS

Oakland, Calif.
April 1, 1901

Dear Cloudesley:—

The novel [*A Daughter of the Snows*] is off at last, and right glad am I that it is. The very first thing I shall do, now, will be the "Salt of the Earth." I do not know whether it will be a success (from standpoint of writing), and if it is I do not know whether I can find publication. But if these things come out all right, you'll then have your chance to fire back at me. But there are others. Almost everyone I know very intimately, are threatening to come back at me on the same thing. So there should be something doing.

You have heard me speak often of Strawn-Hamilton, the genius, tramp, socialist, etc., etc. He has been back some time now, and has gone into the labor movement. Two months ago he organized the cooks and waiters of San Francisco. To-day they are seventeen hundred strong, with six thousand dollars cash in the treasury. He is their walking delegate (business agent), and gets five dollars a week carfare and a hundred a month salary, besides having an assistant secretary, etc. So things move along.

I never can understand why it is you cannot leave go that Postoffice. How is it?

I send herewith a letter from *Town Topics*. They are paying two dollars for jokes now, and if you have any it wouldn't be a bad idea to send them along. I do not know much about joke writing, but I wouldn't send jokes in a bunch. I sent four triolets (the only four I ever wrote), to *Town Topics*. They took one, and sent three back. Later I re-sent one of the triolets: they took it. Later I re-sent another; they took it. But they balked on the fourth.

Yes, I should like ever so much to have some of those pastescraps—the more the merrier.

Your remarks concerning my stuff in the *Writer* ["The Question of a Name"] was the first I had heard of its being published. I did not know what to make of your criticism, and bided judgment until I had read what I had long before written—written long before I was married. I have just now read the stuff and cannot see that your criticism is merited. Pray where am I "illogical and unscientific"?

You remember my advice long ago (this is not apropos of the previous paragraph, but of your letter in general)— By all means shake Harold, and come somewhere and live in the center of things. In this day one cannot isolate oneself and do anything. Get you a big city anywhere, and plunge into it and live and meet people and things. If you believe that man is the creature of his environment, then you cannot afford to remain way off there on the edge of things.

                                                                    Jack London

To ANNA STRUNSKY

                                                            Oakland, Calif.
                                                            April 3, 1901

Dear Anna:—

Did I say that the human might be filed in categories? Well, and if I did, let me qualify—not all humans. You elude me. I cannot place you, cannot grasp you. I may boast that of nine out of ten, under given circumstances, I can forecast their action; that of nine out of ten, by their word or action, I may feel the pulse of their hearts. But of the tenth I despair. It is beyond me. You are that tenth.

Were ever two souls, with dumb lips, more incongruously matched! We may feel in common—surely, we ofttimes do—and when we do not feel in common, yet do we understand; and yet we have no common tongue.

Spoken words do not come to us. We are unintelligible. God must laugh at the mummery.

The one gleam of sanity through it all is that we are both large temperamentally, large enough to often understand. True, we often understand but in vague glimmering ways, by dim perceptions, like ghosts, which, while we doubt, haunt us with their truth. And still, I, for one, dare not believe; for you are that tenth which I may not forecast.

Am I unintelligible now? I do not know. I imagine so. I cannot find the common tongue.

Large temperamentally—that is it. It is the one thing that brings us at all in touch. We have, flashed through us, you and I, each a bit of the universal, and so we draw together. And yet we are so different.

I smile at you when you grow enthusiastic? It is a forgivable smile—nay, almost an envious smile. I have lived twenty-five years of repression. I learned not to be enthusiastic. It is a hard lesson to forget. I begin to forget, but it is so little. At the best, before I die, I cannot hope to forget all or most. I can exult, now that I am learning, in little things, in other things; but of my things, and secret things doubly mine, I cannot, I cannot. Do I make myself intelligible? Do you hear my voice. I fear not. There are poseurs. I am the most successful of them all.

Jack

To Cloudesley Johns

Oakland, Calif.
April 8, 1901

Dear Cloudesley:—

Thanks for slips. I'm open to as many as you can spare. I am using them for precisely the same thing you do, so thanks for the idea, too.

I am sending you herewith pictures of the youngster at three weeks and two months.

Every man, at the beginning of his career (whether laying bricks or writing books or anything else), has two choices. He may choose immediate happiness, or ultimate happiness. This is a fact you nor nobody else can deny. He who chooses ultimate happiness, and has the ability, and works hard, will find that the reward for his effort is cumulative, that the interest on his energy invested is compounded. The artisan who is industrious, steady, reliant, is suddenly, one day, advanced to a foremanship with increased wages. Now is that advance due to what he did that day, or the day before? Ah, no, it is due to the long years of industry and steadiness. The same with the reputation of a business man or artist. The thing grows and compounds. He is not only "paid for having done something once upon a time," as you put it, but he has been paid for continuing to do something through quite a period of time. Is this not true of the veriest gambler, who first loses to his victim, deferring payment for such expended energy until the end?

However, Cloudesley, I grasp what you meant to say. You meant "unethical" instead of "unscientific." Science deals with the things which are; ethics deals, usually, with the things which ought to be. Ethically, perhaps (only perhaps), it might be better to have only immediate happiness; but *actually,* ultimate happiness is a potent thing which must be considered.

O no. My "incentive" is not the "assurance of being able some day to sell any sort of work on the strength of a name." Every year we have writers, old writers, crowded out—men who once had names, but who had gained them wrongfully, or had not done the work necessary to maintain them. In its way, the struggle for a man with a name to maintain the standard by which he gained that name, is as severe as the struggle for the unknown to make a name.

Jack London

To Anna Strunsky

Oakland, Calif.
July 24, 1901

My Little Collaborator:—

Yes, and the Yellow[1] is dead—at least for some little time to come. For all I know, I may be doing prize fights next.

Explanations are hardly necessary between you and me, but this case merits one I think. Didn't get home till the middle of the day, Monday. Went to see my mother, sister, etc. Tuesday went to Santa Cruz to speak. Came back Wednesday and pitched into work on back correspondence. All the time intending to take up reply to Dane Kempton's last and surprise you with it. But the *Sunday Examiner* rushed me Thursday to have a freak story in by Friday noon. And Thursday also the *Daily Examiner* clamored to see me instanter. Put *Daily* off, finished *Sunday* work on time, and on Friday also went to see *Daily Examiner.* They proposed the "Schuetzenfest" to me. Saturday I started reply to Dane Kempton and paid bills. And on Sunday took up the "Schuetzenfest" and have been at it steadily for ten days, publishing in to-day's *Examiner* the last of that work. My whole life has stood still for ten days. During that time I have done nothing else. Why, so exhausting was it that my five and one-half hours would not suffice and I had to sleep over seven.

And just now, to-day, as I sat down to send you greeting, along comes yours to me. I kind of looked for you to be over to-day, though little right had I to, and I have now given up that idea.

And further. I find I must do something for *McClure's* at once, or they will be shutting off on me. So I am springing at once into a short story, which will be finished by end of week, and then the letters. You know I have striven to be on time, so forgive me do this once. Tell you what I'll do, if you don't expect to be out—see you on Friday afternoon. Won't be able to stop to dinner, though, for have to go to 6:30 supper. If I do miss the supper, will be dropped from the rolls, for it will have been my third consecutive absence.

Haven't finished "Aurora Leigh" yet, but it is fine, greater, I think, than Wordsworth's ("Excursion" is it?) from the little you read me of it.

Jack

[1]His reference to his completion of the "Schuetzenfest" articles which he considered to be "yellow journalism."

To Cloudesley Johns

Oakland, Calif.
Dec. 6, 1901

Dear Cloudesley:—

Nothing doing. Am hammering away in seclusion, trying to get out of Alaska. Guess I'll succeed in accomplishing it in a couple of years.

By the way, the book of letters is not based upon your proposition at all. Said proposition is merely a phenomenon of love, of which there be many phenomena. The book goes down deeper, and my side, at least, shows why very many other things are besides your proposition. And, in fact, when I say your proposition, I do not mean to say that we have used your characterization of that proposition, and when I say that I mean to say that the phenomenon your proposition characterized is a very old one and has been recognized and put into print many times ere you and I were born. Leaving out the evolutionists, I can refer you to Max Nordau's[1] essay on Love which occurs in his *Paradoxes*. The same thing is handled there at length.

And yet furthermore, the particular proposition or epigram upon which "The Theorist" is founded, in our letters will occur among so many many other propositions that it can not hurt in the slightest any subsequent publication of your book. Not that your epigram has been used at all. For it hasn't.

In trying to give you a comprehension of the nature of the letters, I recollected your epigram and knew that by mentioning it you would get the whole point of view it stood for. That was all.

Wyckoff[2] is not a tramp authority. He doesn't understand the real tramp. Josiah Flynt[3] is the tramp authority. Wyckoff only knows the workingman, the stake-man, and the bindle-stiff. The profesh are unknown to him. Wyckoff is a gay cat.[4] That was his rating when he wandered over the States.

Well, good luck on the way to Cuba! Wish I were with you. I am rotting here in town. Really, I can feel the bourgeois fear crawling up and up and twining round me. If I don't get out soon I shall be emasculated. The city folk are a poor folk anyway. To hell with them.

Jack London

---

[1] A Zionist leader, favoring Herzl's plan for a Jewish National Home in East Africa.
[2] Prof. of Sociology at Princeton University, frequently lived with workers and unemployed and wrote *A Day With a Tramp and Other Days*.
[3] London dedicated *The Road* to Josiah Flynt, a hobo acquaintance.
[4] "Gay Cats are short horns, chechaquos, new chums or tender feet. A Gay cat is a new comer on The Road who is a man grown, or at least youth grown." . . . "The profesh are the aristocracy of The Road." *The Road,* p. 173.

To ANNA STRUNSKY

Oakland, Calif.
Jan. 5, 1902

Dear, Dear You:—

Your greeting came good to me. And then there was the dear little token for Joan. And it all impresses me with how much I am and always shall be in your debt. You do not know—you, you!

You look back on a tumultuous and bankrupt year; and so I. And for me the New Year begins full of worries, harassments, and disappointments. So you? I wonder?

I look back and remember, at one in the morning, the faces I saw go wan and wistful—do you remember? or did you notice?—and I wonder what all the ferment is about.

I dined yesterday, on canvasback and terrapin, with champagne sparkling and all manner of wonderful drinks I had never before tasted warming my heart and brain, and I remembered the sordid orgies and carouses of my youth. We were ill-clad, ill-mannered beasts, and the drink was cheap and poor and nauseating. And then I dreamed dreams, and pulled myself up out of the slime to canvasback and terrapin and champagne, and learned that it was solely a difference of degree which art introduced into the fermenting. And I thought of you, and I wondered.

Sordid necessities! For me Yorick has not lived in vain. I am grateful to him for the phrase. Am I incoherent? It seems very clear to me.

And now to facts. Bessie wants me to ask you, if, on January 12th., we can stop all night, and if we can put Joan to bed also. You see, in Piedmont here, we have to leave San Francisco an hour earlier than we used to on account of the street cars. And Bessie cannot bring herself to be away from Joan a whole night.

Jack

To Cloudesley Johns

Oakland, Calif.
Jan. 6, 1902

Dear Cloudesley:—

But after all, what squirming, anywhere, damned or otherwise, means anything? That's the question I am always prone to put: What's this chemical ferment called life all about? Small wonder that small men down the ages have conjured gods in answer. A little god is a snug little possession and explains it all. But how about you and me, who have no god?

I have at last discovered what I am. I am a materialistic monist, and there's damn little satisfaction in it.

I am at work on a short story that no self-respecting bourgeois magazine will ever have anything to do with. In conception it is really one of your stories. It's a crackerjack. If it's ever published I'll let you know. If not, we'll wait until you come west again.

As regards "effete respectability," I haven't any, and I don't have anything to do with any who have . . . except magazines. Nevertheless I shall be impelled to strong drink if something exciting doesn't happen along pretty soon.

My dear boy, nobody can help himself in anything, and heaven helps no one. Man is not a free agent, and free will is a fallacy exploded by science long ago. Here is what we are:—or, better still, I'll give you Fish's definition: "Philosophical materialism holds that matter and the motion of matter make up the sum total of existence, and that what we know as psychical phenomena in man and other animals are to be interpreted in an ultimate analysis as simply the peculiar aspect which is assumed by certain enormously complicated motions of matter." That is what we are, and we move along the line of least resistance. Whatever we do, we do because it is easier to than not to. No man ever lived who didn't do the easiest thing (for him).

Or, as Pascal puts it: "In the just and the unjust we find hardly anything which does not change its character in changing its climate. Three degrees of an elevation of the pole reverses the whole jurisprudence. A meridian is decisive of truth; and a few years, of possession. Fundamental laws change. Right has its epochs. A pleasant justice which a river or a mountain limits. Truth this side the Pyrenees; error on the other."

Nay, nay. We are what we are, and we cannot help ourselves. No man is to be blamed, and no man praised.

Yes, [W. H.] Cosgrave[1] wrote me instanter about the letters. I am afraid they're not for him. They would be utter Greek. Say, Cloudesley, did you ever reflect on the yellow magazinism of the magazines? Cosgrave says I ought not to write for the *Examiner*. And in same breath he says he will take what I write if I write what he wants. O ye gods! Neither the *Examiner* nor *Everybody's* wants masterpieces, art, and where's the difference in the sacrifice on my part?

You mention Sedgewick of *Leslie's.* Do you mean weekly or monthly *Leslie's?* And what are his initials?

Well, in six days I shall be twenty-six years old, and in nine days Joan will be one year old. Did you know we had named her Joan?

Jack London

[1]An editor of *Everybody's* Magazine.

To George P. Brett[1]

Oakland, Calif.
Jan. 30, 1902

Dear Mr. Brett:

My hearty thanks for *Little Novels of Italy*[2]—a favorite book of mine which I did not possess. I think "A Madonna of the Peach Trees" one of the world's short story masterpieces.

Unfortunately, I haven't any copy of the stories already written of *The Children of the Frost*—that is, no *readable* copies, as witness my fist[3] in this letter.

The idea of *The Children of the Frost,* is the writing of a series of tales in which the reader will always look at things from the Indian's point of view, through the Indian's eyes as it were. Heretofore the viewpoint in my Northland stories has been that of the white man's.

Thanking you for your kind interest and hoping that California may soon open her arms to you, I am,

Sincerely yours,
Jack London

[1]President of the Macmillan Co.
[2]By Maurice Henry Hewlett.
[3]The letter was handwritten.

To Anna Strunsky

Oakland, Calif.
Feb. 11, 1902

Dear You:

It is because you are "dear you" that it is made very hard for me. I am unable to express the counter impulses and dictations which run riot in me at this moment. Impulses—to grant. Dictations—to deny. Believe me, it is far far easier to yield to the impulses than to obey the dictations. The woman in me pleads, but my manhood reasons. And, strongest of all, over and above your dear face I see myself, demanding me to be true to myself, to be consistent. I am sure your esteem for me would be less were I untrue to myself in order to be true or kind to you. Do you catch me? I know not why, but the thing so shapes itself that it is not you I must face and consider, but myself. All that I have stood for, and preached and thought (which is I), rises up before me to judge. And I, careless and wanton though I may have always appeared, do secretly respect myself. Without that respect I go to pieces. And believe me, for one of my mould I realize how easily I may go to pieces.

But I cannot say my thought. I become incoherent. Possibly you may grope and catch me. I pray you do, though you remain unconvinced. To strive to answer, as I have just given over striving, were the truer way, but I fail of it.

Superficially, I may easily say many things. If I believed it were wrong, I should not go.[1] Believing it right, honestly believing it right, dare I not go? I do thank you for one thing: you do not ask for your sake. It would make it harder than it is. But you are generous enough to put the request on the fairest possible basis. But it does hurt to be told that I do not stand close enough; that I must always believe my way is far enough from yours never to run counter. And it is not the statement, but the truth of the statement that hurts. And there's the paradox—why do I, who am so little of you, find so much in you? And we are coldly independent of each other. But, as I think, it seems not so. Possibly in no way have I affected you, possibly in only a little way have you affected me. But a little way with some, in the very nature of things, turns out to be a great deal.

Behold! I have lived! Ah, but don't you see? We are so different, that to live we must live differently. Is it necessary that we should be like to be friends? Is it not well that we should reach out hands to each other, like captains of great hosts, in alliance?—neither of us compromising, neither of us giving over or diminishing? Surely such things can be, and are. Is it meet that friends lose themselves in each other? Away with such friendships!

And how have I lived? Frankly and openly, though crudely. I have not been afraid of life. I have not shrunk from it. I have taken it for what it was at its own valuation. And I have not been ashamed of it. Just as it was, it was mine. And as I have not been afraid of life, so have I a frankness with death. I am not afraid to die, and for that reason I am not afraid to see men die. And by "afraid" I do not mean the ordinary meaning of fear. I am not afraid that it will hurt me to see men die. I have seen men die. It was of value to my living that I should see them die. And whatsoever I take I am willing to give. All the world, if it so wishes, may come and see me die.

I am a sentient creature. To live is to experience sensations. To see living is to know living—so dying. I shall be unable to reflect upon my own death, even though I, too, ripen and fall from a gallows tree. And being denied the intellectual value of my own death, I must seek to get those values before my death from the deaths of others. There is such a wonder in it all.

You have not faith enough in me. You fear that if I should see a man sordidly die that it will pollute me—"coarsen" you said. Possibly you meant it. How coarsen? My whole life rises up and says no. I have seen far worse and viler than a legal execution. The legal execution could only be anticlimactic. If I am coarse (as I am), then I am. The worst has been wreaked upon me. What is done, is done.

O God! you can't understand. My manhood to your womanhood may be all wrong, but to stand up, on my two feet, and face life as it is, to have no fear, to see death come to others with as calm and equal poise as when I shall see it come to me, to be unafraid, undismayed, to have no poltroonery, no femininity (which is mawkish in a man though good in a woman), to not cover up my eyes but to look bravely out, to take life and the things of life just as I know myself to be a mere thing of life—but you cannot understand; nor can I tell you. How can I tell you?—tell you of the things slowly and subtly grown in me, of the long upbuilding of what I am, of my last and inmost self from which I cannot get away. Why to tell you this, were to have you live with me from the cradle, to dream with me my boyhood's fancies, to do things with my hands, and face things with my face, to buck with men, to think as I have thought at masthead or solitary wheel, to drink long nights and days away, to sleep under blanket with men that were MEN, to learn to grow sick at cowardice and to honor a brave man above an honest man, to honor men unafraid—and how can you understand when I cannot tell you.

On the other hand, I fail to see the difference between laughing and joying in a system wherein a man is hanged, than in seeing that man hanged. And you and I—we all laugh and joy. When you dare to walk home by sidewalks lighted by the Law, then are you a party to the crime committed by the Law when it hangs a man. Nothing remains but to find some mountain top or coral reef utterly outside the domain of man's Law, or else to quit living. But if you dare accept the gaslight on the corner then you must accept the murders the Law commits, for you are part of that Law, by your accepting the gaslight on the corner and the policeman on the crossing you live in this community of people, and by living in this community of people you help to support the Law which this community makes, and when you help to support the Law it means that you pay your share of the rope which is bought to hang the man. Quit or stay with it—that's the proposition. I, for one, stay with it, and staying with it I am neither afraid nor ashamed of it. I do not purpose to live in the front parlor with the blinds drawn. I want to see the kitchen and the scullery. By God! the man who is afraid to take the fish off the hook or the guts from the bird he expects to eat is no man at all. Neither the fish nor the bird were intended for him. He has no right to them. Let him quit eating. Or, if he will eat, let him get in and unhook and gut. We are no cleaner because we have someone else to do our dirty work for us.

Do we want fruits and vegetables? Well and good. Let us work for them.

But while we are working for them we must eat fish and birds? Very true. Then, so long as the fish and birds are good enough for our bellies, let them be not unclean for our hands. And rest assured that the Law that protects you from insult and assault on the open street is stained with the blood of the man it hangs at San Quentin. What if that man's eyes rest on you or me? Do they not rest upon us five miles or five thousand miles away? I am not afraid to look that man in the eyes. Why should I be afraid? Do I coarsen by looking him in the eyes? Then do I coarsen more by staying away afraid to look him in the eyes, afraid that I will be hurt by looking him in the eyes. Believe me, only a bastard sympathy can be generated on couch cushions. "Tender feelings" after all are pleasurable. I should rather look with my own eyes and feel sick. Then I might feel sick ever after when a man is hanged.

But why go on? Am I bending to convention by baring my soul? I only wax heated anyway. The primordial beast lifts up its head and roars—of what good?—ten thousand generations seem to separate us. And anyway, though you may point the way to the New Jerusalem, I shall build the road thereto. And while you eat your fish and birds, and though you despise me, I shall unhook and gut. And it will taste good in your mouth and your hands will be as dirty as mine.

I did not write the letter I intended to write. I went astray somehow. I wished to meet your sweetness with sweetness, and instead have called upon all that was harsh and unlovable in my nature. I am grateful, and I do appreciate that you care enough for me to wish me not to do anything no matter how great or small. But—but possibly the first page of this letter, is, after all the clearest expression of what I mean. I cannot. Had you, before I dreamed of going, said "Never go to a hanging," I would have promised to please you. But coming afterward, the whole thing seems changed. I should be ashamed of myself. I would rather go, and then, to make it easier for you, never see you again, than to not go and have your favor showered upon me a thousand-fold. Not that I hold a hanging above your favor, much less your favor a thousand-fold; but that there is something else which I must hold above all if I would hold you or anyone or anything at all.

Jack

[1]London was invited to witness an execution at San Quentin.

To Cloudesley Johns

Piedmont, Calif.
Feb. 23, 1902

Dear Cloudesley:—

Behold! I have moved! Therefore my long silence. I have been very busy. Also, I went to see a man hanged yesterday. It was one of the most scientific things I have ever seen. From the time he came through the door which leads from the death-chamber to the gallows-room, to the time he was dangling at the end of the rope, but 21 seconds elapsed.

And in those twenty-one seconds all the following things occurred: He walked from the door to the gallows, ascended a flight of thirteen stairs to the top of the gallows, walked across the top of the gallows to the trap, took his position upon the trap, his legs were strapped, the noose slipped over his head drawn tight and the knot adjusted, the black cap pulled down over his face, the trap sprung, his neck broken, and the spinal cord severed—all in twenty-one seconds, so simple a thing is life and so easy it is to kill a man.

Why, he made never the slightest twitch. It took fourteen and one-half minutes for the heart to run down, but he was not aware of it. ⅕ of a second elapsed between the springing of the trap and the breaking of his neck and severing of his spinal cord. So far as he was concerned, he was dead at the end of that one-fifth of a second. He killed a man for twenty-five cents.

You ask what else beside matter moves. How about force? Waves of light, for instance?

We'll have to reserve the free will argument till God brings us together again. I've got the cinch on you.

Did you go in on the *Black Cat?* I went in for a couple of stories, though I have little hope of pulling down even the least prize. I imagine I can sell the stuff somewhere else, however.

Lord, what [a] stack of hack I'm turning out! Five mouths and ten feet, and sometimes more, so one hustles. I wonder if ever I'll get clear of debt.

Am beautifully located in new house. We have a big living room, every inch of it, floor and ceiling, finished in redwood. We could put the floor space of almost four cottages (of the size of the one you can remember) into this one living room alone. The rest of the house is finished in redwood, too, and is very, very comfortable. We have also the cutest, snuggest little cottage right on the same ground with us, in which live my mother and my nephew. Chicken houses and yards for 500 chickens. Barn for a dozen horses, big pigeon houses, laundry, creamery, etc., etc. A most famous porch, broad and long and cool, a big clump of magnificent pines, flowers and flowers and flowers galore, five acres of ground sold the last time at $2000 per acre, half of ground in bearing orchard and half sprinkled with California poppies; we are twenty-four minutes from the door to the heart of Oakland and an hour and five minutes to San Francisco; our nearest neighbor is a block away (and there isn't a vacant lot within a mile), our view commands all of San Francisco Bay for a sweep of thirty or forty miles, and all the opposing shores such as San Francisco, Marin County and Mount Tamalpais (to say nothing of the Golden Gate and the Pacific Ocean)—and all for $35.00 per month. I couldn't buy the place for $15,000. And some day I'll have to be fired out.

Jack London

To George P. Brett

Piedmont, Calif.
April 16, 1902

Dear Mr. Brett:—

Here's some idea of the *Children of the Frost:*

Nam-Bok the Unveracious	3,500	words.
Li Wan the Fair	6,500	"
The Sun Folk[1]	8,000	"
In the Forests of the North	6,800	"
The Law of Life	2,700	"
Keesh, the Son of Keesh	4,000	"
The Master of Mystery	4,100	"
The Death of Ligoun	3,700	"
The Sickness of Lone Chief	3,000	"
	45,000[2]	"

The first four are sold and waiting serial publication. The fifth and sixth have received serial publication, the seventh is seeking serial publication, as are the eighth and ninth which were written within the past month. I expect shortly to write one or two more, when the collection will be complete. It should be in your hands by early fall. The two previous collections, *The Son of the Wolf* and *The God of His Fathers,* contained respectively 49,000 and 50,000 words.

In connection with *The Children of the Frost,* I should like to know if it is in line with the Macmillan Company's policy to sometimes make an advance on royalties? And if so, could two hundred dollars be advanced me now on the royalties of *The Children of the Frost?* Now I do not mean this as a guarantee necessary before the book can go to you. Whether you can make any advance or not, the book goes to you, for I have said it. The point is, that if you can make the advance, things will be made easier for me. And this is the reason: I have no income, and my expenses are about $150 per month. This sum I manage to get from my magazine work. But, beginning next week, I shall put in about thirty days writing and revising a book manuscript, so that during that time I shall be earning no ready money. This book,[3] by the way, has been promised to Bliss Perry for the *Atlantic,* (if serially available), and for Houghton, Mifflin & Co., which firm brought out my first book.

It hardly seems necessary for me to state that two previous collections of short stories have earned me much more than two hundred dollars apiece.

The tramp story, which you mention, is only the first one of a series which I have discontinued. It is with the *Atlantic* just now, or I would let you see it, though, really, I have become chary of letting anyone see it. As for sea novels, I am waiting to make a lucky strike some time, when I can devote a few months to them. You see, though once a sailor myself, I have gone stale on sea men and sea atmosphere, and I have control enough not to attempt such work until I have refreshed myself. My plan is, when I can see expenses clear for half a dozen months, to take passage on sailing vessel almost anywhere, and with typewriter and paper along, to do my work in the thick of it.

Thank you very much for Mrs. Atherton's new book [*The Conqueror*], which I have just received and which I look forward to reading with pleasure.

Yours very sincerely,
Jack London

---

[1]Was not included in first edition. "The League of Old Men" and "The Sunlanders" were.
[2]The addition is apparently in round figures.
[3]Unidentifiable.

To George P. Brett

Piedmont, Calif.
April 28, 1902

Dear Mr. Brett:—

I am returning you herewith the signed agreement of *The Children of the Frost*. It is eminently satisfactory. I am now at work on the last story in that series, and will have it off to the magazines ere another week is out. Also, within a week or ten days I shall be able to dispatch to you duplicates of nearly all, if not all, the stories, so that they may be available for illustration and for copyrighting in England. I will enclose with them a list of the ones which are to receive serial publication in England.

I feel very confident that the complete manuscript will be in your hands in time for October publication. The Century Company expects to bring out a book of mine [*The Cruise of the Dazzler*] this fall, a boy's story expanded from one to be published soon in *St. Nicholas,* and Lippincott's are bringing out a novel [*A Daughter of the Snows*] I wrote a year ago, this fall or winter. In England, Isbister & Co., are bringing out *The God of His Fathers,* and they have bought the English copyright of *Son of the Wolf* from Ward, Lock & Co. and expect to bring same out this fall or winter.

That's the way I stand with my work just now, with, in addition, the book [*The Call of the Wild*] I am at present working on and which Houghton, Mifflin & Co., have been promised the first sight of.

I do not know whether *Children of the Frost* is an advance over previous work, but I do know that there are big books in me and that when I find myself they will come out. At present I am just trying to find myself and am busy gripping hold of life.

Yours very sincerely,
Jack London

To CLOUDESLEY JOHNS

Piedmont, Calif.
July 12, 1902

Dear Cloudesley:—

You must have been having one hell of a time. Aren't you disgusted with metropolitan life? If you aren't you ought to be. I am, and I've never seen it.

This world is made up chiefly of fools. Besides the fools there are the others, and they're fools, too. It doesn't matter much which class you and I belong to, while the best we can do is not increase our foolishness. One of the ways to increase our foolishness is to live in cities with the other fools. They, in turn, would be bigger fools if they should attempt to live the way you and I ought to live. Wherefore, you may remark that I am pessimistic.

Speaking of suicide, have you ever noticed that a man is more prone to commit suicide on a full stomach than on an empty one? It's one of nature's tricks to make the creature live, I suppose, for the old Dame knows she can get more effort out of an empty-bellied individual than a full-bellied one.

Concerning myself, I am moving along slowly, about $3000 in debt, working out a philosophy of life, or rather, the details of a philosophy of life, and slowly getting a focus on things. Some day I shall begin to do things, until then I merely scratch a living.

Between you and me, I wish I had never opened the books. That's where I was the fool.

Well, someone is going down town, so I'll shut off and give them a chance to mail this. I am just staggering along under an attack of "grip."

Jack London

To ANNA STRUNSKY

R.M.S. Majestic
July 31, 1902

Dear You:—

I am thinking of you to-day, as you speak at Pacific Grove.

It is 6:30 p.m. here, which is 3 p.m. with you, and possibly you are speaking at this present moment. Well, good luck be with you, comrade. I know you will do well.

I sailed yesterday from New York at noon.[1] A week from to-day I shall be in London. I shall then have two days in which to make my arrangements and sink down out of sight in order to view the Coronation from the standpoint of the London beasts. That's all they are—beasts—if they are anything like the slum people of New York—beasts, shot through with stray flashes of divinity.

I meet the men of the world, in the Pullman Coaches, New York clubs, and Atlantic-liner smoking rooms, and truth to say I am made more hopeful for the Cause by their total ignorance and non-understanding of the forces at work. They are blissfully ignorant of the coming upheaval, while they have grown bitterer and bitterer toward the workers. You see, the growing power of the workers is hurting them and making them bitter, while it does not open their eyes.

"There are many to-morrows my love, my dove; but there is only one To-day."

This may be bettered. "There are many To-morrows, my love, my dove, and we will make them all To-days."

I am doing quite a lot of essay work aboard ship, and so, until you hear from me in London,

The Sahib

---

[1]The American Press Association asked London to go to South Africa to write a series of articles on the Boer War and the political and economic situation in the British Colonies. However, his plans were altered before he reached New York and he made tentative arrangements with Macmillan to publish a sociological study of the London slums. The result was *The People of the Abyss*.

To George and Carrie Sterling[1]

London, England
Aug. 22, 1902

Dear George and Carrie:—

How I often think of you, over there on the other side of the world! I have heard of God's country, but this country is the country God has forgotten that he forgot.

I've read of misery, and seen a bit; but this beats anything I could even have imagined. Actually, I have seen things and looked the second time in order to convince myself that it was really so. This I know, the stuff I'm turning out will have to be expurgated or it will never see magazine publication. I won't write to you about the East End and I am in the thick of it. You will read some of my feeble efforts to describe it some day.

I have my book over one-quarter done and am bowling along in a rush to finish it and get out of here. I think I should die if I had to live two years in the East End of London. Love and regards to everybody.

Jack London

---

[1]Sterling was a well-known Californian poet. Carrie was his wife.

To George P. Brett

Texas
Nov. 9, 1902

Dear Mr. Brett:—

When I left you Thursday, I went to the American Press Association to get ms. of *People of the Abyss*. I found that they had, after all, submitted it for serial publication. However, should it come back to them, they will at once forward it to me.

In the meantime, I have duplicate copy in my baggage. As soon as I arrive in California I shall get hold of it, revise it at once, and forward to you. So you will receive it by November 20th, if not a day or so sooner.

By N.Y. letters (which I have just opened on the train), I learn that Miss Anna Strunsky is now on her way to New York. She is my collaborator in the *Letters*. She will come and see you, for she wishes to re-write the last two letters of the book and to do some general revising.

I am sure you will find her charming. She is a young Russian-Jewess, brilliant, a college woman, etc.

By the way, I feel inclined somewhat to differ with the idea that the *Letters* may not make a hit. They are just the sort of stuff to arouse a whole lot of interest and agreement and disagreement among the critics; and this once aroused, the subject (Love), is likely to make the book go far with the reading public. The thing with the book, as I see it, is that it will hit big or not hit at all.

Well, in four days I shall be in California and hard at work again.

Very truly yours,
Jack London

To George P. Brett

Piedmont, Calif.
Nov. 21, 1902

Dear Mr. Brett:—

A couple of days ago I expressed you the revised duplicate manuscript of the *People of the Abyss*. The slight delay in dispatching it was due to the fact that I was out on a newspaper detail—buckling down to the grind as soon as I won home.

This *People of the Abyss,* as you will speedily learn on looking over it, is simply the book of a correspondent writing from the field of industrial war. You will notice, while it is often unsparingly critical of existing things, that it has proposed no remedies and devoted no space to theorizing— It is merely a narrative of things as they are.

Ere this you will have met Miss Anna Strunsky, and been pleased with her I am sure. Of course, she will be one of the contracting parties in getting out this book of letters, though she is content to let me arrange the thing for her.

Now concerning myself and the work I wish to do, I should like to have a good talk with you. The hurry and bustle and unwonted confusion of traveling and racing around post haste is over with, and I think I can say what I wish to say somewhat more coherently than when I was rushing through New York.

In the first place, I want to get away from the Klondike. I have served my apprenticeship at writing in that field, and I feel that I am better fitted now to attempt a larger and more generally interesting field. I have half a dozen books, fiction all, which I want to write. They are not collections of short stories, but novels. I believe I can turn out a novel now. The novel Lippincott's published this fall [*A Daughter of the Snows*] was written by me over two years ago, at the beginning of my writing. At that time the twenty short stories I had written constituted my literary experience. Not only was that novel my first novel, but it was my first attempt at a novel. I have done a great deal of studying and a great deal of thinking in the last two years, and I am confident that I can to-day write something worth while.

Besides others, for which I have been gathering material a long while, I have three books which I should like to write as soon as I can get at them. The third book, with which I shall bid for a popularity such as Bellamy[1] received, (yet a quite different popularity), I shall write last, in the meantime preparing for it while I write the other two. The first of these two I have thought of calling *The Flight of the Duchess*. It will be in the Here and Now, and though situated in California, it will not be peculiarly local, but will be really a world-story which might take place anywhere in the *civilized* world. It will end happily. The second is a sea story, or, better, a sea study. I have thought of calling it *The Mercy of the Sea,* though I am not altogether satisfied with the title— It will be almost literally a narrative of things that happened on a seven-months' voyage I once made as a sailor. The oftener I have thought upon the things that happened that trip, the more remarkable they appear to me. Looking back, they hardly seem real. I can no more say that this story will end happily than can I say that it will end unhappily. It is, in fact, a sea-tragedy, and not to end it as it did end would be a distinct disappointment to the reader.

Now here comes the rub. I have no income save what my pen brings me in the magazine and newspaper field. Just as you advanced royalties to me on *The Children of the Frost,* so the royalties have been advanced on my other books recently brought out. In the four months I have been away, my stock of articles and stories has been disposed of to the magazines; so I return home without these assets, without income, and with nothing before me but to sit down and write up another stock of magazine articles and stories. Of course, this means the work of months, and then continual work to keep the stock replenished. Without a certain sure income, it is impossible for me to sit down and write a book. The returns from a book, from the moment of beginning the first chapter, do not arrive for a year or two, but the tradesmen's bills arrive the first of each month.

That you may understand how I happen to be thus situated, let me give you a brief biographical note. When I was ten years of age I was selling papers on the street. From then on, I worked for my living. At fifteen I left home to shift for myself. I worked with my hands at many things. I grew up to an early manhood without any education to speak of. When I first began to write I had no art-concepts whatever. So I have mainly educated myself in the last several years while at the same time I was learning to write, and on top of it all, trying to get a living from my writing. When I returned from the Klondike I began to write. But when I returned from the Klondike I found my father dead and my mother in debt. I was a young fellow who had never been rash enough to anchor himself by marrying. Nevertheless I found myself with a household on my shoulders. I buckled down and began to write to support that household and at the same time to educate myself. Finding myself anchored with a household, I resolved to have the compensations of a household, and so I married and increased my household or the weight of my anchor. But I have never regretted it. I have been well compensated— Nevertheless, as a result, I have no income save what I earn with my pen from day to day, and the tradesmen's bills are larger and more insistent than they would be were I all by myself in the world.

We live moderately. One hundred and fifty dollars per month runs us, though we are seven,[2] and oft-times nine when my old nurse and her husband depend upon us. Now, if I am sure of this one hundred and fifty dollars per month, I can devote myself to larger and ambitious work. And here is the proposition I wish to advance for your consideration. If you find it practicable to advance me $150. per month for one year, say beginning with December 1st., 1902, I guarantee to have in your hands *The Flight of the Duchess* and *The Mercy of the Sea* by December 1st., 1903. In addition, I shall by that time have completed two other books which are now nearly done.

One book is a collection of Klondike stories, similar to the ones I have already brought out. 33,000 words of it are already written, all of which, save the last story written, have been published in the magazines. They were written off and on during the time *The Children of the Frost* was being written. To complete them I have but 17,000 words to write, and nearly half of this amount I owe to *Ainslee's Magazine* in return for the story they gave up so that *The Children of the Frost* should not be delayed.

The other book is a series of connected boys' stories, *The Fish-Patrol Stories,* which I had nearly completed for the *Youth's Companion* before I went to England last summer. A couple of weeks' work will finish them. This book will compare favorably with *The Cruise of the Dazzler,* a juvenile which the Century people are bringing out this fall and which is going well.

140

So the account, if you met my proposition, would stand something like this on December 1st., 1903:

From you.	From me.
$1800.	New Collection of Klondike Stories.
	Fish-Patrol Stories.
	The Kempton-Wace Letters.
	The People of the Abyss.
	The Flight of the Duchess.
	The Mercy of the Sea.

That is to say, against your $1800. I will balance six books. Granting an average earning power of $300. to each book, the six books will equal the $1800. Of course, either *The Flight of the Duchess* or *The Mercy of the Sea* may sell well enough to wipe out the $1800. Also, from the way I shall write *The Flight of the Duchess* I know that it will have a serial value of a thousand dollars at least—this in case its serial sale be necessary to balance the account. On the other hand, *The People of the Abyss* already has $150. advanced on it, and the royalties from the *Kempton-Wace Letters* will be divided between Miss Strunsky and myself. These last two items I do not think will alter the balance when it is considered that I have placed the average earnings of each of the six books at $300.

My idea is this: balancing the books against the $1800. does away with financial risk on your part and gives me a year's trial with the experiment. Please let me know what you think of my proposition as soon as you conveniently can.[8]

Of course, my hope, once I am on my feet, is not to write prolifically, but to turn out one book, and a good book, a year. Even as it is, I am not a prolific writer. I write very slowly. The reason I have turned out so much is because I have worked constantly, day in and day out, without taking a rest. Once I am in a position, where I do not have to depend upon each day's work to keep the pot boiling for the next day, where I do not have to dissipate my energy on all kinds of hack, where I can slowly and deliberately ponder and shape the best that is in me, then, at that time, I am confident that I shall do big work.

While this letter is traveling to you, I shall work on the sort of story magazines buy. Should you view my proposition favorably, telegraph me, and I shall at once start to work on *The Flight of the Duchess.*

There was one matter upon which I wished to speak with you, but I forgot it in my rush West through New York. In England, I found Mr. H. Perry Robinson, President of Isbister & Co., most enthusiastic over my work. Every book I had written he had brought out or got possession of, with the one exception of *The Children of the Frost.* He had pioneered the English market for me. The copyright of my very first book had been bought by an English house, which seemed afraid to publish it. All the English houses seemed afraid, or, at least, they were all loth to play pioneer. But Mr. Robinson got hold of my second book and made the initial attempt. And he worked hard that I might get a good hearing. He ploughed the ground, he was the first to plough it, and he ploughed it well. Then he bought the first book, which had been lying around England for so long, and brought it out. Since then he has procured the English rights of my other books and is preparing to bring them out. When I met him, he put the case fairly and squarely before me. He was the first to take me up in England; he had performed the labor of introducing me; in order to introduce me well he had foregone immediate profits, sinking them into the publishing, with the idea of building up greater mutual profit for both of us; and because of all this he looked upon my future work as honestly his to publish.

Now I have explained to you the errors and confusions through which I have waded in acquiring what little experience I have of publishing. Living out here on the edge of things, utterly ignorant of the whole thing, I simply butted around blindly in the dark till I knocked holes through somehow and saw daylight. I believe, now, that the first period of my career has been completed, and that I am about to enter a second period. And on the publishing side of this second period, I think I shall be able to avoid the errors into which I previously blundered. I think I am starting off without being handicapped by my own confusion and ignorance and by all that confusion and ignorance entail. What I want is to have everything clear and straight, and in the following statement I hope to get everything clear and straight:

To have Macmillan Company, and no other house, bring out my American books (if they should wish to). To have Isbister Company, and no other house, bring out my English books. In the case of Isbister, I had much rather it had been the Macmillan Company too, but it seemed to me to be Isbister's by right of work performed. I give over to them from a sense of justice. In their favor, I may say that they agree to give me the same royalties, whatever they be, that I receive in America.

In trying to be just to Isbister & Co., I do not think I have been unjust to the English Macmillans or to you. As I understand it, the two houses are quite separate, financially separate, though they work together in a friendly way. So that I do not financially hurt the American Macmillans, who interested themselves in me, when I give the English rights to the Isbisters; nor do I wrong the English Macmillans, who did not interest themselves in me as the Isbisters did. You know the difficulties that oft-times beset the author in dealing with publishers, and this is, I hope, my last difficulty.

My difficulty this fall of three books coming out at the same time, was unavoidable, and was because I was ignorant and had no definite arrangement with anybody. The Lippincott novel, written long previously, was altogether out of my hands. While the Century juvenile was a serial written a good while before for *St. Nicholas* (written before the novel, even). And when the *St. Nicholas* people bought it, at that early date, they asked for and received the book rights for the Century Company. So it happened that these two books, written at different dates and altogether out of my control, unfortunately came out at the same time you brought out *The Children of the Frost*. Not only was the simultaneous publication of these three books unfortunate from a standpoint of sales, but it gave rise to a feeling that I had become unduly prolific and was turning out regular machine stuff.

In conclusion, I can only hope that I have not wearied you with this lengthy recital. Also, I want to say, "Keep an eye on those *Kempton-Wace Letters.*" There is a bigger chance for a hit in them than they are given credit for. First, the subject, love, is one that possesses not only undying interest, but the most wide-spread interest. We are given more to an analysis of our emotions these days than ever before, while the tendency of the American reading public is so strong towards things scientific, that a scientific discussion of love is bound to arouse interest. Further, though I may be wrong, it is my belief that the book is quite original in both its treatment and subject matter.

Sincerely yours,

Jack London

[1]Edward Bellamy, author of *Looking Backward*.
[2]The seven included London, Bessie, Joan, Bess, London's mother, his sister Ida, and Johnny, Ida's son.
[3]Macmillan accepted the proposition but extended the time to two years, during which time they published *The Kempton-Wace Letters*, May, 1903; *The Call of the Wild*, July, 1903; *The People of the Abyss*, Oct., 1903; *The Faith of Men*, May, 1904; *The Sea Wolf*, Nov., 1904. *The Flight of the Duchess* and *The Mercy of the Sea* were never written.

To Anna Strunsky

Piedmont, Calif.

Dec. 6, 1902

Dear Anna:—

I am so glad you like Mr. Brett, and overjoyed to hear the readers' opinions of the *Letters*. You see, I came through New York in too great a rush to hear those opinions. Of course they are "eminently publishable," etc., etc. Quite agree with them; but if only Mr. Brett can raise the faith in their making a hit, why I am confident that they will make a hit. You see, Mr. Brett's faith is necessary, not that they may be published, but that they may be *pushed* after they *are* published. There is a chance for them to make a hit without being pushed, but being pushed will greatly increase this chance.

Every letter I write to Mr. Brett I insist upon their large chance for success. I remember writing to him in my last letter, (written sometime before I [received] yours, in which I learned that he thought I had lost interest in the *Letters)*—in this last letter I remember opening a *spurring* paragraph thus: "Keep an eye on those *Kempton-Wace Letters*. There is a bigger chance for a hit in them than they are given credit for."—and then I went on to show why there was that bigger chance for a hit.

Concerning title and a precedence of authors' names, Anna, I leave to you. You know I want you to appear in the manner which will be most advantageous to you. That is my wish in the matter. But, recollecting back, I do not know whether you wanted your name to appear before mine or after mine. Also, whether it should be *Kempton-Wace* or *Wace-Kempton* Letters. I leave this to you. Let me know upon what you decide.

By the way, can't you think out a better title for the book? Not only better commercially, but better artistically. I have been vainly racking my brains for that title. There is such a title, if we can only find it.

To my mind, it seems absolutely impossible to interlard a series of Hester's letters. You see, the book would be neither one thing nor the other. As it is, it is a straightforward, consecutive series of well-argued letters on Love. It is not Love Letters. To interlard love letters would not only not make it a book of Love letters, but would destroy it as a book of Letters on love. It would be a broken-backed, unconsecutively argued hodge-podge. Do you see what I mean?

Further, and mark well, the public is sated with *Love Letters,* while that same public has not had any letters on Love at all.

All goes well. I am hard at the grind again. Though I have just received a telegram from Mr. Brett which makes me financially secure for some months to come. I am getting ready to write a novel to be called *The Flight of the Duchess*. Similar motive to Browning's.

I enclose a letter from a Hollander I met in Latin Quarter, to whom I sent a couple of my books. How would you like to know him?

Jack

To George P. Brett

Piedmont, Calif.
Dec. 11, 1902

Dear Mr. Brett:—

I am sending you herewith signed contract. I cannot say how glad I am that you have made the period of contract two years instead of one year, giving me a year to a novel instead of six months. In token that I am taking it seriously, carefully, and without haste, I shall deliberate long over *The Flight of the Duchess,* and over the two or three other motifs for novels. Some time in January I shall send you the scenario of *The Flight of the Duchess,* or whatever else I may decide upon in place of it, or maybe two or three scenarios for you to select from.

You have the full list of books by me, written, or partly written, or projected, and there is none in other publishers' hands, nor have I any arrangements with other publishers whatsoever concerning above books and future work.

Collection of Klondike Stories—I have already brought the 33,000 words written up to 43,000 words. This leaves me only about 7000 words left to complete the book. So I shall certainly have the manuscript in your hands by July, 1903. There is, of course, a chance that it may be short, say one story; but even in this case, virtually the whole manuscript will be in your hands.

The Fish-Patrol Stories—I shall finish them, and have manuscript in your hands by July, 1903. It comes in conveniently that you do not expect to bring them out till the fall of 1904, or till 1905, because the *Youth's Companion* I do not think will run them till 1904. You see, they like to make announcements a year ahead, especially of anything like a series of stories, and as they are not yet completed, and as they are unannounced for 1903, there is no chance for them before 1904 for serial publication. Of course, I am quite willing to have an additional clause put in the contract, agreeing (in event of discontinuance of contract), to publish no books elsewhere till these six books or their equivalents have been brought out by you. If you wish to put in such a clause, I am perfectly willing to sign it. I am prompted to this solely by the *Fish-Patrol Stories,* for the *Youth's Companion* sometimes holds stuff a long time before it brings it out.

Kempton-Wace Letters—Miss Strunsky has written me that she is about starting to work to add about fifteen thousand words from the woman, Hester Stebbins. I am thoroughly in accord with this plan of hers. It is excellent. In the book, as so far written, two fundamental aspects of love have been presented; but she will cap them by presenting the third aspect, which is, from what I understand from her letter, the intuitive aspect—the heart-love of woman as opposed to the two different kinds of head-love of the men. I am confident that there is nothing published that will be anything like it. I am overjoyed that you have so far decided to bring it out in the spring.

People of the Abyss—I see you have set this off till next Fall. Being correspondent-stuff, I believe that serial publication, far from hurting it, should enhance its value when published in a book. If you have no objection to the plan, I should like to submit it to a couple of publications. And if you have no objection, will you send the manuscript in your possession to the *New York Independent?* I shall write them to-day advising them of its possible coming. By the way, I have a few photographs which may go to illustrate it should you so decide, and possibly that very tough picture of me in East End garb might not make a bad frontispiece.

I have a copy of the *People of the Abyss* manuscript, which is now on its way west to me. If you wish it, I can revise it and put it in your possession in place of the one I am asking you to send to the *New York Independent.* However, I should like to keep this duplicate copy in my possession, for I am sometimes called upon to give lectures out here, and I have matter for a number of lectures in it—social reform lectures, etc., you know.

I have several thousand words to do to finish this Klondike short story I am now at work upon. Then I shall put my undivided thought upon *The Flight of the Duchess* and other motifs for novels till I have made my choice. Depend upon it, I shall put the best that is in me into the work of the next two years; and the one thing, above all, that I shall avoid, is haste.

Sincerely yours,

Jack London

To George P. Brett

Piedmont, Calif.
Feb. 16, 1903

Dear Mr. Brett:—

Am sending you herewith "The Story of Jees Uck." It is something like ten thousand words in length, and I think may possibly be suited for your series of small booklets. It was published in the *Smart Set* some time ago. I had intended it for next collection of Klondike tales, which, as you know, is nearly complete. This collection of tales, the title of which I am thinking of making *A Hyperborean Brew*[1] (so named from the title of one of the stories), you will not be able to publish for nearly two years; so, bringing out "The Story of Jees Uck" in your series of booklets—will it prevent it later on being included in the larger collection?

I hope you will like this "Story of Jees Uck." At the time it was published serially I was gratified to receive a letter from a man who had lived wild life, and who was so convinced by the story that I could not unconvince him that I had never lived with a native wife, for only by so living, he contended, could I have got the experience necessary to write the story.

According to your request, I am also informing you that I have this day expressed the revised copy of *The People of the Abyss* to you, so that no delay may occur in rushing it into print.

I have wholly cut out the references to the King of England in the Coronation chapter, have softened in a number of places, made it more presentable in many ways, and added a preface and a concluding chapter. In this concluding chapter I have surely been optimistic (as I really am), though I have seriously challenged the political managing class of England. The point I make, that political machinery racks itself out and must be replaced by newer and improved political machinery, I have also touched [on] in the preface.

Do you remember that photograph of myself I sent you in my slumming clothes—would not this photograph make a good frontispiece?

Also, I have a few photographs, which I took, which are now with the copy being serially published. Later on, when we see how these photographs reproduce, would it not be well to consider the advisability of putting a few of them in the book?

Again advising you that *The People of the Abyss* has been expressed to you to-day for purposes of immediate copyright.

Very truly yours,
Jack London

[1]The collection came out under the title *Faith of Men.*

To Corresponding Editor,
Youth's Companion

Piedmont, Calif.
March 9, 1903

Dear sir:—

Your letter of March 4th. enquiring about actual conditions upon which were built the *Fish Patrol Stories*.

Let me frankly state, first of all, the knowledge from which I write. I, when a young fellow of from fifteen to seventeen, was for a good while one of the oyster pirate fleet. My sloop, the *Razzle Dazzle* was an oyster pirate sloop. With the rest of the fleet, grown men, convicts, and what-not, I have raided the oyster beds when I was fifteen and sixteen, both in my sloop, and, when she was wrecked, in the actual sloop *Reindeer* with one, Nelson, a man who was shortly afterward shot by officers of the law at Benecia. He was shot and killed upon another sloop, which, at the time, he was running.

In fact, the oyster bed raid I have described in one of the stories, is almost literally a narrative of an actual raid. The watchmen had been placed on the beds as the tide was falling, and left there without a skiff. When the oyster pirates, in small boats, which they dragged a long distance across the mud, arrived, they forced the two watchmen off into the water, but did not molest them. The only departure from truth is that the raid was successful and that not one of the pirates was captured.

Later on, this Nelson and myself, in the *Reindeer,* were up in Benecia with a load of oysters, when we were approached by one of the Fish Patrolmen with a proposition which caught our fancy, and for some months afterward the *Reindeer,* Nelson, and myself, took an active part in the raids on the law-breaking fisherman. The way we captured the big Chinese fleet of shrimp-fishers in the first story "White and Yellow," again almost a literal narrative of what actually happened, even to the refusal of the Chinese to bail the *Reindeer* until she was just about ready to sink.

Big Alec, the King of the Greeks, in story by that title, was an actual man. I have not even changed his name, or nickname. He had a record of several men killed by him, but, aided by all the Greeks, with money, etc., he beat the cases. He actually came down to Benecia with his ark, told Charley and me that he was going fishing Chinese Sturgeon-line in the Bight at Turner's Shipyard; but, such was his reputation, Charley and I left him alone, instead of, as in story, capturing him. Later on, Big Alec (I was in Japan at the time),[1] killed two sailors, under most dramatic circumstances, escaped the authorities, and has never been heard of since. Let me give you the facts of this killing. A feud was on between these two English sailors (deserters), and Big Alec. Everybody knew of this feud. The people on the wharf at Martinez, in broad day, saw Big Alec sailing along in one direction, and the two sailors sailing along in an opposite direction. The point where the two boats would pass was hidden from the people on the wharf by a wheat ship lying at anchor. The people saw the two boats disappear behind the wheat ship. After a while they saw Big Alec's boat appear as he continued on his way. They watched for the boat with the two sailors to appear. It never appeared. In the short space of time while behind the wheat ship, Big Alec had killed these two men, sunk their boat with them in it, and gone on as though nothing had happened. Charley told me the details of this affair when I returned from my voyage to Japan. He had dragged for and finally recovered the scuttled boat with the two dead occupants.

"The Siege of the Lancastershire Queen" is founded on a certain amount of fact. Charley and I, in the salmon-boat of a captured Vallejo Greek, came upon the two men with the sturgeon line outfit, chased them round and round a wheat ship, and lost them by having them sheltered by the captain of the wheat ship. We gave them up, the story captured them. But, we captured other fishermen in the same water, for the same offense, sailing along our side of the triangle in a faster boat. Also, we have had them beat us ashore, when we returned, dragged for their line, and raised it with over a thousand pounds of sturgeon on the hooks. And when the men claimed their line we arrested them and convicted them.

"Charley's Coup" is imaginary insofar as the story goes, but is based upon the fact that it was an old trick of the fishermen to leave their nets drifting and go ashore, and when the Fish Patrol attempted to confiscate their nets, to fire with their rifles from the shore.

"Demetrios Contos" is a fiction which exceeds the truth. For, in point of fact, Demetrios Contos would have left me to drown had the story actually occurred. But the pride in a fast boat, and the flaunting of the Fish Patrol is certainly true to life.

"Yellow Handerchief" is a fiction insofar as he chased me around through the mud. But I actually did take the helm of his junk, outpoint the *Reindeer,* have them cast off the tow-line, and beat them into San Rafael Creek. Yellow Handkerchief, however, did not escape, but went to jail with his crew.

I have written of the years 1891 and 1892 in San Francisco Bay and up the rivers. The fishermen were then a wild crowd, as they still are a wild crowd. The oyster pirates are gone. The Chinese shrimpers remain, for, backed by the powerful Seven Companies, which hired for them the best legal talent to be obtained, they beat all our efforts to convict them by carrying the cases from court to court and by outgeneraling the mediocre city attorneys who usually fought our cases for us.

There is not so much shooting, etc., going on now among the Greeks and Italians as formerly, and they have been pretty well brought under the heel of the law. Though, as I say, they are a wild lot yet. George, one of the cowardly patrolmen mentioned in first story of series, was stabbed, after I left the Fish Patrol, by a revengeful Greek. In the old days dead fishermen were brought in lying across their nets, and pitched battles, such as was fought around Big Alec's ark, were fought.

I know that Charley, three other men, and myself, have raced for our lives down the Martinez wharf, pursued by a howling mob of fishermen, because we had just arrested two of their number red-handed. We escaped in our salmon boat, and when the trial later took place in Martinez, we attended with a reinforcement of fighting men in case of trouble. But the trial was a farce. Martinez was to a large extent a fishing town, fishermen innumerable were challenged by us, but a solid jury of fishermen remained at the end, and brought in "Not Guilty" without leaving their seats, when as I say, the culprits had been caught red-handed.

So I certainly do vouch for the conditions which obtained among the fishermen ten years and more ago, and I should be glad to have all letters of enquiry referred to me. By the way, there in the East with you, the Chesapeake oyster pirate war is not yet forgotten.

Sincerely yours,

Jack London

[1]This would be 1893 when he shipped as a seaman on the sealing vessel, *The Sophie Sutherland*.

TO GEORGE P. BRETT

Piedmont, Calif.
March 10, 1903

Dear Mr. Brett:—

I am glad you like the *Call of the Wild,* but, unfortunately, I cannot accept your offer for all rights in it. You see, the *Saturday Evening Post* bought the American serial rights of it, and already have sent me over half of the proof-sheets; while Watt & Son are handling the English serial sale of it.

The whole history of this story has been very rapid. On my return from England I sat down to write it into a 4000 word yarn, but it got away from me & I was forced to expand it to its present length. I was working on it when you came to see me in January. At the time I had made up my mind to let you carry the uncompleted duplicate away with you; but somehow the conversation did not lead up to it & I became diffident. Then I sent a copy to the *Saturday Evening Post* and they at once accepted it.

They have paid me three cents a word for the American serial rights. This was the money I intended dividing between my debts and my South Sea trip. But when it arrived last week, my debts loomed so large & the South Seas loomed so expensive, that I compromised matters and bought a sloop-yacht [the *Spray*] for San Francisco Bay. It is now hauled out & being fitted up. I shall live on it a great deal, and on it I shall write the greater part of my sea-novel. The sloop is old, but it is roomy & fast. I can stand upright in the cabin which is quite large. I'll send you a picture of her some time.

I did not like the title, *The Call of the Wild,* and neither did the *Saturday Evening Post.* I racked my brains for a better title, & suggested *The Sleeping Wolf.* They, however, if in the meantime they do not hit upon a better title, are going to publish it in the *Post* under *The Wolf.*[1] This I do not like so well as *The Sleeping Wolf,* which I do not like very much either. There is a good title somewhere, if we can only lay hold of it.

The *Saturday Evening Post,* as first buyer, reserved the right of setting date for simultaneous serial publication in England & America, so they would be the ones to write to in this connection. Of course, they will illustrate it.

I should have been glad to close with your offer, both for the sake of the cash & of the experiment you mention; but, as I have explained, the serial right has passed out of my hands. As a book, however, under the circumstances as they are, you may succeed in getting a fair sale out of it.

I shall shortly make a rough sketch of the map for frontispiece of *Fish Patrol Stories.* The difficulty with *Youth's Companion* is that they may not publish it serially for a good time to come.

Will you please send me five copies of *Children of the Frost* (if they have not already been sent), and also, one copy of *Guns, Ammunition, and Tackle,* & charge to my account.

Sincerely yours,
Jack London

[1]*The Saturday Evening Post* used the title *Call of the Wild.*

TO GEORGE P. BRETT

Piedmont, Calif.
March 25, 1903

Dear Mr. Brett:—

I have telegraphed you to-day accepting your offer for *The Call of the Wild.*[1]

I had thought, previous to receiving this last letter from you, that my already having disposed of serial rights had knocked in the head whatever plan you had entertained for the publishing of the book. I cannot tell how glad I am to find that I was mistaken.

I am sure that pushing the book in the manner you mention will be of the utmost value to me, giving me, as you say, an audience for subsequent books. It is the audience already gathered, as I do hope you will gather in this case, that counts.

Concerning title, I must confess to a sneaking preference for *The Call of the Wild*. But, under any circumstance, I want the decision of the title to rest with you. You know the publishing end of it, and the market value of titles, as I could not dream to know.

You may send the contract along at your convenience for me to sign. And I cannot convey to you the greatness of my pleasure at knowing that the book has struck you favorably; for I feel, therefore, that it is an earnest of the work I hope to do for you when I find myself. And find myself I will, some day.

Concerning the *Kempton-Wace Letters,* I am rushing the proofs through as fast as they arrive.

The covers you mention sending will probably arrive in this afternoon's mail, when I shall at once state my preference.

As the *Letters* come out anonymously, they should not collide with the dog story at all.

Sincerely yours,

Jack London

P.S.—Do you remember what I told you of the nationality of Joseph Conrad? It was correct. He was a Polish boy who ran away to sea from Poland.

---

[1]Brett offered London $2000 for publishing rights (outright sale), no royalties. London received $700 from *The Saturday Evening Post*. So for a book that has sold nearly 2 million copies, London received $2700.

To Cloudesley Johns

Oakland, Calif.
July 11, 1903

Dear Cloudesley:—

Yes, I shouldn't mind living for a while in Los Angeles; but, you see, I'm settled, am three months behind in all my work, letting my contracted work go and hammering away at hack in order to catch up with a few of my debts, and do not see my way to getting even with my work for all of a year hence.

Hard-a-lee with me will not affect my work—in fact, I am confident it will be far otherwise.

I laugh when I think of what a hypocrite I was when, at the Bungalow,

I demanded from you your long-deferred congratulations for my marriage—but, believe me, I was a hypocrite grinning on a grid.

Concerning your affair, let me say this: it's all right for a man sometimes to marry philosophically, but remember it's damned hard on the woman.

Jack London

To George P. Brett

Oakland, Calif.
[c. Sept. 2, 1903]

Dear Mr. Brett:

Concerning my separation from Mrs. London,[1] I have really nothing to say except the *Kempton-Wace Letters* have nothing whatever to do with it. That the causes of the separation have been operative long previous to the writing of the book. As the reporters could not ascertain the real reason, they dug one out of the book, that is all. So far as the public is concerned I have no statement to make except that the *Kempton-Wace Letters* play no part whatever in the separation.

I am enclosing herewith an amplification of the synopsis of the sea novel [*The Sea Wolf*], also a copy of the synopsis, so that both may go to Mr. Gilder[2] together. I shall return you his letter in a couple of days if I may be permitted, or pardoned, rather, the liberty of holding it that long.

He has my full permission to blue pencil all he wishes, and, while it is practically impossible to give any synopsis of such a novel as this, I have striven to show him that the situation, because of the characters themselves, will not permit of anything offensive. Furthermore, in this there is no alteration of my original conception of handling the story. I elected to exploit brutality with my eyes open, preferring to do it through the first half and to save the second half for something better. I am taking plenty of time on the book and shall not rush it. In fact, because of the changes in my life which have just been occurring, yesterday morning is the first actual work on the book I have done in a month. But there are no more interruptions in sight, and I shall now proceed steadily with it. I shall have it finished by the first of Dec.

Mr. Gilder's offer for the serial rights is satisfactory. If he should take the book, I can have the final copy of the first installment in his hands in a month, or in two months, just as he elects.

Mr. Gilder speaks of rough drafts. I do not make any. I compose very slowly, in long hand, and each day type what I have written. My main revision is done each day in the course of typewriting the manuscript. This manuscript is the final one, and as much time is spent on it as is spent by many a man in making two or three rough drafts. My revisions in proof-sheets are very infrequent, chopping a word or a phrase out here, putting in one or the other there, and that is all. So that, for me, a rough draft is an impossible thing.

You can say to Mr. Gilder, however, that I shall be very amenable to any suggestions he may make concerning the serialization of the novel. I am absolutely confident myself, that the American prudes will not be shocked by the last half of the book.

Cosgrave is the most conservative and conventional of editors. He wrote me concerning the novel and I thought I'd make him shy at it. Work of mine he has refused for *Everybody's,* I have sold promptly, and right on top of it, to the *Atlantic.*

Personally, and outside of money considerations, I should greatly like to see the novel serialized in the *Century.* It means much in the way of advertisement and of bringing me into the notice of the clique of readers peculiar to the *Century.*

Very truly yours,

J. L.

---

[1]In a letter of August 27 Brett asked if there was any truth in the newspaper accounts that the *Kempton-Wace Letters* had been the cause of his separation from Bessie. The divorce became final in November of 1905.
[2]R. W. Gilder, Editor of *Century.* Mr. Gilder had some misgivings about the realism of the first half of *The Sea Wolf.*

To George P. Brett

Oakland, Calif.
Sept. 10, 1903

Dear Mr. Brett:—

I am enclosing herewith Mr. Gilder's letter which you asked to have returned. I have also, this day, sent you telegram giving permission to print authors' names on title page of second edition of *Kempton-Wace Letters,*[1] and giving permission to Mr. Gilder to use *The Triumph of the Spirit* as serial title for sea story, but suggesting, in place of it, *The Sea Wolf* or *The Sea Wolves.*

Frankly, I do not like Mr. Gilder's title at all. The very thing he feared about the last half of the sea novel (the making of a tract of it), I fear about his title. It seems to breathe a purpose, an advertisement of a preachment; in fact, it might do for the title of a tract—or, at least, that is the way it strikes me.

The Sea Wolf is a strong and brief title.

I have also expressed you to-day that collection of essays, which I have thought of calling *The Salt of the Earth.*[2]

I am indeed grateful to you, Mr. Brett, for your efforts in behalf of my sea story. It is a good thing to have it come out in the *Century,* and I hope the additional synopsis I forwarded will clinch the matter.

Sincerely yours,
Jack London

---

[1]The first edition was published anonymously.
[2]Published under the title *War of the Classes.*

To Marshall Bond

Oakland, Calif.
Dec. 17, 1903

Dear Marshall:—

Lo and behold! I am just reading your letter of Oct. 12th.

About that time I jammed my unopened mail into a gun-case and pulled out on a duck-hunting cruise of six weeks. During this cruise of course, I opened my gun-case correspondence & answered it. Then I was gone for a few days. During which time gun-case remained on the yacht. Last Monday pulled out on another cruise. Are now in lower end of the Bay near Alviso. Today my partner, cleaning guns, discovered your letter, crumpled up at very bottom of the case where it had been jammed by the gun. It is a miracle that it was ever found. Might have remained there for years.

Yes, Buck was based upon your dog at Dawson and of course Judge Miller's place was Judge Bond's—even to the cement swimming tanks and the artesian well. And don't you remember that your father was attending a meeting of the Fruitgrowers Association the night I visited you, and was organizing an athletic club—all of which events figured with Buck if I remember correctly. As you say you expect to be in S.C. [Santa Clara] for Christmas I'll mail this to you there. Hope to see you soon. Have received a couple of letters from Del Bishop & Charley Meyers[1] looked me up recently.

Sincerely yours,
Jack London

P.S. Was it a boy?

---

[1]Two of London's acquaintances of Klondike Days.

To George P. Brett

Seoul, Korea
April 3, 1904

Dear Mr. Brett:—

I hear that Isbister and Co. has failed. If this is so, and they're out of business, somebody else will have to handle my books in London. Isbisters were giving me same rates I received in America. It would not be unfair for me to receive same rates from whatever other English house takes up my books. May I leave this to you?

I can't do anything myself out here.[1] Haven't received a letter for a month and don't know what has become of all my mail. As yet, all I have received from Isbisters is ten pounds. I wonder if anything is coming to me.

The Son of the Wolf,	they bought from Ward, Lock Co., so nothing to me from that.
The God of Their Fathers,	they got on an arrangement from McClure, Phillips, so nothing there.
A Daughter of the Snows	same arrangement.

But *The People of the Abyss*
Kempton-Wace Letters
Cruise of the Dazzler   they owe me for. The first two on same rates I have with you, and *Cruise of Dazzler* on similar arrangement. Anything you can do in straightening this out will be appreciated I can tell you of course, if they have failed and all the rest. I merely heard it as a rumor.

Now, concerning that book of essays of mine, *The Salt of the Earth*. From the way you spoke (in San Francisco) I had the feeling that you had read only the title essay. If this is so, would you mind glancing at some of the later-written essays, "The Scab," "The Class Struggle," "The Tramp," etc., with the object of a change of conclusion regarding the expediency of not issuing as a book for an indefinitely long time to come. The later-written essays, to me, seem to have timely importance. I'll abide by what you say, but just give a second thought to them.

At this late date, all the correspondents are still held back from the front. While the rest remained in Tokio, I made a dash for the front, traveled up the west Coast of Korea in sampans (8 days and 2 hard blows), and on horseback through the snow from Seoul to Ping-Yang, and from Ping-Yang to Sunan—which latter place, even now, a month after I was there, is only a half-day's ride from the fighting line. I was right up with the fun when arrested and ordered back by the Japanese military authorities.

155

Am now waiting in Seoul (under instructions), for the correspondents in Tokio to get permission to start and to overtake me. Then I may go on. Believe me, it has all the appearance, now, (so far as we are concerned), of a personally conducted Cook's Tourist proposition.

When the *Faith of Men* is issued, please send twenty copies of same to my Oakland address, where I shall get them on my return.

Sincerely yours,

Jack London

P.S. I'm going to try, later on, to get accredited to the Russian side, and go over and see how they do things.

---

[1]London became a correspondent for the Hearst papers, covering the Japanese-Russian War, and sailed Jan. 7, 1904, on *S. S. Siberia* for 'Korea.

To Charmian Kittredge[1]

Anju House (Korea)

April 17, 1904

Plugging along in the race for Japanese Headquarters. Four men ahead of me, but expect to overhaul them, though I am bringing my packs along and they are traveling light. The rest of the bunch is left in the rear.

Beautiful long hours in the saddle, and beautiful mud. Had Belle in up to her shoulders more than once to-day.

Am prouder than a peacock—for I am able to keep her shoes on her, to tighten them when they get loose, and to put on a shoe when she casts and loses one. Of course, it is cold-shoeing, but they *work!* they *work!*

Wÿn, April 24th.

Well, I didn't overtake the four men ahead of me, though I caught up with them where they were stopped farther back along the road, and arrived here with them, where we shall stop for some time.

Now, to business. As I understand it, Macmillan's expect to bring out the *Sea Wolf* late this fall. I shall not be able to go over the proofsheets. And you must do this for me. I shall write to Brett telling him this and asking him to get into communication with you.

In the first place, before any of the book is set up in print, you must get from him the original ms. in his possession. Much in this ms. will have been cut out in the *Century* published part. What was cut out I want put back in the book. On the other hand, many *good* alterations have been made by you, and George, and by the *Century* people—these alterations I want in the book. So here's the task—: Take the Macmillan ms., and, reading the *Century* published stuff, put into Macmillan ms. the good alterations.

Furthermore, anything that offends you, strike out or change on your own responsibility. You know me well enough to know that I won't kick.

Haven't received a letter from you—and, for that matter, a letter from anyone for I don't know since when.

I hope to get hold of them in a month or so.

In previous letter I told you certain things, and on chance that it may not have reached you, I tell them again.

Register yourself at telegraph office at Newton, Iowa, as "Mate,"—also, your house address.

Thus, I may cable you any time.

Also, when I am pulling out for California, I'll cable you. If it suits you, you could take your comfortable time in pulling back for California and yet be there a good time before I arrive.

Say I telegraph: "Mate, am coming," from the field here. It would take me between 30 and 40 days to get to 'Frisco. You, receiving this cable, could be in California between 3 and 4 weeks before I arrived. And then I could see you at once, on landing. Can you guess what that means to me?

Now, when you get back to Berkeley, register your name and address there as "Mate"; and, from last point of departure, say Japan, I could again cable you, giving this time the name of steamer on which I sail.

Presumably arriving in Oakland some time in the day, I should be out that evening to you. Will you occupy your old quarters? Or maybe go to Glen Ellen? Let me know. If Glen Ellen, register yourself there.

And now I'm off in haste to get this censored—a good 2-mile ride to headquarters and back 2 miles more.

Nevertheless, I dare to say I love you, love you, love you.

Jack

P.S. As I told you before, your letters to me are not read, so be kind as ever.

P.S. A little, red rubber stamp on envelope will show the censor's mark.

---

[1]After his separation from Bessie, London became a friend of Charmian Kittredge. Before leaving for Korea he made an arrangement with Charmian and George Sterling to proofread his Mss.

To George P. Brett

Wija (Korea)
April 24, 1904

Dear Mr. Brett:—

Here I am, on the banks of the Yalu, waiting for the first big land fight. Dare say I know a lot more about horses than when I started out.

As I understand it, you expect to bring out Sea Wolf late this year. I shall be unable to prepare same for printing, or to go over proofsheets. This, I shall have to put in Miss Kittredge's hands.

Much that *Century* cut out I should like in book; and on other hand, many *Century* alterations I should like to retain. So the thing to be done is this: Do you send the ms. you possess to Miss Kittredge, and she will put in the *Century* alterations for the better. Then, when this is printed, please send her the proofs.

I am writing her this mail advising her fully what is to be done and promising her that you will enter into communication with her. Her address is:

> Miss Charmian Kittredge
> Care Mrs. Lynette McMurray
> Newton, Iowa.

If you will mail me a copy of the *Faith of Men,* I shall be highly pleased. Address it to

> Jack London
> War Correspondent,
> Headquarters,
> First Japanese Army,
> Japan.

There it will be forwarded to me.

> Sincerely yours,
> Jack London

P.S. Any other good new novel to read would also give me joy.

To George Sterling

> First Japanese Army
> Antung, Manchuria
> May 8, 1904

Dear George:—

How often I think of you and the fresh California days in the open, the while I swelter here in a Chinese city breathing alike the dust of the living and the dust of the dead.

I am clean disgusted. My work is rotten. I know it, but so circumscribed am I, so hedged about with restrictions, that I see little, hear but little more (and that unsatisfactory and ofttimes contradictory), and in no way can manage to get in intimate touch with officers or men. I am an outsider, pent in one portion of the machine and from that restricted view watching the machine work. The result: Rot.

My love to Carrie—with due hesitancy I offer it.
To you my love with no hesitancy at all.

Jack

To George P. Brett

Seoul, Korea
June 4, 1904

Dear Mr. Brett:—

Yours of Jan. 23rd just received. Am now turning back to the States, quite disgusted with the world situation so far as it concerns a correspondent getting material. Our treatment has been ridiculously childish, and we have not been allowed to see anything. There won't be any war-book so far as I am concerned.

I am glad I shall be able to revise the *Sea Wolf,* though I can't make up my mind, now, as to whether it would be advisable to shorten the description of the remasting of the schooner. I'll be better able to decide when I get back to white-man's land.

Yes, I have thought often of that Indian race-story, but it's a stubborn thing, and the get-at-ableness of it has so far eluded me. It's a big thing—if it can be done, and if I can do it.

If all goes well, by the time you receive this I should be in California.

Sincerely yours,
Jack London

To Charmian Kittredge

Oakland, Calif.
July 6, 1904

The fight is on. Am too busy to write love. Knew that George (Sterling) had telegraphed you. Had no time to write. Bess is adamant. Tell you the case in a nutshell. Bess brought suit before the year was up. Couldn't therefore bring suit on ground of desertion, so brought it on ground of cruelty, etc., etc. She wanted to bring suit in order to get injunctions on all I possess, before I arrived on the spot, and so hold all I possess tied up until full year elapsed, when she could bring suit for separation and maintenance and have court give her a whack at all I possess in division of community property.

She never intended to press suit for divorce, for she will not give me my freedom.

She offered to withdraw complaint for divorce if I would contract to buy her land and build her a home and give regular monthly support. When I asked for freedom she said nay. Then I said nay. There it stands.

159

Now this is the case. For the first time in my life I have a couple or four thousand dollars above my debts. She intends fighting for cash. You know I don't give a whoop for money. She has started the expense of law, I'll help run up said expense of law. Result, neither she nor I shall see a penny of it. The several thousand will be dribbled out amongst the lawyers.

My English publishers have failed, all my American publishers have injunctions served upon them, likewise the *Examiner,* the Central Bank, the *Spray,* my books, carpets, everything.

Now there is to be no suit for divorce—from present indications. You were not mentioned by name in complaint for divorce, (said complaint being only a bluff anyway). I see no reason why you should not return to California, for my troubles with Bess are bound to continue for a weary long while. You may crop up in the midst of it, you may never be mentioned. But elect to do as you see fit. If you remain away till divorce is granted, you may remain away for years, you may die and be buried away.

With this mail I shall send letter for transportation for you to California. If you should decide to come, let me know and I shall telegraph to New York for them there to forward you transportation (which above mentioned letter will have already arranged for).

In this matter I cannot impress upon you too strongly these several things: (1) Bess will not sue for divorce. (2) Quite a time must elapse before lawyers can get my few dollars and I go insolvent. (3) Though no divorce is sought your name may be brought in and a big scandal may be made of it. (4) Your name may not be brought in at all. (5) I shall almost believe that I am wild to see you. And, sixth and last, you must decide for yourself, for your own good, and not allow any thought of me and my selfish desire for happiness to influence you.

Mate

Write me at Flat if you can see your way to it.

To MR. FRANK PUTNAM,
National Magazine

Oakland, Calif.
July 6, 1904

Dear Mr. Putnam:—

Somewhere along in February or March, 1903, you will remember we had a correspondence concerning payment for my story "The One Thousand Dozen." In your letter of March 16th of that year, you stated that you could pay me in transportation, which same you had over several roads.[1] It was a couple of hundred dollars worth of transportation coming to me, I believe. And I said to let it go until I needed it. Now I need it. I want transportation, first class, for Miss C. Kittredge, from Newton, Iowa, to Oakland, Calif.

Can you let me have it? Will you telegraph me immediately?

And if you can arrange it, and telegraph me to that effect, when you in turn receive telegram from me will you at once send transportation to: Miss C. Kittredge, Care Mrs. Lynette McMurray, Newton, Iowa.

Sincerely yours,

Jack London

[1]Some magazines such as *National* and *Sunset* paid for stories with railroad transportation.

To George P. Brett

Oakland, Calif.
July 11, 1904

Dear Mr. Brett:—

Concerning the book publication of the *Sea Wolf,* I hardly see how you can bring it out in October. I have just sent back the October proofs to the *Century,* and it was patent that there must be a couple of installments to follow. All of which is merely by the way. I don't care myself, and if you can arrange it with the *Century* well and good.

Haven't you issued a paper-cover edition of *People of the Abyss?* And if so, couldn't I get several copies of same?

Also, please have sent to me and charge to my account the following:—

3 copies *Kempton-Wace Letters.*
3 copies (cloth) *People of the Abyss.*
5 copies *Faith of Men.*
5 copies *Call of the Wild.*
3 copies *Children of the Frost.*

By the way, is the *Call of the Wild* still selling to any extent? You know, I don't know what has been happening during the last six months.

And now, if you think my selling-power has increased sufficiently to warrant such an advance, I'd like to know if you can let me have $250.00 per month. If you can, please do it as follows:

Send my wife a monthly check for $75.00, and me ditto for $175.00.

Frankly, this is what I am doing for my wife. In addition to check from you, I shall (and have been doing same in past), personally pay all unusual expenses such as Doctor bills, nurses, outings, etc., etc.

Also, with what I have earned as correspondent, plus what *Century* pays for *Sea Wolf,* I am setting about buying land and building her and the children a home after her own plans. This will take all my little capital above mentioned, and also put me a bit into debt. But it will all be straightened up inside a year or so.

If an injunction has been served on you, it will soon be raised.

If you can see your way to the $250.00 per month, I'd like to have it begin the first of August.

Will you please have your bookkeeper send me the earnings of my different books up to date, and royalties advanced on same—in fact, full account.

And now, another idea for you to consider. The *Sea Wolf* will make my tenth published book. If I can go on and develop in the next few years, and turn out a few successful books, there will be a good string of books and a fair possibility for uniform editions. Therefore this suggests itself: Why shouldn't you get the copyright on the several books you haven't published? I do not know enough about publishing to know whether it would be worth while or not.

The books are:

The Son of the Wolf—Houghton, Mifflin & Co.
The God of His Fathers—McClure, Phillips.
A Daughter of the Snows—Lippincott's.
The Cruise of the Dazzler—Century Co.

Please let me know what you think of all this.

You have arranged with Heinemann for *Faith of Men* and *Sea Wolf*. Do you think I could now get a fair advance from them?

And by the way, I want to ask your advice. Isbisters are paying 6 shillings on the pound.

Isaac Pitman (or some similar publishers) who have taken hold of Isbisters, offer to take over my Isbister books and pay, not 6 shillings on the pound, but all that is coming. Their offer seems to imply, also, my future dealings with them. Now what do you think—would it be wiser for me to accept the six shillings, and get the books for myself? or to turn them over to Pitman? I may here state that Isbisters own outright *The Son of the Wolf,* having bought it off Ward, Lock & Co., who bought it from Houghton, Mifflin.

I do not know how much is due me from Isbisters, but shall write to learn this mail.

Sincerely yours,
Jack London

To Anna Strunsky

Oakland, Calif.
July 23, 1904

Dear Anna:—

Your 2 letters just to hand. You see, Cameron's letter to me gave me to understand that he was acting for you, and the content was such as to require an answer such as I gave. I am sorry, also amused as regards my telling or hinting of my approaching marriage.[1] Either he imagined it, or you imagined it, or else he had some outside information which is news to me and which I should like to hear.

I do most earnestly hope that your name will not be linked any more with my troubles.[2] It will soon die away, I believe. And so it goes. I wander through life delivering hurts to all that know me. And so one pays for the little hour—only, it is the woman who always pays.

Unspoilt in your idealism? And think of me as unsaved in my materialism. And why should we forget each other yet awhile? Why should we not always remember and know each other?

However, I am changed. Though a materialist when I first knew you, I had the saving grace of enthusiasm. That enthusiasm is the thing that is spoiled, and I have become too sorry a thing for you to remember.

Jack London

---

[1]During London's separation from Bessie and before his divorce in 1905 many rumors spread concerning his personal life. See footnote on page 168.
[2]Bessie London at first named Anna Strunsky as corespondent and later retracted it; however, rumors continued to circulate.

To ANNA STRUNSKY

Oakland, Calif.
Oct. 13, 1904

Dear Anna:—

The movement of this is too rapid and sketchy. It is too much in the form of a narrative, and narrative, in a short story, is only good when it is in the first person.

The subject merits greater length. Make longer scenes, dialogues, between them.

And then you quit too suddenly, too abruptly. It is not rounded to its end, but chopped off with a hatchet.

You should elaborate the development of his apparent madness, his own psychology, the psychology of the cruelty of the East Side idealists—as you did for me by word of mouth.

My criticism is, in short, that you have taken a splendid subject and not extracted its full splendor. You have mastery of it (the subject), full mastery, —you *understand;* yet you have not so expressed your understanding as to make the reader understand. And this same criticism I would make in general of all your short stories.

Remember this—confine a short story within the shortest possible time-limit—a day, an hour, if possible—or, if, as sometimes with the best of short stories, a long period of time must be covered,—months—merely hint or sketch (incidentally) the passage of time, and tell the story only in its crucial moments.

Really, you know, development does not belong in the short story, but in the novel.

The short story is a rounded fragment from life, a single mood, situation, or action.

Now don't think me egotistical because I refer you to my stories—I have them at the ends of my fingers, so I save time by mentioning them. Take down and open *Son of the Wolf*.

The first eight deal with single situations, though several of them cover fairly long periods of time—the time is sketched and made subordinate to the final situation. You see, the situation is considered primarily—"The Son of the Wolf" in beginning is hungry for woman, he goes to get one; the situation is how he got one.

"The Priestly Prerogative" is the scene in the cabin—the rest is introductory, preliminary.

"The Wife of a King"—not a good short story in any sense.

"The Odyssey of the North"—covering a long period of time, in first person, so that long period of time (the whole life of Naass) is exploited in an hour and a half in Malemute Kid's cabin.

Take down and open *God of His Fathers*.

First story, single situation.

"Great Interrogation"—single situation in cabin where whole past history of man and woman is exploited. And so on, to the last story, "Scorn of Women"—see in it how time is always sketched and situation is exploited— yet it is not a short story.

And so forth and so forth.

Am sending you "The Nose" ["A Nose for the King"] for a wee bit of a smile.

Jack London

To George P. Brett

Oakland, Calif.
Nov. 17, 1904

Dear Mr. Brett:—

Gee! the advance sales of the *Sea Wolf* make me feel good. Your letter telling of same caught me at a fiercely hard-up moment, with Christmas staring me in the face, heavy annual insurance on half a dozen policies waiting for me to pay first of January, and a few other debts. Will it be possible for you to advance me on *Sea Wolf* sales, right away, say about three thousand dollars?

Now as to the business talk you mention. I don't think I'll be in New York for a long time to come. On the other hand, I may run off, as a sort of recreation, next January, for six weeks, and give a few lectures in the middle west.—All this, however, is in the air. Possibly, we could have the talk by letter. What do you say?

This I must say for myself. As my earning capacity increases, my output diminishes. With all the top-notch magazines offering me from 8 to 10 cts. per word, I am writing nothing for them. *The Game* is not a magazine story —I don't expect to find a magazine that will dare touch it.

This play I am experimenting with (to be three acts) I shall in two days more have completed the second act, in 2 weeks the third act. Then a trip on the *Spray* and duck-hunting.

What did you think of our socialist vote?

And by the way, not to utterly forget the *Salt of the Earth,* why couldn't that book be brought out this summer, after *Sea Wolf* has run its run?— That is, if it can be brought out without loss to you. You know I have a sneaking liking for it, and I have waited pretty patiently while my favorite child was set aside for my mongrel fiction children.

And also, would it be expedient, some time in the future, to bring out *People of the Abyss* in paper cover to sell for 25 cts. or fifty cents?

It's good propaganda to commence with. On the other hand, there is a likelihood that it may become a sort of sentimental-radical-reformer's classic. If it could be more generally read in paper cover, it might react and increase future sales again in cloth-cover. Tell me what you think of the idea.

And by the way, I don't know whether I've told you already why I am hard up. At any rate, (so that you may not think I am dissipating, blowing myself), my cash has principally gone to buying land and building and furnishing a home for my children and their mother. Also, in legal tangle (brought about because of my absence in Far East), the lawyers got hold of my wife, and as a result they waded into me good and hard for the cash.

Sincerely yours,
Jack London

P.S. On next page I give several books published by you I'd like sent to me and charged to my account.

P.S. Some time ago a Mr. Peluso wrote to you about translating *Call of Wild* into French.

Can you tell me how the correspondence turned out?

Jack London

To GEORGE P. BRETT

Oakland, Calif.
Nov. 19, 1904

Dear Mr. Brett:—

Mr. Georges Dupuy is a Frenchman, an artist, a journalist, and a man

165

who knows Alaska better than I do. He has lived the life. He feels that he can make sympathetic translations into French of say *Faith of Men* or *Children of the Frost.* Incidentally, if no arrangements have been made for *Call of the Wild,* he'd like to tackle that.

He will write you this mail.

Will you please talk it over with him, the business arrangements, etc., and see what can be done.

I called him an artist, and by the word I mean not "painter" but "temperament." He *sees.*

From my talks with him I see that he has the romance, the fire, the color, the idiom of the land.

This last thing, the idiom, is vastly important in the translation of any of my stuff. The mere scholar-translator, or literary-translator could never render the spirit of my language into another language.

Mr. Dupuy is on his way to Paris. I have taken the liberty of inviting him to call on you when passing through New York.

Sincerely yours,
Jack London

To George P. Brett

Oakland, Calif.
Dec. 5, 1904

Dear Mr. Brett:—

I'm dropping you a line hot with the idea. I have the idea for the next book I shall write—along the first part of next year.

Not a sequel to *Call of the Wild.*

But a companion to " " " " " "

I'm going to reverse the process.

Instead of the devolution or decivilization of a dog, I'm going to give the evolution, the civilization of a dog—development of domesticity, faithfulness, love, morality, and all the amenities and virtues.

And it will be a *proper* companion-book—in the same style, grasp, concrete way. Have already mapped part of it out. A complete antithesis to the *Call of the Wild.* And with that book as a forerunner, it should make a hit.

What d' ye think?[1]

Jack London

---

[1]The letter refers to *White Fang.*

To George P. Brett

Oakland, Calif.
Dec. 8, 1904

Dear Mr. Brett:—

Received your check for $3000.00 on account of general royalties, and I can tell you it came in handy for Christmas.

Concerning *Salt of the Earth,* I'm glad you'll bring it out in the spring. If you'll return it to me I'll get in shape at once. I may possibly take out the "Salt of the Earth" essay, and change title.[1] Also, I'll bring the matter of the other essays right up to date—and also revise thoroughly. Taking out "Salt of Earth" essay, will still leave 40,000 words. Also, I'll write a preface. On the strength of the vote we socialists cast the other day, and also on the strength of the aroused interest in socialism, there is a chance for a fair sale of the book. I can have the copy in for you early in January—if you send it on to me right away.

The *People of the Abyss,* like *How the Other Half Lives*[2], etc., is more of a popularly written book than *Benevolent Feudalism* and *Social Unrest.* You see, it is largely narrative, and is certainly popular in treatment. Also I imagine I am better known to the reading public, because of my fiction, than [W. J.] Ghent or [J. G.] Brooks, who have done no fiction. I was thinking of a fifty-cent paper cover edition. The kind they sell on trains, etc., etc.

The Game I think is sold to the *Metropolitan Magazine.* They've made an offer, and we're now dickering. But concerning adding 3000 or 4000 words to the *Game.* It's the hardest kind of work to do that adding, but I believe I can do it—simply recast the first portion of it, keeping a grip in accord with the last portion, which cannot be added to. You ask me to add and then you'll make estimates of it. Why not make estimates, on the basis that I have added (I'll do my end all right), and let me know what you think you can do with it?

It may interest you that I've won a *Black Cat* prize—a minor prize, for it was a skit ["A Nose for the King"] written, typed, and sent off in one day.

I'm wondering how my companion story to *Call of the Wild* has struck you.

Say—if I should want to get an automobile somewhere along the first of next year, would it be decent for me to ask for another advance on royalties?

Sincerely yours,
Jack London

---

[1] He did both; the book was published as *War of the Classes.*
[2] By Jacob A. Riis.

To George P. Brett

On Board *Spray*
Feb. 21, 1905

Dear Mr. Brett:

Yours of Feb. 8 just received. Yes, I cut out the trip East, and have gone off for a couple of months on the *Spray*. Am just starting in *White Fang*.

Can you give me an idea of *Sea Wolf* sales.

I am having difficulty in selling *White Fang* serially. The leading magazines are willing to give me 10 cts. a word for serial rights, and *Harpers* offer that much for American serial rights alone; but all of them append the proposition that they are to publish the book. So in each case, so far, it is all off.

I see you have not congratulated me upon my engagement to Blanche Bates.[1] Why this cold unregard?

Concerning that remittance on account. I want it for an automobile, but I can't get the time to buy the automobile. One has to study up the proposition first. So just let that remittance go for a while. Will it be all right for me to wire for it when I want it?

Sincerely yours,

Jack London

[1] Blanche Bates was an actress in a company directed by David Belasco. A rumor that she had become engaged to London was started as a publicity stunt, because the show was not doing well.

To George P. Brett

Oakland, Calif.
Mar. 13, 1905

Dear Mr. Brett—

Concerning pamphlet "The Scab"[1] in your letter of March 3rd. No, I do not think that pamphlet publication of same can hurt sale of *War of Classes*.

On the contrary, it reaches people who never read, or, rather, who never buy $1.50 books.

The first paragraph of your letter explains this very point—you say "These concerns (socialist publishing houses), do not seem to be very successful in selling any considerable quantities of the high-priced publications."

That's the very thing. Their patrons are the cheap-publication-buyers.

Of course I may be wrong in all this, and if so, am sorry and won't do it again.

But just the same I'd almost believe I'd like to bet a dollar against a dollar that no 5-cent-sale of "Scab" will ever knock a $1.50-sale of *War of the Classes*.

By the way, when complimentary copies of *War of Classes* are sent me, can 20 additional copies be sent me charged to my account.

I received a letter from *Everybody's* asking to see *White Fang,* and I thank you for your kind offices in this. I don't remember whether I have already told you, but *Outing* has agreed to take serial rights only. So that's settled.

I may say that—

(1) I am running for mayor of Oakland.[2]
(2) I am not going on the stage.[3]
(3) I am not going to marry Blanche Bates.
(4) I am going lecturing next fall (thought I'd have one try at it).[4]
(5) And I am not going to do any of the other things mentioned in the papers.

Have been having a great time on the *Spray,* and have hardened up some. You ought to see my hands! And my broken nails—I carry no sailors.

Am going to bring the *Spray* back to her moorings now, and go up into the mountains until next fall—no telephones, no people, no engagements, nothing but work, sunshine, and health.

Sincerely yours,

Jack London

[1]First printed in *Atlantic Monthly* and reprinted and sold for 5 cents by the Charles H. Kerr Co., a Socialist publishing house, in Chicago. Neither the *Atlantic Monthly* essay nor the pamphlet contained the excerpt quoted by Phillip S. Foner in his book *Jack London, American Rebel,* page 57.
[2]Ran for mayor on the Socialist ticket; he was defeated.
[3]At various times rumors were circulated that London would play a role of one of his characters on stage or screen.
[4]In fall of 1905 he toured the Midwest and East on a lecture tour under the management of the Slayton Lyceum Bureau.

To CHARLES F. LUMMIS

Oakland, Calif.

April 4, 1905

Dear Mr. Lummis—

You and I are both fighters, and single-purposed fighters, too. So I am sure you will understand my position.[1] If I have ten dollars a year to spare, I'd sooner put it into my fight than your fight.

Besides, you can get capitalists to contribute to your fight, but I'm damned if we can get capitalists to contribute to my fight.

I'm willing to give my countenance to your fight, but not to give my time nor my money.

Sincerely yours,

Jack London

[1]Lummis had invited London to be a member of The Archaeological Society of America. London declined: "Not because of lack of interest in your cause but because of too great interest in my own cause, which is the Socialist revolution."

To Editor, *The Atlantic*

Oakland, Calif.
May 6, 1905

Dear sir:—

Please find herewith, essay, "Revolution." Before reading it, I wish you would take this one thing into consideration: It is an essay composed of facts. There is not one bit of prophecy in it. The number of the Revolutionists is a fact. The Revolutionists exist. Their doctrines exist just as much as they themselves exist. Their doctrines are facts. You will note that I do not say their doctrines are *right*. I merely state what their doctrines are, in the process of describing things that exist.

In conclusion, please remember that this essay is composed of facts.

Sincerely yours,
Jack London

To George P. Brett

Glen Ellen, Calif.
May 26, 1905

Dear Mr. Brett:—

As I am up here in the hills, away from all my letter-files and business papers, I don't remember exactly what time of the year the contract calls for, for a settlement of account. But I have a hazy recollection that it is somewhere along in the spring of the year. I should like to get from you a statement showing how much royalties has been advanced, the respective earnings of the various books, and how much is now coming to me.

I'll tell you why: For a long time I have been keeping steadily the idea in mind of settling down somewhere in the country. I am in a beautiful part of California now, and I have my eyes on several properties, one of which I intend to buy, so I want to know how much money I possess in order to know to what extent I may buy.[1]

Also, the situation is such, other men desirous of buying in at low figures, (and they have been waiting for years, some of them), etc., that I'd like to have a few thousands on hand in order to close immediately with any proposition that may be made. If I had to delay the putting up of the cash for the ten or twelve days necessary to get the money from you, there would be opportunity for the word to be carried to the rival would-be purchasers, and they might snap up the property themselves. So, I'd like to arrange with you, if possible, the two following things: (1) For you on receipt of telegram from me, to reply by telegram that money was being forwarded, and also, to forward money by mail. (Your telegram I could use to raise money upon immediately with some bank, and I guess, that would be cheaper than telegraphing a large sum directly to me. That's one thing I do not know much about—telegraphing money. It might not be as dear as I think, and it might be more expedient and practical for you to telegraph me the whole sum.)

(2) If the time is up or past for the annual settlement of account, I should like you, not only to send statement, but to send me balance due me along at the same time. And for that matter, if it is anywhere around time for settlement of account, and if you could find it in line with your policy, I should like the balance due me to accompany the statement of account.

I should prefer getting the money this way, in my hand, to the depending upon telegraphing for it.

Please let me hear as soon as you can, concerning the whole matter.

Sincerely yours,

Jack London

P.S. I have just received the proofs of *The Game* and I want to tell you how pleased I am with the way it is being illustrated, page by page. The effect is splendid. This running illustration of the text, in my belief gives life to the impressions of the reader. In short, I like it immensely.

---

[1]He purchased at this time the Hill Ranch of one hundred and thirty acres—the beginning of his famous "Beauty Ranch."

To George Sterling

Glen Ellen, Calif.
May 28, 1905

Dear Greek:[1]

Be sure and let me know when to look for you when you come up. Let me know in advance what train you are coming on, and let me know well enough in advance, so that in case I am not going to be there, I can head you off.

You see, I am planning to go down to see Mrs. Fiske[2] some time during her stop in San Francisco, which will be somewhere in the first part of June, but precisely where in the first part of June, I do not know.

Regarding [Harry] Lafler's scheme[3]—I think it's all right. I am willing to work for it, I am willing to write for it, and to pony up a share of the money necessary to start it. But on the other hand, plans of mine which have been maturing for some time would render it impossible for me to be the angel for the enterprise. I have long since given over my automobile scheme;

171

it was too damned expensive on the face of it, and I have long since decided to buy land in the woods somewhere and build. I have just written Macmillan Company to get whatever balance I have coming from them, and also to find out how much more they can advance me on future work, in order to put through my land-buying and house-building enterprise. Of course, dear Greek, all the foregoing is between you and Lafler and me.

For over a year now, or rather, since my return from Korea, which is just under a year, I have been planning this home proposition, and now I am just beginning to see my way clear to it. I am really going to throw out an anchor so big and so heavy that all hell could never get it up again. In fact, it's going to be a prodigious, ponderous sort of an anchor.

To return to the question. While I am willing to get in and work for Lafler's paper should he start it, you will readily see I could not go in for being the main-finance-guy of it without smashing my already matured plans. It's up to Lafler and any enthusiastic co-workers he can gather immediately around him to hustle for the sum total of money necessary to start this paper and keep it going for the many months which in the nature of things are bound to intervene before it can attain a paying basis.

It's this way, George: I feel that I have done and am doing a pretty fair share of work for the Revolution. I guess my lectures alone before socialist organizations have netted the Cause a few hundred dollars, and my wounded feelings from the personal abuse of the Capitalist papers ought to be rated at several hundred more. There is not a day passes that I am not reading up socialism and filing socialistic clippings and notes. The amount of work that I in a year contribute to the cause of socialism would earn me a whole lot of money if spent in writing fiction for the market.

So now you see the situation as regards other plans, as well as my feeling in the matter, and I know you understand. Don't forget to let us know several days in advance, when you expect to come up.

Wolf

---

[1]Sterling dubbed London "Wolf," and London retaliated by calling him "Greek," because of his profile.
[2]The well-known actress. Cousin of Bessie London.
[3]Lafler (one-time literary editor for the *Argonaut*) and Sterling planned to publish a Socialist periodical which they hoped London would finance or underwrite.

To George Sterling

Glen Ellen, Calif.
June 1, 1905

Dear Greek:—

Nay, nay, I don't think you misconceived my financial status insofar as you thought that the *Sea Wolf* had made me at least $20,000. I guess the *Sea Wolf* made me about $15,000. Your misconception lies in how much of it I have on hand. You take advance royalties such as I am receiving from the Macmillan Company—$300.00 per month, or $3600 per year—and figure about how rapidly they will eat into $15,000. Yea—yea, and figure how rapidly no end of other things will eat into $15,000. I have just come through hospital myself, and I guess I dropped a couple of hundred right there. I have just put one of my sisters through five weeks of hospital; it is not the first time I have done this for her, nor will it be the last. The doctor's bills that I have paid for Bessie and the two children have run up into many hundreds of dollars in the last year, to say nothing of nurses. My Mammy Jenny has to send for a doctor once in a while. I pay for it. My mother has to send for a doctor now and again. It's up to me. I haven't said a word about dentists for myself and other people. I'll mention in passing the several hundred dollars that Bessie's lawyer hooked me up for. And I could go on for a half dozen more blessed pages reciting where my money has gone. Yesterday, for instance, I sent off a $10 check to help out a new Socialist paper that is struggling for existence in Toledo, Ohio. Just now I am coughing up $30.00 for the printing of the Appeal to the Supreme Court of an ex-convict who is lying in the County Jail with a sentence of fifty years over his head. And so on, and so on—it just leaks away.

As the situation now is, I hope to be able to scrape enough money together to buy merely the land; then I'll either wait for a year or so to build, or else mortgage the land in order to build. I haven't made up my mind yet.

I have been giving you all this hash of stuff in order that you may see my position and just how I stand. You're the only person in the world that I'd take the trouble for. The rest could go to the devil and I wouldn't care. But you, dear Greek, you I do want to know.

Oh, the little item of life-insurance comes into my head—I am carrying $20,000 insurance. It is in the endowment form. And if you know what Endowment means, you can see how heavy that little item is.

I don't care a red how much the Lazar-sheets roast me. It was merely in a humorous way that I decided that my hurt feelings were worth something.

I am sorry to hear that you are not coming up. I don't know when I am coming down. I have to go to see Mrs. Fiske, but we have not yet arranged date of meeting. From your repeated trips to Carmel, it would strike me that something is doing down there. How is it? Have you got the land in sight yet, or are you still prospecting? Let me know.

I have given your final line to Charmian, and she tells me she got a letter off to you day before yesterday.

No, I am afraid the dream was too bright to last—our being near to each other. If you don't understand now, someday sooner or later you may come to understand. It's not through any fault of yours, nor through any fault of mine. The world and people just happen to be so made.

As ever,
Wolf

To George P. Brett

Glen Ellen, Calif.
June 7, 1905

Dear Mr. Brett:

Yours of the 1st just received. Now I'll tell you what I have done and what I want. I have found the land I want, and have closed the deal by paying $500.00, binding the bargain for a few days, when I must pay the balance, $6,500.00. The place was a bargain, one of those bargains that a man would be insane to let slip by. The entrance is a half-mile from a small town and two different railway stations. An electric road is soon to be constructed, when the running time to San Francisco will be cut down to an hour and a half. At present it is something like two hours and a half by the railroad. There are 130 acres in the place, and they are 130 acres of the most beautiful, primitive land to be found in California. There are great redwoods on it, some of them thousands of years old—in fact, the redwoods are as fine and magnificent as any to be found anywhere outside the tourist groves. Also there are great firs, tan-bark oaks, maples, live-oaks, white-oaks, black-oaks, madrono and manzanita galore. There are canyons, several streams of water, many springs, etc., etc. In fact, it is impossible to really describe the place. All I can say is this—I have been over California off and on all my life, for the last two months I have been riding all over these hills, looking for just such a place, and I must say that I have never seen anything like it.

Woodchoppers were already at work when I snapped up the place. It had to be snapped up. Twenty years from now I'll wager it will be worth twenty times what I am now paying for it. In a few days I shall have to pay over the balance of $6,500.00. This I want to get from you as soon as you receive this letter. Also, I want you to telegraph me at above address as soon as the money is dispatched.

Now to business: I have made a rough calculation upon royalties advanced, and upon earnings of books. I say "rough calculation," because all my papers are down in Oakland; but I also made it a conservative calculation. Outside the regular monthly advances, I have received, I believe, a couple of thousand. Subtracting all royalties advanced from what I figure to be the royalties earned, there should be coming to me say $10,000—in this calculation I have taken no account of what the English earnings of a couple of the books would be, *The Sea Wolf* and *The Faith of Men*.

Now in the past, you made me advances on unearned royalties. The present situation is different; I am asking an advance on *earned* royalties. Of course, I understand according to contract that in present instance I am not supposed to touch the royalties of *The Sea Wolf* until nearly a year afterward. So I am compelled to call upon your good-nature to help me out.

I don't care to bother with getting San Francisco banks to discount your note; so you can arrange it any way you wish, discounting your Note there in New York, and sending me the $10,000 as soon as you possibly can.

I say "as soon as you possibly can," because just now every moment counts. I have to go away in October, and between now and then, with all the usual irritating delays, I must start building; when I have paid out that $7,000.00 for the place, there won't be very much left with which to build. But I can at least put up the barn and live in that until I can get the money together to put up the house. Incidentally, today, according to agreement with present tenant who is leaving in order to put me into possession, I am to pay him something like $600.00 for his several horses, a couple of cows, mountain wagon, harnesses, plows, harrows, etc., etc. So you'll see I am pinching my ready cash down and shall be flat-broke until I get remittance from you.

This is to be no summer-residence proposition, but a home all the year round. I am anchoring good and solid, and anchoring for keeps, and it means a great deal to me. My lasting regret, in case the thing fell through, would be not the loss of the money already advanced, but the loss of the place itself. I could never find another place like it again, and I who am a Californian, tell you this.

Sincerely yours,
Jack London

P.S. In reading over this letter, I notice an ambiguity. In one place I mention your dispatching me $6,500 (for payment of the place), and later on I mention your sending me $10,000. Now what I want is the $10,000.00.

To GEORGE STERLING

Glen Ellen
June 24, 1905

Dearest Greek!

If Hillquit[1] and Hunter didn't put it all over Bierce—I'll quit thinking at all.

Bierce's clever pessimism was nowhere against their science. He proved himself rudderless, compassless, and chartless. Bierce doesn't shine in a face to face battle with socialists. He's best at long range slinging ink. He was groggy at the drop of the hat, and before they got done with him was looking anxiously around and wondering why the gong didn't ring.

All he did was to back and fill and potter around, dogmatize and contradict himself. When they cornered him, he went off on another tack, wherefore they'd overtake him and lambaste him again.

175

Bierce, with biological and sociological concepts that crystallized in the fervent heat of pessimism a generation ago, was—well, pathetic. And more pathetic still, he doesn't know it.

Wolf

[1]Morris Hillquit was a prominent Socialist leader and labor lawyer, author of *History of Socialism in the United States,* etc. Hunter was apparently a fellow Socialist.

TO GEORGE P. BRETT

Glen Ellen, Calif.
Aug. 1, 1905

Dear Mr. Brett:

In reply to yours of July 11. First of all, I want you to thoroughly understand my situation and point of view. You know I am pretty much of a hermit. I have never knocked around amongst writers nor publishers. About the ins and outs of the trade I know practically nothing. I have never received any information from anybody. I have simply stayed out here in the West and butted around, by correspondence, finding out things for myself. I have never known, for instance, what were the best royalties paid to writers. In this case, you have told me, and if I hadn't butted around after increased royalties, I wouldn't have got this information from you. You see, I have to find out, and the only way I can find out is by letter.

Now, as regards royalties: You tell me that I am getting 20%. Yes, and no. I am getting 20% on all over 5,000 copies of any book, and 15% on the first 5,000. Now why can't we put it on a basis something like this—15% on any book of mine (regular cloth-bound book) that sells less than 5,000; and 20% on every thousand of any book of mine that sells more than 5,000? You see what I am driving at is to avoid robbing you on a small-sale book of mine, one that sells less than 5,000, out of which sales the whole of the initial cost to you must come. But a book that sells more than 5,000, as I understand it, does not have a greater initial cost, and with a larger sale gives an increase of profit.

One thing must be considered in my favor, as regards advertising, and that is namely, that I am so peculiarly constituted that I manage to get a whole lot of advertising from sources other than my book-publishers, and which nevertheless conduces to the sale of my books. Just consider the amount of advertising I got out of the Hearst newspapers with their millions of circulation, in the course of the six months I was away in the Orient for them.

Going on the basis that *White Fang* is the long novel referred to in previous agreements, and that according to those agreements there is owing you in addition one book of short stories, then we shall have to consider that *The Game* is a book thrown in on the side. This is quite agreeable to me. Also, I thoroughly realize and appreciate your kindness to me in allowing me to be practically a year behind in fulfilling my agreements, and not saying anything about it. Anyway, as I understand the feeling that exists between you and me, these agreements are now more a matter of mere business form,—at least that's the way I feel about it, because I do not feel that there is any liability on my part of rushing away to some other publisher.

Now as to the new Agreement for the year beginning Dec. 1, 1905: I take all your suggestions as follows: I am to receive for that year $300.00 per month on account of general royalties; I am to give you for publication *White-Fang* and a collection of short stories; you are to retain, in addition, book-rights for America in all other work completed by me during the year beginning Dec. 1, 1905.

As I say, all the foregoing suggestions from you for the new Agreement are perfectly satisfactory to me, and I now make one suggestion to you, about royalty, and that is, namely, 15% on any book of mine that sells less than 5,000, and 20% on every thousand of any book of mine that sells more than 5,000.

I have just read *A Publisher's Confession*[1] and found it interesting and instructive, and have learned a lot out of it that I did not know about the relations of publishers and writers.

According to my present lecture-itinerary, I should be in New York somewhere around next December.

Sincerely yours,
Jack London

P.S. Oh, by the way, I've got another big project in view. After I have settled down and enjoyed my mountain ranch for about five years, it is my firm intention to build a boat about 40 feet long,[2] and go off on a several years' cruise round the world. Now, don't think I am joking. I mean it. I have never more ardently desired to do anything in my life. I don't care very much for ordinary travel anyway, and this certainly would be everything but ordinary. And Lord! Lord! think of the chance to write without interruption when I am between-ports. First rattle out of the box, 2100 miles sailing from San Francisco to Honolulu, and then the long stretch down the South Seas, and some time ultimately, the stretch across the Atlantic to New York City!

---

[1]By Walter H. Page, at that time Editor of *The World's Work*.
[2]London built the boat in 1906 and called it the *Snark,* after the creature in Lewis Carroll's mock heroic poem, "The Hunting of the Snark"—a portmanteau word of "snake" and "shark." He sailed for Honolulu in April, 1907.

LETTERS FROM JACK LONDON

To EDITOR OF *The New York Saturday Times*

Glen Ellen, Calif.
Aug. 18, 1905

As one interested in the play of life, and in the mental processes of his fellow-creatures, I have been somewhat amused by a certain feature of the criticisms of my prize-fighting story, *The Game*. This feature is the impeachment of my realism, the challenging of the facts of life as put down by me in the story. It is rather hard on a poor devil of a writer, when he has written what he has seen with his own eyes, or experienced in his own body, to have it charged that said sights and experiences are unreal and impossible.

But this is no new experience, after all. I remember a review of *The Sea Wolf* by an Atlantic Coast critic who seemed very familiar with the sea. Said critic laughed hugely at me because I sent one of my characters aloft to shift over a gaff-topsail, and that he knew what he was talking about because he had seen many gaff-topsails shifted over from the deck. Yet, I on a seven-months' cruise in a topmast schooner, had gone aloft, I suppose, a hundred times, and with my own hands shifted tacks and sheets of gaff-topsails.

Now to come back to *The Game*. As reviewed in *The New York Saturday Times,* fault was found with my realism. I doubt if this reviewer has had as much experience in such matters as I have. I doubt if he knows what it is to be knocked out, or to knock out another man. I have had these experiences, and it was out of these experiences, plus a fairly intimate knowledge of prize-fighting in general, that I wrote *The Game*.

I quote from the critic in *The Saturday Times:*

"Still more one gently doubts in this particular case, that a blow delivered by Ponta on the point of Fleming's chin could throw the latter upon the padded canvas floor of the ring with enough force to smash in the whole back of his skull, as Mr. London describes."

All I can say in reply is, that a young fighter in the very club described in my book, had his head smashed in this manner. Incidentally, this young fighter worked in a sail-loft and took remarkably good care of his mother, brother and sister.

And—oh, one word more, I have just received a letter from Jimmy Britt, lightweight champion of the world, in which he tells me that he particularly enjoyed *The Game,* "on account of its trueness to life."

Very truly yours,
Jack London

To the Central Labor Council,
Alameda County

Glen Ellen, Calif.
Aug. 25, 1905

I cannot express to you how deeply I regret my inability to be with you this day. But, believe me, I am with you in the brotherhood of the spirit, as all you boys, in a similar brotherhood of the spirit, are with our laundry girls in Troy, New York.

Is this not a spectacle for gods and men?—the workmen of Alameda County sending a share of their hard-earned wages three thousand miles across the continent to help the need of a lot of striking laundry girls in Troy.

And right here I wish to point out something that you all know, but something that is so great that it can not be pointed out too often, and that grows only greater every time it is pointed out,—*and that is, that the strength of organized labor lies in its brotherhood.* There is no brotherhood in unorganized labor, no standing together shoulder to shoulder, and as a result unorganized labor is weak as water.

And not only does brotherhood give organized labor mere fighting strength, but gives it, as well, the strength of righteousness. The holiest reason that men can find for drawing together into any kind of an organization is *brotherhood* and in the end nothing can triumph against such an organization. Let the church tell you that servants should obey their masters. This is what the church told the striking laundry girls of Troy. Stronger than this mandate is brotherhood, as the girls of Troy found out when the boys of California shared their wages with them. (Ah, these girls of Troy! Twenty weeks on strike and not a single desertion from their ranks! And ah, these boys of California, stretching out to them, across a continent, the helping hand of brotherhood!)

And so I say, against such spirit of brotherhood, all machinations of the men-of-graft-and-grab-and-the-dollar are futile. Strength lies in comradeship and brotherhood, not in a throat-cutting struggle where every man's hand is against every man. This comradeship and brotherhood is yours. I cannot wish you good luck and hope that your strength will grow in the future, because brotherhood and the comrade-world are bound to grow. The growth cannot be stopped. So I can only congratulate you boys upon the fact that this is so.

Yours in the brotherhood of man,

Jack London

To CARRIE STERLING

Glen Ellen, Calif.
Sept. 15, 1905

Dear Carrie:

I have been a long while getting around to your letter. It caught me just before I went down to see the fight, and ever since I came back from the fight I have been catching up with back work.

I wish you were here opposite me where I could talk to you, and where you could ask me a thousand-and-one questions which would naturally crop up and demand answers in the course of such conversation. However, here goes to do my best by letter in a limited space of time:

As regards Charmian's deliberately breaking up my family, I am upon known ground. I know the ground myself, pretty close to every inch of it. And I am going to tell you what I know.

During the time I lived in the Bungalow, Charmian was often at the house. There was not the least iota even of flirtation between us. During that time I was tangled up with Anna Strunsky—in fact, during that time (and Bessie kept me informed of it), Charmian was very solicitous on Bessie's behalf. I never gave Charmian the first thought, much less a second thought. During all the time that I was away in England, Charmian was a great deal with Bessie, cheering her up and bolstering her up, and telling her that everything would come out all right regarding the Strunsky affair.

Now, I come to the year 1903, the year of my separation. Somewhere in the latter part of June, 1903, Bessie and the children came up to Glen Ellen, camping. I was shortly to follow them. Up to this time there had never been a word exchanged between Charmian and me, nor a look. Just a short time previous to this, several weeks at the outside, one Sunday at your house, in the midst of the Crowd, I felt my first impulsion toward Charmian. (This, of course, I have since told her about.) But this she knew nothing about at the time. I gave no sign of it, and as I say, it was my first impulsion toward her. My first feeling about her in a sexual way. I, myself, gave no immediate further thought to it.

Bessie came up, as I have said, camping at Glen Ellen the latter part of June, to be followed by me later on. In the meantime, I was going to take the *Spray* out on a cruise. Up to the time of Bessie's departure from the Bungalow on this camping-trip, I repeat, nothing had passed between Charmian and me,—not a word nor a look.

About this time I was not in a very happy state. You will remember yourself, the black moods that used to come upon me at that time, and the black philosophy that I worked out at that time and afterwards put into Wolf Larsen's mouth. My marriage was eminently unsatisfactory. I was preparing to go to pieces. Said going to pieces to culminate in my separation from Bessie. While she had started on her camping-trip up here, I was going out on the *Spray* to have a hell of a time with any woman I could get hold of. I had my eyes on a dozen women—not alone in connection with the *Spray* cruise, but in any way that I could get hold of these women. It was then that my thoughts turned to Charmian amongst the rest. I was not in love with her, had never flirted with her, but I decided that she was a warm enough proposition to suit me in an illicit way. (By "warm proposition" I don't mean to say the easy proposition that a woman of loose career would mean, but by warm proposition I mean just a good warm human woman, as you are, for instance.) As I say, my thoughts turned to Charmian as one of the dozen likelihoods. On the other hand, she was not a likelihood sufficiently impelling for me to go out after her then.

Now, here's the situation: Bessie is camping at Glen Ellen, and I go out to your camp in the hills from Saturday night to Monday morning. I have not seen Charmian nor had a word with her nor a look with her. On Monday morning I get into the rig and drive into town with the rest of the Crowd coming in. My plan is to set about at once with the outfitting of the *Spray,* and to sail in a couple of days. No woman picked out yet. That was part of the outfitting! Coming in, in the rig on Monday morning, the fifth-wheel carried away, I lost a few inches of skin, had seven different bandages upon my carcass, and a stiff knee. I had had stiff knees before, and I knew that the last place in the world for a stiff knee was on a rolling and plunging boat. So I decided to go up to Glen Ellen until I could get myself in shape for the cruise.

This was on Monday morning. That evening Charmian telephoned to find out if I was coming up to Glen Ellen, because Bessie had commissioned her to get some things for her to send up by me whenever I went up. These things Charmian said she had all ready for me to take. I told her I was packing that night and would start early next morning. She said she would come out right away with them. My knee was stiff, I was sick and miserable. All the places where the skin was off had stiffened up so that it was a grievous pain for me to move my arms or legs. I was looking on, directing, and [Frank] Atherton was packing my trunks for me, when Charmian arrived. She lent him a hand, packing in the things also that she had brought.

Here was my chance,—one of the likelihoods happened opportunely to hand. But I was too darned sick and miserable to go after it very hard. I wanted to get to bed,—alone. For possibly twenty minutes or half an hour, on the porch as Charmian was leaving, we talked. We talked philosophically, and at the same time personally. I believe I was busy telling Charmian some of the things in her that I didn't like. That was all. At the end of the talk, which was unsatisfactory as I had not succeeded in explaining to her what the things were that I didn't like, as Charmian was going, I took hold of her and kissed her; and that was all, absolutely all. The conversation had no connection whatever with the kiss. It was the conversation that relieved my own miserable feelings caused by the accidents of that day. The kiss was my sole effort to go after this one likelihood in a dozen.

I went up to Glen Ellen. I dropped a line to Charmian, rather a letter, apropos of the conversation we had had.

(You see, Carrie, what I'm trying to do? I am trying to give you, just as it actually was, the working-up of my relation with Charmian from its very first inception, when I decided that she was one of a dozen likelihoods.)

Now, don't forget the basis of my life at that time. I had made up my mind to go to pieces,—to deliberately and intentionally go to pieces. Before my first trip down to town from Glen Ellen, I wrote a letter to Charmian asking to see her when I came down. Incidentally I came down. I saw her. I began to grow pretty desirous for her. At the same time that I was down, I met a girl, another man's wife, whom I had not seen for some years. I made a date with her. She was to start in a few days for Stockton and Sacramento, for a week or ten days' vacation, ostensibly to visit friends. We made it up to go together,—to go up [on] one of the river steamboats. Charmian and I came out to your camp on a Saturday afternoon. We returned on a Sunday afternoon. You will remember Charmian's and my conduct together at the camp-fire at your camp that Saturday night. We were just beginning to come together good and hard. On Sunday afternoon when we went in, I did my best to get Charmian to go out to Hayward with me that night. She said if I wanted to see her, I had to come to her house. And out to her house I came that evening in Berkeley. It was during this period, Saturday night and Sunday, that I was proceeding to fall in love with her, only I did not yet know it. I simply thought that I was growing more desirous of her, and more desirous for her to be my mistress.

I went back to Glen Ellen. Bessie was jealous and suspicious at that time. She feared every woman. She was jealous of the nurse-girl, a scabby-faced maid. Jealous of everybody. Going through my wastepaper basket constantly, and piecing torn shreds of letters together, etc., etc. And I not caring a whoop to hell about anything she did in that way. For instance, the girl I was going up to Stockton and Sacramento with, wrote me several times (incidentally, I wasn't bothering about this girl, because I was falling in love with Charmian and didn't know it; and that took up all my interest). I did not reply to this girl's letter. Finally, came a telegram,—my last chance before she started, to let her know that I would accompany her on the trip. I received the telegram while I was eating supper. Bessie came around and wanted to see the telegram. I told her that it was for me and that I didn't think it would be good for her to see it. I had not yet read the telegram, but was tearing open the envelope. Bessie said she thought it was from her folks. I told her I thought it wasn't, and that if it was, I'd let her know. She insisted on looking at it as I opened it. I turned myself sideways so as to prevent her reading it. She moved around behind me so that she still could read it. And then I quit,—and let her read it. The girl's name was not signed, but the whole trip was given away. (I am giving you this to show you my frame of mind, and to show you that I was getting ready for a separation from Bessie).

I went down to Oakland on a second trip. I called Charmian up at Berkeley, I being at the bungalow. Incidentally, Charmian told me that Bessie had gone through my waste-basket and pieced together several shreds of the letter she (Charmian) had written me in reply to my request to see her (Charmian) and in which Charmian had told me to come to see her at Berkeley. As it was typewritten, Bessie did not know who the woman was, and had no suspicions of Charmian. All this information had come to Charmian through her aunt, as so much gossip, for to her aunt promptly had Bessie gone to relate the discovery she had made in my waste-paper basket. (It was always Bessie's way to shout all things from the housetop.)

In this talk over the phone with Charmian, in which I made mention of the fact of trouble arising if Bessie discovered the identity of the person who had written the letter, Charmian said she would be "game" for her share of the trouble. And in that moment, it came to me, without warning, for the first time, that I loved Charmian. And in that moment, on the very instant, spontaneously, without even thinking, I answered, "Then you'll be game for *all* of it!" The thought I had in mind was, that I would marry Charmian.

Now, don't forget my basis. All during this period, from before the beginning of the camping in Glen Ellen, I had made up my mind to go to pieces and get a separation. This without being in love with anybody, but from sheer disgust in life, such as I was living it.

I came back to Glen Ellen. There was hell to pay. Bessie was suspicious of everybody. She broached the letter to me that she had got from my wastepaper basket. She didn't know but what it was from the girl from whom I had received the telegram. I was careful to steer her clear of Charmian. I had intended to bring about the separation after the camping trip was over, and when Bessie had returned to the Bungalow. But this letter which she had discovered in the wastepaper basket, plus the telegram, and her discussing the matter with me, precipitated the separation. She asked me if I loved somebody else. I told her that I did, though I refused to tell that person's name. And I told her frankly that it was because of the trouble she would make for that person, if she learned that person's identity. So the separation was thus precipitated. The story is all told.

Now, the source of this story that Charmian broke up the London household, is due directly to Bessie. It is the gossip of Oakland at the present moment. You say in your letter to me, that from things Bessie had said, etc., etc., you made up your mind that Charmian had broken up the household.

Now, Carrie, I have never made a defense of my actions in this matter before to anyone, nor explained the course of events as they really happened, —and all this in the face of a countless number of lies that have been circulated. I am making this explanation to you, and you are the first one to whom I have made an explanation. I don't think you have ever heard me breathe a word against Bessie, nor anybody else ever heard me breathe a word against Bessie. Nevertheless, I now tell you that Bessie is one of the most colossal and shameless liars I have ever encountered. I'll give you but one instance. At the present time and for many months past, it has been going the rounds of Oakland gossip that financially I have treated Bessie shamefully, so shamefully that she was compelled even to sell her furniture in order to feed her babies.

Let me give you the real facts of the foregoing lie: When I went away to Korea, Bessie received from my publishers, the first of every month, $65.00 —maybe it was $75.00 a month, I don't remember. In addition, all extraordinary expenses, doctor bills, nurse bills, etc., etc., were charged to me and paid by me. In addition to this I made arrangements with my publishers before I left, that if Bessie wanted money at any time, all she had to do was to write them or telegraph them, whereupon they would send her the money. This Bessie understood, and this she utilized while I was away. Bessie decided to go to Los Angeles for a while. She stored some of her furniture, and she sold some of it. The reason she gave me for selling it, was that she didn't want it any more. She wanted better. She got better, and I paid for it.

Now, Carrie, very little reliance can be placed upon any person who would circulate so shameless a lie about her husband, as Bessie did in the foregoing.

Do you remember how Bessie dragged Anna Strunsky's name through the mire? Through all the newspapers and pink-tea councils at the time of my return from Korea?

Do you wonder that I wanted to shield Charmian from the moment I knew that I loved her and wanted to marry her? I believe I shielded Charmian fairly well. In order to save Charmian from Bessie's shameless and lying tongue, at the time of my separation I counseled Charmian not to break off entirely from Bessie, but to see her occasionally. This she did no oftener than was absolutely necessary, seeing Bessie in the six months between my separation and my departure for Korea, but four or five times.

The one person before the separation, during the separation, and after the separation, who was practically above suspicion in Bessie's mind, was Charmian. And Charmian was practically above suspicion, because Charmian's conduct in the London family had been most exemplary. Remember Bessie's eagle eyes; remember the eagle eyes of any married woman so far as her husband is concerned, with other women in the house. During all this time Bessie never suspected Charmian once—BECAUSE THERE WAS ABSOLUTELY NO REASON TO SUSPECT HER, WHILE THERE WERE MANY REASONS FOR NOT SUSPECTING HER. During the time in the Bungalow, Charmian had a love-affair of her own with somebody else. Hints of this were given by her at the time to Bessie and carried on from Bessie to me. I know the ins and outs of this love-affair, myself, now, and during the whole of the period that Charmian dropped in at the Bungalow, she was badly tangled up with somebody else.

So well did I shield Charmian, that at the time of my departure for Korea,

Bessie did not have the slightest suspicion that she was the woman. My sister, who has been uniformly loyal to me, at that time slipped and played me false. My sister said to Bessie, "I am going over to the steamer to see Jack off. And I know that I shall there discover who the woman is." She did, and she promptly came back and gave Bessie the news. This was the first inkling Bessie had as to who the woman was.

Now you've got it all in a nut-shell. With an eagle-eyed, jealous wife in the house, the woman doesn't live who can go into that house and cut out that eagle-eyed, jealous wife's husband from under her nose, without that eagle-eyed, jealous wife getting some suspicions. I say again, the woman doesn't live who could accomplish that feat, and you know it yourself, Carrie. Again, and in connection with this, let me point out to you the fact that Bessie did not have the slightest suspicion as to Charmian's being the woman, until six months after the separation, and then, the news was carried to her by my sister.

Carrie, I have given you in downright frankness my love-affair with Charmian, its beginning and its culmination when I first became conscious that I loved her; I have pointed out to you that the separation had already been decided upon by me before I knew that I was in love, and before I had ever had a single thought about Charmian. I have been frank, almost too frank in the matter, and if I hadn't cared for you I wouldn't have been frank with you at all, nor told you a word of it.

In conclusion, I want to tell you this: that according to my code, I don't consider it a crime for any woman, no matter what the circumstances, to attempt to cut out a man from under the guns of another woman. All women are so made, all women do these things,—at least all women who have the temptation. And if a woman loves a man so circumstanced, it *is* a temptation.

It happens in this case however, that the conduct charged against Charmian by you is considered a most heinous crime of conventional society. And, it also happens, that in this case Charmian is absolutely Not Guilty. It merely happens so; but it makes your mistake the more egregious insofar as you have made that mistake public. And public you have made it, because already, and for weeks past, the gossip has been dribbling back that the Crowd dropped Charmian because Charmian broke up the London family.

You say in your letter that "as a man and as Charmian's possible sharer in whatever blame is connected with this affair, you are in honor bound to find excuses for her in the matter." Your reasoning is fairly good if you fit it to the average man. The average man is not as truthful as I am, and you know it. The average man is more of a chivalrous liar than I am. If you will take my last bunch of correspondence with you, you will find that I was not chivalrous enough to lie in order to save other women or any woman. My rule of conduct is for every man to stand on his own legs, and for every woman too. In this last big correspondence with you and the rest of the Crowd, I made Charmian stand on her own legs, and I made every other woman stand on her own legs. I said the time was past for any beating about the bush and we threshed it out without any chivalrous lying, everybody standing upon their own legs.

I know that this is a very inadequate way to give to you all the events and all the psychology of the time before, during and after my separation from Bessie and my love for Charmian; and so I am quite willing, and not only willing but anxious, to answer any questions from you which may throw additional light on the matter;—light that I have forgotten to shed myself.[1]

Jack

[1]Divorce from Bessie was made final Nov. 18, 1905; London married Charmian the following day.

To Carrie Sterling

Glen Ellen, Calif.
Sept. 29, 1905

Dear Carrie:

This is a long-delayed reply to your letter of Sept. 19. I have read your letter through carefully, and in order to show you that every statement of fact you have made in it coincides with what I wrote to you, I make the following quotations:

(1) "We all knew and felt sorry for her (Charmian) as we thought it hopeless."

(2) "When George charged her (Charmian) with it once, (loving me, Jack) she did not deny him."

(3) "When Charmian went East, we thought it was to forget her love for you. Even Isabelle and Mother Sterling, at the time, spoke of C.'s infatuation for you, and how she used to, when up there, talk of no one but you—before you and Bessie separated."

(4) "The only time I (Carrie) ever saw anything which led me to believe there was aught between you, was one Saturday night and Sunday, in June, at our camp."

(5) "Again, the faithful friend who dallied enough with the husband to cause disgust to an old reprobate like Joaquin Miller."

(6) "Then the night of your accident, she (Charmian) told me that she felt so sorry for you that while on her horse she put her arms around you."

Now let me reply to the foregoing quotations from your letter:

(1) You did not any of you know, nor feel sorry for Charmian, until after the separation.

(2) George charged Charmian out at Dingee's, after the separation. Charmian told me about it at the time.

(3) Charmian went East many months after the separation. As regards Isabelle and Mother Sterling's statements that Charmian talked of no one but me before Bessie and I separated, this may well be correct. I was a

protege of Charmian's family; her Aunt Netta in particular, and the whole family was particularly enthusiastic over me.

(4) This reference I covered in my letter to you. It was at the very moment of separation, when I was trying to get Charmian to be my mistress, and before I knew I was in love with her.

(5) Same date as (4),—at the very moment of separation.

Still referring to (5): I wonder if you sincerely mean precisely what you said as there quoted. I remember the Sunday very well. I spent a great deal of time—practically all the time—while Joaquin was present getting drunk, in fooling with the girls. I washed Kate's face with cherries and dirt, if you will remember, and it took some time, all that squabbling around with Kate. I poured a lot of water over Charmian; also, when Carlt and Charmian got to fooling with the box of powder, Carlt threw the box of powder into the brush, and I spent a good while getting said box out of the brush. Said box had fallen down through the brush into a creek, a dry creek, and we were all a long time locating it. Then part of the time I listened to Joaquin Miller and Austin Lewis recite, and altogether Joaquin Miller wasn't there a couple of hours. For a few minutes only, Charmian and I had our heads in your lap, together. Then for a time we lay feet touching feet, and heads in opposite directions, so that our heads came pretty close to being nine and ten feet away from each other. We did not lie alongside of each other at all. I am not denying that Joaquin made this remark. But anent this remark of Joaquin's, I am putting it up to you. Go over that day in your memory, and find out if Charmian's and my conduct MERITED such a remark from Joaquin Miller or anybody else.

(6) This also was at the very moment of separation.

Now, concerning all the foregoing. All the facts that you have stated occur within the time stated by me in my letter to you,—at the very moment of separation, or subsequent to the separation.

Now, Carrie, you know yourself that you had no suspicions whatever against Charmian, and so you have stated, prior to the separation or at the time of the separation. Why did you fail to have these suspicions? Because Charmian's conduct and mine had never given you cause for such suspicions. And you can go over every member of the Crowd on this point, and find a similar consensus of opinion. It was not until after the separation that any of you began to suspect that Charmian cared for me.

You mention at the time Bessie went up to Glen Ellen, Charmian's coming with a tearful message that it was a shame the way I was treating Bessie. She told me about this message, before I went to Korea. Incidentally, no finer proof could be given that there was nothing between Charmian and me than this same message which you have instanced. As I had kept my mouth shut with all of you, concerning Bessie and my life with Bessie, so had I kept it shut with Charmian concerning Bessie and my life with Bessie. And while Charmian liked me for a certain comradeship that was mine, and for the work I was doing in my writing, etc., etc., she none the less listened to the lies Bessie told about me, and believed those lies. Hence the tearful message instanced by you. She believed it at the time.

Now, concerning this tearful message: It was caused by my not going down to the train to see Bessie off to Glen Ellen. Bessie had told this same tearful story at Glen Ellen, of my ill-treatment of her in not coming down to see her off, and it had been believed. And everybody at Glen Ellen was righteously indignant about my conduct. Now let me give you the facts: There were two babies to be taken to Glen Ellen, and a lot of luggage. The luggage I paid an express company to handle. The two babies had, to carry them, Bessie and a stout nurse-girl, one baby to each, and one of the babies able to walk. Those are the facts of it, and said facts must be taken in conjunction with one other fact, namely, that if I had accompanied Bessie I would have lost my whole morning's work writing. And who in hell was to pay for the express-wagon, and the railroad tickets, and the nurse-girl, if I wasn't?

I now quote from your letter: "I know of three parties who left your house in disgust at three different times, because of the actions of you and Charmian before Bessie." Now, Carrie, let me give you straight talk and plain talk. Never, in my house, have I romped nor cut up in any way with any woman, girl or child whatsoever, to the extent that I have done all these things in your house with yourself, and about every woman who was ever in your house while I was present,—except Charmian. And I am sure, that in this cutting up with you, and girls in your house, nothing so very reprehensible was thought of my conduct. There's no use in naming all the girls, with all the hugs and all the kisses, and all the rest of it. You know, you absolutely know, and you know that I know that you know. Now, one of two things concerning these three people who left my house in disgust because of my conduct with Charmian. Either these people lie, or else they are damn finicky. Practically the only cutting up, at least that I can remember, that I had with Charmian, was boxing. Also, I boxed with Ida Brooks, Anna Strunsky, the servant-girls, Bessie, and anybody who would put the gloves on with me.

Still anent my disgraceful conduct with Charmian in my house: I want to ask you a couple of questions, Carrie, and I want you to please answer them. First, do you think that I made a practice of putting on company manners when you were at my house, with the Crowd?; and second, did you, yourself, ever see any conduct of mine with Charmian that disgusted you, or that was likely to disgust anybody worthy to enter your house or mine? And before you answer these two questions, let me make the statement that I never in my life in my house put on company manners for anybody, and pray God I never shall.

Concerning the talk of people of the sort that say they were disgusted at what they saw in my house, let me give you the following, which was brought to me shortly after my separation, and which went the rounds of Alameda

188

gossip. Namely: That other visitors at my house, eye-witnesses, had seen me offer personal, physical violence to Bessie. And this was told by the eye-witnesses themselves at Alameda dinner-parties and pink-teas.

In conclusion. After reading your letter, your statements, and your objections, the case stands just as I stated it in my letter to you. And in addition let me again assure you that I know, personally and convincingly, of the fact that right up to within a short time of my separation, a very short time, Charmian had a deep and tragic love-affair with somebody else. I know who this person is, though at the time I did not even guess. At the time, however, I did know that Charmian did have this affair with somebody, and that it was causing her all kinds of worry and trouble. Once again let me say, that I am as certain that Charmian had this love-affair, as I am that I am sitting on this chair,—that I am certain this love-affair extended up almost to the moment of my separation, and was settled but a short time before.

Now, a little information, Carrie. This affair of Charmian's with somebody else, tragic and full of worry and anxiety, as I have told you, extended through about a year's time. Finally, and during Charmian's vacation in the first part of June, up here in Glen Ellen, she thought it all over and made up her mind to quit. Then it was that the affair was *settled*. She was a free woman again, and ready for any sort of a joyful action that could come along. It was at this time, as Charmian was coming back from her vacation, and Bessie was going up to take her vacation at Glen Ellen, that I came along Charmian's way, looking for a mistress. As I say, Charmian was ready for any kind of a joyful reaction that could come along. I came along, and it was a case of speedy falling in love for both of us. I have told you all this in my preceding letter.

As I told you before, I am not only willing, but anxious, that you should thoroughly understand the situation, and not allow a false judgment to rest upon anybody. And so, I not only am anxious, but glad, to have you ask any questions, the answers of which may explain things that appear contradictory or obscure in your mind. Please, Dear Carrie, ask these questions, and state any further objections that you may have to the explanations that I have given.

Sincerely yours,
Jack

To Cloudesley Johns

Glen Ellen, Calif.
Oct. 4, 1905

Dear Cloudesley:
I'd like to have seen that trial. Must have been great!
Now to business.

To buy the ranch and build barn, I had to get heavy advances from Macmillan. I had already overdrawn so heavily that Macmillan's asked me, & in common decency I agreed, to pay interest on these new advances made.

At present moment my check book shows me $207.83 to my credit at bank.

It is the first of the month & I have no end of bills awaiting me. Prominent among which are!

My mother $55.00
Outfit of tools
for ranch 57.60
Rent here at Glen Ellen $24.00
The smaller bills will total $50.00

Now, I have to pay my own expenses East. Lecture Bureau afterward reimburses me. But immediately I must pay my way and Manyoungis'[1] way to Chicago. Charmian follows me inside 24 hours. There are her expenses.

I haven't a cent coming to me now from any source, & must borrow this money in Oakland.

Also, in November I must meet between seven & eight hundred dollars insurance.

My mother wants me to increase her monthly allowance. So does Bessie. I have just paid hospital bills of over a $100.00 for one of my sisters.

Another member of the family (whom I cannot refuse) has warned me that as soon as I arrive in Oakland they want to make a proposition to me. I know what that means.

I have promised $30.00 to pay printing of appeal to Supreme Court of Joe King, a poor devil in Co. Jail with 50 yrs. sentence hanging over him and who is being railroaded.

And so on, & so on, and so on—— Oh, & a bill for over $45.00 to the Bay press.

So you see that I am not only sailing close into the wind but that I am dead into it & my sails flapping.

Wolf

[1]Houseboy Jack brought home from the Orient, who remained with him until the sailing of the *Snark*.

To Charmian Kittredge

New York City
Nov. 12, 1905

My Mate—

I have told *Outing* to forward my check to Newton.[1] Keep track of it. It should be for $3,700—½ of what they are to pay for American serial rights.

Not so bad, is it?—$7,400 plus what I get from English serial rights, plus book royalties (which are bound to be larger still) all for a couple of months work.[2]

Save *all* letters I send you. Some of them I want for my collection.

If you have not forwarded foto to me already, please forward it directly to

Mr. Jack Barrett,
   Editorial Rooms
     S. F. Examiner.

Seal & register the photograph, writing your name on back of fotograph.

All mail that comes to you for me, hold until I get there.

What does Aunt Netta[3] mean by saying that "all her moments" "are given to the work Jack set" her?

I don't understand. Forwarding mail—yes. Keeping mice out of my clothes—yes. But what else?

Building house? But that's her business. Tell me if you can.

Don't exactly appreciate the "luxury" of the washstand, seeing, according to Aunt Netta's plans, that you & I are to be in the annex only for meals.

First, Aunt Netta gives all the details of the "luxuries" she is preparing for our enjoyment. And then she gives all the details showing us that we shall not be able to use them. She's a corker!

We'll need bedding for the yacht anyway, so explain to Aunt Netta that I'll get necessary bedding.

Yes—the death lines in "all Gold Canyon" came from my experience with the "little death in life," "the drunken darls," "the sweet thick mystery," etc.

[James B.] Pinker[4] has *White Fang* you know.

Portrait attachment—in pigeonholes *in* cottage.

I *love* your letters.

And I read them again and again, & love them over & over.

Expressed you four or five.

I read your writing like print.

Be sure & save the Des Moines clipping. It is rich!

My God! these Iowa people who look upon a cold bath in the morning as a hobby!

Dear, dear Wolf Mate, the 25th is very near—and very dear. Dear wife!

                                             Wolf

[1]Charmian was staying with friends at Newton, Iowa.
[2]This refers to *White Fang*.
[3]Ninetta Eames, Charmian's aunt.
[4]His English agent at this time.

To George P. Brett

Newton, Iowa
Dec. 2, 1905

Dear Mr. Brett—

In reply to yours of Nov. 29th.

I have not enough Klondike stories to make a volume by themselves, and I don't care to mix them up with other stories. I shall complete the volume of Klondike stories next summer. I find that I can't write that set of "Created He Them" sketches, while traveling around.

I have just glanced at the preface of Henry George's[1] book which you so kindly sent me, and I know that I shall enjoy reading it, agreeing with his destructive criticism while disagreeing with his constructive theorizing.

Please hold the parcel marked glass and all express packages; but forward mail according to directions in my last letter.

Am going to run down to Jamaica last part of December, from Boston, and shall arrive back in New York the middle of January.

I suppose you have learned from the papers ere this, that I've got married. This time I cannot deny. I plead guilty. It's true. As my wife is here to see what I write, I am enobled to explain to you that I got married in order to have one more member in the crew for the trip around the world.

Sincerely yours,
Jack London

---

[1] 19th-century writer on economics and social problems.

1906-1909

THE YEARS OF THE *SNARK*

CHRONOLOGY

1906: The Building of the *Snark*.

Published: *Moonface and Other Stories,* The Macmillan Co., September (collected stories).
White Fang, The Macmillan Co., October (novel).
Scorn of Women, The Macmillan Co., November (drama).

1907: April. Left San Francisco on the voyage of the *Snark*. From San Francisco to Hawaii, to the Marquesas (early December), to the Society Islands, Tahiti (late December).

Published: *Before Adam,* The Macmillan Co., February (novel).
Love of Life and Other Stories, The Macmillan Co., September collected stories).
The Road, The Macmillan Co., November (tramping experiences).

1908: Continued the *Snark* voyage. From Tahiti to the Samoan Islands (May), to the Fiji Islands (early June), to New Hebrides (mid-June), to Samoa (late June), to the Solomon Islands (Guadalcanal). Left the Solomons in November for Sydney, Australia.
Purchased the Lamotte Ranch, Glen Ellen, Sonoma Co., California (110 acres).

Published: *The Iron Heel,* The Macmillan Co., February (novel).

1909: Hospitalized in Sydney, Australia. Left Sydney in May. Returned from the *Snark* voyage on an English tramp ship, the *Tymeric,* from Sydney to Ecuador, to the Panama Canal, to New Orleans (July). Arrived in Glen Ellen in early August. Purchased the Fish Ranch, Glen Ellen, Sonoma County, California (17 acres).

Published: *Martin Eden,* The Macmillan Co., September (semi-auto-biographical novel).

To Bailey Millard[1]

Glen Ellen, Calif.
Feb. 18, 1906

Dear Millard:

The keel is laid. The boat is to be 45 feet long. It would have been a little bit shorter had I not found it impossible to squeeze in a bathroom otherwise. I sail in October. Hawaii is the first port of call; and from there we shall wander through the South Seas, Samoa, Tasmania, New Zealand, Australia, New Guinea, and up through the Philippines to Japan. Then Korea and China, and on down to India, Red Sea, Mediterranean, Black Sea and Baltic, and on across the Atlantic to New York, and then around the Horn to San Francisco. You can take a look at the map and get an idea of the different countries I'll stop at along the way. I shall certainly put in a winter in St. Petersburg, and the chances are that I shall go up the Danube from the Black Sea to Vienna, and there isn't a European country in which I shall not spend from one to several months. This leisurely fashion will obtain throughout the whole trip. I shall not be in a rush; in fact, I calculate seven (7) years at least will be taken up by the trip.

This boat is to be sailed by one friend[2] and myself. There are no sailors. My wife accompanies me. Of course, I'll take a cook along, and a cabin boy; but these will be Asiatics, and will have no part in the sailorizing. The rig of the boat will be a compromise between a yawl and a schooner. It will be what is called the ketch-rig—the same rig that is used by the English fishing-boats on the Dogger Bank.

Shall, however, have a small engine on board to be used only in case of emergency, such as in bad water among reefs and shoals, where a sudden calm in a fast current leaves a sailing-boat helpless. Also, this engine is to be used for another purpose. When I strike a country, say Egypt or France, I'll go up the Nile or the Seine by having the mast taken out, and under the power of the engine. I shall do this a great deal in the different countries, travel inland and live on board the boat at the same time. There is no reason at all why I shouldn't in this fashion come up to Paris, and moor alongside the Latin Quarter, with a bowline out to Notre Dame and a stern-line fast to the Morgue.

Now to business. I shall be gone a long time on this trip. No magazine can print all I have to write about it. On the other hand, it cannot be imagined that I shall write 50,000 words on the whole seven years, and then quit. As it is, the subject-matter of the trip divides itself up so that there will be no clash whatever between any several different publications that may be handling my stuff. For instance, here are three big natural, unconflicting divisions: news, industrial, and political articles on the various countries for newspapers; fiction; and finally, the trip itself.

Now the question arises, if you take the trip itself (which will be the cream), how much space will *The Cosmopolitan* be able to give me? In this connection I may state that *McClure's* and *Outing* are after me; and, as I am throwing my life, seven years of my time, my earning-power as a writer of fiction, and a lot of money, into the enterprise, it behooves me to keep a sharp lookout on how expenses, etc., are to be met. And one important factor in this connection that I must consider, is that of space.

And while I am on this matter of space, I may as well say that it is granted, always, that I deliver the goods. Of course, if my articles turn out to be mushy and inane, why I should not expect any magazine to continue publishing them. I believe too much in fair play to be a good business man, and if my work be rotten, I'd be the last fellow in the world to bind any editor to publish it. On the other hand, I have a tremendous confidence, based upon all kinds of work I have already done, that I can deliver the goods. Anybody doubting this has but to read *The People of the Abyss* to find the graphic, reportorial way I have of handling things. (Between ourselves, and not to be passed on, I gathered every bit of the material, read hundreds of books and thousands of pamphlets, newspapers and Parliamentary Reports, composed *The People of the Abyss,* and typed it all out, took two-thirds of the photographs with my own camera, took a vacation of one week off in the country—and did it all in two months. That's going some, now, isn't it?)

While on this matter of space, I may also state that it is not so much the point of how large the space is in a given number of the magazine, but how long a time the story of the trip can run in the magazine.

Another thing to be considered is, that I am a good photographer (you know my photographs of the Japanese-Russian war for the Hearst newspapers). And so far as the magazine public is concerned, the story of the trip will be enhanced tremendously by its being adequately and sympathetically illustrated with photographs taken by the writer.

Still another thing must be considered. This is something that has never been done before. No writer of prominence, in the days of his prominence, has ever gone sailing around the world. Even Stevenson, in his South Sea cruise on the *Casco,* took a large boat and carried Captain and crew; was himself the veriest passenger. But here I take a small boat, and with one friend, a man sixty years of age, navigate this boat around the world. There will be no sailors whatever; there will be no sailing-master whatever. This friend, who is my wife's uncle, and I, will do all the navigating and all the sailorizing ourselves. We expect lots of action, and my strong point as a writer is that I am a writer of action—see all my short stories, for instance. Another point is, that while I am a writer, I am also a sailor, having spent years on the water and before the mast; and a still further point is, that I am an acknowledged and successful writer of sea-matter—see *The Sea-Wolf, The Cruise of the Dazzler,* and *Stories of the Fish Patrol.* In short, I end this paragraph as I began it: there never has been anything like this done in the history of the writing world.

I have dealt with space, and now comes the item of pay. In the first place, here is a traveler-correspondent, and traveler-correspondents are usually expensive, because their traveling expenses are paid by their employers. But in my case I'd pay my own traveling expenses. I build my boat, I outfit my boat, and I run my boat.

Another point in the matter of payment arises. It's going to cost me a lot of money to build this boat, to outfit it, and to get instruments, charts, etc. So, in whatever conclusion we arrive at, it must be stipulated that I receive in advance, in the course of the building of the boat, say $3,000.00 (Three thousand dollars).

To boil this whole letter down: You know, roughly, what the trip is to be. You know my ability as a writer and as a photographer. The two main points to be determined upon between us are space and price. The advance is incidental to the foregoing. And in passing, it may as well be noted that to *The Cosmopolitan* will be sold the American serial rights only. The English serial rights, of course, are reserved. Please let me hear from you at your early convenience.[3]

Sincerely yours,
Jack London

[1]Editor, *Cosmopolitan Magazine.*
[2]Roscoe Eames, husband of Charmian's Aunt Ninetta.
[3]This same letter was sent to Mr. Collier, *Collier's Magazine,* Feb. 19, 1906; to Mr. McClure, *McClure's Magazine,* Feb. 19; to Mr. Whitney, *Outing Magazine,* March 23. The only changes occur in paragraph five where the names of the magazines are altered according to the addressee.

TO BAILEY MILLARD

Glen Ellen, Calif.
April 3, 1906

Dear Mr. Millard:

I agree to furnish the *Cosmopolitan Magazine* a series of exclusive articles descriptive of my voyage in my sailboat, which voyage is to extend, if possible, around the world. I reserve the English serial rights for the publication of these articles, guaranteeing that no English or other foreign publication shall be made of any of them before they are printed in the *Cosmopolitan Magazine.* These articles are to be four thousand words each, for the first three, and not to exceed thirty-five hundred words each for the others, except as may be ordered by the editor of the *Cosmopolitan Magazine.* The rate of payment for the articles will be ten cents a word. The number of articles will not exceed ten unless more are ordered by the editor of *The Cosmopolitan.*

The *Cosmopolitan* has advanced to me the sum of two thousand dollars, receipt of which is hereby acknowledged, as part payment for the articles. The payment for the other articles of the series not covered by the two thousand dollars is to be made from time to time before the series is concluded in the magazine, the understanding being that if I need money after the fifth article has been submitted I can draw upon *The Cosmopolitan* up to the sum of fifteen hundred dollars, in addition to the two thousand dollars already paid. In case I fail to furnish the articles, I agree to provide in lieu thereof acceptable short stories at the same rate, within one year.

I also agree to furnish photographs to illustrate the articles, on condition that *The Cosmopolitan* shall provide me with a small camera and sufficient films and agree to pay for the developing and the printing expenses.

The manuscript and the photographs will be sent to the *Cosmopolitan Magazine,* promptly as circumstances may permit on the voyage.

Very truly yours,

(Signed) Jack London

I agree to the foregoing terms for the *Cosmopolitan*.

(Signed) Bailey Millard,

Editor of the *Cosmopolitan Magazine*.

To Robert Collier, Jr.[1]

Glen Ellen, Calif.

April 8, 1906

Dear Mr. Collier:

In reply to yours of April 2. In my previous long letter to you, dated Feb. 19, I did not propose the description of the boat-trip to you because I did not think you would be able to afford the space. The description of the boat-trip I have arranged to furnish *The Cosmopolitan*. But what I did propose to you was "events of large news-value" that I might run up against, such as, for instance, if I were at the present moment in Naples, I could write a thousand words or so and furnish photographs of the new eruption of Vesuvius. Or, if I managed to survive a hurricane such as wrecked all the war-vessels at Samoa some years ago. Or, if I happened to be knocking around the Panama Canal. Or, I might be near some place that you decided had the big news-value, and you could cable to me to go and do it.

For instance, the description of a Fiji-Islander's house, family, and culinary arrangement, would not be proper stuff for *Collier's*. Such description, however, would be just the thing for the *Woman's Home Companion;* and with the *Woman's Home Companion* I am putting through an arrangement for such articles.

Now, on top of all the foregoing, I want to say that if I were going on a six-months' trip, I would do only one thing, and that for one publication. But I expect to be gone at the very least seven years, and maybe longer. If I should remain in California and should go away on seven six-months' trips in seven years, and write up each trip for a different publication, it would be somewhat similar to what I am doing when I go on this long, continuous trip.

Sincerely yours,
Jack London

¹Of *Collier's Magazine.*

TO HAYDEN CARRUTH¹

Glen Ellen, Calif.
April 8, 1906

Dear Mr. Carruth:

In reply to yours of April 3 *The Cosmopolitan* is to get from me a description of the boat-trip itself, handling, managing, and sailing of the boat. This *The Cosmopolitan* understands. And if it doesn't understand, it ought to understand, from the letters I have written to it. (To read *The Cosmopolitan* announcement, one would think *The Cosmopolitan* were sending me around. But, by golly, I can't check in advance and prevent everything that everybody is going to write about me)!²

You wrote to me suggesting articles describing home-life amongst the different peoples. And this was what I had in mind when I replied to you. However, and in addition to home-life articles, I imagine from time to time I could furnish you other descriptive articles suitable for your pages, about the places in which I find myself.

You ask if I propose doing anything for any other periodical besides *The Cosmopolitan* and yourselves. The chances are I shall. I am negotiating now with *Collier's* for the furnishing, from time to time, of events of large news-value, political and industrial articles, for example.

I shall be gone a long time on this trip. No magazine can print all I shall have to write about it. On the other hand, it cannot be imagined that I shall write 80,000 words on the whole seven years, and then quit. As it is, the subject-matter of the trip divides itself up so that there will be no clash whatever between several different publications that may be handling my stuff.

On top of the foregoing, I want to say that if I were going on a six-months' trip I should do only one thing, and that for only one publication. But I expect to be gone at the very least, seven years, and maybe longer. If I should remain in California and should go away on seven six-months' trips in seven years, and write up each trip for a different publication, it would be somewhat similar to what I am doing when I go on this long continuous trip.

There is nothing exclusive about it—that is to say, no one publication is going to publish the whole thing to the exclusion of other publications. It will be just as though I remained in California and wrote from time to time for different publications.

There is, however, a certain sort of exclusiveness. That is to say, the description of the boat-trip itself, sailing and handling of boat, etc., will be exclusive for *The Cosmopolitan*. Home-life articles, etc., whatever is determined upon in contract, will be exclusive for the *Woman's Home Companion*. Events of large news-value, industrial and political articles, etc., will be exclusive for *Collier's*. That's the idea of it.

As you suggest in your letter, my giving you a definite statement of the nature of *The Cosmopolitan* series, will enable us to plan a totally different series for the *Woman's Home Companion*.

As to rate, I would say my regular ten cents (10¢) per word. As to photographs,—while I have done lots of photographing for the Hearst newspapers, etc., I have never yet sold any photographs, so I have no idea of what would be a fair remuneration. I do know that cameras, films, developing and printing, are frightfully expensive; so whatever you say about remuneration for photographs, will go with me.

I am trying to answer your letter in detail, and now I come to the paragraph in which you want to know when my initial article will appear in *The Cosmopolitan,* and suggest that my first article with you should appear at least simultaneously. My first article for *Cosmopolitan* will describe the boat, the crew and the plan of the voyage. This is the only kind of an "initial" article that one could possibly write about the trip. This will probably appear in the November *Cosmopolitan,* seeing that *The Cosmopolitan* goes to print so long in advance of the first of the month.

Now, it would be impossible for me to write, before I sail, about home-life, etc., in the places I expect to visit. So I cannot see how a corresponding initial article could be published in the *Woman's Home Companion.* I've got to get somewhere in order to write about it. I could promise definitely, however, a first article, say descriptive of home-life in Hawaii. Hawaii, as you know, is my first port of call.

I may give you a brief idea of the trip. From Hawaii, we shall wander through the South Seas, Samoa, Tasmania, New Zealand, Australia, New Guinea, and up through the Philippines to Japan. Then Korea, and China, and on down to India, Red Sea, Mediterranean, Black Sea, Baltic, and on across the Atlantic to New York, and then around the Horn to San Francisco. We shall not rush ourselves, and shall have no schedule of places to visit. If the whim strikes us, we'll go off to a thousand different and remote places that no tourist ever heard of. If it takes a dozen years, instead of seven years, well and good. You can take a look at the map and get an idea of the different countries we shall stop at along the way, as well as of many additional places we are likely to visit. For instance, if it is possible to get permission from the Chinese Government, we shall spend several months on the Grand Canal and the great rivers of China. We shall certainly put in a winter at St. Petersburg, and another in the South of Italy.

If it is possible, we shall go up the Danube from the Black Sea to Vienna. There are great canals across Europe, France, Germany and Holland that we shall go through, if arrangements can be made with the various governments controlling those canals.

There isn't a European country in which we shall not spend from one to several months. I am putting a 40-horse-power engine into the boat, to be used in cases of emergency, and also for going into the interior of countries. For instance, when we strike Egypt, we go up the Nile, traveling through the heart of the land and living on board the boat. There is no reason at all why we should not in this fashion come up the Seine to Paris, and moor alongside the Latin Quarter with a bow-line out to Notre Dame and a stern-line fast to the Morgue.

Sincerely yours,
Jack London

[1]Editor, *Woman's Home Companion*.
[2]In the "Magazine Shop-Talk," in the issue of *Cosmopolitan* just prior to this letter, the following statement appeared: "When *The Cosmopolitan* learned that Jack London was planning for this voyage its editor immediately arranged with him to let this magazine have the exclusive story of his wanderings about the world.

*   *   *

"We are able to lay before our readers some of Mr. London's characteristic comments on his proposed adventure as contained in letters to the editor." And following this statement was London's letter to Bailey Millard of February 18, 1906, printed verbatim.

To S. S. McCLURE[1]

Glen Ellen, Calif.
April 10, 1906

Dear Mr. McClure:—

In reply to yours of April 3. Life is so short and people so silly, that from the very beginning of my career, when I first began to get newspaper notoriety because of my youthful socialism, I made it a point to deny nothing charged against me in the newspapers. On the other hand, I have made it a courtesy to deny such things when requested to do so by my friends. Wherefore, because of your request, I am now making this explanation of the similarity between my "Love of Life" and Augustus Bridle's and J. K. MacDonald's "Lost in the Land of the Midnight Sun."

It is a common practice of authors to draw material for their stories, from the newspapers. Here are facts of life reported in journalistic style, waiting to be made into literature. So common is this practice that often amusing consequences are caused by several writers utilizing the same material. Some years ago, while I was in England, a story of mine was published in the *San Francisco Argonaut*. In the *Century* of the same date was published a story by Frank Norris. While these two stories were quite different in manner of treatment, they were patently the same in foundation and motive. At once the newspapers paralleled our stories. The explanation was simple: Norris and I had read the same newspaper account, and proceeded to exploit it. But the fun did not stop there. Somebody dug up a *Black Cat* published a year previous, in which was a similar story by another man who used the same foundation and motive. Then Chicago hustled around and resurrected a story that had been published some months before the *Black Cat* story, and that was the same in foundation and motive. Of course, all these different writers had chanced upon the same newspaper article.

So common is this practice of authors, that it is recommended by all the instructors in the art of the short story, to read the newspapers and magazines in order to get material. Charles Reade swore by this practice. I might name a lengthy list of the great writers who have advised this practice.

All the foregoing merely to show that this practice exists and is generally employed by story-writers. Now to the "Love of Life," which the *New York World* so generously paralleled with "Lost in the Land of the Midnight Sun." "Lost in the Land of the Midnight Sun" is not a story. It is a narrative of fact. It was published in *McClure's Magazine*. It tells the actual sufferings of a man with a sprained ankle in the country of the Coppermine River. It is not fiction, and it is not literature. I took the facts of life contained in it, added to them many other facts of life gained from other sources, and made, or attempted to make, a piece of literature out of them. There was another narrative of suffering that I used quite as extensively as I did "Lost in the Land of the Midnight Sun." This other narrative was a newspaper account of a lost and wandering prospector near Nome, Alaska. On top of this, I drew upon all my own personal experience of hardship and suffering and starvation, and upon the whole fund of knowledge I had of the hardship and suffering and starvation of hundreds and thousands of other men.

If you will turn to the end of my "Love of Life," you will find that my rescued hero becomes suddenly fat. This abrupt obesity was caused by his stuffing under his shirt all the spare hardtack he could beg from the sailors. Now I did not invent this. It is a fact of life. You will find it in Lieutenant Greely's narrative of the Greely Polar Expedition. I scarcely see how I could be charged with plagiarizing from Lieut. Greely; and yet if I plagiarized from Augustus Bridle and J. K. MacDonald for some of my material, I must have plagiarized from Lieut. Greely for some more of my material. And I must have plagiarized from the newspaper correspondent who described the wanderings of the Nome prospector, and I must have plagiarized from the experiences of scores and scores of Alaskan prospectors whose accounts I have heard from their own lips.

The *World,* however, did not charge me with plagiarism. It charged me with the identity of time and situation. Certainly the *World* is right. I plead guilty, and I am glad that the *World* was intelligent enough not to charge me with identity of language.

But little remains to be said. It might be well to explain how that half-page of deadly parallel was published in the *World*. In the first place, SENSATION. Sensation is the goods demanded by a newspaper of its space-writers. The suggestion of plagiarism is always sensational. When a half-page of deadly parallel is run in a newspaper, plagiarism is certainly suggested. The loose meaning of words in the average mind would make ninety percent of the readers of such a parallel infer that plagiarism had been charged.

Secondly, the space-writer writes for a living. I hope for his own soul's sake that this particular space-writer also writes for his living. His newspaper wanted the goods of sensation, and by refusing to charge plagiarism, while leaving the inference of plagiarism to the reader, this space-writer sold half a page to the *World*.

In conclusion, I, in the course of making my living by turning journalism into literature, used material from various sources which had been collected and narrated by men who made their living by turning the facts of life into journalism. Along comes the space-writer on the *World* who makes his living by turning the doings of other men into sensation. Well, all three of us made our living; and who's got any kick coming?

Sincerely yours,
Jack London

P.S.
   Dear Mr. McClure:
   You are at liberty to use the whole foregoing letter any way you see fit. I should like to see it published in the *World,* incidentally. But I should not like to see it "revised."

¹Of the *New York World*.

To S.S. McClure

Glen Ellen, Calif.
April 25, 1906

Dear Mr. McClure:

In reply to yours of April 17. I hope *The World* will publish that letter I sent you, concerning how I got my materials for "Love of Life." By the way, a couple of weeks after I sent this letter to you, I received a letter from Toronto from Augustus Bridle, who wrote "The Land of the Midnight Sun," asking me to explain. I sent him a duplicate of the letter I had sent you, and also told him to turn it over to the editor of one of the Toronto newspapers for publication—said Toronto newspaper having published already an interview with Bridle on the subject. I figured that the two-weeks intervening time would not hurt in any way the use you had intended for the letter.

You ask when you are going to see another short story. I sent you a weird decadent one, "When God Laughs." I won't get a bit excited if you don't see your way to publishing it. It is preposterous, untrue and impossible—in fact, it's speculative.

Incidentally, I may say that I am one-third of the way through with a short-long-story (about 40,000 words), which I expect to call *Before Adam*. The situation of this story, in the biological sense, is really before Adam; it is the most primitive story ever written. It is vastly more primitive than Stanley Waterloo's *Story of Ab*, and Gouverneur Morris' "The Pagan's Progress." It goes back before the cave-man; before fire; before the wearing of clothes; before the use of weapons—to a time when man was in the process of Becoming. When he spoke no language, and used sounds instead of words. In short, as I said before, it is the most primitive thing ever written, and I think I am doing it in a lively and interesting fashion. There is a love-motif! a hero! a villain! rivalry! and a literary reproduction of the landscape and conditions of the Younger World. Would you care to have a look-see at it for publication in the magazine?[1]

Sincerely yours,

Jack London

[1]McClure apparently rejected it. The story was first serialized in *Everybody's* and Waterloo charged London with plagiarism.

To George Sterling

Glen Ellen, Calif.
May 31, 1906

You Blessed Greek!—

As usual, your criticisms are right up to snuff. I think, as I go around the world, I'll have to send all my proofs to you just the same—if you'll let me.

I wouldn't dare to lock horns with Bierce. He stopped growing a generation ago. Of course, he keeps up with the newspapers, but his criteria crystallized thirty odd years ago. Had he been born a generation later he'd have been a socialist, and, more likely, an anarchist. He never reads books that aren't something like a hundred years old, and he glories in the fact.

Have you a copy of *Harper's Weekly*, containing Whitaker's Earthquake story? If so, can you lend it to me? Hopper's[1] article in *Everybody's* was great. Best story of the quake I've seen. My congratulations to him . . . only I don't know where to find him.

Lute[2] and I, in an automobile, last Tuesday morning passed Coppa's—and there we saw Monte!

Sure, you and Carrie come and stop at time of Jinks,[3] as long as you can —and any other old time, too. I guess you're pretty crowded there now. And besides, I'm busier than hell.

Remember Ban, my saddle-horse? Got in barb-wire, sawed a leg half off —had to shoot him yesterday.

I'd tackle Bierce by mail, through a magazine, all right—and I think I could give him a run for his money.

Wolf

[1]Jimmy Hopper, a member of the "famous fraternity of writers and artists" that flourished in Monterey and San Francisco during this period. Other members included Anna Strunsky, Herman Whitaker, George Sterling, Gelett Burgess, Mary Austin, Austin Lewis, Colonel Edwin Emerson.
[2]Lute Pease, editor of the *Pacific Monthly*.
[3]The Bohemian Club of San Francisco, founded in 1872, the oldest and the most enduring of the Bohemian Clubs in America, held its summer outing on the Russian River north of San Francisco and called this event the "High Jinks." Sterling and London were both members.

To MRS. M. SELINGER

Glen Ellen, Calif.
July 1, 1906

Dear Madam:

I have learned that I am a personal friend of yours, and that you have known me for a number of years. I have learned also of a remarkable attachment of mine for a Mrs. Stenberg, formerly of Fresno, now of Sacramento. I have learned that you have been a sort of go-between between us. I have learned a great many things also, about the Hindoo, and his and my persecution of Mrs. Stenberg through you.

Now I am writing to you for information. I am the real Jack London. I don't know you. I don't know the Hindoo. I don't know Mrs. Stenberg, much less love her. Was this all a concoction of yours, or did you really know some fellow who claimed that he was Jack London? I should be very grateful for a reply at your early convenience.[1]

Very truly yours,
Jack London

[1]One of many such letters concerning doubles. During his lifetime London received at least fifty letters concerning people who posed as "Jack London," or as relatives.

To BAILEY MILLARD

Glen Ellen, Calif.
July 16, 1906

Dear Bailey Millard:

In reply to yours of July 9. Your idea of sealed letters to be opened at sea, is simply great.[1] I really envy you the idea. Why didn't it occur to me: You can depend upon it that I shall make the most of these letters. It is simply delightful. I grin all over with anticipation every time I think of it. My congratulations.

I am inclosing you half a dozen photographs.

No. 1, is of Mr. Roscoe L. Eames, my wife's uncle, and co-navigator with me. (By the way, neither of us knows anything about navigation. Mr. Eames is going to study it up, if he gets time, before we start, and I am so dreadfully busy that I do not expect to study it up until after we start.)

No. 2, I should by all means recommend publishing this photo of the boat. You see, when we want to emphasize the smallness of the boat by photography, the last thing we should do is to photograph the boat out of water. If you will notice amidships the longitudinal scantling, second from the top, you will discover our water-line. In the water, all below this will be out of sight, and the boat will look light and delicate. But when you take the boat out of the water, down the whole depth of its keel, it looks a monstrous thing. I especially recommend this photo for reproduction, because of the fact that there are no clews in it that will give an idea of the size of the boat. The boat is 45 feet on the waterline, and will draw 6 feet of water. But on the ways, it looks like the hull of a full-rigged ship.

No. 3, I should scarcely recommend publishing this view of the boat, though it is a good one.

No. 4, is not so bad, showing Mr. Eames, Mrs. London and myself.

No. 5, Yours truly in the foreground. This is not so bad for reproduction.

No. 6, Neither is this. I am taking a photograph of her myself.

We are going to call her the *Snark*.

She will look like a toy when in the water, and trust to me for a good photograph of her at that time.

This damned earthquake is just beginning to show up the delays it caused. There is scarcely a thing we want, that we can buy in the local market.

Sincerely yours,

Jack London

---

[1]Millard wrote: "I am arranging to have a number of letters written to you to be opened while you are on your voyage. They will come to this office, and will then be sealed and marked according to the wishes of the writers. They will be from such good folk as Edwin Markham, Admiral Dewey, Gorki, Elbert Hubbard, John Muir, John Kendrick Bangs and others. These letters will be superscribed 'To be opened while sailing out of the Golden Gate,' 'To be opened on the approach of a storm,' 'To be opened in your moment of highest elation,' 'To be opened in your saddest hour,' etc. I have devised this scheme in order that all the big writers shall take an interest in this adventure and be on the lookout for your series." The scheme never materialized.

To James Randolph Walker[1]

Glen Ellen, Calif.
July 29, 1906

Dear sir:—

In reply to your telegram of July 28. I'll tell you what I can do. I have just finished a short story, entitled "The Wit of Porportuk."[2] It is an Alaskan story, and though I have never made a practice of praising my work, I must say that I would rank it among my best half-dozen Alaskan short stories. If you say so, I'll send it along to you.

Now, as to rates. I am receiving from fifteen to twenty cents per word for the American serial rights of my short fiction—and from twelve and a half to fifteen cents per word for the American serial rights in a long serial.

"The Wit of Porportuk" is longer than the average short story, wherefore I am willing to let it go at fifteen cents per word. Your initial number, I hope, will not be published so soon as to prevent me getting simultaneous serial publication for the story in England.

Please let me know how soon your initial number comes out. Please telegraph me on receipt of this, if you want me to mail "The Wit of Porportuk" to you. Telegraph if you do *not* want me to mail it to you. In the meantime, I hold it waiting your telegram.

Of course, it is understood that your telegram to mail it on to me does not imply acceptance. It's up to you to reject it if you do not find it suitable.

Sincerely yours,

Jack London

[1]Editor, *Times Magazine*.
[2]London sold the story to *Times Magazine* for $1,000. It was published December, 1906, in the first and only issue of *The Times*. London never received his money.

To the Editor,
Seattle Post-Intelligencer

Glen Ellen, Calif.
Aug. 2, 1906

Dear Sir:—

I have just noticed, in the *Post-Intelligencer* for Saturday, July 28, the discrediting of my story "The Unexpected," published in August *McClure's* —or rather, the discrediting of the statement made that the story had a foundation in fact.

If you will turn to your file of the *San Francisco Examiner* for October 14, 1900, you will find there an account of the double-murder committed by Michael Dennin, and of his hanging by Mrs. Nelson and her husband Hans. I quote from that article the following:

"The United States Court, before whom Mrs. Nelson and Hans laid the whole matter of the crime and execution of Michael Dennin, has decided that the hanging of the murderer was a judicial execution."

Of course, this was news from a newspaper, and the quotation I have just made is made from the columns of a newspaper. Now, if no hanging occurred at Latuya Bay in the winter of 1899, then the whole story as published in *The Examiner,* with many of the thumb-marks of verity, is all a newspaper lie written by newspaper men. In which case, it's up to you, not to lambaste me, as you have done, but to turn loose and lambaste your fellow-newspaper-men who are responsible for this.

Very truly yours,
Jack London

To Bailey Millard

Glen Ellen, Calif.
Aug. 13, 1906

Dear Bailey Millard:

In reply to yours of July 23. I haven't sold a story to *McClure's* for so long that I can't remember when. "Love of Life" and "The Unexpected," the only two stories of mine they have published in several years, have been held by them for several years. I especially remember selling "Love of Life" to them before I went off to the Japanese-Russian war.

I'll tell you what I'll do. If the rate is all right, I'll send you a crackerjack between now and the time I sail. *Collier's, Everybody's, Woman's Home Companion,* etc., etc., are paying me 15 cents a word now for my fiction. I have just sold a 40,000-word story [*Before Adam*] for 12½¢ a word for American serial rights. This was to *Everybody's.*

I never thought about naming the boat "Cosmopolitan." The only objection to that name is, that boats, like horses, should have names of one syllable. Good, sharp, strong names, that can never be mis-heard. There's only one thing that would make me change the name "Snark" to "Cosmopolitan," namely, the presentation of the *Snark* to me as an out-and-out present. She is costing me $10,000.00, and by golly, it would be worth $10,000.00 worth of advertising to the magazine. In return for such a present, not only would I put up with the five-syllable "Cosmopolitan," but "Magazine" to be appended. That would make eight syllables. Why, I'd even take subscriptions and advertisements for the magazine as I went along!

Joshing aside, I'm glad to hear that the sea-letters are coming in, and bully for Markham and the poem he is writing. And say, while we're on this sordid matter of dollars, I wouldn't sell my chance to go around on the *Snark* for less than $20,000.00. In which case I'd be able to build another *Snark* and start a year later.

Really, I don't see how you, with all your nature-love, can possibly stick it out in New York City. I'd commit suicide in three months, if I lived there.

Please let me know that you have received the photographs I sent you, as well as the first article.

Sincerely yours,
Jack London

208

To W. H. Cosgrave[1]

Glen Ellen, Calif.
Aug. 21, 1906

Dear Cosgrave:

In reply to yours of August 14. Well, I guess we'll just have to let it go at that, anyway. If I write up something that I think you'll want, I'll let you have a look at it. All the itinerary I have so far, I have already sent you, and that is not hard and fast. There is nothing hard and fast in this trip. You might want me to make a study of the Mikado, and I might not want to make a study of the Mikado. And suppose I did make a study of the Mikado, you might not want it after I had written it. And there's no telling where I'll be at any given time. I may stop at Hawaii for three weeks or three months, and I might head straight for Samoa, or I might be six months in getting to Samoa; in the meantime cruising around in other and undreamed-of islands.

Of course, as regards short stories and other fiction, shall be glad to let you have a whack at them now and again.

I am glad you fellows liked *Before Adam*. I've got a sneaking kindly place in my heart for that yarn, and I'm very curious to see how the public will take it.

What kind of a time did you have in Europe? And do I understand aright, that you got married? Or was it that I understood you *ought* to have got married?

Sincerely yours,
Jack London

[1]Of *Everybody's Magazine*.

To A. L. Babcock

Glen Ellen, Calif.
Sept. 21, 1906

Dear Sir:—

I am inclosing you herewith a photograph of myself. Please tell me if this double of mine looks anything like me. I was only in Montana once in my life, and that was last February, when I came through to the Pacific Coast on the Northern Pacific without getting off.

This double of mine is always getting me into trouble. Last year, while I was in Cuba, he was in Washington, entering into an engagement to deliver a lecture at the Congressional Library. Of course, he jumped the lecture, and I got the blame for being an "erratic genius," from the newspapers.

When I was East in January of this year, he was making love to a married woman with two children in Sacramento, in my own State. And now I have his love-troubles on my shoulders, too.

When I was in Boston last year, he was in San Francisco, my native city, entering into engagements with school-teachers to gather data for a volume on Education that he was writing.

When I was in California, he was lugging away armfuls of books from the Astor Library in New York, on the strength of his being I.

When I was in California, in 1900, he was in Alaska, and when I was in China, in 1904, I was meeting the people who had met him in Alaska in 1900.

These are only a few instances of this miserable double of mine. I don't know what to do with him. Up to date I have congratulated myself upon the fact that he had never raised money in my name. Yours is the first instance of his having done so, that I know. I should be deeply appreciative of any advice you could give me on how to put a stop to this impostor. I am scared to death, now that he has begun raising money, because he will find it so easy that he won't stop with the $50.00 he got from you.

I should also appreciate all data you can furnish me about this man, from what you know of him.

Regretting the occurrence,[1]
Believe me,

Sincerely yours,
Jack London

[1]On July 14, 1906, on the letterhead of Yellowstone National Bank of Billings, Montana, Babcock protested to London that his draft for $50.00 had been returned unpaid. He also enclosed some newspaper clippings with headings such as "Jack London, Famous for His Stories, Enroute to Park," "Noted Novelist Here." See following letter.

To A. L. BABCOCK

Glen Ellen, Calif.
Oct. 2, 1906

Dear sir:—

In reply to yours of Sept. 28. The registered letters which you sent to me under care of *The Cosmopolitan,* have also arrived.

Now, concerning this man Seffner.[1] He must have been dreaming, or else exaggerating profoundly. I have never been a newspaper-reporter in my life. I have been a war-correspondent. Also, after I had received recognition as a novelist, I occasionally did *special* work for the *San Francisco Examiner,* such as, for instance, interviewing Governor Taft on his return from the Philippines; or writing up some interesting case in criminology; or doing a special article on sociology. But this work was not done at the *Examiner* office. I have been in the *Examiner* office possibly half a dozen times in my life. If this Seffner was a reporter on the *Examiner,* he may have seen me, he may even have been introduced to me, but I do not remember him; but the one thing he never did do, was to work alongside of me. Then, here again, there is the very slightest chance for the foundation for his exaggeration, namely, when I did something special for the *Examiner,* say when I interviewed somebody, the *Examiner* always detailed a couple of reporters to go along and break ground for me. He might possibly have been one of those reporters. And there is still one other very slight chance for a foundation for his exaggeration, namely,—once, I wrote up a national "Schuetzenfest" for the *Examiner;* this man Seffner might have been at that "Schuetzenfest." I remember a dinner was given to the newspaper men at that time, and I attended the dinner. Possibly Seffner attended the dinner.

Certainly this man Seffner knew me so little as to be deceived by the impostor.

In June I was in Glen Ellen, California. I have not been out of California since the middle of February.

Where did Seffner say he had worked with me?

And now, to tell the truth, I don't know how to go about running this impostor down. I don't know which way to turn. I do not know what first step to take. I should be indeed grateful for any advice from you on the subject.

Is there not some system of the Banks for running such impostors down when they pass worthless paper on the strength of being somebody else who is well known?

Thanking you in advance for any advice you can give me,

Sincerely yours,
Jack London

[1] In Babcock's reply he explains that Seffner, a local newspaper man to whom the impostor introduced himself, believed the man to be Jack London.

To Bailey Millard

Glen Ellen, Calif.
Oct. 20, 1906

Dear Bailey Millard:—

Magazine editors are sharp and unprincipled business men. And I have never known one of them to fall down in living up to this reputation. It is because I think you will agree with me in the foregoing that I tell you that you ought to have jumped Vance of *The Woman's Home Companion,* before you jumped me. You might have found out, before you read me the riot act, you might have just inquired, you know; and saved the vials of your wrath for Vance's head. As it is, you've broken said vials on my head, and by the limitations of physiology, you will be forever unable to accumulate so large a supply of wrath on the same subject to empty on Vance's head. That's where you lose.

I contracted with *The Cosmopolitan* to give it the story of the boat-trip itself.

I contracted with *The Woman's Home Companion* to give it articles on the various phases of life I would see in the course of my travels. I quote the following from said contract:

> "These articles are to be upon home life and social conditions in a broad sense of the term (as outlined in Mr. Vance's letter to Mr. London, dated May 12, 1906), of the various countries visited by the said Mr. London. And upon these subjects he agrees that he will not write for any other periodical."

Having read the foregoing quotation, it's up to you to go out and have a scrap with Vance for making the announcement he did in the October number. I am inclosing you herewith a letter I am sending Mr. Vance by this mail.

It occurs to me, when I read the first lines of your letter, that possibly the November *Woman's Home Companion* has come out, and that you have read my letter therein, in which I give an idea of what I am going to do for *The Companion*. And that you base your complaint upon said letter. In which case, all I can tell you is, that you've got your feet in the trough.

Speaking now in connection with contents of foregoing paragraph, I want to know what in hell you think 35,000 words will cover! Do you think 35,000 words will cover a tithe of the boat-trip itself, much less all the things I expect to do and see in the course of seven years?

There is absolutely no conflict between these two contracts that I have signed. That's flat.

Magazine editors are all the same. I have made a practice of not noticing their misdeeds against me; but now that you jump me for the misdeeds of one of your brethren, namely Vance, why I'm going to jump back. Don't you think I've got a kick coming for the way you have advertised me as going around the world for *The Cosmopolitan?* Going around for *The Cosmopolitan*—hell! Everybody thinks *The Cosmopolitan* is building my boat for me, and paying all my expenses, and giving me a princely salary on top of it,—and this impression by your manner of advertising you have spread broadcast, all on the foundation of your miserable guaranteed 35,000 words that you have agreed to take from me. 35,000 words at 10¢ a word means $3500.00, and the initial cost of my boat is running past the $12,000.00 mark, to say nothing of expenses of running said boat.

Again, no one but a brute of a magazine editor would have quoted that portion of my private business letter to you wherein I said that "no writer of prominence" had ever gone sailing around the world, etc., etc. This has been quoted against me by every newspaper enemy I have, and nasty remarks about it are already coming back to me in my English clippings.

I have said that the boat is costing me past twelve thousand dollars. Those are the figures up to date, and they're still going up. San Francisco is mad.

Prices have climbed out of sight. I pay $200 for a bit of iron work on the boat, that should cost $40. Everything is in this order. The outlook is now, that I shall not sail before January. Weeks go by without a tap of work being done on the boat. Can't get the men. All my stuff is coming from the East because the earthquake destroyed the local market; and freight is congested. The Southern Pacific at the present moment is refusing further freight in the East, while its freight cars loaded with goods for San Francisco are piled up on sidings all over the State.

Now, the next time you go out looking for trouble, be sure you jump the right man.

And for God's sake, don't tell me that Hearst is "very much wrought up" about me and my affairs. I read different accounts of Hearst in the newspapers. He lets his lieutenants do his worrying for him. And surely he has no worry coming on $3500 worth of Jack London. But if Hearst is really wrought up, tell him that he owes me $200 that I can't collect from his lieutenants, and that I am very much wrought up over it.

Sincerely yours,
Jack London

To ARTHUR T. VANCE

Glen Ellen, Calif.
Oct. 20, 1906

Dear Mr. Vance:

Bailey Millard is throwing fits all around the shop, as near as I can make out because of the way you worded your announcement of what I was going to do for you in the November number. That announcement is so worded that it would lead every reader to believe that I was going to write the story of the boat voyage for you. Now, that is not in accordance with our contract. It is unfair to Millard—but that's his trouble. And it is unfair to me, because it has got me into trouble with Millard. And that is my trouble, and that is why I am writing you.

Sincerely yours,
Jack London

To STANLEY WATERLOO

Glen Ellen, Calif.
Oct. 20, 1906

Dear Stanley Waterloo:

I have just read in a San Francisco paper, what I take to be an Associated Press Dispatch. In this dispatch you are quoted as saying a number of uncomplimentary things about me, and about my story *Before Adam,* first installment of which has been published in *Everybody's Magazine.* I guess it will be better for me to give you the words that you are alleged to have said: Here they are:

"I am not personally acquainted with Mr. London. But I am convinced that he is a clever writer when he uses other people's brains. He has accomplished in six weeks what it took me fifteen years of deep study and investigation to produce. *The Story of Ab* was my pet, and I worked on it for fifteen long years. Jack London not only starts out with the same proposition I based my work on, but he employs in some instances practically the same language."

Of course, I am not sure that you said a word of the foregoing. If you did not, why of course you can tell me so, and we'll let it go at that. But if you did say the foregoing, I want to say a few things to you.

In the first place, don't you think that it is mighty rash to talk that way about a whole book, on the strength of having seen only the opening installment?

And don't you think that it is a case of getting your feet into the trough, when you arrogate to yourself the whole field of the primitive world for exploitation in fiction? At that rate, when one man describes a sunset, no other men are ever to describe sunsets; when one man writes a historical novel based on the Civil War, no other men are ever to write historical novels based on the Civil war; when one man writes a journey-to-other-worlds story, no other men are ever to write journey-to-other-worlds stories.

The only resemblance between your *Story of Ab* and my *Before Adam* is that both deal with the primitive world. If you preëmpt the primitive world, and would keep others out by virtue of priority of exploitation, then you'll have to get out yourself, for [H. G.] Wells was on that ground before you, and so was Andrew Lang. I might point out also that Kipling and a few score others, have exploited that same primitive world before you.

If you return then to the proposition of similarity of treatment, then let me tell you that your story and mine are as wide apart as the poles in treatment, point of view, grip, etc. Why, I wrote my story as a reply to yours, because yours was unscientific. You crammed the evolution of a thousand generations into one generation—something at which I revolted from the time I first read your story.

This last, in the foregoing paragraph, strikes me as very funny. Here I fall out with you because of your unscientific treatment of the primitive world, and therefore write a reply, and then have you say that in six weeks I took all I knew from you.

You say that you worked fifteen long years. How long do you think I have been working in my study of science? Read my *Kempton-Wace Letters,* my *Call of the Wild,* my *War of the Classes,* (especially these three)—read everything I've written, and you will find that I am firmly grounded—not

214

in Stanley Waterloo—but in the same scientific writers that Stanley Waterloo is grounded in.

If you did say the words quoted on the preceding page, then an investigation on your part is due me, and when you have finished, I believe you will agree with me that an apology is also due me—an apology as widely public as was your original statement.

Awaiting a reply at your early convenience,

Sincerely yours,
Jack London

To ARTHUR T. VANCE

Glen Ellen, Calif.
Oct. 23, 1906

Dear Mr. Vance:—

I take it all back. I have just seen the November *Cosmopolitan,* wherein Millard has claimed everything I am to do for you. It's tit for tat. You're a precious pair, the two of you, claiming everything in sight. I retire. You can scrap it out between yourselves.

Sincerely yours,
Jack London

To BAILEY MILLARD

Glen Ellen, Calif.
Oct. 23, 1906

Dear Bailey Millard:—

I have just seen your claims in the November *Cosmopolitan.* You're as bad as Vance. Find herewith copy of letter I have just sent Vance, which shows the position I take in the matter.

Sincerely yours,
Jack London

To GEORGE P. BRETT

Glen Ellen, Calif.
Oct. 31, 1906

Dear Mr. Brett:—

In reply to yours of Oct. 22. Many thanks for the check for $5000.00. I think I already wrote you how much I like the appearance of *White Fang.*

215

It is a splendid companion-book for *The Call of the Wild,* in every way. Somehow, I think I like it even a bit better than *The Call of the Wild.*

I shall be only too glad to take advantage of your offer to lend me a hand in getting serial publication for *The Iron Heel.* More of this, later.

Final proofs of the play [*Scorn of Women*] have been returned to the printer,—or, rather, a card has been dropped to the printers to the effect that the proofs are OK.

Am glad to hear that you think there will be no difficulty in arranging to use the design from *Everybody's* for the cover of *Before Adam.* The more I think of it, the more I am convinced that it will make a most effective cover.

Now, as regards my itinerary. It is very indefinite. I shall go wherever the mood strikes me to go, and stay as long as I want. So that it is impossible for me to outline such a trip. But this is the arrangement I have made. I shall always cable my next address to Mrs. Ninetta Eames, Glen Ellen, California. A telegram to her, any time, will bring to you my most recent address in case you want to cable to me. If you write to me, just mail the letter to Glen Ellen, from where it will be forwarded.

Monthly check—please forward it to Mrs. Ninetta Eames, Glen Ellen, California. She will handle all my business affairs while I am away, and she will have Power of Attorney so that she will be able to endorse the monthly check and apply to payment of bills, etc.

When we do get you out here on the ranch, the one thing that we would like would be to have you stay just as long as you want to—months. Then we could show you something of our country, and I'll wager a few things that you never saw when you were here before. Mrs. London and I now know this country like a book. We have been exploring it everywhere on horseback, and where there aren't trails, we make our own trails.

Another thing that I think would delight you when you come to visit us, would be the fact that willy-nilly you would be compelled to take half of each day by yourself, I never see any of my visitors until the afternoon. I do my day's work before I get sociable. And also, if you wanted a whole day to yourself, you could have it. There is only one thing that we require of our visitors—promptness at meals!

Sincerely yours,
Jack London

To Perrington Maxwell[1]

Glen Ellen, Calif.
Nov. 1, 1906

Dear Mr. Maxwell:

In reply to yours of Oct. 27. Yes, Bailey Millard did write to me upon the matter of "distributing my cabbages in several baskets," and I must confess that he got me rather hot in the collar. What of the size basket he had furnished me and thought would hold all my cabbages,—the crop of seven years in a 35,000-word basket!

I am inclosing you a copy of the letter I sent him in order to save myself the trouble of making the whole explanation over again to you.

Since writing this letter to Mr. Millard, I wrote him another calling the turn on him for doing just what Vance had done, namely, claiming everything in sight so far as my seven-years' voyage is concerned. *The Cosmopolitan* said that practically my total output would go to it, concerning lands, people, etc., that I would see.

The mental processes of editors are beyond me. I fought with Millard for more than 35,000 words, and couldn't get it out of him.

I am glad to learn that the balance of $26.70 due on "Just Meat" is being forwarded to me. I can less afford to lose that amount of money than *The Cosmopolitan* can afford to save it.

When are those letters to be opened on the voyage—when are they to be forwarded to me?

If *The Cosmopolitan* will pay for guards at $5.00 per shift, day and night, to prevent photographs being taken of the boat at the shipyard; why there won't be any photographs taken of the boat. But I'll be darned if I'll pay for the guards.

Will you please return the photographs I sent you, and which you say you are unable to use.

Sincerely yours,
Jack London

¹Of *Cosmopolitan Magazine.*

To Arthur T. Vance

Glen Ellen, Calif.
Nov. 11, 1906

Dear Mr. Vance:

In reply to yours of Oct. 29. Since writing my earlier letter, when I saw how Mr. Millard was trying to hog it all, I took all of my first letter back. Of course, what I referred to was not to my preliminary letter that you published, but to what you said on your announcement page. It was so worded as to lead people to believe that I was going to do the boat-trip for *The Woman's Home Companion;* but all is squared, because Millard made his announcement as though I was going to do all the lands and peoples for *The Cosmopolitan.*

There are fourteen men at work at the present moment on the boat. The labor conditions are so frightful here that I have taken the building of the boat out of the hands of the shipyard and am going on with it myself, paying a dollar a day extra to each man. Barring accidents, we shall certainly be away by the middle of December. There is the engine, however, that is somewhere in a freight car between New York and San Francisco. If there should be a smash-up on the railroad, and that engine should be destroyed, I should be delayed months, because it took months to build that engine, and would take months to build another like it.

Sincerely yours,

Jack London

To MARTIN E. JOHNSON[1]
[Telegram]

Glen Ellen, Calif.

Nov. 12, 1906

MARTIN E. JOHNSON,
INDEPENDENCE, KANSAS.
CAPACITY OF COOK ALSO DO TRICK AT WHEEL TWENTY FIVE DOLLARS PER MONTH CAN YOU COOK WHAT IS YOUR WEIGHT TELEGRAPH REPLY

JACK LONDON

[1]Martin Johnson, who later established fame as a big game hunter, adventurer and writer, signed on the *Snark* as a cook but could not cook.

To MARTIN E. JOHNSON

Glen Ellen, Calif.

Nov. 17, 1906

Dear Martin E. Johnson:

In reply to your letter. All right.

And now for some details of what you are in for. In the first place, the boat is 45 feet on the water-line, 57 feet over all, and 15 feet beam. Draws 7 feet of water. It is the strongest boat ever built in San Francisco. We could go through a typhoon that would wreck a 15,000-ton steamer. Primarily it is a sailing-vessel; but it has a 70-horse-power gasolene engine. This is to be used in going up the great rivers in the different countries we come to, in making harbors, and in getting out of ticklish positions. Otherwise we shall do nothing but sail. Practically, for every week that we are on the ocean, we will be a month in port. For instance, we expect that it will take us three weeks to sail from here to Hawaii, where we expect to remain three months—of course, in various portions of the Islands.

218

Now to the crew: All of us will be the crew. There is my wife, and myself. We will stand our watches and do our trick at the wheel. Incidentally, a large portion of our time will be used in working in order to pay the expenses of the trip. My wife's uncle, Mr. Eames, will act as co-navigator with me, and devote himself mainly to the engine, and the deck,—the sailorizing, in short. The fourth member is a young fellow of your own age, an all-round athlete from Stanford University.[1] He is shipped, in reality, as an after-thought, and largely to do that portion of the sailorizing that would otherwise fall to me. You see, I could not do my full share of the sailorizing and at the same time do the writing and keep the pot boiling. The fifth member of the crew is the cabin-boy, a Japanese boy[2] of your own age, who has been with us all summer. He is as brave as a lion, and as gentle as a lamb—in fact, he is the soul of gentleness. He is to serve as cabin-boy, serve the meals from the galley, set the table, keep things clean down below, and pay attention to the personal needs of myself and Mrs. London.

And now, comes the sixth member of the crew, which, it seems, will be yourself. The galley is next to the main cabin, in which we shall eat. Beside the cooking, you will merely have to pass the food to the cabin-boy. You can imagine it won't be much trotting around on such a small boat. For cold weather there will be a wood-stove in the galley but we shall be practically all the time in hot weather, and cooking will be done on Primus stoves which burn kerosene, and are odorless.

When it comes to doing the trick at the wheel, I want to explain that this will not be arduous as it may appear at first. It is our intention, by sail-trimming, to make the boat largely sail herself, without steering. Next, in bad weather, there will be no steering for then we will be hove-to. But watches, or rather lookouts, must be kept at night, when we are sailing. Suppose we divide day and night into twelve hours each. There are six of us all-told on the boat. Each will take a two-hour turn on deck.

Of course, when it comes to moments of danger, or to doing something ticklish, or to making port, etc., the whole six of us will then become the crew. I will not be a writer, but a sailor. The same with my wife. The cabin-boy will be a sailor, and so also, the cook. In fact, when it's case for all hands, all hands it will be.

It must be thoroughly understood that when we are on duty, the relations existing will be that of Captain and crew. Off duty, is another matter. We can then be friends, or enemies, or not speak when we pass by! But the point is, on duty is on duty. You've had enough experience knocking about to know what that means.

From the present outlook, we shall sail out of San Francisco Bay on Dec. 15. So you see, if you accompany us, you will miss your Christmas at home. I should like to have you arrive not later than December 10. There must be a little breaking-in before we get started—trial-trips, etc.

Please let me have an immediate reply telling me how the proposition strikes you. I shall also want you to send me a telegram the day you start.

219

Send the telegram to 490 27th street, Oakland, California. I shall be at that address after December 1. Up to December 1, I shall be at the present address, which is Glen Ellen.

As regards the cooking, we expect plain cooking,—in fact, cooking with a minimum of grease. We shall use oil instead of lard and such things. Now, don't think I am some sort of a food-crank, for I am not. I'll eat anything in sight, when I have to; but when I don't have to, why then I have my preferences.

Oh, if you have a bad temper, don't come, for it'd be the only one on the boat! Incidentally, if you like boxing, I may tell you that all of us box, and we'll have the gloves along. You'll have the advantage of us on reach. Also, I may say that we should all of us have lots of good times together, swimming, fishing, adventuring, doing a thousand-and-one things. On the other hand, when we are in some ports, my wife and I will be making excursions into the interior, or will be entertained ashore, so that the crew will be thrown upon its own resources as far as entertainment is concerned. You can depend upon me giving good opportunities for shore-liberty, to all members of the crew.

As regards photographs, I am glad to hear that you are 'way up in the matter. Mr. Stolz (the Stanford man), has been making all preparations for doing my developing and printing, etc. But you can certainly lend him a hand and I know give him much good advice. Since you are a photographer, undoubtedly you will want to bring your camera along. That's all right, bring it. And ashore you can take what photographs you want. But you must not take photographs of ourselves and boat, and use said photographs in magazines, etc., without my first seeing them and giving permission for said use. You see, I have contracts with certain magazines and it would scarcely be the fair thing for me to allow those contracts to be violated by those who go along with me. You can understand the situation, I am sure, without my going into further details in the matter.

Now, about clothes. Remember that the boat is small, also that we are going into hot weather and shall be in hot weather all the time. So bring a small outfit, and one for use in warm weather.

Give my regards to your good father, and my thanks for the kind letter he inclosed with yours.

Sincerely yours,
Jack London

---

[1]Bert Stolz, Stanford student who later became a Rhodes Scholar.
[2]Manyoungi didn't go on the *Snark,* as it turned out.

To GEORGE P. BRETT

Glen Ellen, Calif.
Nov. 17, 1906

Dear Mr. Brett:

Does this[1] belong to you? I am getting puzzled. This is the second one of these things I have received, and I have never received them before. Please let me know. You see, I have a double who is continually going around over the country getting me into all kinds of trouble from borrowing books from libraries on my name, and agreeing to give lectures which he never gives, to passing worthless checks in my name, and also to making love to other men's wives. He keeps cropping up everywhere, and in so many strange guises that I never know what his next stunt will be. For all I know, he may now be copyrighting things in my name.

Sincerely yours,
Jack London

---

[1] A copyright notice that London could not account for. Brett said, "The card which you enclose refers only to the separate publications in *Everybody's Magazine* which is copyrighted in your name as each installment appears."

To ARTHUR T. VANCE

Glen Ellen, Calif.
Nov. 18, 1906

Dear Mr. Vance:

In reply to yours of Nov. 12. First of all, to get rid of this matter of bad faith with *The Cosmopolitan,* I am inclosing you a copy of a letter which I am sending them this mail, which same please return. For two cents I'd throw up the whole proposition and let everybody sue my mortgaged ranch for what they could get. I can make more money writing fiction, anyway. And to have behaved as I have, with the highest honor, and keenest integrity, and then to be up against a bunch of squalling editors, makes me sick. I haven't got it in for you as much as I have for *The Cosmopolitan.* Your big sin, and the one you are guilty of without discussion, was in the wording of your announcement, from which I quote the following:

"Jack London is going to take you on his spectacular trip around the world in a little boat he calls the *Snark*—in other words, he is going to tell you in a series of important articles, about the trip he and Mrs. London are about to take."

Now, there's no discussing it, in those words just quoted you certainly gobbled precisely what was contained in my contract with *The Cosmopolitan.*

In short, I've been handled pretty nastily. But as I said before, I haven't it in for you as badly as I have for *The Cosmopolitan.* They have gone the limit.

When I, in my letter to *The Cosmopolitan,* which I inclose herewith, mention their blatting my "bad faith" about New York, it is not a betrayal of your letter to me which you call confidential. The charges of "bad faith," blatted by *The Cosmopolitan* people around New York City, are already in print in the scandal weeklies of the Pacific Coast.

Just put yourself in my place, and imagine how you'd feel about the whole thing. I have already replied to Mr. Carruth's letter of Nov. 5.

If it weren't too late, I'd be glad if you could buy out *The Cosmopolitan* and take the whole works yourself. But it IS too late, worse luck, for the Christmas number of *The Cosmopolitan* is already out.

I don't know what I can do in this matter of arranging a simultaneous publication of my first two articles from Hawaii. I know that *The Cosmopolitan* would not give you any courtesy in the matter whatever. It's darned easy to shake responsibility on the publication where a horde of editors is coming and going all the time.

Better let me cool down a bit, and get out on the ocean, and then some light on the situation may come to me.

In spite of your big sin mentioned previously, the *Cosmopolitan* has been so superlatively mean that I am sure of one thing and that is that I will do my very best work for *The Woman's Home Companion.*

I'll tell you what I will do. I'll write *The Cosmopolitan* letter and hold it as you suggest; and whether your April or May number will be the one to publish my first letter, I'll give you a month's start of *The Cosmopolitan.*

Sincerely yours,

Jack London

To EDITOR, *Cosmopolitan Magazine*

Glen Ellen, Calif.
Nov. 18, 1906

Dear Sir:

First of all, I want to know who *is* the editor of *The Cosmopolitan.* I do not know with whom I am dealing, and I suppose that's the reason why my letters are not answered. If I can only get hold of the real editor of *The Cosmopolitan,* why then I shall have some hope of straightening matters up.

It would be much fairer, and certainly more logical and trouble-saving, to answer my letters instead of blatting around New York City charging bad faith on my part.

Now as regards this bad faith. I contracted to do the boat-trip for *The Cosmopolitan.* There can be no misunderstanding as to what constitutes the narrative of the boat-trip, because, in my letter to Bailey Millard, dated Feb. 18, 1906, I distinctly say the following: "I shall be gone a long time on this trip. No magazine can print all I have to write about it. On the other hand, it cannot be imagined that I shall write 50,000 words on the whole seven years, and then quit. As it is, the subject-matter of the trip divides itself up so that there will be no clash whatever between any several different publications that may be handling my stuff. For instance: here are three big, natural, unconflicting divisions: News, industrial and political articles on the various countries for newspapers; fiction; and, finally, the trip itself."

The foregoing was thoroughly understood before the contract was entered into. *The Cosmopolitan* was to get the boat-trip itself.

All the foregoing has been fully elaborated in my letter of Oct. 20, to Bailey Millard (unanswered). In my letter of Oct. 23 to Bailey Millard (unanswered). And in my letter of Nov. 1, to Perrington Maxwell (unanswered).

Now to other matters. When are those letters, to be opened on the voyage, —when are they to be forwarded to me? I've got to have them soon, or not at all. The outlook is now that I shall sail about Dec. 15.

Now to photographs. On April 3, I wrote Bailey Millard. If you will refer to that letter, you will see what I have to say about photographs. I have received no answer to that. In my letter of May 16, I asked again for an answer on this matter of photographs, and to date I have still received no answer. In the meantime, I have spent several hundred dollars for cameras, lenses, films, developing materials, etc. Now, I want definitely settled what the remuneration for these photographs is to be. I want to know whether it will be worth my while to go in for photographs or not. And since there are so many editors on *The Cosmopolitan,* with no one apparently responsible, I simply MUST have this matter definitely settled NOW. Furthermore, I am being pushed for money. Reference to previous letters will show how much more my boat is costing me than I expected. I am mortgaging my ranch in order to pay for the boat. Wherefore, it's up to you to make an advance now, of $250.00, upon the photographs that I am to furnish you, to help me pay, now, for the preliminary cost of cameras, lenses, films, developing materials, etc.

And while we are about it, there is a claim of mine against you for $26.70, balance due on my story "Just Meat." In a letter from Perrington Maxwell dated Oct. 27, I am told that this sum is being forwarded to me. It hasn't arrived.

Sincerely yours,
Jack London

To EDITOR, *Cosmopolitan Magazine*

Glen Ellen, Calif.
Nov. 19, 1906

Dear sir:—

I have just received from you, along with a rejection-slip, two poems, one

"An Epitaph," and the other "A Dirge," which have evidently been submitted to you over my name. Now, I didn't write these poems; neither did I submit them; but I'm darned anxious to get a line on the person who did. Any information will be gratefully received.

Sincerely yours,
Jack London

To *The Appeal to Reason*[1]

Glen Ellen, Calif.
Nov. 22, 1906

Dear Comrades:

In reply to your telegram of Nov. 20; first of all, I don't know whether or not I can succeed in serializing *The Iron Heel* in some one of the big magazines. If I can do so, and get $10,000 for it, why I'll certainly do so. I am mortgaging my ranch in order to build my boat, and such a deal would help me out. Also, some very excellent socialist propaganda will be thereby spread.

On the other hand, there is a large likelihood that the stuff will be too strong for any of the conventional magazines, in which case I shall be only too glad to have *The Appeal to Reason* serialize it. But in the meantime, let me try to dispose of it to two or three of the big magazines. And in the meantime, let me know (in case you should like *The Iron Heel*) what arrangements you can make.

I'll tell you what I'll do. And this will be in the meantime. As soon as *The Iron Heel* is finished, I'll send you one copy of the MS to read. It will be a little less than 100,000 words in length, and I am on the home-stretch now.

Yours for the Revolution,
Jack London

[1]A free-lance socialistic periodical published at Girard, Kansas, under the editorship of J. A. Wayland.

To EDITOR, *Cosmopolitan Magazine*

Glen Ellen, Calif.
Nov. 24, 1906

Dear sir:—

I have just seen the Christmas number of *The Cosmopolitan*. You got the article out beautifully, and you are featuring it splendidly, for which two things you have my congratulations and thanks. But on top of that, I have a howl coming—the regular long wolf-howl. I don't like the way you have taken liberties with my copy. Any tyro can cut a manuscript and feel that he is co-creator with the author. But it's hell on the author. Not one man in a million, including office-boys, is to be found in the magazine offices, who is able properly to revise by elimination the work of a professional author. And the men in your office have certainly played ducks and drakes with the exposition in the first half of my first boat-article.

The men in your office are certainly most unfit for such work. For instance, I have just finished reading the proofs of "Just Meat." In one place I have my burglar say, "I put the kibosh on his time." Some man in your office changed this to, "I put a crimp in his time." In the first place, "crimp" is incorrect in such usage. In the second place, there is nothing whatever in the connotation of "kibosh" that would prevent its appearing in the pages of your magazine. "Kibosh" is not vulgar, it is not obscene. Such an action is wholly unwarranted and gratuitously officious. Did this co-creator of mine, in your office, think that he knew what he was doing when he made such a ridiculous substitution? And if he does think so, why in the dickens doesn't he get in and do the whole thing himself?

In our contract, I take your right of revision to consist in rejecting an article as a whole, or in eliminating objectionable phrases. Now I have no objection to that. I have no objection to your truckling to Mrs. Grundy, when, for instance, you cut out swear-words or change "go to hell" to "go to blazes." That's the mere shell. In that sort of revision you can have full swing; but that is a different matter from cutting the heart out of my work, such as you did in my first boat-article. You made my exposition look like thirty cents.

I WEAVE my stuff; you can cut out a whole piece of it, but you can't cut out parts of it, and leave mutilated parts behind. Just think of it. Wading into my exposition and cutting out premises or proofs or anything else just to suit your length of an article, or the space, rather, that you see fit to give such article. Who in the dickens are you, any of you, to think that you can better my work! Don't you see my point? If the whole woven thing—event, narrative, description—is not suitable for your magazine, why cut it out—cut out the whole thing. I don't care. But I refuse to contemplate for one moment that there is any man in your office, or in the office of any magazine, capable of bettering my art, or the art of any other first-class professional writer.

Now I want to give warning right here: I won't stand for it. Before I'll stand for it, I'll throw over the whole proposition. If you dare to do it with my succeeding articles (and I'll know shortly after the article in which you do it is published) I'll not send you another line. By golly, you've got to give me a square deal in this matter. Do you think for one moment that I'll write my heart (my skilled, professional heart, if you please) into my work to have you fellows slaughtering it to suit your journalistic tastes? Either I'm going to write this set of articles, or you're going to write it, for know right here that I refuse definitely and flatly, to collaborate with you or with anyone in your office.

In order that this letter may not go astray, I am sending copies to each of the three men[1] who, in my present hypothesis, I think may possibly be editor of *The Cosmopolitan*.

And I want, at your earliest convenience, an assurance that the sort of mutilation that I am complaining about, will not occur again.

Sincerely yours,
Jack London

[1]Bailey Millard, Perrington Maxwell, John Brisben Walker.

To George P. Brett

Glen Ellen, Calif.
Dec. 1, 1906

Dear Mr. Brett:

In reply to yours of Nov. 22. This is the last letter I send from Glen Ellen. We have said Good Bye to the ranch and are now packed up and just on the eve of starting for Oakland.

Yes, I saw the many advertisements with which you are shoving along *White Fang*. It does my heart good to see them, for you've no idea how much I am pinning my financial faith and hopes upon that book. In fact, the unexpected and exceeding expense of building the boat has caught me hard. And I sail away from California in great trepidation financially. To cap it all, I am squabbling with *The Cosmopolitan* people, who are to publish the boat-voyage, and who have treated me scurvily, and the outlook is now (if they don't come to time), that I shall throw the whole proposition overboard. Of course, this means an immediate loss of money in the first months of the voyage, during which time things will be just nip and tuck with me. Wherefore, I want to throw myself upon your good nature and ask that you inform me by mail if the sales of *White Fang* happen to pick up. You see, I am rather desperate, and the prompt receipt of good news like that will mean a great deal to my peace of mind.

Mrs. Ninetta Eames, of Glen Ellen, will be left with Power of Attorney for me. She will transact most of my business, etc. Now, in case she should need money suddenly, I'd like to have the assurance that she could call upon you for an advance up to $1,000.00, at any time.

You see, this request has much behind it. There are various families and people that I am taking care of, and I have arranged it that said families and people can call upon Mrs. Eames for extra money in case they should be in trouble and need it. Since I have arranged the sums they may call for, varying from $100 to several hundred dollars, if they should suddenly and simultaneously need those sums, and if Mrs. Eames should have in her possession practically no balance belonging to me, why there'd be hard times. If, on the other hand, Mrs. Eames in such a case of need or in any other emergency, should be able to call upon you for the advance requested, it will make me feel safer out on the ocean.

I like exceedingly the way you've brought out the play *Scorn of Women*. It's a pretty little solid volume, and it makes me glad when I look at it.

I shall barely have time to receive a reply from you before I sail—that is, barring accidents in the last work on the boat. That miserable engine has not yet arrived, and everything is now hanging upon it. But we expect it from moment to moment.

Sincerely yours,
Jack London

To PERRINGTON MAXWELL

Glen Ellen, Calif.
Dec. 1, 1906

Dear Mr. Maxwell:

Your feeble, evasive letter of Nov. 26, at hand. I see that you have tried the ancient ruse of invading the enemy's camp in order to repel attack. But you don't do it cleverly. The situation being that a number of my important letters have not been answered by you, you reply by charging me with not having answered your letters. You mention two of your previous evasive, equivocal letters as being unanswered, and demand why I haven't answered them. Yet all you can think of that you wanted answered in them, was my sailing-date. I have given that to you—some time ago, as January 1; and a little later, as about December 15. I can say now that it will be somewhere between those two dates.

And now to business. Either we're going to work together, or we're not. Frankly, I'd like to call the whole thing off. Nothing would please me better; for you, or, rather all of you, have disgusted me. I have never been treated so in my life. If you can't see your way to calling it off, then it's up to you to find some basis for us to work upon. And if you don't find the right basis, it will be called off willy nilly.

We have a choice of two bases; first, a fair and square basis; secondly, a technical basis. If you choose the latter, on your head be it. I'll neither give nor take quarter. And if you ever get called onto the carpet for it, hell will freeze over before you succeed in explaining all things away.

We will just do a little back history, in order to feel our way up to a fair and square basis. In your letter to me of Oct. 27, you speak of writing me in the "name of justice, fair play and good business." In my letter in reply, dated Nov. 18, which same please refer to, I gave you excerpts from correspondence and contract, showing conclusively that there has been no bad faith on my part whatever—all of which you ignore in your letter I am now answering, and airily reply, "I think none of us need worry any more about that matter." That's the way you stall, when it's up to you and your whole bunch to show whether you possess "justice, fair play, or good business."

Now, take it from me straight from the shoulder: You can't charge me, around New York City, with bad faith, and when I have shown you conclusively that your charge is without foundation and absolutely false, airily reply, "I think none of us need worry any more about that matter." You've got to take back this charge of bad faith, or you'll find a pretty big wad of worry still coming to you.

In short, you and your office, so far as I am concerned, will have to undergo a radical reform, and undergo it quick. I have given you your choice of two bases. If you want to be technical, I'll deal with you on a technical basis. I'll give you 35,000 words, and drop you flat. If you don't want a technical basis, but a fair and square basis, if you want more than 35,000 words, it's up to you to decide now. If you decide that you do want more, you can forward me by return mail a contract for a second 35,000 words with a stipulation in that contract, that in neither my first 35,000 words, nor my second 35,000 words, will you play the pranks of revision that you did play in my first boat-article published in the Christmas number. You have my letter on this point. Refresh yourself on it.

You've treated me scurvily, and are treating me scurvily. This is the first squabble I ever had in my life with a magazine. I hope it will be my last, but I'll make it hum while it lasts.

Your proposition to me, to render an itemized bill for my photography expenses is a hair-raiser. Do you realize, my dear Mr. Maxwell, that that $250.00 is not an expense item that is being stood by the *Cosmopolitan Magazine?* That is an advance payment on photographs that I am to send *The Cosmopolitan.* I am standing the expense, and don't think for one moment that I am any kind of a tu'penny dub to furnish itemized accounts to you of my own expenses.

Now, send that $250.00 right along; and with it, send me definite and satisfactory scale of payments for photographs—this latter I have been trying to get from your bungling, slipshod office for many weary months. Nor have you shown yourself a bit less slipshod in the matter than the rest of your bunch. You ignored flatly that particular, emphasized point in my letter. This is the last time that I shall ask for the scale of payment for photographs.

You want to know when my next article will be sent to you. There are a few things that I want to know first, and I've got to know them in a satisfactory way, or else you never will know when that second article will be sent to you; you'll think the Day of Judgment is a whole lot quicker in coming, than that second article.

Reply, and reply as quickly as your self-respect will let you, and give me the basis that we are to go on. War or peace. Take it or leave it. It's up to you. Everything must be settled *now.* And for fear that you may not know what I want settled, I'll give you a resumé. I want settled, first of all, what basis we're to go on. Fair and square basis, or technical basis. Next, I want assurance that my copy will not be pawed over and revised by your office. I want $250.00 advanced on photography expenses. I want a satisfactory scale of payments for my photographs. I want a contract for 35,000 additional words. If you don't send said contract, that places us irretrievably upon the technical basis, which means that you either get precisely 35,000 words and be dropped, or that you won't get any words at all. And finally, I want a retraction from you of your charges of bad faith.

I want an answer. I want that answer quick. I want it to the point, and I want it to every point. Selah.[1]

Jack London

[1]Sometime later London sent a copy of this letter to Vance with the following statement: "Dear Mr. Vance:—This was my letter that fetched them. . . ."

To B. W. BABCOCK

Glen Ellen, Calif.
Dec. 3, 1906

Dear Mr. Babcock:

In reply to yours of Nov. 27.[1] First of all, I want to tell you about two letters I sent off, and the answers received. When I read in the papers the charges made by Mr. Waterloo and Mr. Bandlow (I don't know how his name is spelled, but he is one of the officers of the Chicago Press Club and is the man who sent the frenzied telegram to *Everybody's Magazine,* calling me a "clumsy kleptomaniac"), I wrote to both men giving them a few salient facts and asking for an apology. Mr. Bandlow wrote me a lengthy epistle, which, epitomized, was to the effect that he was going to give me a fair trial, but that he was quite certain in advance that I was guilty. Mr. Waterloo's reply was not to the point, was quite vague—and, in fact, was a confession that he did not know what he *had* said when making the original charge of plagiarism. In fact, I received two very unsatisfactory replies to my straightforward letters.

This charge of plagiarism is so absurd that personally I do not care to have anything more to say about it. However, since you request it, I will say this much: I wrote *Before Adam* as a reply to the *Story of Ab,* because I considered the latter unscientific. Mr. Waterloo crowded the social evolution of a thousand generations into one generation. The whole point of *Before Adam,* on the other hand, is to demonstrate the excessive slowness of social evolution in the primitive world. Also, I tried to reproduce the primitive world in an artistic form, which same Mr. Waterloo did not do. His whole story is full of meat, and interesting; yet, through the use of an awkward form, Mr. Waterloo failed to create the convincing illusion that is proper to any work of fiction.

When a man has handled the primitive world unscientifically and awkwardly, are all other men to be forever debarred from handling the same subject? I think not so. At any rate, I refuse to be debarred, let Mr. Waterloo and Mr. Bandlow splutter and protest as they will.

I never remember what I have written, when it is off my hands. So I do not know what you mean when you speak of the initial incident of Ab that I have been charged with plagiarizing in my third chapter. I don't know what's in that chapter, and I have not a copy of the MS at hand from which to find out. I imagine, however, that the "plagiarized" incident must be the clinging of the child to its mother when the mother climbs up a tree. If such be plagiarism, one cannot avoid it when dealing with so meager a subject as primitive man. Now, in the modern world, a woman with a baby threatened by some danger, has a thousand ways of escaping. She may call a policeman, she may jump into a canoe and paddle away, she may catch a street-car, she may run into the kitchen and slam and lock the door, she may draw a revolver and shoot the danger that threatens her, or she may leave it to the nursemaid to save the baby. In fact, the ways in which a modern woman with a baby can escape danger, are endless; but in the primitive world there is only one way for a woman with a baby to escape danger. She can climb a tree. She has to use her hands in climbing a tree. There remains only one way for the baby to co-operate in being saved, namely, to hold on to the mother while the mother climbs.

You ask me for my views in general upon plagiarism. I think the whole subject of plagiarism is absurd. I can conceive of no more laughable spectacle than that of a human standing up on his hind legs and yowling plagiarism. No man with a puny imagination can continue plagiarizing and make a success of it. No man with a vivid imagination, on the other hand, needs to plagiarize.

I feel like being speculative for a moment. Let us suppose a bona fide case of plagiarism. Here's a man who has written something and written it well. Another man plagiarizes from him. Considering that the original is written well, how under the sun is the plagiarism going to get anywhere. Suppose, however, the plagiarism is so eminently great that it outshines the original. Who has any complaint coming? The world is better off for the bigger creation. The original creation stands where it was, and it's ridiculous for the original creator to yowl because somebody else has made a bigger mudpie. I have a vision of the first child in an alley making a mud pie, then announcing to the rest of the children in the alley "Thou shalt not make bigger mud pies." On the other hand, suppose the original mud pie to be a failure, to be a mess. Are all other children to be denied the right of attempting to make mud pies? Oh, I don't know—the whole subject is so ridiculous that I can't help being anything else but non-sensible when I think of it. That's all plagiarism is—nonsense. The real question of plagiarism is not Did he do it the way I did it—but is, Did he do it better than I did it? And if he did do it better, why, take off your hat to him.

Somewhere in Egyptian history there is a story of a queen who fell in love with an incorruptible young Hebrew who refused to be seduced by her during her husband's absence. This queen promptly tore her clothes and called the guard. She reminds me very much of the type of man who cries Plagiarism.

Sincerely yours,

Jack London

[1]Babcock, on *New York Times'* letterhead, wrote to London an inquiry concerning Waterloo's charge of plagiarism of *The Story of Ab* and said: "I should be pleased to have you write me at such length as may be necessary your views on this matter, on plagiarism and charges of plagiarism in general."

To Roscoe Eames

Oakland, Calif.

Dec. 11, 1906

Dear Roscoe:

In reply to yours of Dec. 10. The *Sophie Sutherland* was not quite so large as a man-o'-war, nor quite so small as the *Snark*. She had two captains on board. The owner was Captain Sutherland. He was a little shriveled shrimp of a fellow. He didn't know anything about navigation. And he performed no duties whatever on the vessel. Nevertheless, he was Captain of the *Sophie Sutherland*. The other Captain on board was Captain Scott. Scott's rating, in spite of his being a Captain, was that of Sailing-Master. It did not seem to worry him at all,—his rating, I mean. All the yachts sailing on the bay have for captains their owners. If I am not to be Captain of my own boat, what the devil am I to be?—only the "angel?" In fact, your proposition strikes me as a very peculiar one. I had given the matter no thought whatever, and when you first mentioned it to me in Glen Ellen, on the spur of the moment I suggested that you would be Sailing-Master. You would be known everywhere as Captain Eames, and would be called Captain Eames socially, and would be introduced by me as Captain Eames; but nevertheless, it is my firm and abiding intention to be myself Captain of the *Snark*.

I shall not mention myself as Captain of the *Snark* in my articles. I shall not mention you as Captain Eames in my articles. I shall not mention Charmian as Mrs. London in my articles; and the only formal titles by which I shall designate anybody in my articles will be ridiculous and undignified titles. I am a little too old to revolutionize my whole being and suddenly become formal. I put up with no more formalities than I have to. At the present moment I have no recollection of how I referred to you in my *Cosmopolitan* article, otherwise than that I called you Roscoe as I called Charmian, Charmian. I shall continue so to call you, unless you ask to be left out, in which case I shall be courteous enough to leave you out, though thereby I shall sacrifice some of the material for writing whereby I hope to pay expenses. My regret is that this feeling of yours upon the subject has come up at so late a date. In fact, this feeling of yours upon the subject is not only disconcerting, but perturbing. It cannot but make me fear for the future. When, for instance, there has been absolutely no constraint whatever on my part in introducing you to my friends; and when, because of your private feelings over the formality of designation, you imagine there is constraint on my part in introducing you to my friends; why, I find myself up against the old, eternal proposition of having people interpret my acts by projection of their own psychological processes. This is dangerous. It always is dangerous. I have seen more trouble caused by that than by anything else in the world. It's the one thing a man cannot guard against. How is a man to know what private feelings a friend is fomenting, and be able to guard his actions so as not to hurt those private feelings? It's the proposition at which I always throw my hands down. When people inflict me with projections of their own psychological processes, and charge me therefore with doing things I never dreamed of doing, I quit. Now, with you, it's different. I do not quit, I merely tell you that whatever constraint you have seen on the part of my introducing you to my friends has been a reflection from some inner vision of your own.

Now, as regards facetious remarks dropped by Charmian as to her being Mate,—all I can say is, that they were facetious. She is MY Mate, but she is not Mate of the *Snark,* and never will be.

The lines with which you refer to that remark of Charmian's, in connection with the rest of the letter, would seem to lead [me] to believe that you think "Mate" is a higher formal designation than is Sailing-Master. In which case, why, take Mate for your formal designation—that is, if you want it. Personally, I always thought that Sailing Master was higher than Mate, but I'm rather shaky on such things.

I hope you can see your way to the situation. It is rather too ridiculous for me to be anything else than Captain of my own boat. And that not from any standpoint of formality, but because I couldn't avoid being it. It just happens to be a custom, Roscoe, that's all. You refer to my calling you my co-navigator, as being a nondescript office. I called you my co-navigator out of tactful consideration. I made you my equal; did not refer to myself as Captain (never have referred to myself as Captain). I spoke of you and me navigating the *Snark* around the world. We were to be co-navigators. I thought that that was the sweetest and easiest way to arrange it. Your letter, however, has convinced me of my mistake.

Your letter has impressed upon me the necessity for formality. It never entered my head that there was going to be any trouble about who was Captain at all. "Co-navigator" satisfied me. Your letter shows me that co-navigator does not satisfy you—that there must be a Captain. Therefore, I have to be Captain of the *Snark.*

Affectionately yours,
Jack London

To THOS. MASSON[1]

Oakland, Calif.
Dec. 15, 1906

Dear sir:

Your request that I should tell you about the book I have read during the last year which has instructed me most, entertained me most, and inspired me most, rather took me aback. For some little time I could not think of which book had done all these things to me in the superlative degree. Then I remembered all I had been reading about myself in the newspapers, and the book flashed into my mind at once. It is Stanley Waterloo's *Story of Ab*. That it instructed me as no other book has done, I have Stanley Waterloo's own word. For he has stated that I got from his *Story of Ab* in six weeks what it had taken him fifteen years to get.

The entertainment the *Story of Ab* afforded me goes with the saying. It was, honestly, the most entertaining book.

The inspiration the *Story of Ab* afforded me goes with the advertising. I read in all the papers that it so inspired me and so filled me with desire that others might know of it and receive the same pleasure and profit, that I lifted its content and put it into my *Before Adam*.

Yes, without a doubt the *Story of Ab* is the book of the year that most instructed me, most entertained me, most inspired me and most profited me.

Sincerely yours,
Jack London

P.S. Oh,—I made a mistake. I have just recollected that it was six years ago that I read the *Story of Ab*.

---

[1]Masson was literary editor of *Life* at this time.

To EDITOR, *The Times Magazine*

Oakland, Calif.
Dec. 15, 1906

Dear sir:—

I have never been so puzzled in my life. I can't understand the treatment I have received and am receiving at your hands. In the latter part of July, this year, Mr. James Randolph Walker, representing your magazine, requested me by telegraph to let your magazine have a short story of mine. You will observe that I did not solicit *The Times Magazine*. I had never heard of *The Times Magazine*. I was solicited for my short story, by *The Times Magazine*.

On August 7, in response to the request mentioned in preceding paragraph, I sent to *The Times Magazine* my story "The Wit of Porportuk." After some telegraphing, *The Times Magazine* agreed to pay me $1,000.00 for the story. This agreement was by telegram dated Aug. 20. On Aug. 21, I accepted the offer by telegram.

From that time on, your Magazine became dumb. Three different times I wrote your Magazine, asking payment for my story. I wrote you on October 11, on Oct. 30, and on Nov. 16. These letters of mine were ignored.

On Dec. 5, I telegraphed your Magazine as follows: "AM DEPARTING PLEASE MAIL IMMEDIATELY THOUSAND DOLLARS FOR MY STORY ALSO REPLY BY TELEGRAM."

I received no reply to the foregoing telegram. On Dec. 8, I telegraphed as follows: "HAVE NOT RECEIVED REPLY TO MY TELEGRAM DATED DECEMBER FIFTH."

I received no reply to that telegram. On Dec. 11, I telegraphed as follows: "WILL YOU DO ME THE COURTESY TO REPLY TO MY PREVIOUS TELEGRAMS?"

Nor did I receive a reply to that telegram. In fact, from the moment you arranged to take my story I ceased to exist so far as any recognition of me by you is concerned.

After reading the foregoing, can you wonder that I am puzzled? I see *The Times Magazine* on the news stands; I see its advertisements; it receives my telegrams, (I know this because they are not returned to me), and I cannot but conclude that *The Times Magazine* is still in existence. What puzzles me is why it ignores my existence. It solicited me for a story. I furnished the story; and now, when in pressing need of the money, *The Times Magazine* will not even do me the courtesy of replying to my letters and telegrams.

I am to sail in a very few days now, and as I have stated in my previous letters to you, I am terribly pressed for money. I can assure you that your check for $1,000.00 would be deeply appreciated. And I appeal to your manhood for a prompt reply to this letter. A telegram from you, on receipt of this letter, announcing that you are forwarding check at once by mail, would ease me quite a deal in the present financial straits that are pinching me.[1]

Very truly yours,
Jack London

[1]London never received payment.

To GEORGE P. BRETT

Oakland, Calif.
Dec. 15, 1906

Dear Mr. Brett:

In reply to yours of December 7. There's no use in my telling you how keenly I appreciate your sending me that check for one thousand dollars. Honestly, I wasn't going to ask you for any further advance, so your check landed like a bombshell of joy. Its coming was especially grateful because of the fact that it had finally been made clear to me that I had lost just a thousand dollars with *The Times Magazine* of New York City. *The Times Magazine* last summer bought from me one of my best long-short-stories, and was to pay me $1,000.00 for it. The initial number of *The Times Magazine* was the December number. In it was published my story. Ever since the middle of last summer I have been trying to collect the $1,000.00, and up to date have failed to receive even a reply from them. Telegrams and letters I have wasted on them. No sooner did they get the story than they ceased to exist so far as I am concerned. Up to date I have sent them five letters and three telegrams. To none of which have I received a reply. Can you give me any information about this magazine? Has it collapsed? gone bankrupt? Its address is 500 Fifth Avenue, your city.

It seems now that we shall not be able to sail before the 1st of January. So for the next several weeks please address me as above.

I do hope *White Fang* will make a hit. I am really pleased by the reviews I have seen. I courted fate in the first place when I dared to write a companion-piece to *The Call of the Wild*. But God was with me! For at any rate I have escaped the fate I courted.

I sent you two days ago by express a complete Manuscript of *The Iron Heel*. This, of course, you can get into print as soon as you wish. Now tell me what you think of it. I don't care how frank you are. I think the tie that is between us (while it has never been exuberant nor bombastic), is nevertheless a tie that is close enough to admit of all frankness between us. Personally, I think from a pseudo-scientific standpoint the situation of *The Iron Heel* is plausible. Practically, from a business standpoint, considering the widespread interest in socialism at the present moment, I think there is a fair chance of *The Iron Heel* making a hit. I originally told you that *The Iron Heel* would be 100,000 words long. You will find that it is only 90,000 words long. I didn't dare an anticlimax after The Chicago Commune. So I cut it short right there.

By the way, just to interest you, I am inclosing you a letter I received a few days ago from Caspar Whitney.[1] Please return this letter to me. I merely told Mr. Whitney that I regretted the barb-wire fence he had put between us, but that I didn't think he would esteem me so well if I came over to him, as he would if I didn't. In fact, his method of doing business may be business, but it's not sportsmanlike. "Finis" was a long-short-story Alaskan study. I submitted it to *Outing Magazine,* and Whitney said it was great, and that he'd like to have several more similar studies in order to make a series of them. I told him I would be willing, and told him my rates for American serial rights; whereupon he promptly came back with the letter I am inclosing.

Again thanking you for your kind forethought in sending me what I wanted, but which I would not have asked for (honest!).

Sincerely yours,

Jack London

---

[1] An editor of *Outing Magazine*. Whitney wanted book rights as well as serial rights for *White Fang* and other stories.

To EDITORIAL DEPARTMENT,
Cosmopolitan Magazine

Oakland, Calif.
Dec. 17, 1906

Gentlemen:

Yours of December 10th just to hand. I hasten to accept your agreement to terminate the contract. I have just gone over the number of words printed by you of my first article. I find 3,558 words were printed. This will come to $355.80. Cut out the 80 cents. Seven photographs at $5.00 each, is $35.00. $355.00 plus $35.00, makes $390.00 You advanced me $2,000.00. $2,000.00 minus $390.00, equals $1,610.00, the balance I owe you.

As you surmised, I am not prepared at the present moment to return to you this $1610.00 in cash. So I take advantage of the offer you make in your letter, namely, that I place in your hands, by the 1st of January, articles or short stories from my pen (subject to your approval), to be paid for at the rate of fifteen (15¢) cents a word, in amount equivalent to the $1610.00 I owe you. These stories and articles are to be ones that have not been previously submitted to other publishers.

Now, it happens that I have just finished my novel, *The Iron Heel,* and have just begun work on the first of a series of tramp reminiscences. I have 2,000 words of the first one of this series completed, entitled "Confession." In this series I am giving true personal experiences of mine of the days when I was a tramp. At the rate of fifteen (15¢) cents a word I can have the equivalent of $1610.00 in your hands by January 1. Of course, these reminiscences will be subject to your approval. If, on reading the manuscript, you find this series eminently acceptable, why I am quite willing to extend them beyond the $1610.00 worth, if you are willing. On the other hand, I can cut them short at the $1610.00 worth. Also, if this series does not meet with your approval after you have examined it, of course you must then give me time to furnish you with further material.

Please give me a reply to this letter at your early convenience. I have no objection to addressing "all communications in future simply to the Editorial Department *Cosmopolitan Magazine.*" And your wishes in this matter will be observed. On the other hand, I do object as a business man, to receiving letters from you, the signatures of which are type-written, and indefinitely in terms of *"Cosmopolitan Magazine,* Editorial Department." In future, please sign in ink the signature of the authorized representative of the *Cosmopolitan Magazine.*[1]

Very truly yours,

Jack London

[1]*Cosmopolitan* accepted London's offer and published all of the series which Macmillan published in Nov., 1907, under the title *The Road.*

To ARTHUR T. VANCE

Oakland, Calif.
Dec. 17, 1906

Dear Mr. Vance:

Never been so happy in my life. The state of affairs with *The Cosmopolitan* became practically impossible, and I made a proposition to them that they must either meet me in a decent manner, or call the whole thing off. To my delight, they have come around to my view and called it off. I have just received their letter, and am inclosing you herewith a copy of my reply to them.

Now, the boat-trip is the cream of all the work I shall do on my voyage. I have now the American serial rights of the boat-trip in my own hands again. And I want to make you one of two propositions.

First,—Suppose you take the boat-trip for *The Woman's Home Companion.*[1] Take it not in addition to what I have contracted to give you, but take it as a substitution for what I have contracted to give you. If you should take it as a substitution, I should be quite willing, now and again, to send you articles of the nature described in our original contract—you know, just the things I should see amongst strange peoples and conditions that would strike me hard with an irresistible desire to write up.

Secondly,—In case you do not care to take the boat-trip, let me keep my contract with you just as it is. In this case, I shall wait a year and then sell the boat-trip to some other magazine.

There are certain advantages, if you should accept my offer of the boat-trip as a substitution. In the first place, you would have practically the exclusive account of my voyage. In the second place, you should somehow be able to avail yourself of the immense amount of advertising that the *Cosmopolitan* has given to my boat-trip—not only in its own advertising pages, but in the pages of all the Hearst newspapers all over the land. You could advertise in flat, precise terms, that you have arranged to get from me all that *The Cosmopolitan* was to publish, etc.

Now if you accept my proposition of taking over the boat-trip, I should like to have you advance me $1500.00 more. You see, between now and the 1st of January I have to return to *The Cosmopolitan* $1610.00 worth of fiction. This fiction, if it were not for that, I could sell elsewhere for cash. And I need cash badly just now. In these insane times in San Francisco, the boat has more than doubled upon itself. In fact, at the present moment, the sum-total cost of building and outfitting, runs past the $15,000 mark.

I don't think we have come to any definite arrangement as regards payment for photographs. You will notice that *The Cosmopolitan* is giving me $5.00 a photograph.

If you should see your way to accepting my proposition of giving you the boat-trip, I should like to have you make out a contract embodying the new conditions, mentioning the $1500 additional advance, arranging remuneration for photographs, etc. Send me this contract as soon as you can, in duplicate, so that we can sign up—that is, of course, if my proposition is acceptable.

No matter what you may decide to do, please telegraph me at earliest possible moment your acceptance or rejection of my proposition. Let your letter follow.

From sheer inability to get men to do the work, our departure is now delayed until somewhere in the first week of January.

In great haste,

Sincerely yours,

Jack London

P. S. I am so happy!

---

[1]The boat-trip articles make up *The Cruise of the Snark*. *Woman's Home Companion* published four of the series: "A Royal Sport," "The Lepers of Molokai," "The Nature Man," and "The High Seat of Abundance."

To Valdemar Blad

Glen Ellen, Calif.
January 2, 1907

Dear Sir:—

In reply to yours of December 26. Since my publishers, the Macmillan Company, have suggested to you that you communicate with me before you send the manuscript of your translation of *The Call of the Wild* to Copenhagen, I assume that they, my publishers, are willing, if I am willing. In which case, of course I am willing.

As to the percentage of royalty. I think I understand thoroughly the situation. I am quite confident that if you can do no more than publish *The Call of the Wild* at space-rate in Danish newspapers, that you will yourself be very poorly paid for your work. So I don't want any royalty at all on that. On the other hand, if you should succeed in having some Danish publishing house bring the story out in book form, I am willing to abide by any royalty you may decide upon, at least if you do not make that royalty too big. Now, don't think I am laughing. I'm speaking seriously. I know the copyright situation on the continent, and especially in the Scandinavian countries. I'll take a royalty, if you make it small enough,—more as a token of good-fellowship between you and me.

I have another stipulation that I must insist upon. If *The Call of the Wild* is published in bookform in Denmark, you must send me a couple of copies of it.

Wishing you all the luck in the world,

Sincerely yours,
Jack London

To EDITORIAL DEPARTMENT,
Cosmopolitan Magazine

Oakland, Calif.
Feb. 12, 1907

Gentlemen:

In reply to yours of February 7. As regards the count of words in the three articles, it seems to me that the difference of agreement as regards the number of words is due to what we consider words to be. I have always counted compound words, for instance, as two or more words. Abbreviations I have always counted as two words. For instance, when "was not" is abbreviated to "wasn't," in colloquial use, I have always counted it as two words. You certainly print it as two words in your magazine. You merely substitute an apostrophe for the "o" in "not," and print that abbreviation separately. And so forth, and so forth. I could go on at length, pointing out the causes of the disagreement in our count of words. It is the first time I have ever had the method of count questioned. But I am willing to be easy-going on this matter, and am willing to accept your method of count for these three articles.

You say that you have ascertained that the rate of fifteen (15¢) cents per word that you are paying me is higher than that of any other magazine. You have more ascertainment coming. Out of my memory I shall give you some data, and you have my full permission to go to the editors and cashiers of the magazines mentioned, to verify what I say. For instance, take *Collier's Weekly*. It is not so long ago that I turned down an offer of twenty (20) articles, which I was to prepare in the course of two years for *Collier's Weekly*. They offered me $1,000.00 per article of 5,000 words. If that isn't 20¢ per word, I'll eat my hat. I turned down the offer for me to do the twenty articles, because I thought it would keep me away too much from my fiction, and from the articles I would prefer doing. This last summer, I sold a short story to *Collier's Weekly*. It was entitled "A Day's Lodging" and was 5,000 words long. For this article I received $750.00, for American serial rights only. This is 15¢ per word. They have not yet published the story, but if you will see them about it, they will verify what I say. The last article published by *Collier's* I received payment for at the rate of 20¢ per word. Incidentally, I may state that at the present moment I have a contract with *Collier's* for news articles, for which I am to receive fifteen (15¢) per word, and all expenses.

Sometime during this past summer, *Everybody's* published a 5,000-word story of mine entitled "Brown Wolf," for which they paid me $750.00, which is at the rate of 15¢ per word. Their books will certainly show the price they paid for this story. I sold 40,000 words to *Everybody's* this past summer, in the serial they have just finished publishing, for which they paid me $5,000.00, which is at the rate of 12½¢ per word—a wholesale rate that was mutually agreed upon. Remember, that in all these stories and articles I am mentioning, including the news articles for *Collier's,* the rates paid are for American serial rights only.

At the present moment I have a contract to deliver two (2) 5,000-word stories to *Success,* for $750.00 each, which is at the rate of 15¢ per word. In fact, I'm not going to bore you with any more instances on the subject. You can verify the statements I have made, and if you want more of them, I'll send them to you.

On the other hand, do not forget for a moment that sometimes a fellow gets stuck,—writes a crackerjack good story that no magazine would dare to publish; that he couldn't get a magazine to publish if he paid them 15¢ a word to publish it. Then there are other instances, when in an easy-going way I let a story go for 10¢ per word to a magazine, when my rate was 15¢. An editor says to me, "It was a year and a half ago when you agreed to let me have that story. At that time your rate was 10¢ per word. Therefore, I think I ought to pay you that 10¢ per word, and not what your rate is now." And I let it go. I am not such a frightfully stiff proposition, except when I get my dander up. I let "Just Meat" go to you at 10¢ per word, at a time when my rate was 15¢ per word. If you will refer to our correspondence at that time, you will see how easy-going I was, and the reasons that I myself gave you for letting it go to you at 10¢ per word.

And now that I have shown you, at the risk of boring you, that you have some more ascertainment coming, let's get down to business. I am willing to accept your count on the three articles now in your possession, namely, "Pictures," which you count at 4,473 words, "The Pen," which you count at 5,491 words, and "Pinched," which you count at 5,296 words. According to your suggestion, on receipt of my agreement to the foregoing, you will send me check for the three articles.

Your suggestion of a general title for the series of articles is all right. It is my intention, later on, to publish the collection in bookform, under the title *The Road,* with the sub-title, "Tramp Reminiscences." Why could you not publish the series under the general title *The Road,* with the sub-title "Underworld Reminiscences," or any other sub-title you wish to select for yourselves?

And now, just to be easy-going, I have four (4) more of these tramp articles completed. These four articles complete the series. They are as follows, and should be published in the order given:

"Hoboes That Pass in the Night,"	6,910 words.
"Road Kids and Gay Cats,"	5,433 words.
(In this article I tell how I first went upon the Road.)	
"Two Thousand Stiffs,"	4,750 words.
"Bulls,"	6,865 words.

Now, I'll tell you what I'll do. In order to let you have the whole series, I'll offer these four to you at 10¢ per word,—YOU TAKING MY COUNT OF WORDS. I will say this—that some of the very best articles in the series are in these remaining four.

If you care to consider this offer of mine, send me a telegram to my Oakland address, and I'll immediately mail the four articles to you.

Of course, it is thoroughly understood that in all these articles, I am selling you the American serial rights only.[1]

Very truly yours,
Jack London

[1]*Cosmopolitan* accepted the offer and published all the sketches.

To GEORGE P. BRETT

Oakland, Calif.
March 7, 1907

Dear Mr. Brett:

In reply to yours of February 28. No, if you put before me good evidence that the publication of *The Road* would be likely to damage the sale of my other books, it would not affect the question of my desire for you to go ahead and publish it. Though you have not stated your reasons, I think I apprehend them. And while it is possible that just immediately the sale of my other books might be slightly damaged, I believe ultimately there would be no damaging effect at all. And I want to say this, apropos of *The Road* in particular, and of all my work in general:

In *The Road,* and in all my work, in all that I have said and written and done, I have been true. This is the character I have built up; it constitutes, I believe, my big asset. As my character has developed through my work from time to time, there have been flurries of antagonism, attacks and condemnations; but I pulled through them all, and the consistent and true picture of myself is by that much more clearly limned.

I have always insisted that the cardinal literary virtue is sincerity, and I have striven to live up to this belief.

If I am wrong in the foregoing, if the world downs me on it, I'll say "Good-bye, proud world," retire to the ranch, and plant potatoes and raise chickens to keep my stomach full and strength in my body.

I am willing to grant the chance that I am wholly wrong in believing that sincerity and truthfulness constitute my big asset. I am willing to grant the chance that I am wholly mistaken in my reasoning. Nevertheless, I look back on my life and draw one great generalization: IT WAS MY REFUSAL TO TAKE CAUTIOUS ADVICE THAT MADE ME. At the very beginning, had I taken the advice of the magazine editors, I'd have been swiftly made into a failure. *McClure's Magazine* gave me $125 per month, and held the bread-and-butter lash over me. Phillips[1] said, "Write such and such stories for our magazines. Quit writing the stories you are writing." In short, he wanted to make me take the guts and backbone out of my stories; wanted me to make an eunuch of myself; wanted me to write petty, smug, complacent bourgeois stories; wanted me to enter the ranks of clever mediocrity and there to pander the soft, fat, cowardly bourgeois instincts. It was because I refused his advice that I broke with *McClure's*. In fact, Phillips fired me, and took away the $125 per month. I had a hard time for a while. You will remember that in New York I was compelled to come to you to borrow my railroad fare to California; but in the end I pulled through and did better by far than if I had taken Mr. Phillips' advice.

And so, in the present case (being cussedly made, I suppose), I feel compelled to follow my own judgment. I am indeed grateful, however, for your solicitude, not merely in mentioning the contingency that may arise from the publication of *The Road,* but for the delicate way in which you did mention it. In fact, it is I who have taken the liberty of forestalling the objection you did not state.

The Road has been sold to *The Cosmopolitan Magazine*. The first article will be published in May number. I suppose they will continue until the series is completed. Incidentally, I may state that I got between $6000 and $7000 for it.

I note, by the way, in your bulletin of new books, that *Love of Life* is scheduled shortly to appear. There are two stories in that collection, one of which I know has not yet appeared serially, and the other of which I am in doubt about. "The White Man's Way" was sold to The Associated Sunday Magazines [Syndicate], 52 E. 19th St., your city. A line or a telephone to them will ascertain whether or not they have published it. The other story, "A Day's Lodging," was sold to *Collier's Weekly,* and I know that they have not yet published it. Please make sure that these two stories have been published serially before the book comes out. You see, I have been paid nearly $1500.00 for the American serial rights in those two stories, and if the book anticipates the serial publication of same, I'll have to refund the money.

Had the boat out on her second trial-trip, last Sunday. She is a sheer delight to me. I could not ask for any alteration in her. Shall not be able to get away until after April 1. I no longer set definite dates of departure.

Sincerely yours,

Jack London

[1]John S. Phillips, later with *American Magazine*.

To Arthur T. Vance

Oakland, Calif.
March 14, 1907

Dear Mr. Vance:—

In reply to yours of March 9. I am a pretty good correspondent. I answer all letters and all telegrams. I answered immediately your recent telegram. The telegram you mention having sent two weeks before that one was never received by me. It's up to you to make a kick to the Telegraph Company.

I wish I knew, myself, why it is that I do not get started. I am paying out $1000 a month wages to workingmen, alone, without taking into account the cost of material. And still the building of the boat drags on. A boat that at the outside should have cost no more than $7,000.00, has already cost me more than $20,000.00. Post-earthquake conditions, and the power of organized labor, are responsible for this. At the present moment there are seven men working on the boat—that is, they are being paid for working on the boat; and if I don't like their way of working, why there are plenty of other jobs for them. The carpenters are getting ready to demand $8.00 per day for an eight-hour day.

I really don't know when I shall get started. I say now, sometime in April;[1] but I wouldn't be surprised if it were April 1908! I left the ranch on Dec. 1, expecting to sail on Dec. 15,—and I'm still here. It would require just ten hundred thousand words to give you the history of the building of the boat and the causes of the delay. On March 28, the boat goes on the ways again—she has leaked ever since she was launched, and now we'll have to strip the copper off and find the leak. I am not happy. I won't be happy until I get away. and I'm going to get away as fast as God, earthquakes, and organized labor will let me. I'm sorry it throws your magazine arrangements out; but great God, think of the way it throws me out. You've got a bed of roses compared with what I have.

Yours with a grouch against the multitudinous causes of delay,

Jack London

[1]The *Snark* sailed from San Francisco April 23, 1907.

To George P. Brett

Honolulu, T. H.
May 28, 1907

Dear Mr. Brett:—

Since I have always drawn pretty well in advance on my royalty, I have never got into my head the date of the yearly payment of royalties; so I do not know when the next yearly payment is due, and I do not know how much, if any, is due. Also, I carefully filed away, in Glen Ellen, my contract with you, so do not have access to it. So will you please send me a brief accounting, up to date. You see, I am so hard up that I want to know where I stand.

To finish the building of the boat in San Francisco became absurdly and grotesquely impossible. With the boat half completed, one coat of paint outside, and no paint inside, the engine a wreck, and a multitude of things undone, I bundled everything aboard and came down here. And down here I find myself at the end of my resources. I borrowed $5,000.00 on my Oakland home, or, rather, my mother's home in Oakland, in order to pay off the San Francisco pirates before I sailed.

So I have to finish building the boat down here, and need money. Now, I do not know just how I stand with you, but I think the sales of *White Fang* and *Before Adam* must amount to something. Also, I want to tell you how I am situated with regard to the future. I have much material on hand, and many part-completed books.

There are three (3) unpublished books of mine now in your hands namely: *The Iron Heel, Love of Life,* and *The Road.* Of these three, *The Iron Heel* may make a considerable sale.

At present moment I have on hand the following part-completed books: I have a collection of Klondike short-stories, 38,000 words of which are already written. Two stories, each 6,000 words in length, will complete this collection. I have half a book of miscellaneous short-stories, all written within the past year; I have three-fifths (3/5) of a collection of what I call Future stories, all written within the past three months, and I have a third of the first volume of my boat-trip, written.

Incidentally, I have already gathered much material for work in the future, down here in the Hawaiian Islands. Also, I have a new book in my mind which I shall write somewhere in the not too distant future, namely, *A Book of Sharks.* I have a dozen of the stories for this book already filed away. And so forth, and so forth.

And now to come to the point. I should like to have advanced to me $5,000.00, on account of royalties, and if you care to, I should be only too glad to sign a contract that will cover the various before-mentioned books, completed, incomplete, and projected. In case I should die, all the afore-mentioned books could be brought out just the same, with the exception of the boat-trip, which, of course, wouldn't be completed, and *A Book of Sharks.*

It is very important that I should hear from you immediately, and, if possible, I should like to have the check and contract come along at the same time.

I just wish to say a word in explanation of my precarious financial situation. The building of the *Snark* has been the cause of it all. I expected to pay about $7,000.00 for the completed boat. Never mind the horrible and monstrous causes. The result is, that at the present moment, the *Snark* has cost me $25,000.00. Naturally, this has absorbed money as fast as I could earn it, and a bit faster. That is why I had $6,000.00 advanced from you, and raised $5,000 on my Oakland house. If the building of the boat had not all been inconceivable and monstrous, I should have had a few thousand dollars in my pocket at the present moment, and [been] perfectly safe as regards the future. But now that this tremendous initial cost has been gone through with, I have nothing to do in the future but begin to pull even again.

You see, hand in hand with the building of the *Snark,* I have gone on with the building of the ranch in Glen Ellen. I have a magnificent barn on it, all paid for, and also thousands of dollars worth of improvements in the way of orchard, vineyard, wild trees (that I planted), fences, etc. You see, if I had shut off on the building of the barn, even the monstrous and inconceivable building of the *Snark* would not have put me in the hole.

And by the way, I have also another projected book, a sea story, which I shall entitle *The Mercy of the Sea.*[1]

Please let me hear from you at the very earliest moment.

Sincerely yours,
Jack London

[1] Neither *The Book of Sharks* nor *The Mercy of the Sea* was ever written.

To George P. Brett

Honolulu, T.H.
July 11, 1907

Dear Mr. Brett:

I am sending you, inclosed herewith, the signed Contract for 1908, and I cannot thank you too heartily for your kindness of forwarding me the $5000 on account of royalties.

Has there been any news from that $1000 which your business manager has kindly undertaken to collect for me from *The Times Magazine?* Has *The Times Magazine* gone out of existence, or is it still publishing?

Believe me, I thoroughly appreciate your point of view in the matter of the publication of my tramp experiences, and that your letter did not offend me in any way, I beg of you to refer to the letter I wrote at the time in reply to it. As regards the clipping[1] you have sent me, in which some man gratuitously attempts to order my life for me, I can only say that I have received dozens of similar gratuitous letters, all of which, however, have been in praise of my series of tramp articles. Dog-on-it! This many-headed public is a thing that no man can really understand or keep track of.

I am still firm in my belief that my strength lies in being candid, in being true to myself as I am to-day, and also in being true to myself as I was at six, sixteen, and twenty-six. Who am I, to be ashamed of what I have experienced? I have become what I am because of my past; and if I am ashamed of my past, logically I must be ashamed of what that past made me become.

Mrs. London and I are just back from a five-days' visit at the Leper Settlement on Molokai, where we mingled most freely with the lepers, and had a disgracefully good time; and to-day I have just finished a 5000-word article on the subject ["Lepers of Molokai"]. We are departing to-morrow for a ten-days' or two-weeks' trip to Maui, and the great extinct crater of Haleakala.

By the way (though I do not remember whether or not I told you I canceled the story of the boat-trip with *The Cosmopolitan Magazine*)—what I started to say, is that *Harper's Monthly,* I believe now, are going to publish the story of the boat-trip. And I must confess that I like the treatment from *Harper's Monthly* much better than that I got from *Outing. Harper's* cabled and wanted to know if they could have book-rights, and I cabled that The Macmillan Co. had them, and made up my mind that that would be the last I'd hear from *Harper's.* And after some more cabling, lo, they accepted four chapters which they had not yet seen, at my rate, and said that upon reading said four chapters they would let me know their views upon accepting the rest of the series as yet unwritten by me. All of which I think is very fine on the part of *Harper's Monthly,* and The Harper's Book-publishing Co.

Sincerely yours,

Jack London

¹*New York Times Saturday Review of Books:*

"A man who has risen from the status of a common tramp to that of a successful novelist deserves much credit, and should be proud of his achievement. Jack London is evidently proud of his achievement, for he is now exploiting his experiences in the 'underworld' in a well-known monthly magazine, ('My Life in the Underworld,' *Cosmopolitan,*) but there is nothing of modesty in his pride. He glories in the facts that he lived by begging, stole rides on trains, and was skillful in eluding the police. These memoirs are certainly not praiseworthy, and will, I think, detract from his literary reputation. It is deplorable that he should so far debase his art."—E. F. Allen.

TO NINETTA EAMES

Honolulu, T.H.
July 25, 1907

Dear Aunt Netta:—

In reply to yours of July 2, July 11, and July 15. The vouchers from the BANK were forwarded directly to me, and arrived some time after I wrote you about them. There is a missing check-book, precise date of which I shall send you later. This missing check-book may come up to you from Oakland in the things Eliza is sending you in the trunk. And anyway, when I later write you, giving you date of said book, you can write and ask her about it.

And now about Eliza. She is terribly diffident and formal with people she

Jack London and his first wife, Bessie, early in their marriage.

Anna Strunsky.

Jack London
Piedmont
Alameda Co., Calif.

April 24/03

Dear Anna :—
            This is the first
writing I have done for some
time. Easter Sunday I elected
to cut off the end of my
thumb, and not finding
the piece, have had a
painful wound to heal.

        Mabel Applegarth has been
spending a couple of weeks
with us ——— likewise
Cloudesley Johns.

        Am glad you liked the
dog story. Have a heart beating
in the end of my thumb,
so ——

                Jack London.

3.

Jack and Bessie London at home in Oakland.

6.

Above: Jack London at the time of his trip to London in 1903. Below: in 1905, with his husky, "Brown Wolf," during the writing of *The Sea Wolf*.

7.

London's daughters, Bess and Joan, in 1905. Below: with their father.

10.

Two portraits of London—right: by the well-known photographer Arnold Genthe; above: by a friend of London, Xavier Martinez.

11.

2. Part of the Carmel group, including (bottom, left to right) George Sterling, Jimmy Hopper, Jack London and Carrie Sterling. At top left is Charmian, London's second wife.

Jack and Charmian frequently mugged for the camera. Here, they are at their ranch, in 1905. Below: London, who was fond of putting on the gloves with all comers, in a bout with Charmian.

15.

London aboard the *Snark* in Oakland, 1907, as sailing day approaches. At the right is Roscoe Eames.

The Londons "aboard" the *Snark* in 1906, before its completion.

16.

17.

Trial run of the *Snark* on San Francisco Bay, 1907. Below: The *Snark* on sailing day in April, 1907.

18

19.

The Londons in Honolulu, 1907.

London in a costume of human hair during the cruise of the *Snark* in the South Seas.

20.

21.

London riding on "The Beauty Ranch." Below: The bungalow where the Londons lived. Jack died in the sunroom at the right.

22.

3.

London aboard the *Roamer* with Nakata, 1914. Below: On the *Roamer* four
years earlier.

24.

25.

The ruins of "Wolf House," overlooking Sonoma Valley. Below: The architect's sketch of "Wolf House."

26.

27.

London with his daughter Joan, in Oakland, about 1912.

From left: George Sterling, Stewart Edward White and London at the Bohemian Grove.

28.

29.

The Londons in
Hawaii, 1916.

30.

JACK LONDON DIES IN HIS "VALLEY OF THE MOON"

PHYSICIANS' BULLETIN AFTER DEATH

"At about 6:30 p. m., November 21, 1916, Mr. Jack London partook of his dinner. He was taken during the night with what was supposed to be an attack of acute indigestion. This, however, proved to be a gastro-intestinal type of uraemia. He rapidly entered coma and died at 7:45 p. m., November 22, 1916.

"W. S. PORTER, M. D.,
"A. M. THOMSON, M. D.,
"W. B. HAYS, M. D.,
"J. WILSON SHIELDS, M. D."

AN EARLIER BULLETIN ISSUED BY DOCTORS

"London Ranch, Glen Ellen, Calif., Nov. 22, 1916, 6:30 P. M.
"Mr. London is in a state of uraemia following an error in diet, causing a faulty elimination of the kidneys. His condition is serious. Further bulletins will follow. "Signed,

"J. WILSON SHIELDS, M. D.,
"A. M. THOMSON, M. D.,
"W. B. HAYS, M. D."

(Continued from Page One)

Mrs. Shepard and the others who are near and dear by family ties.

LOVED HIS RANCH HOME

Many years ago now, Jack London came to be a resident of Sonoma county and bought the farm on which he died near Glen Ellen. He immediately began intensive farming. He started in to raise the best breeds of cattle and to see that they were splendidly housed. Then he developed the planting of thousands of trees and began the improvement of the ranch in many other ways. At the time of his death—to use his own words expressed here a few days since

early days when what he made as a "cub" meant so much to him. Upon the occasion of his last visit here Mr. London mentioned to the writer that he would go east the first week in December and would stop at Chicago to attend the international stock fair and would probably buy some more fine blooded stock to ship to London ranch. Then he was going to New York to pay off an election bet in a dinner to about two hundred friends of the man with whom he wagered.

SO MUCH COULD BE WRITTEN

So much could be written about the life of Jack London from a street urchin following a few years on his

London, with C. D. Wright
of Honolulu, a few days
before his death. Above:
A bulletin which appeared
in a Santa Rosa news-
paper.

31.

does not know very well, and is ridiculously scrupulous in striving to avoid stepping over the mark in any way. Her diffidence and her scrupulousness combined, have undoubtedly been the cause of the slight hitch as regards the selling of the Oakland house.

As regards the selling of the Oakland house: if the market at any time appreciates so that it can be sold at $10,000.00, let it go. Otherwise, don't sell it—this, however, is all dependent on whether or not I receive the $5000 for *The Iron Heel*. If that sale falls through, and I do not receive that $5000, why go ahead and sell as cheaply as $8000.

That $5000 check from Mr. Brett, came straight thro to me, and I now have it in bank at Honolulu.

I have just received the cable from you and Edward.[1] The code-book is down in Pearl Harbor so I do not know contents of cable; but I feel pretty sure that the cable is to the effect that I am to withhold pillorying Roscoe until I get word from you and Edward. That's all right—I don't bother my head about pillorying him now. I am not going to pillory him until I bring out The Voyage of the *Snark* in book-form, when I shall do it in a foot-note. There won't be anything vicious in what I shall say in said foot-note, but merely a brief statement of the surpassing grotesqueness of Roscoe's handling of the *Snark*.

Dear Aunt Netta, can't you understand that my complaint against Roscoe is not that his inefficiency cost me thousands of dollars, but is, that he didn't wash the decks; that he didn't keep a log-book; that he was never over-worked at all, because he practically did no work at all. He didn't do one-fifth part as much as Charmian did on the trip down. With the exception of four hours, Charmian stood just as many night hours at the wheel as Roscoe did, while she spent scores of hours more of day-watches at the wheel than Roscoe did. On top of that, she cheered and livened things up; took a hand down below when the cook and cabin-boy were sick; wrote her Diary and personal correspondence, typed all my manuscripts (and I was doing a day's work every day), and took all my letters by dictation. As regards Charmian's not approaching Roscoe upon his wholesale dereliction, I especially forbade her from "butting in." I intended to get rid of him anyway, and I didn't want any family quarrel on hand. My God—if Roscoe was unable to work because of the dirt on the boat, why in hell didn't he clean it up? I waited days for him to wash the decks and finally washed them myself. I let that boat lie ten or twelve days in Pearl Harbor, during which time Roscoe never washed the decks at all; and in every way was letting twenty-odd thousand dollars' worth of property belonging to me, go to rack and ruin, by simply doing nothing. And when he finally left the boat, he left his stateroom the filthiest pig-pen I ever saw. Lack of sleep?—he slept more than any two of us on the boat put together, the whole trip down. Only twice did he stand four-hour watches on the trip down, and Charmian stood two four-hour watches, which was all that he did. Every night, he had two hours on deck, and the rest of the night was below; and blessed well he stayed below until I routed him out for breakfast in the morning (I didn't purpose to have a restaurant run on the *Snark* for his convenience, while Charmian grew gray trying to get him to the other meals on time, and even then did not always succeed). Roscoe was not expected to do "housework," and furthermore he didn't do one tap of "housework." His navigation was just as rotten as Bert Stolz' and mine; and Bert and I started in and taught ourselves navigation. Roscoe certainly did not perform any of the duties of engineer. Bert Stolz did all the engineering that was done. The only time Roscoe did any engineering was at Pearl Harbor in the launch, which Martin had running nicely, and which Roscoe promptly put out of commission.

As for plumbing, Roscoe tackled it once, after earnest and repeated requests, ended his one attempt in failure, and announced that plumbing wasn't his trade anyway. He certainly did not perform any duties of sailing-master—a man who won't wash the decks isn't performing the first duty of a sailing-master. Nor did he perform the first duty of a navigator, which is to keep a log. Believe me, Aunt Netta, neither Roscoe nor anybody, was overworked on the run down. The run down, so far as working the ship was concerned, was a fat and lazy time. The only hard work at all, on the run down, was the four hours spent in trying to heave the *Snark* to, and this hard work was done by Bert and me. Bert and I did all the heavy pulling and hauling. Roscoe did the superintending. Roscoe's talk about overwork is simply the absurdest whine I ever heard. From what I know of Bay yachting, I am confident that Roscoe never spent a Sunday on the Bay in his own boat, that he didn't work four times as hard as the hardest day we had on the run to Honolulu, and there was only one such hard day. Roscoe's bowels may have been out of order; but it wasn't for lack of the proper food I bought and paid for from the Sanitarium nor was it from lack of sleep, nor was it from lack of eating. Charmian says she never saw him eat so much as he did on that trip—usually three square meals a day. And let me tell you one thing, Aunt Netta—when a man eats more heavily than is his wont, and sleeps half the time, and loafs seven-eighths of the remaining half of the time, that man's going to get constipated. Roscoe's conduct contaminated Bert Stolz. And Bert Stolz was hopeless on the run down, and all the time Roscoe was on board at Pearl Harbor. As soon as Roscoe left, Bert became another man, and pitched in and worked like a good fellow, and was his old self in every way. And furthermore, he twice apologized to Charmian and me, for his behavior on the way down, namely, his shirking of work, and, as he explained himself, it was inexplicable to him that he had behaved in that fashion. This was Bert's polite way of explaining away the contamination he had received from Roscoe. Whatever Roscoe may have been in the past, he utterly and absolutely went to pieces long before the voyage of the *Snark* began. This going to pieces began to dawn upon me during the last months of the building of the *Snark*. But I never dreamed how absolute it was until we started on the voyage. And I want to say, furthermore, that when Roscoe ate my bread (Sanitarium grub!), and drew pay from me, for those many days at Pearl Harbor, and all the time allowed the boat to go to rack and ruin, that he was unqualifiedly vile. When I asked him, on the last day, if everything was in good condition on the *Snark,* he said "Yes." When I asked him if there was anything that needed to be done, he said "No." And then I said to him: "Then everything is in first-class condition on the *Snark,* in every way?" And he said "Yes." And at that very moment he knew, and I knew, that there were ten thousand things that ought to have been done upon the *Snark:* that the decks had not been washed for 12 days, and were opening up; that big hawsers were lying rotting on the deck in the tropic heat and moisture. That the big mainsail, hung above the awning instead of under the awning, was mildewing and rotting. That the masts should be scraped; that there were blocks and ropes hanging by shreds in the rigging, that should be renovated. That costly railings of teak were going to rack and ruin for lack of oil—I say he knew all these things, or else he was the damnedest imbecile that ever trod on God Almighty's footstool. But never mind what he said—the fact is that he was eating my food, and drawing $50 a month from me, knowing in what fierce financial straits I was, and was letting the thousands of dollars of property go to rack and ruin.

And don't forget, that Roscoe did not have to do this work himself. He had Martin and Bert, who were both willing to do it. And don't forget further that Roscoe had told you nothing but a mess of lies from start to finish—the lies of a crank, an imbecile, or a scoundrel, take your choice. And then he writes a most contemptible letter to Charmian, in which both she and I are repeatedly and most vilely insulted, and dares to threaten that if we don't watch out, he is liable to open his lips to the reporters in self-defense! Self-defense, forsooth—when I, from the start, have been defending him from his mean wretched self. The very day he sailed on the *Sierra,* the reporters were hot-footed after me to find out why he was leaving. And I told them because he was getting old, and because his wife was sick and he wanted to get back to her! And then the newspaper lies went out, over the United States, and to England, everywhere, giving me a notorious reputation for bad temper and quarreling, etc., etc. And I swallowed it all, and never said a word. And then, to have him dare to threaten me—if I didn't watch out, he'd talk in self-defense!!!

And now, no more of Roscoe, dear Aunt Netta. For the first time I really appreciate what you have endured. And I cannot help calling you a silly, sentimental fool for having endured it for so long, as you have. And again, enough. I love you just the same as ever, and more than ever, and I do not care how you feel about this matter. If you elect to believe that Roscoe is more truthful than I, go ahead,—and I'll love you just the same. But if you do believe him, then let me tell you that he's a damn liar and you're a damn fool!—And now, and for the last time, enough of that detestable creature.

There is one thing at least, upon which you and I agree—namely, the character of my mother. I chortled with joy at every word you uttered anent your interview with her. Let me tell you right now that you have not seen one thousandth part of the real devil that she is.

I am glad that Wiget has bought a good span of horses. And the situation is this: I want to go ahead with the ranch in every possible way. If I should go broke on this yachting-trip, I shall have all the better refuge to retreat to! And if I don't go broke, so much to the good, anyway.

You certainly did the right thing regarding acceptance of Reynolds' proposition for the serial sale of *The Iron Heel*.

Give my love to everyone in camp—all the children, I mean.

You did right about paying interest on the mortgage out of my bank account in Oakland.

There is liable to be a check for $750 coming to me from *Success* [Magazine]. When that check comes, it would be well for you to capture it and deposit it in your own bank account so as to be ready for the Fall premiums on my life insurance. As you possibly know, the Fall premiums are very heavy.

And now, since we are just back from two weeks on Maui, and I have a heavy correspondence to get off, take lots of love from me, and also love for Edward.

Jack London

[1]Edward Payne, Ninetta's second husband.

To George Sterling

Hilo

Sept. 27, 1907

Dearest Greek:—

Poor Gene![1] He couldn't make good. He caught a glimpse, in some metallic, cog-like way, of the spirit of adventure, and thought to woo her—Adventure, who must be served whole-souled and single-hearted and with the long patience that is so terrible that very few are capable of it. Gene came to woo her—a shirk, a liar, a betrayer, and a poor little embezzler.

He came on world-adventure in a small boat, expecting sheets, table-cloths and privacy, with no work to do except to draw money, with servants to take care of him, and his host to entertain him.

He shirked on everybody; betrayed his friend, (yours truly), when he told his friend, leaving Honolulu, that the engine was in first-class condition. He either was stupid about gasoline engines, or else he was deliberately criminal in his neglect of my engines, which neglect has already cost me hundreds of dollars.

He sinned against me as only a friend can sin; and then grew sullen as a dog—forsooth because he had behaved like a brute—and treated me, my wife, and my Captain, as if they were dirt under his feet.

And finally, after he left, (see clipping inclosed),[2] he gave my voyage a black eye, prophesied early termination of same, and lied about Martin,—about Martin, who had even defended Gene against me, Martin who has the soul of a gentleman and a man (which Gene has not). See clipping, and note that I tell you that at the time Gene left, I was even a few dollars in debt to Martin.

Gene was not made for adventure; nor was he made for manhood. He is a paradox. With the body of a primitive, of a gorilla; he has the guts of a louse and the soul of a chicken!

Gene might save your life some time at the risk of his own, as you suggest. I agree. He might easily do it, if it were a sudden peril—but to save your life by slow sacrifice, to bleed and suffer, toil and sweat for you through long days and nights, in order to save your life, (even for pay!), believe me, he hasn't the guts nor the manhood to do it. He is too selfish; he is an egomaniac—all "sensitive plants" are egomaniacs; they are colossally stuck upon themselves.

Gene may, as you say, be a sailor, a carpenter, and a mechanic. But on the boat, he showed himself to be one thing only—namely, a first-class shirk.

And so Gene passes. If you want to, show him this letter, along with lines anent Gene, which I dictated to Charmian in her letter to Carrie.

O Greek, great Greek, noble Greek—my greatest friend in the world, than whom there will [not] be another who can approach within a million miles of you—you are head-and-shoulders in the stars compared with the puny earth-men who dare to yawp at your power of beauty! I am a whole lot angrier over the clippings[3] you sent me *(Wine of Wizardry),* than if the thing, a thousand times worse, had happened to me. You convert me more and more to your point of view on the magazines, and the fact that there are only swine for whom to create beauty.

No, I don't correspond with Ella Wheeler Wilcox, and I don't want to.

Tear out page of Gans-Britt fight, Admission Day, and mail to me.

I forgive Emerson . . . because you ask me to. Write and tell him so, though he is many things that are not nice, and I see by his swinishness that he has got the whole thing played up big in the S.F. papers just now.

But don't ask me to forgive Gene. He is without soul, is possessed of a mechanical religion, and is nothing but a shameless cadger.

Gene had no hardship on the boat. I have gone through ten thousand times worse for years on end. Gene began squealing from the moment he arrived at Honolulu. He is a huge, mighty-muscled cry-baby.

Damn Gene! I keep reverting to him. I did not intend to mention him to you at all, but I changed my mind at the last moment.

I hope to sail on Sunday, Sept. 29.

Poor Jimmy [Hopper]! Nobody should blame him for anything he does these days. He's sweating in hell. I went through it once, and I hadn't a tithe of the artist-nature that he has to suffer with! Give him my best love, and tell him that if he wants to live, I advise him to do what I did.

Gee! I'd like to be out with you one day for a muscle-feed.

Love to Dick and Carlt and all the crowd.

When I saw that Gene, the last friend on board, had cheated and betrayed me, the people of Hilo nearly had some entertainment. I was damn near to taking the *Snark* out into deep water, and burning her. Then Charmian and I would have taken the first sailing vessel into the South Seas, and gone on alone in one way or another, around the world.

Charmian landed on Emerson neatly. Emerson had charged you with being at fault for reading her diary before people. She said that the only person you had been at fault about reading the diary before, was Emerson!

Gene complained of lack of congenial company on the *Snark*. Tell him to buck up, and learn how to be congenial himself, first. And then he may find congeniality in others—a sullen brute can never rest in bed of roses. We have found Martin and the Captain, and Frank, the sailor whom Gene corrupted (and evidently found congenial enough to corrupt)—we have found them all to be quite congenial fellows—all except Gene.[4] I want to add to my description of Gene, by saying that he is a cad and a snob, and you can find proof of same in clipping inclosed herewith, from Honolulu paper, —"when you are with a crowd you do not know, etc."

I return clippings—you may need them.

Beauty! Beauty! Beauty!

Wolf

[1]Gene Fenelon, friend of George Sterling, who replaced Stolz on the *Snark* at Honolulu and left at Hilo.

[2]The clipping was from the Honolulu *Star* and reported that Fenelon would have left the *Snark* sooner except for the fact that he had to work out what he owed London on advances; also, that Martin Johnson would have been let out (for not being able to cook) if it were not for his owing money.

[3]Attacks upon Sterling's book of poems, *Wine of Wizardry*.

[4]When London left Hilo he had as a crew Captain J. Langhorne Warren (a paroled murderer who was pardoned by the Governor of Oregon after London's intercession); Martin Johnson; Frank Herman; Wada, an Oriental, as cook; and Nakata as houseboy. Nakata returned to the States and served London for some years, later becoming a dentist in Honolulu.

To GEORGE STERLING

On Board the *Snark*
126° 20′ W. Long.
6° 47′ N. Lat.
Nov. 24, 1907

Oh, you Greek:

Just a line or two, to make up for that blast I sent about Gene. He deserved it all, and you deserved to receive it, for I had just received a letter from you in which you wanted to know why I didn't write you more of Gas Engine troubles, etc.

252

I haven't received a letter for two months, and two months more will probably elapse before I pick up a mountain of mail in Papeete. You know what my mail is—think of four months of it coming in one swat!

Forty-nine days next Monday since I last saw Hilo and land, and we're in the Doldrums now, hundreds of miles away.

Did anybody ever tell you that it's a hard voyage from Hawaii to the Marquesas? Anyway, you tell the next fellow so, if he's tackling it in a sailing vessel. The *South Sea Directory* says that the whaleship captains doubted if it could be accomplished from Hawaii to Tahiti—which is much easier than to the Marquesas. We've had to fight for every inch of easting in order to be able to make the islands when we fall in with the S.E. trades, which we expect to pick up anywhere from 30° to 50° north of the line.

The first two weeks out of Hilo we met the N.E. Trades well around to the east and even at times a bit south of east. Result was we sagged south (across a westerly current) and made practically no easting till we struck the Variables, 8 to 10 N. Lat.

But I'm working every day!

Say, you've seen dolphins. Think of catching them on rod and reel! That's what I'm doing. Gee! You ought to see them take the line out (I have 600 yards on the reel, and need it all). The first one fought me about twenty minutes, when I hauled him to gaff—four feet six inches of blazing beauty.

When they strike, they run away like mad, leaping into the air again and again, prodigiously, and in each mid-leap, shaking their heads like young stallions (trying to shake out the hook).

I find it hard to go to sleep after catching one of them. The leaping, blazing beauty of it gets on my brain.

I never saw Dolphins really until this trip. Pale-blue, after being struck, they turn golden. On deck, of course, afterward, they run the gamut of color. But in the water, after the first wild run they are pure gold. I am going to write up the voyage of the *Snark* and entitle it: "Around the World with Three Gasoline Engines and a Wife."

Love, love to you and Carrie, and remember me to everybody.

Wolf.

P.S. Talk about luck! I have played poker and I have now lost the ninth successive time, eight out of the nine times being the only loser. You can't beat that, you ever-blessed Greek!

Wolf

To Eliza Shepard

On Board "The Snark"
6° 19′ N. Lat.
125° 21′ W. Long.
Nov. 25/07

Dearest Eliza:—

A long voyage, this one—49 days to-day since we sailed from Hilo; 1200 miles from our destination, and sailing away from it every moment. Nothing but head winds all the time.

But what of it. My work goes on every day and every day. I have 95,000 words written on a new novel, which will be about 120,000 words long—the longest one I have written. Shall entitle it *Success*[1] perhaps.

Feeling fine—am in great condition. Lots of fun catching fish and losing at poker—also studying navigation.

At present moment I am well able to navigate a ship anywhere in the world.

When I get back, if I want to, it will be a snap to get my captain's papers.

I'm not writing news—for you get Charmian's diary. And Charmian is proving herself a "blowed-in-the glass," A No. I, crackerjack.

Expect to get a wad of letters in Papeete . . . when we get there. Then shall write again.

With an armful of love from your brother Jack. Best love to Irving. Remember me to Mr. Shepard and everybody.

Jack

[1]Published under the title of *Martin Eden*.

To George P. Brett

Papeete, Tahiti
Jan. 16, 1908

Dear Mr. Brett:—

In reply to yours of Sept. 18, 21, 27; Oct. 5, 21, 29; Nov. 7; Dec. 2, Dec. 3, and Dec. 16. I am now on board the *S. S. Mariposa,* bound for San Francisco, and some four or five days before you read this, you will have received a telegram, which I intend to send you upon landing at San Francisco. I shall only be in San Francisco eight (8) days, sailing from San Francisco on Monday morning, February 3, on the *S. S. Mariposa,* for Tahiti, where we rejoin the *Snark,* and continue our voyage around the world.

I cannot tell you how much I appreciate the splendid way in which you brought out *The Road.* I like those photograph illustrations very much, and was glad also to see that you included the drawings from *The Cosmo-*

politan. In the last mail I received quite a number of clippings of reviews of *The Road,* and thought from them that the book was being most favorably received. I did not notice any contemptuous or sneering notes such as you anticipated, and, to tell you the truth, which I myself anticipated to a certain extent. Of course, I do not know really how the book has taken; but from the few reviews I have seen, it seems to have been received most genially and goodnaturedly.

Concerning *The Iron Heel,* I think that this is the psychological moment for it to appear, and that, what of the panic, the general trade depression, and the general situation in the United States for the past year, that the public is just ripe to boost *The Iron Heel* along into large sales. As I say, and as I repeat, this is the psychological moment for *The Iron Heel* to appear.

I have finished 120,000 words of my new novel, which I believe I shall entitle *Success,* and which I think will be at least 10,000 or 15,000 words longer. I simply could not write it inside the space of 100,000 words. I couldn't trim sail without capsizing; so I am rounding her up slowly and carefully to the mooring buoy. (The foregoing is certainly heterogeneous metaphor, but it sounded good while it sounded.)

As usual, I am dictating this letter to Mrs. London. You should see us at this moment. We are in the dining-saloon of the *Mariposa,* half a gale is blowing, most of the passengers, men and women, are seasick, and somewhere off to the south of us a hurricane is raging. And every day and every day, since we left Papeete, I complete a thousand words on my novel in the morning, and spend the afternoon dictating letters to Mrs. London.

We were only sixty days in going from Hilo, Hawaii, to the Marquesas! —and altogether, we found over ninety days' mail waiting for us at Papeete. Mrs. London, by the way, spends what time I am not dictating to her, in writing a diary. This diary is an account of the voyage of the *Snark* around the world, from a woman's standpoint. I have read what she has written of it, myself, up to date, and I confess that I find it most interesting reading, and I am confident that it will prove interesting reading to large numbers of people. I am going to make a try of it for serial publication. Also, I am wondering if you would care to consider it for book publication.

Yes, as you suggest, I am mighty glad to get off at a little distance from the swine struggling in the financial trough in the United States, and watch them calmly from afar. A pretty spectacle for any rational human being.

The royalties due me in November, 1907, turned into drafts reached me safely at Papeete. And I must thank you for your kindness in helping Mrs. Ninetta Eames out with my affairs in California. Things happened fast and furious with her for a while, and several payments I had expected from various sources failing to materialize, while the panic most successfully materialized, she was pretty hard-pressed.

I hope to get my new novel off to you before I leave San Francisco on my return-trip to Tahiti.

Also, I must thank you for all the trouble you have taken in trying to collect that $1000 for me from *The Times Magazine*. Since there seemed to be no financially responsible persons connected with the magazine, it does not seem practical for me to go to the expense of suing them. So I don't know what I shall do. I must confess that they robbed me pretty coldbloodedly.

Tahiti—well, wait till you read Mrs. London's Diary on it. We enjoyed it there very much; but we enjoyed even better Nuka-hiva in the Marquesas. The climate there is delightful. Also, from Taichae, in the Marquesas, we rode over on horseback to the valley of Typee—you remember Herman Melville's *Typee*. This was the historic valley.

Sincerely yours,
Jack London

To Hayden Carruth

Papeete, Tahiti
Feb. 15, 1908

Dear Hayden Carruth:—

I am just writing you a howl. If you will remember, there were two reasons that impelled me to cancel my contract with *The Cosmopolitan* for the boat-trip of the *Snark*. One reason was their blue-penciling of my work; the other and major reason was, because they were advertising that they were sending me around the world. Now, here you are, doing precisely the same thing—advertising that you are sending me around the world; giving the public to understand, clearly and definitely, that you are putting up for this voyage of mine. You know that this is absolutely untrue, and you should know that it is unfair to me. *The Woman's Home Companion,* it is true, advanced me a thousand dollars, upon a contract to take a certain number of words from me relating to the places I visited in the course of my voyage. If I had not written the two articles that you have already received and published, I should have written a couple of short stories instead, and financially have been just as well off. *The Woman's Home Companion* is not sending me around the world. By the time I had sailed from San Francisco, the *Snark* had cost me $30,000.00, and it has cost me a few thousand dollars since then. And everywhere I have been, the prices have been raised and stuck into me and broken off, all upon the understanding that I wasn't spending my money, but that I was spending the money of a rich magazine in the United States. Your miserable and untrue advertising has cost me more than the sum of money you advanced to me. And it has put my voyage, in the eyes of my friends, and in the eyes of my public, upon a totally different basis from its true basis. This is not a square deal at all that you are giving me, especially in view of the fact that it was thoroughly known, in the *Home Companion* office, that I had broken off with *The Cosmopolitan* because it had done that very thing. Now, I don't know what you are going to do to rectify it, but rectify it you must, somehow.

Sincerely yours,
Jack London

To CLOUDESLEY JOHNS

Papeete, Tahiti
Feb. 17, 1908

Dear Cloudesley:—

I got both your letters and the papers. You seem to have been raising particular hell down your way.

Oh, you can't lose the *Snark*. By the time Charmian and I had arrived in Frisco we were both saying: "Me for the *Snark*." We were honestly homesick for her. We're a whole lot safer on the *Snark* than on the streets of San Francisco.

Wish, often, you could be with us in some of our jamborees and adventures. We sail from here in several days for Samoa, the Fijis, New Caledonia, and the Solomons. Have just finished a 145,000 word novel [*Martin Eden*] that is an attack upon the bourgeoisie and all that the bourgeoisie stands for. It will not make me any friends. *The Iron Heel* ought to be out by now. I wonder what you will think of it.

Have just finished Austin Lewis' "American Proletariat." It's good stuff.

Gee! You certainly found yourself in the Socialist movement. Charmian joins me in sending love to you and Mrs. Cloudesley.

Jack

To GEORGE STERLING

Papeete, Tahiti
Feb. 17, 1908

Oh You Greek!—

This is just a line to let you know that you were right and I was sick when I denied having a Bierce letter. Find it herewith. I am also sending you Constance Skinner's parody on Porter Garnett.

Your long letter missed the other steamer, came down in the mailbags on our steamer and was delivered to us here.

I can't get a line on why you wish I hadn't written *The Road*. It is all true. It is what I have done, and it is part of the process by which I have become. Is it a lingering taint of the bourgeois in you that makes you object? Is it because of my shamelessness? For having done things in which I saw and see no shame? Do tell me.

257

Was sick all the way down on the steamer—so was Charmian. Also we buried one horse at sea and one man.

Engine not yet running. We expect to get away in a week. Will you write and tell Mr. Brett (Macmillan Co.) where proof-sheets of new novel are to be mailed to you. This novel, *Success,* 140,000 words, will be mailed to Brett on next *Mariposa,* five weeks hence.

Am mailing off several "Testimonies" this steamer, with good things about you written inside.

Charmian sends loads of love. I send you all mine.

Wolf

To Ninetta Eames

Hobart, Tasmania
July 3, 1908

Dear Mother Mine:—

In reply to yours of March 6 and May 21.

All mail came safely to hand at Panata. Please find inclosed, copy of amount from Pinker dated Mar. 31, 1908. It is certainly not the information that I was after. I had that information before; but what I was after was the DATES OF PUBLICATION. I have not yet received any dates of publication.

Who is Theodore T. Dowdle, Architect? Is he the one who designed Mama's house?

Glad you liked Jack Johnson's photo.

Whatever plans you are making about Wake Robin Lodge are all right.

One is in absolute harmony with Nature's laws when a yellow-fever mosquito bites. He is in absolute harmony with Nature's law when as a result of that bite yellow-fever develops in him. He is in absolute harmony also, when, as the result of the fever, much albumen will be found in his urine and he suffers various other perturbing and disconcerting afflictions. And still in absolute harmony with Nature's laws will his heart-action die down, and he shall cease to be, all on account of that yellow-fever. Nature is just about as much interested in killing live creatures as it is in curing them —in fact, that constitutes the vast harmony of Nature. No alleged harmony with Nature's laws will make a humpback straight or render immune a man who has a predisposition toward yellow-fever.—This all apropos of your statement in your letter in which you said the cure of any disease, and underlined *any.* Once again, I rise to inquire, *WHY SHOULD HALF SUFFER!*

Gee! There'll be a lot for us to see when we get home—the new ranch; the big tank; and all the rest. Can't tell you how glad we are to get back. Hurrah for the cook! She'll be well broken in by the time we get there.

Please order for me, from the Tabard Inn Book Company the following books: Tell them to send by express, and you can pay the expressage when it arrives.

Biography of a Prairie Girl,	25¢
Aladdin O'Brien,	25¢
Her Washington Experiences,	25¢
The Kempton-Wace Letters, 5 copies,	25¢ each, $1.25
The 13th District,	25¢
Reminiscences of a Dramatic Critic,	50¢
Saints and Sinners,	35¢

Hold these books until I arrive home.

If, by the time you have received this, no check for me has come to hand from the *New York Herald,* for the prize-fight article I cabled them from Sydney,[1] why please write to the Editorial Department of the *New York Herald,* telling them you are my business agent and have been advised by me to collect for same. (Don't make any mistake in writing to the *S. F. Call* for payment. The *Call* bought its right to publish, from the *N. Y. Herald,* and you are to collect from the *N.Y. Herald.*) I can't tell you what amount to expect to· collect, because no arrangement was made as to amount. That'll be up to the *N. Y. Herald.*

The Calendar has just come to hand, and it is the sort of thing I like to have around my desk. It was immediately impressed into use.

With lots of love, dear Mother Mine.

Jack

P.S. We are down here in Hobart in 43° South Latitude, in what is equivalent to the month of August in California. Yet the air is crisp and cold, with a touch of frost in it. My hands, which, with one exception, during all their period of sickness, have not sweated. They are improving in this cool weather, and just now the very lightest perceptible sweat is to be seen. I can scarcely tell you how I hailed it with delight. Charmian is beginning to look like herself again, and to have more zest in life than she has shown for some time. She has a tomato-soup-and-graham-bread appetite that is something shameful. She has had a pretty hard pull herself the past three months. And let me tell you that malarial fever, like Solomon Island sores, and other things, can be contracted by the purest blooded, purest-living persons in the world.

[1] Jack Johnson–Tommy Burns heavyweight bout, Dec. 31, 1907.

To George P. Brett

Penduffryn, Guadalcanal
Solomon Islands
Oct. 25, 1908

Dear Mr. Brett:—

Just dropping you a line from the Solomon Islands. I have just returned here from a voyage on the *Snark* up to Lord Howe and Tasman Islands. We were gone over two months on the trip, during which the *Snark* was a hospital ship. There was never a time when some of us were not sick, and most of the time most of us were sick. Fever was the principal affliction, from which none of us escaped. One of my native sailors, a Tahitian, nearly died of it, and incidentally was crazy for a while. The cook, a Japanese, from sheer funk over the general sickness and over the fear of being eaten by the natives, went crazy and left us at Meringe Lagoon, on Ysabel Island, where he remained over two months before he could get away. I don't know whether I told you or not of the book I had been thinking of writing, sometime ago, namely, *Around the World with Two Gasoline Engines and a Wife*. I am now contemplating another book: *Around the World in the Hospital Ship Snark*. I am the navigator these days, and the doctor, and a whole lot of other things as well. Mrs. London ably performs her part as chief nurse and A.B.[1] She has been standing not only her own watches but some of the watches of the sick men. And all the time I think I've been the sickest of anybody on board, at least, I have accumulated several new and alarming diseases, two of which have been utterly unheard-of by any white man I have met in the Solomons.

Speaking seriously about books, I have just been casting up what I have on hand. Which is as follows:

Lost Face,—	52,000 words, containing my latest Klondike short-stories. It will be the last collection of Klondike short stories I shall ever bring out.
Revolution, and Other Essays,—45,000 words—similar to *War of the Classes*.	
When God Laughs,—	42,000 words,—all late miscellaneous short-stories, to which a couple more will have to be added to make a book.
Tropic Tales,— [*South Sea Tales*]	(so-called for want of a better title, which I may find later), 53,000 words, consisting of South Sea short-stories.
The Snark Book,— [*Cruise of the Snark*]	81,000 words, covering the voyage of the *Snark* from San Francisco to the Solomons, inclusive, and which will conclude the voyage of the *Snark* in the Pacific, for from here we go on into the East Indies. This collection consists of articles, special articles, handling

particular phases of the voyage, such as "The Amateur Navigator," "The Amateur M.D.," "Cruising in the Solomons," "A Pacific Traverse," etc., etc. It also includes special articles of particular things ashore, such as "The Nature Man of Tahiti," "The Leper Settlement at Molokai," "The Stone-Fishing of Bora Bora," a visit to the Valley of Typee, etc., etc. Of course I will see that there are photographs to go along with this.

Also I have 30,000 words of Hawaiian short-stories written [*The House of Pride*], and [as] I can't figure out any more Hawaiian short-stories I am wondering whether I should combine these 30,000 words of Hawaiian short-stories with 20,000 words of short-stories written on other parts of the world, or if the book could be brought out as a wholly Hawaiian collection of stories, in which case, being 30,000 words long, it might be sold at a dollar instead of $1.50. Please let me know your judgment concerning this.

And I have now 20,000 words written on a short Solomon Island novel —love-story and adventure [*Adventure*]. I am working on this novel now, and should have it finished in the next two months.

Of course, all the foregoing books have not received serial publication yet. In the *Lost Face* collection there are three stories yet to receive serial publication. Two of these have been bought by the *Century Magazine,* but I do not know whether they have yet been published. The third, "Lost Face" itself, written last, is seeking serial publication. And so on and so on with the other collections. As fast as they have received their serial publication, I shall turn them over to you.

I sail now in about five days on the steamer to Sydney. I am leaving the *Snark* in the Solomons with the sails unbent, to ride through their northwest season, which is one of calms and gales. I am going to Australia to go into a hospital for an operation, and then I expect to fool around several months in Australia, New Zealand, and Tasmania, and, of course, shall go on writing.

Sincerely yours,
Jack London

¹Able-bodied seaman

To NINETTA EAMES

Penduffryn, Guadalcanal,
Solomon Islands
Oct. 26, 1908

Dear Aunt Netta:—
I haven't received any of the Batavia mail yet, but in the Macassar mail

have received a check from Pinker for 284.14/5 [pounds]; and I have received original drafts, 10 in number, 9 of which are for 100 each, and one of which is for 126.13/11. Also I have received duplicates 5 in number, Nos. 3578-9-80-81-82. I assume that the other 5 duplicates have gone on to Batavia, and as I have not received any Batavia mail, I expect to receive said duplicates in that mail.

If I have not yet told you, please keep track and let me know the dates of publication and in what magazines of all my stuff in the United States and England. You see, I have with me account-books into which I put said data.

Always let me know when you ship boxes for me, where you ship said boxes, when, how many boxes, and roughly what the contents are, and also Bills of Lading for same. Of course, up to all the Macassar mail that I have received, you may not have shipped any boxes. You speak vaguely in your letter of getting boxes ready to ship; but at present moment I have no clew as to whether or not you have shipped any boxes at all to me at Macassar.

I am replying herewith to the last bunch of your letters received, which are dated April 2, May 22, June 9, June 14, and August 4. In all the time covered by these letters you have sent me my monthly account for the month of May only under date of June 15. In all the Port Moresby letters received by me, a couple of months ago here in the Solomons, you sent me only one monthly account, for month of February 1908. I am driven to conclude one of two things—either a lot of your letters containing the missing monthly accounts have gone astray, or else you have not sent them. Anent the foregoing, the letter dated June 14 is addressed to Charmian, not to me.

In a letter of yours to Charmian, you speak of freight in New Guinea, wishing that we could get into our boxes there. The only New Guinea port I asked you to send freight to was Port Moresby, and I understood from you later on that you had sent no freight to Port Moresby. Is this an error, or have you really sent freight to New Guinea somewhere?

Whenever you receive shipments of curios, etc., etc., from me, be sure to tell me if the right number of boxes has been received, the condition of the goods, the freight you have had to pay, the duty you have had to pay, etc. I sent you quite a shipment of curios from Tutuila, Samoa, via Apia. I have no letter from you acknowledging receipt of this shipment at all. Of the shipment of curios from Suva, Fiji, you mention the fact of having received them, and that a couple of war clubs were missing, but you have not told me freight, duty, etc.

As regards raising money on insurance policies made out to Bessie as beneficiary, I think she has got me on a technicality on our agreement arranged preceding the divorce. So it would be impossible to get her to sign any papers allowing me to raise money on said policies. However, I am proceeding to fight this out with her, and I shall let you know the outcome.

The one copy of *The Iron Heel* you speak of sending me by last mail (in your letter of April 2) has not arrived. Where did you send it? To Port Moresby?

Be sure that you do not continue the ruinous policy of paying 5¢ a clipping to the Authors' Clipping Bureau. See previous instructions of mine to you prior to leaving California in which I state that I am paying $30 per 1000 clippings, in advance.

In your letter of April 2, you state that you are sending me packages of clippings, many of them about *The Iron Heel*. I have received one package of clippings, in which there are four mentions of *The Iron Heel,* only.

Mildew in boxes shipped by us is practically unavoidable. Hence the extreme necessity of unpacking said boxes when received, and airing the contents and stowing away in a dry place.

Please note this clearly: I have an English Clipping Bureau, and an American Clipping Bureau. I have given repeated instructions to the American Bureau, that is the Authors' Clipping Bureau, that they are not to send me English clippings at all. Just now they are sending me practically nothing but English Clippings; all of which are duplicates of clippings sent me by the English Bureau. I am inclosing you herewith a bunch of said duplicates, which you will please send to the Authors' Bureau, reiterating my instructions, and asking them to credit my account to the extent of that number of clippings. In my letter files, you should find a record of some of my more recent letters to the Authors' Clipping Bureau, stating that they were to send me American clippings only.

Concerning the Stewart negatives—I don't know whether I had them stored in Oakland or whether I had them stored up on the ranch.

As regards book-translations, the only thing to do is let me handle them personally; so when you get any letters regarding translations, be sure to forward them to me.

Anent Miss Roseboro's statement that [Paul R.] Reynolds was hawking my stories from one editor to another as though he were handling merchandise, I can't exactly see what Miss Roseboro is getting at. All stuff sold to magazines is handled just precisely like merchandise. It doesn't matter whether Reynolds does the hawking, or Mrs. Ninetta Eames does the hawking, or Jack London does the hawking; it is handled as merchandise. The big majority of the stuff written by well-known writers in England and America to-day, is "hawked" by their literary agents. There is no writer to-day, of importance, who does not use, either steadily or sporadically, literary agents for the sale of his work.

From the time I started my first manuscripts to the magazines, up to the time I left California, I never inclosed a personal letter with the manuscripts. I put the manuscript into an envelope and sent it off without any letter at all. And I should advise you to do the same thing; then if the editor writes, it's up to you to write back. You say in your letter of May 22:

"Anyway, I'm not urging a price on your matter, but just ask the editor what he will give for the inclosed story by Mr. Jack London." I am afraid this is bad psychology from the standpoint of my pocket. You put the manuscript into an envelope and send it to the magazine, and don't make the mistake of inclosing any stamps. This will save you time, and I think will pay better. At any rate it has always been my policy. Possibly once in a hundred times when I am sending manuscript to an editor that I know, and in which case am most likely filling an order, do I ever inclose a letter.

Will you please find out from the Oakland bank, and let me know, the sum of money I have to my credit there.

You did just right in selling *Martin Eden* to the *Pacific Monthly*. I like the change of name very much. The title *Success* did not strike me.

When I started on the *Snark* voyage I told you to set your own price on your time. You set $10.00 a month. When you asked for $20.00 a month, I gave it to you, dating the raise back to the time when you asked for it. When this time you decided $30.00 was all right, you saved me the trouble of dating back the raise. And now I say all right. I have given you a free hand at determining what your time is worth, and have no complaints whatever to make about what you have done, while on the other hand I have much praise.

You have written frankly to me about the matter, and, having stated my thorough satisfaction with what you have done, I shall now write to you frankly about the matter. I may be altogether wrong, but I am sure, had I not been Jack London, but Tom Jones, and had I read your letter to Jack London mentioning the need for the raise to $30.00, and the many reasons that went to constitute that need—I, Tom Jones, could only have concluded that Jack London was not paying you enough, and furthermore, that he was rather a stingy fellow who overworked those in his employ. Mark you, I am merely choosing this method of conveying to you the impression I get from your letter. And I must confess that I was rather finished off when I read in your letter: "The hundred you allowed me for commission." I did not allow you any hundred for commission. I sent it to you as a present. When I take a schooner, pay all expenses of said schooner, supply it with food and diving-suits and boats, and hire divers at a monthly salary, and go to a pearl lagoon and one of my divers finds an unusually large pearl, he does not get any commission on that pearl. And so, with the $100 I sent to you. You were not a literary agent, you were my agent; and had you not been my agent, Mr. Brett would not have turned over to you the correspondence or telegrams from *Pacific Monthly* in which they stated that they wanted to get hold of *Martin Eden* for serial publication. The $100 to you was a present, a bonus, a voluntary increase in salary, in appreciation for work well performed.

Now, please don't misunderstand me. I am writing this in frankness, and because my feelings have been somewhat hurt by the impressions I got from your letter of the situation. And while I am about it, let me point out this: Had you not been my agent, the chance to sell *Martin Eden* would not have come to you, and had you not sold *Martin Eden,* the $100 would not have come to you. Therefore, that $100 must be looked upon as a perquisite of your office. If I should string that $100 out through the year, it would come to $8.50 a month. Adding this to the thirty dollars a month salary you are receiving, we get $38.50 a month. And if this is not enough, if you feel that I am overworking you and underpaying you, why it's up to you to do what I have told you to do from the beginning—to set your own price upon your time.

And now to other things. The thought strikes me that in the earlier bunch of letters, to which I replied some two months ago, there may have been the monthly statements of account which I filed separately. The more I think of it, the more I am sure that this is so.

But of the bunch of letters I am answering now (find dates of same in earlier part of this letter), I am absolutely sure that there was but one accompanying monthly statement, that for the month of May, dated June 15.

Please don't type your letters to me on both sides the paper. Not only is it exasperating, but it is time-losing. One of the reasons I can get through so much work is that I insist upon not being hampered in such and a thousand similar ways.

No matter how hard up you may become, don't call in the loan to Eliza. And of course, charge her no interest.

In glancing through your paragraphs relating to your request for the raise to $30.00, I find sentences like the following, which should go far to explain to you the impression I got from your summing up of the situation: "If you feel that the work I do is worth a living wage." Don't you see the connotation to that is not nice? Tom Jones, reading that letter, would be quite sure that Jack London was not paying Ninetta Eames a living wage. Now there is one wage that is less than a living wage, and that is the wage that is paid to sweated labor. Ergo, I sweat my labor. No, I'm quite sure you don't mean all this; but still, that and the other things will show you how my feelings have come to be hurt. One of the things I have prided myself on since I have had a dollar to spend, has been that everybody that ever did anything for me has always been well paid.

I try to read between the lines, and make out whether or not you are averse to going on handling my affairs. You don't say that you are; but IF you are, please do say so. Don't, in good American slang, pass the buck to me. I am satisfied, and I want you to be satisfied. But if you are not satisfied, please do not put the responsibility upon me by making me say Quit. That is for you to say.

No, I'm going to have no more captains on the *Snark*.[1] I find that I can navigate a whole lot better than they can. I have just shipped, however, a white mate who will take a lot of the overseeing and sailorizing off my hands. The *Snark* shall never again be turned into any man's hands to handle.

You are absolutely right in not letting Mr. Jones publish in his advertising that I considered it my best novel. Even if I did so consider it, neither you nor he could have been aware of the fact, and it would to all intents and purposes have been a lie. I am delighted with the advertising they are doing.

Be sure, in most of the correspondence that you carry on for me, and even in the seemingly unimportant stuff, to make carbon copies, so that you have always a set of all the letters you have written, on hand. It will save lots of trouble in the end. This, of course, will include your letters to me.

Be sure that a file of the *Pacific Monthly* is sent me.

You ask for advice concerning the stories of mine which you have sent the rounds of all the paying publications. Don't offer them to the newspapers unless I tell you to. Newspapers never pay anyway. Of course, if you should receive a good newspaper offer for any of them, why go ahead; but don't offer them yourself. File them away and hold on to them. Sometimes requests come in from magazines, and from new magazines, just starting, for stories. Then you have some stock to draw upon. In the meantime, send me a list of the manuscripts that have gone all the rounds, with the list of magazines to which each one has been sent.

Please write to the editor of *Papyrus* merely mentioning that I am away off on the other side of the world on the *Snark,* and that it would be better, under the circumstances, to let the subscription expire.

As regards Mr. Brett's letter of June 11, 1908, which I am returning to you herewith, you can write him and say that I do not know what Mr. Pinker has done in the matter of *Martin Eden.* That if Mr. Pinker has sold *Martin Eden* and has not sold the Colonial rights, it would be well to write to him telling him that I should be glad indeed to have him see that those rights are turned over to me so that I can utilize them by way of Mr. Brett's proposition. On the other hand, if Mr. Pinker has not yet sold the book-rights of *Martin Eden,* it might be told to him that I request said Colonial rights for Mr. Brett's purpose, but that while I REQUEST, I do not command. I imagine this is the best I can do in the matter. I have had so many complications over these Colonial rights now that I am afraid of further entanglements.

You would better write to Mr. Pinker telling him to change the title to *Martin Eden.*

With lots of love,

Jack

---

[1]London dismissed Captain Warren in Suva.

To Bessie M. London

Penduffryn, Guadalcanal
Solomon Islands
Oct. 27, 1908

Dear Bessie:—

I have just received your two letters, one dated March 24, and one dated July 30. I must confess that they surprise me. I am afraid I am a dreadfully easy-going fellow. You ought to know that pretty well yourself. But on top of my easy-goingness, I am a fighter, and you ought to know that, too. Your two letters are a challenge to fight.

You should have had better sense than to think that I wanted the $2000 out of the house that Charley put into it, in case the place was sold before twenty years were up. I did not know anything about what you intended to do with the house after you bought it, in the way of fixing it up; and here is the way I shall fix it up. On the day that you and Charley are married,[1] or, rather, on the day that you and Charley buy the house, you sign a contract or you and Charley sign a contract, rather, granting me, for the space of twenty years, the right of refusal on the house, at the price of four thousand five hundred ($4,500.00) Dollars, plus the improvements made by Charley's money. All you and he will have to do will be to have your receipts for additional improvements on the house, and they will be paid by me in addition to the $4,500.00 Dollars.

Now I have pointed out clearly to you that I do not wish to make a profit out of you and Charley. And, furthermore, if your marriage should prove a happy one, so that you and Charley are living together twenty years after your marriage, the increased value of the property from the day I bought it and improved it, to the day of your marriage, which said increased price is the cause of the present trouble, will go to you and Charley. That certainly shows that I am not trying to make a profit out of you. I flatter myself, what of the household furniture at which you sneer, plus the increased value aforementioned, that will go to the two of you when you have been married twenty years, is a pretty nice wedding present to a man's first wife upon marrying her second husband. I am very sure that nowhere in my recollection is stored the memory of any wedding-present given by you to your first husband when he married his second wife.

It amuses me to see the way, in both your letters, that you reiterate the firm foundation upon which you stand, namely, that you are observing the letter of our agreements. Of course, in my own mind, there is a very strong suspicion that you are *not* observing the letter. But that is beside the point. The point is, as you naively make it yourself, that you go in for the letter of things, and not the spirit. Has it ever entered your mind that possibly that phase in your character will explain why you and I were not happily married?

In all your dealings with me, it has been nothing but letter, letter, letter,

letter. I, on the other hand, have always exceeded the letter. I have always done better by you than I agreed to do. I have always given you more than was laid down in the letter of the contract. You yourself know thoroughly the spirit of my intention as regards you and the children, whether it was in agreements we made and conversations we held, or wills that I made. You know that you, Bessie London, were not to be considered at all, according to said wills, agreements, and conversations, from the moment that you contracted a second marriage. You know that in this you were placed in the same category with my second wife and with my mother. You know, absolutely, according to my will, that the moment my second wife or my mother married again, that they ceased, flatly, from participation in one cent of my money. You know that according to my will, as fast as any one of the three of you should marry, that the money that had been their share was to go to the children. And now, in the face of all this, you come back on me and try to spring a technicality about the insurance—in fact, in virtuous and magnanimous free-heartedness, point out that by all the gods you are going to have that insurance. Well, we shall see what we shall see.

Let me point out another thing to you. As regards the children, whether I live or die, they are amply provided for. This insurance, this endowment insurance, rather, and the increased value on the house, represents sums of money which you are trying to drag out of me, not for the children, but for you and your second husband to spend or invest. Surely, your second husband will be able to take care of you without any such assistance from me.

Then comes the funniest thing of all in your letter. You threaten, that if I do not accede to the dragging out of me of aforementioned sums of money for the benefit of you and your second husband, that you will be danged if you will get married. Why, my dear child, I don't care a whoop in high water whether you get married a second time or not. I should like to see you happily married for your own sake, but I regret that I cannot genially contribute money to finance that second marriage. I can't possibly imagine what was working in your brain that impelled you to make such a threat to me.

I quote the following from your letter of March 24: "Now, another thing I do not think you have thought about. When I marry, your little girls will have their share of Charley's estate just the same as they have of yours. DO BE JUST, JACK."

I confess that the preceding quotation rather puzzles me. I do not see where I can be unjust in the matter. And let me tell you now that I do not and shall never require any money from you or Charley for the taking care of my children. And I do not see that Charley's willingness to make my little girls his heirs, plus all the other little girls and boys that will be his and yours, is sufficient inducement for me to be just, or for me to allow, at the present moment, you and your future husband to drag money out of me.

You tell me that the day after I signed that contract you consulted a lawyer. I was agreeably surprised by this decent delay, until I remembered that I had signed the contract on Sunday. The lawyers are not usually in their offices on such a day.

In your letter you say, "Now, Jack, I am not buying this place for investment. I want a home. We Madderns have always had a home. I want mine."

Now, anent the foregoing, I'm surely not standing in the way of your having a home. I have kept you in a pretty good home myself, and I am even allowing you and Charley to get this present home at less than it is worth, at less than I could sell it on the open market any time. I kind-of think I'm a pretty good home-provider myself. Furthermore, as you say that you are not buying the place for an investment, but for a home, it seems that I am working no hardship on you and Charley when I stipulate that for the first twenty years of your marriage that you consider the place a home and use it for a home, and not as an investment out of which you will extract the increased value of which I am making you a present. Furthermore, if you are anxious for a home or an investment, and you don't like my terms, go out in the market and buy one on more favorable terms.

Your letters call for frank speech from me. Like the majority of women you have two failings. The first is that of voluble asseveration of your own truthfulness. The second is your constitutional unveracity. There is no discussion about this. I have had to swallow a few lies myself from you, and let me tell you that when you say that when "I signed away my rights to your royalties, etc. (which was community property) with the understanding I was to have the insurance instead,"—let me say that you lie. And let me say it again—that you lie. Without saying one word to me when I was away in Japan, while you were selling the clothes I had made you presents of and which you had never made up, when you were receiving regularly from me your monthly allowance, when you were calling upon my New York publishers for additional money (according to my volunteered permission), and when you were sowing the impression broadcast that you were starving —you turned loose on me, filed most horrible charges against me, attached everything I possessed, and I found myself, upon my arrival in San Francisco off the steamer, without a penny that wasn't tied up. You did this on the advice of a lawyer. I don't know just exactly the letter of the law or agreement you were living up to when you did it, but you undoubtedly did it. Now, why didn't you carry out the program? Why didn't you get in and mulct me of the few books and the several hundred dollars that I possessed? Why did you, on the other hand, sign away your rights in royalties, etc., as you say in the quotation just given? You did it because you knew me well enough to realize that you would get nothing at all out of me—that the lawyers would swallow up what little I had and that you would be compelled to get down on your knees to me for bread and butter. You knew that you were beaten. You knew that I held the club over you of my own careless disregard for money when a fight was on and injustice was being dealt out to me. That is why you signed away your royalties, etc. And then for you to come and say that you signed away with the understanding that you were to be treated better than my mother or my second wife, who were not to have any of my endowment insurance in the event of their marrying again! Once more, let me tell you that there was no such understanding, and that when you say there was, it is a lie.

I quote from your letter of March 24: "Surely I deserve something besides a little household furniture." I think you've got a whole lot more out of me than a little household furniture. Which is beside the point, however. No matter how virtuous and noble and exalted you have been in the past, that is no just reason that I should be putting up money for you and your second husband to spend.

You keep saying in your letters: "Treat me white." It is the first time I ever heard that "white" treatment of a divorced wife consists of a first husband helping to support a second husband.

You tell me that you have not written this letter in anger. It was quite unnecessary to say this. It sticks out all over the letter that you were writing it in acquisitiveness.

You keep telling me the things I said that Sunday morning while we talked over your marriage with Charley—the day I sailed for Tahiti—you keep telling me these things, and I find that I look at them for the first time. I am willing to confess that I was a bit too drunk on the whiskey you gave me that morning to remember much of anything that was said. But just the same, if I stood before God's Throne, I'd stake my immortal soul against ten thousand centuries in hell that I never said those things.

You say: "Jack, if I wanted to sell this place, for what earthly reason would I want it so badly! I want a home." That being so, why under the sun are you raising all this tempest because I refuse to let you and Charley drag out of me the increased value of said home, when, if you use it as a home, at the end of twenty years the increased value will be yours and the home can then become an investment, and you can pocket the money I have given you?

You tell me in your letter of July 30, that when you had me draw up the agreement, for once in your life you did the right thing at the right time. Let me tell you that when you started to drag this money out me for the use of yourself and your second husband, that you have done the wrong thing at the wrong time, and that you've tackled the wrong man as well.

I sometimes wonder if you have one atom of love in your nature. Pride I know you do not possess. But there are many prideless women who possess love. I quote from your letter of July 30: "I shall not marry until we come to some sort of an understanding in regard to this." Just analyze this sentence. It means that you care more for the few dollars you think you can drag out of me than you care for Charley. You will not be happily married if you balance your husband off against a few paltry dollars, and overbalance him with said paltry dollars. I am compelled to repeat my remark made earlier in the letter, namely, that I do not care if you never get married.

Now I am going to sum up. I have treated you all through the past and up to the present in an open, free-handed way. I have always given you more than any agreement we had ever called for. And all you had to do was ask me for more, and you got it. I have met you in excess of the letter, which is more than I can say you have done for me. And as the case now stands, in spite of all that I have done, you have mapped out a program whereby you think you can mulct me of several thousand dollars for the use of yourself and your second husband. I tell you now, flatly, that I shall not stand for it. You can go to law and lawyers all you want. I'd sooner give law and lawyers ten dollars for every dollar you're trying to rob me of than see you get those dollars you are trying to rob me of. You can begin fighting any time you want; and let me promise you one thing, that it will be fight, fight, fight, day and night, month in and month out, year in and year out, until either you or I cease to be. And I tell you furthermore, that I will fight, fight, fight until there is not a penny left for anybody to get. And I promise you solemnly, here and now, that you will never touch one penny of the sum you contemplate robbing me of. I'll fight you in the courts, but I'll carry the case farther, and fight you in every newspaper in Christendom. And let me tell you one thing, that a great ha! ha! will go up over the world at the spectacle of Jack London's first wife trying to bleed money out of Jack London for the use of her second husband. You were once so faithful and trusting where lawyers were concerned that you put down on paper, and swore to the vilest calumnies, the most damnable and horrible lies, that any woman, no matter how low, could think of. That these damnable lies, not only blackened your husband, but blackened you and blackened your two children. That the shame and disgrace is publicly recorded, right down in the county court house in Oakland, California. And let me tell you that when I start fighting, every last horrible, damnable lie in that document will be made public by me. And I won't even have to go to the courthouse for it—I've got my copy filed away.

If you think you can drag this money out of me that does not belong to you, can use it for the benefit of your second husband and yourself, why go ahead and fight for it.

I am sending carbon copies of this to Mrs. Eames, to Eliza, and to Charley, reserving, of course, copies for myself. I am sending also to my people in California who represent my interests, additional data that will equip them to start the fight the very instant you deliver the first blow.

You talk to me about my investing the $4,500.00 in that house. Let me tell you that if I had my hands on it, I'd be spending it very lively these days. I have had a big slump in all my book-sales in the States partly due to the panic, and partly due to my socialism, and I am so pinched that I scarcely know where to turn. Furthermore, I am going down to Sydney, Australia, in several days, to go on the operating table, and I shall also then be in touch with California by cable, in order to direct proceedings the moment you start the ball rolling. What it is going to cost me to get through hospital I do not know. I have tied the *Snark* up in the Solomons where she will lie for months while I am in Australia. I have got to tie her up in order to maneuver around and get money to go on with the trip. I am so heavily overdrawn with the Macmillan Company now that I shall be unable to get money from them for a couple of years to come. My stories are not selling. In the past year 19 out of 20 of the stories I have written have been rejected by every magazine in the United States. And because of the financial pressure that is now on me, I am proceeding to retrench in every way. One of my acts of retrenchment is the tying up of the *Snark*. Another will be that for some months to come, until I have a better financial outlook, I shall be compelled to cut down your allowance from One hundred ($100.00) Dollars to Sixty-five ($65.00) Dollars, provided you are still single. Of course, you will not suffer—in case I go temporarily to pieces for the next several years and cannot advance you that $65.00 a month, you will have to allow 519 31st to be mortgaged and to live off of the money so raised at the rate of $65.00 a month. In this case, both you and Mrs. Eames, who has my power of attorney, will have to sign the mortgage.

I guess that is all I can think of now.

Very truly yours,
Jack London

[1]Bessie never married a second time.

To GEORGE STERLING

Guadalcanal, Solomon Islands
Oct. 31, 1908

O You Blessed Greek:—

In all these months no letter from you. Don't know how Charmian and I would have survived had it not been for Carrie's splendid long letter. I am answering this mail letters that are 8-9-10- and even 11 months old, and all of which have just come to hand.

I have yet to receive my mail forwarded from Batavia, and I imagine you've a couple of good long letters for me in that bunch.

I haven't written any letters for months and months—with the exception of one long-delayed one to Whitaker.

For the last three or four months the *Snark* has been cruising about the Solomons. This is about the rawest edge of the world. Head-hunting, cannibalism and murder are rampant. Among the worst islands of the group day and night we are never unarmed, and night watches are necessary. Charmian and I went for a cruise on another boat around the island of Malaita. We had a black crew. The natives we encountered, men and women, go stark naked, and are armed with bows, arrows, spears, tomahawks, war clubs and rifles. (Have Fiji and Solomon war clubs for you. Won't be able to give them to you till I get back home.) When ashore we always had armed sailors with us, while the men in the whale-boat, laid by their oars with the bow of the boat pointed seaward. We went swimming once in the mouth of a fresh-water river, and all about us in the bush our sailors were on guard, while we, when we undressed, left our clothes conspicuously in one place, and our weapons hidden in another, so that in case of surprise we would not do the obvious thing.

And to cap it all, we got wrecked on a reef. The minute before we struck not a canoe was in sight. But they began to arrive like vultures out of the blue. Half of our sailors held them off with rifles, while the other half worked to save the vessel. And down on the beach a thousand bushmen gathered for the loot. But they didn't get it, nor us.

And during all these months in the Solomons, the *Snark* has been a hospital ship. We have all had the fever more than we like to remember, as well as half a score of worse afflictions. The Japanese cook and one Tahitian sailor went crazy—from funk at sickness. The Jap's lunacy was also caused by fear of being eaten by the natives. When we careened the *Snark* on Ysabel there were times when only one man of us was able to go overside into the water and work. And I have had to doctor all of them, as well as myself, write stories and articles, and navigate the boat. You know I'm my own navigator now, and I have no man I can trust on deck in squalls.

Am leaving here in two days to go to Sydney, where I go into the hospital for an operation. And I have other afflictions, from a medical standpoint vastly more serious than the operation, which latter means only a few days in bed. The foregoing will serve to explain somewhat why I'm not writing letters these days. But that's no reason that you shouldn't write me good long ones. I have a lot of other curios for you, but have not time to indicate them. So they will have to remain stored up on the ranch till I get home. With love all around,

Wolf

To R. W. GILDER

Sydney, N.S.W., Australia
Dec. 22, 1908

Dear Mr. Gilder:—

I have been sick for many weeks now,[1] am just out of hospital and pretty weak and wabbly, with a mass of correspondence piled up that almost gives me a collapse every time I look at it. Somewhere in that mountain of letters is a bunch of correspondence relating to "To Build a Fire."[2] I cannot find it, and shall have to go on memory.

A long, long time ago I wrote a story for boys which I sold to the *Youth's Companion*. It was purely juvenile in treatment; its motif was not only very strong, but was very true. Man after man in the Klondike has died alone after getting his feet wet, through failure to build a fire. As the years went by, I was worried by the inadequate treatment I had given that motif, and by the fact that I had treated it for boys merely. At last came the resolve to take the same motif and handle it for men. I had no access to the boys' version of it, and I wrote it just as though I had never used the motif before. I do not remember anything about the way I handled it for juveniles, but I do know, I am absolutely confident, that beyond the motif itself, there is no similarity of treatment whatever.

I can only say that it never entered my head that there was anything ethically wrong in handling the same motif over again in the way I did, and I can only add that I am of the same opinion now, upon carefully considering the question. Please let me know how you feel about the matter.

Sincerely yours,

Jack London

P.S. My sickness is of so serious a nature that I am compelled to abandon the voyage of the *Snark* and to return to my own climate of California. The doctors in Australia can do nothing for me, because they do not know what is the matter with me. My trouble is nervous in origin; and all I can prescribe for myself is to return to an environment where I maintained a stable nervous equilibrium, in the hope of regaining that equilibrium.

¹With a strange skin disease.
²Published in *Youth's Companion,* May 29, 1902, under the same title.

To the Editor, *Collier's Weekly*

Sydney, N.S.W., Australia
Dec. 22, 1908

Dear sir:—

Some years ago I submitted to COLLIER'S an article entitled "Revolution." For this I received five hundred ($500) Dollars. The years went by. *Collier's Weekly* wouldn't publish it. It was a timely article, its statistics, etc., right up to date of the moment of selling it. But the several years that you have held it have destroyed its timeliness. The article as an article, has perished. Recently I wrote you, or had my agent in California write you, asking you to return it. My idea in asking for its return was two-fold. First, I wanted it to do some good for the socialist cause, and so desired to have it issued by the *Appeal to Reason* in pamphlet form. For this I would receive no remuneration whatever. Second, I wished to have the article so that I could include it in a new collection of essays to be brought out by The Macmillan Company.

I now learn that you have returned the article to Mrs. Eames, my California agent, and that you have asked in return for payment of the $500.00. I cannot see the equity of this. Granting that the article was worth $500, you allowed its value to perish in your pigeon-hole. I cannot see the fairness in making me pay for this loss of value, which was occasioned not by my act, but by your act.

A long time ago, when I first began to write, I sold a similar socialist article to *McClure's Magazine*. They did precisely what you did, held it for years and allowed its timeliness to perish. They, in the end, returned it to me, without having published it, so that I might include it in a collection of essays to be brought out in book-form. But they did not make me repay them the money they had paid for the article.

As you can see, the two occurrences are identical. In both articles I poured out my innermost convictions at white heat in the hope that said convictions would speedily be put before the public eye. But in both cases I was disappointed. In both cases the timeliness of the articles perished in the editorial pigeon-hole. Please let me know your opinion in the matter of my paying you $500 for the return of "Revolution." I may add that if *Collier's* had not bought and pigeon-holed the article, in all likelihood I should have been able to dispose of the article to some other magazine. But *Collier's* purchasing and pigeon-holing of the article destroyed all chances of disposing of it elsewhere.[1]

Sincerely yours,
Jack London

P.S. Concerning that article of mine, "The Other Animals," I have to get down on my ham-bones and beg forgiveness. When I wrote the article I remembered only one fight in *White Fang,* between a wolf-dog and a lynx. On re-reading *White Fang,* I discovered at least three fights. In the first place, I had a wolf proper killed by a lynx, I had White Fang's mother kill a lynx, and I had White Fang himself, in later fights, killing lynxes before paid audiences. I confess that my field observations, so far as the text of my own book is concerned, are rotten. In extenuation, all I have to say is, that the big fight in which White Fang's mother killed the lynx, occupied a great deal of space, while the killing of the wolf proper by the lynx occupied a mere line and was merely mentioned in passing.

---

[1]*Collier's* suggested that London send them a story for publication in lieu of the five hundred dollars. Apparently London never complied.

To George P. Brett

Sydney, N.S.W., Australia
Dec. 22, 1908

Dear Mr. Brett:—

In reply to yours of May 4, 1908, which has been tangled up in the Dutch East Indies and has finally come to hand, or, rather, it has been to hand for a couple of months, but I have been lying sick in hotels and hospitals, and been unable to reply to it or any other letters.

This sickness has led up to a change in my plans. In some way my nervous equilibrium has been overthrown, and for about four months now I have been suffering from an obscure nervous affliction which defies all the doctors of Australia. Not only have the biggest specialists here stated that they have never seen anything like it in their experience, but they further state that no line describing such an affliction is to be found in all their medical libraries. I am at times practically helpless, unable to cut a piece of cold meat with a knife and fork. Of course, in this condition, it would be impossible for me to travel on the high seas in the *Snark* unless I were strapped down in my bunk. In case of a roll I should be unable to seize a rope to hold on.

Because of all of which, and with deep sorrow on Mrs. London's part as well as my own I am compelled to abandon the voyage. I shall sell out the *Snark* in Sydney and go back to California to the climate where I have always succeeded in maintaining a stable nervous equilibrium, in the hope that my equilibrium will be restored. I expect to be in California several months from now.

Please find herewith signed contract for 1909.

I think when all is said and done, your choice of *Martin Eden* for title of my novel is the very best.

Concerning Mrs. Eames writing you about striking out certain portions of the text of *Martin Eden,* I can say I am very glad that you took the position you did.[1] I have written Mrs. Eames that the particular portion of the text that offends her will remain in the book.

My deepest thanks for advancing that last $5,000.00, which has come safely to hand. Since I am returning home, affairs will be easier with me, and I do not imagine that I shall be compelled in the future to throw myself so remorselessly upon your kindness in the matter of making heavy advances on royalties.

Since my last letter to you telling you of the various books I had completed or nearly completed, I have not written one line. I have been too sick. I have not even been able to write letters. I am just now out of hospital where I had a successful operation performed. This operation, however, had nothing to do with the vastly more serious nervous trouble from which I am suffering.

The funniest thing about this nervous trouble is that it displays itself only on certain parts of my body and in a physical way. The rest of my body is all right, I am in good health otherwise, nor is my brain afflicted in any way.

It isn't Mrs. London's fault that *The Log of the Snark* hasn't reached you before this. I have been holding it for the purpose of going over it, and have been unable to get around to it.

Sincerely yours,

Jack London

[1]The portion referred to is the scene where Martin Eden goes to the editorial offices of *The Transcontinental Magazine* and by physical means collects his five dollars. London had had a similar experience with *Overland Monthly*. Mrs. Eames felt that the scene was too thinly veiled.

To GEORGE STERLING

Sydney, Australia
March 3, 1909

Dear (dearest) Greek:—

Find here a sample of Australian wool. *Snark* has just arrived from Solomons. Shall sell her for any sum, no matter how small, get away to New Zealand, and then head for California.

One month cold weather in Tasmania helped me wonderfully. While not cured, this mysterious malady of mine is much better. Cool weather seems the best. Since return to Sydney warm weather no further improvement.

Just think!—one phase of it (happily past) was thickening of toe-nails till they were thick as they were long.

Your sonnet to Nora May French[1] splendid in its feel. "Sonnets to Oblivion" the real thing.

Be back in three months. You must save a *Wine of Wizardry* for me.

For heaven's sake don't you quarrel with Ambrose [Bierce] about me. He's too splendid a man to be diminished because he has lacked access to a later generation of science. He crystallized before you and I were born, and it is too magnificent a crystallization to quarrel with.

Your point about *The Road,* namely that it "gave the mob a mop to bang" me with. What of it? I don't care for the mob. It can't hurt me. One word of censure or disapproval from you would hurt me a few million myriads of billions times more than all the sum total the mob would inflict on me in one hundred and forty-seven life-times. I thank the Lord I don't live for the mob. (You damned Greek! If I ever get back to California I'll play cards with you and I'll curse God and the devil and you twice as hard as you can curse God and devil and me, when the luck goes against me.)

You were absolutely right in not changing part in *Martin Eden* about *Overland.* Your changes of club names O.K. The only reason I used real names of several clubs was that I said nothing nasty about them.

Charmian says to send her love to Greek and Greekess and all the Crowd. Same for me.

Wolf

[1]A young poetess in the Carmel circle who had committed suicide.

277

To George Sterling

Onboard *S. S. Tymeric,* between
Australia and Ecuador, and on
this day, May 2, 1909, off Pitcairn Island.

(Blessed) Greek:—

O you of little faith! Both your letters of Jan. 31 and Feb. 10th came safely to hand, as well as the *Wine of Wizardry.*

Am not writing a long letter, as we'll soon be home. Took this opportunity of voyaging on a tramp steamer. The voyage will last forty days, and the only land sighted is Pitcairn, which we picked up this morning.

We'll run up to Quito, see a bull-fight, and get home somewhere in July.

Oh, Greek—you should see Charmian play cards! She's as bad as you. After I won $160.00 from her at Casino, and after she'd sworn a dozen times that she'd played her last game, she tore up the deck. Later on she said that at last she knew just exactly how you felt when you had a run of bad luck.

We're playing cribbage, now, at ten cents a game. (Casino was five dollars a game.) (Yes George, and I "skunked" him twice today! C.L.)

Am already planning for California. We shall live at Wake Robin this summer and fall, while four guest cottages are going up on the ranch.

Then, next winter, we shall live in the guest cottages, and next summer build the house.

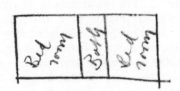

The above is plan of cottages. Guests will have quarters to themselves, while in house proper will be the living rooms. What do you think of the idea?

You and Carrie must come up this summer, or we won't go down and eat one damned Carmel-by-the sea mussel.

By Golly! we'll have some great times!

When you come up to see us you'll have to work at your trade (because I work at mine every morning.) Never you mind [Joseph] Noel and all the other little bats, but go on hammering out beauty. If the urge comes from within to write propaganda, all right; otherwise you violate yourself. There are plenty who can do propaganda, but darned few that can create beauty.

Some day you may see your way to fuse both, but meanwhile do what your heart listeth.

"Memory" is great! I've read it aloud a dozen times. (You should see us, George, when you send us a new poem! We sit and read it with tears in our eyes!)

Am boxing every day now—with the first, second and third mates—all husky young Englishmen. The first has a couple of beautiful black eyes I gave him. My straight left to the Second precipitated a gumboil that raised his face four inches and kept him from boxing for a week. And the straight lefts I presented to the Third, yesterday, have swollen his nose to twice its normal size. O, I'm doing nicely, thank you. I've got two game thumbs, and my face has divers discolorations, and I get cramps in my legs while fighting —but I'm getting into condition. Haven't had a drink for a month. But I think they know how to make dry Martinis in Guayaquil.

Love to Carrie. Tell her I've some splendid Samoan tapa for her when I get back and unpack it—and a war-club and spears for you—to say nothing of a clitoris, dried with appurtenances attached and strung on a string for an ear ornament—procured in Solomon Islands.

Charmian joins in love to both of you. Remember us to the rest.

Wolf

To WM. JAMES GHENT

S. S. Tymeric, Australia to
South America
May 7, 1909

Dear Ghent:

Your open letter to [Upton] Sinclair, dated February 9, 1909, and entitled "In Re Comrade Sinclair's Revised 'Manifesto,'" came to hand just as I was leaving Australia, and this is my first opportunity to answer. In the first place, I must say that I agree with the points you make in objection to the "Manifesto," especially where you refer to the fact that the signatories speak with an authority of influence which is after all an assumption. This "authority of influence" gets me, for one, very keenly, because of all untrue and egotistic positions to find oneself in, this is certainly the limit. I think you were quite right in your contention that the paper or "Manifesto" be submitted to the National Committee.

In the second place, I didn't sign my name to that "Manifesto" anyway. Some of my friends did it for me. I am not a bit angry because they did so, because I believe their intentions were of the best; but nevertheless I wish they hadn't.

It seems to me, if there is anything in party-organization and party-discipline, that no more ridiculous spectacle could be presented than that of

279

a group of young hot-heads issuing independent "Manifestos" on their own. One of the hardest things that I had hammered into my head was party-discipline; but it has been hammered in so thoroughly that at this late day you will find me the last man in the organization to jump over the traces.

Sincerely yours,

Jack London

To *S. F. Examiner*

    L. A. Examiner

    Vanity Fair, LONDON

COPY TO PINKER

Canal Zone, Panama

July 1, 1909

Arriving at Panama from South America, after being four months away from newspapers and letters, I got in touch with my mail and found the usual charge of plagiarism awaiting me. Mr. Frank Harris,[1] using the deadly parallel column, has published in *Vanity Fair* an extract from an article written by him in 1901, and an extract from *The Iron Heel* published by me in 1909. Line by line, and paragraph by paragraph, he proves conclusively that I have lifted from him bodily fully a thousand words of his own composition. On the face of it I should be hanged. That is the way we used to have of dealing with horsethieves in the Wild West. Of course, occasional horsethieves were hanged on strong circumstantial evidence, and afterwards found to be not guilty. I do not know whether I am guilty or not, but I shall state my side of the case to the public, and let it judge.

Mr. Frank Harris says: "A great meeting was to be held at Westminster Town Hall for the promotion of public morality. The Bishop of London presided. *** It occurred to me that it would be amusing to picture what would be the effect on the meeting if the Bishop of London had suddenly become a Christian. I wrote it all down."

Now in 1901 I found Mr. Harris's composition published in an American paper. To it was affixed an introduction by an American journalist, in which he said that these quoted words of the Bishop of London had been taken from the one London publication that had had the courage to print what the Bishop of London had actually said. Now I had never heard of Mr. Harris; I did not know that the unknown English journalist had perpetrated a canard; I don't think the American journalist knew that Mr. Harris had perpetrated a canard. He took Mr. Harris's article in good faith. And I certainly took it in good faith. I took what I saw in the newspaper as the quoted words of the Bishop of London uttered on a public platform. I thought I had a human document, and it made such a striking impression upon me that I filed it away for future use. Years afterwards, in writing *The Iron*

280

Heel, I resurrected the clipping. And with much glee I used it word for word, and again filed the clipping against the possibility of being charged in the future with having stretched realism and human probability. I smiled to myself at the thought that when such a charge was laid at my door I would bring forth the clipping—the human document containing the publicly-uttered words of the Bishop of London. And behold, it was a canard!

Mr. Harris made a canard that fooled an American journalist, and that through the American journalist fooled me. Mr. Harris baited his hook and caught me. I was what we call a sucker. But Mr. Harris, instead of gaily crying "Sucker!" gravely cried "Thief!" I am afraid that Mr. Harris is a very precipitous and guileless young man, or else dreadfully desirous of getting free advertising. If somebody else who did not know all the ins and outs of the affair had called me "thief," then Mr. Harris could have enjoyed a further and hearty laugh at my expense. But Mr. Harris himself, the man who made the canard and who caught me with it, carried the joke to the further extent of calling me a thief, and in so doing exceeded all decent limits of humor. Mr. Harris either has no sense of humor or, I repeat, is a very guileless young man.

The laugh is on me. I confess to having been fooled by Mr. Harris's canard. And I have but one regret, namely, that Mr. Harris did not make sure of his ground before he made a sensational public charge. Mr. Harris came out of the affair all right. Thanks to me he has managed to sell the same composition at space rates twice, and has received a lot of advertising. I do not come out of it so well. Not being content with having hooked me with his canard, Mr. Harris has publicly branded me as a thief, and has done so in a pert and patronizing way.

Jack London

---

[1] The English critic and writer.

To ALICE LYNDON[1]

Glen Ellen, Calif.
July 29, 1909

Dear Alice Lyndon:—

In reply to yours of July 12, which I received just as I was leaving New Orleans. I have been traveling ever since, and have been unable to answer until now, when I have arrived home.

Had a jolly time in New Orleans, and liked the people and the place very much.

Along about the time you said you had wild notions of coming out to California, I was very much in love with the one who was to become my wife, and who, odd to relate, I am more in love with than ever, in spite of the fact that I've had more than two years in which to overcome the "spasm."

We live and learn, and in this connection I will say that I've learned a few myself. And I've had some jolly good living while I was learning it.

Of course, I may be going to pieces as you suggest; but I'm living so damned happily that I don't mind if I do go to pieces. I prefer living to writing. Incidentally, I'd like to ask you a question or two. Since I was in the throes of the present love "spasm," I have written a number of books. In fact, I have now nine books waiting to be published, one of which is *Martin Eden.* I wonder if you have read any portion of it as it has appeared serially in the magazines. Personally, I believe it's the best book I have ever written. Also, I want to know if *White Fang* was particularly rotten. If *Before Adam* was particularly rotten. If *The Iron Heel* was particularly rotten. And so on down through the several books written and published during the past several years. To tell you the truth, I'm afraid I'm going to die in this present "spasm," even if I live to be a hundred and forty years old.

For heaven's sake tell me about this "Love's Sacrifice," the Tale of Lucy the Leper, printed in the *Redbook.*[2] It seems the ultimate irony that the only story of recent years of mine that you have seen was one that I have never written nor heard of. Can you tell me the number of the *Redbook* in which this story appeared?

You swatted me in good fellowship and frankness, and believe me, it is in the same spirit that I have swatted back.

Jack London

[1]An unknown fan.
[2]London published a short story entitled "Good-by Jack" in *Redbook* in June, 1909, in which a character is called "Lucy the Leper." Charmian has a note in London's copy, "He never heard from her [Alice Lyndon] again."

To Arthur Stringer[1]

Glen Ellen, Calif.
Aug. 2, 1909

Dear sir:—

I have just returned home after two years and a half of wandering through the South Seas, on which portions of the earth's surface men will be found, no doubt, who will rise up and say that I have never been in the South Seas and do not know what I am writing about. Having just returned, I have for the first time read your article entitled "The Canada Fakers," and published in the October number of *Canada West.* And now a word with you.

You have charged me with various Canada fakes, and I shall take them up in the order given by you. (1) When "Love of Life" was originally published in *McClure's Magazine,* the charge was then made that only an amphibious fish could have got from one pool of water to the other pool of water. I replied to this at the time, and gave eminent satisfaction to the be-puzzled inquirers. Now I am not going to explain to you how that fish,

282

without being amphibious, escaped from one pool to the other; but I will make you a proposition in two parts, said proposition to be a test of your cocksureness in the matter. On the one hand, I will bet you $200, and on the other hand, I will bet you $2000.00, that I will demonstrate before any committee of professors of physics selected by you, that under the circumstances precisely narrated in my story, the fish did escape from one hole to the other, through the crevice, and that it could escape by swimming, and that the man could bail the one pool dry in a few minutes and that the other pool into which the fish escaped, could not have been bailed by him in half a day. In this connection, it is up to you either to recant or to make your bet with me and prove yourself a physics-faker.

(2) You raise a great laugh at my expense because I have a water-hole open at a very low temperature, said water-hole remaining unfrozen. This is such an absolute literary fakerism that I wonder either at your audacity in promulgating it, or at your colossal carelessness. The water-hole at issue, according to my story, was first approached by the man who arrived first at the cabin. What takes place I now quote from my story: "The dogs had stopped beside a water-hole, not a fissure, but a hole man-made, chopped laboriously with an axe through three and a half feet of ice. A thick skin of new ice showed that it had not been used for some time." The time of the action of the story that takes place in the cabin is a matter of but few minutes, during which time first one man and then the other man goes out to the water-hole. At the end of the few minutes of action inside the cabin, one man departs, and departing he casts the sack of gold into the water-hole. Again I quote: "He worked the sack of gold out between the lashings and carried it to the water hole. Already a new skin of ice had formed. This he broke with his fist."

(3) You criticise me for speaking of a birch-bark sled. Such an objection, when the context is considered, is so puerile as to be a matter of marvel that you should be guilty of making it. In *White Fang* I show the method of driving the dogs, and describe the sleds that the dogs haul, so that no man acquainted with the locality would dream for an instant that I meant anything else than a birch-bark toboggan sled. Criticise my use of the word "sled" if you please, but do not abort your criticism until it becomes a criticism of my fact. Such tricks may be all very well in schoolboys' debating societies, but between grown men, and writers of books, they are certainly out of place. In this connection you throw yourself open to the charge of being a logic-faker and an etymology-faker.

(4) You object to my use of the dog-driver's command of "mush on." My Northland stories are practically all confined to the Klondike and to Alaska, and there the only phrase used as a command for the dogs to get up, to go on, to move, is "mush on." There is no discussion about this fact. There is no man who has been in Klondike or Alaska but who will affirm this statement of mine. In this connection, you have made yourself into a Canada-faker, and a self-advertised scholastic Canada-faker at that.

Now what I want to know is, what are you going to do about it? Will you take these charges back as publicly as you have charged them? And if, in the nature of journalism you cannot take them back as publicly as you have charged them, what amends then are you going to make?

Sincerely yours,

Jack London

[1]Writer of adventure stories.

To Lute Pease[1]

Glen Ellen, Calif.
Aug. 14, 1909

My dear Mr. Pease:—

In reply to yours of August 11. I am glad to hear that you are kindly disposed toward the manuscripts I sent you, and I thank you for your frank letter in the matter. The only hitch seems to be that of pride. First of all, let us go over the ground and see what quantity of stuff I sent you. Here are my figures;

"The House of Pride"	5340	words,
"Koolau the Leper"	5991	"
"The House of the Sun"	4898	"
"A Pacific Traverse"	6045	"
"Typee"	5188	"
"Stone Fishing at Bora Bora"	2404	"
"The Amateur Navigator"	5804	"
"Cruising in the Solomons"	7434	"
"The Amateur M.D."	6572	"
	49,676	words.

Now I don't know anything about magazine affairs, but as a tyro it seems to me that certain advantages ought to accrue to *The Pacific Monthly* through publishing this stuff. You did the Jack London advertising while you were bringing out *Martin Eden*. This advertising, to a certain extent represents so much ploughed ground. I should imagine that the simplest sort of announcement to the effect that you had practically a year's supply of further matter from Jack London would be sufficient seed for the aforesaid ploughed ground. Of one thing I am sure, that those of my admirers who subscribed on account of *Martin Eden* would certainly renew upon your promising another year's run of my stuff—and especially of my *Snark* stuff. Don't forget this: that *The Cosmopolitan Magazine* advertised the *Snark* trip most extensively, and that this is so much ground already ploughed for you without any expense. Furthermore, there has been a great deal of general

Snark-trip advertising in the news columns of all the newspapers of the United States.

Now, as to the matter of price. Suppose you make me the best offer you can, for these 50,000 words, and remember the photographs. Between the cost of the cameras, the loss of films and chemicals, etc., through deterioration in the tropics, and leaving out of account any personal work on my part in taking the photos, my photographic expenses for the voyage have been over $1500. Now I am not suggesting this $1500 as a price to you—far from it; I am merely pointing out that the photos *are* worth something. In this connection, more of my films are arriving within a few days (in baggage that was sent from the Isthmus of Panama to South America by mistake). When these films arrive I shall be able to dig up some more good illustrations for the article.

One thing, namely: whatever offer you make, it must be cash on acceptance. My reason is this: there are a couple of hundred acres of land adjoining my land that can be purchased by me inside the next thirty days at a bargain. I have had my eyes on this land for years, and now is my opportunity. So I am gathering all the cash that I can in order to buy in.

Sincerely yours,
Jack London

[1]Of *Pacific Monthly Magazine.*

To EDITOR, *Vanity Fair*

Glen Ellen, Calif.
Aug. 16, 1909

Dear sir:—

I have just received through my clipping agency a clipping from *Vanity Fair* under date of July 28, 1909, in which Mr. Frank Harris is so incredibly stupid as to call me a liar and to insinuate that I do not possess the clipping I referred to in my letter to you of July 1.

In my letter to you of July 1, having been two years and a half away from the United States, and being then at the Panama Canal on my way home from South America, I had to write wholly from memory. I told you, as nearly as I could remember, how I had read Mr. Harris's composition published in an American paper, in which form it had affixed an intro-duction by an American journalist to the effect that only one London publication had had the courage to print what the Bishop of London had actually said. I told my story from memory, simply and sincerely. I never dreamed that my word would be doubted in the affair, as Mr. Frank Harris has publicly doubted it.

Upon my return home to California I went up to my ranch, and in the barn, resurrected a large box labeled on the outside with *"Iron Heel* Clippings." Running through these clippings I found the one Mr. Harris said

I lied when I stated I possessed it. Here is the clipping, with my marks on it, and my notes made at the time when I utilized it for *The Iron Heel.*

But Mr. Frank Harris has proved himself so suspicious a man, so prone to impute evil to others, that he will doubtless aver that this clipping is not a clipping, but that I have had it privately printed at this late day. In a reply to any such anticipated move, I may as well say that if Mr. Harris be guilty of it, that he will render himself beneath my contempt and beyond my notice.

If, on the other hand, Mr. Frank Harris be honorable enough to accept this clipping as *bona fide,* and to take my explanation of July 1 as a true explanation, then there will be owing to me a sincere apology from Mr. Frank Harris. This apology, in the nature of the case, must be as public as has been his violent charges concerning my veracity, my honesty, and my sanity.

The rest of Mr. Harris's argument published in your columns on July 28 is so beside the question that I need not refer to it. I can only say regarding his treatment of me that his methods are unfair. He is a bully of the pen and the printed page. He is a yellow-journalist. But even a bully of the pen, with the taint of yellow in him, cannot override facts. I have presented my facts. First, my explanation contained in my letter of July 1, and, second, the clipping referred to. It seems to me, as regards this clipping, that it should be published in your columns entire, including the remarks of the American journalist which were appended to the quotation and not prefaced as was my faulty memory of it.

Very truly yours,
Jack London

P.S. Will you please see that this clipping is returned to me. Also, will you please mail to me a copy of *Vanity Fair* in which this letter is published? I can say in addition that I do not know where in the United States the *Socialist Spirit* was published, nor when, nor by whom. But if necessary, by writing to all the large cities, I am sure that I can discover all the facts concerning this now defunct publication.

To Flora London

Glen Ellen, Calif.
Aug. 30, 1909

Dear Mama:

I just want to give you the figures and reasoning on your bread-baking.

You and Jennie were agreed that the work she has recently been doing in cleaning the house would cost at least $6.00 per month if a Japanese boy were engaged to perform it.

You and Jennie agreed that you worked harder at your bread-baking than she did at cleaning the house.

The conclusion is obvious (1) that the enormous amount of work required by your bread-baking prevents you from doing the housework. (2) that if you had no bread-baking to do, the expenditure of energy on your part to keep the house would be less than the expenditure of energy when you bake bread.

This being so, it is likewise obvious that the cost of $6.00 a month for taking care of the house is a legitimate cost that must be included in your bread-baking.

This being so, let us review the figures of your bread-baking:

In your most prosperous month, you have cleared $7.50. You paid $26.00 for the stove. If, for three months, you devoted your total profits of $6.50 for paying for the stove, you will have worked those three months with no profit to yourself, and at the same time, at $6.00 per month, you will be owing Jennie $18.00 for taking care of the house.

NOW: Having worked for three months to pay for the stove, you find yourself in the following position: The stove is paid for, you are paying Jennie $6.00 a month to take care of the house, and you are clearing the difference between $6.00 and $7.50, or, namely, $1.50.

But, you owe Mammy Jennie $18.00 for housework during the three months in which you were paying off the stove. If, after the stove is paid off, you pay her $6.00 each month for current housework performed, you have left $1.50 which you can apply to paying off the balance of $18.00 you owe her. It will take you 12 months, at $1.50 a month to pay that balance of $18.00.

Thus, having worked hard for three months to pay for the stove, and for 12 months more to get square with Mammy Jennie, (or with whomsoever does do the housework) you will have worked 15 months without having made one cent, and you will then be in a situation thereafter to make a profit of $1.50 per month.

The conclusions are obvious.

Jack

To the Editor,
Cosmopolitan Magazine

Glen Ellen, Calif.
Aug. 30, 1909

Dear sir:—

I am sending you herewith a short story entitled "The Strength of the Strong." If you will remember, some time ago, Kipling made an attack on Socialism in the form of a parable or short story, entitled "Melissa," in which he exploited his Jingoism and showed that a co-operation of individuals strong enough to overcome war meant the degeneration of said individuals. I have written my "Strength of the Strong" as a reply to his attack. What do you think of it?

Sincerely yours,
Jack London

To Robert Lutz[1]

Glen Ellen, Calif.
Oct. 1, 1909

Dear sir:—

In reply to your letter of September 9. I thank you very much for your kind, definite letter. I cannot tell you how much I appreciate straight talk such as you have given me in this letter of yours. Thanks to you, I see the situation very clearly. It is somewhat as follows: The German public cares very little for my work. The best way to get the German public interested in my work, is to get them to read some of my work. According to your judgment, the way to get the German public to read some of my work is to spoil two of my books by taking several stories from each of them and publishing them in German.

Now, let me give you my views on the subject, just as simply and directly: In the first place, literature being at such a low ebb in Germany as regards authors' remuneration, I am not particularly interested in having anything to do with the German market. In the second place, I believe you are far from right in the selection of stories from the two books you have named—these would be just about the last stories of all, in my opinion, with which to make a bid for popularity with the German reading public. And, lastly, since the German market is not excitingly remunerative to an author, I think more of my books than to have them gutted in the way you suggest.

If *The Call of the Wild,* for instance, did not incline the German public favorably toward me, I am quite confident no miscellaneous and aborted collection of my short stories would have any better effect.

I may tell you, in passing, that I have just succeeded in having the contract with Mr. Hellmann[2] canceled, and I am writing to him to that effect by this mail.

Sincerely yours,
Jack London

---

[1]German publisher of Bret Harte, Mark Twain, Helen Keller, Conan Doyle, *et al.*
[2]A publisher in Fauer, Germany, who sold Lutz three of London's stories.

To Frank Harris

Glen Ellen, Calif.
Nov. 15, 1909

Dear Mr. Harris:—

I have just received clipping from *Vanity Fair* of date of October 27. There seems nothing more to be said so far as the public discussion is concerned. The charge of knavish, idiotic and impudent plagiarism against me has been satisfactorily disproved. So this is just a letter to you. Believe me, throughout this correspondence I have been absolutely sincere, and all I cared for was that my sincerity should be accepted.

But, just good-naturedly of course, it seems to me that you have got yourself into several logical tangles. The first of these is your request that I should have apologized to you for having been deceived by an American journalist. (See second sentence in penultimate paragraph of your last article.)

While your demand that I should pay you for the portion of your work used by me was cleverly facetious in its origin in your mind, it seems that in the intervening time you have taken your own facetiousness seriously. Of course I have no objection to that, and merely mention it in order to lead up to another tangle of logic, namely, your refusal to apologize to me for having doubted my word (euphemism for liar), until I paid you your share of *The Iron Heel*. This is a queer admixture of ethics, commercialism, and facetiousness.

But why go any further with the tangles! I think you realize by this time that I was innocent of deliberate plagiarism.[1]

Sincerely yours,
Jack London

P.S. Are you the Frank Harris who wrote *The Bomb*—a book recently published in the United States? I haven't read it yet; but if you are the author, I shall. There! That shows you how good-natured I am.

[1]Harris wrote a facetious letter to Charmian after London's death ending the correspondence on the note that he believed that he (Harris) was in the right.

To William English Walling[1]

Glen Ellen, Calif.
Nov. 30, 1909

My dear Walling:—

In reply to yours of Nov. 24. I am writing you immediately. Having been buried down in the South Seas for a couple of years, I am not now closely in touch with the socialist movement in the United States, so that everything in your letter has been news to me. I am forwarding your letter immediately to various socialists in California.

Depend upon me for one thing. I am a hopelessly non-compromising revolutionist, and I shall stand always for keeping the socialist party rigidly revolutionary. Any compromise such as an affiliation with the American Federation of Labor would be at this time suicidal. Australia is a splendid example of this. They started a splendid socialist movement there, began to compromise in order to gain strength, and then became lost in the political organized labor movement, so that to-day, in my opinion, from the socialist viewpoint, Australia is more backward and far worse off than the United States. There is a little handful of struggling revolutionists down there and some pretty good fighting-men; but they are all too few. The labor-party swamps them out.

If the socialist movement in the United States goes in for opportunism, then it's Hurray for the Oligarchy and the Iron Heel, or, speaking seriously, it would mean a set-back of twenty years to the movement, at least, and heaven only knows how much more serious such a catastrophe would be.

Yours for the Revolution,
Jack London

---

[1]Anna Strunsky's husband, sometimes referred to as a millionaire Socialist.

1910-1916

THE YEARS OF THE BEAUTY RANCH

CHRONOLOGY

1910: Began serious development of the Beauty Ranch. (Purchased the Kohler Vineyards, Glen Ellen, Sonoma Co., California. This 800 acres joined the Hill, the Lamotte, and the Fish Ranches.) Birth and death of first daughter by Charmian. Purchase of the *Roamer*.

Published: *Revolution*, The Macmillan Co., April (sociological essays).
Burning Daylight, The Macmillan Co., October (novel).
Theft, The Macmillan Co., November (drama).

1911: June to September. The four-horse driving trip through Northern California and Oregon.

Published: *When God Laughs*, The Macmillan Co., January (collected stories.)
Adventure, The Macmillan Co., March (novel).
Cruise of the Snark, The Macmillan Co., June (essays).
South Sea Tales, The Macmillan Co., October (collected stories).

1912: Began construction of the Wolf House.
February to August. The Cape Horn voyage on the *Dirigo*.
After return from Horn trip, bought the Freund Ranch, Glen Ellen, Sonoma Co., California, which connected with the Kohler Vineyards and increased the Beauty Ranch to about 1300 acres.

Published: *A Son of the Sun*, Doubleday, Page and Co., May (collected stories).
The House of Pride, The Macmillan Co., March (collected stories).
Smoke Bellew Tales, The Century Co., October (collected stories).

1913: Burning of the Wolf House. Balboa-Bosworth Copyright Trial.

Published: *The Night Born*, The Century Co., February (collected stories).
The Abysmal Brute, The Century Co., May (novel).
The Valley of the Moon, The Macmillan Co., May (novel).
John Barleycorn, The Century Co., August (semi-autobiographical novel).

1914: April to June. Correspondent for *Collier's Magazine* in the Mexican dispute.

Published: *The Strength of the Strong*, The Macmillan Co., May (collected stories).
The Mutiny of the Elsinore, The Macmillan Co., September (novel).

1915: February to July. Trip to Hawaii.

Published: *The Acorn Planter*, The Macmillan Co., February (drama).
The Scarlet Plague, The Macmillan Co., June (novel).
Star Rover, The Macmillan Co., October (novel).

1916: March to August. Trip to Hawaii. Death, November 22, 1916.

Published: *The Little Lady of the Big House*, The Macmillan Co., April (novel).
Turtles of Tasman, The Macmillan Co., September (collected stories; last book published before his death).

Published posthumously: *The Human Drift*, The Macmillan Co., February, 1917 (collected essays).
Jerry of the Islands, The Macmillan Co., April, 1917 (novel).
Michael, Brother of Jerry, The Macmillan Co., November, 1917 (novel).
The Red One, The Macmillan Co., October, 1918 (collected stories).
On the Makaloa Mat, The Macmillan Co., October, 1919 (collected stories).
Hearts of Three, The Macmillan Co., October, 1920 (novel).

To EDITOR, *Honolulu Advertiser*

Glen Ellen, Calif.
Jan. 7, 1910

Dear Sir:—

Is the Territory of Hawaii to become part of the Twentieth Century World, or is it to remain provincial, like any backwoods settlement? I am prompted to make this query because of "The Bystander" who, on the staff of *The Advertiser,* has made some most provincial and untrue remarks about me. I do not make reference to the letters of subscribers and readers, wherein I have been assailed, because a newspaper is supposed to publish communications from its subscribers and readers, even though they be lunatics or feeble-minded *cretins.*

But "The Bystander" is on the staff of *The Advertiser.* He sells his wit and *The Advertiser* buys, because it considers his wit is modern, worthwhile and up-to-date.

Here is some of the abuse which has been heaped upon me by "The Bystander": I am a "sneak of the first water, a thoroughly untrustworthy man, and an ungrateful and untruthful bounder." Also, I am a "dirty little sneak." Not only is the flavor of "Bystander's" vituperage essentially that of the backwoods, but so also are the untruths against me which he states and upon which he bases his vituperation.

"Bystander" accuses me of having been granted privileges by the authorities to visit the Leper Settlement at Molokai, and then having abused those privileges by writing sensational and untrue short-stories about Molokai.[1]

Now, here are the facts: by the consent of the authorities, I visited Molokai, and I wrote an article on Molokai that was so satisfactory to the authorities that the stamp of approval was given to it for publication to the world.

Incidentally, I wrote a couple of short-stories[2] dealing with leprosy, locating one on the Kona Coast of Hawaii, and the other on the Island of Niihau. Both these stories were avowedly stories, things of fiction; and furthermore, they did not deal with Molokai, nor with any of the knowledge that I had gained while I was at Molokai. I have been interested in leper settlements for years, and have visited other leper settlements and lazar-houses before I ever came to Hawaii. Not only have my two short-stories nothing to do with the leper settlement on Molokai, but no data in those two short-stories was gathered on Molokai. And when "Bystander" says that I violated my promise to the authorities, made when I went to visit the leper settlement on Molokai, why said "Bystander" not only lies, but deliberately lies.

It is the perfect provincial note, to state absolute untruths concerning a stranger's visit to one's backwoods section, and upon this basis to rear an edifice of abuse. This is what "Bystander" has done, and has been countenanced in doing by the editor of the *Advertiser.*

And now, Mr. Editor, let me give you a few facts of my visit to Hawaii. I came to Hawaii on my own, subsidized by nobody; nor did Hawaii subsidize me, nor did I ask Hawaii to subsidize me. I paid my way; I paid my way on the steamer to Molokai, and I paid my way back on the steamer from Molokai. I spent a few thousands of dollars in Hawaii, and there is no man in Hawaii who can lift up his voice and say that I owe him one cent. On the other hand I can lift up my voice and say that the citizens of Hawaii owe me, and owe me a great many cents—that the dwellers of Hawaii, instead of subsidizing me, some of them, at any rate played very deft and gentlemanly games of robbing me.

On the other hand, I want to say that I was gloriously entertained by a number of persons in Hawaii; that I received a height of hospitality that cannot be excelled anywhere else on the earth; and that my heart goes out in love and appreciation to numerous friends that I made in Hawaii. But I wish to point out this weakness of Hawaii: namely, of elevating every chance visitor to its shores on a pedestal, seemingly for the purpose of casting potsherds at him. I had scarcely left the shores of Hawaii myself, when the papers let loose with an attack upon me charging me with having issued worthless checks. "Bystander" says that I was treated like a lion. All I can say is that it was a darned funny way to treat a lion. Again, I reiterate, this is the provincial note struck by Hawaii. And the sooner Hawaii gets over it the better. Of what use is a Promotion Committee, and of public broad-minded citizens, when they allow a set of mediocre reporters to set their ethical newspaper pace for them and mould their opinions for them? So long as Hawaii is satisfied with the opinions of men of the caliber of "Bystander," just that long is Hawaii contented to be provincial.

Sincerely yours,

Jack London

[1]"The Lepers of Molokai" and "Good-by Jack."
[2]"The Sheriff of Kona" and "Koolau the Leper."

To Lorrin A. Thurston[1]

Glen Ellen, Calif.
Feb. 1, 1910

Dear friend:—

I have just finished reading your reply to my letter, published in the *Sunday Advertiser,* January 23, 1910. And first of all, let me say that I have only kind appreciation for the kindliness of the tone of your letter. On the other hand, I cannot but deprecate the logic of your reply.

There were two ways in which you could have replied to me. (1) You could have replied to me and the points I made, or (2) you could have replied holding in mind the effect of what you said on the reading public.

In this latter respect, the newspaper man is incorrigible. So it was in this latter way that you replied—that is to say, you replied neither to me nor to the points I made, but you had your eyes on your reading public all the time you were replying. In this reply of yours, my resentment of "Bystander's" abuse was handled facetiously; while Hawaii's resentment of my short-stories was handled seriously. Now, from a standpoint of logic and of fair play, you cannot mix oil and water this way. This facetious reply to my resentment was just the trick of debates of which any newspaper man would be expected to be guilty. It is purely a trick of debate, you know, and I think you also know that I scarcely need to point it out to you.

Now, to some more of your illogic. In my original letter, I said that Hawaii was provincial because of the habit she had of elevating every chance visitor to her shores on a pedestal seemingly for the purpose of casting potsherds at him, of receiving a guest with open arms, and of abusing him roundly as soon as he had departed. In my particular case, I was called a "sneak of the first water," "a thoroughly untrustworthy man" and "an ungrateful and untruthful bounder." Also I was called a "dirty little sneak." I pointed out clearly that it was this behavior on the part of Hawaii that incurred the charge of her being provincial. Nevertheless, by a clever shift on your part in your reply, you gave your readers to understand that I based the charge of provincialism upon the fact that I had been robbed by some several of the citizens of Hawaii. Now, Mr. Thurston, this will do for the reading public, but I leave it to you if you think it will do for me. Mind you, I am only asking you if you think such illogic will do for me.

In my original letter, in reply to the charge of being ungrateful, I pointed out that Hawaii owed me nothing; that Hawaii had subsidized me not one cent, and that if it came to a showdown, when it came to a matter of dollars and cents, Hawaii had got the best of me. This was particularly apt modern business rottenness at the hands of some several of Hawaii's citizens. It certainly was not provincial. My point in making it was that I was not indebted to Hawaii, and therefore could not have incurred the charge of ingratitude. I was not squealing about my experiences in Hawaii; I was merely pointing out that I was not the various vile things that "Bystander" had asserted I was. It strikes me that Hawaii began to squeal first of all, through the mouth of "Bystander," and turned then to deliberate lying abuse. Nor am I squealing now about this abuse. I am merely trying to point out to Hawaiian newspaper men the way of their feet through the fields of logic.

In another place in your letter, you regret the harshness of "Bystander's" remarks. "Bystander" called me "a dirty little sneak," "a sneak of the first water," "a thoroughly untrustworthy man," and "an ungrateful and untruthful bounder." Now, Mr. Thurston, you do not in your letter say that these epithets of "Bystander's" are untrue. I am driven to conclude that, while you judge them unduly harsh, they are nevertheless true, and that I am a dirty little sneak, bounder, etc. Maybe you were letting "Bystander" down easily. If so, you did not let me down easily. Either I am or I am not these various things. I want to know where I stand in your estimation. It's up to you.

This is merely another favorable trick of debate, namely, the sliding out of a difficult position under the seeming of fair speech while granting or recanting nothing.

One other thing: suppose the Irish should object to the telling of funny Irish stories, and that the Jews should object to the telling of funny Jewish stories, and the Dutch, and the Swedes and the English, and the Scotch, and all the rest of the nationalities; immediately would result a paucity of funny racial stories. By the same token, if Hawaii should hold that her most salient characteristics should not be exploited in fiction, and if Ireland and England and South America, and Africa, and Asia, should take a similar stand—well, fiction would go glimmering, that's all. Because, by the same token, every man and woman in every walk of life, trade, or profession, could make a similar objection to having his walk of life, trade, or profession exploited in fiction.

I think Hawaii is too touchy on matters of truth; and while she complacently in her newspapers exploits the weaknesses and afflictions of other lands, gets unduly excited when her own are exploited. Furthermore, the several purely fictional stories on leprosy written by me have not shaken the world at all, Hawaii's fevered imagination to the contrary. My several stories haven't stopped one person from going to Hawaii, nor one dollar from being invested in Hawaii. Believe me, Stevenson's "Father Damien Letter" has had more effect in a minute, and will go on having more effect in a minute, than all the stories I have written or shall ever write.

And, finally, while I can sympathize with the excessive irritability and excitability of Hawaii on the matter of its leprosy, I do object to Hawaii's unfairness in slinging billingsgate. Argument is argument, but abuse is ever dastardly. And whenever you get your opponent abusing you, believe me it is a sign you've got him going. I love Hawaii, I'm not afraid of Hawaii, its citizens, or its afflictions. But I should like to see the newspaper end of Hawaii buck up a bit, cease its provincialism, and strive to be at least as logical as the newspapers on the mainland.

Sincerely yours,

Jack London

P.S. Dear Kakina:[1] Really, you've laid yourself open to the above, because your reply was hopelessly illogical, and you brazenly shifted the bases of the points of argument. But anyway, if I get 25¢ a word, think of all the words the *Advertiser* is getting for nothing! And by the way, don't fail to mail me a copy of the *Advertiser* in which the foregoing is printed. I was indebted to a chance letter from a person in Honolulu for a copy of your reply. None was mailed me by your office.

[1] A writer for the *Honolulu Advertiser*. Thurston and his wife were friends of London and Charmian from the time of the *Snark* voyage. They all took Hawaiian names. Thurston's name was Kakina; his wife's name was Kakina Wahine; London's name was Lakana; Charmian's, Lakana Wahine.

To OLGA NETHERSOLE[1]

Glen Ellen, Calif.
Feb. 9, 1910

Dear Miss Nethersole:

In reply to yours of January 30. In addition to our brief, and on my part toothachy conversation, I should like to have you give me, if you can, with greater definiteness, your rough idea of a motif for the play. Given this, after mulling over it for forty-eight hours, I couldn't make up my mind whether or not I should be able to handle it. (In this connection, I'd vastly prefer the scene laid in America for the reason that I am stale on things English, and I am so hopelessly a realist that I'd have to travel to England and soak atmosphere for a year, if the scene were laid in England.)

As to terms—such as any first-class playwright gets. I have data of same, and am not bothering to look it up just now.

I should, of course, prefer to do the play myself rather than in partnership; yet in this connection, let me add that I should be most willing to receive all help, suggestion, etc., you could give, and also to give public recognition of same. Let me here explain that I am the everlasting marvel of the magazine-editors of the United States, because of the fact that I always give them an absolute free fist in blue-penciling my manuscripts. I never have any passions or excitements over interferences and changes in my work. The reading of the proof-sheets of my books I usually turn over to my most amiable friends. I never know what the cover-design of any of my books is going to be until I get advance-copy of the market edition. I never know whether or not my books are to be illustrated, nor how. All of which goes to show that I am the least finicky of writers when it comes to being prejudiced in favor of anything I do, and all of which goes to show that if I did get to work on a play for you, you yourself would have a free fist in suggesting, altering, and remodeling.

If I can get from you a suggestion for a motif, or of the meat of a motif, which, after mulling over, I decide I can do, I could arrange to join you between March 18th and April 2,—unless, of course, your personal convenience should not be consulted by this particular choice of dates.

Sincerely yours,
Jack London

[1] Well-known actress of the time.

To C. S. STANTON

Glen Ellen, Calif.
Mar. 7, 1910

Dear sir:

In reply to yours of March 1, asking me to do the Prizefight between Jeffries and Johnson,[1] for *The Examiner*. Please let me tell you the situation. The first and only newspaper work I ever did was for the Hearst newspapers, and whatever work I did for the Hearst newspapers was done directly through *The San Francisco Examiner*. For years I did a sort of special work, answering any call *The Examiner* or the Hearst papers sent out to me. I had never considered any of the offers that I received from other newspapers. I was faithful to my employ and my salt. I used to receive $100 for every book-review I gave. Jack Barrett, one day, wrote me telling me to go ahead and write a review of Sinclair's *Jungle,* which was just coming out. I did so. Before *The Examiner* could publish it, the New York end of the Hearst newspapers telegraphed for that review to be immediately forwarded to New York. It was published in one or the other of the New York Hearst papers. I never got paid for it. The New York and the San Francisco end continued to pass the buck back and forth. At about the same time Jack Barrett, acting under instructions from the New York end, got in touch with me by long-distance telephone and wanted me to go to Idaho to report the Moyer-Haywood trial.[2] This I found I was unable to do. Again communicating with the New York end, he came back with a proposition for me to write an article on the Moyer-Haywood situation. This I did. I never got paid for this, either. The S.F. end and the N.Y. end passed the buck back and forth on this.

In spite of the fact that $200 were owing to me, I remained faithful to my employ. A little over a year ago, I was in Australia, at the time of the Burns-Johnson fight. I cabled to the *San Francisco Examiner,* asking them if they wanted me to do the fight. I received no reply whatever to my cable. I then cabled to the *New York Herald,* and I did the Burns-Johnson fight for the *New York Herald*.

Now, I leave it to you, in consideration of the foregoing, what was I to do when the Jeffries-Johnson fight began to impend? I had been turned down by the paper I had been faithful to—by the paper which owed me money which it refused to pay, by the paper which refused me the courtesy of replying to my cable. For the first time I had done work for another paper, the *New York Herald*. When the Jeffries-Johnson fight began to impend, I cabled the *New York Herald* and for fully three months have had all arrangements made to do the fight for the *New York Herald*.

You can see the situation. I was turned down and rejected by the only newspaper I had ever worked for, and it was up to me to get a billet elsewhere. And I am still curious, and shall always be curious, to know why it is that the Hearst papers adopted a deliberate course of refusing to pay me for work performed by me and solicited by them.

Believe me, this letter is not written in any unfriendly spirit. I know the rush and chaos of newspaperdom, and I am merely writing this letter to you so that you may clearly understand my point of view in the present situation.

Sincerely yours,

Jack London

[1] Jack went to Reno June 22, 1910, and for ten days wrote daily articles about the two fighters and then his final account of the fight.
[2] The famous trial which grew out of the bombing murder (Dec. 30, 1905) of Frank Steunenburg, former Governor of Idaho. Clarence Darrow was the defense attorney.

To GEORGE P. BRETT

Glen Ellen, Calif.
Apr. 1, 1910

Dear Mr. Brett:

I have just signed a contract with Nelson & Sons for the publication of my story *Adventure,* which long since has been in your hands. Nelson will publish *Adventure* some time in 1911. In the meantime the story is seeking serial publication in England, and will be published serially by *The Popular Magazine* in the United States. My English agents are Curtis Brown & Massie, 5 Henrietta Street, Covent Garden, London W.C. They will communicate with you regarding the arrangement of a practically simultaneous publication of the book in both countries.

In the meantime, I have plenty of other books to keep you busy without there being any need for *Adventure.*

I am not dead sure yet, but it looks probable that the *New York Herald* will buy *Burning Daylight.*[1]

I have just finished a 20,000-word pseudo-scientific story entitled *The Scarlet Death* [*The Scarlet Plague*].

Just now I am at work on a play for Olga Nethersole.

Also, I have just planted 16,000 eucalyptus trees, and am preparing to plant 25,000 more next year. If I could get you out here and tell you the profits of eucalyptus-growing, you'd quit the publishing business.[2]

Also, I am in hopes that there will be a Jack London, Jr. in Glen Ellen along in next June.

Sincerely yours,

Jack London

[1] They did and paid London eight thousand dollars for American serial rights. Seven years earlier (June, 1903) *The Saturday Evening Post* paid him seven hundred dollars for the same rights for *The Call of the Wild.*
[2] The venture proved a total failure.

To Lillian Collins[1]

Glen Ellen, Calif.
April 26, 1910

My dear Lillian Collins:—

In reply to your good letter of April 22. I don't know whether to take your letter as an unconscious compliment to me, or as a subtle compliment to me. I quote from your letter: "He was not physically able to defend himself. He was heart-sick; the nerves of action paralyzed by enormous strain, the power to weigh and analyze, compare and select, submerged under an overwhelming sense of loss."

From the foregoing, and much more that you have said in your letter, you point out to me that I did succeed in showing the inevitableness of his death. I was no more treacherous to Martin Eden than life is treacherous to many, many men and women. You continually point out to me where I took unfair advantages of Martin Eden, "cramming his newly-awakened mind with abstractions which his crude mental processes were not able to assimilate." Granted; but do not forget that this was MY Martin Eden, and that I manufactured him in this very particular, precise and peculiar fashion. Having done so, his untimely end is accounted for. Remember that he was MY Martin Eden, and was made by me in this fashion. He certainly was not the Martin Eden that you would have made. I think the disagreement between you and me lies in that you confuse my Martin Eden with your Martin Eden.

You say: "I look upon Martin Eden's selfish individualism as a crudity adhering from the boy's early habits of life—a lack of perspective which time and a wider horizon would correct." And you complain because he died. Your point is that if I had let him live, he would have got out of all this slough of despond. Again, to make a simile which I know will be distasteful to you, let me point out that the case is exactly parallel with that of a beautiful young man, with the body of an Adonis, who can not swim, who is thrown into deep water, and who drowns. You cry out, "Give the young man time to learn to swim while he is drowning, and he will not drown, but will win safely to shore." And the queer thing, reverting to the original proposition, is, that you yourself, in sharp, definite terms, point out the very reasons why Martin Eden couldn't swim, and had to drown.

You tell me that I asserted that love tricked and failed Martin Eden, and that you know better and that I know better. On the contrary, from what I know of love, I believe that Martin Eden had his first big genuine love when he fell in love with Ruth, and that not he alone, but that countless millions of men and women, have been tricked in one way or another in similar fashion. However, you are unfair in taking such an assertion and making the sweeping generalization that I deny all love and the greatness of all love.

Then, it is an endless question. I don't think you and I have so much of a quarrel over Martin Eden as we have on account of our different interpretations of life. Your temperament and your training lead you one way—mine lead me another way. I think that right there is the explanation of our difference.

Thanking you for your good letter,

Sincerely yours,
Jack London

[1]An unidentified critic.

To GEORGE P. BRETT

Glen Ellen, Calif.
May 5, 1910

Dear Mr. Brett:—

I don't know how my account stands, but I imagine I should be somewhere roughly around square. It is a long time since I have written to you for a lump of money in advance, and I should not be writing to you now except that I am buying seven hundred acres of land that rounds out and connects my present two ranches, giving me miles of frontage on three big creeks, and some magnificent mountain land, to say nothing of timber—real wild country where they shoot several deer each season.

I have been expecting to sell the *Snark,* which still lies for sale down in Sydney. Had this occurred, I should not have called for this advance from you even.

What I need and must have in my hands by June 1, is five thousand ($5,000.00) dollars.

Among the half-dozen books of mine now in your hands, and as yet unpublished, there are two that should make good sales. One is the adventure novel entitled *Adventure,* and the other is *Burning Daylight*. I have just recently sold the American serial rights of *Burning Daylight* to the *New York Herald,* for $8,000.00, and I think that is a good earnest that the story should sell well in book-form.

I think the outlook is such that it will be a long, long time, and possibly never, when I call upon you for another heavy advance.

Sincerely yours,
Jack London

(If Mr. Brett is away in Europe or anywhere else, will you please immediately cable him the import of this letter.)

To George P. Brett

Glen Ellen, Calif.
May 25, 1910

Dear Mr. Brett:—

In reply to yours of May 19, and acknowledging receipt of check for Five thousand ($5000.00) Dollars. Now, you and I have always been dreadfully frank with each other. We have wasted little time on trimmings. Do you remember, a number of years ago, when I sat in your office and borrowed $150.00 to get back to California on? We hitched up with each other then, and we've been hitched up ever since. You have been frank with me, and I have been frank with you. On the whole, the most excessive frankness has come from you, especially instance the time when I was heaven knows where down in the South Seas on the *Snark,* and you scared my agent, Mrs. Ninetta Eames, nearly to death, by telling her that the monthly advances would cease—all because a lot of mail had miscarried in those far stretches and gone to the Dead Letter Office at Washington, said mail containing contract for the next year between you and me, and which contract had not been signed and returned to you because I had not received it. Now, I did not go up in the air over that. I don't think I ever bothered you with mentioning that I considered it cavalier treatment. I said to myself: "We know each other so well that we can afford to be dreadfully frank with each other." And I let it go at that.

Now, this is the first time, in the telegram I sent you, that I have been really dreadfully frank. I made no threat and never dreamed of making any threat of severing our relations. I merely told you the truth—because I wanted the money, and wanted it badly—namely, that another American publishing house had offered an immediate advance of $10,000 for the American book-rights of *Burning Daylight,* which I was then just in process of finishing. The reason I gave you this information was to show you that you would be justified in making an advance of $5000 on said book.

That miserable, invidious "if" with which you began the second paragraph of your letter of May 19, leads me to believe that you rather don't believe that a financially responsible publisher is willing to pay $10,000 down on advance of royalties, etc. I have looked up my file, and I find that the original letter I have sent off to England, in the course of dealings over there. I am inclosing you herewith, however, a carbon-copy of the reply Mrs. Eames sent to B. W. Dodge & Co. Unfortunately, the sum of money is not stipulated in this reply of hers. But I fancy you have found me straight enough in the past to accept my word when I say that the sum stipulated by B. W. Dodge & Co., as advance-payment of royalty, was $10,000.

I am afraid that I have settled down to accepting you as my publisher for as long as I live, or as long as The Macmillan Company remains in business —unless you fire me. On the other hand, I shall always expect that I be not accepted as a mere permanent, steadfast appurtenance whose books will sell so many copies to a certain public, and will therefore not be pushed and urged as would the books of a new-comer to your house. I think you see my point without further explanation.

I think, from the time you published my first book, that I have delivered the goods and that I have continued to deliver the goods, all ominous prophecies of my going to pieces to the contrary. I know I have been rather stiff-necked and stubborn to handle where my judgment came up against the judgment of others who, while they knew more about the publishing business, did not know as much about me and my own personality as I did myself; but still, I have delivered the goods, and I am a long way from being dead.

But say—I did need that money. And some day when you get out here, and cut the Palace Hotel from your itinerary and come up and spend some weeks on the ranch, and ride over with me, you will say that you are damned glad that you sent me the money, and you will wonder why I didn't make ten times as big a howl for said money as I did.

Sincerely yours,
Jack London

To JOHN S. PHILLIPS[1]

Glen Ellen, Calif.
May 26, 1910

Dear Mr. Phillips:

In reply to yours of May 20. Now I am more puzzled than ever. You say that you could never see the sense of paying by the word. I wish I could discover your formula so that I wouldn't have to write by the word. It takes me just so long to do so many words. And it takes me three times longer to do 9000 words than it does to do 3000, and five times longer to do 10,000 than to do 2000 words.

Why, the material in that story of "Samuel" cost me at least $250 hard cash to acquire, and 43 days at sea between land and land, on a coal-laden tramp-steamer. Also, it took me two weeks to write. And my wife threw in 43 days of her time helping me in making a study of the vernacular, and in writing it down and classifying it. How the dickens I could sell that story for $250 and make both ends meet is beyond me.

Don't forget another thing: I don't know anything about your personal history, but I imagine that you have a higher standard of living to-day than you had when you were a young man of twenty years of age. Why or how you got that higher standard of living is beyond the question. The point is, you are a success, and success inevitably breeds a higher standard of living. And you are just a sample of the process. Every successful man, inevitably develops a higher standard of living. It is a process that is universal and that cannot be explained away or nullified by an inability to see the sense of paying by the word. Would you cast me out of this process? Am I different from all the other men who have succeeded? Surely not. I certainly have a higher standard of living; yet you offer me, for what you call a "remarkable," a "wonderful" story, a rate no greater than what you gave me when I was an absolute unknown with a very low standard of living. Nay—worse than that, considering the rise in prices, you offer me less, for with that money I cannot come anywhere near purchasing what I did a dozen years ago. Why, I simply cannot afford to sell such a story for $250.

Here's another way of looking at it. It has been the custom, since publishing began, to pay the known writer, the arrived writer, carrying with him his public, etc., higher prices than to the unknown and the unarrived. Do you likewise cast me out of this process? I want to go on selling you stories, and I'll give you a look-in from time to time; but really, it will have to be on a different basis from that which led you to offer the price you did for "Samuel."

Sincerely yours,

Jack London

---

[1]Of *American Magazine*.

To EDITOR, *The Workingman's Paper*

Glen Ellen, Calif.
June 5, 1910

Dear Comrade:

In your issue of May 28, you have an article entitled "A Little Debate," in which Comrade Armstrong holds that I am a Socialist, and in which Manley insists, from his reading of my book, *Martin Eden,* that I am not. Wherefore, I am impelled to send you the reply I made to the Rev. Charles Brown, when he misinterpreted *Martin Eden*. Please return this copy.

Yours for the Revolution,

Jack London

To THE REV. CHARLES BROWN
[Open Letter]

Since hearing the Rev. Charles Brown's sermon last night on *Martin Eden,* I can understand why for two thousand years the Church has been rent with dissension over the interpretation of the Scriptures. Mr. Brown gave last night a splendid sample of the churchman's capacity of misinterpretation.

Mr. Brown interpreted Martin Eden as a man who failed because of lack of faith in God. I wrote *Martin Eden,* not as an autobiography, nor as a parable of what dire end awaits an unbeliever in God, but as an indictment of that pleasant, wild-beast struggle of Individualism of which Mr. Brown is not among the least of the protagonists.

Contrary to Mr. Brown's misinterpretation last night, Martin Eden was not a Socialist. Mr. Brown, in order to effect a parallel with my own life, said that Martin Eden was a Socialist. On the contrary, I drew him a temperamental, and, later on, an intellectual, Individualist. So much was he an Individualist, that he characterized Mr. Brown's kind of ethics as ghetto-ethics and Mr. Brown's kind of Individualism as half-baked Socialism. Martin Eden was a proper Individualist of the extreme Nietzschean type.

Now to my parable, which I thought I had expounded lucidly in the pages of this novel. Being an Individualist, being unaware of the needs of others, of the whole human collective need, Martin Eden lived only for himself, fought only for himself, and, if you please, died for himself. He fought for entrance into the bourgeois circles where he expected to find refinement, culture, high-living and high-thinking. He won his way into those circles and was appalled by the colossal, unlovely mediocrity of the bourgeoisie. He fought for a woman he loved and had idealized. He found that love had tricked him and failed him, and that he had loved his idealization more than the woman herself. These were the things he had found life worth living in order to fight for. When they failed him, being a consistent Individualist, being unaware of the collective human need, there remained nothing for which to live and fight. And so he died.

All this is so clearly stated in the pages of the book I am compelled to quote the following, which occurs when Brissenden asks Martin to go down with him to the Sunday night meeting of the Socialists. Brissenden says to Martin:

"Outsiders are allowed five-minute speeches. Get up and spout. Tell them what you think about them and their ghetto-ethics. Slam Nietzsche into them and get walloped for your pains. Make a scrap of it. It will do them good. Discussion is what they want, and what they want you want, too. You see, I'd like to see you a Socialist before I am gone. It will give you a sanction for your existence. It is the one thing that will save you in the time of disappointment that is coming to you. You have health and much to live for, and you must be handcuffed to life somehow."

I cannot comprehend how, after reading such lines, that Mr. Brown conceives Martin Eden to be a Socialist, nor how Mr. Brown failed so lamentably in grasping the thesis I have expounded.

Martin Eden failed and died, in my parable, not because of his lack of faith in God, but because of his lack of faith in man. Even Mr. Brown will agree that he cannot get to God except through man. Martin Eden failed because he did not get even to man. He got only as far as himself, and the rest of humanity did not count.

Unfortunately, Mr. Brown's sermon was not on *Martin Eden,* but on Jack

London, and Mr. Brown was woefully unacquainted with the subject. He said that I was Martin Eden. Let me point out the vital weakness of his parallel—Martin Eden killed himself; I am still alive.

Why am I alive? Because of my faith in man, a faith which Martin Eden never achieved, and a faith which Mr. Brown evidently did not know appertained to his subject, namely, Jack London. Yet my faith is most readily accessible to all men; my books are in the Public Library. Mr. Brown should have read up on the subject before he expounded it. Let me here quote some of my faith. I take the following from my *What Life Means to Me.*

"I look forward to a time when men shall progress upon something worthier and higher than his stomach, when there will be a finer incentive to impel men to action than the incentive of today, which is the incentive of the stomach. I retain my belief in the mobility and excellence of the human. I believe that spiritual sweetness and unselfishness will conquer the gross gluttony of today. And last of all, my faith is in the working class. As some Frenchman has said, 'The stairway of time is ever echoing with the wooden shoe going up, and the polished boot descending.' "

Again I quote my faith, this time from the preface of my *War of the Classes:*

"He must learn that Socialism deals with what is, not with what ought to be; and that the material with which it deals is the clay of the common road, the warm human, fallible and frail, sordid and petty, absurd and contradictory, even grotesque, and yet, withal, shot through with flashes and glimmerings of something finer and Godlike, with here and there sweetnesses of service and unselfishness, desires for goodness, for renunciation and sacrifice, and with conscience stern and awful, at times blazing imperious, demanding the right—the right, nothing more or less than the right."

Jack London

To Lorrin Thurston

Glen Ellen, Calif.
June 11, 1910

Dear Kakina:—

Many thanks for your published reply to me, and also for your good letter of May 25. Don't bother about printing this reply to you. What's the good? We get nowhere anyway.

If there is anything that inclines me to the pessimism (you censure) more than any other thing, it is this very spectacle of you and me, both honest and sincere, yet unable to understand each other on an impersonal question. You believe you are right and I am wrong. I believe I am right and you are wrong. The abysmal futility of it is appalling.

Yet, you do not find me morbid in my personal life and character,— though you do find, what you miscall morbidity, in the stories I make in order to earn my living. As well might I call you morbid because you exploit murder and arson, conjugal infidelity and infamy, in the columns of your newspaper. As well may I call you unfeeling and brutal because you exploit said afflictions of your fellow men in your newspaper. The point of the foregoing is for no other purpose than merely to point out that you do continually stray from the path of logic.

Your last published reply is a splendid example of this illogic. I dare not flatter you (as I did previously) by inferring it as deliberate. You won't stand for this, so compel me to charge you with a congenital lack of logic. An instance of this is where you attempted to turn back on me the illustration I used of the various nationalities objecting to funny stories being told about their own nationality. If you will go back and look at my use of this illustration, you will find that the funny racial story part was merely a step in the course of building up the wider conclusion that if any particular country should object to her most salient characteristics being exploited in fiction, then by the same token every other country should be entitled to object, and that there wouldn't be any fiction written about the salient characteristics of any country. Now that was the entire illustration that I used, and you took the illogical liberty of ignoring the big, wide conclusion, and of balancing the woes and afflictions of Hawaii on the one side against the funny fun of funny racial stories on the other. I don't ask you if this is fair; I don't ask you if this went down with your readers, because you know that it did, but I only ask you if you think it is logical.

The way you parried me by charging me with carrying the war into Africa, was a clever retort, and I know that it went down with 999 out of every 1000 of your readers; but really, it didn't go down with me, and I doubt if it has gone down with you. The lack of balance and equity in this retort can be shown convincingly by paralleling the epithets. I herewith parallel them:

Sneak of the first water . . .	Incorrigible newspaper man
A thoroughly untrustworthy man . . .	Trick of debate
An ungrateful and untruthful bounder . . .	Keeping eyes on the reading-public
A dirty little sneak . . .	Illogical, etc.

Perhaps your lack of understanding is due to the fact that, your mental processes being muddled by your local patriotism, you fail to apprehend the question at issue. The question at issue is really literature. What constitutes a short story, or the stuff of a short story? Go over the great short stories that are classics, and you will find that they deal, ninety-nine times out of a hundred, with the terrible and tragic. I have written whole articles on this very topic, and I refrain from boring you here with the content of said articles.

Historically, let me ask you why one of Captain Cook's officers, in his

Log of the voyage, mentions the *leprous* native priest swimming off to the ship the night after the day on which Captain Cook was killed. I am very curious to get your conclusion upon this, because it has been my experience in reading the histories of nations, to find that every nation laid every vile and loathsome disease at the door of some other nation.

Logically, now, why is it that these stories of leprosy are so saliently in the mouths of your dwellers in Hawaii—if said tragedies of leprosy are not salient high lights of Hawaiian life? No sooner had the *Snark* anchored in Hawaii, than the Hawaiian papers published the statement that the father of one of my sailors had been killed by Koolau. I have written three leper stories, every one of which was told me by you Hawaiians—"The Sheriff of Kona," "Koolau the Leper," and "Good-by Jack." And let me tell you that these three are only three out of scores and hundreds of leper stories that were told to me.

You say I ought to write of the brightness of Hawaii. Well, haven't I? Take "The First Landfall," "Surf-Boarding," "Haleakala," "The Lepers of Molokai."

If you want the jolly time of your life, and if I am wrong in believing that you deliberately and consciously shift your logical bases, why read Schopenhauer on "The Art of Controversy," and there find tabulated and exposited a few of your tricks of debate, and all the other tricks of debate you have encountered among other men.

I cannot get away from your sincere fear that I am too much devoted to pessimism and morbidity. Wherefore I quote to you the following lines:

> "We write of sorrow and of death,
>   And yet, perhaps, that day,
> The lips we love have smiled at us,
>   And hope has passed our way."

Knowing myself, and catching glimpses of you, I dare to say that I am more continually happy than you. I laugh more than you; I have always laughed more than you. I laugh at smaller things than do you; also, do I laugh at the little-big things that you take seriously; and also do I laugh at the big-big things that all men take seriously. You are simple—I am simpler. You are ideal, I am more ideal. Your ideal has consisted of conventional statecraft, conventional morality, and conventional material exploitation. My ideal, on the other hand, has been that of a cleaner, better, nobler world, more immediately accessible for all humanity than you could ever dream to hope for. Hope? Ay, I have more hope than you; and as a man thinks, and hopes, he is. Morbid? Pessimistic? Believe me, dear Kakina, you are more morbid than I, and more pessimistic. You, who know humanity in all its deepest depths of vilest degradation far less than do I. You believe humanity to be more base, more hopeless, more unimprovable, more mire-spattered, than do I. As a man thinks, he is. As you think, you are. And you certainly think less of humanity than I do.

310

To know the naked facts of life is not to be pessimistic. Your contention that we must ignore certain unpleasant facts, and dwell on the nice facts, is a sign that you are afraid of a portion of life. And insofar as you run away from a portion of life, by that much will you be ignorant of life. As a man thinks, he is. You are more abnormal about life than I. You are more morbid about life than I. I couple your two formulas together: First, As a man thinks, he is. Second, Think only of the bright things. Well, a nice squint-eyed vision of life such a lopsided man must see.

To your saying, As a man thinks, he is, let me add a rider, As a man is, so is the world. Thus in the eyes of a man who has just dined, all the world is well-fed. Make your own application.

Believe me, Lakana Wahine only likes you and loves you, and would never pepper your wounds. Also, she knows you and honors you so well as not to believe that you would be wounded anyway. She has chortled with delight over this discussion. And right now, let me tell you that as I look at her taking this dictation on the eve of her visit from the Stork, I rather incline to the belief that it will be the last dictation she will be able to take.

To show you that you are not alone in missing the motif of *Martin Eden,* I enclose you my reply to the Rev. Charles Brown, who sermonized in somewhat similar fashion. If you will remember, I began *Martin Eden* while we were visiting with you.

And also to show you that while I am not afraid to look the facts of life clear-eyed in the face, I am not appalled by them nor made pessimistic, I inclose you a MS, recently completed, called "The Human Drift." Please return both these MSS to me.

Affectionately yours, with love to Kakina Wahine,

Lakana

To CHARMIAN LONDON[1]

Glen Ellen, Calif.
July 24, 1910

Dearest Mother-Woman—

Your two boo'ful letters!

Did my 1000 words today, went swimming twice, and rode Gert with Mexican bit. She's a dandy piece of horseflesh. Not as wild as when she was in heat, but still fresh enough to keep one busy all the time.

Jan Jones[2] says he's struck it rich. He's already borrowed five from me. Has been drunk for two weeks. Arrived with a quart of whiskey to sober up on, and drank said quart today and asked me to send him down another pint this eve. I told him to go to hell, and yet I like the poor devil.

Edward is a Joy.

Mrs. Selby voluntarily contributed 10.00 toward the dam.

Best swimming pool we ever had—a dandy.

Remember all details about Greek. Poor Carrie!

It is now 7:45 P.M.—I've seen Jan to bed, and am now going to bed myself. Last night was in bed at eight.

Take good care of yourself, among other things that you may run more quickly to my arms.

If you only knew how often these days I congratulate myself that I'm married to a *good* woman who knows most everything and is a dead game sport.

Father-Man

[1]The first of a series of letters written to Charmian while she was in the Fabiola Hospital following the birth of their first child, June 19. In a letter to Brett, July 12, Jack said "the stork came and brought a beautiful perfect little girl that lived only 38 hours. Its death was due to the exhaustion consequent upon a protracted birth."

[2]One of the many unfortunates that found a haven at the Ranch.

To CHARMIAN LONDON

Glen Ellen, Calif.
July 25, 1910

Dear Mother-Woman:—

If those several letters (they are the first I wrote you) and one contains clippings of "A Wicked Woman," have not come to hand, telephone me. If they have, write me. I sent several hundreds of dollars in same mail to deposit in bank.

Didn't get any letter from you this A.M. Suppose it will come this evening.

Here is a horseshoe made by Fitzsimmons[1] and sent to you, via me.

Am going swimming now with Jan. Jones, and then give him a drive and get shaved.

Father-Man

[1]Bob Fitzsimmons, prize fighter, Heavyweight Champion of the World, 1897-1899. He lost the championship to Jim Jeffries.

To CHARMIAN LONDON

Glen Ellen, Calif.
July 27, 1910

Dearest—

Sketch arrived and off. That last stenographer was the most hopelessly rotten ever.

Herewith letter from Armine.[1] I *dared* to open it on the chance they were immediately arriving in California.

Rode Gert 12 miles yesterday. To-day skin off inside of my legs. Today drive Gert & Fritz & take Nakata along to look at trees at Laundale.

Read your "first thoughts" and two of your later letters to Eliza last night and both she and I were in tears.

Going swimming.

Your own Father-Man

[1]Armine von Tempsky, Hawaiian author.

To CHARMIAN LONDON

Glen Ellen, Calif.
July 28, 1910

My Heart's Dearest:—

Another booful letter from you, which I have just finished.

And I have just finished enclosed open letter to Judge Samuels. Please have ten copies made of it—two originals and four carbons each.

Don't delay to discuss the advisability of it with me, but dispose of the open letters as follows:

Mail in evening, with special delivery stamps on every envelope, one copy each to:

Judge Samuels,
Police Court
City Hall,
Oakland.

Editorial Department of
Examiner
Call
Chronicle
Bulletin
Post
Oakland Tribune
Oakland Enquirer

And the two remaining copies to me.

Also, get me copies of above papers on dates letter would be published.

Also, get me copies of to-day's morning papers, July 28, including *Examiner,* and of evening paper of July 27 or 28, whichever may contain accounts of Mrs. Muldowney's suit for divorce. Cut out clips of same and send to me.

Enclose with Samuels' letter, the Muldowney clipping I enclose you herewith.

Dear Woman, the more I think of that cowardly, oily Jew, the angrier do I get about it. I'm going after him and if I don't do anything else, someday I'll bankrupt him in the business game. Watch my smoke.

Mate Man

313

To Police Judge Samuels

Glen Ellen, Calif.
July 29, 1910

Dear Sir:—

You will remember that you treated me rather scurvily in your little courtroom a few days ago. You will notice, by enclosed clipping from yesterday's paper, that the man whose perjured testimony you accepted as equal to mine, and whom I charged with wantonly and unprovokedly beating me, assisted by half a dozen of his creatures, is now accused of beating his wife, of manhandling a woman.

You will remember the straight and simple story I told on the witness stand, of the beating I received—a story that was unshaken in every way, except by the perjured testimony of Muldowney and his assistants, which perjuries were so palpable and gross that the whole courtroom roared with incredulous laughter when they were uttered.

You know yourself, from what you already knew, and from what you gleaned privately ere the case came before you, the odorous reputation of said Muldowney and his tenderloin resort.

You knew, in your heart of hearts, unless you were incredibly stupid, that the story I told on the witness stand in your courtroom was the simple truth.

Nevertheless, and for reasons I need not suggest to you, you decided to give a "draw" decision, in the affair between Muldowney and his vile crew and me. Never mind what you were convinced of in your heart of hearts, you were determined to give this decision. You gave it. Both Muldowney and myself were discharged. You found by convenient and cheap judicial verbiage, that each of us had been so manifestly truthful as to prove the other a liar, and that we being both guilty of a squalid fight, were not guilty before the law of anything.

Very good. For all the foregoing I have no quarrel with you. I recognize the economic necessity that drives men to action. You have your political, judicial, and bread-winning career to make. Well, in my particular case you made them all. You delivered the goods. You squared yourself with your bread-and-butter and career problem. The cheap and easy verbiage of your decision was all that was necessary. Muldowney, who lives and has his being in a tough part of Oakland, was acquitted. I, who live up country, was acquitted. Your ends were served. To find us both not guilty, considering Muldowney's unsavory reputation and unsavory means of getting a living, was tantamount to finding me guilty. You knew that, you did it, and you served your ends. And still I have no quarrel with you. Nor do I challenge in any way the eminent legality of your decision.

But was it necessary, Judge Samuels, was it necessary, for you to play the bully with me? Was it necessary for you to play a myriad times more

314

cowardly a part than did Muldowney when his crowd held me in while he beat me up in a back room a hundred and fifty feet from the street?

I ask, Judge Samuels, was it necessary? You took a grosser advantage of me than did the dive-keeper Muldowney. Entrenched in your miniature high place, under the sacred panoply of the law, with behind you the policemen's clubs, the city prison cells, and the right to punish for contempt of court (fine or imprisonment), you elected to bully me. You could strike, and not be struck back. You knew it, and you struck. You knew you could do it because so often before, with impunity, you had done it to the poor devils who appeared before you.

And thus I have a quarrel with you. As safe as if behind a thousand machine guns, you bullied and ill-treated me. Was it necessary for you to ruff and rough me the way you did as soon as I got on the stand? I had a solitary witness, who was ready to testify to my sobriety and to the fact that Muldowney and his crew were perjurers. Was it necessary for you to ruff and rough him, like a pickpocket hustling and bustling an honest man? I was irresistibly reminded of it at the time, as I watched you, the judge, ably assisted, ruff and rough my poor one witness.

So now you understand my quarrel with you. You played the cheap, unfair, bullying game that police judges and magistrates have played in the Anglo-Saxon world for a score of generations before you and yours entered said Anglo-Saxon world and embraced its unfair practices.

And in conclusion, let me tell you this: Someday, somewhere, somehow, I am going to get you. I am going to get you legally, never fear. I shall not lay myself open to the law. I know nothing about your past. Only now do I begin to interest myself in your past and to keep an eye on your future. But get you I will, somewhere, someday, somehow, and I shall get you to the full hilt of the law and the legal procedure that obtains among allegedly civilized men.

Most sincerely yours,
Jack London

To CHARMIAN LONDON

Glen Ellen, Calif.
July 30, 1910

My Own Woman:—

I wish you were here. I'll come down to you if you say. Ay—and I'll cut out the Jinks if you say so. Let me know.

I figured on writing a letter that would not lay me open to criminal or civil libel nor to contempt of court. I think I succeeded, but there is no telling. Samuels, a sheeny shoe peddler! Bah! My blood boils. I can make him sick that he ever locked horns with me.

As long as you have me, and deem me worthwhile, you have no license to be blue.

Mate-Man

To Charmian London

Glen Ellen, Calif.
Aug. 2, 1910

Dearest My-Woman:—

The papers were slow in getting started because my signature to open letter was typed and they feared it was a fake.

But, honestly, I believe I've got Samuels' *goat!* He's afraid to come back.

It's election time, you know, and I think enough votes will be swung to defeat him.

Also—hush—mention it not—I got a tip from Noel to-day, which remains to be investigated and proved, namely (1) Samuels is partly interested in Muldowney's dive—how, I do not know. And, (2) one of Samuels' relatives owns the ground and the building rented by Muldowney. Noel is looking it up.

Election—the waterfront, other places, there are any number of men, not socialists, who will remember me and scratch Samuels' name from the ballot.[1]

Incidentally, Muldowney goes on getting more public notoriety for his place, and is sorry he ever met me. He'll have a job living down (police) the notoriety I've given him.

There is a daily published in Oakland named *The Mail,* I believe. Look up and send me what it said yesterday. Don't forget to-day's *Call* and *Chronicle.*

Two letters, on strength of evening papers' publication of letter, show how some votes will swing.

I am saving all your letters. I only destroyed one—the "blue" one in which you worried about me and Samuels.

Your Own Man

[1]He was defeated in the election.

To Police Judge George Samuels

Glen Ellen, Calif.
Aug. 9, 1910

Dear Sir:—

For some time, now, my mail has been burdened with letters from persons in Oakland. These were letters of advice. One and all, they informed me that if I looked up the records for the property of 362—7th street, I should find something of interest.

Now 362—7th street is the Tavern, a tenderloin resort of which Timothy Muldowney is proprietor, and wherein, by the aforesaid Timothy Muldowney and his assistants, I was beaten up a short while ago. (You will remember the case, since you yourself tried it in your court.) According to the records in the Assessor's Office of the County of Alameda, 362—7th street is assessed to George Samuels.

In the telephone directory of Oakland there is only one George Samuels, and that is Judge George Samuels. So I am writing to you to ask if you are the George Samuels who is assessed for Muldowney's tenderloin resort at 362—7th street.

If you are not the George Samuels in question, I apologize here and now for entertaining even for a moment the idea that a judge of rectitude should own such a low place and derive revenue from it, and at the same time try a case between a non-resident like me and a revenue-paying, vote-swinging tenant like Muldowney.

Truth was, I was unprovokedly beaten up in Muldowney's resort. If Muldowney had been found guilty by the police court decision, his license would have been endangered and, also, would have endangered the revenue of the owner of the place. No judge, in common sense and equity, being so interested, could try such a case. You tried the case between Muldowney and me.

I repeat. If you are not the George Samuels who owns Muldowney's tenderloin resort, I apologize for entertaining the suspicion. But if you are the George Samuels who owns that resort of low repute, then what have you to say for yourself?

Very truly yours,
Jack London

TO ROBERT FITZSIMMONS

Glen Ellen, Calif.
Aug. 11, 1910

Dear Bob:—

In reply to yours of August 3. I have been away from home, up to the Grove Jinks of the Bohemian Club, and have only just got back. And I am hastening now, first to thank you for the beautiful watch-fob, which I shall cherish all my life and leave to my children after me. You know you have always been a hero of mine, and at the time of your fight with Corbett at Carson City, I don't believe there was a person in this world who pulled harder for you in spirit than I pulled. I tell you this, so that you may know how I appreciate the watch-fob.

Now for a moment of business. As regards the sketch,[1] I leave everything up to you. Whatever price you want to name will be acceptable to me. I won't even discuss nor question it. Whatever you say, goes.

This is the first letter Mrs. London has taken by dictation from me for many weeks, and she and I both join in asking you and Mrs. Fitzsimmons, when you plan your next itinerary to the Coast, to leave time and space in it for a good visit to us up here on the ranch. We are only a couple of hours by train from San Francisco, and we have some of the most beautiful country to be found in all this world. If you and your wife ride, we've got horses for you; if you drive, it is the same thing. In summer we always have a dandy swimming-pool, and at the right time of the year you can catch trout here, or shoot deer. Don't forget, I'd like us four to get together some time on that visit.

Mrs. London was delighted with your remembrance in the shape of the little horseshoe, and takes this opportunity to thank you for it.

Affectionately yours,

Jack

---

[1]Jack wrote a vaudeville sketch for Fitzsimmons and his wife called "Her Brother's Clothes."

To W. B. VAN DER WEYDE[1]

Glen Ellen, Calif.

Aug. 12, 1910

Dear sir:—

In reply to yours of July 29. I have been away from home, and have only just returned, and am sending this off to you in a rush:

Had the noble Ferrer[2] been killed in any other century than this, he would have been but one of the host of martyrs. But to be killed as he was killed, by a modern state, at the end of the first decade of the twentieth century, is to make his martyrdom not only an anachronism but a most startlingly conspicuous historical event.

It were as if New England had, in the twentieth century, resumed her ancient practice of burning witches.

This killing of Ferrer is inconceivable and monstrous. And yet it happened. And we stand aghast, and cannot quite believe. We know it did happen, and yet it is too impossible to believe.

Jack London

[1]Van der Weyde and a group including Leonard Abbott, Charles Russell, Upton Sinclair and others organized a movement to honor Francisco Ferrer.
[2]Professor Ferrer, founder of the modern schools of Spain, was court-martialed and shot by the Spanish Government of Barcelona, Oct. 13, 1909. The reason given: "The modern schools were a menace to church and state."

To E. C. BECKWITH

Glen Ellen, Calif.
Aug. 24, 1910

Dear Mr. Beckwith:

I thank you heartily for your good letter of recent date. I cannot begin to tell [you] how your liking for *Martin Eden* has delighted me. My own judgment is that *Martin Eden* is far above my more popular books, and yet no one else seems to think so. With rare exception, the critics have hated it and abused it.

I wonder if you have read "The Somnambulists," contained in my last collection of essays under title of *Revolution*. Perhaps we are all sleep-walkers. That, at any rate, is the only explanation I can get for the critics' and the public's rejection of *Martin Eden*.

Very sincerely yours,
Jack London

To CHURCHILL WILLIAMS[1]

Glen Ellen, Calif.
Oct. 4, 1910

My dear Williams:

In reply to yours of September 22, like 90% of my stories, "The Benefit of the Doubt" is based upon an actual experience, but is so entirely modified, added to, and changed, that there is very little likelihood of its being recognized. In my actual experience, the Judge was really and truly, legally and officially, and in every other way, the owner and tax-payer of the tenderloin resort; so that if that Judge should by any possibility recognize himself, he would be the last man in the world to "come back."

Furthermore, and consider this letter a legal contract or agreement to same, I hereby guarantee and pledge myself to stand for and pay all damages in any way whatsoever incurred by any suit or "come-back" that anybody may bring against *The Saturday Evening Post* on account of said story. Of

319

course, there isn't one chance in a thousand million billion, of such a "come-back."

Don't get frightened if I send you a string of stories in the next several months. I write short-stories only in spells. Having finished a long novel [*Burning Daylight*], and then a play [*Theft*], I am taking a time off for the writing of short-stories. Then I shall plunge into another novel or so, and a year may elapse before I write any more short-stories.

Say—the next time you come out here, I've got a trail to ride you over that'll make your hair stand up, and your esthetic backbone thrill with the beauty of it. I have had a bunch of men at work on it for the past few months, building it into the mountains. Mrs. London is looking forward to riding over that trail with you.

Sincerely yours,
Jack London

---

[1]Of the *Saturday Evening Post*.

To JUSTUS SCHARFF, ESQ[1]

Glen Ellen, Calif.
Nov. 1, 1910

Dear Sir:—

In reply to your good letter of Sept. 26. I am indeed glad to learn that at last luck is coming our way as regards the sale of the *Snark*. There are absolutely no claims whatever against the *Snark*. Just before I sailed from San Francisco, at the beginning of the voyage, a San Francisco ship chandler having got the idea into his head that we were going to sail some days before we really did sail, got into a panic and libelled the *Snark*. This libel, of course, was promptly cleared. It was for a matter of £40. This is absolutely the only claim there ever was against the *Snark,* and it was cleared up. And please hereby take this letter from me as a personal guaranty to indemnify you for any possible claims that may ultimately be presented against the *Snark,* and for which, according to the arrangements of the sale you are conducting, you may be held responsible.

Congratulating you upon your success in selling the *Snark*[2], and assuring you that all things concerning same shall be held confidential by me, and hoping to have you or any of your firm visit us on our California ranch.

Sincerely yours,
Jack London

---

[1]Business agent in Sydney, Australia.
[2]The *Snark* was sold, for a mere fraction of her cost, to an English syndicate, which operated her, trading and recruiting, in the New Hebrides.

To George Sterling

Glen Ellen, Calif.
Nov. 16, 1910

O you Greek!

Your showing "The First Poet" to Heron and Williams, and then coming on and asking me to father it, is equivalent to exposing your penis to a couple of 90¢ alarmclocks, and then trying to rape a quail. I'm the quail. And if I let you rape me, both alarm clocks would immediately go off and tell the news to the world.

"The First Poet" is DELICIOUS. I'd be damnably proud to have written it. And I'd be willing to father it for you, if it weren't for the aforesaid alarm clocks.

The best I can do is to change a comma and agree to collaborate with you in it, and attempt to market it that way.

But far better than that, I should like to see you put it out under your own name. It's one of the best things you've done in the way of good popular satire. Mitchell Kennerley would publish it in *The Forum* over your name as a matter of course. And yet I would consider *The Forum* as a last resort, financially. I'd try all the other big magazines first.

You make me sick. You ought to be castrated—writing things like "The First Poet" and the "43 Chapter of Job," and then not wanting to put your name to them or wanting anyone to know you have written them. Talk about the gladiator amongst the eunuchs!— you're a gladiator all right; but you go crawling around sideways and byways trying to emasculate yourself all the time. I want to tell you I'd be prouder than hell to have done either of these two things of yours. And I want to tell you furthermore, that if you insist on your emasculatory foolishness, that I'll father your stuff if you don't let a soul see it!!! And still furthermore, and beforemore and alwaysmore, I insist that it's not fair to ask me or anyone to father such good stuff, and it's up to you to get sensible and practical and father it yourself.

When are you and Carrie coming up to see us? We're home any time for you now. And when you do come, I'm going to turn loose and give you hell because of compelling me to write the foregoing letter. You damned Greek!

Lovingly yours,
Wolf

To Lute Pease

Glen Ellen, Calif.
Nov. 19, 1910

Dear Lute Pease:

In reply to yours of Oct. 28. I am wondering what you are thinking of the play.

Oh, well, we had enough ducks to eat on our voyage anyway. But we didn't have any to give away. Mrs. London is feeling quite strong again since the trip.

Glad you liked the Bull Fight story ["The Madness of John Harned"] in *Everybody's*. I am afraid that personally I was guilty of some of the sensations my hero experienced at his bull fight. I know, among other things, that I jumped up, and in the tense silence cheered when the bull was getting the matador. And I didn't intend to, at all. I suddenly discovered myself doing it.

Funny about "The House of Pride." I wonder if some of the disinclination for it is due to the fact that I didn't kill anybody in it. You know my reputed formula for a short story is to start with three characters and to kill four before the end. Possibly I erred in not killing anybody in "The House of Pride." The situation of the story itself was true. The story is real. What more could I say? Of course, I could have done more; I could have had them drown themselves in the surf, or murder each other; or fall on each other's necks in brotherly love. The only trouble is, life so rarely works out that way.

Now, look here, Lute, don't you cast any sneers upon Californian waterways. I can sail from San Francisco Bay 30 odd miles south. I can sail from San Francisco north 120 miles. I can sail, on the various bays of San Francisco, its rivers and its sloughs, for hundreds and hundreds of miles. And if you don't believe it, and if you think it isn't excitingly interesting, you come down here some time on a vacation and let me take you out.

Sincerely yours,

Jack London

To Henry W. Noyes[1]

Glen Ellen, Calif.

Nov. 19, 1910

My dear Mr. Noyes:—

In reply to yours of Oct. 30. First, let me apologize for and explain my delay in answering. I have been away from home for over a month, and have only just returned, to find a mountain of MSS and letters awaiting me. I hardly know how to reply to you. I am divided between sentiment and my appreciation of what is beautiful and true on the one hand, and my practical knowledge of the publishing business on the other hand.

Nobody makes any money out of poetry in the United States. I may state flatly and absolutely, that today in the United States no man writing serious poetry makes the expenses of publication. There are one or two men, such as Wallace Irwin, writing humorous verses and doggerel for the magazines, who make a living and a good living. And that is all.

Here is where I have to bring my practical, experienced judgment to bear, and tell you that there is not one chance in a million for you to make two cents out of your collection of poetry. I have a friend [George Sterling], whom I believe to be the greatest living poet in the United States. He has published three volumes of great poetry. They have never brought him a cent. The average poet of the day who brings out a book of verses, pays for the publication of the same in advance, and never gets his money back. This is a sweeping statement I am making, and it is a true one.

And now, a warning. Whatever you may do with your verse, do not ever let a publisher bring it out who compels you to pay for said publication in advance.

I have been in jail a few times, and I feel that I am able to appreciate no end of the good work you have put into these poems. Yet I, who do appreciate this, have spent quite a few years writing for the public and discovering that said public appreciates or understands damn little of the life I have delineated as I knew it. Again and again I have opened up leads of true life and found that it was wholly misunderstood by my reading public, and been compelled to abandon them.

And again I do not know what to say. Recognizing how you must be situated, I am willing to do anything and everything in my power to be of assistance to you. I do not know what to do with them. On the other hand, pray consider me at your service in any and every way you may suggest as regards handling said poems.

Please, please do not consider this a cold letter. It is only a hard-headed, practical letter of one who knows. There is no need of my giving you a "jolly." The intrinsic value of the poems is not to be considered. If they were as great as Shelley's, the publishing situation in the United States to-day would still be the same. This poet friend of mine whom I mentioned, cannot sell his big poems to the magazines. The magazines won't look at them, preferring instead to publish a lot of ephemeral rot. Years ago, angered by what I considered my friend's slothfulness, I jumped in and tried to market some of his poetry for him. I failed utterly. I never made one sale. And, pardon me, his poetry was even better than yours. So you see the situation.

Is it possible for me to send you a couple of my own books to read? If so, please give me full instructions for the sending of same, and tell me what you have already read, and, if possible, what you would care to read.

And again believe me,

Yours to command,

Jack London

[1]At the time of this letter Noyes was a prisoner in San Quentin; later he was transferred to Napa State Mental Hospital.

To Japanese Ambassador, Washington, D.C.

[Telegram]

Glen Ellen, Calif.
Nov. 24, 1910

AS A LOVER OF LIBERTY AND A CITIZEN OF THE WORLD I DO MOST EARNESTLY PROTEST TO YOU, AND THROUGH YOU PROTEST TO YOUR COUNTRY, AGAINST THE UNJUST CONTEMPLATED EXECUTION OF DOCTOR KOTOKU, HIS WIFE AND THEIR TWENTY-FOUR COMRADES. I SIGN MYSELF ONE OF THE GREAT ARMY OF INTERNATIONAL SOLDIERS OF FREEDOM.[1]

(Signed) Jack London

[1]*The New York Times,* Nov. 10, 1910, carried a story under the headline "Plotters against the Mikado to die." According to a Tokyo dispatch, 26 persons were found guilty, including the ringleader Kotoku and his wife, of an attempt to assassinate the Emperor. They were executed.

To Rev. Charles R. Brown

[Open letter]

Glen Ellen, Calif.
Dec. 2, 1910

Dear Sir:—

It may seem unfair to "jump" a man when he is in trouble. But the desire to point a moral is human. You have done both these things to me, in spite of the fact that you know nothing about me except what you read in the newspapers. It is for this very human reason that I feel impelled now to write you this Open Letter.

Once only in my life I sat under you, in your First Congregational Church of Oakland. It was a Sunday night. Your full congregation was present. You were supposed to speak on a book of mine entitled *Martin Eden.* Instead, you made me your subject. I sat with my dearly loved wife, my Mate, beside me. You attacked me, and my Mate beside me, making invidious references to the "sanctity of the home," and to the fact that I "had the love of two wives both of whom were still living."

I can only ask you now, under the present circumstances, and in the light of your own recent experiences, in Stevenson's beautiful logic: "Was it wise? Was it kind? Was it true?"

Very truly yours,
Jack London

P.S. I earnestly desire you to reply to this. I don't believe everything I read in the newspapers. Do you believe everything you read in the newspapers?

What did you know about me, when you publicly attacked me, save what you had read in the newspapers.

To A DOUBLE, "JACK LONDON"

Glen Ellen, Calif.
Dec. 23, 1910

Dear Jack London:—

I've traced you down the Arkansaw River, when you caught the big catfish. I've run you over the 101 Ranch. And through Kremlin, Oklahoma. And now listen to me. You know who I am, and you know who wrote the stuff that has appeared above my name. Now, I'm a good fellow, and I don't bear you any ill-will whatever. The thing that I am intensely curious about is to know the various ways in which you have run the game on me, and on the people you have met. So here's a free and open-hearted invitation to come and visit me here on my ranch in California. We ought to have a jolly good time together. We've been over the world, both of us, and we've a lot of experiences to swap. And again, let me repeat, I am dreadfully anxious to have you tell me the ins and outs in the game you have been playing. Believe me, you're not the only Jack London that's wandering over the country. There are several of them. But you are the only one whose address I have been able to get. Therefore you are the first one to whom I have addressed this invitation to visit me. You've read my stuff. I know it. I know you know it like a book; therefore, I am confident that you will know that this is a straight deal I am giving you. I want to meet you, as a visitor at our ranch, where you will be genially and jovially entertained, and behind this entertainment there is no ulterior motive. All that I want to see you about, I have stated in this letter. I am sure we'll like each other.

Sincerely yours,
Jack London

P.S. Hell, man—there's a real Jack London fifteen years of age, whose father is a druggist and who lives at Bendigo, Western Australia, and he's a bona fide Jack London.

To JOHN STRYBER

Glen Ellen, Calif.
Dec. 28, 1910

Dear sir:

In reply to yours of December 25. I have just now finished making out and signing the "Agreement to Employ a Paroled Prisoner." And I have sent it off by this mail to the County Clerk of Sonoma Co., to have him vouch for me as a resident of good standing in this county.

As soon as the County Clerk returns the paper to me, I shall forward it immediately to you.

Now, first of all, let me tell you that I am leaving in several days for a month's stay in Los Angeles. However, my ranch and a number of my people are here. I shall see about making arrangements to receive you, before I go to Los Angeles. You, in turn, must keep me informed of when you expect to arrive.

If you arrive while I am in Los Angeles, I wish you would write to my sister, Mrs. Eliza Shepard, Glen Ellen, California, telling her the train you expect to arrive on, and the day, so that she may be at the station to meet you.

Now, here is the way I am situated. I have got a ranch of 1000 acres here, but I have not yet built my house on it. As a result, I am renting a small house outside of the ranch for my own use. This house is too small and crowded, and this year I am starting to build. As a result of the present situation, however, there is no place for you in this small house; but on the ranch I have a small comfortable cabin in a beautiful spot. This was last occupied up to several months ago by a friend of mine [Strawn-Hamilton], a scientist and a philosopher, who wrote several books there. This is within a quarter of a mile of the farmhouse on the ranch, where my ranch foreman lives with his family. While working for me, you will have to "bach" it in this cabin. I shall leave instructions with my sister, in case you arrive in my absence, telling her to arrange for groceries, supplies, etc.

Now, please keep me informed as to when to expect you, etc., etc.

Very truly yours,
Jack London

To C. F. Lowrie[1]

Glen Ellen, Calif.
Dec. 28, 1910

Dear Comrade Lowrie:—

In reply to yours of Dec. 20. First of all, my thanks for the subscription-cards to *THE COMING NATION*.[2]

Now about Miss Katherine Dopp:[2] I don't know the lady. This is no discourtesy on my part, for I usually forget the persons I casually meet or casually correspond with. I don't remember meeting her. If she says so, I certainly did meet her; in which case I am curious to know, as she asserts, what material she verbally presented me with. Likewise am I curious to know what material she presented me in writing or by way of correspondence.

I wonder if the dear lady at issue is aware that this is the most unfortunate book I ever wrote; if she is aware that I have been long since charged with plagiarizing *Before Adam* from Rudyard Kipling and Stanley Waterloo, and other writers who died a generation before they were born.

Here is the chronology of *Before Adam:* It was finished June 7, 1906. It was written in forty (40) days. It was accepted by *Everybody's,* by telegram July 19, 1906. Its publication began in the October Number of *Everybody's,* 1906.

It might be well to look up and find out if the lady comrade published her work prior to that date. I saw her stuff published subsequently in *The International Socialist Review.* My little private query at the time, uttered only to myself, was to ask if she had gleaned the primitive idea from me. Of course, I made no noise about it. I never dreamed of knocking a comrade.

As regards her charges, they are so unfounded that they are to me more astounding than if she had charged me with raping her. I thought, years ago, when all the charges of plagiarism had been slammed into me, that the end of the affair had come. Now comes this lady comrade, whom I don't know, telling me that what I know was learned from her. If she will pardon me, I'll name my teachers as Darwin, Huxley, Spencer, and all the school of evolutionists, who, I hope, had promulgated their theories before she was dry behind the ears. Really, she vexes me, and reminds me of the abnormal females described by Havelock Ellis and other specialists. No other explanation can I reach of her charge that I have intellectually raped her.

Take it or leave it, I didn't bother over bourgeois knockers and traducers; but to have a female comrade jump into the game leads me to doubt and to consult my shelf on psychopathic mania.

I wonder if the lady comrade cherishes the idea that her ideas have been evolved out of her own subliminal self?

I am returning herewith my letter to you dated February 24, 1909. By all means, show it to her. Better yet, make a copy of it and let her have a copy. Also, show her this present letter of mine.

By all means, go ahead with your enterprise.

Sincerely yours,
Jack London

---

[1]A contemporary Socialist who attempted to dramatize *Before Adam*.
[2]Katherine Elizabeth, who wrote many books for children on history and pre-history.

To George P. Brett

Glen Ellen, Calif.
Dec. 29, 1910

Dear Mr. Brett:

In reply to yours of Dec. 21. I am returning herewith the Supplementary Agreement, asking you to sign same and return to me.

Also, it will be necessary for you to tell me the titles of the several books for which you have granted translation-rights, and also the languages of said translation-rights and the names and addresses of the men possessing said rights—of course, all this is necessary for me to keep my own books straight.

Oh, you New Yorkers! I've got you all skinned to death. *Burning Daylight* lives with Charmian; Charmian is my wife:

Now who the devil am I?

Sincerely yours,

Jack London

P.S. And in reply to yours of Dec. 22:

I am of the firm conviction that of all the titles for collections of short stories that I ever achieved, *When God Laughs* is the best. It gives the cue to every story in the volume. Without this as a collective title, there is no rhyme nor reason for the collection.

When I read that the dealers who specialize in religious books are afraid to list this book because of its title, I feel so confident that said dealers are so absolutely the reflexes of the minds of their patrons that their patrons wouldn't buy the book no matter under what title it was listed.

I cannot conceive of this collection of stories being published under any other title. And in this collection I have only a past distressing experience to call upon. When *The Sat. Eve. Post* proceeded to publish serially *The Call of the Wild,* the editor wrote me, told me that it was a bully story, but that the title was rotten. I told him I couldn't think of a better, to invent one, and go ahead and use it. He evidently failed in this, and reluctantly used my title. When you came to the book-publication of this story, you wrote me the very same proposition: The yarn was bully, but the title was rotten. I told you the same thing I had told the editor of *The Sat. Evening Post*. You failed in getting another title, and reluctantly used my title. And I'll be damned if that very muchly-rejected title didn't become a phrase in the English language. This is only one of many experiences concerning titles, wherein editors, booksellers and publishers absolutely missed.

I believe that the *When God Laughs* collection of stories is the best collection I have ever written. I believe that the title-story itself is one of the three best short-stories I have written. I believe that no more adequate title for the title-story and for the collection, could be worked out in a thousand years by a thousand editors, booksellers and publishers. I believe that the

328

intrinsic imprudence and catchiness of this title will make up in sales with the profane booksellers far more than will be lost by the refusal of the religious booksellers to list same.

To Bessie London

Los Angeles, Calif.
Jan. 8, 1911

Dear Bessie:—

In reply to yours of January 4.

First of all, let me tell you that I am in the thick of hard times. I have mortgages of over $30,000.00, upon which I am paying interest. In addition to this I have something like $10,000.00 in debts.

When you figure repairs of house, painting, taxes, etc., dancing lessons, music lessons, railroad passes (I work for them), etc., you will discover that you are getting more than $100.00 a month, in addition to the free rent of a house.

As regards my writing, I am not making the money I was making a few years ago. My socialism, my going out of vogue, and my natural and inevitable deterioration as a writer, have reduced the price I have received from the magazines, and have reduced the sales of my books.

I am making the effort of my life at the present moment to provide for the future. I am planting eucalyptus trees. My laborers' wages for the month of Jan. will amount to over $1,000.00, and this does not include my horses, my feed for my horses, my wagons, my harnesses, plows and harrows, and expenses of repairing same; nor does it include a thousand and one other expenses. Do you think this is for myself? I can live on $20.00 a month. Do you think this is for Charmian? She can do the same. This is for all of us. This means Grandma, Jennie, Johnnie, doctor bills, houses, taxes, life-insurance, etc., and all in addition to you and Joan and Bess. For years I have fed, clothed, and sheltered quite a number of people. I have to work and provide for all these people. You are not the only one. You tell me in your letter that you owe Dr. Majors. So do I—not for myself, but for Mammy Jennie. You and Joan and Bess are not the only ones who have doctor bills.

Now, I am working like hell. What am I getting for it? A rare chance to see the children, and in the most unnatural conditions of being a visitor I have no opportunity of getting acquainted with them. What chance have I? I live in the country. At long intervals I come to the city, and then I am too busy to do anything more than take a passing look at them.

As usual, and as of old and always, I am putting up and getting nothing in return. Please don't think for a moment that you're the only person who loves Joan and Bess. And don't forget this danger: The less I am acquainted with my children, the less I shall know my children, the less I shall be interested in my children. And insofar as you stand between me and knowing my children, by that much will my interest be lessened, and by that much will what I shall do for them be lessened. Don't forget that the program that I have permitted you to employ for some years now, is a process of alienation of me from my children, a process that leads to lack of knowing my children and lack of interest in my children.

I can sacrifice—but I must get something for it. I have long since learned that you Madderns drive the hard bargains. Very well, here's a bargain: Let my children part of the time visit me. Let me have something of the children that have cost me thousands of dollars and many weary days of toil. Do you think that you are so uniquely made that you only can have a love and interest and care for our children? If you think you want the children as strongly, as you say you do, how strongly do you think I want them part of the time?

Your narrowness is the narrowness of the narrowest cell in all hell. I have yielded to this narrowness a long time. I am a philosopher. But the time has come, and in fact it is long since due, when I should have something of my children; and I refuse further to sacrifice all of my father-love and interest in order to satisfy the narrow prejudice of your narrow mind.

What is your narrow prejudice? You are suffering from what you deem a sex-offence. You blame me for that sex-offence, never deeming for a moment that it is due to your own sexual shortcoming.

Your attitude is not that of a co-partner in the procreation of our children. It is the attitude of a separate individual female, sexually offended because I found a woman who could make me happy as you never made me happy and never could make me happy.

You Madderns are a narrow, mean crowd, and I know the whole boiling lot of you. In you Madderns is condensed all the narrowness of the narrow peasant mind. I refuse further to sacrifice myself to this narrow peasant mind.

Are you so much wiser than I? Am I so stupid, so vilely rotten, that I cannot have some hand in forming my children's minds and souls? Let me warn you that you are playing the part of a dog-in-the-manger when you insist by your past and present attitude in dwarfing my children through their lack of me—and all because Charmian has proven herself a better wife and mate for me than you proved yourself.

Remember, that when I asked you to marry me, and you accepted me, that it was there and then stated explicitly by me that I did not love you. You accepted me on that basis. Long afterwards I found somebody whom I could love.

Do you think Charmian wants to alienate my children from you? Please don't forget that no woman is particularly enthusiastic about taking any hand in raising another woman's children. Yet Charmian is noble, Charmian has no peasant-mind, and Charmian is willing to meet me and go any distance with me in this matter at issue.

And another thing that you must not forget, is: That over half of my work is done by Charmian. That for every dollar you receive from me, Charmian has earned over 50 cents of it; that every piece of bread and butter or chunk of meat you put in your mouth, Charmian has paid more than half of the same. And yet, you are willing to eat this bread and butter and meat, and ask for more, and at the same time deny me any acquaintance with my children, because you are a sexually-offended, jealous female creature.

Are you a woman? Or are you a mere sexual beast, filled with such sex-jealousy and hatred that you will sacrifice your children and your children's father to your own morbid hatred? Wild Indians, headhunters and cannibals, have sometimes in their deepest depths of degradation, been like this: Are you willing so to classify yourself?

I've watched you, and waited for you to show your better self. It's high time you did, if you've got any lingering shreds of it in you.

I want you to answer this letter by a letter. I don't want any drawing up within your narrow, prejudiced sacredness of isolation (as you have done in the past); I want you to verify my assumptions of you in this letter, or to prove to me that you have developed into a something finer and higher and nobler and more civilized than a mere jealous sexually-offended, unmotherly, peasant-minded female.

Jack London

To KARL EDWIN HARRIMAN[1]

Los Angeles, Calif.
Jan. 10, 1911

Dear Mr. Harriman:

In reply to yours of the 31st. Since it will take me a week of mulling to get a clear conception of my character, and that each story will also require its own particular mulling, it would be inexpedient of me to give you in advance a scenario of the first three stories. I ain't got no first three stories. And I am not going to spend the many days of mulling on an idle correspondence adventure. When I start in to do it, I am going to do it, but I'm not going to run the chance of wasting a lot of time doing it in advance.

I can promise you some good stories. I can promise you a good hero character that will move through all the stories. They will be in the South Seas. Time, the present. From time to time I keep catching glimpses of my hero, and making sporadic notes. But I certainly shall not attempt to realize him nor his adventures until I really start to realize him. I've three or four stories in his fashion already up in the air, with slight notes taken on them. But I never compose a story, outline a story, until I actually set to work upon it. Then I take my period of mulling, and immediately follow this mulling with the actual writing. And I am unfortunately so made, that if ever I soak myself in a thing, and then let any time whatever elapse, I am done with that thing forever. I can never again realize it. When I get soaked, then I pitch in immediately to do the work.

I can deliver you the goods with six ripping stories; but I must have the contract in hand before I turn loose on these stories. Since you wish it, a 10¢ flat rate will be acceptable. I am so cussedly made that this will not influence me one way or the other in the length of the stories I shall deliver.[2]

Sincerely yours,
Jack London

[1]Editor, *The Red Book Magazine.*
[2]London never published any stories in *Red Book* after this date.

To C. F. LOWRIE

Los Angeles, Calif.
Jan. 13, 1911

Dear Comrade Lowrie:

In reply to yours of Jan. 5. I certainly must have met Miss Dopp, because she says so, and I see my mistake of mixing her up with Mary E. Marcy; but if Miss Dopp could only realize that in the course of the year I meet several thousand people whom I never meet again, she would understand how impossible it is for me to remember her.

I wrote *Before Adam* because I quarreled with the science of Stanley Waterloo in his *Story of Ab.* In one generation he had his primitive men discover fire, domesticate the dog and the horse, invent the bow and arrow and the spear, and achieve an intricate tribal development. To myself, I said this was impossible. Primitive man developed very slowly. Therefore I wrote *Before Adam* to show two things, (1) the mistakes and lost off-shoots in the process of biologic evolution; and (2) that in a single generation the only device primitive man, in my story, invented, was the carrying of water and berries in gourds. Gosh—if you knew all my troubles with persons of the Miss Dopp variety, you would not soothingly suggest to me that I should not lose "any more sleep over the matter." Believe me, I sleep like a babe, these people jump into me, I slam back, and the thing is forgotten the next instant.

Yours for the Revolution,
Jack London

To Sydney Pawling

Los Angeles, Calif.
Jan. 22, 1911

Dear sir:—

In reply to yours of January 5. I sometimes wonder if you think that in your dealings with me you feel that you are compelled to play a sharp and baffling game of business enterprise. As a business man and a horse trader, these things might go with me; but being neither a business man nor a horse trader, but just an ordinary common-sense sort of a man, they don't go. I have no patience with bafflement nor with cleverness.

Your letter of January 5, as a direct reply to mine of December 21, has all the shortcomings and deficiencies as laid down by me in the foregoing paragraph. For instance, you tell me that you consider you are serving my best interests by not rushing out books at too short intervals. At the same time you have a contract with me under which you are to publish all my books. At the present moment, of books unpublished by me in the United States but finished, and of books published in the United States which are not published in England, you are precariously close to ten (10) behind the schedule. If, despite the contract, which covers all my books, you cannot keep up with this schedule, the best thing for both sides to this matter is to quit the arrangement. A better thing would be to let me deal with Mr. Heinemann directly. You, Mr. Pawling, may be a very excellent Englishman; but you're not the right kind of an Englishman to meet an American like me. I am quite confident that I can deal with Mr. Heinemann, but I cannot deal with you. There is a smack of the shop and of petty cleverness about you, and of small caddish ways, that turns my gorge. From the beginning of my correspondence with you, after I finished my correspondence with Mr. Heinemann, you have dealt with me in the spirit of a Jew Pawnbroker trying to buy several moth-eaten undershirts from an impecunious sailor. Now, we can't go on this way. Personally, my feeling is that if ever I should meet you, I should pull your nose.

Pray believe me that the foregoing statements are made by me not in a spirit of crude harshness, but out of a wide experience in dealing with publishers and editors. In my experience I have dealt with more publishers and editors than you have with writers. And in all my experiences you stand alone as a unique challenge to the decency of the cosmos. You irritate me. I have no contempt for you, but I am aware of a constant irritation at your smallness.

Now there are two things to be done. Either I must get a square deal, or I shall have nothing further to do with you and your house.

If I cannot be treated by your house as I have been treated by every house with which I have dealt, why the only thing for me to do is for me to quit your house. I don't care how your house may decide to accord this treatment, but I cannot possibly receive it from you, nor through dictation by you to some underling go-between. Let me deal with Mr. Heinemann. Let me deal with a man. Let me deal with somebody who has enough decency to tell me what is being done with my stuff, what books are being published, what books are proposed to be published, etc., etc.

Please take this letter as the expression of one who is temperamentally not akin to you. You and I live in different worlds and talk different languages. I care never again to howl on your door-step, and I wish never again to have you slink under my window when I'm trying to sleep.

Kindly show this letter to Mr. Heinemann, and deliver to him the rest of our correspondence from A to Z. If you don't, I'll see that I get to Mr. Heinemann by other means. As it is, I refuse further to be treated in the absurd and preposterous way in which you treat me.

Very truly yours,
Jack London

P.S. I shall consider it a great favor from you if in the meantime you send me at least one copy of the shilling edition of *The Sea Wolf,* which you, at this late day, in response to a prod from me, inform me has been published and is selling well.

To John Stryber

Los Angeles, Calif.
Jan. 29, 1911

Dear friend Stryber:

In reply to yours of Jan. 22 and 24. First of all, please find inclosed herewith the signed Monthly Report of a Paroled Prisoner. According to your suggestion, I leave the filling out of this blank to you. Of course, we shall have to get together and talk before I can reach a conclusion as to what arrangements will be made between us. The main thing was to get you paroled as soon as possible; and I did this before I left for Los Angeles. It has of course caused you some trouble and confusion; but I guess that was unavoidable. It was unfortunate that Mrs. Shepard was down in Oakland at the time you arrived. I think the fault of the misconnections was due to the way they handled it from the Warden's office end of it.

Please make a copy of the filling-out of this monthly report, and send said copy to me.

We expect to be home in a couple of weeks now.

Did Noyes give you any message of me? It's too bad the way the deputy sheriff told Glen Ellen. But what the hell of it! So long as you are happy in the open air and freedom again, why what do a lot of village people amount to?

Your adventure with that Christian scientist in San Francisco was very amusing. Also irritating. Miss Blanche Partington *is* a friend of mine.

I can readily understand how the rain on the roof and the loneliness of the cabin must affect you. But you'll get over this more quickly than you think.

I only have about forty letters to write, so you'll excuse my not making this any longer.

Very truly yours,
Jack London

To H. A. HANNER

Los Angeles, Calif.
Jan. 29, 1911

Dear Mr. Hanner:—

In reply to yours of January 25, 1911. Here are several brief ideas: You've got philosophy of life, and have thought about life and the world and things. You lack method. Study Jimmie Hopper's method, and imagine how he'd have written this story. I'd be willing to bet you $10.00 that he'd pay you $10.00 for the idea in this story. Heavens—I'd pay you $10.00 myself for it! All of which means to show that Jimmie Hopper and I have mastered our tools. With artisanship we could shape this idea of yours into a story that would sell. Do you get the point?

Take your time; study the stuff of the other fellows who've mastered the trick—study until you can turn the same trick. Take your time; elaborate; omit; draw; develop. Paint—paint pictures and characters and emotions—but paint, paint, draw, draw. And take your time. Spend a day on a paragraph, or on ten paragraphs. Grab your motif, master it. Make it LIVE, and spout blood and spirit and beauty and fire and glamor.[1]

Sincerely yours,
Jack London

[1]In his letter to London, Hanner wrote, "have had lots of Ms. returned by magazines but haven't much respect for their opinion."

To HERBERT FORDER[1]

Los Angeles, Calif.
Feb. 3, 1911

Dear Herbert Forder:

In reply to yours of recent date. First of all, let me say that your letter goes to my heart, and, secondly, that I'm in a hell of a position.

I am very heavily in debt, and am only just now beginning my first feeble attempts at building a house for myself. That is to say, I am chopping down some redwood trees and leaving them in the woods to season against such time, two or three years hence, when they will be used in building the house. I have four households running all the time, and am taking care of a number of persons besides my own relatives. In fact, because of my lending a hand in so many different directions, which amounts to many thousands of dollars every year, I am thus in debt and unable to build a house for myself.

Now, as regards collaboration, it's not a case of my meeting the wrong kind of person. The point is, I'm the wrong kind of person. It's nobody's fault but mine—this inability to collaborate.

Now, to come back to my general situation. Everything I can raise and scrape I am sinking into the planting of eucalyptus trees. I have no Americans working for me. With the exception of my German-Swiss ranch-foreman, I employ nothing but floating labor, and this is practically entirely Italian. At the present moment there are some 20 Italians planting trees for me. Of course, this work for such a number of men lasts only during a couple of planting months. Several men are kept on throughout the year, plowing, watering, cultivating, caring for the trees; but it is all cheap, unskilled labor.

I pay these Italians $1.75 a day. They board and lodge themselves. They get paid when they work, and don't get paid when they don't work. During the last month, they have not worked more than two weeks on account of heavy rains. They got paid accordingly. I have no need nor use for any other kind of workmen.

Incidentally, I had one small cabin on the ranch, an affair of one room, but since I left on my trip to Los Angeles, one paroled convict has arrived at the ranch, and taken up his residence in that cabin, and a second paroled convict is expected soon to join him. I have to stand sponsor with the prison authorities for these men. They are sick, miserable, broken old men, of no use to me, and on the contrary a burden to me.

Still on the situation: There is the ruins of an old winery on the ranch, which is owned by the California Wine Association. Also, there is an old farm cottage belonging to the Cal. Wine Ass'n. I don't know whether this old cottage is habitable or not. I have never been inside of it. I have written this mail to the Cal. Wine Ass'n, offering to take over the care-taking of their property, in return for the use of the cottage. There is no furniture in this cottage.

Now, if you're up against it terribly hard, the foregoing explains what I could do,—that is, if the Wine Ass'n will let me have the cottage.

There isn't much work in this valley. I could give you $1.75 a day, and turn you into that cottage; but you would have to take orders from the ranch-foremen. Also, I don't know how your wife and children would like living in this place. It is lonely, it is a mile from where I am living at the present moment, and a great deal of the time I am not at home. And when I am at home, I am pretty well up the neck with my work. And when I'm not working, I am usually out on horseback with my wife.

There is nothing here but a country school, and the children are principally those of the Italian laborers.

I am outlining the situation, not with the idea of making it a tempting proposition, nor with the desire that you accept it; but wholly with the idea of letting you know, if you go up against the game to an absolute finish, that here is a lean, scrawny anchor in a fissure of rocky ground. It will hold, but I know so thoroughly well that it is not up to your standard of living, nor your wife's, nor your children's; that you, if driven to such an anchorage, would not stay in it any longer than you had to. On the other hand, I am absolutely unable to offer what would come up to your standard of living.

In fact, I am on such shaky legs myself just now, that with interest on mortgages overdue, taxes unpaid, and heavy month's bills coming in from everywhere, I was compelled to flee here to Los Angeles so as to stall off payment for a while. I haven't paid my ranch foreman's salary for three months. I managed to raise the wages for the first of February for the laborers, and they're the only ones that I've paid.

And there's the everlasting hell of it. I'd like to lend you a hand; I'd like to finance you for a year or two in your struggle. But I simply cannot do it.

In hopes that better things will shortly heave in sight for you,

Sincerely yours

Jack London

---

[1]Pen name, John Dathan Landor. Landor made the proposition to London that, "if you will transport myself, wife, and two young children to the neighborhood of Glen Ellen and allow me to collaborate with you, I will agree to train you every day, the curriculum to consist of boxing, wrestling, physical training and bathing."

To WILLIAM HEINEMANN, ESQ.

Glen Ellen, Calif.

Mar. 1, 1911

Dear Mr. Heinemann:—

In reply to yours of February 11, 1911. If a man goes through an earthquake or a boiler explosion, he is very liable to have an "unaccustomed want of restraint" in his communications to others of his kind. Pray consider your Mr. Pawling as such an earthquake or boiler explosion, and you will understand what you have seen fit to call my "unaccustomed want of restraint." I note with keen appreciation that it is not your habit to receive communications such as the one I addressed to Mr. Pawling. I need scarcely tell you that if you read the content of that letter thoroughly, you would have discovered that it was not my habit to write such communications. In fact, I have never written a letter like that particular one in my life.

Now I am not going to waste the time necessary to make an abstract of all the correspondence I have had with your Mr. Pawling. I shall proceed immediately to give you your choice of three positions in which you have placed yourself:

First: You have not read the correspondence that has passed between Mr. Pawling and me.

Second: You have read this correspondence, but you are of the same caliber as Mr. Pawling.

Third: Or I am a lunatic.

Number Three is inadmissible, because out of all my experience I have never been compelled to write as severely as I wrote to Mr. Pawling; because, out of all my experience with publishers of books and magazines, with literary and dramatic agents, all over the world, I have never received any hint of the treatment that has been accorded me by your Mr. Pawling. No, I am not a lunatic.

Therefore, you must place yourself either in the first or second positions. Either you have read the correspondence, and you are like your Mr. Pawling, or else you have swallowed your Mr. Pawling whole and I am causing you indigestion.

I feel impelled to tell you a little story that occurred down South. A Northerner who had never seen a skunk, was inquiring as to what a skunk looked like. The white master said that a skunk looked like a pussy-cat—in fact, he thought, if anything, the skunk was handsomer than a pussy-cat. And he referred the matter to his Negro servant, who replied: "Well, Massa, you may think a skunk is handsomah than a pussy-cat, but I say that handsome is as handsome does." Pray pardon me, but if your Mr. Pawling stinks, who that are overtaken by the smell may not announce that they have smelled him?

If, in line with the whole of the foregoing letter, you still elect to swallow your Mr. Pawling whole, without reading the correspondence, then the only thing that remains is to sever our relationship. I am too old a writer and dealer with men to continue such a relationship. I am now open to receive suggestions from you as how best to proceed with the annulment of our relationship.

Very truly yours,
Jack London

P.S. By your favor of February 7, 1911, I learn that four of my stories have been sold and published. In spite of the many reiterations on my part of my desire to keep my account-books straight, which required information from your Mr. Pawling as to where stories were published and when they were published, I am now compelled again to ask information as to where and when these four stories were published mentioned by you in your letter of February 7.

P.S. By yours of February 18, 1911, you tell me what a bombshell it was to you to learn that Nelsons were to publish my *Adventure*. And this in spite of the plain fact that during the dickering your Mr. Pawling compelled me to go through, he got it from me in black and white that Nelsons held my *Adventure*. I never gave a copy of *Adventure* to your house afterwards. You never had a peep at the manuscript nor a shred of it. Your complaint was that I had too many books for you to publish, I urged upon your Mr. Pawling that these books had to be published, he sweated and fumed and explained, and then in spite of the plethora of books that he had a right to publish, unknown to me, without informing me, in spite of my letter telling him that Nelsons had this manuscript, despite the absence of any such manuscript in his own hands, unknown to me and by privy means he persuaded my American publishers to send him proofsheets and try to rush out an English edition of the book, in violation of all decency and courtesy between men, in his efforts to hog it both on me and on the Nelsons. Talk about a bombshell! I was getting a cash advance from Nelson, equivalent to the total yearly advance your house makes me. And your Mr. Pawling damned near hogged me out of it. Bombshell? What do you think it was to me—a zephyr?

P.S. I am still waiting, despite my previous correspondence unread by you, for a copy of the cheap edition of *The Sea-Wolf,* which you at this very recent date tell me you have got out.

P.S. And now, last of all, reiterating my belief that the only thing for us to do is to sever our relations, as man to man, and never mind discrepancy in ages, let me give you some straight advice: (1), Either do your own work yourself, or (2), get a man to do that work for you—a man that is a man, not a cad, nor a Petticoat Lane Huckster.

To L. W. CALLAHAN

Glen Ellen, Calif.
March 2, 1911

Dear Sir:

In reply to yours of January 18,1911.[1] And some persons never grow up. They retain their childish belief in the newspapers. Then, to demonstrate their innate malignity, say nasty things to those they read about in the newspapers. I have been in Carmel twice in my life on brief visits. The last time I was there was over a year ago. I never heard of the dog mentioned in the newspaper canard, nor of the dog's owner. I don't know that the affair ever took place.

Now, what do you think about It? And what do you think about yourself?

Very truly yours,
Jack London

P.S. In my life, I have eaten dog. I see no reason why I should not eat with a dog. And if I ever get a chance, I'm going to eat with a dog. And what do you think of that?

[1]Callahan wrote to London: "I have a newspaper article before me under date of January 8, 1911, headed, 'London Breaks Bread with Society Dog.' The article goes on to say that the doggy's name is Fluffy Ruffles, the dinner being given upon the occasion of her second birthday and attended by a few mere humans of both sexes."

To William Teichner

Glen Ellen, Calif.
March 6, 1911

Dear sir:—

In reply to yours of February 27, 1911, asking a few lines from me concerning the subject of Prisons and Prisoners:[1]

I have gone through prisons with the stripes on me, marching the lockstep. I have, as a trusty, shown visitors around, (and I knew darned well what to show them and what not to show them).

Also, I have gone through prisons as a visitor, and all the time in my mind's eye I was seeing what the trusty did not show me. Everything he showed me was lovely. He didn't dare show me anything that wasn't lovely. What does the average innocent minister know when he is shown around?

Let me tell you that the average warden, holding down a political job, knows very little about what goes on inside the prison over which he nominally and politically has charge.

I've gone through a few, and seen a few, and let me tell you, my dear Mr. Teichner, that the convicts are few and far between who come out and dare to peep a word of what they know. And they are dead right for keeping mum. Otherwise, under our present wild-animal police and penitentiary system, they would be worse than dead. I have known ex-cons who became dead for peeping. I know one who got fifty years for peeping. There is a pleasant little system known as "railroading." Every ex-con knows all about this little system. Keep mum? Wouldn't you?

Sincerely yours,
Jack London

[1]The Warden of Marquette had been accused by Detroit ministers of inflicting physical punishment upon prisoners. Teichner wanted London's opinion, apparently for newspaper publication.

To J. Maiewsky

Glen Ellen, Calif.
Mar. 30, 1911

Dear Comrade Maiewsky:

In reply to yours of January 17. I should have replied sooner, only I have been laid up in bed with a long sickness. I like all that you have proposed in relation to the Russian publication of my books. Will you make up a contract, embodying the terms suggested by you in your letter. Of course, concerning my books already published in the United States and not yet published in Russia, your royalty of 2½ % on the sales would be satisfactory. Concerning future books, I shall arrange with my publishers to send you proof-sheets of same as soon as they are printed in the United States. These future books of mine would be embodied in the contract under the 5% royalty suggested by you.[1]

As regards the twenty-six (26) books already published, a list of which I am sending you herewith, suppose you put into the contract a provision that they must be published inside of five (5) years—said five years subject to renewal on my part when it has expired. Also, concerning books of mine not yet published, suppose you put in a time limit of one year after publication in the United States. That is to say, that the contract ceases to be operative at the end of five years with books already published by me, and during which five years you have failed to publish, and that the contract ceases to be operative at the end of one (1) year, in the case of books of mine which are to be published in the United States in the future.

Before Adam is the only book of mine for which I have given permission for a Russian translation.

Will you please do me the favor of purchasing such books of mine as have already been published in Russian, and of sending me a copy of each of same. Of course, as soon as you have informed me of all costs of same, I shall promptly remit.

Suppose you yourself write for me my letter to the Russian publishers, asking them not to issue any more of my works, because I have contracted with you. You are far better fitted to write such a letter than I am. Send me such a letter, and I shall typewrite it here and sign and return same to you.

I have no autobiography published. A book of mine, called *The Road,* has been published, but this contains only a few of my reminiscences during the period in which I was an American tramp.

I am inclosing herewith photograph, autobiographical data, etc. This, of course, you will not need to return.

I am writing this day to my publishers, The Macmillan Company, 66 Fifth Avenue, New York City, asking them to send you any books of mine you may order, and that I shall guarantee the bills to you for said orders.

I am quite certain, that if you wrote to Anna Strunsky Walling, Care The Macmillan Co., 66 Fifth Avenue, New York City, they would be able to forward your letter to her address. I do not myself know her address.

Very truly yours,
Jack London

P.S. Please send me the contract in DUPLICATE, one copy of which you will sign. This I shall retain; the other copy I shall sign and return to you.

[1]More copies of London's books have been sold in Russia than in any other country, but he never received any income from Russia, nor has his estate.

To H. S. Latham[1]

Glen Ellen, Calif.
April 7, 1911

Dear Mr. Latham:—

In reply to yours of March 4, 1911. I am this day sending you, by express, prepaid, valued at $150.00, the corrected proof-sheets of *The Cruise of the Snark,* and also, included in same package, the wreckage of the illustrations.

Let me tell you that you certainly have got my proud goat. If you know anything at all about my work, you know that I have never been consulted about the illustrations of one of my books, nor about the book-covers of one of my books. You will know that I never revise. You will know that I never go over my track again. And you will also know that the wildest, maddest thing I ever did was carefully, painstakingly, heartbreakingly, dismally, to arrange the photographs, by chapter, by consecutive order in chapter, and by legend accompanying each film or print, for *The Cruise of the Snark.* I cannot reiterate, nor can I find enough adjectives to describe the perfection of orderliness with which I arranged these illustrations, and forwarded them to you. And then you threw me down. As I said at the beginning of this letter, you got my proud goat. When I found the mess that had been made of the whole thing, I very near abandoned the book. Remember, I never do things a second time. I am not proud of the fact; I am so made, that is all.

You returned me reproductions with the envelopes missing. You returned me envelopes with the reproduction missing. You capped the whole mess by so forwarding the empty envelopes with the legends written on them, that the postmaster refused to deliver same to me until I came down to the Post Office in person and accepted the parcel, signing off responsibility of the Post Office in the matter. God knows how many of these envelopes, every one vitally important if I untangle the mess, had been inclosed in a cheap, large envelope. The cheap, large envelope, naturally, had burst into pieces. And from New York to Glen Ellen, every mail transfer point had been littered with a lost inclosed envelope.

342

You say: "The result is that they had to take all the films from the envelopes, and there is no one who is able to identify which legend goes with which illustration but yourself. I think you will see how this was brought about, and agree with us that it could not be prevented."

Now the foregoing quotation from your letter sounds all right to the uninitiated. But you do me little credit to think that I can accept it for a moment. Suppose I were Jesus Christ, just being crucified, and that my illustrated autobiography had just been forwarded to you. Now this would be a nice big book. Do you think you would illustrate it because I, Jesus Christ, was dead on the Cross? No. You would have worked out a system by which every legend on every envelope would have been identified with every film or print that went to the electroplaters. Possibly you don't know it, but as a professional photographer of fifteen years' experience, let me tell you that every print, film, and plate can be marked legibly and without harm (for identification) with a mere lead-pencil. Why this was not done in my case, was beyond me, and up to you. You made of the whole thing chaos thrice confounded. Now, I'm not kicking to anybody but you, but let me tell you that you have given me one hell of a time. And let me tell you, that the best dinner New York can provide will not make amends for quite all the havoc you have wreaked on me in this mere matter of simple details.

Now to business: There are a number of important missing reproductions, and a number of important missing envelopes. Of the important missing envelopes I have no clew whatever. But the important missing reproductions have their clews given by the empty envelopes which I am returning you in aforementioned package. For instance, here are some of the legends: "The air we breathed was heavy with the perfume of flowers," "Sea Wolves," "Florida Island," "Careening the Snark."

The last legend, "Careening the Snark," has attached to it the statement by me that two or more films or prints were inclosed, and that a choice was to be made from them. I desire to have the illustration under this legend more than any other illustration in the book.

If you can locate any of the missing ones, for heaven's sake stick them in where they belong. You've got to do your best by me in this matter, because I've got a wild wolf howl coming at the way I've been treated.

I am afraid this whole thing has been done unthinkingly on the part of you or your office. For instance, the frontispiece, "The Snark Lying at the Wharf at Suva, in the Fijis." This was plainly put in a separate envelope and marked as "Frontispiece." Yet you had it reproduced in the proportions of a dinky little marginal decoration. Certainly you must take this film and make a big decent frontispiece out of it.

One other thing. Let me reiterate that it is my desire that you return the films and prints to me—and that they be not scattered at every mail-transfer point between New York and Glen Ellen. Please make a decent, common-sense package of them.

And finally, you've got to do your best by me with this particular book, from now to the time it leaves the press. And let me warn you that the very best that you may do, multiplied ten thousand times, will not save you from the dinner you've got to buy me the next time I come to New York.

Sincerely yours,

Jack London

¹Of the Macmillan Company.

To Lute Pease

Glen Ellen, Calif.

April 22, 1911

Dear Lute Pease:—

In reply to your good letter of April 12, 1911. I am afraid you will have to send "Samuel" back to me. I ran into a similar predicament with those two stories with *The American Magazine*. Mr. Phillips wanted "Samuel," and I wouldn't let it go unless it was accompanied by "The Sea Farmer." Also, there was some other one of the big eastern magazines that tangled up with me on the same proposition. I shall just hang on to "Samuel" and "The Sea Farmer," and start them traveling eastward again.

Far be it from me to rub it in—but we are once more out cruising on our magnificent Bay. At the present moment, as I dictate this to Mrs. London, we are lying high and dry on a mud flat, up the Alviso Slough, at the very southeasternmost end of San Francisco Bay. It happened this morning, shortly before eight o'clock. I was sailing down the slough with a nice fair wind, when I missed the channel and went aground on a fast-falling tide.

We expect to finish this cruise in a couple more weeks, and then, the latter part of May, we shall throw four of our saddle-horses into harness, hitch them to a light Studebaker trap, and, with Nakata, whom you will remember, a couple of saddles, and a couple of suit-cases and a type-writer, head over to the Coast, then follow up the Coast clear into Curry County, Southern Oregon. And there we expect to head east through the Modoc country and into Nevada. We intend to stop off, hunt and fish, and throw the saddles on our horses for the wilder trails, and so have given ourselves three months for the trip.

With best regards to you and Mrs. Pease,

Sincerely yours,

Jack London

To Comrade J. H. Seymour[1]

Glen Ellen, Calif.
May 16, 1911

Dear Comrade Seymour:—

In reply to yours of April 17, 1911, which has just caught me on my return home. Hurrah for the hobo newspaper! I wish there'd been something like that afloat when I was knocking around on the road. Now your request for me to contribute an article, is a very embarrassing one. You can imagine that I am compelled to decline some similar request for contributions every day in the year. I simply couldn't do it. But you have my full permission to go through all my books and pamphlets, and make excerpts from same. They would carry my name, and would enable you to advertise me as a contributor if you wanted to.

Your running into that Sailor Jack written on the ceiling of an old Grand Trunk box, is very exciting. I'm afraid that any car I may have ridden in seventeen years ago, will have wandered as much as I have since. I wonder if I wrote that "Sailor Jack."

Yours for the Revolution,
Jack London

[1]Hobo, Socialist and poet, who was instrumental in establishing a Hobo Newspaper in St. Louis. In his letter to London asking him for an article, he wrote, "I feel that your brand of sanctimoniousness is just the sort needed in this priest infested social cancer . . . St. Louis."

To George P. Brett

Glen Ellen, Calif.
May 22, 1911

Dear Mr. Brett:—

In reply to yours of May 16, 1911. Whatever you do with Curtis Brown & Massie is all right. They are my accredited English Agents.

Now concerning the Milwaukee mix-up and the "bill of health."[1] I don't know how to do it. The paradoxical and lunatic mix-up of modern life and interests has long since compelled me to throw up my hands in despair, saying to myself, "Let her slide." In short, I couldn't do a darn thing with this Milwaukee crowd. Years ago I was nearly expelled from the Socialist Party because I did not at that time believe in equal suffrage. I have had to fight the Socialists and the Labor Unionists every time I had a story published in a magazine with a scab printing establishment. I just settled a labor strike yesterday on the ranch where I am starting to build my house.

By the way, some ten years ago Owen Wister jumped on me, in a letter to you, criticising me because I did not confine myself to pure fiction, and that I once in a while got in and aired my socialistic views. The gods love me. I have just finished reading Owen Wister's preface in his last collection of short stories [*Members of the Family*] published by you. He has certainly aired his views on politics, ethics, and insurgency, and a few other things entirely irrelevant to the collection of short stories that follows. At least, when I aired my views, I aired them; and I do believe I was never so irrelevant as Owen Wister has been in this preface of his. The only conclusion I can draw is this: I, in my early youth, discovered that the thing worth while to one was the thing one must talk about. Wherefore I expounded my views on all subjects. Owen Wister has taken twenty years longer to reach the same conclusion, and I fear me beginning so late in life that he does it with no fine Italian hand.

Sincerely yours,

Jack London

P.S. Please, this Owen Wister section is in confidence between you and me.

[1] The Macmillan Co. had been attacked by socialist interests in Milwaukee in connection with the sale of their school books in the schools. Mr. Brett stated that Macmillan had published more socialistic books than any other publisher and had printed them in union shops; he asked London to give Macmillan a clean bill of health in Milwaukee.

To G. W. FOWLENER

Glen Ellen, Calif.
May 22, 1911

My dear G. W. Fowlener:—

In reply to yours of May 11, 1911. Will you please tell me what it's all about? I have no niece by the name of Myrtle London,[1] much less any niece who has the right to sell manuscripts of mine. Will you please give me the full details of the transaction that has occurred between you and Miss Myrtle London. The California address given to you by her is not my address. I have never lived on Mortimer Street, nor do I know where Mortimer Street is. I live up here at Glen Ellen on my ranch.

Can you tell me precisely what is meant by "manuscripts"? Do you mean stories for publication, or do you mean the manuscripts of stories which have already been published? You will do me a very, very great favor by letting me know all that has taken place between you and this Miss Myrtle London.

Sincerely yours,

Jack London

[1] Fowlener had written, "Will you please tell me why I have heard nothing from your niece in regards to Mss. for which I paid first payment. It has been over two months now

and I have not seen sign of any return for my money." On June 2nd Fowlener wrote to London: "that a clever young woman who claimed to be your niece Myrtle London" exchanged several pages of what she alleged to be part of the Ms. of the *Sea Wolf* for some curios. She maintained that most of London's Mss. had been disposed of and that the "value of the remaining Mss. would rise." See Loodiet letters.

To ROLAND PHILLIPS[1]

Glen Ellen, Calif.
May 30, 1911

Dear Mr. Phillips:—

I am planning a serial [*Valley of the Moon*], the motif is back to the land. While, for once in my life, the story will not be offensive to bourgeois business ethics, it will at the same time be something of which I shall absolutely and passionately believe every word.

It will be about 90,000 words long.

I take a man and a woman, young, who belong to the working class in a large city. Both are wage-workers, the man is unskilled—a driver of a brewery wagon, or something of that sort. The first third of the book will be devoted to their city environment, their meeting, their love-affair, and the trials and tribulations of such a marriage in the working class. Comes hard times. The woman gets the vision. She is the guiding force. They start wandering penniless over the country of California. Of course, they have all sorts of adventures, and their wandering becomes a magnificent, heroic, detailed pilgrimage. After many hints and snatches of vision, always looking for the spot, they do find the real, one and only spot, and settle down to successful small-scale farming.

I am starting to-morrow morning with my wife on a three-months' driving-trip. We have broken four saddle-horses to harness, and are carrying our saddles with us as well. I dearly love California, so much so that you never see me East, and I shall gather up in these three months all sorts of data and atmosphere for this story.

Next October 1, 1911, I shall be ready to begin the story.

Will you consider this story?[2] Will you, on the strength of the thin description I have given of it, beginning October 1, 1911, advance me $500.00 per month for five months? If, on reading the manuscript, you reject it, let it be arranged in contract that I shall then give you the equivalent of the $2500.00 advance, in short-stories or serial novel work that will be acceptable to you, and that said equivalent shall be given to you in one year.

As regards the reason for making this request, let me explain: It is very simple. I am building my dream-house on my dream-ranch. The latter is already mine, the former I am starting to build. I want the work to go on, and at the same time I want to stop my short story stunt for awhile and write a novel that I have close to heart. This is such a novel. As regards rate of payment, suppose we say 12½¢ a word; and if I exceed 90,000 words, the loss shall be mine,—and so help me, being so made, I shall certainly exceed the 90,000 words. During the past I have always done so.

For security or guarantee, I offer the statement that in past years I have had many advances from many editors and publishers, and that at present instant, casting up the balance of all such dealings from first to last, I owe no publisher any work; while, on the other hand, there is something like $4000.00 owing me.

My last novel, *Adventure,* is only a skit, after all. I have had no proper novel since *Burning Daylight.* I have no other novel under way. This particular novel I am writing you about would be complete by March 31, 1912, and it would be the first novel of mine published in two years.

Sincerely yours,

Jack London

[1]Of *Cosmopolitan Magazine.*
[2]*Cosmopolitan* serialized it April-December, 1913.

To H. S. LATHAM

Glen Ellen, Calif.
May 31, 1911

Dear Mr. Latham:—

In reply to yours of May 23, 1911. I telegraphed you to-day, telling you that the photograph in question of Mrs. London[1] must go into the book, and go in large, no matter what the delay to the book. Pardon me, but I can't see what is wrong with that photograph. Possibly it is because I am not a New York man. I know that I am just a Californian savage, so is my wife. The editors of *The Pacific Monthly* must also be Pacific Coast savages, because they published this photograph enlarged in their magazine. It's beyond me why the half-dozen other people "not finicky," to whom you showed it, should have passed adverse judgment on it. It is beyond me that the engravers should have passed adverse judgment on it. Who in hell are the engravers that they should pass judgment on anything that they engrave? Whose book is this? Whose wife is it? When I am not even consulted in such a matter as the leaving out of a photograph which I put in, I am compelled to wonder what is the need of my writing books at all. I might as well let the New York end do the whole thing, and collect royalties just the same. Really, Mr. Latham, you're hipped back and forth on this book again.

Sincerely yours,

Jack London

[1]The photograph appeared in the first edition of *The Cruise of the Snark* with the caption "Charmian goes to market."

To G. W. FOWLENER

On Four Horse Driving Trip
July 27, 1911

Dear Mr. Fowlener:

In reply to yours of June 27, 1911. I am interested in arrow-heads, skinning-knives, tomahawks, and stone hatchets.

Look me up in *Who's Who in America, Who's Who in England,* and *The International Who's Who,* and you will find that my address is Glen Ellen, Sonoma County, California.

I have never sold nor disposed of a manuscript in my life. My wife does all my typewriting for me, and so she retains my manuscripts as wages. And she has all of my manuscripts. If you and I put a trade through, it will be the first one of my manuscripts to go out. I have argued with my wife, assuring her that I shall continue to write for some several years to come, and pointing out that she can easily spare a manuscript, in order that I may get some of your curios.

Now here are two troubles: I don't know what your curios are worth, and I don't know what a manuscript is worth.

An average short story of mine runs between fifty and eighty pages of handwritten manuscript. Of course, the writing is not handsome, but it is mine.

I shall not be home for about six weeks. But suppose you, in the meantime, send me by express, to Glen Ellen, where my manager will receive and hold the package—suppose you send me the arrow-heads, skinning-knives, tomahawks, and stone-hatchets. Also, you can give me some idea of the value of same, and what you think ought to constitute an equitable trade in manuscripts.

If you see your way to sending this express package, it would be very well to insure same with the express company.

I cannot recognize anybody of my acquaintance who answers to your description of Myrtle London. And I can assure you positively and absolutely that nobody in this world has any of my handwritten manuscripts for sale.

Sincerely yours,
Jack London

To Mr. Ricks[1]

Medford, Oregon
August 17, 1911

Dear Mr. Ricks:

I am indeed grateful to you, in yours of July 22, for sending me the two clippings of the advertising in the *Arcata Union* and the *Humboldt Times*. Not only is it the first I have heard of it, but had you not sent them to me, I should not have heard of it at all. It is indeed a very curious and stupid perpetration of a stupid and unthinking man. Concerning this advertiser, he evidently must have paid for this advertising. I can only call to mind the old adage that "A fool and his money are soon parted."

I do not know exactly how to understand your very evident surprise at discovering that I am a socialist. This is a matter of such common knowledge with all the world that I cannot conceive how you have missed hearing of it. I have something like eight (8) books published on socialism. All my other books ooze socialism, and there are some twenty-eight of them on the market, not to speak of numerous socialist pamphlets. Eighteen years ago I went to jail fighting for socialism. I was the first president of the Intercollegiate Socialist Society. I have spoken to audiences of from 3,000 to 5,000 people on the subject of socialism, in all great universities of the United States. I have been boycotted and blacklisted by stupid capitalists on account of my socialism, and made to lose more money on account of my socialism by these same stupid capitalists, than they themselves possessed. I have paid through the nose for my socialism to the tune of hundreds of thousands of dollars. I tell you the foregoing because this is the day of dollars. I interpret my actions to you in terms of dollars. It is somehow strange that you were so unaware that I am a socialist.

And yet it seems to me that you must have had some glimmerings, because if you will remember, as I distinctly remember, we had not been face to face in your house for two minutes before you earnestly and nervously requested me not to speak of socialism in your house.

What more can I say? Surely a man's political persuasion and sociological concepts need not stand in the way of friendship. Mrs. Jack and myself like you and yours very much. We had a delightful time at the hands of your hospitality. Friendship, as I understand it, has nothing whatever to do with even so simple a thing as identity of agreement on the merits or demerits of the multiplication table.

I should advise you, however, to read up on socialism. It is very interesting.

Mrs. Jack and I have been having a delightful time, and have only just now returned to Medford from a trip to Crater Lake. To-night we shall be entertained by the socialists of Medford in the Opera House, to-morrow we are going to try our hand at catching steelheads and the next day we pull

south for California and home. We still expect to get back to Glen Ellen
before the fall rains.

I read in to-day's paper that your son-in-law has given me a black eye,
and that my wife has deserted me! In yesterday's paper I read that I had
been fishing in a Washington lake for Beardslee trout with a diamond stud
attached to my troll for lure. One reads very many things.

Sincerely yours,

Jack London

¹A casual friend the Londons met on their four-horse driving trip.

To Mrs. Jack London

Redding, Calif.

Aug. 27, 1911

Dear Madam:

I am just wondering. I have been on the Pacific Coast all summer. To the
best of my knowledge and belief, my wife, Mrs. Jack London, has been with
me. Not a day nor a night has she been away from me. Yet behold! I read
in the New York City *Herald* of July 30, 1911, that Mrs. Jack London is
spending the month of August at the Watch Hill House, Watch Hill, Rhode
Island. And in the Providence, R.I., *Journal,* I read that "Mrs. Jack London,
wife of the author, is a guest at the Watch Hill House."

I am sorely puzzled. Can you clear this riddle for me?

Sincerely yours,

Jack London

To Editor,
*The American Hebrew and
Jewish Messenger*¹

Redding, Calif.

Aug. 27, 1911

I have made villains, scoundrels, weaklings, and degenerates, of Cockneys,
Scotchmen, Englishmen, Americans, Frenchmen and Irish, and I don't know
what other nationalities. I have no recollection of having made a Jew serve
a mean fictional function. But I see no reason why I should not, if the need
and the setting of my story demanded it. I cannot reconcile myself to the
attitude that in humor and fiction the Jew should be a favored race, and
therefore be passed over, or used only for his exalted qualities.

I have myself, not as an American, but personally and with the name so little different from mine that it was not even a thin disguise, been exploited before Jewish audiences in the most despicable of characters. The only sensation I experienced was regret at not being able to be present to enjoy the fun.

Finally, I am a terrific admirer of the Jews; I have consorted more with Jews than with any other nationality; I have among the Jews some of my finest and noblest friends; and, being a Socialist, I subscribe to the Brotherhood of Man. In this connection, let me add that it is as unfair for a writer to make villains of all races except the Jews, as it is to make villains only of Jews. To ignore the Jew in the matter of villainy is so invidious an exception as to be unfair to the Jews.

Sincerely yours,

Jack London

[1]In the issue of Sept. 22, 1911, was an article entitled "The Jew in English Fiction," a symposium. London was asked to contribute.

To Harry H. Ryan[1]

Glen Ellen, Calif.

Oct. 18, 1911

Dear Ryan:—

I received the postcard and letter, forwarded from Alma. If you will notice, the postcard is in a woman's handwriting, was addressed to one, "Dear Babe," and was signed "Babe." Now, I don't know this "Babe" lady; but don't you think you were rather precipitate in having such things forwarded to my home-address, knowing I was married, and not knowing but what I was tangled up with a "Babe." If I HAD been so tangled, wouldn't I have had the dickens to pay with Mrs. London here in Glen Ellen when she saw postcards like that coming through the mail, forwarded by my dear friend Harry:

Hey, you! Buck up!

Some time when you are in Alma, will you inquire around and see if you can find out if a hatter, by the name of Jack London, was not drifting around Alma the last weeks of September or the first week of October. This man is causing me lots of trouble, and he seems to move about pretty freely on the Pacific Coast. So far, I have succeeded in locating an address of his in Aberdeen, Wash., and I have received the information that his family lived in San Francisco, but I don't know where.

With regards to the wife, in which Mrs. London joins, (and not "Babe").

Sincerely yours,

Jack London

[1]Casual friend of the Londons. Ryan did not forward the postcard; he merely returned it to the post office, and the postmaster sent it on to Glen Ellen.

To EILEEN MORETTA[1]

Glen Ellen, Calif.
Oct. 18, 1911

My dear Eileen Moretta:—

But why—just because I kick against your ardent exploitation of the popular and optimistic inane, do you come back with nothing but resounding slaps against Socialism?

I cannot follow you, save on the hypothesis: Woman, thy name is Eileen Moretta.

"Ah, bah! You admire the woman who picks up life and looks at it wide-eyed."—But who the devil was talking about women or the admiration of women? You took the initial slam-bang at me on account of my unhappy ending of a short story. This was quite abstract and impersonal. I replied with an abstract thesis only, and here you come, lugging in as a dogmatic assumption the kind of woman I admire. Really, it seems to be difficult for Eileen Moretta to keep sex out of argument. I took for granted that Eileen Moretta was a woman. What need or excuse for her to shout her sex through the abstractions of an art-controversy challenged and precipitated by herself?

Really, it's more dignified to screech about the unhappy endings of human affairs, than it is to yawp sex at every clatter, and then to exploit the mediocre for the consumption of mediocrity at so much exultantly per.

Why such a tirade against Socialism? I am more and more appalled, paragraph by paragraph, as I read your letter. What in the dickens has Socialism to do with it? All that I can conclude is that folks who are Socialists have hurt you. But what bearing your onslaught has upon the original discussion is beyond my ken.

Sometime, when you're out in California, run up and visit my wife and me on our ranch, and we'll show you what comradeship, mateship, and connubial happiness are. And I, for one, will give you the dangdest abstract thrashing that you ever heard tell of! There's one chance in a million that I might do your soul good. You see, you've got temperament and empiricism. But you wofully lack in scientific and sociologic knowledge of the world up to date.

Sure—I don't mind anybody shouting out when they've landed a publisher for a hundred dollars; but I do hate to have my attention called to the matter by receiving a smack in the face.

Sincerely yours,
Jack London

---

[1]Unidentified. This letter is an answer to her criticism of "The Night Born."

To Jack McGlashan

Glen Ellen, Calif.
Oct. 18, 1911

Dear Jack McGlashan:

In reply to yours of Oct. 12, 1911. One of the things that bothers me with this other Jack London, is that I keep receiving letters and postcards in a woman's handwriting, mailed from San Francisco, calling me "Babe," and signing herself "Babe." Now, that's all right, except when it comes to the postcards. I live in the country, and I'm married, and it bothers other people a whole lot to think that I've got a woman addressing me as "Babe," and signing herself "Babe." The worst of it is that I cannot find this woman because she puts no address in these letters. I know she lives in San Francisco, and that's all. Now, if you could get a letter to this Jack London, and could you tell him my predicament, and tell him I'd like to write to him? Do you think you could find his San Francisco address for me?

Thanking you for your good letter,

Very truly yours,
Jack London

To Maurice Magnus[1]

Glen Ellen, Calif.
Oct. 23, 1911

Dear Maurice Magnus:

In reply to yours of September 21, 1911, which has only just now come to hand, having been forwarded to me via various comrades in the Socialist movement.

Nay—but I have always imagined Wolf Larsen and Burning Daylight as "knowing" women—but I did not think it necessary explicitly so to state in my writing.

You are certainly right. A certain definite percentage of men are so homosexual, or so nearly homosexual, that they can love another man more than they can love any woman. But then, I dare say, no homosexual man is qualified to say whether a fictional woman is real or not to a normally sexed man. A man who is normal sexually conceives of women in ways repellant to a homosexual man.

Surely, I have studied the sex problem even in its "most curious ways." I, however, have drawn men-characters who were sexually normal. I have never dreamed of drawing a homosexual male character. Perhaps I am too prosaically normal myself, though I do know the whole literature and all the authorities of the "curious ways."

I think I know the problem you suggest, and I think I know it fairly thoroughly and scientifically. Unfortunately, those who figure vitally in that problem constitute too small a percentage of the human race to be an adequate book-buying inducement to a writer.

I think I get your point of view. Am I wrong? Do you get my point of view? Flatly, I am a lover of women.

Sincerely yours,
Jack London

[1]Contemporary writer, author of *Memoirs of the Foreign Legion.*

To George P. Brett

Glen Ellen, Calif.
Oct. 26, 1911

Dear Mr. Brett:—

In reply to yours of Oct. 20, 1911. Concerning the miscarriage of the introduction of Dana's book, just as you say yourself that you do not know just how it happened, so I must say the same thing, not only concerning that but many other things during the past year or so. I am afraid that I have been less in touch with you and not at all in touch with your careless staff who had dealings with me. I have been repeatedly outraged by outrageous carelessness. *The Cruise of the Snark* alone was a personal crucifixion to me. No money could buy prints and films that were forever lost; while days and days of needless repetition of work were caused me by the same carelessness on the part of those in your office. There is little use of going into details— there are so many of them. In fact, I no longer see anything but first proofs. Then I receive a telegram asking me to forego further submission of proofs. I acquiesce in this; but instead of earning me gratitude, it seems to get me into trouble later on. Indeed, in all the mechanical work between your house and me, this has been the rule for quite a long time. I do not know how your interests have suffered in the matter; but I know that mine have suffered.

Sincerely yours,
Jack London

P.S. Please do not bring me up personally in this matter with any of your staff, because it is very patent that I would further financially suffer for it. Human men are only human men, and it was because of this concept that I was acquiescent in a lot of carelessness in the hope that the careless ones would cheer up and treat me more decently.

To V. C. GILMAN

Glen Ellen, Calif.
Nov. 14, 1911

My dear Mr. Gilman:

In reply to yours of November 4, 1911.[1] You dwell upon authority. I dwell upon utility. This is just another token of how diversely men are made.

Nay—I do not fight sophistically because I disagree with you. If you will read over my letter, you will find that I fight with a club. You must not be so unfair to me nor to the English language as to style my club a stiletto. To do so is to misuse thought and fact.

And I don't disagree with all you say, at all. As near as I can get at it, the difference between us is that we believe differently. You are sincere, you are not sophistical. I am sincere, I am not sophistical.

My kind kicks authority out of the path. Your kind puts mine in jail for violent assault on authority. My kind makes the living language. Your kind preserves the language my kind makes. Your kind and mine are always at war. We have been so in the past, and we shall be so in the future as long as languages *live* upon the planet. This is not sophistry; it is clubbing home the science of language, and is deeper than the deepest generalizations of the purist and the vulgarist.

Think it over.

Sincerely Yours,
Jack London

[1]Gilman, in a long letter, criticized London's language and particularly the word "fetch."

To COMRADE ARTHUR SCALES[1]

Glen Ellen, Calif.
Nov. 20, 1911

Dear Comrade Scales:

Oh! You were the man who wanted to borrow ten dollars. You see, amongst the many letters from strangers, I answer about five begging letters each day. Surely, I could not be expected to remember them all. That is how I failed to remember you when you got in and everlastingly cussed me.

It is manifestly impossible for me to lend money to these multitudes of strangers who beg me for money by mail. I have tried it just about one hundred times, and have never heard from any one of them since, except from the percentage that tried a repeat begging letter.

And anyway, just between one fellow who knows the world, and another, a more sufficient inducement must be presented to me than a mere snappy letter, in order to get me to part with my cash. What money I have to spare goes into the Socialist movement, and not to individuals.

I regret your harsh letter. I thank you for your good letter.

Yours for the Revolution,
Jack London

---

[1]A Socialist and somewhat of a writer. Scales' first letter to London, Sept. 8, 1911, is a panegyric of London as a writer and ends by asking to borrow $10.00. London declined to lend it. Scales' next letter, Oct. 19, 1911, begins, "Just a few lines to let you know you are a fraud," and continues to berate London. The third letter was an apology for the second.

To CHURCHILL WILLIAMS

Glen Ellen, Calif.
Dec. 17, 1911

Dear Churchill Williams:

I am sending you by this mail, REGISTERED, under separate cover, an unfinished manuscript entitled *The Assassination Bureau*.[1] These 30,000-odd words I am submitting to you, will give you an idea of the farcical nature of the thing. I expect there will be something like 15,000 words more to bring the story to a close.

Now the reason I am sending you this unfinished manuscript is, that I am shortly departing for New York, in order to take passage on a four-masted, skysail-yarder, for a voyage around the Horn to San Francisco. I shall be unable to finish this *Assassination Bureau* until after I am on board and at sea. I can forecast the ending, which will be happy for the pair of lovers, and which will end ridiculously in the death of the last surviving member of the Assassination Bureau. There is a lot of farcical mental pabulum in the yarn.

Please hold the manuscript until you hear from me; but please telegraph me whether or not *The Saturday Evening Post* would care for it; and please telegraph me quickly.

I shall be about six months on the voyage, including delay in catching the vessel, and margin of time for slow passage. Of course, Mrs. London, and the Japanese boy Nakata, go with me.

Sincerely yours,
Jack London

P.S. I need hardly state that the typewriter machine also goes along.

---

[1]On a plot supplied by Sinclair Lewis. London never finished it, but it was completed by Robert L. Fish from London's notes, and McGraw-Hill published it in 1963.

To ELIZA SHEPARD

New York, New York
Jan. 18, 1912

Dearest Eliza:

Sweet birthday cards received. I am still rushing around and as yet there is nothing doing. In case I do not send you any money for the first of February, remember that you will receive a check from The Macmillan Co. the first week of February for $1000. The January check for $1000 I had you forward to me, and which I am holding to clinch my passage for the voyage around the Horn. The thousand dollars which comes the first week in February you will use to pay the January wages.

Please stop *The Examiner* and the local county papers, and ask them to keep the accounts open until my return, when the service will be renewed.

Is there any line yet about when the stone masons will finish the work on the house?

I'm having such a time here just now, under circumstances and conditions that I shall not take the time to tell you about, that you may in a way prepare yourself for some shortening down of ranch expenses in the near future. I *don't* think this will happen at all, yet there *may* be a chance that it will happen. But I've had the goat of New York all the way from California for fourteen years, and I think I shall continue to keep my hand on the goat of New York.

Charmian will write you about some elk horns, the shipping expenses of which you will pay.

Any of the freak letters that you can answer with the stereotype around the Horn letter, why do so, and keep the letters for me.

With an armful of love,[1]

Jack London

P.S. Your numbered letters are coming along all in order so far.

J. L.

---

[1]London's sister Eliza replaced Ninetta Eames Payne as his business manager.

To ROLAND PHILLIPS

New York, New York
Jan. 18, 1912

Dear Roland Phillips:

I am glad you like the opening stride of *The Valley of the Moon.* Still rambling around and fooling away time in this part of the world. I have been compelled largely to stop writing on the novel. But I drive out a thousand words or so every little while. In a short time I shall send you another later batch of the manuscript. I am firmly convinced that I am going to write some book here. With equal certitude I agree to eat my hat if it resembles any other book in the ruck of the books or in the exception of the books. It may be rotten—God knows; but at least it will be different. And I'm going to pick up some raw facts of life in it, and turn them over.

Thank the Lord that your adult policy for an adult magazine will enable one to handle sex frankly and cleanly in the Anglo-Saxon way.

In the months to come, when I am away on my windjammer, please forward checks to me as a matter of course, at my California address. My ranch superintendent and business agent has full power of attorney, will cash those checks, and pay off the men working on the ranch, as well as buy forty dollar a ton barley and twenty dollar a ton hay for my 30 horses. So, please send the monthly check to the end of the *Smoke Bellew* stories, to California. Also, as you love me, please make *Nash Magazine* come across with the $1300 from England; and have that sent to California. Believe me, that beauty ranch burns up the shekels.

I shall drop in to see you before I sail—and it may be some time before I sail, because my ship is now overdue, and will soon be posted. If she never arrives, I have another one picked out, because around the Horn I'm bound.

Sincerely yours,

Jack London

To Henry Lanier[1]

New York, New York

Jan. 18, 1912

Dear Mr. Lanier:

A rather belated reply to your good letter of January 9. I have been out of town and have only just now got back to tackle the correspondence which has heaped up on me.

I cannot begin to tell you how sincerely sorry I am that we failed to get together. I don't know what was the matter with your house, but I do know that my financial trouble was because I had been building a house, and that this was complicated by my desire to move house.

I wonder if you know how the California farmers plant hops. One season a few plant hops; the price goes up; the next season, all plant hops, and the price goes down. There is a sort of herd psychology in this, and I am wondering if our publishers are not also subject to the same herd psychology. Just now their hops are novels, as I see it. Cent percent, they discount the art of literature and the art of the short story; but if I were convinced that the publishers were able to kill and bury the short story, I'd quit the whole snide game. And when no longer able to buy my passages on windjammers, I'd sign on before the mast.

Believe me, the foregoing is not meant harshly. It is a mere passing commentary on a passing phase.

Mrs. London joins me in thanking you for your good wishes for our voyage. We are both looking forward to the time of our lives.

Indeed, and I should like to see a novel of mine come out from the presses back of the patio garden, but so strangely complicated are the ways in which we build our houses in this modern world, that the presses which bring out my novels in the years to come will belong to some house that has helped me to move house because I was lethargically unable to move house myself.

Sincerely yours,
Jack London

P.S. Big stuff in me! Hell, I haven't started to write yet.

[1] Of Doubleday, Page and Co.

To George P. Brett

New York, New York
Feb. 21, 1912

Dear Mr. Brett:

I remember your kind offer to advance me money if I needed any in New York. I did not need it, and I do not need it. My passage around the Horn is already paid for, and the ranch expenses are fixed up for the next six months.

However—you will remember the invention I spoke to you about. Mr. Unger,[1] I understand, says that it is not the same thing of eight years ago that you apprehended, but that it is something new. As I understand it, he has glimpsed not the whole of it but only the outermost fringes of it.

Now, and to the point of this letter. I shall be out of communication with the world for from five to six months. There is a possible need for some money in the matter. Hence my present request to you, namely, that you advance for me, against my account, up to $1000.00. This advance will be to Mr. Joseph Noel,[2] whose address is Marguerite Villa, Bensonhurst, L.I., N.Y. The way I should like to arrange it, if you are agreeable, is $300.00, subject to immediate call from Mr. Noel, and $700.00, if possibly needed any time after the next thirty days. If you will drop me a special delivery you will catch me inside the next two days. The ship at the present moment is towing down to Baltimore, the ice having broken on Chesapeake Bay sufficiently to let her in.

Since I understand Mr. Unger's conclusion that this is an entirely new invention, a mechanical invention, and not a composite one, I have firmer faith in it than ever. I think there is a pot of money in it,—not merely for me, but for you. And, after hearing what Mr. Unger has to say, I should be glad if you would select other experts and go further into the matter. To me it is a terrifically big thing, and if you can find other experts who agree with Mr. Unger that it is new and not old and that it does not infringe any previous patents, it is my hope that you will then feel yourself justified personally to investigate. If we can cut the time and labor expense of a big portion of the reproductive processes in half, and beat the Ben Day Co. to its knees and make it join with us, we shall get many a dollar for every dollar we put in.

If you care to go further in the matter, if you feel that expert report justifies you in going further in the matter, why communicate with Mr. Noel. He is a very dear, very old, and very trustworthy friend of mine. It has been due to his labor that the Millergraph[3] has been brought from California to New York and put on its present basis.

I shall proceed to keep an eye on this new writer[4] we spoke of, and if I can't develop him into a winner, then nobody can. I for one am confident that he has the power in him.

Under separate cover I am mailing to you a book manuscript by Benjamin De Casseres,[5] whose address is, 11 West 39th Street, or, Proofroom in *The New York Herald*. This man is really and truly the American Nietzsche. I, as you know, am in the opposite intellectual camp from that of Nietzsche. Yet no man in my own camp stirs me as does Nietzsche or as does De Casseres. The manuscript I am sending you is entitled *Chameleon: Being the Book of My Selves*. Please, if you feel interested, glance over the manuscript. In any event, accepting or rejecting, communicate with De Casseres. I shall be away on the sea.

Sincerely yours,
Jack London

P.S. I am inclosing you herewith a "Prelude" of his to another book. It has nothing to do with the book manuscript I am sending you. Nevertheless, his "Prelude" will give you an idea and a feel of him.

---

[1]Ford Adam Unger, an expert lithographer.
[2]Newspaperman and author of *Footloose in Arcadia*.
[3]A man by the name of F. R. Miller had invented a new lithographing process, in which London became interested along with Joseph Noel and George Sterling, and London was instrumental in organizing the Millergraph Co. The venture failed, and along with it, the friendship of London and Noel came to an end.
[4]Probably Sinclair Lewis.
[5]Contemporary writer and translator.

New York, New York
Feb. 22, 1912

Dearest Eliza:

Please go into my manuscript boxes and get a complete set of the *Smoke Bellew* manuscript and express same to Mr. W. B. Parker, Century Company, Union Square, New York City. George Sterling will handle the proofsheets of this as they come out. Any proofsheets that come from anywhere, send to him, and keep in touch with where he is. At present he is in Carmel.

Concerning the Millergraph. Use your power of attorney for me, and follow Joe Noel's lead in whatever he asks you to do. Not only will there be the Millergraph business, but there will be other and independent companies which we are forming. Follow Joe Noel's lead in whatever he asks, whether it comes to selling my Millergraph stock for a song, or for a whole lot more than I paid for it. Whatever he tells you to do in the way of handling stock, selling it, transferring it, etc., why obey. Of course this does not include his getting money out of you. He has no instructions to get money from you. But whatever he says or asks of you, let it go.

I have a moving picture deal on hand. The woman's name is Bernadine Risse Leist.[1] Her addresses are Care *Dramatic Mirror,* New York City, and Hotel Marseilles, 103d Street, New York City. Whatever contract she may send you for signing, you will sign, in relation to moving pictures. She understands that she is to forward all moneys to you, and you can repeat that same proposition to her. If the thing goes through, it will mean $5,000 cash advance and $500 apiece for at least ten stories. Her commission will be ten (10) percent.

Let Sydney Ayres and his moving picture proposition go to hell. If he writes or telegraphs you, tell him that you are in power to do nothing in the matter.

I am inclosing you herewith a letter that is virtually a contract with Mrs. Leist. I am writing her by this mail telling her to forward to you immediately all moneys that may be advanced.

Inclosed you will find some correspondence about my Jersey cow Ramona. Look up my previous correspondence on the subject and you will find it was agreed that I was to receive a registered pedigree. Refer Mr. Stowe to our correspondence, and insist upon getting this registered pedigree.

Keep pursuing the stuffed deer heads of Oregon, and the furs of Los Angeles.

My arms are about you.

Jack

[1]She wanted to do some of London's stories for Kinemacolor Company of America. The plans did not materialize.

To WM. W. ELLSWORTH[1]

Glen Ellen, Calif.
Sept. 7, 1912

Dear Mr. Ellsworth:

In reply to yours of August 12, 1912. I am now at last really at home and settled down to work.[2]

Some time ago, I sent a telegram to The Century Company, and the Century Co.'s reply seemed to evidence a misunderstanding of this situation. I am trying to avoid writing any more short stories than I can help; and you know you publishers abhor short stories.

I am at present at work on *John Barleycorn,* which will be 50,000 or 60,000 words long. It is a book the sub-title of which might aptly be called, *Alcoholic Memoirs.* It is the personal autobiographic discussion of the drink question from A to Z. *The Saturday Evening Post* is giving me 15¢ a word for it, for American serial rights.

I did not mean, in my telegram to Century Company, that this book was to be immediately published. It can take its time after *Smoke Bellew,* and after any other of my books you want to bring out first. In fact, *The Sat. Eve. Post* wouldn't be done with the serial publication for some time.

I need scarcely tell you that an advance of say a couple of thousand dollars from The Century Company, would make the writing of *John Barleycorn* an easier matter with me. That the book should sell big, I have all the confidence in the world. You see, I am running an expensive ranch —said ranch being expensive because of the fact that I am heavily investing in it. I am planting eucalyptus trees, and at present moment have a hundred thousand trees in. Each year I plant from 20,000 to 40,000 trees. This makes rather a tidy wage-list, when, for months at a time, there are fifty men on the pay-roll. Then is the time when I rush in and write short stories for $1000 per story for the magazines. Which is the very thing I am trying to get away from. I don't want to write short stories. I want to write long stories.

As a sample of my long-story work, you will remember there was one novel, as yet unwritten by me, which was to be published by The Macmillan Company. This novel The Macmillan Co. advanced me $6000 on. I wrote it after I left New York, in the course of my voyage around the Horn. I have just received a telegram from *The Cosmopolitan* that they have accepted it serially, paying me $12,000 for 100,000 words. When I arrived in California at the conclusion of the voyage around the Horn, I found that the $6000 advanced me by the Macmillan Co. had already been earned by royalties on other books, and that I had a favorable balance with The Macmillan Co. I imagine the Macmillan Co. will publish this novel in book form, entitled *The Valley of the Moon,* somewhere around October, 1913.

363

But the point of the foregoing paragraph is, that my long stuff is pretty good at money-earning, and that's a thing I want The Century Co. to help me to. I am confident that it will be mutually profitable. And that is why I suggest that a couple of thousand dollars advance at present time on *John Barleycorn,* to be published by The Century Co. whenever it sees fit, after *The Sat. Eve. Post* has published it serially, would come in very handy for me and help me toward doing longer work.

Sincerely yours,
Jack London

[1]Of the Century Company. London became unhappy with Macmillan about 1912 because of their mishandling of photographs for *The Cruise of the Snark* and because he believed they were not promoting his books adequately. He turned to the Century Company, who published his next four books.
[2]London was on the Horn voyage until late August, which accounts for the absence of letters from February until September.

To JOHANNES LOODIET

Glen Ellen, Calif.
Sept. 15, 1912

Dear Mr. Loodiet:—

In reply to yours of August 23, 1912, which recently came to hand. Your handwriting is so absolutely mine, so frankly modeled after mine, that it was a great surprise to me when I saw your envelope.

About two years ago, this alleged niece of mine, Miss Myrtle London, showed up in Indiana, where she was trying to sell alleged genuine manuscripts of mine. Now, no one has any manuscripts of mine to sell. I have never sold any of my manuscripts, nor have I ever deputed anybody else to sell any of my manuscripts.

So you can see that I am curious as to what propositions this Myrtle London made to you. It would seem, apparently, that she was trying to get you to make copies of my manuscripts—all this, of course, with the understanding on your part that my permission had been obtained for the transaction.

Now, will you please let me know what this Miss London looks like, and what the propositions were that she placed before you. I have no idea of how I can find her, but I wish to learn all that is possible about her, in case she tries to get me into a scrape with manuscript collectors. I will esteem it a great favor if you will give me the fullest information in the matter.

Sincerely yours,
Jack London

To Johannes Loodiet

Glen Ellen, Calif.
Oct. 25, 1912

Dear Mr. Loodiet:—

In reply to yours of Sept. 30, 1912. There can be no objection to two men having handwriting as similar as yours and mine are.

If you will go to the library and look me up in the following books: *Who's Who in England, Who's Who in the United States,* and *International Who's Who,* you will find that my home is in Glen Ellen and that I am really Jack London the writer.

In my letter to you of Sept. 15, 1912, I asked you for information concerning this woman "Myrtle London." I asked you to let me know what propositions she had made to you. Will you please give me this information?

I do not know Myrtle London. Nor can she have any of my manuscripts in her possession. Yet she has in the past tried to sell manuscripts of mine.

After reading your letter and Laura Herkimer's letter I should very easily believe this to be a practical joke on your part, except for the fact that this Myrtle London appeared a couple of years ago in Indianapolis and tried to sell forged manuscripts of mine.

Please give me full information about this Myrtle London at your very earliest convenience.

Sincerely,
Jack London

P.S. What work did Myrtle London want you to do? What were you taking notes of?

P.S. If Laura Herkimer is so anxious to punish Myrtle London, then get Laura Herkimer to advise you to give me the information I am asking for.

Why do you not give me your address?

Please also give me a description of Myrtle London.

To Roland Phillips

Glen Ellen, Calif.
Oct. 25, 1912

Dear Roland Phillips:—

My wife is in hospital.[1] In lieu of her, my Japanese boy (who sailed cabinboy on the *Snark)* typed the new form of contract enclosed herewith. And now my Japanese boy is away, hence this scrawl. Here go explanations of some of changes I have made in the contract.

100,000 words minimum for novels. If you will remember, you offered me $15,000 for 125,000 words of *Valley of the Moon*. That was before it was written. When I delivered the manuscript, you offered $12,000 for 100,000 words. Now, in 5-year contract you are offering $12,000 for 125,000 words. Don't you see the whipsaw you've passed me?

Now, if you want 125,000 words of each novel alter the contract to that effect and include in the alteration $15,000 for said 125,000 words.

6000 words average minimum of short stories. Really, as a writer, I can't wholly emasculate my art by selling length without regard to strength, which latter is *form*. I might write you a gem of a short story that was 5000 or 5500 words and that would be ruined by being made 6000 or 7000 words. You know that. I make this change merely as an artistic precaution, because, on the other hand, my short stories average between 7000 words & 8000 words right along, year in & year out.

Your contract was an *impossible* one, in its demand for machine-like regularity of delivery of manuscript. My little daughter is ill with typhoid at the present moment. Suppose, next year, I come down on my back for eight weeks with typhoid. So far as I was concerned, the contract would be smashed through my inability to deliver. Hence, I have included a margin of delivery of three months.

I had to change delivery of first short story to Oct. 1, 1913. You know of my year agreement with the *Monthly Magazine Section,* which expires somewhere around Oct. 1, 1913. I'd be in a hell of a mess, if I agreed to deliver short stories to you before that time. But after that time they'll land on you in lumps and clumps.

I simply must insist on ten per cent for English language serial rights outside of the United States. You know I am retaining those rights on present thousand dollar short stories with other editors. Why I should sign an exclusive with you for less than I'm getting on the open market is beyond me. At present moment I'm correcting proofsheets of what will be at the end 70,000 words and for which, American rights only, *The Sat. Eve. Post* is paying me 15 cts. per word. Also, the *Post* is clamoring right along for more short stories, & you know my rate with the *Post* is now a thousand dollars per story for American serial rights.

I've had to reserve the right to publish serially in England old stories long past written by me, and now sold & being sold in England.

As I see it, the essence of this contract is exclusiveness and not quantity. I am tying myself up to give you my fiction exclusively for five years. As you had the contract worded, if I became an invalid unable to work more than half time or quarter time, or if I got so prosperous that I didn't care to work more than half time or quarter time, then you'd have my fiction exclusively tied up for ten or twenty years. So I have made the essence of this contract exclusiveness for a period of five years.

In the foregoing connection I can only assure you that I have no investments except in the eucalyptus on my ranch, from which no returns can be expected for fifteen years. My one source of income is my writing. So never fear, I'll turn out the fiction. Besides, I've got the habit. Look how steadily I've written since the year I began, 1899. 33 books published, and 6 books finished & waiting their turn to be published. 39 books in 13 yrs., or 3 books a year. Why, my maximum contract with you would reduce my future output to two books per year. The signs are propitious that I'll press the maximum of the contract for the next five years if somebody doesn't die & leave me a million dollars.

Sincerely yours,

Jack London

P.S. *Important*. Please note that my wording on page 1, in paragraph three, is vague. This should be changed by you so that in the proper place in the body of that paragraph, and in the body of later paragraphs relating to amount & method of payment it should read to the effect that 100,000 words for $12,000 dollars, and 12 cents per word for all over 100,000 printed by you. (In this connection, you could arrange that all money due me in excess of 100,000 words, can be applied to the yearly balancing on Feb. 1, which I have suggested.)

Jack London

P.S. In contract it must be flatly stipulated that any rights in my non-pictured fiction are untransferable, untranslatable, unassignable, & remain wholly my property.

My pictured fiction of course is transferred as fast as it is pictured and sold.

---

[1]The occasion was the birth and death of the second child.

To Professor Philo M. Buck, Jr.

Glen Ellen, Calif.

Nov. 5, 1912

My Dear Professor Buck:

I have just read your "American Barbarian."[1]

Will you mind my telling you that your critical conclusions are at the same time very naive and very complimentary to me?

You see, all the lessons I've hammered home in my fiction, (my motifs), you've grabbed and crucified me with.

I was a socialist before I was a writer. I believe in a culture far beyond present-day culture. I do not believe in war. I am not an individualist. *Sea Wolf, Martin Eden, Burning Daylight,* were written as indictments of individualism. Martin Eden died because he was an individualist. Individualism failed him. For heaven's sake re-read the book.

How about my *People of the Abyss, War of the Classes, White Fang, Before Adam, Iron Heel, Revolution,* etc., etc.?

Don't you see? All my conclusions, all my place and fight in life for higher civilization and culture, so utterly miss you that you take my data (which leaves the conclusion to the reader), and pillory me upon it.

Now, really, you owe me and yourself something—and the public.

Very truly yours,

Jack London

---

[1]Prof. Philo M. Buck, Jr., published in the *Methodist Review,* Sept., 1912, an article entitled, "The American Barbarian," to which London took exception. For complete treatment of the controversy, including all correspondents, see *Creator and Critic,* Utah State University Press Monograph Series, Vol. 8, No. 2, March, 1961.

To CHARMIAN LONDON

Glen Ellen, Calif.

Nov. 19, 1912

Dear Woman:—

Telephoned you to-day. You were elsewhere. From the way you gallivant around—well, you could almost gallivant around that way on the Ranch.

No; I told Eliza, George is no go. First time in his life he was ever in the country.

As for Hamilton, I get more sheer pleasure out of an hour's talk with him than all my inefficient Italian laborers have ever given me. He *pays* his way. My God, the laborers *never* have.

The Ranch has never lost very much money on Hamilton, and George, and Spiro, and Seymour, and "Lone Wolf," and all the rest of the fellows who've had a few meals and beds out of me. The Ranch has lost a hell of a lot on the weak sticks of $1.75 cash per day laborers who've fattened off of me and on me.

Please don't forget that the Ranch is *my* problem. Netta and Edward never helped me; Wiget never helped me; Eliza never helped me. It was I, when I was ripe, and when I saw a flicker of intelligence in Eliza, who proceeded to shake things down. What all these various ones have lost for me in cash is a thousand times more than the price of the few meals and beds I've given to my bums. And I give these paltry things of paltry value out of my heart. I've not much heart-throb left for my fellow beings. Shall I cut this wee bit thing out too?

Cosmopolitan wired me it's mailing revised contract. So that deal still struggles along. If it doesn't go through, we don't get in the house next fall, maybe—though I could turn loose and earn the money other ways.

Anyway, it's raining and blowing, and I'm going to quit now and play pinochle with Jerry Carlin.

You mean more to me than you can ever guess, and I'll be damned if I tell you.[1]

Wolf-Man

[1]Charmian added the following note to the original letter: "After losing 2nd chance of a child."

To WILLIAM ELLSWORTH

Glen Ellen, Calif.
Jan. 30, 1913

Dear Mr. Ellsworth:

In reply to yours of Jan. 10, 1913. Find inclosed herewith receipt for $1000.00 advance payment on royalties, and signed contract for *John Barleycorn*.

In the matter of the *John Barleycorn* contract, I am questioning paragraph 6. What does this "even division of profits on Canadian editions and on cheap reprint editions" mean? Does it mean that you furnish the plates and I furnish the matter, and we divide the profits, or does it mean that we divide the profits after you have made a profit to yourself on the sale or rental of the plates?

Now, Mr. Ellsworth, my books have always been a great deal unlike one another. *John Barleycorn* being as unlike *Smoke Bellew* as *Smoke Bellew* is unlike *The People of the Abyss,* as *The People of the Abyss* is unlike *The Iron Heel,* as *The Iron Heel* is unlike *White Fang,* as *White Fang* is unlike *The Cruise of the Snark,* and as *The Cruise of the Snark* is unlike the *Sea Wolf*—means nothing.

Of course, *John Barleycorn* is unlike. I'm not only a teller of bear stories, I can tell snake stories and fish stories.

I may venture to point out that *John Barleycorn* is unlike any other book ever published anywhere in this world.

I dare venture further and assert that if *John Barleycorn* is handled right (being a totally different book from any other book ever published, and covering a very vital topic), it can go into as many editions as you may want to print it.

On the other hand, if you shy at it, if you don't play it up, you'll get the public to shy at it and it will never fall flat because it will never have received impetus enough to achieve any fall at all. For goodness sake, don't let's have a still-born of it.

If you are going to shy at it because it is "different," depend upon it you will make the public shy too.

At the present moment I have 15,000 words done on a sea novel [*The Mutiny of the Elsinore*], and I'm swinging along a thousand words a day on it. And I rush right in here to tell you that this sea novel will be quite different from any other novel I ever wrote, and it will be quite different from any

369

other sea novel ever written by anybody else. *The Cosmopolitan* will publish it serially, and you will have the book publishing of it. I haven't got a title for it yet.

Will you please assure me that I may rest easy and depend upon you to arrange the book publishing of *John Barleycorn* with Hughes Massie, 17-21 Tavistock Street, Covent Garden, London, W.C., England, so that the protection of international copyright will not be slipped up.

Sincerely yours,

Jack London

P.S. Could you give me any idea of sales of *Smoke Bellew* up to date.

To Hartwell S. Shippey[1]

Glen Ellen, Calif.

Feb. 7, 1913

Dear Shippey:—

In reply to yours of Jan. 10, 1913. First of all, find herewith a couple of bunches of clipping stuff, which same please return. Whatever you do, do not fail to return me as immediately as you can, the Jules de Gaultier article. I think you'll like it.

I am ordering direct from Houghton Mifflin the 2 vols. of George Cabot Lodge.

Quite sub rosa, I don't mind telling you that the only reason I am permitted to remain in the socialist party at present moment is the fact that I have never taken any part in the policy of the party. I have never spoken out in meeting. I've just been a propagandist. But all I can see to-day is that our beautiful American Socialist movement is headed along a very lovely sidetrack. It seems doomed to become the bulwark of conservatism. I believe in direct action, and syndicalism, and all that goes with it. But heavens on earth! we can talk these matters over—not write about them. Life's too short.

Please remember that you started in the writing game somewhat later than I did, and that even yet you haven't reached my attitude on the matter of writing for the dear public. No, there is nothing tragic about it at all. It's a damned good way to make a living. It's the best way I know to make a damned good living. You won't think there's any tragedy about it when you come to see what I am trying to do with the soil, and with hogs, and with beef-cattle, and dairy-cows, and draft-horses. I am trying to master this soil and the crops and animals that spring from it, as I strove to master the sea, and men, and women, and the books, and all the face of life that I could stamp with my "will to do."

I should like to send you a MS entitled *John Barleycorn,* which will begin running serially in a short time in *Sat. Eve. Post.* All I want to get from you is a safe address to which I may send it. You see, I have only one spare copy, and I want it back in order to send to other friends. What bothers me and compels me to ask this safe address, is the fact of your fall-out with *The Citizen.* Oh, that was only to be expected.

Sincerely yours,

Jack London

[1]Of *Citizen's Magazine.* In a letter to London, dated Jan. 9, 1911, Shippey wrote, "You may or may not have heard of me as I.W.W., jailbird and writer of idiotorials, of the *Industrial Worker.* Never again. Yours for Ours."

To EDITOR,
The Bookman

Glen Ellen, Calif.
Feb. 24, 1913

Dear Sir:—

In the February number of *The Bookman,* I read that in former years I "suffered greatly from insomnia, and kept a little supply of food at the head of my bed," since I found that eating tended to produce slumber. Of late years I learn that I have been relying upon riding, yachting and shooting to keep me in good writing trim.

Now, my old friend Bailey Millard has got the thing turned just precisely about. I have never in all my life suffered from insomnia, and in fact have been so good a sleeper all my life that I am compelled to have something to nibble on as I lie in bed reading and working late at night in order not to put myself to sleep but to keep myself awake. Sometimes it seems that this is the chief trouble of my life—my gorgeous capacity for sleeping. I could do ever so much more work if I did not have to sleep so much.

Sincerely yours,

Jack London

To ROLAND PHILLIPS

Glen Ellen, Calif.
Feb. 27, 1913

Dear Roland Phillips:—

Yesterday I replied to your letter of Feb. 20, 1913, with a long telegram explaining the situation to you. In my letter to you of Sept. 20, 1912, I explained the whole situation concerning my writing and writing arrangements at that time. Among other things, in the last paragraph of the first page of that letter of Sept. 20, I told you as follows: "At the present moment my price with the *Sat. Eve. Post* is $1000 per short story, and here is my present situation with that publication: It is paying me 15¢ per word for 50,000 words of personal reminiscences (no fiction). If the 50,000 words of reminiscences proves unavailable, then the $2000 advance to be paid by me within the year by two (2) short stories at the rate of $1000 per story."

You see, first having explained so fully to you, I am surprised at your present surprise; and, secondly, *John Barleycorn* is not fiction at all. It is bare, bald, absolute fact, a recital of my own personal experiences in the realm of alcohol.

When I was in New York last winter, as you will remember, I approached you with various things, three of which I now remember. There was the narrative of my voyage around the Horn in a windjammer, which I was on the verge of making; there was the Ed Morrell convict story [*The Star Rover*] of a California penitentiary which I gave you at length; and there was *John Barleycorn*. My feeling concerning these three was, that they did not interest you; and when you will remember that in all the subsequent months, up to the present time, you mentioned no one of these three to me again, it just about clinches the certitude of my conviction at the time that they did not interest you.

I am swinging along on my Horn novel [*The Mutiny of the Elsinore*]; somewhere along about 40,000 words are now completed. And let me tell you, it will be quite a different sea novel from any sea novel ever written.

Sincerely yours,

Jack London

P.S. *The Semi-Monthly Magazine Section* did not see its way to using the short story "Samuel" I wrote you about some time ago. I have turned it over to *The Bookman*. If you should object to this, please drop me a wire, and I shall promptly recall it.

To George P. Brett

Glen Ellen, Calif.
March 1, 1913

Dear Mr. Brett:—

By account you rendered me of April 30, 1912, I see that at that time I had a balance unearned and earned by me of $16.03. I should imagine that in the intervening time my various books have earned quite a bit.

And now to my troubles, or my needs rather—my needs being I verily believe extravagances.

First, the house: Some eight or nine years ago I bought the land on which our house-site is situated. Some six or seven years ago I planted the house orchard, the house vineyard and the hedges around the house-site. These have been growing ever since. Two years ago I started to build the house.[1] By working very hard and very expensively this summer, we hope to be into the house this fall, not later than October 1. When I tell you that all these years we have been without a house; that I have been without space sufficient to shelve all my books, and that we have waited nine years for the completion of our house to approach, you will see that we have been very patient. As regards my library, it has been mostly stored away in boxes in the various barns on the ranch. Yet these books were my tools and are my tools. Most frequently, when I desire a reference, and look over my limited shelves, I find that the books which I need are stored away in some of the barns.

I am inclosing you herewith a brief article that was published a couple of years ago, outlining the house that I was just starting to build. Incidentally, I may mention that at the present moment I am building three other houses. One is in the hills back of Oakland for my first wife and the children. The second house is for my sister here on the ranch. My sister is a capable business woman who takes charge of the ranch in my absence. The third is a house in a remote outlying portion of the ranch, which I intend renting to summer campers at about $50 or $60 a month. This is an immediate asset, because I calculate at least 20% return on the money invested in that house. The fourth is the stone house I have already told you about.

And there are two other extravagances, or sane extravagances, of which I have been guilty. I have crowned the ranch by the purchase of 500 more acres that cover the most beautiful spots of the ranch and some of the most fertile spots of the ranch, and that march alongside of the ranch clear to the top of Sonoma Mountain, 2200 feet above my head. Also, I have just bought a stallion[2]—oh, not a thoroughbred racing stallion nor trotting horse stallion nor a saddle horse stallion, but the finest draft horse stallion I have ever seen. It is an imported English Shire, and I have paid $2500 for it. Also accompanying this stallion I have paid $750 for an imported Shire mare in foal. You see, I have some 15 or 20 work horses or work mares on the ranch, and in this out of the way valley have been hard put to find proper stallions to which to breed these mares, in order to turn out the right kind of draft horse stock for the San Francisco market.

And now to my immediate need for money: The roof on the stone house I am building is to be of Spanish tile, and will cost all-told $3500.00. The first carload of tile is already on the way here.

Since ten months ago I was squared up with you, since in the intervening time my various books must have earned quite a sum, since you still have waiting to be published *The Valley of the Moon,* a good money-earning long novel, I should most gratefully and pressingly like to have you advance me $3500.00 in the following manner: $1500 by the end of the third week in March; $1000.00 in first week in April; and $1000. in first week in May.

Sincerely yours,

Jack London

IN THE EVENT of Mr. Brett's absence in Europe, will whoever is in charge of The Macmillan Company, please either forward my letter to Mr. Brett, or, better, cable to him at my expense the gist of its contents.

Sincerely yours,

Jack London

---

[1]The Wolf House. The house was nearing completion when on August 22, 1913, it mysteriously burned, evidently the work of an arsonist.
[2]Neuadd Hillside, an imported shire stallion that died one month before London.

To ROLAND PHILLIPS

Glen Ellen, Calif.
March 14, 1913

Dear Roland Phillips:

My Cape Horn novel swings along. I am now some 65,000 words along with it, written and typed.

Say—I have a splendid motif for a novel. Have spent the past three days making notes and assuring myself of my grip on it. And now, I've got it in both my hands.

Three characters only—a mighty trio in a mighty situation, in a magnificently beautiful environment. Each of the three is good; each of the three is big. It will be a winner.

It is all sex, from start to finish—in which no sexual adventure is actually achieved or comes within a million miles of being achieved, and in which, nevertheless, is all the guts of sex, coupled with strength. Oh, my three are not puling weaklings and moralists. They are cultured, modern, and at the same time profoundly primitive.

And when the tale is ended, the reader will take off his hat to each of the three of the trio: "By God! he was some man!" or "By God! she was some woman!"

As I go over this novel, I am almost led to believe that it is what I have been working toward all my writing life, and now I've got it in my two hands.

Except for my old-time punch, which will be in it from start to finish, it will not be believed that I could write it—it is so utterly fresh, so absolutely unlike anything I have ever done.

What I should like, is your permission to substitute this novel for the series of short stories, so that you will publish it following upon *The Valley of the Moon*.

Oh, of course, I can do the short stories in the cold, calm confidence and surety of the trained craftsman; but here, with this novel, I am hot. It will be big stuff. It will offend no one, and it will hold suspense to the last page.

And—it will be just about 100,000 words and no pruning nor condensing necessary for serial publication. It will be a cleancut gem, even in serial form —a jewel of artistry. You will not need to subtract a word.

Oh, hell! I am not going to talk any more about it.[1]

Jack London

[1]The letter refers to *The Little Lady of the Big House*.

To GEORGE STERLING

Glen Ellen, Calif.
Mar. 18, 1913

Blessed Greek:—

Am sending you to-day the complete manuscript of *John Barleycorn*. Please read and return as soon as you can.

Oh, hell! I don't mind being a member of anything so long as there are no dues, no duties and no responsibilities.

Am wondering when you are coming up along with Jim Hop.

I am so tied up with the ranch these days that I can't find time to go away from it even in order to visit a dentist. I had the first tooth pulled yesterday in over 20 years—just because I couldn't take the time off to go to Oakland and have the tooth fixed up. Oh! I am real stuck up on the ranch just now. Am stuck on the ranch and stuck to the ranch. The only chance I ever get to go away is when I rush off to buy a Jersey cow, or to look at a silo, or to buy a stallion or an angora goat herd or a shorthorn bull or such truck. Anyway, the quicker the better for you and Jim Hop to come up here, for goodness knows how long I shall remain stuck here. Your Laddie is some Laddie. In the photo you sent me of you and Laddie, will you please tell me on which side you were standing?

Thine,
Wolf

To: WINSTON CHURCHILL
  ROBERT W. CHAMBERS
  LLOYD OSBORNE
  OWEN JOHNSON
  GEORGE BERNARD SHAW
  H. G. WELLS

Glen Ellen, Calif.
March 23, 1913

Dear sir:—

I live in California—when I am not farther afield—I have published thirty-three books, as well as an ocean of magazine stuff, and yet I have never heard the rates that other writers receive.

If it is not asking too much, may I ask you to tell me (confidentially, of course) what top rates, average rates, and minimum rates, you receive from (1) English magazines, (2) American magazines, (3) English book-publishers, (4) American book-publishers.

Sincerely yours,
Jack London

To CORDIE WEBB INGRAM[1]

Glen Ellen, Calif.
April 9, 1913

Dear Cordie Webb Ingram:

In reply to yours of April 2. Please remember one thing: any time you are in doubt and want any advice, write to me. I do detest being asked general advice, because, in reply, I must do one or two things: (1) Either write two or three books handling the replies or (2) damp the replies by giving only a few short sentences.

What I mean is, any time ask me for particular specific advice, and I shall be only too glad to place myself at your service.

Please remember that I write thousands of letters every year to unknown correspondents. And please remember, (1) that I do not like to write for a living, even; that if I had my way I should not write a single line; and that (2) therefore, when I have written all the books that I have written and upon which I work every day, that I am so tired of writing that I'd cut off my fingers and toes in order to avoid writing.

Why, I have a phonograph here, into which I talk all my letters. And you may find me at midnight, or two in the morning, or at six in the morning, or at midday, or at two and four and six in the afternoon, talking my replies as quickly as I can and as briefly as I can, into the phonograph—and still I cannot keep up with my correspondence.

Anyway, please remember that you can call upon me any time for SPECIFIC, PARTICULAR advice on any subject.

Sincerely yours,

Jack London

[1]An aspiring writer from Texas. In an earlier letter London advised her to read Kipling, O. Henry, and de Maupassant, and "attempt to, in a way, imitate, and grow less wordy if possible."

To WILLIAM ELLSWORTH

Glen Ellen, Calif.

April 9, 1913

Dear Mr. Ellsworth:—

In reply to yours of March 31, 1913.

Really, I am dreadfully puzzled to answer your letter. Now, we don't want any mistakes in a relationship which, I hoped, when I entered into it, would endure through the years. The one thing we do not want is mistakes of any sort. I am sure The Century Company would not wish such a thing to happen any more than I would wish it to happen.

Right at the start, for a foundation, I wish to say that it is my firm belief that The Century Company understands the publishing game better than I understand it. Next, I want to say that it is my firm belief that The Century Company does not understand the publishing game in relation to me as well as I understand it.

To begin with the immediate, namely, my sea novel on which I now have some seventy [thousand]-odd words completed. Perhaps The Century Company is right in its judgment (I refer it to its letter of March 31, 1913). Perhaps this sea novel of mine is just something real, something "almost like an account of an actual happening." Perhaps it is just the sort of a Horn novel no writer would write who has never been around the Horn. But, surely, The Century Company has had access to enough of the world's literature to know that some writers sometimes write something that is "almost like an account of an actual happening."

And now to a more general statement of the situation. Here is some data to go on. (1) No publisher has ever lost money on me. (2) I have always failed to get along with any publisher who was an office man and a flat-floor man and a cent percent man, and who, in dealing with me who never lost money for him, could not be as careless as I. (3) It has always been give and take with me. I have never haunted New York nor worried publishers with personal contact. My dealings have been conducted with the New York publishers from all quarters of the world where I might happen to be at any time.

When I framed up the present contract with The Century Company, the ordinary advances as stated in that contract were considered as ordinary advances. Mr. Scott knew that I was accustomed to receive extraordinary advances on novels—because I told him so, and in that contract allowance was made for the possibility of said extraordinary advances—not in my words, however.

This general situation I understood clearly in my careless way, that was so careless that I fear me I did not insist it be stated most explicitly in the words and phrases of the contract—namely, that I understood at the time of making and signing the contract that I was agreeing to a cut of five ¢ royalty on all my books. It was somewhere around that time or shortly before that the old $1.50 retail price on a book was changed to $1.30 net and to $1.25 net. For years I had been getting 20% royalty, and 20% royalty on a $1.50 book means 30¢. 20% royalty on a $1.25 book means 25¢—a difference of 5¢ per copy in royalties on my book. "Well and good," thought I, "understanding that from time to time I shall require advances which in publishing houses are figured at cent percent, I shall let, under this new arrangement, the difference go of 5¢ per copy on my books, which, in my careless way, I thought would surely pay interest on any advances my publishers made me. 5¢ is one-sixth of 30¢, or 16⅔%. In my careless way I agreed, tacitly, to pay interest on advances of 16⅔% of my royalty earning power.

Very well. Remembering the foregoing facts, the present situation stands this way: (1) I shall always want heavy advances. (2) The Century Co. seems averse to giving heavy advances. (3) I thought I had arranged, by reducing my royalties 16⅔%, an interest paid in advance on all advances.

All this being the situation, don't you think it would be better, if we can possibly arrange it, to escape future misunderstanding by nullifying our present contract. We can do this in all good friendliness, I am sure.

I was puzzled, when I began this letter, as to how to answer your letter. Now it all seems clear and plain. I think that inside of thirty days I can raise the money from outside sources, to pay up the sum total of my indebtedness to The Century Company. The idea that comes to my mind is this. Balance our accounts, and tell me what the present balance is against me, of unearned advance on my books. Inside this thirty days I shall put this sum of money into your hands. In return, you will give me back my books unpublished by you—of course, including *John Barleycorn*. In the case of *John Barleycorn,* of course, seeing it is so far along in print I should take from your hands the same contract which you have with your printers, paying your printers the same as you pay them. This, of course, includes illustrators, etc.

If the foregoing proposition seems all right to you, will you kindly immediately wire me the full details, giving me your permission to go ahead and attempt to raise the money outside, and to pay it to you inside the following thirty days?[1]

Sincerely yours,

Jack London

P.S. Please, before you make your telegraphic reply, take into consideration the peril we run of future misunderstandings if our relationship be continued. I do not want these misunderstandings, and I am sure you do not want these misunderstandings.

---

[1]Century did not accede to London's request. In a letter dated May 29, 1913, London agreed to Century's demands to publish *John Barleycorn* and then sever the relationship.

To George Sterling

Glen Ellen, Calif.
April 20, 1913

Dearest and Only Greek:

I am so damned glad for your good words for "The Unkissed." I am sending your letter on to Margaret Smith Cobb. I want to tell you a lot about her when you get up here—if you are ever going to get here. Great Christ! It isn't even very far to walk from Carmel to Glen Ellen, and I don't think the S.P. has raised its rates.

Yes, I have agreed to your several suggested changes in "The Unkissed." I have agreed to every one of them, and I am, as I say, forwarding your letter to Margaret Smith Cobb, and am quite sure she will accept the changes. She is a wonder. She is fifty years old. She is a mountain woman. When we were in her mountain home a couple of years ago, her sixteen year old daughter had never seen a railroad train. Her knowledge of poetry is limited to half a dozen of the older poets, and yet she turns out a thing like this!

I did have all sorts of qualms of conscience when I thought I had turned over to you over one-quarter of a million of words of proof-sheets. But you came through and did it like a little man. All hail to you, you hero!

When are you and Carrie and Jimmie and Jimmie's wife coming up?

Thine,
Wolf

To George P. Brett

Glen Ellen, Calif.
April 22, 1913

Dear Mr. Brett:—

In reply to yours of April 2, 1913. I have delayed thanking you for your advances and delayed replying to you, because I have been and still am trying to get back to you.

Inclosed correspondence will speak for itself. It will give you a grasp of the situation with The Century Co. I do not know what the outcome will be, but I have hopes that I can sting them into a sense of manhood.

Here are a few of the pledged books with The Century Company. My Horn novel, 70,000 odd words of which are completed. It is going to be a sailing ship voyage around the Horn in the year 1913. Everything is brought right down to date. And it will be unlike any sea novel ever written.

John Barleycorn—this is bound to be a terrific winner. Every day and every day the clippings and the letters come in to me from all over the United States. It is cutting up and down and crosswise clear through society. There is not a sort of person of any classification who is not falling in one way or another for *John Barleycorn*. Scarcely was the first week's copy published in *The Saturday Evening Post,* when the Prohibitionists in California were copying from it and bringing out pamphlets based upon it.

I have *The Abysmal Brute* completed, which should sell for from $1.00 to $1.25. It is a short-long story.

Also, there are some four other completed collections of short stories.

Now for the future, beginning with the past. In over one and one-half years I have not written a short story. In the next five years, made safe by my *Cosmopolitan* contract, I shall turn out at least ten (10) novels, and a couple of volumes of reminiscent stuff like *John Barleycorn*—one, for instance, my writing-autobiography; another, for instance, my farming-autobiography. Both will be good stuff. I am starting in on another stage of my writing career—and I am going to do things.

The advances with the Century or from The Century Company, are something like $10,500 or $11,000 at the present moment. These cover the foregoing books. I mean the foregoing books, not the novels I am going to write in the next five years. I figure that *John Barleycorn* alone will more than pay the $10,500 or the $11,000 advances. *John Barleycorn* will be a killer, a winner. I have gone and am going on the basis that you will put up this advance and let me come back to you. If not, wire me immediately.

At any rate, immediately return to me all the Century correspondence and telegrams which I am inclosing you herewith.

If I go back to you, I'll stay with you forever, but I'll go back only on the understanding that your personal eye will be on me, and that you personally will treat with me. I am hugely disgusted with the new generation of flat-floor young men who are without vision or romance or imagination, and who chaffer and bicker in quite similar ways to those I have seen in Petticoat Lane.

As regards the next five years, here is the situation: I am made safe for the writing of the ten novels as well as other books, because of the fact that my contract with *The Cosmopolitan* for serial rights in the United States and England bring to me some $2200 each month, paid regularly. It will enable me to leave short stories alone. Unfortunately, this contract will prevent me from resurrecting that other young writing man I told you about. It would be impossible for him to do anything, because this contract demands everything over my own name. I am forced to cut this letter short in order to catch the mail, without saying all I want to say.

In any event, return to me the Century correspondence immediately, and telegraph me how you feel about the matter. Why, man, I have not yet begun to write.

Sincerely yours,

Jack London

To Edward Broadley[1]

Glen Ellen, Calif.

May 10, 1913

My dear Mr. Broadley:—

In reply to yours of April 29, 1913. First of all, I hardly know what to say. You have been very frank to me, and I know that I must meet you in equal frankness; and yet, and yet—I do not know what to say.

The confidence that you have reposed in me I shall keep. Nobody shall ever see the letter you have written me. By the same token, I request of you to let no one see the letter I am now writing you; and, furthermore, not to tell anybody, not even Mrs. Gilbert, of its contents. This is between the two men of us.

I am only very slightly acquainted with Mrs. Gilbert. I have met 100,000 persons as intimately as I have met Mrs. Gilbert. She has been in my house while I was there, two or three times. I do not know that she ever had a meal at my table, and I am certain she never slept a night in my house. I know she did have a cottage near my ranch, and that on several occasions she called on my wife and me at our house. I know that several times driving up and down the country roads I met her, and that is about all. After she left this part of California, she wrote to me and asked me if I would stand for this advertising stunt of hers of going around the world on a wager.[2] Of course, I said "Anything to help anybody; go ahead." I have never said a word in public about the true inwardness of this wager, which has really never been made. It arose in Mrs. Gilbert's mind, and I fell for it merely for advertising purposes for her.

There is the whole situation in a nut-shell. So far as Mrs. Gilbert is concerned, I am not under the slightest obligations to her. On the other hand, she has never asked me for a dollar, nor have I helped her in any way save in this matter of the fake wager about going around the world.

I have so many other persons on my hands whom I am helping at the present time that I cannot see my way to helping her out with anything. This is not a matter of choice nor of desire but of simple financial expediency. I have too many on my hands at the present time.

I have enjoyed your clean, manly letter, and I like the spirit you have radiated through every line of it. Any time you should be in California, Mrs. London and I should be glad to have you look us up on the ranch.

Then we could talk a great deal more than we could possibly write in a thousand letters.

Most sincerely yours,
Jack London

[1]Of the Gaiety Theatre, Manchester, England.
[2]In September, 1914, a San Francisco paper printed the following: "Mrs. Hilda Gilbert arrived in San Francisco five months ahead of schedule. Trip result of wager. Novelist wins five thousand dollars by backing ability of American girls. Mrs. Hilda Gilbert won for Jack London, the novelist, a bet of five thousand dollars when she arrived in San Francisco yesterday on the steamer *Matsonia*. The wager was made nearly four years ago. London declared that the average American girl would not find it difficult to work her way around the world. A friend disputed the assertion and London selected Mrs. Gilbert, a neighbor of his near Glen Ellen, to prove he was right. Mrs. Gilbert sailed from New York on the *Lusitania,* February 28, 1911, and was to have four years to make the trip eastward through San Francisco. She was to do Europe, India, South Africa, Australia, China, Japan, Honolulu. When she reached here yesterday, she was just five months ahead of her allotted time and asserts that she has fulfilled scrupulously all the conditions of the wager."

To Jack London

Glen Ellen, Calif.
May 10, 1913

My dear Jack London:

In reply to yours of Apr. 29. I first of all turned your letter over to my sister and asked her to write you about my family. She knows more about our family than I know. I find my letter back here on my desk, so I can see that Mrs. Shepard, my sister, has already written you.

To show you how many Londons there are in the world, a week ago I was in Los Angeles and got something into my eye and went to a doctor's office. While waiting for the doctor, who was working on another man, I discovered that the name of the man he was working upon was Matt London. Then when the doctor finished with him and brought me in, we were introduced,—Matt London and Jack London. This Matt London, by the way, was a Swede.

I remember, often, hearing my father speaking of a grandmother, a French grandmother, whose name was Miss Champion before she married into the London family. That looks like some sort of a connection right there.

Hell!—I have nothing to be proud of. I'd acknowledge relationship with any man, woman, or child in this whole universe, if they had relationship. Suppose you look it up and find out more about yourself and whether or not we are related and how much we are related. *Of course* I'd acknowledge the relationship.

382

I'm afraid there is no work on the ranch just now. We have a full supply of workmen here. Furthermore, I never hire nor fire anybody on the ranch. All that I leave to my sister, Mrs. Eliza Shepard, who is ranch superintendent. All I have to do is the simple task of paying the bills.

Concerning grammar, composition, vocabulary, etc., etc., I am sending you a bit of the literature of the Editor Pub. Co. I found this of greatest advantage to me when I started in to write, a number of years ago. Of course I need not assure you that I have no money invested in this Editor Pub. Co. enterprise, and receive no remuneration nor commissions from them whatsoever; but I think you will do very well if you get in touch.

Sincerely yours,
Jack London

To Emanuel Julius[1]

Glen Ellen, Calif.
May 21, 1913

Dear Comrade Julius:—

In reply to yours of May 15, and thanking you for the copies of *The Western Comrade* which you so kindly sent me.

Now, in reply to your request that I send you a letter at once telling you that I like your story. Between you and me, how can I?

You see, I gave you a chance for a very good story. Your methods were so careless that you had to devote the major portion of your story to talk about moving pictures, to quotations from my book entitled *The Road,* erroneously ascribed by you to Bailey Millard, and to absolutely misquote, because devoid of context and place and time, quotations from my serial running in *The Saturday Evening Post* entitled *The Iron Heel.*

After looking over your story and your hotch-potch methods, and your carelessness, and your lack of knowledge of what constitutes mood and unity, I am almost compelled to believe that I am an artist. Why in hell did you bring in all this extraneous and misapplied and misquoted stuff? I gave you plenty of stuff for your article.

Another thing: just a word of advice from an old man to a young man. Get over, as quickly as you can, being provincial and insular. In the first place, a sombrero is not an abominable head-gear—except to a provincial, insular, ghetto Easterner such as you are. Second, I do not wear a sombrero. The hat you saw me wearing in Los Angeles was not a sombrero. Don't you see how utterly you lost out on all your counts? And why in hell did you want to bring in the sombrero anyway. What had that to do with me? What does the public care how you estimate a sombrero? Don't you see, my boy, hell and newspaper offices are full of men who do careless work such as you did, and who are as insular and provincial as you are. Of course, the connotation of provincialism and insularity is egotism. My boy, I'm giving you a lesson here that should be worth everything to you if you can take it to heart and head.

Either one of two things: Either you did not understand the socialism I talked to you, and the socialist situation, or else you deliberately shied from the point at issue, which I exposited to you concerning my position in the socialist movement to-day. Again, I think it was due to carelessness. You must straighten up. Don't try to do too much; but what you do do, do well.

Because I am weary with your point of view in the socialist movement, does not make me a pessimist. Don't you see that? Again yourself. This was not really an interview with Jack London; it was an exposition by Emanuel Julius of Emanuel Julius. I was in the newspaper game before you were dry behind the ears, and I made interviews of bigger men than I am, and I kept myself out of the interviews. I interviewed these men. I put these men down for what these men were. I did not put myself down. I was merely the medium. If you want to do anything big, cut yourself out of the proposition entirely. And, getting down to brass tacks, there is where the money lies. The fellow who cannot forget his ego when he is interviewing other men, who cannot forget that a sombrero that is not a sombrero is abominable to him because he does not like sombreros and does not know what sombreros are —that fellow will work for twenty-five dollars per week, and wonder why the fellow who wears the sombrero that is not a sombrero, gets five thousand dollars a week.

Just a line on your whole interview, will you notice how you stole the curtain at the end of the interview? You actually, absolutely, shamelessly stole the curtain in the last line in the published interview. I'll tell you what: Publish this letter. There's a dare and a challenge.

Sincerely yours,
Jack London

P. S. The funniest thing is, that I am not a pessimist at all. Why, I exploited to you that love is the biggest thing in the world, and held out my arms to you and to all the world in love while I was talking to you this stuff. No man who is a lover can be a pessimist. When you have grown a few years older, you will realize that a man who disagrees with your political, economic and sociological beliefs, does not necessarily have to be a pessimist—especially if he be a self-proclaimed lover.

---

[1]Emanuel Haldeman-Julius, who took the name Haldeman from his wife and is best known as the publisher of *The Little Blue Books*.

To George P. Brett
[Telegram]

Glen Ellen, Calif.
May 30, 1913

IN AUGUST BARLEYCORN LAST BOOK OTHER COMPANY PUBLISHES. DO YOU WANT TO RESUME RELATIONS ON OLD BASIS SAVE THRESHING OUT MINOR POINTS SUCH AS SECOND SERIAL RIGHTS. IF WE RESUME RELATIONS YOU MUST SEND ME CHECK FOR TWENTY FIVE HUNDRED WHICH I SHALL PAY TO OTHER COMPANY FOR HORN NOVEL. EIGHTY THOUSAND WORDS HORN COMPLETED. YOU WILL FIND FULL DATA IN PREVIOUS TELEGRAMS AND LETTERS. TELEGRAPH REPLY.[1]

(S) JACK LONDON

[1]Brett agreed and published the rest of London's books, including the posthumous ones.

To Cloud Le Dare[1]

Glen Ellen, Calif.
May 30, 1913

My dear Cloud Le Dare:—

In reply to yours of the 14th inst. Yes, but what is it all about? I do not know what you ask of me. I have read your letter twice over. I find you do not ask anything of me. I do not know what you are driving at. You challenge me, you tell me that originally my life ran parallel with yours, but that you have your doubts—namely that the Jack London of today is the shell of yesterday; that I have lost my vim and fire and youthful energy; that I am now different from you. I get all that very clearly, as a sort of challenge. I accept the challenge and read the rest of your letter and I don't find what the challenge is, namely, that once upon a time I was like you and now I am not like you. But where is the challenge? What do you want me to do. What do you want me to do for you that you cannot do for yourself? What do you want me to do for you that you cannot do for yourself that is in some way similar to what no one else did for me, and what I did for myself?

Do you get my drive? In short, what are you after? What is the meaning of this letter to me? Come through. Come across. Tell me in plain words just what you want of me and I shall do my best to fulfill what you want of me.

Most sincerely yours,
Jack London

[1]Cloud Le Dare, alias C. L. Marriott, Milford, Ohio. Le Dare was 19 years old. Later he addressed London as "Dear Humphrey Van Weyden" and signed himself "Cloud Le Dare, alias Wolf Larsen."

To Max Eastman

Glen Ellen, Calif.
May 31, 1913

Dear Max Eastman:—

Just a few lines of appreciation of your *Enjoyment of Poetry*.

It is a splendid presentation of the poet's case, especially so in view of the fact that the book is as full of common sense as it is of delicacy and distinction. In all of the book there is no nonsense, none of the absurd notions about poetry that have set most persons treating it in critique—notably Mr. Hudson Maxim. You are, moreover, fully sensitized to the poetic atmosphere, and show unerring taste in your convictions and likes (in my judgment likes and convictions being one and the same thing).

It seems to me that you reach your high-water mark on pages 116, 117 and 118. It would be hard to find elsewhere in literature a finer insight into matters that elude ordinary terms and dissections.

Again thanking you for your splendid contribution,

Sincerely yours,
Jack London

To Charles Menges[1]

Glen Ellen, Calif.
June 6, 1913

My dear Mr. Menges:—

In reply to yours of May 31. I have already had a lot of talk and correspondence with Mr. Ayres about *John Barleycorn,* and I think I have Mr. Ayres brought around to my opinion, namely, that *John Barleycorn* should not be used in moving pictures until it has made an ascertained strike as a book. Also, that it should be used as a play before it is used in moving pictures. In this connection, I had a short conversation with Mr. Horkheimer at the time I was in Los Angeles.

I agree with you that *John Barleycorn* has immense possibilities. My mail is loaded down these days with newspaper clippings from all over the United States, as well as with letters from the Y.C.T.U. [Young Christian Temperance Union] and the Prohibition Party, and as well with many requests for me to come and lecture, in the cause of prohibition. The thing is going to make a big strike, not only with the Prohibitionists, but, as you say, with the suffragists.

But in the meantime, we must keep off the matter until, first, the book shows what kind of a strike will be made, in order that we may adequately ride it in the moving pictures, and secondly, until there is a chance to exploit it on the stage as a properly acted play.

I have not as yet received the *Martin Eden* scenario.

Sincerely yours,
Jack London

¹Of the Balboa Amusement Co.

To WILLIAM T. HOYT

Glen Ellen, Calif.
June 17, 1913

Dear Friend:—

In reply to yours of June 7, 1913. My situation here in California is very unusual. I have practically no personal contacts with the people of California. Either I am away traveling over the wild places of the earth, or I am settled down here in my mountain ranch in Glen Ellen. I have no touch with the Prohibitionists, the Y.M.C.A., nor the Y.C.T.U.

I am absolutely convinced, in my own mind and practical, hard-headed judgment, that the No-Drunkard plan is the finest thing that has yet been presented, considered in the light of all circumstances, for the abolition of drinking. Also, I am quite willing to be a Vice-President from the State of California, in any organization that you now have or that you are planning to form, on the lines of the No-Drunkard proposition. On the other hand, being so peculiarly situated as regards the people of California, and having given up public speaking for over three years now, I should be unable to take an active talking-part in the organization. But in the matter of writing, I should back the organization to my full ability.

Sincerely yours,
Jack London

To MARGARET SMITH COBB

Glen Ellen, Calif.
June 21, 1913

Dear Margaret Smith Cobb:—

I am sending you a rush line, accompanied by check for $40.00 from *The Century Magazine,* by The Century Magazine's letter, and by a copy of the letter I sent to The Century Magazine along with your poem "Unkissed."

You will notice that *The Century* desires to publish my letter along with your poem. This personally am quite willing to grant, if you can see your way to granting it. I have struck out one phrase only in the letter. Any changes you wish to make in the letter, please do so and send same back to me.

Of course, I need not tell you that *The Century Magazine* is an absolutely first-class culture magazine in the United States and in the world. No higher recognition to one's poetry can be given than by magazine-publishing in *The Century*. Ranking equally with *The Century* comes *Harper's Monthly*, *Scribner's* and *The Atlantic Monthly*. These are the four top culture-magazines in the United States, and far be it from me to say that any one of the four ranks higher than any other of the four.

So, please, if you see your way to letting the letter go through, make any changes you wish to make in it, and return same to me. You will notice how nice and prompt *The Century Magazine* has been in sending the check upon acceptance of the poem. I so loved that poem that I wanted to see it get first-class publication; and now we have got it.

In a wild rush,

Sincerely yours,
Jack London

To Fred Berry[1]

Glen Ellen, Calif.
June 26, 1913

My dear friend:—

Please remember:

I average a receipt of 100 gold-mine propositions a year.

I average a receipt of at least 100 perpetual motion and other inventors' devices per year, including all sorts of disease cures.

I average, per year, at least 300 manuscripts, novels, short stories, and plays, which I am supposed to correct, and most of the writers of which desire me to rewrite said manuscripts and to sell and publish over my name, and divide up with the writers thereof.

I average at least 300 propositions a year to take care of people, furnish college educations to orphan boys, endow old ladies' homes with libraries, muck-rake the powers that be from one end of the world to the other, and contribute to every bazaar that ever was got up by a ladies' aid Society.

I have endless applications to assist struggling geniuses such as painters, sculptors, writers, musicians, composers, and singers; such as men who want to leave on my hand their mothers, wives, children, grandparents, etc., while they pursue their own favorite phantoms.

I have had men by the score who wanted to die on my ranch from tuberculosis of the lungs, of leprosy, and of cancer. I have had on my hands men by the score who wanted to send their wives here on the ranch to be confined while they shoved their muzzles into their own favorite lard-pail.

—Oh, hell! I have not time to enumerate further the flotsam and the jetsam that swamp this ranch ten-deep year in and year out and all the time.

I am sending you a Le Gallienne letter. He, too, has had some sort of experience in the game. Let it burn its way into your appreciation; and try for a moment to appreciate my situation and the penalty I pay for being decent to the tens of thousands of persons who write to me all the time. Each one pursuing his favorite phantoms. Each one with his muzzle in his particular lard-pail. All sorts of love to you and Ray,

Jack London

P.S. Of course, you realize that I must protect myself against this flood that pours upon me.

J. L.

P.S. Of course, Mrs. London types this letter. She types many thousands of my letters every year.

J. L.

[1]Berry returned London's letter, having written on it: "This letter is not for me. I should not care to have it found on me or in my possession. So am returning it. With a little more forethought in its use it may yet be made to serve its intended purpose.

"I have not sunk so low in the scale of human depravity as to acquiesce in the terms of your generalized classification. I have made a mistake. I thank you for having helped me to discover it. For all success may bring; for all the glory that may shine down upon the Gods who achieve and sit at the summit of the bone pile, if it be attainable only at the cost of one of my heart's poor possessions, I would say: take 'success' and with it go to hell. Your words of love and friendship, however, have lifted me up."

To J. J. HAWLEY

Glen Ellen, Calif.
June 26, 1913

Dear friend Hawley:

If God created a perfect man in his own image (which means precisely like God); and if man, being so perfect, had volition of right and wrong; then God, being of the same image as man, with volition of right and wrong, may do right and wrong, and, therefore, who are we that we should be greater than He in order to judge whether or not what he has done is right or wrong?

Your basic premise breaks down on the face of it. Of course man is not free to do as he will. To commence with—and one need not go further than the commencement—man is not free to will that he be born or not be born. He begins with his slavery to antecedent conditions beyond his will and prior to his own existence.

I breed too many horses, cows, pigs, sheep and goats, on my ranch here, to accept for a moment your baseless assertion that evolution is wrong and is not.

Sincerely yours,
Jack London

To Emanuel Julius

Glen Ellen, Calif.
June 28, 1913

Dear Comrade Julius:—

In reply to yours of 20th inst. Why, bless your heart, my original kick was that in your interview you did scamp work and cheated on me. You told neither the truth about my stuff nor your stuff.

I offered love (militant love, of course) to the world with arms outstretched. You turned all this into terms of pessimism, in accordance with some predisposition of yours concerning me.

To clear up one thing. By "antecedent slavery" I did not mean "slave ancestry." I meant the antecedent slavery of your own life which you placed before me in your letter as a plea.

Well, anyway, from an oldster I tried to hammer some discipline of writing into a youngster.

Now suppose we get really acquainted. Any time that you have the time and want a vacation, come up and visit us. Circular inclosed will tell you all about how to get here and about our ranch and how to get here. Remember this, that if you want to work, here is a good place.

Your Bob Wagner interview is all right. You did carry out, from start to finish, the note you struck at the start.

Well, come up and let us talk and fight for a while.

Yours for the Revolution,
Jack London

To John S. Phillips

Glen Ellen, Calif.
June 30, 1913

Dear Mr. Phillips:—

In reply to yours of 23d inst. I, too, am surprised.

As I understand the situation, the first serial rights precede book publication; second-serial rights succeed book publication; and you bought first serial rights on a basis of publishing serially inside of six months. Because my book publishing plans happened to change, as I see it, does not alter the situation. You know what it is to have unavoidable things arise to change certain of your plans.

I have never been able to understand you. You, when I was an unknown, having never published a book and having no name whatever as a writer— you paid me in advance $200 on a socialist essay of mine entitled "The Question of the Maximum." Afterwards, you got cold feet; you delayed the publication of it. You never did publish it. You killed the thing, and year by year you used to charge that $200 against my account with you and S. S. McClure,[1] and then, you always gave in when I repeated the situation as it was to you.

As I say, I have never understood you. Our very correspondence in this matter of "Samuel" convinced me all over again that I never understood you. When other top writers were getting $1000 a short story, and I was ranked as a top writer, you considered my "Samuel," said it was one of the best stories I had ever written, and gave me a paltry sum for it. Please remember that I accepted this paltry sum on a six-months' basis. By my own lights, I do not understand you; and by the lights of ordinary business, I do not understand you.

When you accept a limit of six months for serial publication, I understand that you accept a limit for six months' serial publication. Should I, afterward, face a change of plan that compels me to eat that manuscript and chew it up and swallow it page by page, still I cannot see how it affects your six-months' limit accepted by you and paid for by you accordingly, at a cheap rate.

Should the thing be horses, or gold mines, or any other article of commerce, see what six months means. A manuscript is a similar article of commerce.

Of one thing I am certain: I do not surprise you any more than you surprise me.

Very truly yours,
Jack London

P.S. I do earnestly desire of you to go through our correspondence covering the manuscript "Samuel" from start to finish.

[1]Phillips, of *The American Magazine*, was with S. S. McClure at that time.

To Eliza Shepard

Oakland, Calif.
July 16, 1913

Dearest Eliza:

You should shortly receive a check for $2500.00, from The Macmillan Co.—it will come, of course, in my mail. You indorse said check and deposit it in your Santa Rosa account. The chances are that I shall have to mail this same sum of money to The Century Co., inside several days; in the meantime I am dickering with The Century Co. trying to get them to charge the $2500 I owe them against *John Barleycorn*.

If, within five days, you do not receive a check for $2000.00 from *The Cosmopolitan,* send a telegram to Roland Phillips, Cosmopolitan Magazine, 381 Fourth Ave., New York City, as follows:

"HAVE NOT RECEIVED JULY TWO THOUSAND I NEED IT QUICKLY."

(S) "Jack London."

I have an entirely new deal on with the moving pictures, and the chances are that I shall run down to Los Angeles for several days before I return to the ranch. I leave hospital to-morrow, Wednesday, and shall most likely start for Los Angeles Saturday night or Sunday night. In case Charmian's judgment or mine is needed for anything about the house-building, the next several days would be the time to catch us on the matter.

Be sure that Forni starts a couple of men at the block-making, etc. The overseeing of that block-making must be part of Forni's job.

I never got around to a conclusion with you concerning feeding the pigs in pasture. By all means see that they are fed.

From now on is the time to have every work horse working, and every colt being fed in addition to pasturage.

Tell Summers he's got to get Hillside trained to driving, and that later on Hillside will have to do his exercise harnessed up to some gelding, and pulling a farm wagon or something.

Don't you think it is about time to stop the Hillside service advertisement in the local papers? The season must be over now.

In hauling the stones that are to make the stone wall alongside the orchard, on the driveway—be sure that the men haul only large stones. There are plenty of large stones with which to make a beautiful stone wall. If they haul small stones they will make a measly stone wall. Also, the small stones can be used where they lie, for top dressing for the road. They're the ones that are easiest to run through the rock crusher.

Keep me fully informed of what is going on at the ranch.

I have hope of getting some money fairly soon out of this new moving picture deal.

With lots of love
Jack London

To George P. Brett

Glen Ellen, Calif.
July 29, 1913

Dear Mr. Brett:—

Here I am, back on the ranch. Three weeks ago to-day I was operated upon, for appendicitis. To show how good was my condition, let me make my little brag. Six days after the operation, the stitches were drawn. Seven days after the operation, I walked. On the eighth day I left the hospital and went home to my house in Oakland. On the eleventh day I went to Los Angeles where I spent a hard week of business concerning putting my stuff into moving pictures. And now I am here back on the ranch. In a couple of days I start for the Midsummer Jinks of the Bohemian Club, where I shall stay a week. Then I shall come home and take up my writing again.

Had it not been for my appendicitis, I should have finished the Horn novel ere this. As it is, I shall not have the Horn novel completed until about the end of August or a few days before. Whereupon, I shall immediately start the writing of another novel.

What this novel is to be, I have not yet decided. I have half a dozen good ones already worked out, and am withholding my choice until I am ready to begin.

What I am now writing to you for, is to see if I can get an advance of $2500.00 on my next novel, which I shall begin at the end of August. I should like to have this advance soon.

If the moving picture proposition turns out at least one fifth as good as present expectations, I shall not have to bother you for advances during the next several years. Ready money has been raised in these tight times to start the project. The first picture to be made will be *The Sea Wolf*[1] on which they are starting now, and on which at least $6000.00 will be spent in the production. This does not mean that the $6000.00 is to be spent for cameras, machinery, studios, etc., but is to be spent directly on the production of the *Sea Wolf,* such as for actors, properties, etc. I have put no money into the adventure; I receive 50% of the net earnings, and I am in every way exempt from Liability. *The Sea Wolf* is to be produced in five (5) films of 1000 feet each, and the calculations of my share of the earnings are hair-raising, such share being estimated anywhere between $10,000 and $50,000. Also, it is calculated that this money should begin to come in on me by October.

And by October, or the middle or end of October, I hope to be moved over into the new house. Said house goes on apace, and I am well proud of it; but my! it does cost money. But when it is done, I shall be really comfortable for the first time in my life. And I have been pretty patient with the building of that house—not rushing matters in the slightest. Nine years ago I bought the land and picked the house site; so I surely have not shown any undue haste in the matter of housebuilding.

Sincerely yours,
Jack London

---

[1]First filmed by Bosworth Co., with Hobart Bosworth as Wolf Larsen.

To Joan London

Glen Ellen, Calif.
Aug. 24, 1913

Dear Joan:—

I feel too miserable to write this at my desk. I am sitting up in bed to write it.

First, please remember that I am your father. I have fed you, clothed you, and housed you, and *loved* you since the moment you first drew breath. I have all of a father's heart of love for you.

And now we come to brass tacks. What have you done for me in all the days of your life? What do you *feel* for me? Am I merely your meal-ticket? Do you look upon me as merely a creature with a *whim,* or *fancy,* or *fantasy,* that compels him to care for you and to take care of you?—because he is a fool who gives much and receives . . . well, receives nothing?

Please answer the foregoing questions. I want to know how I stand with you.

You have your dreams of education. I try to give you the best of my wisdom. You write me about the demands of the U.C. in relation to selection of high school courses. I reply by (1) telegram, (2) by letter. And I receive no word from you. Am I dirt under your feet? Am I beneath your contempt in every way save as a meal-ticket? Do you love me at all? What do I *mean* to you?

Answer above queries of mine.

My home, as yet unoccupied, burns down—and I receive no word from you. When you were sick I came to see you. I gave you flowers and canary birds.

Now I am sick—and you are silent. My home—one of my dreams—is destroyed. You have no word to say.

Your education is mixed up by conflict between high school and university. You write me. I reply by telegram and letter. I spring to help you with my wisdom in your trouble, in the realization of your dream.

I say, very sadly, that when my dream is ruined, I do not notice that you spring to me.

Joan, my daughter, please know that the world belongs to the honest ones, to the true ones, to the right ones, to the ones who talk right out; and that the world does not belong to the ones who remain silent, who, by their very silence lie and cheat and make a mock of love and a meal-ticket of their father.

Don't you think it is about time I heard from you? Or do you want me to cease forever from caring to hear from you?

Daddy

To Mr. Nakahara[1]

Glen Ellen, Calif.
Aug. 25, 1913

Dear Sir:—

In reply to yours of August 16, 1913. First of all, I should say, by stopping the stupid newspaper from fomenting race prejudice.

This, of course, being impossible, I would say, next, by educating the people of the United States and the people of Japan so that they will be too intelligently tolerant to respond to any call to race prejudice.

And finally, by [the] realizing, in industry and government, of socialism— which last word is merely a word that stands for the actual application in the affairs of men of the theory of the Brotherhood of Man.

In the meantime the nations and races are only unruly boys who have not yet grown to the stature of men. So we must expect them to do unruly and boisterous things at times. And, just as boys grow up, so the races of mankind will grow up and laugh when they look back upon their childish quarrels.

Sincerely yours,
Jack London

[1]On a letterhead *"Japanese-American Commercial Weekly,* established 1900, only Japanese journal published both in Japanese and English in the United States," Nakahara wrote:

"August 16, Mr. Jack London, Dear Sir: We cannot hand down to our future generation a mutilated romantic relation between Japan and the United States. What should be the best attitude for the people of the two nations, irrespective of the California instance, in order to perpetuate the existing friendship? In behalf of peace and prosperity of the two countries, the *Japanese-American Commercial Weekly* requests you to give us your idea. Your response will be appreciated and treasured in our highest consideration."

To Joan London

Glen Ellen, Calif.
Aug. 29, 1913

Dearest Joan:

Of course, read all your letters from me, to your mother.

This is to reply to yours of Aug. 25, 1913.

No; I neither "see" nor "understand." If you came to see me at Glen Ellen here, you would see me, all the world, and my wife.

When you ask me if I cannot see, if I cannot understand, I answer you that I cannot see, cannot understand what you think you see, and what you think you understand.

Now is the time for us to get right up in meeting on our hind legs and testify to what we see and understand.

WHAT DO YOU SEE AND UNDERSTAND? Now is the time. Tell me. Let me glimpse the face of truth as you glimpse it. Tell me what the face of truth looks like. If you don't tell me, then do you refuse to share truth with me. Then are you not true to me.

And can you or I travel very far together in this world when you refuse to seek anything less than perfect understanding with me?—anything less than full truth shared between us?

Remember that truth is the greatest thing in the world. If you will be great, you will be true. If you suppress truth, if you hide truth, if you do not rise up and speak out in meeting, if you speak out in meeting without speaking the *whole* truth, then are you less true than truth and by that much are you less than great.

Now just what is it that *you* see, and *you* understand, which prevents you from coming to see me on my ranch? Don't be afraid of being harsh. Don't be afraid of being true. What is it you see and understand (which I in truth can neither see nor understand) that prevents you from coming to my ranch?

In all love,
Daddy

To Joan London

Glen Ellen, Calif.
Sept. 5, 1913

But my dear Daughter Joan:—

Truth is no respecter of age, nor of youth, nor of twelve years old.

When Twelve-Years-Old says to her Daddy: "Don't you understand?" then Twelve-Years-Old has in the truth of her heart something true that she expects her Daddy ought to know.

Well, I am your Daddy. I want to know. What is it that you *know,* that you *think* I ought to know, that I *want* to know? Tell me.

Age nor Youth has nothing to do with the matter. Truth is the matter. Now *what* is your truth?

Remember, anything less than the utter truth is a lie and a cheat by you to yourself.

When Twelve-Years-Old suggests a truth to her Daddy, her Daddy wants to know that truth. Twelve-Years-Old, having hit Daddy over the head, as with a club, with what she "understands" as truth, cannot, when her Daddy asks what was the club, reply that "she is only twelve years old and that if he will wait six or eight years she will tell him what the club was that she hit him with."

Don't you see, my dearest daughter Joan, that you cannot play tricks with Truth. Any trick with Truth is a lie and a cheat.

Truth says, if you are to deal fairly with her, that you must in your dealings be as pure as the high heavens, as honest as the bite of frost, as straight as the edge of the sharpest-bladed sword.

Truth says that you cannot hide in a dark alley, hit your Daddy over the head with a brick, and then yell out that you are "only twelve years old."

As soon as you are old enough to use Truth, then are you old enough to be *truthful*. You used truth on me as an insinuation. I ask you what is the truth you insinuated. You reply by squealing that you are only twelve years old.

Dearest daughter Joan, let me tell you that Truth never squeals.

Also, dearest daughter Joan, it is scarcely brave to invoke Truth, and then squeal with fright at what you have invoked.

So thoroughly did you understand something, and so convinced were you that I understood, that you wrote me: "Don't you understand, Daddy?"

Now whatever this thing is, it is clear in your mind. It is *not clear* in my mind. I want to understand. WHAT IS IT?

Oh, Joan, it is so remarkably easy just to tell the truth in this world, that I often marvel that there are so many persons who are so madly foolish, so wretchedly stupid, that they hide truth.

Truth is not merely the *best* policy. It is the ONLY policy.

Now what is it that you took for granted I understood, and which I tell you I don't understand?

Would you prefer to talk it to me? If so, I will come and see you so that you may talk it to me.

Daddy

P.S. Please don't forget that hell, East Oakland, Piedmont, and Mountain View are full of persons who were afraid of truth and who ran away from truth. Also, note that the persons who still live and who have run away from truth are merely the unburied dead who clutter the fair earth with their presence.

Daddy

To FREDERICK H. ROBINSON[1]

Glen Ellen, Calif.
Sept. 5, 1913

Dear sir:—

In reply to yours of August 5, 1913. I am just convalescing from a hospital operation, have had my house burned down, and am hence somewhat delayed in my correspondence. Also, I must be brief.

In reply to your question: "Should criminals and defectives be sterilized?" I believe that it is much wiser to alter an individual before puberty than it is to execute him by hanging or electrocution, or to execute by hanging or electrocution the seed of his loins, because said seed has inherited the criminal and social destructiveness of said loins. I believe that the future human world belongs to eugenics, and will be determined by the practice of eugenics.

At the present moment I am operating a stock farm. If one of my registered Jersey heifers gets through a hole in the fence to an ornery scrub grade bull, I am shocked. I know that the result of said breeding will be bad and not good; will be worse rather than better. This stolid, practical-headed judgment of a stock breeder should apply with equal force to the breeding of humans. Humans breed in ways quite similar to those of animals; and if humans misbreed, the results are misbreds.

Sincerely yours,
Jack London

[1] On the staff of *Medical Review of Reviews*.

To L. Frank Tooker[1]

Glen Ellen, Calif.
Sept. 12, 1913

Dear sir:—

In reply to yours of Sept. 6, 1913. Please find herewith the manuscript of Margaret Smith Cobb's "Unkissed."

Margaret Smith Cobb is now away from home, up somewhere in the back woods of the mountains, and I know it would take a long time to get a letter to her and back again. Whatever must be done, must be decided by you and me. I shall say my say, and then leave the final decision to you.

Although I may be very wrong, I feel firmly convinced that "O" is the proper invocation with which to begin the first line, and that "oh" is not the proper way to begin the invocation. You would not say "Oh God, from Whom all blessings flow"—now, would you? This poem begins as a similar invocation, and, as I say, should begin with "O."

In the first line of the third stanza, "spring" is used in the plural because it particularizes a unit of measure of time. However, in the last line of this third stanza, "spring" is used generically, and should be used in the singular. If you pluralize "spring" in the last line of the third stanza, I shall always believe you made the mistake of your life.

The change you made in the second line of the fourth stanza of "a phantom flame," is a most splendid change. I am with you in this heartily.

And now, to the end of the last stanza, which is the important thing at issue: I would not put a comma after "her eyes," at the end of the third line of the last stanza. To me, the thing reads: ". . . her eyes

Mated the slim hands and the bosom's rise," and in that use of "mated" I see nothing but high poetry, and fail to see any obscurity whatsoever. Please refer back to "slim hands" and "hidden bosom" in the third stanza, and see how "slim hands" and "hidden bosom" are now "mated" by "eyes." However, yours will be the last say in the matter, and whatever you say will go. Nevertheless, please think carefully over the last stanza.

Sincerely yours,
Jack London

[1]Of *Century Magazine.*

To Hobart Bosworth

Glen Ellen, Calif.
Sept. 24, 1913

Dear Mr. Bosworth:—

In reply to yours of Sept. 19, 1913. I have just got back from the State Fair and have just replied to Mr. Garbutt's[1] letter, and have just sent back to Mr. Barker[2] the affidavit, with additional information.

Please be sure to give me warning, as far ahead as you can, of when you expect to be in San Francisco with *The Sea Wolf* film. Mrs. London and I expect to remain on the ranch for at least two weeks longer, at which time we sail for a couple of months' cruise on the bay and up the rivers. We take the two Japanese boys along, the typewriter, and my outfit, so that I do my thousand words every day. It will take anywhere from three or four days to a week on occasion to catch me by telegram, when I get into the tules of the Sacramento and San Joaquin delta.

I get into San Francisco on an average of once a year, at which time I go to the Bohemian Club, and, not being a good rememberer, each time I have to look up the Bohemian Club address in the directory or telephone book— and then ask a policeman what car I must take to get to the Bohemian Club. Therefore, I am not personally in touch, as you will understand, with the newspapermen in San Francisco. Also, in all the years I have been in the writing game, I have observed a rigid policy of never asking a favor of the newspapermen of San Francisco. I should hate to break that policy now. So it will be up to you to assemble the newspaper clan for the exhibition of *The Sea Wolf* films.

I'm glad to hear you are tackling *Martin Eden* next.

The changes you indicate in the *Tales of the Fish Patrol* are entirely acceptable to me. You know I leave all such things up to your own good judgment, although I do like to have you refer them to me in advance. You will find me most easy to get along with in this matter. If I can see you personally when you come up with the films, I can give you quite a bit of information as to what places to go and where to go for the *Fish Patrol* series, and for the *Martin Eden* films.

Please forgive the rush. I took over a week off at the State Fair, and neglected mail, and now I must pay for it.

Sincerely yours,

Jack London

[1]Frank Garbutt, associated with Bosworth in the Bosworth Film Co.
[2]Donald Barker of the Flint, Grey and Barker law firm in Los Angeles, lawyers for Bosworth, London, *et al.*, in the case against the Balboa Amusement Co.

To Jess Dorman

Glen Ellen, Calif.
Sept. 28, 1913

Dear friend Jess Dorman:—

In reply to yours of Sept. 25, 1913. Assuming, to quote you, that you "have in mind an original virile story," that you are "capable of writing it," I should say, if you wrote it, at the rate of 1000 words a day, and sold it as an unknown at an unknown's price (which would be at least 2¢ for such a virile, original, well-written story), I leave the arithmetic to you.

If you are earning more than $20 a day, then leave it alone; if you are earning less than $20 a day, write the story.

Please know that I am answering your letter according to the very rigid stipulations that you laid down to me. Since, as you say, you know my career, you must know that I worked many a long month nineteen hours a day, without sleep, and sold a great deal of my stuff at 75¢ per 1000 words for stories that were not original, that were not virile, that were not well-written.

I plugged. Can you plug this way for 19 hours a day?

You say you cannot so plug. If you say truth, well, far be it from me to advise you to tackle such a game.

If you think you can jump in right now, without any apprenticeship, and lay bricks as well as a four, five, or six years' apprenticed bricklayer; if you think you can jump in on the floor and nail on shoes on ten horses as well as a man who has served a three, four, or five years' apprenticeship at shoeing horses on the floor; if you think you can jump in and nail laths, or spread plaster, or do concrete work, without previous experience, better or as well as the men who have served their three, four, and five years of apprenticeship;—in short, if you think that a vastly better-paid trade than that, namely, the writing-game, can be achieved in your first short story not yet written, or long story not yet written, why go ahead my boy and jump to it, and I'll pat you on the back—pat you on the back! the world will crush you in for the great genius that you are if you can do such a thing. In the meantime have a little patience and learn the trade.

If you know my career, you know that I am a brass-tack man. And I have given you brass tacks right here. If you can beat all the rest of us, without serving your apprenticeship, go to it. Far be it from us to advise you.

Sincerely yours,
Jack London

To T. A. BOSTICK[1]

Glen Ellen, Calif.
Sept. 28, 1913

My dear Mr. Bostick:—

In reply to yours of Sept. 6, 1913. The only trouble, I may say, about *John Barleycorn,* is that I did not put in the whole truth. All that is in it is true; but I did not dare put in the whole truth.

Johnny Heinold still runs the Last Chance[2] on Webster Street, down near the old City Wharf. I was in to see him just the other day. When *John Barleycorn* was appearing serially in *The Saturday Evening Post,* Johnny Heinold wrote to me about it.

Fat and jovial Jessie Harper died about two months ago. She was mentioned in *Barleycorn* by me; and when she died, the papers called her my bosom friend, etc., etc.

Well, at any rate, I assure you that everything in *John Barleycorn* is true; wherefore send along the game birds.

Sincerely yours,
Jack London

[1]A breeder of game birds.
[2]The Last Chance is still (1965) operating on Webster Street.

To H. C. TUCK[1]

Glen Ellen, Calif.
Sept. 29, 1913

Dear Comrade Tuck:—

I think you will remember having known me for about twenty years in the movement. If you do so remember me, I leave it to you if H. H. Caldwell's review of *John Barleycorn* in *The World* of Sept. 6, 1913, isn't something stinking and rotten.

Was this slipped over on you? Or were you privy to printing it in the second column of the editorial page of *The World* of above mentioned date?

Please let me know. I want to know how we stand, and how the Socialist movement stands to-day.

First, have you read *John Barleycorn?* Next, will you, as a favor to me, re-read Caldwell's review before you write to me?

Yours for the revolution,

Jack London

¹State Secretary of the Socialist Party of California and Editor of *The World*, a Socialist magazine.

To EDWARD R. FOREMAN

Glen Ellen, Calif.

Oct. 2, 1913

Dear friend Foreman:

In reply to yours of Sept. 23, 1913. First of all, the worst of all—I am going to quote your last paragraph, merely changing one word: "I notice also in your letter that you refer to yourself as an anthropophagist. This is nonsense. If you will put that perfectly good head of yours at work thinking over this assertion, you will agree with me that this statement is only one of pose. You know very well you are essentially a non-anthropophagist, and you ought to fight any heathen who asserts the contrary."

Now, just for fun, let us substitute some other word for the one word I substituted. Suppose we substitute murderer, forger, liar, thief. Suppose we substitute altruist, philanthropist, good man, and man of God. Read your last paragraph over with these substitutions as indicated by me.

All I can get from this paragraph of yours, is, no matter what the one essential word may be, that if I put my good head to work I shall reach a conclusion similar to the conclusion reached by your good head.

Really and truly, won't you laugh with me—over your last paragraph?

Now the worst being over first, in which I think that if you will exercise your ordinary good, practical, common-sense head for a moment, you will see it is on you—let me thank you for your good words concerning *John Barleycorn.*

Your statement that the President of the Y.M.C.A. of Rochester is a brother elder of the Third Church with you, and a good fellow, and therefore that you hate to knife him, reminds me of another change I might suggest, namely: Christ's saying that it was so easy to die on the Cross, that He declined to die on the Cross.

Sincerely yours,

Jack London

To George P. Brett

Glen Ellen, Calif.
Oct. 7, 1913

Dear Mr. Brett:—

From inclosed copy of letter just received from Mr. Donald Barker, who is my lawyer in Los Angeles, it seems that the time has come for all authors, magazine publishers, and book publishers, to get together and make a fight for themselves. I am now being attacked by a pirate raid which I shall now describe:

Some time back, I entered into a contract with one, Horkheimer of the Balboa Amusement Producing Company, for the purpose of having produced in moving-pictures my various novels and short stories. Said Horkheimer forfeited the contract by direct and explicit violation of the time-clauses. The contract having become forfeited, I made a new contract with Bosworth Company. Said Bosworth Company immediately began to produce my work in moving-pictures.

Horkheimer, however, continued work on my stuff in moving-pictures. We, that is, Bosworth Co. and myself, to prevent Horkheimer from carrying the films East and marketing them, brought a complaint in the United States District Court in the Southern District of California for an injunction and damages and infringement of copyright. When we brought this complaint, our expectation was that Horkheimer would maintain that the contract had not been forfeited. Instead, he sprang the surprise of a pirate raid on us, with Mr. Ligon Johnson, brought especially from the East, to prove that we had no standing in court because we possessed no copyright—in short, because I possessed no copyright in all the stories and novels I have written and published in magazines and in book form in the United States.

The legal intent of this raid is to prove:

(1) That magazine copyright does not copyright contents of magazines, and that the instant anything is published in a copyrighted magazine, said thing becomes public property.

(2) That no book publisher has a copyright to such books the contents of which he has copyrighted, when such contents were previously serially published in a copyrighted magazine.

(3) That no author whose works have been serially published in copyrighted magazines, has any copyright whatsoever in this work.—This means that he has no right in his books, in second-serial publication, in foreign translation, in dramatic and moving-picture reproductions. It seems that this raid upon copyright, that concerns all publishers, magazine publishers and writers, has centered upon me, and is taking place in the remote town of Los Angeles, California. If I am beaten in this attack, all the rest of the writers, magazine publishers and book publishers will have this judicial precedent against them. The instant this precedent is established, all

book publishers, magazine publishers, and writers may look to see themselves raided by pirates of their property.

My idea is that the only feasible thing for all of us to do is to get together on this, the first big fight, and fight it out to a finish. I am sending copies of this letter to Mr. Arthur P. Train, General Counsel for the Authors League of America, and to Mr. George H. Lorimer [*Saturday Evening Post*]. It seems a case for the authors of America, for the periodical publishers of America, and for the book publishers of America, to join in. This is the beginning of a contest that affects all our rights and properties. What I would suggest is, that we get together in the campaign, share the expenses of the campaign, and fight the fight to a finish wherever the pirates raise their heads in the United States.

My lawyer is Mr. Donald Barker, of Flint, Gary & Barker, Suite 1027, Title Insurance Building, Los Angeles, California.

I should like to have The Authors League of America, the periodical publishers and the book publishers, join in with me in this fight.

If, after due conference with your colleagues and comrades, you decide to join in this fight, I should like to have you write replies to me, and also to deal directly with Mr. Donald Barker, and to send to him whatever Eastern special copyright expert attorneys you may see fit to employ.

It seems to me that the present situation is as big as the whole writing and publishing game in the United States. Prompt action is needed, and prompt assurance that you are joining in for the big fight.

Sincerely yours,
Jack London

To Editor, *Century Magazine*

Glen Ellen, Calif.
Oct. 10, 1913

Dear sir:—

At the present time I am undergoing a pirate raid on the part of men who have not given one bit of their brain to create what I have written, one cent of their money to help me write what I have written, nor one moment of their time to aid me to write what I have written. This is a straight, brazen, shameless pirate raid that is being made upon me. My back is up against the wall, and I am fighting hard, and I am calling upon you to help me out.

In the past you have bought work of mine and published it in your magazine. You will know the method of copyrighting you pursued at the time, without my going into the details of this here.

I am asking you now, to assign to me and to send to me the document in which you so assign, any and all rights, with the exceptions of first-serial rights in the United States and Canada, and first-serial rights in Great

Britain and Great Britain's colonies, in all stories, articles, essays, novels and plays written by me and purchased and published and copyrighted by you between the years and months of years beginning January 1, 1898, and ending October 12, 1913, inclusive.

The portion of the period above inclosed in dates, practically covers the days previous to the appearance in the publishing game of second-serial rights, during which time you were publishing my work.

The basis of this request which I am making you in this letter, is that when you copyrighted the various numbers of your publication, you did copyright all rights in the contents thereof, and that you did hold in trust for me all other rights except those first-serial rights already described in the foregoing part of this letter.

If you would kindly have a clerk run through your index for the data, and in the assignment you send to me, specify by title and date of publication, it would be of immense assistance to me in this my hour of rush, in which I am writing some eighty-odd periodicals which have published my work serially since I entered the writing game. Also, I beg of you, because of this necessity for haste on my part, that you will forgive the manner and method of this request I am preferring of you.

If you can see your way to it, please help me out by sending me this assignment at your very earliest possible convenience.[1]

Sincerely yours,

Jack London

[1]London sent copies of this letter to all his major publishers in the United States and a similar letter to his English agent, Hughes Massie.

To Joan London

Glen Ellen, Calif.

Oct. 11, 1913

Dear Joan:

I am in a great hurry. Find enclosed check for $4.00 to pay Whitaker boy for the work he did on the back-yard. The $80.00 for the front steps, and the $185 for the back-yard is too extortionate to be considered by me if I did have the money, and at the present time I haven't any such sum of money. I have inclosed your letter describing the front and back yards to Uncle Ernest [Matthews], and asked him to go and take a look at what is needed. I have told him I haven't the money for the back-yard improvement, and have told him I have no such sum as $80 for the front steps. Also, I have told Uncle Ernest to show the letter I have written him to your mother, so she may know it is all right for him to go ahead and do his best with the least amount of money I can spare at the present time for the front steps alone.

The estimate for the awning comes to $11.50. Do I understand this means canvas alone? Please give me details. What does this $11.50 pay for? Does it pay for the mere canvas, or does it pay for the canvas, for the wood, for the nails, for the rope, pulleys, etc., etc. Also, you failed to tell me what your friend Mr. Thoms will do the work for. How do I know what his work will amount to? Please give me full details about the total cost of this canvas, and of the labor involved in putting the canvas in place, and about what sort of guaranty this Mr. Thoms will give that the thing will work after he put it up. Give me this clearly and immediately, so I may be able to tell you to go ahead and work on it.

In your excitement, you forgot, or did not hear me tell you, that I had sent the order for $3 for renewal of *St. Nicholas* directly to The Century Co. That was done before I came out to Piedmont and saw you.

And now to other things. Please know that silence on your part and a sore hand on your mother's part, means satisfaction on your part and your mother's part with your mother's present policy and attitude concerning the matter I talked over with you on Sunday evening.

And please, please remember what I told you on Sunday evening, concerning the fact that the less I see of you and Bess, the less I would be bound to be interested in you. Just as a token of this state of mind, which is common to all human beings, namely, to be interested in the things one sees and is in some sort of contact with, let me tell you an incident that happened last night: I was thinking this matter over at the table. Nakata, my Japanese boy, was waiting on the table; and the thought so suddenly came to me, and came to me with such strength that I immediately said to Nakata: "Nakata, you know that I have two daughters. When I knew these daughters they were little babies and did not count. I know scarcely anything about them since. Nakata, for six or seven years you have been with me night and day. You have been with me through every danger over the whole world. Storm and violent death have been common in your and my experience. I remember the times in storms when you have stood nobly by. I remember the time when the cannibals assailed us 1500 strong, when you stood on the wreck of our vessel, dashing to pieces on the reef, a rifle in either hand ready to pass me whenever I wanted to use it. I remember the hours of sickness when you nursed me. I remember the hours of fun when you laughed with me and I laughed with you. I remember so many, many of these hours of all sorts, of contact with you, that I know that I know you ten thousand times better than I know my two daughters."

Now, Joan. Remember that the world is populated by big people and by little people. Almost the entire population of the world consists of little people. Here and there are a few of the big people. It is a hard proposition to put up to you at your age, and the chances are that in deciding on this proposition that I put up to you Sunday night, you will make the mistake of deciding to be a little person in a little place in a little part of the world. You will make this mistake because you listened to your mother, who is a little person in a little place in a little part of the world, and who, out of her female sex jealousy against another woman, has sacrificed your future for you. If you join with your mother in this little sex jealousy of a thwarted female, you will doom yourself to grow up in the little environment of the little place called Piedmont, which is populated by little people. On the other hand, I offer you the big things of the world; the big things that big people live and know and think and act. You are now a little woman. You will grow into a mature woman. In the next four or five years your entire future life, so far as your development be concerned, will be determined. The chances are, since you know more about Jim Whitaker, or Jim Whitaker's boys, or your mother, or Uncle Ernest, or Aunt Florrie, or all the other persons about you, than you do know about me, your Daddy—the chances are that you will decide to follow your mother's policy which, as I have already told you, is based upon sex jealousy of a thwarted female. The result will be that when you are a mature woman of eighteen or twenty, you will be merely the little person in the little place in a little portion of the world.

This will be too bad for you, for at about that time you will begin to read with understanding all the books I have written, and you will come to realize the smallness of yourself and of your place. Unfortunately, it will then be too late. You will not then be able to change yourself, you will have been already developed. The developing time is now. From now until you are eighteen years of age. Having developed, you cannot change yourself any more than the leper [sic] can change its spots. You will know your tragedy, you will know what you missed, but you will be unable to remedy it, and so shall I be unable to remedy it for you. And this also will be my tragedy: The thing will have happened to you. You will be as small as the persons around you are small, and it will then be too late for me to lend you a helping hand, because you will have already been fully developed. Also, what will you mean to me when you are eighteen or twenty years old, developed in such an environment? I will know, as a matter of fact, that you are my daughter. But I shall also know that you are a strange sort of a little wizened, pinched, human female creature of eighteen or twenty years, and that it is too late to change you into anything bigger.

Well, anyway, I gave you on last Sunday night several problems. I referred you to the *New Testament* and the study of Christ. Christ was a big man. He was not a little person in a little place in a little portion of the world. If you do not study out these problems, or if in studying out these simple problems I gave you, you come to the wrong conclusion and elect for yourself to become a little person in a little place in a little portion of the world, it will be a great misfortune for which there will be no help. Although it will not avail you any to do so, you will then be able to charge this malformation of you in your development period, this wizening and pinching of you into the little person—you may be able to charge this directly to your mother's conduct in influencing your conduct, because your mother is so small, so primitive, so savage, that she cherishes a sex hatred for a woman who was bigger than she to such an extent that her face is distorted with passion while she talks about it, as it was distorted last Sunday night.

Now, Joan, remember the silence so far has been on your part. If this silence continues, I shall not break it. Any time you want to break it, I shall be here or somewhere in the world. In the meantime, carry my warnings and my problems closely to your heart and head.

Affectionately yours,

Daddy

To George P. Brett

Glen Ellen, Calif.
Oct. 17, 1913

Dear Mr. Brett:—

In reply to yours of October 6, 1913. It seems to me that a document quite similar to the Supplementary Agreement dated January 9, 1911, and signed January 9, 1911, by The Macmillan Co., will cover what I desire from you —with, in addition, the changes suggested by me in the last paragraph of letter to you dated September 30, 1913.

I am just trying to escape away for a cruise on the bay and up the river, which has been delayed for all of a year now. The Supplementary Agreement, dated Jan. 9, 1911, is in my lawyer's hands, Mr. Barker, in Los Angeles, and I have no copy of it here. You have a copy of it in your office, and said copy should cover the whole matter with the exception I have stated in the last paragraph of my letter of Sept. 30.

In reply to your letter of October 9, 1913. First of all, was a notice of The Century copyright, which antedated the Jack London Copyright, printed in the advance paper-edition you copyrighted in my name?

I can only impress upon you the seriousness of this case. I am meeting the brunt of the attack alone. If I go down, look out for a general raid.

I am writing by this mail to Arthur C. Train, of The Authors League of America, advising him to get in touch with you. He has charge of our fight now, in the Eastern part of the United States. His address is 30, Broad Street, New York City.

Who is this Ligon Johnson? He has got himself in very bad company, and is already voluntarily, half-apologetically explaining that it is the first time he has been engaged in such a raid. The raid is so brazen and shameless that some account of Ligon Johnson's conduct should go out in some way to the publishers of the United States. He is attacking them in all truth—I merely happen to be caught in the brunt of his attack, which is really through me on all the book-publishers. Once Johnson establishes his thesis (that magazines own only first-serial rights; that magazines can copyright only what they own; that, therefore, all other rights including book-rights are in the public domain), then all publishers watch out for pirate raids. This point has never been brought up to the Supreme Court of the United States. It is a case where book-publishers and writers must join together and help me in this fight to carry the case up to a final decision before the Supreme Court of the United States. The Authors League, I am sure, representing the writers of America, will join with the book-publishers in such a fight, and such a co-operation is needed at the present time.

Returning to this man Ligon Johnson: Such has been his contamination from the bad company with which he is joined, that already he has descended to the level of blackmail. In the course of our local fight in Los Angeles— my Company having worked weeks in advance of the pirates, and before the pirates began, in the production of *The Sea Wolf* film, was preparing to give the first private exhibition of the finished film. The pirates, esteeming that this would be a technical advantage in our favor, tried to prevent our giving this private exhibition in the Los Angeles Athletic Club. Their method of attempting to prevent such private exhibition was put through by Ligon Johnson. He informed my lawyer that if we did not call off the exhibition, which was for that very evening, he would telegraph East and spread broadcast the information that all my copyrights were invalid, and that this would precipitate a general pirate raid upon everything I possessed. Of course, it did not take my lawyer and my business partners half a minute to tell Ligon Johnson to go to hell with his blackmailing proposition.

I can only repeat that this man Ligon Johnson has fallen into bad company and is behaving very badly, and that in some way his conduct should be made known to the book-publishers and the authors of the United States.

Sincerely yours,
Jack London

To Ernest Matthews[1]

Aboard the *Roamer*
Sunday, Nov. 20, 1913

Dear Ernest:

We're on board the *Roamer* off West Island, which is near Antioch, on the San Joaquin River. It is 6 P.M. and we're lying under the trees, under the weather shore, with three lines fast to the trees. You know how it blew to-day. Alarm went off at 6:30 this morning. *Roamer* slowly dragging anchor on a lee shore.

Nakata and I put one reef in spanker and *three* reefs in mainsail, while Sano cooked breakfast.

Still dragging while we ate breakfast, waiting for ebb tide to start. Eight o'clock we broke out anchor. Set only jib and reefed spanker. Wind too heavy for patch of mainsail (3 reefs). Began head beat, San Joaquin at that point lying east and west.

After an hour's beat, just as we were nearly around bend and ready to slack sheets, *Roamer* missed stays twice in succession and went ashore on lee shore. Carried away portmizzen shrouds.

One hour's hard work repairing shroud and kedging off.

Got around bend and ran to next curve to north. In beating up this curve, carried away jib sheet while sailing with lee-rail continually buried. Had sea room enough to re-rig jib. All the foot-stops of jib, that hold it to jibboom, carried away, so that we sailed rest of day with jib fast only on its three corners.

Talk about wind. On the preceding curve, under only reefed spanker and jib, in small sea, we were buried so deep that a 125-lb. sack of coal, on the aft deck, jammed between mizzen shrouds and the bitt was lifted up bodily and swept overboard. Say— the water was smoking white.

Across the river from us, now, on the lee shore, a scow schooner is pounding.

Charmian was a brick. She lighted about a thousand cigarettes and passed them to me from the cabin. Also, on deck she relayed my orders, and saw them correctly carried out at one end whenever I was at the other end of the boat.

Sano was a dandy. Best sailor-cook we have ever had. He can't swim, but he is absolutely unafraid.

Nakata, always good, was far better than ever. He was just magnificent.

And I take my hat off to the old *Roamer*. I wouldn't trade her (for bay and river cruising) for any yacht I know or ever knew. Yea, and the skiff is a dandy rowing and *towing* skiff. Best skiff I ever dragged astern.

And all the time we sailed, from 8 a.m. to 1:30 P.m., the galley stove kept going without any trouble, and hot coffee—say!

Jack

[1]Brother-in-law of Bessie Maddern London.

To Frank A. Garbutt

Glen Ellen, Calif.
Dec. 5, 1913

Dear Mr. Garbutt:—

Inclosed letter just received, which same please return.

Nine or ten years ago, before ever the question arose of the possibility of moving-picture rights in novels and stories, I signed a contract with Mr. Joseph Noel, an old friend of mine, in which dramatic rights in *The Sea Wolf* were made over to him—of course we were to share royalties between us.

About nine or ten years ago, Mr. Noel's dramatic version of *The Sea Wolf* was staged for a week in Ye Liberty Theatre, Oakland, California. Ola Humphreys, later internationally married to some prince of Egypt, and Landers Stevens were in the cast. I assume that Mr. Noel had his play copyrighted.

Later on, a couple of years ago when I was in New York (the moving-picture proposition in the meantime having arisen), Noel agreed verbally to sign back to me the moving-picture rights in *The Sea Wolf*.

The mention of money paid over, the sum of $500.00, is hot air on his part, but goes to show how eager he is to help me in the matter. I have at home an assignment of the moving-picture rights in *The Sea Wolf* signed by Noel.

In the attack made by Horkheimer, since it antedated even the book publication, and went back to magazine copyright, I never thought to bring up to you or Mr. Barker the fact that the dramatization of *The Sea Wolf* had been run for a week in Oakland.

Now, there are certain court decisions accompanying the rise of the moving-picture rights with dramatic rights.

I am bringing this matter before you in order to find out whether any use may be made of it.

Sincerely yours,
Jack London

To Hughes Massie Esq.

Glen Ellen, Calif.
Dec. 16, 1913

Dear Mr. Massie:

Our copyright troubles in the United States have been settled, and our company takes judgment in all the court cases.

The company that is producing my pictures is BOSWORTH, INC., of which Mr. Frank A. Garbutt is Trustee. At the present moment, some three or four big films are in process of final completion. Only the first film made has been put on the market. It is *The Sea Wolf,* in 7 reels, taking two hours to perform, and it has just completed its opening weeks in San Francisco and Los Angeles. They are going right on playing it through the second week. It has played beyond capacity, and has broken all film records of success in these two cities in which it has been tried out. The last night of the first week in San Francisco the film was played until one o'clock in the morning.

All the foregoing is to show you that Bosworth, Inc., is in every way making most notable films of my work.

I have suggested to Mr. Garbutt your name as a man who might be of possible assistance to us in Europe.

I am inclosing this letter to Mr. Garbutt, who will also write you. Mr.

Garbutt has absolute charge of the entire business of Bosworth, Inc. What Mr. Garbutt will desire to learn is if you can be of use to him, and if you would care to be of use to him. Mr. Garbutt will wish to know what you know of the whole situation of marketing film in Europe, etc., etc.

One thing I desire to impress upon you is that it is a matter of notable film and big business.

I do not know precisely when you expect to make your regular New York trip, and for fear that you may be on your way now, I am advising Mr. Garbutt to address this letter and his letter to you care Galbraith Welch at your New York office, with instructions for Galbraith Welch to read and get to you in the quickest way possible.

Sincerely yours,
Jack London

To Charmian London

New York, New York
Jan. 29, 1914

Dearest My Own Woman:—

Flatly signed up yesterday *John Barleycorn* and received $500 [*sic*] less 10% as an advance, so that I shall be able to finance myself from this end.

"Hee Haw" began night letter I sent you yesterday, apropos of more lawsuits, injunctions, etc., etc.—but this is from the salesman end of the pictures—they are certainly grabbing at all the *Sea Wolf* velvet. But I should worry!

Marking time with Pelton[1] just now. He swears he has absolute trump cards; I say produce them; he says he is sending to California for them; and here we are. At present moment am playing a ticklish game of bluff in lieu of any legal backing. Looks as if Pelton has me; also, my impression is that I have Pelton's goat. Ergo, I may get through by the skin of my teeth plus a nominal sum of money for compromise. My present feeling is that I shall be lucky if I can persuade him to accept $3100. But he doesn't know that.

The trouble with Noel is that he is too *good* to be sensible.

Millergraph outlook excellent. A tremendous amount of original research and invention had been done in physics, chemistry, and metallurgy, and, as a result, present Millergraph is almost unrecognizable. Machine after machine has been invented, to produce. The silver plates we are working on cost $250 each. Our cutting tools are diamonds, and the very machine by which the diamond cuts the silver plate had to be specially invented along with a dozen detail inventions in machine.

Well—can't write, can only talk to you what big work is going on with Millergraph.[2]

Saw *Seven Keys to Baldpate* last night—delicious.

Am mixing up with the "Billtoppers," with the booking agents, the girls creamed from all the country who are succeeding or who are eating out their hearts on Broadway. A book sure will come of it. Was in Van Courtland, after theatre, till one this morning—with Tammany men, prize-fighters, street walkers, managers of theatres, also directors and producers, also leading ladies, kept women, etc., etc., etc. More room for Scandal I guess.

When I kissed Anna yesterday she said "Another Scandal, Jack?" She comes today with Rose and the babies. Tomorrow I lunch with them at City Club where Jane Rolston, (or however name is spelled) will be to meet me.

Darcy is trying to blackmail (business) me on the five stories. May cause me trouble.

I no longer say "To hell with New York." I am here to master New York and to enjoy New York.

Think I'll give Pelton a few days more, and then, (if only I can get legal backing for the case) tell him to go to hell and pull West for you. That will mean war, and a damnable war, but if he won't be decent I'll have to accept war and teach him what war is. Which means that you and I will pay for war, as well as he.

I don't know Merle [Maddern] since she grew up. Glad she's in touch with you. Has she put on any flesh?

Order from Macmillan Company: *Playright and Copyright in All Countries,* by Colles and Hardy.

You write Donald Barker to return my two books on "Copyright," I loaned him—also, to return all letters, documents, etc., no longer essential to Bosworth Inc.

Send me more addressed (to you) envelopes.

"Wolf House"[3]—is most sweet, most beautiful, most true—tell M. S. Cobb the same for me. I care not to utter another word on that sad topic.

Do you know, I look at the women I encounter these days, and always, as I look, is a vision of your sweet, beautiful body, of the spirit that informs it to such quick eagerness to such sureties and certainties of will. Oh, I know your thoroughbredness that is at the one time irk and the highest joy to me. No man may ride a thoroughbred mare without tenseness and irritation along with the corresponding joy that is aroused by the very tenseness and irritation. You've never seen me infatuated with cows. Ergo—my arms are around you, as they shall always have to be around you for love of you and appreciation of you—you damned thoroughbred!

Wolf

---

[1]When, in 1906, London agreed to give the dramatization rights of the *Sea Wolf* to Joseph Noel, Pelton apparently furnished money to Noel with London signing notes as collateral. The play did not succeed and London had to pay Pelton $3835.00. This controversy extended from Feb., 1906, to London's death.

[2]The Millergraph deal was apparently hanging fire at the time of London's death.

[3]A poem by M. S. Cobb entitled "Wolf House," after burning of the Wolf House.

To Joan London

Glen Ellen, Calif.
Feb. 24, 1914

Dear Joan:—

In reply to yours of February 10, 1914. I have just got back from the East, and am taking hold of my business. Please find herewith check for $4.50, according to account presented by you. When I tell you that this leaves me a balance in the bank of $3.46, you will understand how thin the ice is upon which I am skating.

I note by your letter that you have been charging schoolbooks in my account at Smith's. Never again do a thing like this. Never be guilty of charging to anybody's account when you have not received permission from that person to charge to their account. I shall make a point of sending you the money for your schoolbooks when you write to me for same, or, if I have not the money, of giving you permission to charge to my account. If I am away, and if Mrs. Eliza Shepard has not the money, she may also give you permission to charge to my account. Under no other circumstances except those of permission, may you in the future charge anything to any account of mine anywhere. This is only clean, straight, simple business, Joan.

Now I have what most persons would deem a difficult letter to write; but I have always found that by being frank and true, no thing is difficult to say. All one has to say is all that he feels or thinks.

Let me tell you a little something about myself: All my life has been marked by what, in lack of any other term, I must call "disgust." When I grow tired or disinterested in anything, I experience a disgust which settles for me the thing forever. I turn the page down there and then. When a colt on the ranch, early in its training, shows that it is a kicker or a bucker or a bolter or a balker, I try patiently and for a long time to remove, by my training, such deleterious traits; and then at the end of a long time if I find that these vicious traits continue, suddenly there comes to me a disgust, and I say Let the colt go. Kill it, sell it, give it away. So far as I am concerned I am finished with the colt. So it has been with all things in my whole life from the very first time that I can remember anything of myself. I have been infatuated with many things, I have worked through many things, have become disgusted with those many things, and have turned down the pages forever and irrevocably on those many things. Please believe me—I am not stating to you my strength, but my weakness. These colossal disgusts that compel me to turn down pages are weaknesses of mine, and I know them; but they are there. They are part of me. I am so made.

Years ago I warned your mother that if I were denied the opportunity of forming you, sooner or later I would grow disinterested in you, I would develop a disgust, and that I would turn down the page. Of course, your mother, who is deaf to all things spiritual, and appreciative, and understanding, smiled to herself and discounted what I told her. Your mother today understands me no more than has she ever understood me—which is no understanding at all.

Now, do not make the mistake of thinking that I am now running away from all filial duties and responsibilities. I am not. I shall take care of you; I shall take care of Baby B., I shall take care of your mother. I shall take care of the three of you. You shall have food and shelter always. But, unfortunately, I have turned the page down, and I shall be no longer interested in the three of you.

I do not imagine that I shall ever care to send you to the University of California, unless you should develop some tremendous desire to do specific things in the world that only a course in the University of California will fit you for. I certainly shall never send you to the University of California merely in recognition of the bourgeois valuation put upon the University pigskin.

I should like to see you marry for love when you grow up. That way lies the best and sweetest of human happiness. On the other hand, if you want a career instead, I'll help you to pursue whatever career you elect. When you were small, I fought for years the idea of your going on the stage. I now withdraw my opposition. If you desire the stage with its consequent (from my point of view) falseness, artificiality, sterility and unhappiness, why go ahead, and I will do what I can to help you to it.

But please, please remember that in whatever you do from now on, I am uninterested. I desire to know neither your failures nor your successes; wherefore please no more tell me of your markings in High School, and no longer send me your compositions.

When you want money, within reason, I shall send it to you if I have it. Under any and all circumstances, so long as I live, you shall receive from me food in your stomach, a roof that does not leak, warm blankets, and clothing to cover you.

A year from now I expect to have a little money. At the present moment, if I died, I should die one hundred thousand dollars in debt. Therefore, a year from now I may be more easy with you in money matters than I am capable of being now.

I should like to say a few words further about the pages I turn down because of the disgusts that come upon me. I was ever a lover of fatherhood. I loved fatherhood over love of woman. I have been jealous of my seed, and I have never wantonly scattered my seed. I have (we'll say my share at least) a good body and a good brain. I had a father's fondest love and hope for you. But you know, in bringing up colts, colts may be brought up good and bad, all according to the horseman who brings up the colts. You were a colt. Time and fate and mischance, and a stupid mother, prevented me from having a guiding hand in your upbringing. I waited until you, who can dramatize "Sohrab and Rustum," could say for yourself what you wanted. Alas, as the colt, you were already ruined by your trainer. You were lied to, you were cheated. I am sorry; it was not your fault. But when the time came for you to decide (not absolutely between your mother and me)—to decide whether or not I might have a little hand in showing and training you to your paces in the big world, you were already so ruined by your trainer, that you declined. It is not your fault. You were so trained. It is not your mother's fault—she was born stupid, stupid she will live, and stupid she will die.

It was nobody's fault—except God's fault, if you believe in God. It is a sad mischance, that is all. In connection therewith I can only quote to you Kipling's "Toolungala Stockyard Chorus":

"And some are sulky, while some will plunge.
  (So ho! Steady! Stand still, you!)
Some you must gentle, and some you must lunge.
  (There! There! Who wants to kill you!)
Some—there are losses in every trade—
Will break their hearts ere bitted and made,
Will fight like fiends as the rope cuts hard,
And die dumb-mad in the breaking-yard."

Whether or not you may die dumb-mad, I know not. I do know that you have shown, up to the present time, only docility to your trainer. You may cheat and fool your trainer, and be ruined by your trainer. I only think that I know that you are too much of a diplomat to die over anything—result of your reaction over your training, plus your inherent impulse to avoid trouble, kick-up, and smashing of carts and harnesses.

You cannot realize all this letter. You may when you are older. Save it for that time. But I have lost too many colts not to be philosophical in losing you. It might be thought that I am unfair to your youthfulness—yet you dramatized "Sohrab and Rustum," and calmly state to me narrow-minded, bourgeois prejudices (instilled into your mind by your mother). Such as: My present wife, my Love Woman, is all that is awful and horrible in that I do truly love her, and in that she does truly love me.

All my life I have been overcome by disgust, which has led me to turn pages down, and those pages have been turned down forever. It is my weakness, as I said before. Unless I should accidentally meet you on the street, I doubt if I shall ever see you again. If you should be dying, and should ask for me at your bedside, I should surely come; on the other hand, if I were dying I should not care to have you at my bedside. A ruined colt is a ruined colt, and I do not like ruined colts.

Please let me know that you have read this letter in its entirety. You will not understand it entirely. Not for years, and perhaps never, will you understand. But, being a colt breaker, I realize that a colt is ruined by poor training, even though the colt never so realizes.

Whenever you want money, within reason, for clothes, books, spending, etc., write me for it, and if I have it at the time, I shall send it to you.

Jack London

To Joan London

Glen Ellen, Calif.
March 8, 1914

Dear Joan:—

In reply to yours of March 3, 1914. Please find herewith check for $4.70.

It will be well, whenever I am in California, to send me directly what carfare and allowance come to. When I am away Mrs. Shepard will be the one to send to.

Also, whatever school books I pay for I do not care to have charged to your mother's account. You can send to me (or Mrs. S. in my absence) what the necessary books come to and receive check for same.

It is a very good idea to file my letters so that you may read them when you are older. You will be sure to understand them then a bit more. Me of course you will be unable ever to understand, because you have never had an opportunity to be with me. The same will be true of yourself. I shall be unable to understand you. When you are a woman you and I will talk different languages. The thoughts of each will be gibberish to the other.

Jack London

To S. T. Hughes
[Telegram]

Glen Ellen, Calif.
March 11, 1914

THE WORLD AND CIVILIZATION BELONG TO THE RACES THAT PRACTICE MONOGAMY MONOGAMY IS SET SQUARELY AGAINST PROMISCUITY THEREFORE MONOGAMY AS THE CORNERSTONE OF THE STATE DEMANDS A LEGAL FATHER FOR VALLIE ALSO THE FATHER AND THE MOTHER OF VALLIE DESIRE TO MAKE THEIR PARENTHOOD LEGAL THEREFORE THE ONLY LOGICAL THING FOR THE STATE OF ILLINOIS TO DO IS TO MAKE POSSIBLE THIS LEGALIZATION OF VALLIE'S BIRTH AND PARENTAGE OTHERWISE THE STATE OF ILLINOIS STULTIFIES ITSELF BY KICKING OUT THE CORNERSTONE OF CIVILIZATION ON WHICH IT IS FOUNDED NAMELY

417

THE FAMILY GROUP THAT CAN EXIST ONLY UNDER MONOGAMY.[1]

(SIGNED) JACK LONDON

[1]Vallie was an illegitimate child whose father was convicted and sentenced to 30 years in an Illinois prison for seduction of a juvenile. The girl petitioned the State Pardon Board for his release so that he could marry her and give Vallie "a father and a name." The girl's grandfather, who prosecuted the man, also signed the petition for pardon. S. T. Hughes of the Newspaper Enterprise Association solicited an opinion from Jack London.

To ROLAND PHILLIPS

Glen Ellen, Calif.
March 26, 1914

Dear Roland Phillips:

I am sending you by express PREPAID, the complete manuscript of my new novel. I do not know what title to give it. I have thought of calling it the *Star Rover,*[1] also of calling it *The Jacket,* or *The Shirt Without a Collar.* What do you think about one or another of these three titles?

You will find it a curious sort of book. Do not be appalled by it, but read on. I think you will find lots of good stuff in it.

It is a book that cuts various ways. It truly states prison conditions. It is the law to-day that a man can be hanged by the neck until dead, for punching another man in the nose. It is the law in California. It is also legal in California to sentence a man to life-imprisonment in solitary. The Board of Prison Directors has this power on a life convict. The jacket has been legal in San Quentin up to and including almost the entire year of 1913. I understand that in the fall of 1913, the State Legislature passed a law prohibiting further use of the jacket. My hero was executed in the summer of 1913, therefore his jacket experiences occurred during the time when the jacket was still legal. Ed Morrell, Donald Lowrie, Jake Oppenheimer, all these men have testified to the jacket. I have really understated the severity of the use of the jacket.

You will note I have not made the story nor the description of prison conditions grewsome. This is because of the fiction that is wrapped up in it, and the optimism of the story itself, which enables the victim to win to the largeness of the centuries by means of the jacket; which enables the victim to win love, adventure, romance and the life everlasting.

Also note the tricks I have played with philosophy, exposing the power of mind over matter, and making it good accessible stuff to the Christian Science folks, and for all the New Thought folks, and the millions who are interested in such subjects in the United States today. While this is pseudo-scientific and pseudo-philosophic, nevertheless it will make it most palatable to most of the rest of the folk who will read it.

Incidentally, the story is historically correct from start to finish—even

418

back to the old times when, before history was written as we know it to-day, the drifts of men occurred, and they wrote their history in the stars.

The key-note of the book is: THE SPIRIT TRIUMPHANT.

And lovers of love will have no kick coming. The book is a paean of love. It is the glorification of love and of woman.

Don't miss, that in the present reaction against sex-exploitation, here is something clean, fresh, wholesome, new, that expounds the old romantic love and that expounds romantic love in romantic terms, along with philosophical exposition, connotation, and vindication. Being a dissimilar yarn to any that has been published in years, now is the time for it to ride across the back-wash of the recent sex-exploitation in our magazines and books.

Tomorrow I start to mull over my new novel. It shall be either *The Man Who Passes,* or *The Box Without a Lid.*[2] No matter which I elect to write, the novel will be continuous, straight fiction, with a fresh new motif. I have a sneaking idea that I shall tackle first *The Man Who Passes,* which is a New York situation.

Sincerely yours,
Jack London

[1]First English edition was entitled *The Jacket.*
[2]Neither was ever written.

To Dr. Frank Lydston

Glen Ellen, Calif.
March 26, 1914

Dear Frank Lydston:

In reply to yours of Mar. 16, 1914. A prophet is not without honor save in his own country. California is my own country. I was born here, and have lived here, and I make it my home at the present time, and have always made it my home. As a result, I am without honor here in my own state. My socialism has put all the state university people against me from the President down. I would therefore be the last person in the world to do any good in advancing the proposition that you suggested.[1] In token of this I am sending you an interview, which same, after you have laughed over it, please return to me. It will show you that I am at sword's points with everybody in California, and am not afraid to let everybody in California know it.

I am inclosing you herewith a list of my books. Please scratch off the ones you have read, and return this to me.

I have just finished reading your *Sex Hygiene for the Male,* and have thoroughly appreciated it. I like your whole attitude on the whole general subject of sex.

But I think the biggest thing in many a year is your implantation of sex-organs. I shall not begin to tell you how wild I am to hear of the further progress, and of further generalizations from the same.

Please forgive my brief letter. I am just lately home from a six months' absence, and am trying to catch up with many hundreds of letters that have piled up. Incidentally, I am getting ready to start, possibly, for Japan and China in a couple of weeks.

Please don't forget that our house is your home any time you come to California. I want to show you some spots as pretty as you ever saw in California in the old days. Pride forbids me from bragging further in the matter.

Sincerely yours,

Jack London

---

[1]Lydston had acquired a reputation as a scientist and a writer. He felt that, being a native of California, the University of California should recognize him by conferring upon him an LL.D. Degree. He wanted London to "set the machine in motion."

To ERNEST UNTERMANN[1]

Glen Ellen, Calif.
April 11, 1914

Dear Ernest:—

In reply to yours of April 5, 1914. Still it does seem to me that you take an unfair logical advantage of me. I went into the Shaw contest with *The Metropolitan* with as clean hands as you went in.[2] I went in with as much faith in the contest as you went in. It is clear that I came out with more faith in the contest than you came out with.

But we started even, we started, both of us, in all sincerity.

You say: "Everybody expected that you at least would differ from Carnegie and the Chicago editor." The funniest part of the whole thing is that I DID differ from Carnegie and from the Chicago editor. The winner I chose was not the winner chosen by the Chicago editor, and the winner chosen by the Chicago editor was not the winner chosen by Carnegie. Each one of the three of us chose different men for first winner.

What bothers me, Ernest, is that you should make a personal matter of an entirely impersonal matter. I did not even know that you were going to compete when I accepted the judgeship in the contest. You have, in this letter of yours of April 5, been very personal. In one breath, while telling me that you love me sincerely, you, by indirection, insinuate that my hands are not clean, my brains are not clean, and that my heart is not clean. Here are your own words upon that matter: "Believe me, Jack, that I love you sincerely, and that I want to see you come out on top of the shuffle with

420

clean hands, clean brains, and a clean heart."—Now, what in hell have I done to merit such insinuations from you?

You say: "You certainly not have added to your prestige by acting as juror in this contest." Oh,—what's the good of quoting all the attacks you have personally made upon me in your letter!

Dear Ernest, I can only tell you that this letter of yours of April 5, would seem to show conclusively that your dialectic has gone to smash. You seem very hysterical. You bring your and my most intimate personal relations into the feeling of offense that you entertain against *The Metropolitan* people, when you say how much you like me and love me, and when you say that it is a pity that you were broke when I first met you, and when you say that this state of being broke placed you in a very disadvantageous position for real friendship right at the start, and when you say that this condition of being broke gave you a feeling that Charmian never quite outgrew the fear that you were trying to take unfair advantage of my generosity.

The most charitable interpretation I can put on the foregoing sentiment of yours, contained in your letter of April 5th is, that you were drunk when you wrote it. If not, you were hysterical. If you were not hysterical, something at any rate has happened to your dialectic.

Really, Ernest, your letter of April 5 has not hurt me at all, but it has made me solicitous about you. What is the matter with you?—Why should you treat me in such terrible fashion?

Sincerely yours,

Jack London

---

[1]London's friend and a translator.
[2]Untermann asked London if his Ms. had been submitted to the judges. It was apparently ruled out because it did not fit the specified plan.

To CHARLES G. NORRIS
[Telegram]

Glen Ellen, Calif.

April 15, 1914

VANDOVER AND THE BRUTE IS FRANK NORRIS FROM A TO Z IN IT IS ALL HIS RIPE PROMISE WHICH HE SO SPLENDIDLY FULFILLED   VANDOVER AND THE BRUTE WAS TWENTY YEARS AHEAD OF ITS TIME AND TODAY IT IS JUST IN ITS TIME   ALL LOVERS OF FRANK NORRIS WILL HAIL IT WITH DEEPEST SATISFACTION/

(S) JACK LONDON

To E. J. Sisson[1]

Galveston, Texas
April 23, 1914

Dear Mr. Sisson:

If no transport sails before Saturday, I can get away on a fruit boat, if present quarantine complications are smoothed out on Saturday.[2]

There is nothing much doing here; in fact, there is scarcely anything to base an article upon. The United States, so far as Galveston is concerned, is sitting quiet. The transports (loaded the day I arrived here) have only been loaded with ordinary food supplies. Personal baggage and camp equipment ·is being hauled and stored in the warehouses on the docks alongside the transports, but none of it is being put on the transports. The place is as deadly quiet as a New England village in the dog days.

However, I have worked out between 3500 and 4000 words of an article, which, under any circumstances I shall mail to you on Friday, which is to-morrow. If anything should arise, I understand that up to Monday night I can cable you an addition to said article which will have been already mailed.

Now, about the stuff I send you—you may cut, alter, change, do anything you please with it. In the matter of revision, I give you an absolute free fist— just as long as you do not add to my stuff in such a way as to stultify me and negate me. You can even add to my stuff, if said additions do not stultify and negate.

But, please save for me one set of my original articles to you. Please save for me also, original films and photographs I may send you.

METHOD OF SENDING ARTICLES AND FILMS—I shall put ordinary first-class postage with a special delivery stamp, on my articles to you. To register an article means delay in delivery after arrival in New York City. My Japanese boy, Nakata, can operate my typewriter, and unless anything unforeseen occurs, I shall always mail you a duplicate of each article one day after the original is sent, or simultaneously by some other route. Regarding undeveloped films, I may perhaps register them. When I can get my films immediately developed (which in the lowlands of the tropics is imperative once the sealed films are exposed to the air) I shall forward them to you flat, first-class mail, and most likely special delivery.

I have equipped myself with 100 special delivery stamps. If my articles and films mailed should carry a foreign stamp, the special delivery stamp becomes operative after the parcel arrives in New York City.

One other thing: My ranch expense, etc., etc., in California, is all of $2000 each month. Now, I have been receiving, the first of each month, for first-serial rights, $2000 from *The Cosmopolitan*. I do not know what attitude *The Cosmopolitan* will take on my ceasing to write fiction, and departing for Mexico. *The Cosmopolitan* could very fairly, and most likely will, take the position that since I have ceased from writing my fiction for the time being, there is no obligation upon it to continue the monthly advance until such time that I resume writing my fiction. Wherefore, in order not to take any chances, I am making this request to you: Namely, beginning the first of May, to forward the first of each month, for however long time I happen to be away, a check for $2000 to Glen Ellen. This check may be made out in my name, because my sister, Mrs. Eliza Shepard, is the super-intendent of the ranch, handles all my business in my absence, holds my power of attorney, and is absolutely trusted by me. And in order to keep the ranch going, Mrs. Shepard must have this $2000 each month.

In case Mrs. Shepard wants to communicate with me, I have told her to do so by way of *Colliers Weekly*. If she forwarded letters, you, who would have my latest safe address, would reforward same when received. If she should forward important telegrams, asking you to reforward same by telegraph or cable, please do so. Then there is a chance that she might telegraph you by night letter, important matters which when received by you, you would forward by mail. In any event, we will assume that she will describe the manner in which she desires you to forward same.

Sincerely yours,

Jack London

¹Of *Collier's Weekly*.
²London went to Mexico as a war correspondent for *Collier's* during the Mexican fracas of 1914.

To EDITOR,
The Army and Navy Journal

Glen Ellen, Calif.
June 22, 1914

Dear sir:—

First of all, business. Please find inclosed my check for $6.50, for which same please send me (a) a year's subscription to *The Army and Navy Journal*, beginning June 1, 1914; (b) one copy of the Revised Edition of 1914 Field Service Regulations.

I have just received the copies of *The Army and Navy Journal* for May 2 and 9, for which my thanks. Also, I should like to throw myself further upon your good offices by asking you to mail to me one copy of *The Army & Navy Journal* for Dec. 20, 1913, and one copy for Jan. 3, 1914.

After a man, while yet young, futilely tries to nail newspaper lies, he gives up. I gave up years ago. I gave up because I was beaten, not scores and hundreds of lies have gone out about me, but thousands of straight lies and canards. I gave up because I was flatly beaten. I have never yet suc-ceeded in nailing a lie. One of the first lies published about me was that I gave a lecture in the city of Oakland before an ultra-select woman's club, attired in a red sweater. Despite my most strenuous efforts to nail this lie, to this day, after a lapse of sixteen years, that lie is still published.

I remember that on a single day, three news dispatches went out concerning me: The first dispatch stated that my wife had quarreled with me in the city of Portland, Oregon, had packed her Saratoga trunk and departed on a steamer for San Francisco, going to her mother; the second lie was that, in the town of Eureka, California, I had been beaten up in a saloon row by a millionaire lumber man; the third lie was that in a mountain lake resort in the State of Washington, I had won a $100 bet by catching a perfectly uncatchable variety of lake trout. As I say, these three lies were made into press dispatches and sent out on a single day. And on the day in question, my wife and I were deep in a forest reserve in Southwestern Oregon, far from railroads, automobile roads, stage roads, telegraph wires and telephone lines. Now, I never denied any of these three lies. Heavens—I want to have some portion of my life spent in enjoyment. I do not care to spend the major portion of my life in a vain attempt to refute lies.

Please, please forgive a busy wandering man's ignorance of technical journals—I never heard of the existence of *The Army and Navy Journal* until the day I sailed from Galveston on board the United States Army Transport *Kilpatrick*. So, how, under the sun, was I to know that the *Army & Navy Journal's* displeasure had been turned on me in its issue of Dec. 20, p. 487?

Not until I had reached Vera Cruz, did I learn that one, Edwin Emerson,[1] a man who has shared my food and blankets and ridden my horses, had rushed into your printed column, p. 556 of *The Army and Navy Journal* of Jan. 3, 1914, in order to repeat lies about me that he had heard, and further lyingly to defame me?

But the saddest blow of all remained to be dealt to me by you, when you called me a dreamer, when you called me illogical, and when you stated that I was lacking in consistency of reasoning—all on the evidence of Edwin Emerson, who is a child, who never grew up. If he lives a thousand years, he will remain child-minded and childish. I know this man. Do you know this man? I know this man's history. Do you know this man's history?

In conclusion, to show that I am a philosophical sort of a chap, returning very sick from Vera Cruz, as usual I shared my quarters aboard the vessel with Edwin Emerson. I could not quarrel with him because he is a child; and a philosophical sort of a chap cannot demean himself by quarreling with a child, no matter how grievous the child's conduct has been. Of course, I would have done anything in the world for Edwin Emerson, as I will do in the future, as I have done in the past for many children; as I shall always do in the future for other children.

In conclusion, I stand on my known reputation. I have always been a fighter. I have never said anything nor written anything that I have failed to back up afterwards. I have never said anything nor written anything nor published anything, and then denied the saying or the writing or the publish-

424

ing of it afterwards. At the end of it all, I shall go into the darkness, standing by my opinions, and fighting for my opinions. But never fighting lies told against me, and never fighting children.

Sincerely yours,
Jack London

P.S. Merciful heavens—I have not yet read the copy of *The Army and Navy Journal* containing the letter of Edwin Emerson against me. I have only your own account of it, which is an account of only one item of it, and the accounts of several officers and war correspondents who had read the letter as printed by you. And after I had heard these oral versions of what you had printed of Edwin Emerson's letter, I never failed when meeting Edwin Emerson, to invite him to a drink or to invite him to a meal, or to sleep in my quarters.

[1]Edwin Emerson, who was a member of the Monterey group and who professed great friendship for London, wrote a letter to the *Army and Navy Journal* condemning London for "The Soldier's Canard." See letter to Lt. James D. Willson, page 469.

To RALPH KASPER[1]

Glen Ellen, Calif.
June 25, 1914

Dear Ralph Kasper:—

Just a rush line to you. I have come back from Mexico, and at present time am catching up, as usual, with my correspondence, and in addition recovering from an attack of rotten bacillary dysentary, hence, my inevitable, as usual, rush.

I have always inclined toward Haeckel's position. In fact, "incline" is too weak a word. I am a hopeless materialist. I see the soul as nothing else than the sum of the activities of the organism plus personal habits, memories, and experiences of the organism, plus inherited habits, memories, experiences, of the organism. *I believe that when I am dead, I am dead. I believe that with my death I am just as much obliterated as the last mosquito you or I smashed.*

I have no patience with fly-by-night philosophers such as Bergson. I have no patience with the metaphysical philosophers. With them, always, the wish is parent to the thought, and their wish is parent to their profoundest philosophical conclusions. I join with Haeckel in being what, in lieu of any other phrase, I am compelled to call "a positive scientific thinker."

Please forgive rush,

Sincerely yours,
Jack London

[1]Member of the International Typographical Union, Socialist, and a close friend of London's.

To CHARLES BROWN, JR.

Glen Ellen, Calif.
July 28, 1914

Dear Charles Brown Jr.:

In reply to yours of July 24, 1914:

First of all, I must thank you for the copy of *The Marin Journal* you mailed to me and for the pleasure that was mine in reading your story about Bob Wilson.

I have a very poor memory for names. In the course of the year many scores of interesting hoboes drift across the ranch here wherefore, I do not know whether I know your Bob Wilson or not. One thing however you can take straight from me; because of my own tramping experiences you can scarcely find a tramp today in the United States who has not hoboed with me, slept with me, gone to jail with me, etc., etc. Of course they all claim this whether they really have or not, and who am I to say nay to their stories? It was certainly all right for you to use my name in the article the way you did and again I thank you for giving me the chance to read it.

Sincerely yours,
Jack London

To MRS. BOB FITZSIMMONS

Glen Ellen, Calif.
Aug. 4, 1914

Dear Mrs. Fitzsimmons:—

I noticed by the *Minneapolis Tribune* of July 16, 1914, that you are appearing in *Her Brother's Clothes*.

You will remember that Bob, you, and I met each other as old stagers and as old friends, that the request for this sketch was made by you and Bob to me and that I did not bother either of you with such a business formality as a contract. Bob, and you will remember hearing him, promised me my fair whack out of earnings or royalties of this play.

Now I am just as good a fellow as the next and I am willing to listen to anything you have to say in the spirit of good-fellowship. Now, dear Mrs. Bob, if you say that you owe me nothing for having written this play, well and good, but if you think that there may be something coming to me, well and good, in either event, for ever and always, well and good. I shall always love you and shall always love Bob, and remember that any time that you are on the Coast we should be glad to have you make a break in your time and come up and see us on the ranch. No matter how you may decide the question that I have brought up in this letter at any rate give me some sort of a history of the play since last I saw you and Bob. Full of love to both of you.

Sincerely yours,
Jack London

To Hughes Massie

Glen Ellen, Calif.
Aug. 15, 1914

Dear Mr. Massie:

In reply to your letter of July 29, 1914.

I think that Mr. Garbutt made a mistake in failing to inform you of the terms of the compromise between our Company and the Balboa Company. The terms of the compromise were that Balboa could go ahead and market the films it had made of *The Sea Wolf,* but that it could not market them under the title *The Sea Wolf;* but that it could market them under the title of the *Hellship.* Also in the terms of the compromise it was understood that Balboa was not to use my name in any way.

At any rate, we found in our experience in the United States that the *Hellship* film was not recognized by any patron of the "movies" as having been taken from *The Sea Wolf.* Furthermore in Los Angeles, where the scene of the fight occurred, the *Hellship* film was such a "scream" that it only redounded to the popularity of *The Sea Wolf* film which was run in opposition.

Nevertheless Mr. Garbutt made a mistake by failing to inform you of this compromise. At the same time that I am telling you this please to remember not to quote me in this matter to Mr. Garbutt.

Sincerely yours,
Jack London

To Michael Monahan[1]

Glen Ellen, Calif.
Aug. 20, 1914

Dear Michael:—

Thanks be, my hopes that you would like *Martin Eden* are realized.

Yea—Brissenden is largely George Sterling, whom I love greatly.

Say, aren't you ever going to come to California? We've some ranch here waiting for you.

Jack London

---

[1]Literary Editor of the *Chicago Evening Post.*

To Kathleen Norris

Glen Ellen, Calif.
Sept. 10, 1914

My Dear Mrs. Norris:—

I just must drop you a line of acknowledgement of the pleasure your *Saturday's Child* has given me. Your characters have become all friends of mine; and I want to tell you that had I been unmarried, and had your Susan Brown not taken up that Billie Oliver of yours, I surely would have written you for Susan Brown's address.

Saturday's Child makes me home-sick. California is my country. Heavens, I was born here, and all the deliciousness of *Saturday's Child,* and all its essential trueness, really makes me home-sick for the California I knew before the earthquake.

You must be a very happy woman in order possibly to write such a happy, happy book. Congratulations to you for achieving a splendid piece of work.

Sincerely yours,
Jack London

To Mr. Bram Norsen

Glen Ellen, Calif.
Sept. 10, 1914

Dear Mr. Norsen:—

In reply to your letter of September 3, 1914:

No, you will not find "henidical" in the dictionary. The word henid was coined by a crazy German philosopher but I find no substitute for it in the English language. All persons possess henids. A henid is a vague thought which we think is a thought and which is no thought at all, in contradistinction to a real thought which on analysis proves to be a clear concept.

Weininger is the name of the above mentioned German philosopher. He committed suicide when he was about twenty-five years old after writing a book that made quite a stir in the world, entitled *Sex and Character*. It was all about women and was very uncomplimentary to women. I think this man Weininger is the guilty party for whom you are searching.

Sincerely yours,
Jack London

To George P. Brett

Glen Ellen, Calif.
Sept. 21, 1914

Dear Mr. Brett:—

I am just now sending you a telegram asking you please to forward to me the Eighteen Hundred ($1800.00) Dollars that is due to me on November first.

And that is not all. As usual I am plugging away, head over heels with the ranch. If you will only delay your visit to the ranch for a couple of years more I will show you a real ranch when you get here. Just now my pay-roll is averaging $1500.00 a month and of course other expenses are fairly large. I am building, constructing, and making the dead soil live again. My terraces are beginning to show up. I have spent $5000.00 in the last eighteen months on fences and my fence gang is still at work. My first silo is a success and I am building two more silos this winter. I have a fairly decent brood-barn, with liquid-manure tank attached, and I have just finished my concrete dipping tank: and among other things am starting to work to build a piggery that will be the delight of all pig-men in the United States. It will be large and efficient and cheap in relation to the size of it. My first big dam on the place is just finished so that on these poor, old, worked-out, eroded hillsides I shall be able to harvest two crops a year and turn one crop under; in place of the old meagre crop that could be taken off only once in several years. My herds have been forming for some time and now I am compelled to build in order to keep up with them and handle them with a minimum labor expense.

Unfortunately, and as usual, all the forgoing requires money just the same, and I leave it to you, it is a better plan to spend one's money this way than on actresses or racehorses. I have been promising you for some time that I would be easier than ever before in the matter of advances. It is true that never have I been so easy in the matter of advances than at the present time. For the first time in our history I am actually asking an advance from you of something already earned. When I send this telegram today asking for the $1800.00 due in November I am so doing.

This means, that the money advanced by you, the $2000.00 on *The Mutiny of the Elsinore,* has already and some time since been earned by my other book. *The Mutiny of the Elsinore* is just now out on the market. You have in your possession *The Jacket* [*The Star Rover*], another novel, you have just recently published the collection of short stories *The Strength of the Strong.* I am over half way through with another novel, entitled *The Little Lady of the Big House,* which is a California farming novel.

You will observe that I am writing only two books a year now as I promised you some time since. You will also observe that my two books a

429

year are invariably novels. I am not writing any more short stories and I hope so to maneuver that I shall not be compelled to write any more short stories in the next several years.

And now to the point, I want to know if you can find it possible to repeat the $2000.00 advance (long since earned) on *The Mutiny of the Elsinore* and repeat it by the middle of October. Also I want to know if you can by the 15th of November make the first advance of $2000.00 on *The Jacket*.

Among other expenses extraordinary to which I have just been put is the wiring of the ranch all over for electric lighting and electric power.

The reason why I am pinched at the present time is two-fold: first, the business which brought me to New York which required me, to get a settlement, to sign up notes payable every three months for the rest of the year 1914 in order to clear my moving picture rights; and second, the delay by law-suits of money coming from the moving picture enterprise which in itself delayed the putting forth of the films which all the time we were busy making, plus the break-down of the moving picture market in England at the present time due to the GREAT WAR.

I am enclosing you herewith a couple of snap-shots to show you the sort of stock I am breeding.

Sincerely yours,
Jack London

To Ella Wheeler Wilcox

Glen Ellen, Calif.
Sept. 23, 1914

Dear Ella Wheeler Wilcox:—

I cannot tell you how delighted I am to have received your good letter of September 12, 1914.

As regards the unfortunate young man you wrote me about and whose letter you forwarded to me[1]—all I can say is that he is a weak-brother, a sob-brother. If he lives to be one hundred years old he will spend the entire century of his existence leaning on the breast, or chest, of his strong sisters and brothers. He is hysterical, he is a squealer, and he is a fool. Neither you nor I, nor God himself, can help such a poor, unfortunate, mis-begotten creation such as this young man proves himself to be by his written word. You say "he seems intelligent"; permit me, he is not intelligent. He is glib, he is garrulous, he is emotional, he is silly, but the last thing that he can possibly possess is one iota of intelligence.

Now to other and nicer things. Do not forget, for you and your dear husband, that any time you come to California there is a ranch in "The Valley of the Moon" waiting to welcome you.

Please forgive the brevity of this letter and also the rubber stamp signature that will be appended hereto—because of the fact that Mrs. London and I are leaving in a few minutes to catch the train that will take us to our yacht the *Roamer* on which we are bound for a cruise.

With all love from Mrs. London and myself to you and Mr. Wheeler,

Sincerely yours,

Jack London

[1]Mrs. Wilcox had sent London a letter addressed to her by a young man who explained that he had been "in a dreamy, unhappy and pessimistic state for approximately four years. Having placed myself in a very weakened and plastic state of mind through excessive indulgence, and being naturally credulous, I easily became a victim of morbid philosophy in the reading of Jack London's books, particularly that of *Burning Daylight*." Mrs. Wilcox ask London to write to this young man.

To GEORGE STERLING

Glen Ellen, Calif.
Sept. 23, 1914

Dearest Greek:—

Now first of all do not wish in the name of the "blue-eyed Jesus" that you had a rubber stamp for your signature. You are going to get a rubber stamp for my signature to this letter because I am dictating it to the dictaphone and immediately having finished make a wild rush to catch the train, with Charmian, in order to connect up with the *Roamer* and start our winter cruise. Please forgive the busy Wolf.

Herewith find John Masefield, August, 1914. I am sending it to you in the hope that you have not yet seen it; please return.

By the way, I sent you *The Strength of the Strong* to Sag Harbor some time since and I do not know whether or not you have received it.

I am holding off on sending you a copy of *The Mutiny of the Elsinore* until I find out that it is safe to send it to you.

By the way, I have finally been insistently invited to do the 1916 Jinks. Have you any ideas on the subject that you would like to suggest and also all advice whatsoever that will enable me to go ahead and write a Jinks— I mean in dealing with the Jinks committee in relation to the stage etc., etc. Throw your feet and help me out with all sorts of information that you undoubtedly possess from your own experience in writing a Jinks.

I have had the hugest delight in reading the "war sonnets" that you sent me. I cannot believe that you have at the date of your last writing already written thirty-five "war sonnets." They are good stuff and I am astounded that you should at this late day prove so prolific.

For God's sake give me some sort of information about how things are going with the *Millergraph*. I am afraid Joseph J. Noel is a weak-brother.

431

Won't you please try; in order to satisfy my eternal and infernal curiosity, epitomize the discussion of the young fellows at the beach whom you heard talking about me—even though their talk was not entirely uncomplimentary.

To hell with you and the rubber stamp, I know inside of 24 hours a rubber stamp will be affixed at the bottom of this letter to you, dearest Greek.[1]

Thine,
Jack London

P.S. Charmian tells me to say that she wishes she could think up a riddle or a "Spoonerism" bad enough for your corrupt mind.

[1] And the stamp was affixed—upside down.

To George P. Brett

Glen Ellen, Calif.
Oct. 7, 1914

Dear Mr. Brett:—

In reply to your good letter of Sept. 29, 1914. Please, of course, on the advances in question, charge me the regular interest that The Macmillan Co. is itself compelled to pay for such money. This is only fair.

It is dreadfully hard for me to get my friends to understand just what the ranch means to me. It does not mean profit, at all. My fondest hope is that somewhere in the next six or seven years I shall be able to break even on the ranch. The ranch is to me what actresses, racehorses, or collecting postage stamps, are to some other men. From a utilitarian standpoint I hope to do two things with the ranch: (1) To leave the land better for my having been; (2) and to enable thirty or forty families to live happily on ground that was so impoverished that an average of three farmers went bankrupt on each of the five ranches I have run together, making a total of fifteen failures to make a living out of that particular soil.

Next to my wife, the ranch is the dearest thing in the world to me. Heavens! I sit up nights over that ranch; and you ought to see the brass-tack, efficient piggery I am now building!

Sincerely yours,
Jack London

To George Sterling

Oakland, Calif.
Oct. 26, 1914

Dear and Blessed Greek:—

I love you to death for the generous way in which you have recently been writing me. And, as usual, I beg your forgiveness for the miserable way in which I ever write to you or anybody. Incidentally, in extenuation of my present miserableness in this matter, just let me tell you I have been having a hell of a time sailing the boat, writing my 1000 words every day, and battling with barber's itch. It has been weeks on my face, and just now I am convalescing. Charmian has been regarding me with critical and suspicious eye. Charmian also asks me to tell you that she does not like "Jelly Bags."

I won't send you a copy of *The Mutiny of the Elsinore* until I get back to the ranch, where said copies are waiting for my arrival.

The Strength of the Strong stories were written by me before I started on the Snark voyage—with exception of "Sea Farmer" and "Samuel," which were written at sea between Australia and Ecuador.

That rubber signature up-side-down must have been a scream. But it was the only way you could have got the letter at all. I talked a string of letters into the phonograph up to the minute of catching a train, so they had to be stamped up.

Charmian and I yelled over your experience with the temperance-exhilarated sailors.

I am saving "The Tryst" and the "war sonnets" to read aloud to Charmian when we get back on the boat. I have now been dictating to her for some hours, and the sun is setting, and we shall continue this battle with correspondence until it is barely time to rush to the Orpheum. After the Orpheum we are going to eat a duck with a little Liebfraumilch on the side, then go down aboard the *Roamer* and turn in, sailing to-morrow morning at daybreak. Our latest sport has been catching fat and fighting crabs off Angel Island, and catching and eating raw rockcod. We got the finest clams we ever ate, last week down at Alviso.

"The Fish Hawk" I had only read before, but had read aloud a number of times to others.

My private opinion is that Joe Noel is a lunatic. In his inability to believe that he tells untruths, I rank him with Bessie.

Jack

To Max E. Feckler

Oakland, Calif.
Oct. 26, 1914

Dear Max Feckler:—

In reply to yours of recent date undated, and returning herewith your Manuscript. First of all, let me tell you that as a psychologist and as one who has been through the mill, I enjoyed your story for its psychology and point of view. Honestly and frankly, I did not enjoy it for its literary charm or value. In the first place, it has little literary value and practically no literary charm. Merely because you have got something to say that may be of interest to others does not free you from making all due effort to express that something in the best possible medium and form. Medium and form you have utterly neglected.

Anent the foregoing paragraph, what is to be expected of any lad of twenty, without practice, in knowledge of medium and form? Heavens on earth, boy, it would take you five years to serve your apprenticeship and become a skilled blacksmith. Will you dare to say that you have spent, not five years but as much as five months of unimpeachable, unremitting toil in trying to learn the artisan's tools of a professional writer who can sell his stuff to the magazines and receive hard cash for same? Of course you cannot; you have not done it. And yet, you should be able to reason on the face of it that the only explanation for the fact that successful writers receive such large fortunes, is because very few who desire to write become successful writers. If it takes five years work to become a skilled blacksmith, how many years of work intensified into nineteen hours a day, so that one year counts for five—how many years of such work, studying medium and form, art and artisanship, do you think a man, with native talent and something to say, required in order to reach a place in the world of letters where he received a thousand dollars cash iron money per week?

I think you get the drift of the point I am trying to make. If a fellow harnesses himself to a star of $1000 a week, he has to work proportionately harder than if he harnesses himself to a little glowworm of $20.00 a week. The only reason there are more successful blacksmiths in the world than successful writers, is that it is much easier, and requires far less hard work to become a successful blacksmith than does it to become a successful writer.

It cannot be possible that you, at twenty, should have done the work at writing that would merit you success at writing. You have not begun your apprenticeship yet. The proof of it is the fact that you dared to write this manuscript, "A Journal of One Who Is to Die." Had you made any sort of study of what is published in the magazines you would have found that your short story was of the sort that never was published in the magazines. If you are going to write for success and money, you must deliver to the market marketable goods. Your short story is not marketable goods, and had you taken half a dozen evenings off and gone into a free reading room and read all the stories published in the current magazines, you would have learned in advance that your short story was not marketable goods.

Dear lad, I'm talking to you straight from the shoulder. Remember one very important thing: Your ennui of twenty, is your ennui of twenty. You will have various other and complicated ennuis before you die. I tell you this, who have been through the ennui of sixteen as well as the ennui of twenty; and the boredom, and the blaséness, and utter wretchedness of the ennui of twenty-five, and of thirty. And I yet live, am growing fat, am very happy, and laugh a large portion of my waking hours. You see, the disease has progressed so much further with me than with you that I, as a battle-scarred survivor of the disease, look upon your symptoms as merely the preliminary adolescent symptoms. Again, let me tell you that I know them, that I had them, and just as I had much worse afterward of the same sort, so much worse is in store for you. In the meantime, if you want to succeed at a well-paid game, prepare yourself to do the work.

There's only one way to make a beginning, and that is to begin; and begin with hard work, and patience, prepared for all the disappointments that were Martin Eden's before he succeeded—which were mine before I succeeded—because I merely appended to my fictional character, Martin Eden, my own experiences in the writing game.

Any time you are out here in California, I should be glad to have you come to visit me on the ranch. I can meet you to the last limit of brass tacks, and hammer some facts of life into you that possibly so far have escaped your own experience.[1]

Sincerely yours,

Jack London

---

[1]This letter has been published under the title "Letter to a Young Writer."

To C. E. JULIHN[1]

[Aboard the *Roamer*]

Oct. 31, 1914

Dear Mr. Julihn:

In reply to yours of Oct. 13, 1914. I have been away from home for a number of weeks now, and my mail comes to me only semi-occasionally. Also, I have been far behind in my correspondence.

I am returning you your manuscript in the stamped and addressed envelope you kindly inclosed with it.

First of all, as regards your suggestion of my finding something for you to do on the ranch: Right there I am helpless in my domain. I am at home but rarely, and in the past, during the rare intervals when I was at home, I have been responsible for getting a number of persons on the ranch, engaged by me, who drove the superintendent frantic because, while I hired, the superintendent had to do the firing—while I was away merrily over the sea somewhere, out of the trouble. Now the superintendent is also my sister. When she gave me my choice of accepting her ultimatum or of losing her, I surrendered. The terms of my surrender were, that since I was there so little, and never fired, it was up to me to have nothing to do with the hiring. This agreement I have lived up to, and since then all has gone well.

From reading your stories, it is patent that while you have a lot of material in you worth using for the making of stories, you have a lot to learn in the trick of making the stories. Now, I cannot teach you this trick. I have possibly five hundred proposals a year from men and women to have me teach them that trick. When I was younger and more rash than I am now, I did endeavor to teach a few the trick, with the only result that I hurt their feelings and lost their friendship. Not one of them ever got the trick. On the other hand, were I as patient as Job, and did I have forty-eight hours to spare out of each day, I would not have time enough to teach or guide the many who appeal to me for that form of assistance—namely, learning the trick of successful authorship.

I am writing you thus at length, and not about your stories but about myself, in order that you may glimpse how I am situated, and why my attitude has to be what it is.

Let me give you this piece of advice: Under the responsibility of a family, as you are, never, under any circumstances, forsake any position or work you may have and try to go it blind and make a living out of your pen. That road is lined with broken hearts. Do not make an attempt to gain a living solely from your pen until you have some sort of a writing position or magazine connection to guarantee you your living.

I am inclosing a couple of circulars, and would especially recommend that you take a year's subscription to *The Editor Magazine*.

Sincerely yours,
Jack London

[1] A thirty-seven-year-old mining engineer from Virginia City, Nevada, who wanted to settle near London and become a writer with help and criticism from London, in return for working on the ranch at any job any time.

To Hall Caine[1]
[Telegram]

Oakland, Calif.
Nov. 16, 1914

BELGIUM IS RARE. BELGIUM IS UNIQUE. AMONG MEN ARISES ON RARE OCCASION A GREAT MAN, A MAN OF COSMIC IMPORT.

AMONG NATIONS ON RARE OCCASION ARISES A GREAT NATION, A NATION OF COSMIC IMPORT. SUCH A NATION IS BELGIUM. SUCH IS THE PLACE BELGIUM ATTAINED IN A DAY BY ONE MAD MAGNIFICENT HEROIC LEAP INTO THE AZURE. AS LONG AS THE WORLD ROLLS AND MEN LIVE THAT LONG WILL BELGIUM BE REMEMBERED. ALL THE HUMAN WORLD OWES AND WILL OWE BELGIUM A DEBT OF GRATITUDE SUCH AS WAS NEVER EARNED BY ANY NATION IN THE HISTORY OF NATIONS. IT IS A MAGNIFICENT DEBT, A PROUD DEBT THAT ALL THE NA- TIONS OF MEN WILL SACREDLY ACKNOWLEDGE.

JACK LONDON

[1]Caine cabled a number of prominent men for opinions to be used as propaganda for the cause of Belgium—then overrun by the Germans.

To Miss Esther Andersen

Glen Ellen, Calif.
Dec. 11, 1914

My dear Miss Andersen:—

In my opinion, three positive things are necessary for success as a writer. First, a study and knowledge of literature as it is commercially produced today,

Second, a knowledge of life, and

Third, a working philosophy of life.

Negatively, I would suggest that the best preparation for authorship is a stern refusal to accept blindly the canons of literary art as laid down by teachers of high school English and teachers of university English and composition.

The average author is lucky, I mean the average successful author is lucky, if he makes twelve hundred to two thousand dollars a year. Many successful authors earn in various ways from their writings as high as twenty thousand dollars a year and there are some authors, rare ones, who make from fifty to seventy-five thousand dollars a year from their writings; and some of the most successful authors in some of their most successful years have made as high as a hundred thousand dollars or two hundred thousand dollars.

Personally, it strikes me that the one great special advantage of authorship as a means of livelihood is that it gives one more freedom than is given any person in business or in the various other professions. The author's office and business is under his hat and he can go anywhere and write anywhere as the spirit moves him.

Thanking you for your good letter,
Sincerely yours,
Jack London

To C. L. Clark[1]

Glen Ellen, Calif.
Dec. 11, 1914

My dear Mr. Clark:—

In reply to yours of November 28, 1914:

First of all, from my reading of science I cannot believe that man first appeared on earth at the time of the glacial period. I believe that man preceded the glacial period.

Also, I do not believe in God nor in any personal super-interference with the affairs of this world, or of this universe. Therefore you can see that I am not in sympathy scientifically, or philosophically, with your views.

Also, I am compelled to ask you this question. How can you account for man's history of himself, before he was man, as manifested today in the human embryo, 'ere it is born, during which time, anatomically, it recites man's previous history and evolution on earth?

Sincerely yours,
Jack London

[1]Clark had a theory that man was created during the Glacial Period and did not evolve through time. He stated that Thomas A. Edison had written him a "very kind letter," apparently giving approval to the theory. Clark wanted London to weave this theory into a novel in which he (Clark) would receive credit and share in the profit.

To Marion Humble[1]

Glen Ellen, Calif.
Dec. 11, 1914

My dear Marion Humble:—

In reply to yours of October 21, 1914:

Indeed, and in truth, what I have written in *John Barleycorn* and in *The Valley of the Moon* are actually my own experiences as regards Free Public Libraries.

Two wonderful things happened to me when I was a small boy that practically directed the entire course of my life, and I doubt if neither of these two wonderful things had happened to me that I should ever have become a writer.

The first wonderful thing was, when I was a little boy on a poor California ranch, finding a tattered copy of Ouida's novel entitled *Signa*. The end of this book was missing but I read and reread and reread countless times the story of Signa and it put in me an ambition to get beyond the skylines of my narrow California valley and opened up to me the possibilities of the world of art. In fact it became my star to which I hitched my child's wagon.

The second wonderful thing happened to me when, nine or ten years of age, my people were compelled to leave their mortgaged ranch and come to the City of Oakland to live. There I found access to the great world by means of the free public library of the City of Oakland. At that time Ina Coolbrith was the librarian of the Oakland Free Library. It was this world of books, now accessible, that practically gave me the basis of my education. Not until I began fighting for a living and making my first successes so that I was able to buy books for myself did I ever discontinue drawing many books on many library cards from out of the Oakland free public library.

Thanking you for your good letter,

Sincerely yours,

Jack London

---

[1] An instructor in Children's Literature in the Library School of the University of Wisconsin. She was trying to "cross fertilize boys and books" and wanted to learn more of London's actual experiences with books and libraries.

To Mrs. Mary Banks Krasky[1]

Glen Ellen, Calif.
Dec. 12, 1914

My dear Mrs. Krasky:—

In reply to yours of November 24, 1914:

First of all please forgive the brevity of my reply. I have been out cruising and just returned to the ranch last night and I am leaving tomorrow morning before daylight to catch a train for Los Angeles on a business rush.

I fail to see, from the standpoint of a fiction writer employing the medium of a novel, how I could have come out plainer than I did in *The Star Rover*. I have stated names, and have stated facts, and have stated dates. Last year Jake Oppenheimer was hanged at Folsom because he had been found guilty not of murder but of assault. As I understand this he is the first man who has been legally executed in the United States for being guilty of assault. I have used his name flatly in *The Star Rover* and have given Ed. Morrell's name flatly as being a cell-mate of his in "solitary."

As I understand it the warden and the Board of Prison Directors may, in their own judgment, as a matter of prison discipline, condemn a life prisoner for the rest of his life to solitary confinement. As I understand it, still today, at the discretion of the warden, the straight jacket may be used. The present administration of prison officials say that the straight jacket is rarely or never used now but they will not deny that legally they have the right, at the discretion of the warden, to use the straight jacket.

As I said in *John Barleycorn* I am Martin Eden. I would not die but I went largely through Martin Eden's experience. Martin Eden died because he was an individualist, I live because I was a socialist and had social consciousness.

Sincerely yours,

Jack London

[1]A writer who praised *The Star Rover* and hoped that London would tell the plain truth to the women of California so they could start a reform movement.

To GEORGE P. BRETT

Glen Ellen, Calif.
Dec. 26, 1914

Dear Mr. Brett:—

In belated reply to yours of November 18th concerning the matter of making out a new contract.

Suppose first of all that we make the time of the contract for three years.

I have a feeling that now that I am writing long novels again and writing long novels continuously and not writing short stories that some sort of an extra drive might possibly be made at your end of the game in order to get some sort of decent field for said novels. I look at writers like Rex Beach. They are certainly riding the high tide of popularity. They get into the best sellers. I have not seen a best seller of my own for a weary time. Is it because the work of these other writers is better than mine? Is it because the public has soured on me? Or is it because I am accepted by your people as an institution and that no shove is given to my work such as is given to the work of the new men and to the work of the young men? I cannot give the answer to these questions. You are closer in touch with the facts.

Also, cannot, on occasion, a special volume of my work be resurrected from the great mass now published by you? For instance; my first book, *The Son of the Wolf,* was published by Houghton, Mifflin & Company. It was a collection of short stories. It earned me on its own first sales for the first two years something like five hundred dollars. It was then finished as a selling book. Nevertheless, after a lapse of years, Houghton, Mifflin & Company resurrected it, made another printing, or several printings, and earned me a thousand dollars or a couple of thousand dollars more. Again, still later, they made a Christmas book of it, bound it differently, and sold it to the Christmas trade and earned me an additional twenty five hundred or three thousand dollars in royalty. Doubleday, Page & Company did somewhat similar things with their book of mine which they had acquired from the old McClure's Publishing House. This was a collection of short stories entitled *The God of His Fathers*. I have no record of such a re-print or resurrected high-price edition of any of my volumes with you. This is a matter worthy of consideration. Please do not let all of this big body of my work in your possession sleep, or merely receive subsequent cheap edition exploitation.

Now to the matter of second serial rights. Here is the *Cosmopolitan* claiming that it retains the second serial rights of all my fiction published in its columns and in the columns of the other Hearst magazines. Only an expensive law-suit can determine the validity of the *Cosmopolitan* claim. On the other hand, and for some years, in my contract with you the Macmillan Company has been holding, first, entire second serial rights, and, later on, one-half of the second serial rights. Now I flatter myself if I can get the entire second serial rights from you and from the magazine that I can do incredibly better in the handling and sale of same than can you.

Royalties—You know that I live in the far West and that I do not meet nor congregate with writer folk. I have no contact with the general shop talk and business gossip of the writer folk. I do not know what they receive. Wherefore I am now asking you if I am getting the decent top price that I merit. If so, in making out the contract put in the same decent top price that I have been hitherto receiving. If not, please put in what you might think would be my decent top price. Of course this top price, I realize, is determined by all of the factors, stipulations, advances, etc. As usual, I am leaving this up to you.

Copyright—Because of legal technicalities I should like to have it arranged that you take the copyright on all my future books out in my name.

Translations—I want, as I have always enjoyed, the control of all translation rights in my work.

Section 3 of our contract dated the fourteenth day of July, 1913—I should like to balance the privileges of this section to your house by permitting me a reciprocal power.

Section 10 of same contract—This was originally my suggestion. Now it is not clear to me and I am sure the wording of it would puzzle any legal mind in an effort to determine its import. Can it not be placed at a flat twenty per-cent and be done with it?

Your suggestion of no more than four books each year, two of which will be novels, is satisfactory to me. I doubt that I shall ever again have more than three books published in one year and I shall devote myself to writing novels.

Please make up a tentative contract and send same to me.

Sincerely yours,
Jack London

P.S. Please pardon rubber-stamp signature, Mr. London left home for another cruise on his boat before the typing hereof.

To George Sterling

Aboard the *Roamer*
Jan. 13, 1915

Dearest Greek:—

First of all, I am riding out a southeaster on the San Joaquin river, as I am dictating this to Charmian. To-morrow I finish the first act of the Jinks play, which I think I shall call *The Acorn-Planters*. This means that I am over half-way through. I am writing it with a Prologue, two Acts, and an Apotheosis, and without one damn stick of stage scenery. As soon as I am finished, which will be in ten days or two weeks, I shall send you a typewritten copy for you to rip and tear to pieces and make suggestions about. Ye Gods—me writing poetry! The poetry I write is such silly rot. I have crystallized in prose, and imagine me counting meter on my fingers!

I enjoyed your New Year's peregrinations amongst the bums.

Charmian and I have been delighted with the opening instalments of Harry Leon Wilson's *Post* yarn. Shall send you on *The Little Lady of the Big House* in a few days.

Damn the Kaiser! So say I, too.

I wouldn't give a tinker's damn for five shares Common of Millergraph, because I haven't a tinker's damn to give for anything. I never have been so up against it as at the present time, thanks largely to the Kaiser. Damn the Kaiser!

Joe Noel is bugs, in my opinion. He eternally talks honor and honorable actions, and is guilty of the weirdest acts any friend can be guilty of.

Charmian and I are going to stay on the boat for months yet, if we don't get arrested.

All love,
Wolf

P.S. I think the motif of my Jinks play is anti-war. That is as near as I can make it out. I am exalting the Acorn-planters and damning the Warriors, and the Kaiser along with them.

To Walter S. Kerr[1]

Aboard the *Roamer*
Jan. 26, 1915

Dear Walter S. Kerr:

In belated reply to yours of Jan. 14, 1915,—belated because only two days ago did your forwarded letter reach me.

First of all, I haven't anything to do with scenarios or filming of moving pictures. The only scenarios I have ever seen are those which are sent to me in the same way that yours was sent. Save these, I have never laid eyes on a scenario in my life.

The war has hit the whole writing game, and hit it hard. From every side, for months, I have been receiving disaster letters not only from my writing friends, but from scores of whom I never before heard. But their hard times are not a patch on mine. Their hard times started with the war, while my hard times, leading from disaster to disaster, extended over a year and a half, and culminated in the war. Incidentally, instead of winning big at the moving picture game, I am at the present time many thousands of dollars loser, and am doing the most frenzied finance to keep my head above water. I am afraid to go home for fear of having summons served on me. I have been and am being sued right and left. What complicated my serious situation is that, unlike most of you fellows who have only yourselves to care for, I am taking care of many people and running a number of households, all of which people and households are entirely and absolutely dependent upon me for food and shelter. And these expenses of the many others I am compelled to meet every month.

I am starting out now in a wild rush to New York in an attempt to raise the wind. It is sink or swim with me at the present time, and at the present time I am floundering hard.

Sincerely yours,
Jack London

---

[1]Pseudonym, F. F. French. Kerr sent London a scenario and asked for financial help; saying he had been hungry for three months.

To PAUL UNGER

Aboard the *Roamer*
Jan. 26, 1915

My dear Paul Unger:

In reply to yours of January 2, 1915. You certainly have got me puzzled. The major portion of your letter you devote to advice to me about how to comport myself and adjust and regulate my life to a successful culmination. The minor portion you devote to a request that I advise you how best to adjust your life toward a successful culmination. You tell me you cannot concentrate your mind upon the study of steam engineering. Lord! I can't tell you how to concentrate your mind on steam engineering. You say you are twenty-seven years old, have no trade nor profession, and decline to give up five years of preparation for a trade or a profession. You want some short cut that, to save my soul I have no knowledge exists. If I could short-cut men to such success, I'd quit writing for a living and go out and make millions at teaching it. I'd put all the universities out of business if I only had such a magic formula for short cutting. No, I'll be darned if I can advise you.

Sincerely yours,
Jack London

To Dr. John E. Purdon

Aboard the *Roamer*
Jan. 26, 1915

Dear Dr. Purdon:

In reply to yours of Jan. 12, 1915, which has been forwarded to me and which has just reached me. When I tell you that I am hopelessly a realist and a materialist, believing that when I die I am dead and shall be forever dead, you will understand how unable I am to join with you in the prosecution of your most interesting researches.

Please do not think the above paragraph as harshness on my part. Take it, rather, as a concise statement of my attitude on the subject. I was born amongst spiritualists and lived my childhood and boyhood life amongst spiritualists. The result of this close contact was to make an unbeliever out of me. My mother to this day—and she is past seventy years of age—is still an ardent spiritualist.

Thanking you for your good letter,[1]

Sincerely yours,
Jack London

[1]Dr. Purdon had commended London for his understanding of reincarnation as expressed in *The Star Rover*.

To Eliza Shepard

Aboard the *Roamer*
Jan. 26, 1915

Dear Eliza:—

I want you to take the time, any time that suits you best, to make a trip to Dixon and look over the Timm's Dairy. Dixon is only five or six miles west of Davis. Write first to Mr. Timms, apprising him of the day and train of your arrival, so that Mr. Timms will meet you and show you around.

Look especially at:

(1) Use of sand on smooth cement floors of milking-barn, as a sure preventive of slipping.

(2) Feeding of silage in milking-barn while cows are being milked, without tainting milk with silage odors; (a) Is there a difference between the

strength of odor of hay silage and alfalfa silage such as Timms uses, and corn silage? (b) Note also method of feeding grain, bran, etc., at same time with silage and on top of silage.

(3) Notice that inside five minutes after milk is milked, it is reduced to the cooled temperature of freezing-point.

(4) Remember that he is selling certified milk, and keeps no hogs, because he has no skimmed milk, while our plan is to sell only butter-fat and use our skimmed milk or buttermilk on our young calves and hogs.

(5) Get dimensions of troughs behind cows, length of stall-flooring from manger to trough, pitch of floor from manger to trough, elevation of feeding-alley, etc., etc.

(6) Note that he has no litter-carriers to carry manure, whereas my plan still holds of using litter-carriers to dump manure either into manure-pit or waiting manure-spreaders.

(7) Find out if it is practical to spread soft, mushy cow-manure by means of a manure spreader. (In clippings I shall be sending you in a couple of days, you will note another method of handling cow-manure with manure-spreaders from a large manure-pit that is only emptied once a year.)

(8) Write to the various farm authorities to learn how best to spread soft, slushy cow-manure. Also to learn practical methods, etc., for the spreading of liquid manure.

(9) Note (a) his bull-pens; (b) ask him for his past history of experience of having bulls close to milking-cows as they come in and are waiting to be milked.

(10) (a) Note his ice-machine, etc. (b) note his pasteurization processes, including pasteurization machine and pasteurization of utensils and of straining-cloths over the milk-pails.

(11) Note white uniforms of milkers, changed and pasteurized every day.

(12) Note hand-washing basins, towels, etc., in milking-barn.

(13) Ask him about washing the cows' udders before the milking begins.

(14) Note feeding-barns, which are open, and storm-weather sleeping barns.

(15) Plan (after consultation of various dairy-farm buildings we have filed) our own buildings in relation to a brace of silos say for milking fifty cows, and refer same plans to me. Also, try to get some idea of how best to relate these dairy-building plans to our particular location, and to efficiency of moving cows from place to place of roadways, of creamery, etc., etc.

(16) Note that Dixon region is irrigated by pumps at depths deeper than 100 feet, remembering that our irrigation will be done by gravity.

(17) Note that they do not grow corn in Dixon, never forgetting that the demonstrated finest balanced ration is alfalfa hay and corn silage.

(18) And that we *can* grow corn and alfalfa.

(19) Note that these dairies, Timms' Dairy and others, grow merely roughage and always buy the grain.

(20) Note that we must and can grow our roughage, such as alfalfa and

445

corn silage and other hay, and must always buy our grain—in this connection, the problem will be to give the best balanced ration to our animals, along with the least purchased grain.

(21) Ask Timms why he is now raising all his calves, including bull calves—get his statistical experience in this matter.

(22) Get Timms' experience with hand-milking labor conditions, and machine-milking labor conditions, etc.

(23) Note that his cows and bulls are all dehorned.

(24) Get Timms' acreage and number of milking cows (average); number of freshening cows; number of calves, bulls and heifers, being raised; number of active bulls in relation to cow-herd.

(25) Ask Timms (and that it is not for publication) for the wages he pays his milkers, plowman, foreman, etc.

(26) In Timms' silaging of alfalfa and other hays, find out what quantity of water he uses in the process of filling silos.

(27) Find out ground-elevations of milking-barn floor (a) of stall floors, with pitches; (b) of feeding-alleys; (c) of mangers, etc., etc.

(28) Ask why it is that the milking-barn is not made loftier, so that the loft can be used for storage of hay, grain, etc.

(29) And note, not merely in your own head, but write down and refer to me, Timms' answers to all other questions that will arise in your own mind during your visit.

(30) Of course, our system, when we finally determine on it, will be suited to our needs, our location, our landscape, and will be variously different from Timms' system; but from here and there we can gather good ideas to incorporate in our own system.

(31) Especially go over dairy-plans we have filed, for measurements of stalls, etc., and write to authorities such as the Agricultural Press, University of California, etc., for measurements, pitches, etc.

Jack

To Joan London

Glen Ellen, Calif.
Feb. 4, 1915

Dear Joan:—

In reply to yours of February 1, 1915:

First of all, I had Aunt Eliza send you the check for $9.00.

I am astounded at your multifarious activities as stated by you in your letter and as accompanied by clippings from the *Aegis*.

Are you going to the old Oakland High School on Twelfth Street? If you are please remember that I have swept every room in that old High School from garret to basement. Also, that I have hoisted the American flag every high school day for two terms on top of said old High School Building. Also, just for the fun of it, take a walk around the entire block occupied by the High School Building and look up at all the windows from the ground floor to the top floor and just get the idea into your head that every one of those windows I have washed in the past. I washed them inside and outside.

And I did all the foregoing work mentioned by me while at the same time I was doing my studying and my recitations inside the class-rooms during school hours. And, also, that I had a noon-day meal that cost me ten cents —when I had the ten cents. On many a noon I had nothing to eat because I did not have the ten cents and because—I had run a bill so large at the ten cent eating joint that they would not give me credit. And furthermore, another secret, I believe that at the present time I still owe that ten cent eating joint something like $8.50, representing eighty-five ten cent meals which I did not pay for, which I am at the present time unable to pay for because of the fact that many years ago said ten cent eating joint went out of business and I cannot find any responsible party to whom to pay the money I owe.

I now want to sing to you a song:

You are my daughter

You do not know, yet, what that means

Have you no intellectual stir, no mental prod, no heart throb,

Impelling you to get acquainted with your dad?

Oh, my dear, I am very old, and very wise, and I can set you four-square to this four-square world.

I have nothing to offer you in the way of dollars and what dollars can buy.

I have everything to offer you and show you in the way of the spirit and what the spirit never buys, but commands.

Daddy

To George Hough Perry[1]

Glen Ellen, Calif.
Feb. 4, 1915

Dear Mr. Perry:—

In reply to yours of January 29th, 1915:

Yes, you are right, the Panama trip is called off. President Wilson is not going to the canal at all.

So it looks as though I shall be able to do the articles for you.

If I am to do the articles please let me know at your earliest convenience so that I may jump in and do them.

As regards my regular rate, I have just had a copy of a letter made, written by me eight years ago. I am submitting this letter to you in confidence and out of laziness because it will save me the time of going into the matter at length.

In addition to above mentioned letter, copy of which I am sending you, I may add that my last two newspaper agreements have been with the Hearst papers for Panama $1100.00 per week and expenses for one and with the Wheeler Syndicate to do the yacht race which was called off by the European War at the rate of $1100.00 per week and expenses for two, time to begin counting from the moment I leave my ranch to the moment of my return to the ranch.

Awaiting a reply at your early convenience,

Sincerely yours,

Jack London

[1]Director, Division of Exploitation, Panama-Pacific International Exposition, San Francisco.

To Miss Ethel Jennings

Glen Ellen, Calif.

Feb. 5, 1915

My dear Ethel Jennings:—

In reply to yours of January 12th, 1915:

By the way, January 12th, 1915 was my birthday—39 years old, if you please.

I am returning you herewith your manuscript. First of all, just a few words as to your story. A reader who knew nothing about you and who read your story in a book or magazine would wonder for a long time after beginning as to what part of the world was the locality of your story. You should have worked in artistically, and as a germane part of the story, right near the start, the locality of the story.

Your story, really, had no locality. Your story had no place as being distinctively different from any other place of the earth's surface. This is your first mistake in the story.

Let me tell you another mistake which I get from your letter, namely that you wrote this story at white heat. Never write any story at white heat. Hell is kept warm by unpublished manuscripts that were written at white heat.

Develop your locality. Get in your local color. Develop your characters. Make your characters real to your readers. Get out of yourself and into your readers' minds and know what impression your readers are getting from your written words. Always remember that you are not writing for yourself but that you are writing for your readers. In connection with this let me recommend to you Herbert Spencer's "Philosophy of Style." You should be able to find this essay, "The Philosophy of Style," in Herbert Spencer's collected works in any public library.

On page 3 of your manuscript you stop and tell the reader how awful it is for a woman to live with a man outside of wedlock. I am perfectly willing to grant that it is awful for a woman to live with a man outside of wedlock, but as an artist I am compelled to tell you for heaven's sake, don't stop your story in order to tell your reader how awful it is. Let your reader get this sense of awfulness from your story as your story goes on.

Further I shall not go with you in discussing your manuscript with you except to tell you that no magazine or newspaper in the United States would accept your story as it now stands.

It has long been a habit of mine to have poems typed off in duplicate which I may send to my friends. I am sending you a few samples of said poems that I have on hand at the present time. I am sending them to you in order that you may study them carefully and try to know the fineness of utterance, the new and strong and beautiful way of expressing old, eternal things which always appear apparently as new things to new eyes who try to convey what they see to the new generations.

I am enclosing you also a letter to a young writer,[1] a letter that I was compelled to write the other day. His situation is somewhat different from yours and yet the same fundamental truth and conditions underrun his situation and your situation. In line with this let me suggest that you study always the goods that are being bought by the magazines. These goods that the magazines publish are the marketable goods. If you want to sell such goods you must write marketable goods. Any time that you are down in this part of California look up Mrs. London and me on the ranch and I can tell you more in ten minutes than I can write you in ten years.

Sincerely yours,

Jack London

[1] To Max Feckler, Oct. 26, 1914.

To George P. Brett

Glen Ellen, Calif.

Feb. 18, 1915

Dear Mr. Brett:—

I am leaving the ranch tomorrow on my way for a short trip with Mrs. London to Hawaii. I am taking my work with me and shall roll it off steadily day by day.

You will remember *The Call of the Wild* and *White Fang*. My present work consists of two dog stories, each about seventy thousand words long. The first will be entitled *Jerry,* the second will be entitled *And Michael.* These two dogs, Jerry and Michael, are full brothers and, after many adventures, they both come ultimately to the same happy ending, alive and in sunset middle age, as the reader parts from them.

I am making fresh, vivid, new stuff, and dog psychology that will warm the hearts of dog lovers and the heads of psychologists, who usually are severe critics on dog psychology. I think you will like these two books and there may be a chance for them to make a good impression on the reading public.

Sincerely yours,
Jack London

TO MICHAEL MCKENNA

Honolulu, T. H.
April 3, 1915

Dear Michael McKenna:

I am not so much surprised at receiving a letter from a dead man as I am from receiving a letter from a live man whom I have never met and who knows me as well as you know me, and who has eaten and slept with me as often as you have eaten and slept with me.

The only time I was ever in Mexico in my life was last April and May, when I sailed from Galveston to Vera Cruz with General Funston's expedition aboard the transport.

I certainly never was in any part of Mexico except Vera Cruz and Tampico, less than a year ago, and before all the gods I never made that journey with you in Mexico that you in so intimate detail describe.

This man you traveled with made believe he was Jack London. Your letter makes me very curious, and I should be hugely delighted if you would kindly take the time to give me further information about this namesake of mine. Also, and equally hugely, will I be delighted if at any time you are in California, you will visit me upon my ranch. I always have the grub and hard liquor, and the latchstring always out—and some blankets.

Sincerely yours,
Jack London

TO CHARLES C. MCLAREN

Honolulu, T. H.
May 18, 1915

My dear Charles C. McLaren:
Care Empress Theatre,
San Diego, California.

I am astounded, as portrayed in your letter of April 22, 1915, at the ignorance you show of the fundamental, criminal, English and American law. I was born in the United States, my direct ancestors have fought in every war of the United States and of the Colonies before they broke away from England, not only 'way back to the French and Indian wars, but to the coastal scrimmages of old New England. I learned automatically, as a baby boy, that a man was always presumed innocent until found guilty. Not only have you presumed me guilty, as I find from reading your letter published in the *San Diego Examiner,* but you have also imposed punishment upon me; and yet you have made no effort to find out whether I was guilty or innocent. I say that you proceeded to impose punishment upon me when, over your own signature, in the columns of a newspaper, you urged that my bread and butter be taken away from me, and that I be punished by starvation by means of a black-listing of the product I have to sell to the world.

Had you yourself had in the brains and in the blood of you a sense of English law, you would have sought the evidence, considered the evidence, and found me guilty ere you proceeded to agitate for punishment of me.

Had you read, within a year and a quarter, my newspaper denials in toto of having written a line of the canard that was attributed to me, against the soldiers of the United States; had you read, within a year and a quarter, my full-length reply to said canard, published both in *The Army and Navy Journal* of New York, and *The Army and Navy Register,* of Washington; had you read, within a year and a quarter, the series of articles in *Collier's Weekly,* sent by me from Vera Cruz at the time General Funston was there in possession—it would have been impossible for you, unless you were a lunatic or a cur, to have charged me with being guilty of this canard thing circulated about me, much less to have found me guilty, and still much less to have started an agitation for a blacklist to take my bread and butter away from me and my children.

Let him who is without sin cast the first stone. And do you, Charles C. McLaren, draw back that stone you have cast at me, and draw it back as publicly, in a letter to the *San Diego Examiner,* as you found me guilty in your letter to the *San Diego Examiner,* and started a mob movement to starve me to death.

Sincerely yours,
Jack London

To Joseph Conrad

Honolulu, T. H.
June 4, 1915

Dear Joseph Conrad:

The mynah birds are waking the hot dawn about me. The surf is thundering in my ears where it falls on the white sand of the beach, here at Waikiki, where the green grass at the roots of the coconut palms insists to the lip of the wave-wash. This night has been yours—and mine.

I had just begun to write when I read your first early work. I have merely madly appreciated you and communicated my appreciation to my friends through all these years. I never wrote you. I never dreamed to write you. But *Victory* has swept me off my feet, and I am inclosing herewith a carbon copy of a letter written to a friend at the end of this lost night's sleep.

Perhaps you will appreciate this lost night's sleep when I tell you that it was immediately preceded by a day's sail in a Japanese sampan of sixty miles from the Leper Settlement of Molokai (where Mrs. London and I had been revisiting old friends) to Honolulu.

On your head be it.

Aloha (which is a sweet word of greeting, the Hawaiian greeting, meaning "my love be with you").

Jack London

To ALEXANDER G. COTTER

Honolulu, T. H.
June 18, 1915

Dear Cotter:

In reply to yours of May 22, 1915, which has just come to hand. I smile me to myself. I have published some forty-one books. I wish to high heaven you could experience the impossibility of pleasing everyone (including yourself) all the time, when every damn one of them has his muzzle in his own favorite lard-pail, believes his muzzle is the handsomest of all muzzles, and insists that all other lard-pails are rotten and advertise poor taste. The foregoing sentence is a paraphrase of William Cullen Bryant's: "Each pursuing his favorite phantom." I smiled me again when you told me of throwing the magazine into the fire. It is so typical of youth and motion. It is only a heat-rash caused by impatience. You will get over it. We all do. And let me tell you right here that I am proud, damn proud of *The Little Lady of the Big House*. Have you read it? Or have you merely been misled by the illustrations?

By the way, running in the *Monthly Magazine* of the Hearst Newspapers, is another novel of mine, entitled *The Star Rover*. Have you read it? Or am I, after the way of youth and motion, already irretrievably damned?

I haven't been home for the past nine months, and by my present address you will see how impossible it is for me to take advantage of your kind invitation to ride on your mud scow to your bacon and beans.[1]

Sincerely yours,
Jack London

[1] In a subsequent letter, dated Oct. 18, 1915, Cotter explains that he "didn't object to *The Little Lady*. It's her surroundings and the 300 bulls that gets my goat." He read *The Star Rover,* and London was redeemed.

To Joan London

Glen Ellen, Calif.
July 25, 1915

Dear Joan:—

At the end of the first paragraph of your letter to Aunt Eliza regarding the beginning of school:—I am curious to know what grammar school teacher or what high school teacher taught you in grammar to say: "and lunch money and allowance for Bess and I"?

Really, such grammar is horrible.

I have told Aunt Eliza to send you $19.80. You see I have subtracted the $2.50 from the $22.30 you made as a total. I did this because I note that Aunt Eliza, in response to your request for $10.00 for vacation money, sent you an additional $5.00 for the Fair. Aunt Eliza sent you this additional $5.00 on her own responsibility and without consulting with me. This was all right for Aunt Eliza to do, but, after such generosity on her part, I am rather a trifle surprised at your coming back and asking for the $2.50 for the July allowance.

I have also told Aunt Eliza that it is not necessary for you and Bess to have separate accounts at Smith Brothers. You can have the one account and each of you check off the items that you have purchased, and then when both of you have checked off all the items and can certify that the bill is OK, forward the bill as usual to me here at Glen Ellen. I am sorry that your mother's allowance, as well as the allowance of grandma, and Mammy Jenny, is delayed. At the present moment I am very short of money and this delay is unavoidable. None of my bills has been paid either.

No, I am not going bankrupt, I am merely pinched for money at the present time.

Daddy

To Zadel Barnes Gustafson[1]

Glen Ellen, Calif.
Aug. 1, 1915

Dear Zadel Barnes Gustafson:—

I sent you a few days ago a copy of *Martin Eden*. I am enclosing you herewith a carbon copy of my letter to Mr. Brett, President of The Macmillan Company, 34 Fifth Avenue, New York City. I am also, this mail, sending a carbon copy of this letter to you to Mr. Brett, and I am also, this mail, sending your poems and your letter to me to Mr. Brett.

Mr. Brett is a true and tried friend of long years standing. I am sending everything to him under the seal of utmost confidence.

You must let him in with me on this. He is near to you. He can see you.

By carbon copy of my letter to him you will see and understand why I have dared to override your request and let him in. I have not got the money. I have not, even in this month of August, paid the allowances to my mother, my old Negro mammy, my first wife, and my two daughters (both in high school). These allowances should have been paid the first of July. Yet so pinched am I at this time that I am still delayed in paying them. This situation, I know, you will understand.

I am leaving the ranch on rush business that is really acute, and I am going to San Francisco and Los Angeles. I shall be back on the ranch in a few days.

Please forgive the brevity of this letter to you. I am so rushed that I cannot possibly write my heart to you. Also, I have on my desk at the present time possibly three hundred letters that I have not yet read, much less replied to. You see, I have just shortly returned from a five months absence in the Hawaiian islands and all this work has accumulated on me.

Charmian is Dede, and Paula, and somewhat of a great deal of many others of my characters.

Please let Mr. Brett get in touch with you and talk with you and advise you, and do whatever he finds possible for you. Please keep me informed of what result obtains.

Sincerely yours,
Jack London

---

[1] Writer, lecturer, traveler, who wrote to London for money, asking that her request be kept secret.

To GEORGE P. BRETT

Glen Ellen, Calif.
Aug. 1, 1915

Dear Mr. Brett:—

I am enclosing you herewith letters, poems, etc., of Zadel Barnes Gustafson. Will you please return these to me when you have finished with them.

I am also enclosing to you herewith a carbon copy of a letter I have sent to Zadel Barnes Gustafson in this mail.

You can imagine the countless requests for help I receive. I have helped many, against my head, because of my heart, but this is the one great, noble, dignified, imperative letter I have ever received, and it catches me helpless in cash at the present moment. I haven't any thousand dollars, wherefore, I make these propositions to you, whichever of which you select will be absolutely and entirely acceptable to me:

(1) Do you see this dear lady and do what she asks, of yourself, of what good you find is needed for you to do.

(2) Do you do what you can and split, half and half, with me, deducting against my future earnings my half.

(3) Do please do it anyway, and, your judgment not concurring, deduct the entire 100% of what you do for her from my future earnings.

I cannot express myself too earnestly to you in this matter. This is a mad, heroic, prideful case. Treat it, therefore, with utmost delicacy and consideration.

I am enclosing a twenty dollar bill inside an autographed copy of *Martin Eden* to the dear lady so that it will enable her to travel up to see you when you arrange a meeting. Be utmostly delicate. It is her desire to shield herself in this from her five loved ones. Such pride, at such decade of life, demands our consideration. Therefore so shield her, because such is her prideful desire and request. Read the letter she sent to me. Note, not merely the beautiful English and style, that ten thousand young aspiring writers would do well to have and will never have, but also the lucidity of thought and expression of her knowledge, bitter, sweet, painful, wholesome, and always sheer-hammered out of the logic of fine, high, definite, mental processes.

Remember, always, her pride of not having anybody know. Four years ago she wrote me veiled, and I replied, regretting we could not meet nor talk, and requesting, if possible, a statement of what help she wanted. Four years have passed. She now replies. I can only decide, from the lines of her letter and from between the lines of her letter, that her present need is desperate. Lord! Lord! Five dollars a week for six persons for food and clothes.

She has presented her credentials, honorable, intrinsic credentials, which I enclose herewith.

I would suggest that you might have her come up to see you in New York.

Sincerely yours,
Jack London

To Joan London

Glen Ellen, Calif.
Aug. 2, 1915

Dear Joan:—

In reply to yours of July 17, 1915, which I have at the present moment just finished reading.

It is one of a number of hundreds of letters which I am now attacking. In fact I have about two hundred more letters which I have not yet read, much less replied to.

First of all, let me quote to you a sentence from your letter: "I've learned how to play tennis, so I bought a racket and almost every day you could find Bess and I whacking balls down at the court." In lack of a reply to my letter which I sent you a few days ago in which I mentioned your bad

455

grammar, particularly in relation to the objective, I am compelled to ask you again where, under Heaven's name, you get a sanction for such awfulness of grammar? Do your grammar school teachers or do your high school teachers talk such grammar to you, or do your high school school-mates talk such grammar?

In Heaven's name, I repeat, why do you use such awfulness of grammar?

I should like to tell you about swimming but I cannot do it by the correspondence method. I find after all my years of swimming, and I have done some swimming in my time, that I am unable to swim a breast stroke upon the surface of the water. The double over-hand stroke is a good stroke. Do you know how to swim it right? Again, I could not teach you this by correspondence. On the other hand, I would suggest, as the best long-distance swimming stroke of all, you learn to swim on both the left side and the right side, keeping both your arms in the water all the time.

If you are very strong, and are very much interested in swimming, at least to such an extent that you will go swimming frequently, it would be very well for you to learn the "crawl" stroke. This is a very amazing stroke which requires a practical rebuilding by training of all the swimming muscles of your body. It is the fastest swimming stroke in the world and by it all the world's records in swimming have been broken. When I tell you that the present champion of the world, a Kanaka from Hawaii, without using his hands at all in the "crawl" stroke, and merely using his feet in the way his feet are used in the "crawl" stroke, has broken the world's swimming record for women for fifty yards merely by the propulsion of his feet, you may get some idea of what a wonderful thing the "crawl" stroke is.

I should like some time to be able to tell you about the psychology of diving. Diving is first of all a psychological matter, after that, it becomes physical. But the physical in such a matter is a mere slave of the psychological.

The double over-hand is a very good stroke if you know how to swim it. But you can make it the poorest swimming stroke in the world if you do not swim it right. There are different kinds of double over-hand strokes. I should like to show you the one double over-hand stroke that is the best.

I have turned the matter of allowance, etc., over to Aunt Eliza and if there should be any slip-up in the matter write to Aunt Eliza about it. From this letter I thoroughly understand that according to my promise Bess is to get the same allowance that you get from the moment she enters high school.

As regards books, I would suggest that the books that have not been changed in the curriculum of the Oakland high school that such books be used by Bess. You would certainly agree with me that it would be ridiculous and a waste for me to buy a copy of a book for Bess which you yourself possess and have worked through and are finished with.

Sincerely yours,
Daddy

To J. A. KINGHORN-JONES[1]

Glen Ellen, Calif.
Aug. 25, 1915

Dear Mr. Kinghorn-Jones:

I have just this moment read your postal card with amusement, dated March 19, 1915—no, I have deciphered your hieroglyphics and find that it is dated Monday, April 19, 1915.

It is a postal card of amusement on your part at my alert and prompt reply to anybody when anything is coming my way and at my indifference in replying when some man springs the greatest proposition in the world on me which will cost me only one dime, ten cents, or the tenth part of a dollar.[2]

Herewith please receive my reply of amusement. It has been a continual source of amusement to me to contemplate the many persons in this world who make a yard-stick of themselves and measure every other person in the world by their yard-stick. Because it happens that you stay in a sort of permanence in one pigeon-hole for a somewhat long time you are unable to conceive there are other persons in this world who are not at the same time simultaneously remaining in similar pigeon-holes at their post office addresses. The only reason that I have not read your postal cards until this moment is that I have been far and away beyond postal cards and post offices. Your amusement as so stated in your postal card strikes me as provincial and unsympathetic, and non-understanding. How does it strike you?

Sincerely yours,

Jack London

[1]Socialist from San Francisco, who printed pamphlets and booklets which he sold for small sums.
[2]A reference to a booklet for sale entitled "Blot Out Crime, Poverty, Prostitution, War, How and Why." Kinghorn-Jones' answer to the present letter is addressed to "Cheap Jack London" and chastises him for allowing wealth to destroy the finer qualities in a man.

To JOAN LONDON

Glen Ellen, Calif.
Aug. 25, 1915

Dear Joan:

In reply to your good letter of August 6, 1915:

First of all, Daddy must apologize for not having let you understand how busy a man he is. First of all, let me tell you how busy I am. I, personally, write many thousands of letters each year. But that is not all. Many other persons write letters for me, let me name you a few; Jack Byrne, my secretary, writes a very great many for me; so does Aunt Eliza, so does Charmian, so does Nakata, and so does a new boy by the name of Sekine, whom I am now breaking in. On top of this, I have various agents who do a great deal of writing for me in the City of New York, for the United States, in Australia, in England, in Norway, in Sweden, in Denmark, and in the rest of Europe. Now the point is, that while all these other people write these many letters for me, I have to keep track of all the letters they write. Because I am thus occupied, along with my writing, and with my education, and all the other things in the world that I do, you will understand how impossible it is for me to remember what I did with you about vacation money last year.

The only person who is responsible for the mistake this year about the vacation money is your Daddy, and your Daddy got right up on his two hind legs and made his customary roar.

Whenever your Daddy finds he is mistaken he doubles up in order to make even. I am now doubling up, herewith, in order to make even. Please find enclosed in this letter a check for Ten Dollars which is double the sum of money that I contested in my recent correspondence. Take this Ten Dollars and buy the slippers, and also go ahead and spend some of it on Bess.

I am glad to see that you are not overcome by the formalism of the dry-as-dust professors—this in regard to grammar. Of course, when we have a living language the people themselves decide what is right and what is wrong, and let the dry, old professors go hang. However, I almost think you are mistaken in the present question. It is well known to all of us that the subjunctive is passing, and some day will be gone—the subjunctive mood, I mean. Also, it is at the present time on the table whether or not we shall say "it is I" or "it is me." I think it was this very thing you had in mind when you wrote to me your present letter. But the slip-up in grammar for which you were responsible is quite different from "it is I" or "it is me."

I love to hear you say that you "think" in French. That shows you are mastering the language.

Before I forget it, let me give you another warning. I have long since warned you against selecting the stage for a career. There is only one thing worse than the stage that I would think of as a career for you, namely for you to become a school teacher. For you to become a teacher in the grammar school, the high school, the Normal school, the university, or in any private academy or seminary for young daughters of the rich . . . Joan, I tell you straight from the shoulder that that way lies hell.

I am glad and proud to see the part you are playing in high school affairs, and at the same time, in order to give you your proper balance in the world, I must take the liberty of reminding you to look at the windows once in a while and to look at the floors once in a while and to remember that your Daddy washed those windows and swept those floors.

Also, your Daddy would remind you, in order to enable you to keep your normal balance in the world, that on Tenth and Broadway, long before you were born, he was arrested there. Also, since you were born, he was arrested in many other places in the City of Oakland. The only way to know life is by not ignoring life.

You can never wear me out by writing the longest letters you are able to write, are capable of writing, and care to write. Brownie, or Edmund, is a fine looking boy. Furthermore I do not know because I have never seen him. However, I can tell you this, namely, that I know more about men than most men know, and that I know more about men than almost every woman in the world may know. I say this because it is my business to write about men and women. I have to know about men and women in order, successfully, to write about them. Wherefore, some day, some time, I hope we may get together so that I may be able to give you advice in this world about men. You are still a girl and Brownie is still a boy. The world is a big world and there are big men and big women in it.

Only just now have I, in the course of reading your letter, read the last name of Edmund, or Brownie. All the more do I feel the necessity of talking to you about men and women in this world, though at the same time I assure you it is not so material to me as it will be to you.

I think the *Aegis,* as I see the copies of it to-day, is far better and far brighter than it used to be in the old days when I, amongst many others, contributed to the *Aegis's* columns.

O, my daughter, I should like dearly to be able to talk to you about men, and women, and race, and place.

Sincerely yours,

Daddy

To Joan London

Glen Ellen, Calif.
Sept. 18, 1915

Dear Joan:

First of all, I had Aunt Eliza send you the check for $7.00 so that you might buy the two pairs of boots for yourself and Bess.

Second of all, I promised to reply to your letter.

Third of all, and very important, please remember that your Daddy is a very busy man. When you write to society people, or to young people, who have plenty of time, write on your fine stationery and write on both sides of the paper. But, please, when you write to Daddy take any kind of paper, the cheapest paper for that matter, and write on one side only. This makes it ever so much easier for Daddy to read. A two-sheet letter, such as yours that I am now looking at, written on both sides, is like a Chinese puzzle to a busy man. I take more time trying to find my way from one of the four portions into which your two-sided sheet is divided than I do in reading the letter itself.

Some day I should like to see you in your French heeled slippers. Joan, you are on the right track. Never hesitate at making yourself a dainty, delightful girl and woman. There is a girl's pride and a woman's pride in this, and it is indeed a fine pride. On the one hand, of course, never over-dress. On the other hand, never be a frump. No matter how wonderful are the thoughts that burn in your brain, always, physically, and in dress, make yourself a delight to all eyes that behold you.

I have met a number of philosophers. They were real philosophers. Their minds were wonderful minds. But they did not take baths, and they did not change their socks, and it almost turned one's stomach to sit at table with them.

Our bodies are as glorious as our minds, and, just as one cannot maintain a high mind in a filthy body, by the same token one cannot keep a high mind and high pride in a fine body when said body is not dressed beautifully, delightfully, charmingly. Nothing would your Daddy ask better of you in this world than that you have a high mind, a high pride, a fine body, and just as all the rest, a beautifully dressed body.

I do not think you will lose your head. I think, as I read this last letter of yours, that I understand that you have balance, and a woman's balance at that. Never forget the noble things of the spirit, on the other hand, never let your body be ignoble, never let the garmenture of your body be ignoble. As regards the garmenture of your body, learn to do much with little, never to over-do, and to keep such a balance between your garmenture and your mind that both garmenture and mind are beautiful.

I shall not say anything to you about your method of saving, and about Bess's method of saving, but there is much I should like to say to you, and, in the meantime I think a lot about it. You are on the right track. Go ahead. Develop your mind to its utmost beauty; and keep your body in pace with your mind.

Daddy

To Ethelda Hesser

Glen Ellen, Calif.
Sept. 21, 1915

Dear Ethelda Hesser:

In belated reply to yours of August 9, 1915:

I have been away traveling, and have just returned home to wade into a mountain of correspondence. Hence, not only my belatedness, but, also, my asking you to forgive the brevity of this, my reply to your letter.

I am not sure that I agree with you that *The Little Lady of the Big House* is not good work. I am rather proud of that novel, myself. Possibly you have been led astray in your judgment by the illustrations—as you suggested in your letter.

I have two daughters going to high school at the present time and I assure you, in reply to your question, that after having come through all of the game of life, and of youth, at my present mature age of thirty-nine years I am firmly and solemnly convinced that the game is worth the candle. I have had a very fortunate life, I have been luckier than many hundreds of millions of men in my generation have been lucky, and, while I have suffered much, I have lived much, seen much, and felt much that has been denied to the average man. Yes, indeed, the game is worth the candle. As a proof of it, my friends all tell me I am getting stout. That, in itself, is the advertisement of spiritual victory. Thanking you for your good letter,

Sincerely yours,
Jack London

TO ZADEL BARNES GUSTAFSON

Glen Ellen, Calif.
Oct. 12, 1915

Dear Zadel Barnes Gustafson:

I scarcely know what to say to you. I have been away from home fighting law-suits and running around like a chicken with its head cut off, doing frenzied finance in order to keep my head above water. I am now back home and running over our correspondence and your later letter and the last letter from Mr. Brett.

It seems that Mr. Brett has disappointed me. He was out of New York at the time that I first wrote him. He explained, at that, that the letters were forwarded to him, but that, at the time, he was under such circumstances that he was unable to give proper attention to the matter. You see, I did not have the money myself, and I wanted to enlist his pocketbook in the matter. He, after some little time, wrote to me, saying that he would like to have time to look into the matter. He writes me, that, on receipt of my telegram in reply to that statement, on the same day, he received a letter from you absolutely forbidding his mentioning the matter in any way to any person whatever. The result was, as he states it, that he did nothing further actively in the matter. I then stirred Mr. Brett up again, with further letters and further telegrams. I have just now received a check in full for what The Macmillan Company owes me up to date, accompanied by a rather formal letter from Mr. Brett in which he suggests, that, having this money now in hand, which he is enclosing to me, and that, feeling the way he does about the matter—a matter which he cannot adequately investigate without aid of others—that it would be wisest for me to help out from the check he has sent me.

—Good God! While I am getting gray hairs trying to figure out what portions of this check I shall divide between the various pressing creditors who are hounding me.

I am afraid we will have to give Mr. Brett up in this matter. I am looking around trying to find somebody of my acquaintance in California who may be able to do something. In the meantime, with winter coming on, I can suggest that I can let you have one hundred dollars. Say the word, and I will do it, and do it gladly. In the meantime I shall pursue my quest after someone who can lend an adequate hand. Please forgive the rush of this letter.

Sincerely yours,
Jack London

To Hughes Massie

Glen Ellen, Calif.
Oct. 18, 1915

Dear Mr. Massie:

I am glad that I was able to tell you to go ahead and use the "Get the Gun" interview in the *San Francisco Bulletin*.

I can only add this, which I have more than once told my wife: I would rather be a dead man under German supremacy than a live man under German supremacy. If the unthinkable should happen, and England be shoved into the last ditch, I shall, as a matter of course, go into the same last ditch and fight and die with England. I would far rather be a dead man in that last ditch than be the Emperor of Germany when Germany dominated the world. This is not for publication, it is just for you to show you how my life is tied up in the present European War—anti-war canards to the contrary.

Now to mere business. As regards Nelson's offer, as stated by you in your letter of September 21, 1915, all I can say is what I have always said: Go ahead, use your best judgment and do whatever you think best in the matter, and you will never get a complaint from me. Already, in a previous letter, I think I have straightened out a sort of misunderstanding on the part of the old firm of which you once were a member. As I said in that previous letter, I merely forwarded their offers to you in order to show you what they were doing over here in America.

I have no recollection of ever having read a reply from you to my long letter, dated June 18, 1915, and sent to you from Honolulu where I was at the time. I am fairly anxious to know that you received this letter in order that you may know thoroughly your understanding with me in the handling of all my work. Please let me know about this letter. If you will look over your letter of May 18, 1915, you will find that you ventured tentative dates concerning *The Little Lady of the Big House, Jerry, Michael,* etc., etc. In reply to all this, I must again refer you to my letter of June 18, 1915. That left no dates of publication to me whatsoever for my judgment. Just do you yourself go ahead and find out that said dates do not interfere with dates of my American publication according to the suggestions laid down by me in my letter of June 18th.

Sincerely yours,
Jack London

To Mary Austin[1]

Glen Ellen, Calif.
Nov. 5, 1915

Dear Mary Austin:

In reply to yours of October 26, 1915:

Your letter strikes me that you are serious. Now, why be serious with this bone-head world? Long ere this, I know that you have learned that the majority of the people who inhabit the planet Earth are bone-heads. Wherever the bone of their heads interferes there is no getting through.

I have read and enjoyed every bit of your *Jesus Christ* book as published serially in the *North American Review*. What if it does not get across?

I have again and again written books that failed to get across. Long years ago, at the very beginning of my writing career, I attacked Nietzsche and his super-man idea. This was in *The Sea Wolf*. Lots of people read *The Sea Wolf,* no one discovered that it was an attack upon the super-man philosophy. Later on, not mentioning my shorter efforts, I wrote another novel that was an attack upon the super-man idea, namely my *Martin Eden*. Nobody discovered that this was such an attack. At another time I wrote an attack on ideas brought forth by Rudyard Kipling, and entitled my attack "The Strength of the Strong." No one was in the slightest way aware of the point of my story.

I am telling you all the foregoing merely to show that it is a very bone-head world indeed, and, also, that I never bother my head when my own books miss fire. And the point I am making to you is: why worry? Let the best effort of your heart and head miss fire. The best effort of my heart and head missed fire with you, as it has missed fire with practically everybody else in the world who reads, and I do not worry about it. I go ahead content to be admired for my red-blood brutality and for a number of other nice little things like that which are not true of my work at all.

Heavens, have *you* read *my* "Christ" story?[2] I doubt that anybody has read this "Christ" story of mine, though it has been published in book form on both sides of the Atlantic. Said book has been praised for its red-bloodedness and no mention has been made of my handling of the Christ situation in Jerusalem at all.

I tell you this, not because I am squealing, which I am not; but to show you that you are not alone in this miss-firing. Just be content with being called the "greatest American stylist."

Those who sit alone must sit alone. They must continue to sit alone. As I remember it, the prophets and seers of all times have been compelled to sit alone except at such times when they were stoned or burned at the stake. The world is mostly bone-head and nearly all boob, and you have no complaint if the world calls you the "great stylist" and fails to recognize that your style is merely the very heart and soul of your brain. The world has an idea that style is something apart from heart and brain. Neither you nor I can un-convince the world of that idea.

I do not know what more I can say, except, that, had I you here with me for half an hour I could make my point more strongly, namely, that you are very lucky, and that you should be content to receive what the world gives you. The world will never give you due recognition of your *Christ* book. I, who never read serials, read your serial of the *Christ* and turned always to it first when my *North American Review* came in. I am not the world, you are not the world. The world feeds you, the world feeds me, but the world knows damn little of either of us.

Affectionately yours,
Jack London

[1]Contemporary writer and member of the Artist and Writer's Colony of Carmel.
[2]Chapter XVII in *The Star Rover*.

To Joan London

Glen Ellen, Calif.
Dec. 13, 1915

Dear Joan:

In reply to yours of December 11, 1915:

I am afraid that my steamer will start before I have time to catch it. You will understand from this in how big a hurry I am, and how crowded I am for time.

Now, skipping everything else, and getting down to the main point; I do not know anything about furs. I have never worn furs in my life, though I am aware I have bought them for persons of the female persuasion.

You have put up to me a very awkward question, namely, how much and how far I can go in the way of getting furs for you and Becky. I come back and say that I do not know a damn about the prices of furs for girls of your age and of your situation in life. Suppose you come back quick and let me know what you think are the maximum and minimum prices of furs that will suit the two of you.

In a rush, with lots of love,

Daddy

To Edgar J. Sisson

Honolulu, T.H.
March 7, 1916

Dear Sisson:—

In reply to yours of Dec. 16, 1915. First of all, I shall never forgive you if you still persistently decline to tell me whether or not my serialization of *Hearts of Three*[1] is readable or rotten.

Jumping right into the question of short stories: You know that I have written but one short story in the past four years. You know, from our long talk, how I am situated on short stories, and how I hate to tackle any right now. Although you do not remember it, I was really and truly shunted off a while back from the Mexican series of short stories—which was better than well, I believe, for the *Cosmopolitan,* because they were all going to be revolutionary, terrible and tragic short stories—the motives of which were gleaned by me when I was down in Vera Cruz and Tampico.

Another thing at issue is, that I have brought down with me from California no short-story material. When I finish *Hearts of Three* serialization, I shall be totally unable to tackle short stories because all my data for same is in California; and (1) could not be selected out for me by anybody except myself; (2) and I would not dare entrust the sum total of all my short-story material to the risk of transportation down to me by steamer.

On the other hand, I did bring down with me to Hawaii all the notes and data and plots of five novels. When I have finished *Hearts of Three* I should like to go ahead and do one of these novels. I must have your permission to go ahead and do this, as you and I both very well know. Otherwise, I shall have to quit fiction and turn myself loose on non-fiction work. I don't mean this as an ultimatum; I only mean it to show you how hopelessly prejudiced I am under all the circumstances, against tackling short stories at the present time.

As regards Mexico, please tell Mr. Hearst that before I should care to tackle Mexico in the really true and big way of short story writing, I should have to, first of all, really and truly go to Mexico and live there for at least a year or so.

So please go ahead, if you can see your way to it, and send me permission by cable to proceed with a novel when I have finished *Hearts of Three.* Along with this, let me assure you that if at any time in the next couple of months I can start a streak of short stories of some sort or other, I shall willingly and eagerly take hold and bite in. I am cudgeling my head now over a possible bunch of short stories, but I must tell you in advance that this one prospect will not consist of related short stories. Each story is a story by itself—if I can see my way to framing up a bunch of these stories. On the matter of short-story writing you and I pull at cross-purposes. This can be better stated as follows: You demand for your purposes that novels should be broken up in the writing into short story units. You demand that short stories be so related that the sum of a collection of short stories constitutes a novel. That is to say, artistically you are playing hell both with the short stories and with the novels.

I shall await eagerly a cable or permission from you to go ahead with a novel—coupled with this, on a chance if I can see the chance, that I shall try to do a half-dozen short stories for you. In event you cannot see your way to granting this permission, I should suggest the following: Either let me lay off for six months and do some non-fiction work that I am very anxious to do, which will deal with socialism and sociology, and which will not be offered to you; or give me another job of serialization of scenarios in collaboration with Goddard, like the one I am at present doing.

I was very glad to learn from you that Mr. McManus liked George Sterling's poem "Back to Back Against the Main Mast," and wanted to know what he would sell it for. Now, I put myself and Sterling directly into your hands. Let your own judgment decide whether it will be better for Sterling, who certainly needs the money, to sell the song outright, or to go ahead and take a royalty on the sale of the song and music if published and handled by your people. In this connection, I dare to assert that Sterling himself will be able to furnish you a better air and accompaniment than any man you can hire for the job. Please, after you have cabled me on the main proposition of this letter, give me a good letter and a full letter yourself covering the other matters at issue, including the last issue.

I am having a good time down here, and am two-thirds of the way through with *Hearts of Three*.

Sincerely yours,

Jack London

---

[1]London collaborated with Charles W. Goddard on *Hearts of Three*. Goddard wrote a scenario version while London wrote the serialization.

To Members, Local Glen Ellen
Socialist Labor Party

Honolulu, T. H.
Mar. 7, 1916

Dear Comrades—

I have just finished reading Comrade Edward B. Payne's resignation from the Local, of recent date, undated.

I am herewith tendering my own resignation from Local Glen Ellen, and for the diametrically opposite reason from the one instanced by Comrade Payne. I am resigning from the Socialist Party because of its lack of fire and fight, and its loss of emphasis on the class struggle.

I was originally a member of the old, revolutionary, up-on-its-hind-legs, fighting, Socialist Labor Party. Since then, and to the present time, I have been a fighting member of the Socialist party. My fighting record in the Cause is not, even at this late date, already entirely forgotten. Trained in the class struggle, as taught and practised by the Socialist Labor Party, my own highest judgment concurring, I believed that the working class, by fighting, by never fusing, by never making terms with the enemy, could emancipate itself. Since the whole trend of socialism in the United States of recent years has been one of peaceableness and compromise, I find that my mind refuses further sanction of my remaining a party member. Hence my resignation.

Please include my comrade wife, Charmian K. London's resignation with mine.

My final word is that liberty, freedom, and independence, are royal things that cannot be presented to, nor thrust upon, races or classes. If races and classes cannot rise up and by their own strength of brain and brawn wrest from the world liberty, freedom, and independence, they never, in time, can come to these royal possessions—and if such royal things are kindly presented to them by superior individuals, on silver platters, they will know not what to do with them, will fail to make use of them, and will be what they have always been in the past—inferior races and inferior classes.

Yours for the Revolution,
Jack London

To JOAN LONDON

Honolulu, T. H.
March 7, 1916

Dear Joan:—

In reply to yours of February 16, 1916, just to hand.

Glad you like the furs. Hope some day to see them on you before they're worn out. I hope also, twenty years from now, to hear you tell me in your own intellectual maturity, your revised judgment of *The Star Rover*. I hope also, at that time, to find that *The Little Lady of the Big House,* has appreciated in your comprehension. I am glad you like the end of it; it was the only way out—the only clean, decent way out, I mean. Some day, will you take the time off and tell me what books of mine you have read, and what books you have not read. Also, some time, personally, with you, I should like to have you tell me—and I make this as a challenge and a preparation in advance—to tell me what you think about me.

I have told Aunt Eliza to send you the price of the theatre tickets three times each month, when you're not on vacation. I have forgotten to tell her, and so you tell her for me, to send you and Becky the two pairs of shoes, or, rather, the price for same.

I received your forwarded postal, telling me that Becky had come through the operation all right.

Some day, and not very far away, a series of popular films will be run in the moving-picture theatres, entitled *Hearts of Three*.[1] It will take fifteen weeks to see this series of fifteen. The *Sunday Examiner* each week will publish the story as written by me. If you and Becky want to go see these pictures, do so. But you will have to pay the price of admission out of your own pocket money.

Lots of love all round,

Daddy

[1]Never filmed.

To Armind von Temsky

Honolulu, T. H.
June 30, 1916

Dear Armind

After long delay, for which I duly crave forgiveness, I am inclosing herewith the manuscripts.

Now I warned you to expect harsh treatment from me had you been able to come to see me for an hour or two during your last visit to Honolulu. Also, I got your permission to mark up your MSS. I have only marked the first fourteen pages of the "Lionel Pendragon" MS. I have not gone into any question of style, treatment, pitch, taste, handling; I have marked only for one particular thing.

And the harsh treatment I have led you to expect is connected with this one particular thing, which, necessarily, comes before all the other and bigger things in the writing game. This particular thing is slovenliness. There is no other name for it. In this, your case, it is utter, abject, arrant, and impudent. The editor does not exist who would read five pages of any manuscript so slovenly typed as these MSS of yours have been typed. I have in my time read many thousands of beginners' manuscripts. I have never yet read one so slovenly as these of yours.

Such slovenliness advertises to any editor, with a glance at a couple of pages, that you have no sincere regard for literature, no sincere desire to write literature; that either you are an abysmal fool or a very impudent young woman to submit such carelessly typed manuscript; that, in short, you are a self-advertised sloven.

Please believe that still I love you for all your other and good qualities, but that such love for you does not mitigate the harshness of my chastisement of you for what you have done. If anybody ever merited such castigation, you have merited it by submitting such horrible, awful, and monstrous typed manuscript to me!

And further deponent sayeth not.

Affectionately yours,

Jack

P.S. Just the same, you ought to be damned well ashamed of yourself!

To Lieutenant James D. Willson

Glen Ellen, Calif.

Aug. 5, 1916

Dear Mr. Willson:

In reply to yours of June 23, 1916:

I have just returned from Hawaii, last night, hence you will understand my delay in replying.

In reply to your inquiry I will state that I never wrote a line of the "Good Soldier" canard.[1] For years and years I have been denying the authorship of it, in England, in the United States, everywhere, by personal letter, by interview, by telegraph and by cable. There is scarcely a mail that comes to me which does not bring me a letter like yours, wanting to know whether or not I wrote the canard. As far as I can trace the history of this, it was originally published and circulated in Germany, and later on was brought over to the United States, translated and circulated with my name attached. And from there it has spread over the rest of the world. All you have to do is to read my books and newspaper work to find that for the newspapers I have done only war correspondence and prize-fighting, and that in my books I am hailed by the critics as the father of red blood fiction.

My opinion is that it behooves a country or nation like the United States to maintain a reasonable preparedness for defense against any country or nation that at any time may go out upon the way of war to carve earth space for itself out of weaker and unprepared nations.

The dressed fleas which you gave Mrs. London in Vera Cruz are a source of wonder and amusement to our friends to whom we show them.

Remember me to Captain Beach and Doctor Dessez when you see them.

Sincerely yours,

Jack London

[1]This is the letter that was circulated over London's name:
"Young Men: The lowest aim in your life is to become a soldier. The good soldier

never tries to distinguish right from wrong. He never thinks; never reasons; he only obeys. If he is ordered to fire on his fellow citizens, on his friends, on his neighbors, on his relatives, he obeys without hesitation. If he is ordered to fire down a crowded street when the poor are clamoring for bread, he obeys, and sees the gray hairs of age stained with red and the life tide gushing from the breasts of women, feeling neither remorse nor sympathy. If he is ordered off as a firing squad to execute a hero or benefactor, he fires without hesitation, though he knows the bullets will pierce the noblest heart that ever beat in human breast.

"A good soldier is a blind, heartless, soulless, murderous machine. He is not a man. He is not a brute, for brutes only kill in self defense. All that is human in him, all that is divine in him, all that constitutes the man has been sworn away when he took the enlistment roll. His mind, his conscience, aye, his very soul, are in the keeping of his officer.

"No man can fall lower than a soldier—it is a depth beneath which we cannot go. Keep the boys out of the army. It is hell.

"Down with the army and navy. We don't need killing institutions. We need life-giving institutions."

Both the Army and the Navy cleared London of the authorship of this letter. The Navy issued a leaflet entitled *An Old Lie Nailed,* in which it reprinted the foregoing letter to Lt. Willson, together with the canard, and stated "so-called Socialist publications" and "others whose practice it is to misrepresent the Army and Navy of the United States" were responsible. After London's death, Theodore Roosevelt, in a letter to Charmian, wrote that he was convinced of London's innocence in the matter.

To J. L. Jenkins[1]

Glen Ellen, Calif.
Aug. 23, 1916

Dear Mr. Jenkins:

In reply to yours of August 16th, 1916.

Undoubtedly, there must be some mistake. I have known Admiral Moore for many years. Only a little over a year ago, before the Ad Club of Honolulu, I spoke, with opposite me, at the head of the table, Governor Pinkham and Admiral Moore. I spoke upon war and the need for preparedness for war, and when I had finished Admiral Moore and Governor Pinkham shook my hand and agreed with all that I had said. Furthermore, after the said speech at the Ad Club, my wife and I were made guests of honor at a dinner given by Admiral C. B. T. Moore, down at Pearl Harbor, in his own house. The quotation you make from what he said to you, namely—"Get a copy of London's speech before the Navy Club of San Francisco or some other of his damned treason stuff," etc., is too utterly beside the facts for consideration. I never spoke before any Army or Navy Club anywhere in my life.

I have been all my life an intellectual opponent to David Starr Jordan. Especially have I attacked David Starr Jordan on his war theory that we send forth our best men to war, and our second best men, and our third best men, and breed with the men that remain, with the conclusion that the race thereby deteriorates. Somewhere in the last few years I published an article in the *Forum* entitled "The Human Drift." In this article I specifically attacked David Starr Jordan's war theory.

Sincerely yours,
Jack London

---

[1]Editor, *Getting Results.*

To COMRADE CHRIS. H. HILL

Glen Ellen, Calif.
Sept. 1, 1916

Dear Comrade Hill:

In reply to yours of August 28th, 1916:

I never heard of any comrade on the island of Tahiti who offered to give ten acres to any other comrade who might go there. Ernest Darling, who was the "nature man" there, when I was there a few years ago, has left Tahiti and has been away for two or three years. I do not know where he is now. The last I heard of him was when he was somewhere in Southern California. I think he had something like ten acres, but he told me, after he came back to the United States, that he had given those ten acres to another "nature man."

I can say this to you, however, that if you are tired of being a wage-slave, and of answering the whistle every morning, and knocking off in the evening when the whistles blow—if you are tired in this way, you can go to a place like Tahiti and live very comfortably on very little work. Your wants in Tahiti will be simple, and you will have months of leisure on your hands. However, even this did not satisfy Ernest Darling, who gave up Tahiti after a number of years experience there. At any rate, it is worth the fun of trying, and you will not be any worse off to loaf in a place like that for two or three years, even if you have to give it up and come back to the United States because the easy life bores you. Practically all I know about Tahiti I wrote in *The Cruise of the Snark,* which you tell me you have read.

Sincerely yours,
Jack London

To W. H. GEYSTWEIT[1]
[Night letter]

Glen Ellen, Calif.
Oct. 8, 1916

NEVER HAD MUCH EXPERIENCE WITH WINE-GRAPE GROWING. THE VINEYARDS I BOUGHT WERE OLD, WORTHLESS, SO I PULLED OUT THE VINES AND PLANTED OTHER CROPS. I STILL

WORK A FEW ACRES OF PROFITABLE WINE GRAPES. MY POSITION ON ALCOHOL IS ABSOLUTE NATION-WIDE PROHIBITION. I MEAN ABSOLUTE. I HAVE NO PATIENCE IN HALF-WAY MEASURES. HALF-WAY MEASURES ARE UNFAIR, ARE TANTAMOUNT TO CONFISCATION, AND ARE PROVOCATIVE OF UNDERHAND CHEATING, LYING, AND LAW-BREAKING. WHEN THE NATION GOES IN FOR NATION-WIDE PROHIBITION, THAT WILL BE THE END OF ALCOHOL, AND THERE WILL BE NO CHEATING, LYING NOR LAW-BREAKING. PERSONALLY I SHALL CONTINUE TO DRINK ALCOHOL FOR AS LONG AS IT IS ACCESSIBLE. WHEN ABSOLUTE PROHIBITION MAKES ALCOHOL INACCESSIBLE I SHALL STOP DRINKING AND IT WONT BE ANY HARDSHIP ON ME AND ON MEN LIKE ME WHOSE NAME IS LEGION. AND THE GENERATION OF BOYS AFTER US WILL NOT KNOW ANYTHING ABOUT ALCOHOL SAVE THAT IT WAS A STUPID VICE OF THEIR SAVAGE ANCESTORS.

JACK LONDON

¹Pastor, First Baptist Church, San Diego, Calif.

To Bessie London

Glen Ellen, Calif.
Oct. 12, 1916

Dear Bessie—

In reply to yours of October 9, 1916—

I cannot start East quite yet, because I must clear my desk of a number of matters, such as the present new one of yours, which you have resurrected. I want to clean up, and to clean quickly, putting all my affairs in order before I start East. I should have started the twentieth of September, but I am still here working away. So, let me hear your judgment in the matter at issue, in your reply to this letter of mine, as soon as you conveniently can.

You have asked me my reasons for asking you to sign over to me the endowment on the two five hundred dollar policies I carry on your life. I have three reasons.

(1) I pay the premiums each year on this one thousand dollars worth of endowment insurance, and, in case you are not dead when the endowment matures, the endowment should belong to me, and I desire to have this arranged for now by getting your signature to the change in the name of the ultimate beneficiary who will receive this endowment when the policies mature.

(2) I am raising the seventy-five dollars a month to you and the children to one hundred and fifty dollars a month.

(3) My third and final reason is; that you joined with a usurer, by name

Charley ———, whom you permitted my daughters to call "Uncle Charley," whom you planned to marry, and with whom you joined to shake me down, and who, when I stood up on my hind legs and proclaimed war, slunk out because he saw the shake-down of me would not go through, and who then proceeded to shake you down in proper money-lender, interest-collector, rug-peddler fashion.

If you will go over your agreement with me, of many years ago, you will find no mention made whatever in said agreement concerning the two five hundred dollar policies we are at present discussing. So, this particular matter is a question that never before has been raised between us.

I wish you would show me, on these two policies at issue, in your name, that I have kept up, that I agreed that the endowment should go to you.

Concerning the other policies mentioned by you in this letter of yours, to which I am now replying, you claim the old claim that the endowment of said policies at the time of maturity, at the end of twenty years, should go to you. This is what I went up in the air about when Charley ——— and you joined together to shake me down. This was about what I called you at that time in a letter from the Solomon Islands, a harsher name than "unveracious one."

Now that you see it is your way to adhere to the letter of the law, I suggest that you, as the mother of Joan and Bess, follow carefully in your mind the possible insurance of a couple of thousand dollars that you and they could not possibly get if I live five or six years more—to balance this against what you and they won't get if I make a new will, which I solemnly swear I shall make if I do not hear from you soon to the contrary, say within the next eight days, before I start East.

You have always stood for the letter, as against the spirit. If you want the letter, say so, remembering that it is Joan and Bess you are going to trim, and not me.

If you don't want the letter, but the spirit, I shall then submit to you a new agreement concerning insurance, in which you will sign away to me all alleged claims whatsoever on my life insurance policies. Balance, also, the one hundred and eighty dollars a month you and the children will be getting from now on, against the one hundred and five dollars a month and the totality of the life insurance you cannot possibly get.

Of course, if I only live several years more, the life insurance on *my* life automatically ceases, as the endowment policies mature, whereupon I legally draw down the endowment to myself, myself being alive at the time.

Let me hear from you soon. I hate to throw my money away, and it does hurt to throw my money away upon the stupid lawyers such as have advised you in the past. They do not even seem to understand what an endowment insurance policy is. Your lawyer from Sacramento, who drew up the old agreement between you and me, certainly understood, and he drew up the particular paragraph relating to the life insurance policies with thorough understanding. Charley —————— understood, that is why he dropped you, when he found out that I had got up on my hind legs to fight. He, the usurer, knew what an endowment policy was.

I am sending a copy of this letter to Joan and Bess. They have a right to see this letter, because it concerns them very personally, and, also, because the last talk I had with you, a couple of years ago, Joan present, and Bess just outside the door and listening, you repeatedly charged me with "women," despite the fact that I refused to say one word of acknowledgment that I had heard you mention "women" before my daughters.

They did not overlook that particular bet which you offered them, and, if you deemed them ripe enough then to listen to such talk, then, they are certainly ripe enough now to listen, two years later, to the talk in this letter —especially since it concerns their own welfare, about which they are showing themselves solicitous.

Sincerely yours,

Jack

To Edgar Sisson

Glen Ellen, Calif.

Oct. 12, 1916

Dear Sisson—

I am very sorry I frightened you in advance about my three old, one-armed tramps. Long ere this, you should have received "The Princess." I am confident that, after having read it, you could not conclude that it is a horrible story.

I always do feel chagrined, in that you never yet have told me that you liked at all one short story I have written. In fact, you have had such a deterrent effect upon me that now I have abandoned short stories for awhile and am five thousand words along and in full swing on an Hawaiian novel,[1] the heroine of which is named CHERRY. The novel will be anywhere between fifty and sixty thousand words, though I may, before I am done, increase it to a full one hundred thousand word novel. I have only begun to collect possible titles, I shall name you a few—*Cherry; The Screen-Lady; The Screen-Gazer;* and *Fire Dew.*

What in the dickens ever happened to *The Hearts of Three?*

I am still so delayed by work here that I shall not be in New York for another several weeks.

Sincerely yours,

Jack London

[1]*Eyes of Asia,* the story London was writing when he died. *Cosmopolitan* published the unfinished manuscript in Sept., 1924. Charmian finished it for the October number, 1924.

To Loen Weilskov

Glen Ellen, Calif.
Oct. 16, 1916

Dear Loen Weilskov:

In reply to your good letter of March 7, 1916, which was acknowledged by my secretary. I am but lately returned from a seven-months' absence in Hawaii, and am now rushing to catch up with a mountain of correspondence of work that has piled up during my absence; so forgive a brief reply to your letter, which letter I greatly appreciate. Yes, I remember Peder Pederson's letters. Remember me most kindly to him.

As to my favorite of my own books—that is a hard question to answer. I think I put more of my heart into *The People of the Abyss* than into any other book. I like certain of my books for different reasons, and probably have no favorite above all the rest. *The Game* is a particular pet of mine. I like *White Fang* better than I do *The Call of the Wild;* in *The Little Lady of the Big House* and *The Valley of the Moon,* I have expressed much of my heart toward the land. No, I haven't "That Spot." I only have a fine little fox terrier, whom I brought around Cape Horn three years ago on a sailing-ship from Baltimore to Seattle—five months at sea. I am fond of some of my South Sea stories; and, by the way, I hope you can get hold of my wife's book, *The Log of the Snark,* which is published in England by Mills & Boon, entitled *Voyaging in Wild Seas.* It gives all the intimate personal stuff of our two years' voyage in the small boat. Perhaps Martin will publish a Danish translation of this in due time. You will learn from my wife's book the way we love to live, and the way we enjoy adventuring in our own way.

A centerboard? Well, you know what the KEEL of a boat is. Some boats are keel boats and some are centerboard boats—in the centerboard boat the centerboard is a keel that moves up and down. In shallow water this centerboard can be pulled up inside the boat. The use of the centerboard is the same as that of the keel, namely, to enable the boat to beat to windward.

I am very glad you wrote to me. I am very fond of my Danish readers, and hope some day to visit your beautiful country, and renew acquaintance with some of my good friends there.

Forgive my brevity. I am so rushed on account of my long absence from home, and am now trying to get my work done so that I may depart shortly for New York City, three thousand miles away.

Best wishes to you and yours, and thanking you again for your good letter.

Sincerely yours,
Jack London

To Hugo Erichsen, M.D.

Glen Ellen, Calif.
Oct. 16, 1916

Dear Doctor Erichsen—

In reply to yours of recent date, (undated)—

Cremation is the only decent, right, sensible way of ridding the world of us when the world has ridden itself of us.[1] Also, it is the only fair way, toward our children, and grandchildren, and all the generations to come after us. Why should we clutter the landscape and sweet-growing ground with our moldy memories? Besides, we have the testimony of all history that all such sad egotistic efforts have been failures. The best the Pharaohs could do with their pyramids was to preserve a few shriveled relics of themselves for our museums.

Sincerely yours,
Jack London

---

[1] In 1911 London, in a sealed envelope, left instructions for the disposal of his body after death. He wanted no viewing, no funeral, and his remains to be cremated and the ashes spread over the "Beauty Ranch."

To Editor,
Atlantic Monthly

Glen Ellen, Calif.
Oct. 20, 1916

Dear Sir:

I have just received, through my clipping bureau, page 495 of the October number of the *Atlantic Monthly,* so that I am prevented, by being far removed from a newsstand, from knowing the name of the person who wrote the paragraph anent my novel *The Little Lady of the Big House.*

In five and one-half short lines of a column that is a narrow column, because it takes two columns across to make a page of the *Atlantic Monthly*, I find this person has used the following words and phrases— "erotomania," "sensualism," "continence," "voluptuous," "desire," and "ingrowing concupiscence." Two lines further down, this person uses "perverted."

Now I rise up in meeting to say that I never knew an "honest" blacksmith who was honest; that I never met a person proclaiming blatantly that he told the truth, who did tell the truth; that I never met a person shouting a vocabulary of filth in denunciation of what he esteemed filth, who was, himself, clean-minded. Our psychoanalysts have long since classified such persons. I defy any person, in any four-hundred-page novel of mine, or in all the totality of my forty published books of fiction, to collect a total of such words that the critic in your columns managed fecundly to introduce into five and one-half short lines.

But, gee!, the foregoing is not what is bothering me. The person has named the person's pathological pigeonhole. What I rise up in meeting now, the second time, to ask is—who wrote the criticism? I ask because I am infatuated to know the name and sex of the person, possessing such a subtle and active vocabulary, who could conclude such seething criticism with the following query, namely, if I (Jack London, the apostle of red [blooded] school of fiction for healthy wholesome schoolboys), am "too undisciplined for the new impersonal meanings of things?"

I am infatuated with that discipline "for the new impersonal meanings of things."

Is it fish, flesh, or fowl?—I mean the person who wrote it. I simply must know who and what it is, whether it be a he, or a she, or an it.

That discipline, possessed by this person, "for the new impersonal meanings of things"! I don't know what it means. That is why I am infatuated. It sounds almost potent enough to serve as the foundation for a new religion or a new metaphysic. Better cults have been founded on less intelligent propositions. I must know, Please be kind and let me know.

Sincerely yours,

Jack London

P.S. But why the belatedness of the book review? *The Little Lady of the Big House* is long since published and forgotten.

P.S. Dare you publish this letter in your columns, which columns have laid themselves open to much publication by running the discipline "for the new impersonal meanings of things"? I wonder, I wonder; and I wait.

J. L.

To Mrs. H. P. Agee

Glen Ellen, Calif.

Oct. 24, 1916

Dear Mrs. Agee—

In reply to yours, recent but undated—

Why did God make you to love a fountain pen when your handwriting is so hard to read?

The funny thing is that I do not remember the names of the women in *The Merry Widow,* so that I have sort of felt my way about through the names you mention in your letter. Possibly, had the handwriting been more legible, I would not have been compelled to feel my way so much.

I note very carefully that you explain to me what you have already explained to me, namely, that I do not know anything about women. If you were the only woman in the world, I should be compelled to accept your judgment. As it is, you are not the only woman in the world—though far be it from me to be cavalier enough to suggest that I thank my stars that you are not the only woman in the world. I mean not exactly that, when I chortle over the good fortune that has for me placed in the world some other women.

A woman, not greatly daring—please do not misunderstand me—I mean not greatly daring intellectually, who elects to incubate, and hatch, and nurse the small little female subtleties, that are only large and tragic when the petty sum of them can vex a little man, is scarcely the woman who can tell me I know nothing about women, when, forsooth, I have ignored the exploitation of the little female subtleties (be grateful that I have not named them in harsher terms), and have (a) exploited in my work the healthy, wholesome, schoolboy ideal of woman, and (b), kept to myself and not exploited the knowledge of the greatness, and terribleness, of woman.

We live much by ourselves. I have done more than a fair share of living by myself, save when the loosening of alcohol parts my lips in privy talk of woman to woman, which same the woman inevitably resents, being the nature of the two-legged female biped to resent when she encounters a two-legged male biped who refuses to accept her own valuation of herself and sex.

Please show this to your husband, who is a scientist as well as a man, and who will appreciate stuff too baldly stated for boudoir converse.

And now a truce to tilting. Only, I beg of you, to remember and note this, that it is the most favorite stunt of woman to tell a man that he does not know anything about woman, while one never sees or hears a man telling a woman that she knows nothing about man. I call this a favorite stunt. Surely you will agree, if you will go over in your mind the many times you have been aware of other women practising this particular stunt, and, if you go vainly through your mind, trying to remember the one man who practised this stunt.

I am looking forward to the arrival of your new book with keen interest.

Sincerely yours,
Jack London

To GEDDES SMITH[1]

Glen Ellen, Calif.
Oct. 31, 1916

Dear Sir—

In reply to yours of October 16th, 1916—

I have no countryside home. I am a farmer. It is because I am a farmer that I live in the country. I am that sort of farmer, who, after delving in all the books to satisfy his quest for economic wisdom, returns to the soil as the source and foundation of all economics.

What am I doing? In few words, I am trying to do what the Chinese have done for forty centuries, namely, to farm without commercial fertilizer. I am rebuilding worn-out hillside lands that were worked out and destroyed by our wasteful California pioneer farmers. I am not using commercial fertilizer. I believe the soil is our one indestructible asset, and by green manures, nitrogen-gathering cover crops, animal manures, rotation of crops, proper tillage and drainage, I am getting results which the Chinese have demonstrated for forty centuries.

We are just beginning to farm in the United States. The Chinese knew the *how* but not the *why*. We know the *why,* but we're dreadfully slow getting around to the *how*. All of which constitutes my reason for being a farmer.

Sincerely yours,
Jack London

P.S. Please send me as many prints or proofs or whatever you call them of this letter of mine (if you run it); and at least two copies of the *Countryside* in which you publish it.

---

[1]Managing Editor, *The Independent*.

TO WALDO FRANK[1]

Glen Ellen, Calif.
Nov. 3, 1916

My dear Mr. Frank—

In reply to your good letter of October 24, 1916—

Two things prevent me from being kind to you in this matter of manuscripts of short stories which I have filed away on the shelf, and which have not been published.

First, there ain't no such short stories. Second, if there were, my contracts, which are exclusive, and blanket, would prevent me from permitting anyone to publish such stories.

I am replying to your letter immediately, so that I have not yet had the pleasure of reading a copy of *The Seven Arts* which you mention having mailed me.

I do not mind telling you that had the United States been as kindly toward the short story writer as France has always been kindly, from the beginning of my writing career I would have written many a score of short stories quite different from the ones I have written.

Sincerely yours,
Jack London

[1]Of *The Seven Arts* staff.

To Joan London

Glen Ellen, Calif.
Nov. 21, 1916

Dear Joan:—

Next Sunday, will you and Bess have lunch with me at Saddle Rock, and, if weather is good, go for a sail with me on Lake Merrit.

If weather is not good, we can go to a matinee of some sort.

Let me know at once.

I leave Ranch next Friday.

I leave Calif. Wednesday following.[1]

Daddy.

[1]Possibly the last letter London ever wrote. After his death it was found in the letter basket for his Japanese houseboy to mail.

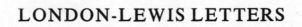

LONDON-LEWIS LETTERS

LONDON-LEWIS LETTERS

In the *Liberty* magazine of October 10, 1931, George Sylvester Viereck published an article entitled "The Ghost of Jack London." His opening paragraph reads:

A "ghost," according to the Standard Dictionary, is "one who does the brain-work for which another person takes the credit; especially in art or literature." Literature is haunted by "ghosts." Nevertheless, it came as something of a shock and a surprise when Liberty discovered that Jack London employed a "ghost," and that his name was—Sinclair Lewis! Thereby hangs a literary mystery.

The article, while interesting and a bit sensational, was false in its basic assumption. The truth is that London bought from Lewis twenty-seven plots. He developed five of these into three stories: "Winged Blackmail," "When the World Was Young," and "The Prodigal Father"; and two novels: *The Abysmal Brute* and *The Assassination Bureau*.

The letters here are the most significant ones of the London-Lewis exchange and reveal the truth of the arrangement.

The Lewis letters are, as nearly as possible, exact replicas of the originals, but we have followed our usual practice of correcting the mechanical errors in London's. The Lewis letters are printed by permission of Ernst, Cane, Berner & Gitlin, Counsellors at Law, executors of the Lewis estate, and Professor Mark Schorer, author of *Sinclair Lewis*.

The Volta Review
Washington, D.C.
Sept. 28, 1910

Dear Jack London:

I was very glad to receive your note suggesting that you are willing to look at some more short story plots, etc. I am enclosing a big bunch, at the completion of which I've been working day AND night since hearing from you. In getting the ideas for such of them as have been suggested to me since I sold you those other plots, I've had you in mind to a considerable extent.

I hope to gawd that you will feel like taking a considerable part of them, because, if you do, it will probably finally give me the chance to get back at the free lancing—nothing but writing—which I haven't done for over a year; can the job and really get at decent work. I've saved up some mun, but not enough yet for a sinking fund. Next spring I shall receive between two and three hundred for a novelette; so that if I get started now I shall be able to hike along nicely, with the novelette money as a safeguard if I don't sell much at first.

I've learned a good many things about this town and this kind of work while here; and ain't sorry I came; BUT I'm pretty damn well able to pass an examination on this particular book, now; and ready for others. So that, I'm hoping these plots will hit you as usable—either now or later; for of course I don't expect you to be interested in them unless they have possibilities for use now or later.

I sure did see your working up of "The Garden of Terror" as "When All the World Was Young," in the *Saturday Evening Post;* and it was GREAT stuff. The use of the girl was excellent. I asked Noyes, my chief here, if he had read the story; and he had, with enough interest to remember it in detail, which is good praise. Please let me know if you use any of the other 14 plots, likewise.

I see that the *Washington Herald* is getting your *Burning Daylite* from the *N.Y. Herald,* and boosting it in great shape.

Please give my regards to Mrs. London. I hear from George, now and then. I was mighty glad to see the *Pacific Monthly* using his long Duandon.

Gawd I'll be glad to get back at writing; for here what I've done—tho it has been a fair quantity—has been only at cost of sleep—which is too cheap and instructive an amusement, is sleep, to be wasted.

Sincerely,
Sinclair Lewis
otherwise
Hal
alias
Red

I enclose a list—sort of index or *invoice* (!) of the plots here.

Glen Ellen, Calif.
Oct. 4, 1910

Dear Sinclair Lewis:

Your plots came in last night, and I have promptly taken nine (9) of them,[1] for which same, according to invoice, I am remitting you herewith check for $52.50.

Some of the rejected ones were not suited to my temperament; others did not suit because I am too damn lazy to dig up requisite data or atmosphere.

I didn't care to tackle the World Police (which is a splendid series), because I am long on splendid novel-motifs of my own, which require only time and relaxed financial pressure for me to put through.

I'll let you know whenever one of your plots is published.

"Winged Blackmail" was published in Sept. number of *The Lever,* a monthly magazine issued in Chicago.

I have 20,000 words done on *The Assassination Bureau,*[2] and for the first time in my life am stuck and disgusted. I haven't done my best by it, and cannot make up my mind whether or not to go ahead with it.

Be sure to send me plots from time to time, with prices attached, and for heaven's sake, remember the ones I take, so that you won't make the mistake of writing them up yourself some time.

In a wild rush,

Sincerely yours,

Jack London

[1]London never used any of the plots. The originals (seven typed and two holograph) are still among his papers. The plots range from 60 to 240 words in length. The following is a typical example:
"GODIVA OF TODAY
Tho' a socialist, she is the wife of a rich manufacturer. He, laughing at her theories, says he will make a certain reform she greatly desires if she will, not ride naked thru the streets, but, say, lecture on socialism at st. crossings and corners. Tho' rather sensitive, and regarded by the socialists themselves with suspicion because she is connected with the disliked mgfr. she pulls it off."
[2]Unfinished at the time of London's death. As noted earlier, the book was completed by Robert L. Fish from London's notes and published in 1963.

The Frederick A. Stokes Co.

New York City

Oct. 12, 1910

Dear Jack London:

Thank you for the check for $52.50 which arrived today. I hope to hell you find the plots of value. I'll keep a keen eye out for others likely to interest you. I certainly do appreciate your using the stuff and hope to hand over value in return.

In order to make it absolutely dead certain that I won't use any thing I've sold you I do two things: destroy my notes on each story, and make a list of those sold, which I glance over now and then.

About 24 hrs. after I wrote you I got an offer from the Stokes Co. to come up here and read MSS. for them. While I'm eager to get at free-lancing, the offer seemed too good to throw down and I took it; so I'll be there for quite a little while at least. Then to it! Meanwhile, I keep rite after the writing, on the side.

The Stokes people evidently regard you as the biggest proposition in the country and would like to handle something of yours—at about your own terms; pushing the sale of it their damndest. Essays, fiction, any thing, so long as it's London. Hope there may some day be a chance of my taking a part in pushing the sale of one of your books as brought out by Stokes.

And then, by God, Jack, rent me a shack under your eucalypts and lemme write and dig dirt and lambaste hell out of you at poker!

Hal

The Frederick A. Stokes Co.
New York City
October 16, 1910

Dear Jack London:

Ever since your last letter saying that, after doing 20,000 words on the *Assassination Bureau,* you feel stuck on the thing, I've been thinking about it.

I wonder if there's too much fantasy and too little Jack London in the plot? and if it couldn't be made a real Jack London plot; one good for a 75,000 word novel? I don't remember just what ending I suggested for the thing, but I've been thinking about one which would make the plot as I outlined it really just the beginning of the real novel. I hope you won't consider the suggestion too fresh. Anyway:

Have your Assassinator, his daughter and son-in-law (the man who gave him contract) finally temporarily safe in some South Sea isle; and then take all that's preceded (even if it's as much as 30,000 words) as merely the BEGINNING of the real story. Make the Assassinator and the other two start a new bureau—of self-protection, rather than assassination, this time —a bureau composed of such savages as the Solomon Islanders. The Assassinator becomes the Napoleon of a strange nation. He fights the chiefs —the nervous wiry Assassinator with infinite nerve and a couple of bombs, facing half a hundred savage leaders. Then, with the semi-hypnotic power he has always displayed, the Assassinator gathers a following of savages, who are sent out on the trail of the Assassinator's trailing sleuths—fire fought with back-fire. Also, he uses a bunch of beach-combers, whom he takes up and makes useful followers. One of these beach-combers might become an important character.

These new, weird agents finally "get" the Chief Assistant Assassinator (—as proud of his work as the Assassinator himself ever was, and hence a tireless chief in the chase of the Assassinator). And the three leading characters are safe in their strange kingdom, where the Assassinator is a kind of Sea Wolf.

All this last part would be Jack London, and Jack London only.

I should think that thus the thing might make a 75,000 word thing, striking, interesting, and most eagerly read—absolutely out of the ordinary run of fiction.

Apropos of this, there are certain questions I want to ask, and would very much like to have answered. I am cooking up a plan which may possibly result in decided commercial advantage to both you and the Stokes Co. I guess you realize that I feel bound in everyway to do whatever may be

486

possible, at any time, to boost *your* cause; and I am coming to feel the same way toward the Stokes Co. To be genuinely allied to both of two parties to a possible deal is a business situation as desirable as it is unusual. I understand, of course, that my plan may come to nothing. In that case, there will be no harm done, however. And if my plan succeeds, there may be big advantages to both sides. Wherefore please let me have this information, so that I can go ahead and see if it will be possible to talk business. The questions are:

(1)—Would it be possible, by following the suggested plan for completion, or some other one, to make a real Jack London novel of not less than 70,000 words out of the *Assassination Bureau?* It is to be understood that, in the not-very-probable case of your wanting my assistance, such assistance may be absolutely counted on. I might be able to suggest some little kink in plot; and could take a good deal of the copy-reading labor off your hands, if you desired. (I copy read two novels which are selling in the thousands today.)

(2)—How much of the *Assassination Bureau* have you now finished (in number of words)?

(3)—To what point in the plot does this bring you?

(4)—If the thing couldn't possibly frame up for a (say) 75,000 word thing, how long could it be made?

(5)—Are you planning any other books not yet finished or disposed of? either fiction, essays or anything else? For instance, is that wonderful thing you read us at Carmel—that character sketch of the Skipper of the Long Absences and the Dialect—intended as one of a series for a book? Or mebbe another volume of short stories and novelettes? or another novel?

PLEASE let me have answers to these five questions. I shall understand that the answers are not final, but subject to change as your plans change.

PS. I ain't writing no articles for no literary journals on "advance dope of Jack London"—not unless you want me to!!!!!!!

I find New York awakening, after being away for two years. It may prove deadening after a while, but it sure ain't just now. And I hope that one of its results may be some good plots to submit to you.

My best regards to Mrs. London, and to Unterman if he is still at Glen Ellen.

Sincerely yours,
Hal
alias
Sinclair Lewis

Glen Ellen, Calif.
Oct. 20, 1911

Dear Lewis:—

In reply to yours of October 10, 1911. Yes, I received the plots some time ago, but have not been home very much. Please find inclosed my check for $15.00 for "The Grit of Doctor Pibbin," "The Deserter," and "Greater Love"! Several reasons prevent me from taking more of them. In the first place, a number of them are regular O. Henry plots. O. Henry could have handled them, and they'd have been great for his style of handling. And then, since the first of the year I've been working quite steadily on the *Smoke Bellew* tales for *The Cosmopolitan,* and the *Sun Tales* in *Saturday Evening Post.* You see, I haven't been using up any outside short story ideas at all.

How would you suggest a possible play out of *The Abysmal Brute?* I can't possibly see any. Frankly, I don't know whether I'm making money or losing money by working up some of those short-story ideas I got from you. Take *The Abysmal Brute,* for instance. I got $1200.00 for it, after it had been refused by the first-class magazines. Had the time I devoted to it been devoted to *Smoke Bellew* or *Sun Tales,* I'd have got $3000 for the same amount of work.

The foregoing is merely in reply to your question. Personally, despite the fact that it did not make a financial killing, I'm darned glad I wrote *The Abysmal Brute.*

Thanks for the tip about the new *Hampton Columbian Magazine.* Luckily, they do not owe me anything. But you can understand how extremely valuable your tip would have been had they been in my debt. Gee! Any time you get a tip like that, send it along.

Sincerely yours,
Jack London

The Frederick A. Stokes Co.
New York City
Nov. 15, 1911

Dear Jack:

Thanks for the fifteen—it is now a part of a winter overcoat, very much needed in these pleasing N.Y. winds.

Now, ask you, could a play be made out of *The Abysmal Brute?* Strikes me as rather easy—for instance, scene: Sam Berger and the new fighter; scene, new fighter's first fight; scene with the girl in training quarters; scene with her after marriage; spectacular last fight—and so on. I may be entirely off, but it struck me, thruout, while reading, as having dramatic possibilities.

No literary news especially that I think of, except that, as I warned you it would, *Hampton-Columbian* has gone up.

Did I chortle, in my last, about the grave business man I am becoming. I shall be wearing a sidewhisker and pushing a baby-carriage before a nice suburban residence in Flatbush, before long, and then I shall at last be respectable.

But would I like it? Oh, that's another question. . . . As a matter of fact, too, I think that my chiefs, if questioned, would still say that I'm a hellion. Every time I'm talking to them and absently reach for my handkerchief in my back pocket, everyone still ducks under the table.

At the same time, I have been on my present job for over a year and probably shall be for many's the moon to come—unless they can me (which, of course, they will do just as soon as they find out what a damn loafer, what an associater with worthless and anarchistic persons like Jack L. and George Sterling and Jimmie Hopper, I actually am!)

By the way, speaking of having been here over a year: I still feel, as I did at the first, that I tremendously wish we had one of your novels to publish. Now that I'm doing publicity—and planting about as much as any press agent in the country—I wish that I had one of your novels to boost. I know that the chiefs are greatly interested in your work, and that they would be willing to pay a great big percentage, as well as push anything of yours actively. Doing big adv. now.

If you ever get at outs with MacMillan, let me know, and I think a good big offer would be made instanter.

Please give my regards to the Sterlings and Mrs. L.

Su servidor, senor splendidissimo,
or words to that effect.
Sinclair Lewis

INDEX

Abbott, Leonard, 319n.
Abysmal Brute, The, 380, 483, 488
Acorn-Planters, The, 442
Across the Sub-Arctics of Canada (James Tyrell), 36
Adventure, 261, 301, 303, 339, 348
Adventures of Miss Gayly (Grant Allen), 60
Aegis, 7, 459
Agassiz, Louis, 41
Agee, Mrs. H. P., *447-478*
Ainslee's Magazine, 117-118, 140
Allen, E. F., 246n.
Allen, Grant, 112 and n.
Amateur M. D., The, 284
Amateur Navigator, The, 284
American Barbarian (Philo M. Buck, Jr.), 367-368 and n.
American Hebrew and Jewish Messenger, *351-352* and n.
American Magazine, 242n., 306n., 344, 391n.
American Press Association, 137n., 138
American Proletariat (Austin Lewis), 257
Anarchy (Edgar Fawcett), 34 and n., 103
And Michael, 449, 463
Andersen, Esther, 437
"Andrea del Sarto" (Browning), 75
Antin, Mary, *see* Grabau, Mary Antin
Appeal to Reason, 224 and n., 274
Applegarth, Mabel, *3-4* and n., *5-11, 12-13, 18-19*
Applegarth, Ted, 4 and n., 8, 12, 13, 18, 19, 73, 105, 106
Arcata Union, 350
Arena, 45, 49n., 50, 87, 90
Argosy, 42
Army and Navy Journal, The, 423-425, 451
Art of Controversy, The (Schopenhauer), 310
Assassination Bureau, The, 357 and n., 483, 485 and n., 486-487
Associated Sunday Magazine Syndicate, 242
Atherton, Frank, 3, 4n., 5, 8
Atlantic Monthly, 45, 50, 64 and n., 68, 72, 79, 87, 88, 96, 134, 153, 169n., *170,* 388, *476-477*
Austin, Alfred, 89
Austin, Mary, 205n., *463-464* and n.
Australia, 261, 271, 273-277
Authors' Clipping Bureau, 263
Authors League of America, 404, 408-409
Ayres, Sydney, 362, 386
Bab Ballads (W. S. Gilbert), 47, 49n., 51, 95, 100

Babcock, A. L., *209-210* and n., *211* and n., *229-231* and n.
Back to Back Against the Main Mast (George Sterling), 466
Baker, Ray Stannard, 54
Balboa Amusement Co., 387n., 400n., 427
Bamford, Frederick Irons, 93 and n., 119
Bangs, John Kendrick, 62, 206n.
Barker, Donald, 399, 400n., 403-404, 408, 411, 413
Barnes, Lillian Corbett, 36
Barrett, Jack, 191, 300
Barrie, Sir James, 95
Bates, Blanche, 168 and n., 169
Beach, Captain, 469
Beach, Rex, 440
Beauty Ranch, Glen Ellen, California, vii, 170, 171n., 172-175, 216, 245, 278, 301, 311, 312n., 313, 318, 320, 326, 329, 336-337, 347, 359, 363, 368, 373-374 and n., 375, 383, 392, 393, 394, 429, 432, 436, 444-446, 476n.
Beckwith, E. C., *319*
Before Adam, 204, 208, 209, 214, 216, 229, 233, 244, 282, 327 and n., 332, 341, 368
Bellamy, Edward, 139, 143n.
Ben Day Co., 361
Benefit of the Doubt, The, 319-320
Benevolent Feudalism and Social Unrest (W. J. Ghent and J. G. Brooks), 167
Benicia, California, 37-38, 147
Bergson, Henri, 425
Berry, Fred, *388-389* and n.
Berry (Cloudesley Johns), 114 and n.
Besant, Sir Walter, 112 and n., 113
Bicyclers and Other Farces, The (Kendricks Bangs), 62
Bierce, Ambrose, 16, 25, 29, 37, 52, 68, 69, 106, 175-176, 204, 205, 257, 277
Biglow, Poultney, 104, 105n.
Bishop, Del, 154 and n.
Black Cat, 13, 14n., 21, 38, 39 and n., 41, 54-56, 90, 96, 99, 102, 106, 133, 167, 202
Blad, Valdemar, *238-239*
Boer War, 64, 66, 105-106
Bohemian Club, 205n., 318, 399
Böhm-Bawerk, Eugen, 36
Bomb, The (Frank Harris), 289
Bond, Marshall, *154*
Book of Sharks, The, 244, 245n.
Bookman, The, 371, 372
Bostick, T. A., *401* and n.
Boston Globe, The, 30n.
Bosworth, Hobart, 393n., *399-400* and n.

491